D1498381

HANDBOOK OF
SEXUAL
and
GENDER
IDENTITY
Disorders

HANDBOOK OF
SEXUAL
and
GENDER
IDENTITY
Disorders

Edited by

DAVID L. ROWLAND
LUCA INCROCCI

WILEY

John Wiley & Sons, Inc.

To my ever-curious and always surprising daughter Clare,
and to the friends, family, and colleagues who have
supported and mentored me over the years.

D. L. R.

To my wife Nicole and my children Jonathan and Carlotta
for their patience and support.

L. I.

CONTENTS

PART II
Gender Identity Disorders 325

Part Editor: Kenneth J. Zucker

Chapter 11
Genetics of Sexual Development and Differentiation 329

Eric J. N. Vilain

Chapter 12
Disorders of Sex Development and Atypical Sex Differentiation 354

Vickie Pasterski

Chapter 13

Gender Identity Disorder in Children and Adolescents   376

Kenneth J. Zucker and Peggy T. Cohen-Kettenis

Chapter 14

Gender Identity Disorders in Adults: Diagnosis and Treatment   423

Anne A. Lawrence

Chapter 15____
Cross-Cultural Issues   **457**

Serena Nanda

PART III
Paraphilias and Atypical Sexual Behaviors   **487**

Chapter 16____
Paraphilia and Paraphilia-Related Disorders:
An Introduction   **491**

Luk Gijs

*Chapter 20*_____

In this volume, we have brought together thoughts and recommendations of notable international experts in the field of sexual disorders, based on their understanding and evaluation of the research literature and on their assessment of current diagnostic and treatment practices. The text is written to benefit mental health clinicians and primary care physicians, as well as specialists in the fields of sex therapy and sexual medicine. The intersection of these multiple perspectives is becoming increasingly inevitable and thoughtful integration is becoming critically important. Health providers from many disciplines, both in and outside the field of sexology, will benefit not only from greater understanding of these merging viewpoints but also from exposure to new developments within their own expert and cognate fields.

The volume is organized around the three major sexual disorder classifications:

Part I *Sexual Dysfunctions,* that is, problems in responding adequately to achieve a sexually satisfying life, usually within the context of a sexual relationship.

Part II *Gender Identity Disorders,* that is, strong cross-gender identification and a general discomfort with one's assigned sex, as usually is biologically determined.

Part III *Paraphilias and Atypical Sexual Behaviors,* that is, strong sexual urges, behaviors, and/or fantasies that involve sexual activity with inappropriate objects or in inappropriate situations.

An underlying assumption of each disorder is that the condition causes significant distress and/or that it leads to impairment in social or interpersonal functioning. Many of the disorders are classified in the *Diagnostic and Statistical Manual of Mental Disorders (DSM;* as well as the *International Statistical Classification of Diseases and Related Health Problems* or *ICD).* We have included an Appendix listing the *DSM* descriptions.

Each part includes a brief introduction, followed by a series of chapters meant to bring breadth to the understanding of the disorder classification. Each chapter addresses a specific aspect of the disorder classification—including an introduction to the issue, definition and description of the disorder, prevalence and risk factors, assessment strategies, and finally, recommendations for treatment. Each part also includes at least one chapter on an emerging issue or alternative viewpoint, selected because it steps in some way beyond the traditional boundaries of sexological inquiry.

We have asked authors to present their topics from a holistic perspective, attending to the multiple audiences of the volume. We encouraged the use of tables, figures, and summary sidebars and bullets to make the information more easily understood and referenced. While some authors responded enthusiastically to these tasks and others had to be coaxed, in the end, because they brought their own discipline-specific perspective and "culture" to the text, we are confident that the overall coverage is fair and balanced. At the same time, we recognize that research and treatment gains have not been spread evenly across perspectives; this results—not surprisingly—in chapters inevitably weighted toward one approach or another (e.g., biological/medical or psychological/ developmental). Our hope is that no matter what the reader's perspective, the material in this volume will both answer questions and raise new ones.

We are grateful to the authors who contributed their time, labor, expertise, and intellectual investment to this handbook. We hope you, the reader, take as much from these chapters as the authors put into them, that you find this volume thoughtful, informative, and useful, whether you are a seasoned expert in the field, a curious professional expanding horizons, or a student embarking on an exploratory voyage into the field of sexology.

The editors appreciate the careful eye, organizational skills, and persuasive communication abilities of Kimberly Wampler—her tireless work with the authors and her calm demeanor staved off many potential panic attacks by the editors. Kathleen Mullen's thoughtful readings and feedback on a number of chapters helped greatly with the progression of ideas within chapters and consistency across chapters. Melissa Fisher's continual formatting and reformatting of chapters, and checking and rechecking this, that, and everything were indispensable contributions to the handbook.

And, of course, we thank our editors at Wiley.

Eric Beauregard, PhD
Department of Criminology
University of South Florida
Tampa, Florida

Yitzchak M. Binik, PhD
Department of Psychology
McGill University
Montreal, Quebec, Canada

Lori A. Brotto, PhD, R Psych
Department of Obstetrics and Gynaecology
University of British Colombia
Vancouver, British Columbia, Canada

Peggy T. Cohen-Kettenis, PhD
Gender Clinic
Vrije Universiteit Medical Center
Amsterdam, The Netherlands

Melissa A. Farmer, BA
Department of Psychology
McGill University
Montreal, Quebec, Canada

J. Paul Fedoroff, MD
Royal Ottawa Health Care Center
Ottowa, Ontario, Canada

Woet L. Gianotten, MD
Hilversum, The Netherlands

Luk Gijs, PhD
Department of Medical Psychology
Vrije Universiteit
Amsterdam, The Netherlands

Louis Gooren, MD, PhD
Department of Endocrinology
Free University Medical Center
Amsterdam, The Netherlands

Goeffrey Ian Hackett, MD
Fisherwick, Lichfield, United Kingdom

Lisa Dawn Hamilton, BA
Department of Psychology
University of Texas—Austin
Austin, Texas

Luca Incrocci, MD, PhD
Department of Radiation Oncology
Erasmus MC-Daniel den Hoed
    Cancer Center
Rotterdam, The Netherlands

Tuuli Kukkonen, BA
Department of Psychology
McGill University
Montreal, Quebec, Canada

Anne A. Lawrence, MD, PhD
Seattle, Washington

Ronald W. Lewis, MD
Department of Urology
Medical College of Georgia
Augusta, Georgia

Mijal Luria, MD
Department of Obstetrics
    and Gynaecology
Sexual Medicine Clinic
Hadassah University Hospital
Jerusalem, Israel

Patrick Lussier, PhD
School of Criminology
Simon Fraser University
Burnaby, British Columbia, Canada

Liam E. Marshall, MA
Rockwood Psychological Services
Kingston, Ontario, Canada

W. L. Marshall, OC, PhD, FRSC
Rockwood Psychological Services
Kingston, Ontario, Canada

Kristie McCann, MA
School of Criminology
Simon Fraser University
Burnaby, British Columbia, Canada

Chris G. McMahon, MD
Australian Center for Sexual Health
St. Leon, Australia

Cindy M. Meston, PhD
Department of Psychology
University of Texas—Austin
Austin, Texas

Serena Nanda, PhD
Department of Anthropology
New York University
New York, New York, and

John Jay College of Criminal Justice
City University of New York
New York, New York

Matt O'Brien, MSc
Rockwood Psychological Services
Kingston, Ontario, Canada

Vickie Pasterski, PhD, CPsych
Department of Psychology
City University
North Hampton Square, London,
    United Kingdom

Michael A. Perelman, PhD
Departments of Psychiatry,
    Reproductive Medicine, and Urology
Presbyterian Weill Cornell
    Medical Center
New York, New York

David L. Rowland, PhD
Department of Psychology
Valparaiso University
Valparaiso, Indiana

Brooke N. Seal, MA
Department of Psychology
University of Texas—Austin
Austin, Texas

Renee Sorrentino, MD
Institute for Sexual Wellness
Shirley, Massachusetts

Jacques van Lankveld, PhD
Department of Medical/Clinical and
    Experimental Psychology
University of Maastricht
Maastricht, The Netherlands

Eric J. N. Vilain, MD, PhD
Department of Human Genetics
UCLA School of Medicine
Los Angeles, California

Run Wang, MD
Department of Surgery
University of Texas Medical School—
    Houston
Houston, Texas

Jiuhong Yuan, MD
Department of Surgery
University of Texas Medical School—
    Houston
Houston, Texas

Kenneth J. Zucker, PhD, CPsych
Center for Addiction and Mental Health
Toronto, Ontario, Canada

SEXUAL DYSFUNCTIONS

Consistent with our peculiarly Western tendency to analyze, organize, and label things, the field of sexology has typically described sexual response as having desire, arousal, and resolution (orgasm) phases. This convenient (with respect to a nosology of diagnosing and treating sexual problems), but misleading characterization of sexual response has, for sexologists, been both a blessing and a bane. It enables us to speak a common language, to investigate more discrete units of analysis, and to thoroughly piece together small puzzles to produce greater understanding. At the same time, such structures impose artificial boundaries on our investigations, limit our abilities to incorporate theories and ideas from outside disciplines, and diminish the creativity with which we go about solving problems in the field.

We editors have complacently and expediently permitted ourselves to fall into this organizational trap, though, of course, differentiating between the responses of men and women. The result is that the various chapters purporting to cover a specific topic cannot do so without making reference to concepts and ideas germane to the other topics. But this is an asset rather than a liability, resulting in the reader sometimes being exposed to similar ideas multiple times through different lenses.

Thus, we include chapters dealing with the normal elements of sexual response and dysfunction on sexual desire (a slippery construct, but one with both a phenomenological reality and ability to help explain the frequency and intensity of sexual behaviors), sexual arousal, and sexual resolution (orgasm and ejaculation in the man). We are certain you will be struck by the substantial differences in approach in the chapters discussing male versus female sexual response. Whether this is a function of differences in the actual phenomena under discussion, in the advances made in each of the fields, in the importance of specific outcomes to treatment or in the perspectives and supporting language of the authors aligned with the issue is not always evident.

Beyond this basic coverage, we have included chapters on emerging or evolving topics, dealing specifically with vaginal pain in women (Is it a sex or a pain disorder?), hormones and aging in men (androgens affect more than just sexual health), aging and menopause in women (the challenge of separating the effects of one from the other), and sexuality and disease (people who are chronically ill lament the loss of their sexuality or face special challenges in realizing it).

Significant advances have been made with respect to men's sexuality, however, there are challenges facing researchers as they try to better understand women's sexuality, work with our current (and even recently modified) models of sexual response, and the systematic exploration of other areas.

Part I has two sections: Male sexual dysfunctions are discussed in Chapters 1 through 5, and female sexual dysfunctions are discussed in Chapters 6 through 10.

Disorders of Male Sexual Desire

Geoffrey Ian Hackett

1

Chapter

Learning Objectives

In this chapter, we discuss the:

- Nature and components of sexual desire.
- Epidemiology of desire problems in men.
- Physiology of sexual desire.
- Medical and psychological factors related to desire disorders.
- Management of hypoactive sexual desire disorder.
- Ethical concerns surrounding treatment.

Low sexual desire in men, clinically referred to as male hypoactive sexual desire disorder (HSDD), is a condition characterized by diminished or absent intensity or frequency of desire for sexual activity. The *Diagnostic and Statistical Manual for Mental Disorders* (*DSM*) first included male HSDD as a sexual disorder in 1977, and most recently *DSM-IV* (American Psychiatric Association, 2004) has defined it as:

> A. *Persistently or recurrently deficient (or absent) sexual fantasies and desire for sexual activity. The judgment of deficiency or absence is made by the clinician, taking into account factors that affect sexual functioning, such as age and the context of the person's life.*

B. *The disturbance causes marked distress or interpersonal difficulty.*

C. *The sexual dysfunction is not better accounted for by another Axis I disorder (except another Sexual Dysfunction) and is not due exclusively to the direct physiological effects of a substance (e.g., a drug of abuse, a medication) or a general medical condition. (p. 541)*

DSM-IV further qualifies HSDD as "acquired" if it develops after a period of normal sexual functioning or "generalized" if it is not limited to certain types of stimulation, situations, or partners.

A number of issues arise from the *DSM* definition. For example, the validity of the statement "unless explained by another medical disorder" has been the subject of discussion for two reasons. First, medical disorders such as depression and erectile dysfunction frequently coexist with low sexual desire, yet even the most thorough sexual history cannot always determine which variable explains the other. Second, it is not always clear when a particular factor affecting sexual desire might be classified as a "medical disorder." For example, testosterone deficiency may contribute to low sexual desire, yet researchers and clinicians have not yet reached a consensus regarding a threshold level for normal testosterone, below which would constitute a deficiency and thus warrant a medical diagnosis of hypogonadism.

Characterizing Sexual Desire and Its Components

Kaplan's (1995) model of the male sexual response concludes that desire in men is innate and spontaneous, leading to arousal, comprising erection and excitement, and further leading to orgasm and detumescence. Today, most experts would regard this view as simplistic because sexual desire is not a singular phenomenon that serves merely as a precursor to the other stages of the sexual response cycle. The *Oxford English Dictionary*'s (1989) definition for *libido*, a term frequently used in the clinical literature to denote sexual desire, hints at the true complexity of this construct. So defined, libido involves spontaneous sexual thoughts and fantasies, as well as attentiveness to external sexual stimuli that may be visual, auditory, or tactile.

Although no broad consensus exists regarding an accepted definition for sexual desire (and, indeed, it may differ for men versus women: see Chapter 6), in an attempt to capture its complex nature, Levine (2003) defines desire as "the motivation or inclination to be sexual" and suggests that this construct be considered in terms of the following components:

- *Drive* is the biological component of desire. Levine suggests that this component might one day be described in terms of a series of specific neurophysiological events. Male sex drive focuses primarily on intercourse and orgasm, whereas female sex drive focuses primarily on intimacy, with sexual activity viewed in this broader context and orgasm seen as optional (see Table 1.1).

- *Motive* is specific to the individual and related to the particular relationship dynamics (i.e., pertaining to the "relationship" reasons for wanting to have sex), as might be considered in terms of "she might leave me unless I have sex with her." Presumably this component is more pronounced in female desire.

- *Wish* refers to the cultural expectations that lead a person to want to have sex; in some instances it reflects the gender expectation of what it means, for instance, to be a "true man."

Hypoactive sexual desire disorder (HSDD), the nomenclature representing a clinical diagnosis of a low-desire problem, is a condition characterized by the absence or noticeable decrease in the frequency with which the man experiences the desire for sexual activity. Whether this condition constitutes a problem for the couple or causes distress within the relationship is frequently related to the desire disparity within the couple. A high level of disparity between partners is likely to distress one or both partners. In contrast, a low level of desire in both parties can be associated with low distress and a satisfactory relationship. As a result, low desire in either partner might never reach the point of clinical diagnosis.

HSDD frequently coexists with other sexual disorders (Meuleman & van Lankveld, 2005). For example, an important distinction concerning the diagnosis of low sexual desire is the exclusion of sexual aversion disorder, a condition where negative emotions such as fear, disgust, revulsion, or anger are expressed

Table 1.1 **Gender Differences in Sexuality**

Men	Women
Genital-focused	Intimacy-focused
Performance-orientated	Sex viewed in a broader context
Orgasm mandatory	Orgasm optional
Visual stimulus has primacy	Visual stimulus often distracting
Tactile stimulus often distracting	Tactile stimulus (not exclusively genital)
	Disparity often the issue

when engaging in sexual activity with a partner or when simply thinking about sex, either with that partner or more generally. Aversion cases are often the result of sexual trauma such as child abuse, conflict about sexuality, or abuse or infidelity by a partner. Such conditions clearly require specific targeted therapy that addresses these primary issues (Leiblum & Rosen, 2000) because low desire in these individuals is a by-product of these other conditions. Both in clinical practice and in epidemiological surveys exploring sexual desire, these components are frequently interwoven. In men, HSDD may also be associated with erectile dysfunction and is frequently erroneously diagnosed and treated as such, often with disappointing results because the primary sexual problem, namely sexual avoidance due to erectile failure, has not been addressed. Such complex situations where comorbid sexual problems exist require both astute diagnostic practices and treatment protocols.

Epidemiology

Prevalence Rates for Low Sexual Desire and Male Hypoactive Sexual Desire Disorder

The 1992 National Health and Social Life Survey (NHSLS; Laumann, Paik, & Rosen, 1999), which surveyed 1,410 men ages 18 to 59 in the United States, reported a prevalence rate of 5% for sexual desire disorders in men, 5% for erectile dysfunction (ED), and 22% for premature ejaculation. The prevalence of desire disorders in the female cohort was 23%. Although this study used suitable statistical methods for generating prevalence rates, the disparity between the low prevalence of ED reported in this study and much higher rates reported in subsequent studies casts doubt on the accuracy of the estimates, including those for sexual desire disorders. One of the potential problems of the NHSLS was that it required the participants' subjective evaluation on an item only indirectly related to low sexual desire: specifically, participants were asked whether they felt "reduced, normal, or higher than average" levels of sexual desire.

More recently, the Global Sexual Attitudes and Behaviors Study (GSSAB; Laumann, Nicolosi, Glasser, Paik, & Gingell, 2005), an international survey of 13,618 men from 29 countries, included a single item as to whether lack of sexual interest occurred occasionally, periodically, or frequently, with self-assessed ranges for these categories occurring between 13% and 28%. Because the GSSAB surveyed almost 10 times the number of men and included more detailed questions than the NHSLS, its prevalence rates are generally considered better estimates. No less important, these rates are more consistent with the clinical experiences of many health providers, and they are consistent with an earlier large United Kingdom population study on men ages 18 to 59 that found 14% to 17% reporting a lack of interest in sex (Seagraves & Seagraves, 1991).

However, self-reported low sexual desire is not synonymous with clinically diagnosed HSDD, and rates for male HSDD are still not clear. In population-based studies, HSDD has been reported in 0% to 15% of men and ED in 10% to 20% (Rosen, 2000). An analysis of 52 studies published between 1990 and 2000 using community samples yielded prevalence rates of 0% to 3% for male HSDD and 0% to 5% for ED (Simons & Carey, 2001). Not surprisingly, prevalence estimates from primary care and sexuality clinic samples have been characteristically much higher.

Covariates of Low Sexual Desire

A number of covariates of low desire have been identified; the NHSLS project found low desire related to such items as "thinking about sex less than once per week"; "having any sexual activity with a person of the same sex"; "partner ever having an abortion"; and "being sexually touched before puberty." In the GSSAB study, risk factors for low sexual interest included depression, high alcohol consumption, emotional problems or stress, and poor general health.

Perhaps the one factor that most consistently predicts low sexual desire is age. Low sexual desire was strongly correlated with age in both the NHSLS and GSSAB study, as well as in other studies (e.g., Dunn, Croft, & Hackett, 1998b). One community-based U.S. study found that 26% of men ages 70 and over had HSDD compared with only 0.6% ages 40 to 49 (Panser et al., 1995).

Gradual decreases in sexual desire are often considered a natural consequence of aging by respondents of many surveys. Decreased desire is less likely to cause distress to an individual if the onset is gradual (as occurs with aging) rather than sudden; many older couples simply adjust to this gradual age-related decline in sexual desire and activity. Nevertheless, at least 25% of men report an ongoing interest in having regular sexual activity (i.e., more often than monthly) into their eighties (Balon, 1996), and many older individuals and couples view sexual activity as an important aspect of individual and relationship well-being. Even though many men suffer a decline in sexual interest and activity, they are often too embarrassed to raise the topic with their physician.

Physiology of Desire and Drive Disorders in Men

While the psychoanalytic concept of libido is now over a century old, the experimental analysis of sexual motivation and drive was first undertaken by Beach in the 1950s. Based on research with male rats, Beach (1956) introduced the concept of the "dual nature of sexual arousal and performance," postulating that sexual behavior depends on two relatively independent processes, one controlling *motivation* (analogous perhaps to sexual desire or libido in humans) and the other *consummation*. Motivation—the use of the term by Beach differs from its use by Levine in the analysis of sexual desire discussed in the previous section—involves a sexual arousal mechanism that determines a male's sexual response to the perception of a receptive female. Its main function is to stimulate the male rat to approach a female and to raise its sexual excitement to the threshold necessary to activate the consummatory elements of sexual behavior, that is, mounting and intromission. Thereafter, the consummatory mechanism controls the intromission and ejaculatory elements of the male rat's sexual behavior, integrating the sequence of mounts and intromissions, thus amplifying the male's arousal until ejaculation occurs. Recent animal research has expanded Beach's model, showing, for instance, that the motivational and consummatory processes involve separate brain regions within the hypothalamic and limbic systems (Hamann, Herman, Nolan, & Wallen, 2004), independently modulated by androgenic and dopaminergic agents (Balthazart & Ball, 1998; Everitt, 1990; Pfaus, 1999). These animal studies suggest an intricate interplay among steroid hormone actions, specific brain regions, and environmental (including partner) stimuli that maintain central sexual arousability. From this, expectations of competent sexual functioning have been developed, including sexual desire, arousal, and performance. However, extrapolation of findings based on animal models to human sexual functioning remains controversial. Although recent work in neural and behavioral sciences has allowed exploration of the many factors that affect sexual motivation and performance in humans, even with this, the understanding of sexual desire in men remains incomplete. The following sections discuss a number of factors that are well-known to affect sexual desire.

Biological and Medical Factors Related to Low Sexual Desire and Hypoactive Sexual Desire Disorder

Research exploring sexual desire suggests that it may be related to any number of sexually specific and nonspecific factors. Some, such as androgen deficiency and relationship conflict, may be spe-

Table 1.2 **Common Factors Associated with Hypoactive Sexual Desire Disorder in Men**

Androgen deficiency

Hyperprolactinemia

Anger and anxiety

Depression

Relationship conflict

Cardiovascular accidents

Antidepressant therapy

Epilepsy

Posttraumatic Stress Syndrome

Renal failure

Coronary disease and heart failure

Aging

HIV

Bodybuilding and eating disorders

cific to the expression of sexual response. Others factors such as anger, depression, and related negative emotional states may entail broad psychological responses that depress sexual interest in general (see Table 1.2). Several factors known to affect men's sexual desire, along with several putative influencers, are discussed next.

Androgen Deficiency and Hypoactive Sexual Desire Disorder

Androgens (see Meston & Frohlich, 2000) are the major hormones regulating the biological component of desire in men (see Table 1.3). Extensive studies have shown that testosterone is necessary for the full-range of sexual responses (Everitt, 1995; Nelson, 2000) and is associated with depression in aging men (McIntyre et al., 2006). The normal physiological range of testosterone is usually above 10 to 12 nmol/L and is considerably higher than that necessary for normal sexual function. Critical testosterone levels for sexual function in males appear to be around 6 to 7 nmol/L (Traish & Guay, 2006), but with large intersubject variation (Nieschlag, 1979; also see Chapter 2, this volume).

Table 1.3 **Relative Potency of Androgens**

Androgen	Ratios
DHT (Dihydrotestosterone)	300
Testosterone	100
Androstenedione (adrenal)	10
DHEA, DHEA-S (adrenal)	5

The effect of androgens on sexual desire is robust and readily reproducible (Gooren, 1987). In hypogonadal patients (i.e., testosterone levels typically under 7 nmol/L), pathological withdrawal of androgens, followed by reintroduction of exogenous androgens, reliably affects variation in such parameters as the frequency of sexual fantasies, sexual arousal and desire, spontaneous erections during sleep and in the morning, ejaculation, sexual activities with and without a partner, and orgasms through coitus or masturbation (Gooren, 1987). However, in eugonadal men with or without sexual problems, the effect of testosterone administration on sexual parameters has received only limited study. In a controlled study of eugonadal men with diminished sexual desire, O'Carroll and Bancroft (1984) showed that, compared with placebo, injections of testosterone esters produced a significant increase in sexual interest; although in most participants, this increase did not lead to a general improvement of the sexual relationship. In other research, when supraphysiological doses of testosterone have been administered to healthy volunteers as a potential hormonal male contraceptive, significant increases in arousal were found, but sexual activity and spontaneous erections did not increase (Bagatell, Heiman, Matsumoto, Rivier, & Bremner, 1994; Bancroft, 1984). Thus, androgens may affect isolated aspects of sexual response in healthy men; but because healthy men typically produce much more androgen than is necessary to maintain sexual function, studies that modify testosterone levels within the normal range have led to the general conclusion that androgens are beneficial primarily to men whose endogenous levels are abnormally low.

Depression and Hypoactive Sexual Desire Disorder

Loss of sexual desire is a classic symptom of major depressive disorders, and therefore depression has played a prominent role in the psychodynamics and therapeutic management of the condition. Systematic studies suggest that low desire is present in up to 75% of depressed patients (Rosen et al., 1997; Spector, Carey, & Steinberg, 1996). Cause and effect are often difficult to ascertain: low desire may be a symptom of depression or may lead to depression as a consequence of its impact on the patient and his relationship. On the one hand, a full assessment of patients with HSDD and erectile dysfunction often reveals mild to moderate levels of depression (Saltzman, Guay, & Jacobson, 2004). Yet, treating the depression with antidepressant therapy is a common cause of HSDD, erectile dysfunction, and ejaculatory problems in men (see Case Study 1.1).

Estrogens and Sexual Desire in Men

Estradiol, the most biologically active estrogen in men, plays an important role on bone formation and serves as the most active

Case Study 1.1

Frank, a 62-year-old long-distance truck driver, was involved in a crash late at night when his truck jackknifed on a frozen road. The driver of an oncoming vehicle was killed, but Frank escaped with only cuts and grazes. For 4 weeks, he was unable to sleep but went back to work after only a couple of days because he felt that it was the best way to deal with his problem. For the next 2 months, he experienced outbursts of temper, poor sleep, and flashbacks of the accident. On several occasions, he had to pull the car over because he was shaking and feeling light-headed. His wife suggested that he see his general practitioner, who prescribed fluoxetine 20 mg. He returned after 3 weeks, and the dosage was increased to 40 mg with some improvement.

Twelve months after the accident, he returned to his general practitioner complaining of erectile dysfunction and was prescribed 50 mg of sildenafil (4 tablets); but he returned 3 months later saying that it had not worked. He and his wife June had always enjoyed a very active sex life right up until the accident. His insurance company had arranged a referral with a urologist to assess the relevance of the accident, the subsequent depression, and its association with his erectile dysfunction. The urologist reported that organic erectile dysfunction could not have been caused by his injuries and diagnosed "psychogenic erectile dysfunction," suggesting that he be referred for sex therapy. The patient requested a second opinion because his case was soon going to court, and he was claiming $60,000 for erectile dysfunction as a consequence of his accident.

A second opinion confirmed that he was in fact suffering from HSDD, secondary to posttraumatic stress disorder. In fact, since the accident, he had made no sexual attempts, avoided all possible sexual contact with his wife, and increased his workload to be away from home. Without telling June, he took two doses of sildenafil 50 mg and experienced no sexual stimulation. His sexual desire was virtually nonexistent from the time of starting fluoxetine.

Observation Points

1. A full sexual history would have elicited the lack of sexual attempts and stimulation.
2. Do not always accept the patient's opinion of his problem.
3. HSDD is often associated with posttraumatic stress.
4. This patient should have been given a full erectile dysfunction assessment for cardiovascular risk, diabetes, hypogonadism, and dyslipidaemia, despite the history. The general practitioner did not put himself in a position to diagnose the patient correctly.
5. The general practitioner could be liable for not assessing the case adequately and not warning the patient about the possible sexual side effects of the fluoxetine on sexual function.
6. Discontinuation of fluoxetine and relationship therapy improved the problem. He was found to have mild Type 2 diabetes, and his erections improved with tadalafil 20 mg, twice weekly, under the severe distress regime. His testosterone and lipids were normal.

metabolite of testosterone, affecting receptors in the brain; this latter function may underlie its possible role on sexual desire in men. Although no significant sexual dysfunction has been observed in men affected by congenital estrogen deficiency (Oettel, 2002), Carani et al. (2005), in a study on two men, observed a synergistic positive effect of estradiol and testosterone on sexual behavior. Yet, under some circumstances, estradiol may have a negative effect on sexual desire in men. In males, 20% of estradiol is formed by the Leydig cells in the testes and 80% in peripheral tissues, particularly visceral fat, from aromatization of testosterone or from adrenal androstenedione. As a result, estradiol levels are generally higher in men with increased visceral fat, as well as Type 2 diabetic patients, resulting in a relative lowering of total testosterone. As sex hormone binding globulin (SHBG) also rises with Type 2 diabetes, free (biologically active) testosterone is further lowered, to the extent that such men may experience reduced levels of desire. Obesity and Type 2 diabetes are also significant risk factors for erectile dysfunction.

Other evidence delineating a relationship between estrogen and male sexual response has been reported, but most is circumstantial to human response or correlational in nature. For example, experiments in male rats (e.g., Srilatha & Adiakan, 2004) have shown that increases in estrogen, including phytoestrogen (i.e., estrogens derived from plant sources), are associated with a reduction in circulating testosterone and erectile insufficiency in rats due to cavernal hypoplasia. In men, a link has been found between sexual dysfunction and exposure to pesticides with estrogenic or antiandrogenic properties (Oliva, Giami, & Multigner, 2002). Elevated estradiol levels have been observed in erectile dysfunction patients with veno-occlusive dysfunction (Mancini, Milardi, Bianchi, Summaria, & DeMarinis, 2005). Despite such associations, evidence is not yet sufficient to justify routine screening for estradiol in men with sexual desire problems or erectile dysfunction.

Dehydroepiandrosterone

Dehydroepiandrosterone (DHEA) is synthesized by the zona reticularis of the adrenal gland. DHEA is a weak androgen (see Table 1.3), available over the counter in many countries, having been reclassified in 1994 as a food supplement. DHEA is converted peripherally to testosterone by 17-beta hydroxysteroid dehydogenase (Siiteri, 2005). Although doses of 50 to 100 mg DHEA have been reported to improve sexual desire in men and women—with a slightly greater effect in women—a recent analysis of all published studies on the effect of DHEA indicates, at best, inconsistent results in men.

Hyperprolactinemia

Increased secretion of prolactin (PRL) may have negative effects on sexual desire by impairing the pulsatile release of luteinizing hormone (LH) and subsequently testosterone (Buvat, 2003). Schwartz,

Bauman, and Masters (1982) reported on a series of patients with hyperprolactinemia (HPL) and isolated HSDD and anorgasmia. Patients with HPL commonly have low or low-normal levels of testosterone, but improvement in sexual function by treatment with the PRL-lowering agent bromocryptine more closely mirrors the lowering of prolactin than the rise in testosterone (T). HPL is also associated with decreased 5-alpha reduction of T to DHT, the more active metabolite, especially on central T receptors. This effect on sexual desire is consistent with that of 5-alpha reductase inhibitors such as Finasteride (Buvat & Bou Jaoude, 2005). The effect HPL has on sexual desire may be mediated by the down regulation of central dopamine receptors; hypothalamic dopamine has been consistently implicated in human sexual desire. Not surprisingly, commonly used drugs that interfere with the prolactin-dopamine pathway may affect sexual desire and erectile function (see Table 1.4). Current recommendations call for the measurement of prolactin levels in conjunction with testosterone therapy in men with HSDD with or without associated erectile dysfunction.

Alcohol

At small doses, alcohol is widely used to relieve inhibitions and to overcome negative influences on sexual desire. At higher doses, alcohol acts as an inhibitor of desire predominantly through effects on the central nervous system and by inducing hepatic conversion of testosterone to estradiol, particularly as hepatic function deteriorates as the result of prolonged alcohol use. Gynaecomastia, testicular atrophy, and visceral obesity are associated with prolonged alcohol use.

Pheromones

Interest in the relationship between chemosensory cues and male desire, arousal, and behavior has developed recently (Cutler, Friedmann, & McCoy, 1998). Although such suppositions are based mostly on animal experimentation, human studies have indicated that, at high concentrations, pheromonal compounds are consciously detected and perceived as body scents and odors.

Table 1.4 **Drugs Likely to Increase Serum Prolactin and Interfere with Sexual Function**

Methadone
Psychotropic drugs especially phenothiazines and tricyclic antidepressants
Anti-emetics, especially metoclopramide
H2 blockers, especially cimetidine at high dose
Antihypertensives, especially Reserpine, methyldopa
Estrogens

Based on "The Neurology of Sexual Function," by C. M. Meston and P. E. Frohlich, 2000, *Archives of General Psychiatry, 57,* 1012–1030.

Presumably, humans show preferences for specific pheromones, can discriminate among them, and show both habituation to them and generalization about them. McClintock's (2006) research on human pheromones has concentrated on the major histocompatability complex (MHC) alleles, which are genetically distinct for each person. In an elaborate study involving women exposed to T-shirts with male odors from their paternal versus maternal side, these researchers concluded that paternally inherited HLA odors might serve as social cues mediating preferences and attraction (Jacob, Garcia, Hayreh, & McClintock, 2002). Although some putative pheromonal compounds have even been marketed in commercially available formulations for the purpose of increasing an individual's desirability to the opposite sex, the role of such compounds in inducing or modulating sexual desire in men remains elusive.

Other Medical and Biological Factors Associated with Sexual Desire

Cortisol appears to have a negative effect on desire, as seen in men with Cushing's syndrome (Starkman, Schteingart, & Schork, 1981). Serotonin usually has a negative effect as well, predominantly associated with feedback from interference with arousal and orgasm, as seen with most nonselective SSRI antidepressants (Montejo-Gonzalez et al., 1997). As suggested previously in the discussion of prolactin, dopamine agonists, particularly apomorphine and l-dopa derivatives, have been associated with increased desire, occasionally causing a problem in elderly male patients with Parkinson's disease who are treated with these preparations. Histamine is thought to have an attenuating effect on desire. The histamine receptor blockers, cimetidine and ranitidine, are associated with erectile dysfunction and estrogenic actions, particularly gynaecomastia (White & Rumbold, 1988). Moderate levels of hyperthyroidism (Carani et al., 2005) can enhance desire, whereas hypothyroidism has been associated with reduced desire in men and women.

Desire and Relationship Dynamics

Relationship dynamics play a critically important role in both general sexual desire and sexual desire for a specific partner. Kaplan's (1995) model for male and female desire describes inciting factors that activate the hypothalamic and limbic sex regulating centers, and suppressing factors, such as specific hormones, drugs, and depression, along with psychosocial inhibitors such as an unattractive partner, negative thoughts, antifantasies, negative emotions, stress, and anger. A common response to lack of desire is sexual avoidance, which may be associated with primary lack of desire or secondary to an associated disorder in men, particularly ED or premature ejaculation. Such problems can disturb the dynamics of the relationship. Although desire disorders are more common in women, low desire in either partner can create a *desire discrepancy* where the low desire partner feels pressure to initiate sex in order to maintain the relationship. In other situations, the partner with the lower desire, particularly when associated with sexual avoidance, often holds the balance of power within the relationship and may use this power as a means of control, punishment, or a way of dealing with hostility toward the partner with the higher desire. The relationship dynamics that evolve under such conditions are complex and usually require significant counseling and communication to untangle them (see Case Study 1.2).

Case Study 1.2

Peter is 54 years old and a successful company director. He suffers from mild hypertension and takes lisinopril 5 mg daily. He complains of total lack of interest in sex for the past 3 years. He gets few spontaneous erections. He blames his lifestyle, with frequent international travel and evening meetings. He rarely takes a holiday and his wife Liz, who is 52 years old, has also lost interest in sex since her hysterectomy 5 years ago. They have drifted apart and feel that they are now just friends. Liz attended a couples' support group, but Peter was too busy to attend.

On direct questioning, it became clear that Peter experienced a couple of episodes of erectile dysfunction over 3 years ago when Liz reluctantly agreed to intercourse not long after her hysterectomy. Around this time, Liz never initiated sex, whereas previously she had been the main initiator. His blood tests show well-controlled blood pressure and cholesterol, normal fasting glucose, and testosterone 11.0 nmol/L.

The clinician initiates treatment with Tadalafil 20 mg on demand, but he takes only one tablet and returns 4 weeks later to say that it did not work. When asked why he did not try more, he states that they have both been busy with work and their daughter's wedding. The clinician adds testosterone gel 50 mg daily for 2 weeks and tells him to take tadalafil regularly every Friday and Tuesday and have intercourse whenever he feels in the mood. The clinician explains to both of them that hypertension can be associated with erectile dysfunction and that low or borderline testosterone can be associated with suboptimal response to therapy. He also explains that relationship problems frequently occur secondary to this and that they need to communicate more, rather than use excuses.

The clinician sees them after 2 months and they have managed intercourse three times with total spontaneity and booked a holiday together. Liz has seen her general practitioner and has started hormone replacement therapy.

Observation Points

1. HSDD is frequently secondary to a change in sexual desire in the partner, creating a "desire disparity."
2. Successful men frequently deal with sexual failure by withdrawing contact, rather than confronting the issue.
3. Low desire in a partner, ED, and borderline testosterone often coexist and focusing on one problem as "the cause" can be unhelpful.
4. A strategy that works is the most important goal and may involve combined medications for both partners and relationship therapy.

Clinical Evaluation of Desire Disorders

General Questionnaires

Currently, no instrument for diagnosing and assessing HSDD has received widespread acceptance (Trudel, Ravart, & Matte, 1993). Sexual health care providers, who wish to be alert to a diagnosis of HSDD, should pose direct and unambiguous questions to patients about their sexual desire and motivation. This point is particularly relevant to men with HSDD, as they seldom reveal sexual problems unless explicitly invited (van Lankveld & van Koeveringe, 2003). Several reliable and valid questionnaires are available for assessing sexual desire problems, with easy-to-follow instructions. The Sexual Desire Inventory (Spector et al., 1996) was designed specifically to measure levels of sexual desire, the International Index of Erectile Function (IIEF) provides a subscale that measures sexual desire (Rosen et al., 1997), and the Golombok Rust Inventory of Sexual Satisfaction (GRISS) provides subscales of sexual avoidance and of infrequency of sexual contact (Rust & Golombok, 1985; ter Kuile, van Lankveld, Kalkhoven, & Van Egmond, 1999).

Patient Questions to Distinguish between Low Desire and Erectile Dysfunction

As indicated previously, the etiology of low desire may be complex, and low testosterone may not, in many cases, explain this condition in male patients. For example, many men with low desire have mean total and free testosterone levels in the normal range (Seagraves & Seagraves, 1991). For the male patient who reports little or no interest in sexual activity, the clinician should determine, at the outset, whether the problem relates to desire or to arousal. For example, a man claiming no interest in sex may be having difficulty getting an erection and therefore is avoiding sex, not that he is not interested in "being sexual."

Such distinctions are important because men with HSDD frequently present with an associated erection problem or premature ejaculation. For example, Corona et al. (2004) reported some element of HSDD in 43% of 428 men with erectile dysfunction. Therefore, the practitioner should ask specific questions of the patient to ascertain whether the desire problem is secondary to another sexual problem (Hoyl, Alessi, & Harker, 1999; Seagraves & Seagraves, 1991). Questions to differentiate a desire problem from another sexual dysfunction might take the following form or tap the following parameters:

- Despite your lack of interest, can you still get an erection?
- Compared to your past, how would you rate your interest in sex?

- If you can get an erection, do you think you would be interested in having sex?
- What is your frequency of sexual activity? (The clinician should realize that sexual activity may be normal, but the activity is done without desire.)
- How often do you have thoughts about sex?
- How often do you have sexual fantasies (whether they include the partner)?
- Who initiates sexual activity in your relationship and has this changed recently?

Additional points that may be useful in assessing HSDD are included in Table 1.5.

Psychological and Relationship Issues

In addition to scores on "desire" scales or subscales of questionnaires, an adequate evaluation takes into consideration the patient's complaint within the context of the his age, lifestyle, emotional disposition, life stressors and transitions, partner considerations and functioning, and relationship dynamics. In instances where male HSDD is suspected, at least one clinic visit with the partner present is highly desirable.

Indeed, obtaining pertinent information on the above parameters often provides insight into problems of low sexual desire and, in some cases, may obviate the need for extensive laboratory testing and/or increase the probability of an appropriate treatment strategy. Whereas general sexual questionnaires (as described previously) may tap such information, a 15 to 20 minute semi-structured interview reveals further information that can assist in determining the subsequent steps in the evaluation process.

The diagnosis of underlying or comorbid depression is often important to addressing low desire issues, and patient medical

---

Table 1.5 **Assessing Sexual Desire:
Always/Usually/Sometimes/Occasionally/Never**

Do you experience pleasurable thoughts about sex?

Do you initiate lovemaking?

Easy to get and stay aroused?

Sexual fantasies?

Responsive to partner's overtures?

Self-stimulation?

Do you miss sex?

histories may cue the health provider to explore this issue further. Questionnaires such as the Hamilton Depression Rating Scale (HAM-D), Hospital Anxiety and Depression Scale (HADS), and Beck Depression Inventory (BDI) may be useful for this purpose.

Laboratory Investigations

Relevant laboratory investigations for men with low sexual desire (Wespes et al., 2006) may include, but not be limited to, fasting glucose, lipids, morning testosterone, LH, serum prolactin, and thyroid function tests (if clinically indicated by the medical history or examination). Although these tests are unlikely to provide any conclusive determination regarding the etiology or cause of a desire problem, they may provide the clinician with insight into potential abnormal physiological profiles that contribute to the problem.

Management of Hypoactive Sexual Desire Disorder

No single "curative" therapy exists for HSDD; rather, most cases require a complex assessment and management strategy that addresses physiological, psychological, and relationship factors. Some men, for example, do not suffer distress from their lack of interest in sex and do not wish treatment—their "medical" compliance is driven by a partner with a higher level of sexual interest. Other contributing issues may need to be explored and assessed as well, including coexisting sexual problems in the partner, especially low desire and vaginal atrophy (Dunn, Croft, & Hackett, 1998a). A comprehensive approach to management of HSDD should include all of the following elements (although not necessarily in the order provided):

- Managing the patient with borderline or low testosterone.
- Addressing associated sexual dysfunctions, most commonly erectile dysfunction.
- Dealing with depression and antidepressant-related HSDD.
- Dealing with psychological and relationship issues, either alone or in conjunction with these strategies.

Managing the Patient with Borderline or Low Testosterone

Testosterone (T) therapy can be effective when hypogonadism is evident by levels of T below 7 to 8 nmol/L on two occasions; such levels have been associated with low desire. Levels between 8 and 12 nmol/L are in the "grey" area and may be treated with a 3-month trial of T, instructing the patient not to expect a response in less than 30 days. Men with levels over 12 nmol/L are unlikely to show improvement of HSDD, and there is no convincing evidence for improvement in erections by treating men with normal testosterone levels (Wespes et al., 2006).

For HSDD patients with low T, studies have shown improvement in sexual desire and ejaculatory and orgasmic function following 6 months of T, with positive effects for some men occurring within 30 days of treatment onset (Wang et al., 2000). Patients should have T levels checked at 3 months and every 12 months thereafter; for such men, PSA and a full blood count should be assessed prior to treatment, with annual checks thereafter (Nieschlag et al., 2005; Wespes et al., 2006). Treatment for established hypogonadism should be viewed as having an indefinite end time, although if the primary reason for treatment was low desire, then cessation of therapy may be negotiated if the circumstances of the couple should change.

Formulations of testosterone commercially available are shown in Table 1.6. Oral therapies are seldom used, due to possible hepatotoxicity and the requirement for doses 2 to 3 times daily. Injection of testosterone undecanoate as Sustanon 100 and 250 causes fluctations outside the normal range over the 2-week period between injections, and, as a result, many partners find the mood changes associated with these fluctuations unacceptable. Furthermore, this preparation causes increased risk of polycythaemia due to intermittent T peaks. In contrast, a long-acting

Table 1.6   **Choice of Testosterone Therapy**

Route	Formulation	Dose (mg)	Frequency
Injectable	T propionate in oil	10–25	Twice weekly
	T cypionate in oil	50–250	2–4 weeks
	T enanthate in oil	50–250	2–4 weeks
	T undecanoate in oil	1,000	10–14 weeks
Oral	T undecanoate	40–80	2–3 times daily
	T undecanoate caps	40–80	Twice daily
	Mesterolone	75–150	Once daily
Buccal	T buccal stem	30	Twice daily
Transdermal	T patch	5	Once or twice daily
	T gel	50–100	Once daily
Subcutaneous	T pellet	600	16–26 weeks

3-month depot injection of 1,000 mg, such as with Nebido™, keeps sustained levels within the normal range and shows promising improvements in desire and erections.

Testosterone gel (50 to 100 mg applied topically daily) is usually the treatment choice of most patients and is well tolerated with excellent efficacy. Patches are equally effective, but skin irritation is a problem in up to 25% of users, and current patches are too readily visible for many men. Any adverse events are readily reversible with these short-acting transdermal formulations, in contrast with long-acting formulations, which are best used only after tolerance and efficacy of the testosterone has been established. Several additional agents are currently under investigation for HSDD, although predominantly in women. Generally, the most promising drugs are those acting as a $5\text{-}HT_{2A}$ and dopamine agonists. Presumably, such drugs would also be effective in men with HSDD.

Testosterone Therapy in Conjunction with PDE-5 Inhibitors in Patients with Cardiovascular Disease

With the development of clear guidelines for erectile dysfunction (Nieschlag et al., 2005; Wespes et al., 2006), the association between erectile dysfunction, hypogonadism, and metabolic disorders (such as diabetes and cardiovascular disease) has received some clarification (see also Chapters 3 and 5, this volume). Hypogonadism has been found to occur in about 20% of erectile dysfunction patients and up to 40% of Type 2 diabetics (Dhinsa et al., 2004). The Health in Men (HIM) Study in Australia indicates strong links between hypogonadism and metabolic syndrome (Mulligan, Frick, Zuraw, Stemhagen, & McWhirter, 2006), and data from the Massachusetts Male Aging Study (Araujo et al., 2004) suggest that low testosterone is associated with increased cardiovascular risk and a threefold cancer risk. Such studies suggest complex and interactive relationships among low testosterone/hypogonadism, erectile dysfunction, and various metabolic disorders. To make the issue of treatment more complex, Type 2 diabetics traditionally have low response rates to PDE-5 inhibitors, such as sildenafil (Viagra; Goldstein et al., 2003; Rendell, Rajfer, Wicker, & Smith, 1999; Saenz de Tejada, Anglin, Knight, & Emmick, 2002). One study suggests a possible alternative to the use of PDE-5 inhibitors. Treating hypertension with Angiotensin II receptor blockers (ARBs) appears to improve both erectile dysfunction and sexual desire levels (Fogari, Preti, et al., 2002; Fogari, Zoppi, et al., 2002). Dusing (2003) studied 3,502 treated and untreated hypertensive patients with the ARB, Valsarten, for 6 months and reported improved erectile function and sexual desire in both groups. Thus, ARBs might improve sexual function and desire in hypertensive males.

Frequently, an element of HSDD coexists with erectile dysfunction. Studies suggest 32% to 50% of patients in this category achieve satisfactory response to testosterone alone and, as might be expected, the response to subsequent use of a PDE-5 inhibitor is typically greater following normalization of serum testosterone. The rationale for correcting testosterone first is:

- Erectile dysfunction improvement will allow for spontaneous sex without requiring additional medication.
- Enhancement of sexual desire is beneficial.
- Improvement in orgasm and ejaculatory function.
- Subsequent prescription of PDE-5 inhibitors is likely to be more effective if testosterone is normalized.
- Testosterone is likely to be reimbursed by insurers.
- Patients would expect clinical abnormalities to be treated rather than "symptomatic" therapy.

In patients with multiple risk factors or with the desire for a quick response, both T and PDE-5 inhibitor treatments may be commenced simultaneously, with the possibility of reducing or withdrawing the PDE-5 inhibitor at a later date.

In support of this strategy, the use of PDE-5 inhibitors by themselves in men with coexisting erectile dysfunction and HSDD may simply not be effective, even when prescribed at an appropriate dose on multiple occasions. Under such circumstances, the clinician's recourse may be to suggest intracavernosal injection therapy, though this treatment is often resisted by patients. Work by Shabsigh, Kaufman, Steidle, and Padma-Nathan (2004), Shabsigh et al. (2006), and Greco, Spera, and Aversa (2006) suggests that nonresponding patients become responsive to oral therapy with the correction of borderline or low-normal levels of testosterone. Thus, in men with erectile dysfunction, the practitioner needs to understand the importance of investigating low desire and possibly low T.

Although PDE-5 inhibitors are generally intended for "as needed" use (taken several hours prior to anticipated intercourse), coexisting erectile dysfunction and HSDD is often best treated with *regular* dosing of a longer acting PDE-5 inhibitor 2 to 3 times weekly. Not surprisingly, men with low desire often find that taking an as-needed tablet prior to initiating sexual activity is problematic, particularly given their low desire for sex. However, by regular dosing, spontaneous erections are more likely to return and to motivate the man to a higher level of sexual interest. This strategy helps eliminate problems reported by some low desire couples that find the requirement to negotiate sex around planned tablet taking unacceptable.

The use of testosterone therapy in this way is now accepted practice for solving the coexisting complaints of lack of desire and erectile dysfunction. Endocrinologists, who do not routinely manage sexual problems, sometimes misunderstand the rationale underlying this approach, and they confuse the use of T in such cases as misguided attempts to overcome problems of aging or a search for a "fountain of youth."

Antidepressants and Hypoactive Sexual Desire Disorder

Antidepressant-induced HSDD has a complex physiological and psychological basis. When caused by depression, the sexual problem usually takes the form of reduced interest and pleasure (Casper et al., 1985), which then leads to reduced sexual arousal and erectile capability, the most common presenting symptom. Most of these sexual functions are mediated through the mesolimbic dopamine pathways; specifically, these pathways are inhibited by the serotonergic input to 5-HT_2 receptors, which are believed to mediate pleasure and reward (Seidman & Rouse, 2001). Abnormal functioning of these pathways is linked with anhedonia and craving for substances of abuse (Rosen, Lane, & Menza, 1999). In simple terms, there is a reciprocal relationship between serotonin (5-HT) and dopamine, with serotonin (or at least this specific subtype of serotonin receptors) tending to inhibit sexual functioning and dopamine tending to enhance it. This relationship explains why selective serotonin reuptake inhibitor (SSRI) antidepressants, such as paroxetine and fluoxetine, which disinhibit the serotonergic pathways innervating the mesolimbic system, can cause sexual dysfunction (Rosen et al., 1999).

Estimates are that about one-third of patients on SSRIs develop sexual problems which, in turn, reduce compliance with prescribed medications (Seidman & Roose, 2001). In addition to problems with sexual desire and arousal, SSRIs can influence ejaculation and orgasm by acting on descending pathways in the brainstem and spinal cord (Seidman & Roose, 2000). The action of the SSRIs on these pathways is thought to explain the increase in genital sensory threshold and the experience of genital anesthesia frequently mentioned by men with HSDD (Ashton, 1998). Sexual problems are seen less commonly with older antidepressants, such as the tricyclics and monoamine oxidase inhibitors (Rosen et al., 1999), and agents that stimulate dopamine can often reverse SSRI-induced sexual dysfunction.

Management Issues in Depression

When the depression is mild, treatment with both PDE-5 inhibitors and testosterone demonstrates improvement in mood and depression scores (Feldman, Goldstein, Hatzichristou, Krane, & McKinlay, 1994; O'Connor, Archer, & Wu, 2004), suggesting a preferred option for both the practitioner and the patient or couple. With more severe depression, appropriate intervention with an effective antidepressant at an appropriate dose should be prescribed, often combined with cognitive behavioral therapy (CBT; Seidman & Rouse, 2001). Sometimes reducing the dose or waiting for tolerance to develop can help mitigate possible effects on sexual function (Seidman & Rouse, 2001).

Certain antidepressants carry less risk of adversely affecting sexual desire, but adequate treatment of the depression is the most important and primary goal. Mirtazepine (Gelenberg et al., 2000) may be the antidepressant with the best profile in such cases, although nefazadone has also been used with some success, largely on the basis of initial reports of prolonged erection with overdose (Seidman & Roose, 2000). Bupropion has been used with success in HSDD in the United States, and two trials reported good results relative to sexual functioning, although primarily in women (Ferris, Cooper, & Maxwell, 1983). Bupropion (Ferris et al., 1983; Labbate, Grimes, Hines, & Pollack, 1997; Roeloffs, Bartlik, Kaplan, & Kocsis, 1996) has been used mainly for smoking cessation in the United Kingdom, and the reported side effects and the lack of a regulatory approval for sexual problems is likely to limit its use in the treatment of HSDD. Tianeptine is an SSRI available in Europe, with neutral or slightly beneficial effects on sexual desire (Bonierbale, Lançon, & Tignol, 2003). Studies involving substitution of tianeptine for other SSRIs have shown improvement in sexual desire and at least in one case, erection as well (El-Shafey et al., 2006). A variety of medications have been used with limited success on depression or antidepressant-induced low sexual desire, including the dopamine agonists amantidine (Balon, 1996) and cyproheptidine (Lauerma, 1996), psychostimulants such as methyphenidate (Roeloffs et al., 1996), and ginkgo biloba (Balon, 1999). However, none of these approaches has achieved widespread acceptance.

Psychotherapy and Sex Therapy

Sex and relationship therapy, either alone or combined with one or more of the previous strategies (Buvat et al., 2006), is frequently helpful or essential, and depends on the clinician's and patient's insights gained through the initial evaluation or, later, through interpersonal developments during the course of treatment. Specific psychotherapy usually includes the following components: (a) affectual awareness to address the sources of negative and positive emotions, (b) insight and understanding, (c) cognitive and systemic therapy, and (d) behavioral intervention.

Common patterns of relationship dynamics are associated with low sexual desire (Leiblum & Rosen, 2000), for example:

- Partner differences in the desired frequency of sexual contact.
- Attitudes toward sexual behavior and arousal.
- Power and control issues related to initiation and type of sexual contact.
- Ineffective communication related to sexuality.
- Conflict in view of sexual contact as a "right to pleasure."
- Sexual interaction bogged down in ritual and routine.
- Issues of privacy.
- Discovery of extramarital relationships.
- Issues related to jealousy and/or possessiveness.
- Issues related to infertility and pregnancy.
- Life cycle changes and the aging process.
- Illness and disability of one or both partners.

For those couples who present with low sexual desire, methodical exploration of some or all of the these aspects of the relationship by an experienced clinician is likely to produce positive outcomes. Usually, this exploration is best carried out with each partner individually, followed by a session involving both partners. However, even in situations that do not lend themselves to extensive exploration of these issues (as is the case when a primary care physician is presented with the problem), a brief inquiry about such issues may be fruitful in determining whether brief therapy might be beneficial to the couple's resolution of the problem. Indeed, it is unlikely that a primary care physician would be able to deliver the full range of therapy required to address these problems without the support of a specialist. Scales such as the Quebec 2000 abbreviated Dyadic Adjustment Scale (DAS) may be used to standardize couples' responses (Begin, Sabourin, Bovin, Frenette, & Paradis, 2002).

Treatment of a low-desire problem may involve general strategies that benefit the relationship, including better communication strategies, normalizing the problem, negotiating the needs of each partner, dealing with generalized stress and time issues, and so on. At the same time, strategies specific to sexual response may also be warranted, including behaviors by the partner that increase attractiveness, incorporating greater variation and stimulation into the sexual situation, and addressing issues of sexual satisfaction and control.

Ethical Concerns

When oral therapies were first developed for erectile dysfunction, the pharmaceutical industry was relieved to learn from clinical trials that these agents did not directly increase levels of sexual desire, specifically as assessed by the IIEF. Despite this, a few high-profile legal cases were brought to court, with claims that the use of these drugs had induced high levels of desire in men that led to infidelity or coerced sex.

The development of drugs or therapeutic procedures that enhance male sexual interest will always be associated with public concerns about sex offenses. Health care practitioners, who prescribe agents or engage in therapies specifically designed to improve sexual desire, therefore need to approach the issue of enhancing sexual drive and desire with an awareness of these concerns.

Summary and Conclusions

As more is understood about the issues of low sexual desire, the current definition of HSDD in males is likely to change in ways that will assist in the management of this problem. In everyday practice, HSDD is most often treated when it causes distress to the patient or his partner; it is also often treated in association with other dysfunctions such as erectile dysfunction and premature ejaculation. However, significant relationship issues might also be involved in the development and maintenance of HSDD, and these need to be explored as well.

Within the medical clinic, erectile dysfunction is the most common presenting symptom and a careful psychosexual and medical history is required to confirm the presence of HSDD. Normalization of testosterone levels in hypogonadal men offers the best hope for success, along with the effective management of the associated coexisting sexual and relationship issues.

Currently, there are no therapies approved by the U.S. Food and Drug Administration (FDA) for HSDD in men, apart from testosterone therapy for associated hypogonadism. Several potential new drugs are under investigation in clinical trials and are likely to be licensed initially for the treatment of HSDD in women. However, practitioners should be aware that by the time most cases appear at a clinical practice, simple drug treatments may not be adequate, and more complex approaches to therapy, including dealing with psychological and relationship issues, may be required.

References

American Psychiatric Association. (2000). *Diagnostic and statistical manual of mental disorders* (4th ed., text rev.). Washington, DC: Author.

Araujo, A. B., O'Donnell, A. B., Brambilla, D. J., Simpson, W. B., Longcope, C., Matsumoto, A., et al. (2004). Prevalence and incidence of androgen deficiency in middle-aged and older men: Estimates from the Massachusetts Male Aging Study. *Journal of Clinical Endocrinology and Metabolism, 89,* 5920–5926.

Ashton, K. (1998). Accommodation to selective serotonin reuptake inhibitor induced sexual function. *Journal of Sex and Marital Therapy, 24,* 191–192.

Bagatell, C. J., Heiman, J. R., Matsumoto, A. M., Rivier, J. E., & Bremner, W. J. (1994). Metabolic and behavioural effects of high-dose exogenous testosterone in healthy men. *Journal of Clinical Endocrinology and Metabolism, 79,* 561–567.

Balon, R. (1996). Intermittent amantidine for fluoxetine induced anorgasmia. *Journal of Sex and Marital Therapy, 2,* 290–292.

Balon, R. (1999). Ginko biloba for antidepressant induced sexual dysfunction. *Journal of Sex and Marital Therapy, 25,* 1–2.

Balthazart, J., & Ball, G. F. (1998). The Japanese quail as a model system for the investigation of steroid-catecholamine interactions mediating appetitive and consummatory aspects of male sexual behavior. *Annual Review of Sex Research, 9,* 96–176.

Bancroft, J. (1984). Hormones and human sexual behaviour. *Journal of Sex and Marital Therapy, 10,* 3–21.

Beach F. A. (1956). Characteristics of masculine "sex drive." In M. R. Jones (Ed.), *Nebraska Symposium on Motivation* (Vol. 4, pp. 1–31). Lincoln, NE: University of Nebraska Press.

Begin, C., Sabourin, M., Bovin, E., Frenette, E., & Paradis, H. (2002). The couple: Pt. 1. Couple distress and factors associated with evaluating the spousal relationship. In Quebec Longitudinal Study of Child Development (QLSCD 1998–2002): From Birth to 29 Months. *Institut de la statistique du Quebec, 2*(11), 19–31.

Bonierbale, M., Lançon, C., & Tignol, J. (2003). The ELIXIR Study: Evaluation of sexual dysfunction in 4557 depressed patients in France. *Current Medical Research and Opinion, 19*(2), 114–124.

Buvat, J. (2003). Hyperprolactinaemia and sexual function in men: A short review. *International Journal of Impotence Research, 15,* 373–377.

Buvat, J., & Bou Jaoude, G. (2005). Hyperprolactinaemia et fonctsexuelle chez l'homme. *Adrologie, 15,* 366–373.

Buvat, J., Shabsigh, R., Guay, A., Gooren, L., Torres, L. O., & Meuleman, E. (2006). Hormones, metabolism, aging and men's health. In H. Porst & J. Buvat (Eds.), *Standard practice in sexual medicine* (pp. 225–286). Oxford: Blackwell.

Carani, C., Granata, A. R. M., Rochira, V., Caffagni, G., Aradna, C., Antunez, P., et al. (2005). Sex steroids and sexual desire in a man with a novel mutation of aromatase gene and hypogonadism. *Psychoneuroendocrinology, 30,* 413–417.

Carani, C., Isidori, A. M., Granata, A., Carosa, E., Maggi, M., Lenzi, A., et al. (2005). Multicenter study on the prevalence of sexual symptoms in male hypo- and hyperthyroid patients. *Journal of Clinical Endocrinology and Metabolism, 90,* 6472–6479.

Casper, R. C., Redmond, D. E., Jr., Katz, M. M., Schaffer, C. B., David, J. M., & Koss, S. H. (1985). Somatic symptoms in primary affective disorder: Presence and relationship to the classification of depression. *Archives of General Psychiatry, 42,* 1098–1104.

Corona, G., Mannucci, E., Petrone, L., Glommi, R., Mansani, R., Fei, L., et al. (2004). Psychobiological correlates of hypoactive sexual desire in patients with erectile dysfunction. *International Journal of Impotence Research, 16,* 275–281.

Cutler, W. B., Friedmann, E., & McCoy, N. L. (1998). Pheromonal influences on sociosexual behaviour in men. *Archives of Sexual Behavior, 27,* 1–13.

Dhinsa, S., Prabhakar, S., Sethi, M., Bandyopadhyay, A., Chaudhuri, A., & Dandona, P. (2004). Frequent occurrence of hypogonadatrophic hypogonadiam in type 2 diabetes. *Journal of Clinical Endocrinology and Metabolism, 89*(11), 5462–5468.

Dunn, K., Croft, P., & Hackett, G. (1998a). Association of sexual problems with social, psychological, and physical problems in men and women: A cross sectional population survey. *Journal of Epidemiology and Community Health, 52,* 12–16.

Dunn, K., Croft, P., & Hackett, G. (1998b). Sexual problems: A study of prevalence and need for health care in the general population. *Family Practice, 15*(6), 14–19.

Dusing, R. (2003). Effect of angiotensin II antagonist valsarten on sexual function in hypertensive men. *Blood Pressure, Supplement, 12,* 29–34.

El-Shafey, H., Atteya, A., Abu El-Magd, S., Hassanein, A., Fathy, A., & Shamloul, R. (2006). Tianeptine can be effective in men with depression and erectile dysfunction. *Journal of Sexual Medicine, 3*(5), 910–917.

Everitt, B. J. (1990). Sexual motivation: A neural and behavioural analysis of the mechanisms underlying appetitive and copulatory responses of male rats. *Neuroscience and Biobehavioral Reviews, 14,* 217–232.

Everitt, B. J. (1995). Neuroendocrine mechanisms underlying appetitive and consummatory elements of masculine sexual behaviour. In J. Bancroft (Ed.), *The pharmacology of sexual function and dysfunction* (pp. 15–31). Amsterdam: Exerpta Medica.

Feldman, H. A., Goldstein, I., Hatzichristou, D. G., Krane, R. J., & McKinlay, J. B. (1994). Impotence and its medical and psychosocial correlates: Results of the Massachusetts Male Aging Study. *Journal of Urology, 151,* 54–61.

Ferris, R. M., Cooper, B. R., & Maxwell, R. A. (1983). Studies of Bupropion's mechanism of antidepressant activity. *Journal of Clinical Psychiatry, 44,* 74–78.

Fogari, R., Preti, P., Derosa, G., Marasi, G., Zoppi, A., Rinaldi, A., et al. (2002). Effect of antihypertensive treatment with valsarten and atenolol on sexual activity and testosterone in hypertensive men. *European Journal of Clinical Pharma, 58,* 177–180.

Fogari, R., Zoppi, A., Poletti, L., Marasi, G., Mugellini, A., & Coradi, L. (2001). Sexual activity in hypertensive men treated with valsarten and carvedilol: A cross over study. *American Journal of Hypertension, 14,* 27–31.

Gelenberg, A. J., MacGahuey, C., Laukes, C., Okayli, G., Moreno, F., Zentner, L., et al. (2000). Mirtazapine substitution in SSRI-induced sexual dysfunction. *Journal of Clinical Psychiatry, 61*(5), 356–360.

Goldstein, I., Young, J. M., Fischer, J., Bangerter, K., Segerson, T., & Taylor, T. (2003). Vardenafil, a new phosphodiesterase type 5 inhibitor, in the treatment of erectile dysfunction in men with diabetes: A multicenter double-blind placebo-controlled fixed-dose study. *Diabetes Care, 26,* 777–783.

Gooren, L. J. G. (1987). Androgen levels and sex functions in testosterone-treated hypogonadal men. *Archives of Sexual Behavior, 16,* 463–473.

Greco, E. A., Spera, G., & Aversa, A. (2006). Combining testosterone and PDE5 inhibitors in erectile dysfunction: Basic rationale and clinical evidences. *European Urology, 50,* 940–947.

Hamann, S., Herman, R. A., Nolan, C. L., & Wallen, K. (2004). Men and women differ in amygdala response to visual sexual stimuli. *Nature Neuroscience, 7,* 411–416.

Hoyl, M. T., Alessi, C. A., & Harker, J. O. (1999). Development and testing of the five-item geriatric depression scale in elderly subjects in three different settings. *Journal of the American Geriatric Society, 47,* 873–878.

Jacob, S., Garcia, S., Hayreh, D., & McClintock, M. (2002). Psychological effects of musky hormones: Comparison of androstadienone with androstenol and muscone. *Hormones and Behavior, 42,* 274–283.

Kaplan, H. S. (1995). *The sexual desire disorders: Dysfunctional regulation of sexual motivation.* New York: Brunner/Mazel.

Labbate, L. A., Grimes, J. B., Hines, A., & Pollack, M. H. (1997). Bupropion treatment of serotonin reuptake associated sexual dysfunction. *Annals of Clinical Psychiatry, 9,* 241–245.

Lauerma, H. (1996). Successful treatment of citalopram induced anorgasmia by cyproheptidine. *Acta Psychiatrica Scandinavica, 93,* 69–70.

Laumann, E. O., Nicolosi, A., Glasser, D. B., Paik, A., & Gingell, C. (2005). Sexual problems among men and women aged 40–80 yrs: Prevalence and correlates identified in the global study of sexual attitudes and behaviours. *International Journal of Impotence Research, 17,* 39–57.

Laumann, E. O., Paik, A., & Rosen, R. C. (1999). Sexual dysfunction in the United States: Prevalence and predictors. *Journal of the American Medical Association, 281*(6), 537–544.

Leiblum, S., & Rosen, R. (2000). *Principles and practice of sex therapy* (3rd ed.). New York: Guilford Press.

Levine, S. B. (2003). The nature of sexual desire: A clinician's perspective. *Archives of Sexual Behavior, 32*(3), 279–285.

Mancini, A., Milardi, D., Bianchi, A., Summaria, V., & DeMarinis, L. (2005). Increased estradiol levels in veno-occlusive disorder: A possible functional method of venous leakage. *International Journal of Impotence Research, 17,* 329–342.

McClintock, M. (2006, March). Human scents and pheromones: Effects on fertility, sexual motivation and mood. *Proceedings of International Society for the Study of Women's Sexual Health,* 133–134.

McIntyre, R. S., Mancini, D., Eisfeld, B. S., Soczynska, J. K., Grupp, L., Konarski, J. Z., et al. (2006). Calculated bioavailable testosterone levels and depression in middle-aged men. *Psychoneuroendocrinology, 31,* 1029–1035.

Meston, C. M., & Frohlich, P. E. (2000). The neurology of sexual function. *Archives of General Psychiatry, 57,* 1012–1030.

Meuleman, E. J., & Van Lankveld, J. J. (2005). Hypoactive sexual desire disorder: An underestimated condition in men. *British Journal of Urology International, 95,* 201–296.

Montejo-Gonzalez, A. L., Llorca, G., Izquierdo, J. A., Ledesman, A., Bousono, M., Calcedo, A., et al. (1997). SSRI induced dysfunction: Fluoxetine, paroxetine, sertraline and fluvoxamine in a prospective multicentre and descriptive clinical study of 344 patients. *Journal of Sex and Marital Therapy, 23,* 176–193.

Mulligan, T., Frick, M. F., Zuraw, Q. C., Stemhagen, A., & McWhirter, C. (2006). Prevalence of hypogonadism in males aged at least 45 years: The HIM study. *International Journal of Clinical Practice, 60*(7), 762–769.

Nelson, R. J. (2000). *An introduction to behaviorial endocrinology* (2nd ed.). Sunderland, MA: Sinauer Associates.

Nieschlag, E. (1979). The endocrine function of human testis in regard to sexuality. In *Ciba Foundation Symposium: Sex, hormones and behaviour* (pp. 182–208). Amsterdam: Excerpta Medica.

Nieschlag, E., Swerdloff, R., Behre, H. M., Gooren, L. J., Kaufman, J. M., Legros, J. J., et al. (2005). Investigation, treatment and monitoring of lateonset hypogonadism in males: ISA, ISSAM, and EAU Recommendations. *Journal of Andrology, 28,* 125–127.

O'Carroll, R., & Bancroft, J. (1984). Testosterone therapy for low sexual interest and erectile dysfunction in men: A controlled study. *British Journal of Psychiatry, 145,* 146–151.

O'Connor, D. B., Archer, J., & Wu, F. C. W. (2004). Effects of testosterone on mood, aggression and sexual behaviour in young men: A double blind, placebo controlled cross-over study. *Journal of Clinical Endocrinology and Metabolism, 89,* 2837–2845.

Oettel, M. (2002). Is there a role for oestrogens in the maintenance of men's health? *Aging Male, 5,* 248–257.

Oliva, A., Giami, A., & Multigner, L. (2002). Environmental agents and erectile dysfunction: A study of consulting populations. *Journal of Andrology, 23,* 546–550.

Oxford English Dictionary (2nd ed.). (1989). Oxford: Oxford University Press.

Panser, L. A., Rhodes, T., Girman, C. J., Guess, H. A., Chute, C. G., & Oesterling, J. E. (1995). Sexual dysfunction of men aged 40 to 79 years: Olmstead county study of urinary symptoms among men. *Journal of the American Geriatric Society, 43,* 1107–1111.

Pfaus, J. G. (1999). Neurobiology of sexual behavior. *Current Opinion in Neurobiology, 9,* 751–758.

Rendell, M. S., Rajfer, J., Wicker, P. A., & Smith, M. D. (1999). Sildenafil for treatment of erectile dysfunction in men with diabetes: A randomized controlled trial. *Journal of the American Medical Association, 281,* 421–426.

Roeloffs, C., Bartlik, B., Kaplan, P. M., & Kocsis, J. H. (1996). Methylphenidate and SSRI induced sexual side effects. *Journal of Clinical Psychiatry, 57,* 548.

Rosen, R. C. (2000). Prevalence and risk factors of sexual dysfunction in men and women. *Current Psychiatry Reports, 2,* 189–195.

Rosen, R. C., Lane, R. M., & Menza, M. (1999). Effects of SSRIs on sexual dysfunction: A critical review. *Journal of Clinical Psychopharmacology, 19,* 67–85.

Rosen, R. C., Riley, A., Wagner, G., Osterloh, I. H., Kirkpatrick, J., & Mishra, A. (1997). The International Index of Erectile Function (IIEF): A multidimensional scale for assessment of erectile dysfunction. *Urology, 49,* 822–830.

Rust, J., & Golombok, S. (1985). The Golombok Rust Inventory of Sexual Satisfaction (GRISS). *British Journal of Clinical Psychology, 24,* 63–64.

Saenz de Tejada, I., Anglin, G., Knight, J. R., & Emmick, J. T. (2002). Effects of tadalafil on erectile dysfunction in men with diabetes. *Diabetes Care, 25,* 2159–2164.

Saltzman, E. A., Guay, A. T., & Jacobson, J. (2004). Improvement in erectile function in men with organic erectile dysfunction by correction of elevated cholesterol levels: A clinical observation. *Journal of Urology, 172,* 255–258.

Schwartz, M. F., Bauman, J. E., & Masters, W. H. (1982). Hyperprolactinaemia and sexual disorders in men. *Biological Psychiatry, 17,* 861–876.

Seagraves, K. B., & Seagraves, R. T. (1991). Hypoactive sexual desire disorder: Prevalence and comorbidity in 906 subjects. *Journal of Sex and Marital Therapy, 17,* 55–58.

Seidman, S. N., & Roose, S. P. (2000). The relationship between depression and erectile dysfunction. *Current Psychiatry Reports, 2,* 2001–2005.

Seidman, S. N., & Roose, S. P. (2001). Sexual function and depression. *Current Psychiatry Reports, 3,* 202–208.

Shabsigh, R., Kaufman, J. M., Steidle, C., & Padma-Nathan, H. (2004). Randomized study of testosterone gel as adjunctive therapy to sildenafil in hypogonadal men with erectile dysfunction who do not respond to sildenafil alone. *Journal of Urology, 172,* 658–663.

Shabsigh, R., Rajfer, J., Aversa, A., Traish, A. M., Yassin, A., Kalinchenko, S. Y., et al. (2006). The evolving role of testosterone in the treatment of erectile dysfunction. *International Journal of Clinical Practice, 60,* 1087–1092.

Siiteri, P. (2005). The continuing saga of DHEA. *Journal of Clinical Endocrinology and Metabolism, 90,* 3795–3796.

Simons, J. S., & Carey, M. P. (2001). Prevalence of sexual dysfunctions: Results from a decade of research. *Archives of Sexual Behavior, 30,* 177–219.

Spector, I. P., Carey, M. P., & Steinberg, L. (1996). The Sexual Desire Inventory: Development, factor structure, and evidence of reliability. *Journal of Sex and Marital Therapy, 22,* 175–190.

Srilatha, B., & Adiakan, P. G. (2004). Estrogen and phyto-estrogen predispose to erectile dysfunction: Do ER-alpha and ER-beta in the cavernosum play a role? *Urology, 63,* 382–386.

Starkman, M. N., Schteingart, D. E., & Schork, M. A. (1981). Depressed mood and psychiatric manifestations of Cushing's syndrome: Relationship to hormone levels. *Psychosomatic Medicine, 43,* 3–18.

ter Kuile, M. M., van Lankveld, J. J. D. M., Kalkhoven, P., & Van Egmond, M. (1999). The Golombok Rust Inventory of Sexual Satisfaction (GRISS): Psychometric properties within a Dutch population. *Journal of Sex and Marital Therapy, 25,* 59–71.

Traish, A. M., & Guay, A. T. (2006). Are androgens critical for penile erections in humans? Examining the clinical and preclinical evidence. *Journal of Sexual Medicine, 3*(3), 382–407.

Trudel, G., Ravart, M., & Matte, B. (1993). The use of the multiaxial diagnostic system for sexual dysfunctions in the assessment of hypoactive sexual desire. *Journal of Sex and Marital Therapy, 19,* 123–130.

van Lankveld, J. J., & van Koeveringe, G. A. (2003). Predictive validity of the Golombok Rust Inventory of Sexual Satisfaction (GRISS) for the presence of sexual dysfunctions within a Dutch urological population. *International Journal of Impotence Research, 15,* 110–116.

Wang, C., Swerdloff, R. S., Iranmanesh, A., Dobs, A., Snyder, P. J., Cunningham, G., et al. (2000). Transdermal testosterone gel improves sexual function, mood muscle strength and body composition parameters in hypogonadal men. *Journal of Clinical Endocrinology and Metabolism, 85,* 839–853.

Wespes, E., Amar, E., Hatzichristou, D., Hatzimouratidis, K., Montorsi, F., Pryor, J., et al. (2006). EAU Guidelines on erectile dysfunction: An update. *European Urology, 49,* 806–815.

White, J. M., & Rumbold, G. R. (1988). Behavioral effects of histamine and its antagonists: A review. *Psychopharmacology, 85,* 1–14.

Male Sexual Arousal Disorder

Ronald W. Lewis, Jiuhong Yuan,
and Run Wang

$\mathcal{2}$

Chapter

Learning Objectives

In this chapter, we discuss the:

- Definition of erectile dysfunction.
- Anatomy and physiology of penile function.
- Pathophysiology and risk factors for erectile dysfunction, including drug interactions.
- Evaluation procedures for erectile dysfunction.
- Management paradigms for the treatment of erectile dysfunction.
- First and second line therapies in the treatment of erectile dysfunction.

With the development of successful oral treatment for erectile dysfunction (ED), there has been an explosion of interest in the basic science of the erectile tissue in the penis and the central and peripheral nerve mechanisms responsible for erection, as well as the clinical correlates and treatment for this disorder, producing a myriad of studies and publications. This chapter summarizes these data by looking at a modern description of this disorder, associated risk factors, an approach to diagnosis in patients who present with this disorder, and the modern paradigms for management.

Definition of Erectile Dysfunction

The *DSM-IV* definition for male erectile disorder consists of the following:

A. *Persistent or recurrent inability to attain, or to maintain until completion of the sexual activity, an adequate erection,*

B. *The disturbance causes marked distress or interpersonal difficulty, and*

C. *The erectile dysfunction is not better accounted for by another Axis I disorder (other than a Sexual Dysfunction) and is not due exclusively to the direct physiological effects of a substance (e.g., a drug of abuse, a medication) or a general medical condition. (American Psychiatric Association, 2000, p. 547)*

Now after two international consensus conferences, the definition has matured, with ED considered an arousal disorder in men consisting of a consistent or recurrent inability of a man to attain and/or maintain penile erection sufficient for sexual activity (Lewis et al., 2004a, 2004b; Lewis, Hatzichristou, Laumann, & McKinlay, 2000). Three months minimal duration should be present for the establishment of this diagnosis except in some instances of trauma or surgically induced ED.

In the context of situational ED, the patient may be interested in addressing treatment for erectile dysfunction that has an impact on a personal relationship; so the ED may, in fact, be intermittent or only occurring in certain specific encounters for him. Such situations are best managed by a trained sexual therapist.

Persistent corpora cavernosal erection in men is also referred to as *priapism* and this rare disorder is often associated with sickle cell disorders, certain medications or treatments for ED, cavernosal trauma with a resultant artery to cavernosal sinus fistula, or infiltrative or metastatic malignancy into the corporal cavernosal tissue. Priapism is a high-flow or low-flow disorder depending on the etiology and the oxygen saturation level in the cavernosal tissue, with the former disorder producing a less rigid, nonpainful penis. Many times this occurs at night or in the early morning and is referred to as *stuttering priapism*.

As with all sexual disorders, a degree of distress or bother to the sufferer would greatly aid the interpretation of data from comparative studies and between or among individual reports of these disorders. Whether ED is lifelong or acquired and whether this disorder is global or situational also aids in the diagnosis and management of this disorder. Including in the description of the disorder the *degree* of dysfunction, such as that afforded by the International Index of Erectile Function (IIEF) erectile function domain scores (EFD: Questions 1 to 5 and 15) or Sexual Health Index in Males (SHIM) scores, has helped immensely in achieving an adequate evaluation of ED (see basic evaluation that follows).

Anatomy of the Penis

General Structure

The human penis is composed of three spongy cylindrical structures, the paired corpora cavernosa and the ventral corpus spongiosum, which houses the urethra and is covered by a loose subcutaneous layer of dartos and skin (see Figure 2.1). The paired corpora cavernosa join together beneath the pubis (penile hilum) and remain attached up to the glans. After they merge, the cavernous bodies communicate with each other through an incomplete septum, which allows them to neurophysiologically function and pharmacologically respond as a single unit. The ischiocavernous muscles covering the penile crura and proximal part of the penile shaft provide additional penile rigidity during the rigid erection phase.

Figure 2.1

**General
Structure of
Penis**

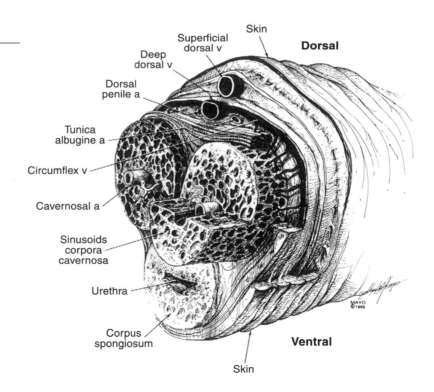

Skin
Superficial
dorsal v
Deep
dorsal v
Dorsal
Dorsal
Dorsal
penile a
Tunica
albugine a
Circumflex v
Cavernosal a
Sinusoids
corpora
cavernosa
Urethra
Corpus
spongiosum
Ventral
Skin

Cavernous Tissue and Tunica Albuginea

The paired corpora cavernosa are the sponge-like cavernosal tissue encompassed by tunica albuginea. The sponge-like cavernosal tissue is composed of a meshwork of interconnected cavernosal spaces, separated by trabeculae (containing bundles of smooth muscle in a framework of collagen, elastin, and fibroblasts and lined by vascular endothelium). The tunica is composed of elastic fibers forming an irregular lattice network with collagen fibers (type I and III; Hsu, Brock, & von Heyden, 1994). The tunica of the corpora cavernosa is a bilayered structure. The inner layer is composed of circularly oriented bundles that support and contain the cavernous tissue. Radiating into the corpora from this inner layer are intracavernosal pillars that act as struts, augmenting the septum that provides essential support to the erectile tissue. The outer layer is oriented longitudinally extending from the glans penis to the proximal crura, inserting into the inferior pubic ramus. Emissary veins run between the inner and outer layers for a short distance, often piercing the outer bundles in an oblique manner and thus can be occluded easily by the shearing action of the tunical layers during erection. The outer layer appears to play an additional role in compression of the veins during erection. The tunica albuginea provides a tough uniform backing for engorged sinusoidal spaces. The cavernosal geometry design gives flexibility, rigidity, and strength (Hsu et al., 1994).

Arterial Supply

The arterial supply to the penis originates from superficial and deep arterial systems (see Figure 2.2). The deep arterial system (main source of blood supply to the penis) arises from the internal pudendal artery, which is the final branch of the anterior trunk of the internal iliac artery. The internal pudendal artery becomes the common penile artery after giving off a branch to the perineum. The three branches of the penile artery are the dorsal, the bulbourethral, and the cavernous arteries. The dorsal artery runs between the dorsal vein and the dorsal penile nerve and with them attaches to the underside of Buck's fascia. The bulbourethral artery supplies the bulb and corpus spongiosum. The cavernous artery enters the corpus cavernosum at the hilum of the penis, where the two crura merge, and then runs through the middle of corpus cavernosum in a slightly medial position to the septum. Along its course, the cavernous artery gives off many helicine arteries that supply the trabecular erectile tissue and the sinusoids. These helicine arteries are contracted and contorted in the flaccid state and become dilated and straight during erection. The cavernous artery is responsible for tumescence of the corpus cavernosum and the dorsal artery for engorgement of the glans penis during erection. Distally, the three branches join to form a

Figure 2.2
Arterial Supply

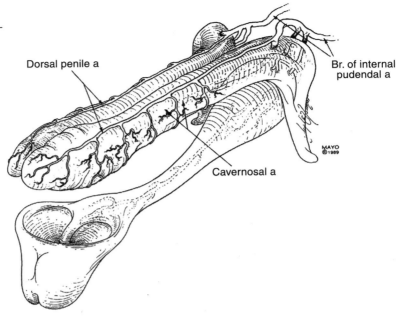

Dorsal penile a

Br. of internal pudendal a

Cavernosal a

vascular ring near the glans and communicate with the superficial arterial system.

Intracorporal Circulation

The cavernous artery gives off multiple helicine arteries among the cavernous spaces within the center of the erectile tissue. Most of these open directly into the sinusoids bounded by trabeculae, but a few helicine arteries terminate in capillaries that supply the trabeculae. The pectiniform septum distally provides communication between the two corpora. The emissary veins at the periphery collect the blood from the sinusoids through the subalbugineal venous plexuses and empty it into the circumflex veins that drain into the deep dorsal vein. With erection, the arteriolar and sinusoidal walls relax secondary to neurotransmitters and the cavernous spaces dilate, enlarging the corporal bodies and stretching the tunica albuginea. The venous tributaries between the sinusoids and the subalbugineal venous plexus are compressed by the dilating sinusoids and the stretched tunica albuginea. The direction of blood flow could be summarized as follows: Cavernous artery→ helicine arteries→ sinusoids→ postcavernous venules→ subalbugineal venous plexus→ emissary vein.

Venous Drainage

The venous drainage system consists of three distinct groups of veins: superficial, intermediate, and deep (see Figure 2.3). The

Figure 2.3
Venous Supply

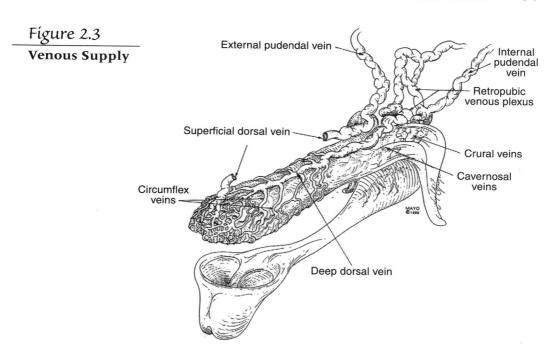

External pudendal vein

Internal pudendal vein

Retropubic venous plexus

Superficial dorsal vein

Crural veins

Cavernosal veins

Circumflex veins

Deep dorsal vein

superficial drainage system consists of venous drainage from the penile skin and prepuce which drain into the superficial dorsal vein that runs under the superficial penile fascia (Colles') and joins the saphenous vein via the external pudendal vein. The intermediate system consists of the deep dorsal vein and circumflex veins that drain the glans, corpus spongiosum, and distal two-thirds of the corpora cavernosa. The veins leave the glans via a retrocoronal plexus to join the deep dorsal vein that runs in the groove between the corpora. Emissary veins from the corpora join the circumflex veins; the latter communicate with each other at the side by lateral veins and corresponding veins from the opposite side. These run under Buck's fascia before emptying obliquely into the deep dorsal vein. The deep dorsal vein passes through a space in between the suspensory ligament and the puboprostatic ligament draining into the prostatic plexus, which then drains into the internal iliac veins. The deep drainage system consists of the cavernous, bulbar, and crural veins.

Nerves
Sexual behavior and penile erection are controlled by the hypothalamus, the limbic system, and the cerebral cortex. Therefore, stimulatory and inhibitory messages can be relayed to the spinal erection centers to facilitate or inhibit erection. Somatic innervation arises from sacral spinal segments S_{2-4} via the pudendal

nerve (Lue, 2002). After giving off the inferior rectal nerve, the pudendal nerve divides into the perineal nerve and dorsal nerve of the penis. The perineal nerve innervates the ischiocavernosus and bulbocavernosus muscles, as well as the skin of genitalia, urogenital diaphragm, and the corpus spongiosum (Lue, 2002). The dorsal nerve of the penis runs along the ramus of the ischium and along the inferior of the pubis with the pudendal artery on the surface of the urogenital diaphragm, and runs the dorsum of the penis accompanied by the dorsal vein and dorsal artery to the glans. Autonomic nerves consist of sympathetics that arise from T_{11} and L_2 and parasympathetics from S_{2-4} (Lue, 2002). The sympathetic pathway travels through the lumbar splanchnic nerves to the superior hypogastric plexus, from which fibers travel in the hypogastric nerves to the pelvic plexus. The parasympathetic preganglionic fibers pass in the pelvic nerves to the pelvic plexus. The pelvic plexus is adjacent to the base of the bladder, prostate, seminal vesicles, and rectum. The cavernous nerves are branches of the pelvic plexus that innervate the penis.

Physiology

Penile Erection and Flaccidity: Physiologic Mechanism

Penile erection is a neurovascular event controlled by corporal smooth muscle tone. In the flaccid state, the corporeal smooth muscle of cavernous arteries, helicine arterioles, and trabeculae are tonically contracted, limiting the inflow of blood to the corpora to a small amount (5ml/min) that enters the penis for nutritional purposes (Wagner, 1992). To obtain penile erection, four physiologic events are needed: intact neuronal innervation, intact arterial supply, appropriately responsive corporal smooth muscle, and intact veno-occlusive mechanics (Rehman & Melman, 2001). Tactile or psychic stimuli caused by erotic activity are processed in the limbic system (medial preoptic nucleus [MPOA], and the paraventricular nucleus [PVN]) and coordinated in the midbrain to generate a neuronal signal, which is carried through thalamo-spinal tracts (Rehman & Melman, 2001). These neural signals leave the spinal cord through nerve roots at T_{11}-L_2 for sympathetic traveling through hypogastric nerves (inhibitory) as well as via S_2 to S_4 for parasympathetic/nonadrenergic noncholinergic (NANC; stimulatory) and travel jointly through the pelvic plexus and cavernous nerve to the penis. The neural signals cause the release of a neurotransmitter that promotes smooth muscle relaxation, leading to dilatation of cavernosal and helicine arteries (fivefold to tenfold increase in flow; Rehman & Melman, 2001). The signal that arrives in the penile tissue spreads rapidly through the corporal tissue by gap junctions, leading to entire corporal smooth muscle relaxation and expansion of the corporal sinusoids. The increased inflow of blood temporarily exceeds the capacity of the veins to drain off the blood. The sinusoids expand and the volume of blood in the corpora increases. Compliance of the sinusoid initially prevents the rapid increase of intracavernosal pressure. When the sinusoidal system is adequately stretched, the intracavernous pressure begins to rise. Venules draining the sinusoidal spaces coalesce into a peripheral plexus below the outer fibroelastic tunica of the corporal bodies. Egress from the subtunical venular plexus is via emissary veins exiting obliquely through the bilayer tunica albuginea into deep dorsal vein in distal two-third and via the short cavernous and crural veins at the base (proximal one-third) of corporal bodies. As the corporeal sinuses or lacunae fill with oxygenated blood, expanding sinusoids dynamically compress the subtunical venules against the inner layer of tunica albuginea. By differential stretching of the two primary layers of the tunica across which the emissary veins exit (elongation and compression of the venules), a large increase in the resistance to the passage of flow through these vessels results and venous outflow is sufficiently decreased to result in turgidity of the corpora (veno-occlusive mechanism; a functional or passive mechanism; Rehman & Melman, 2001).

As the erectile tissue of the penis fills with blood, the outflow is obstructed because of relaxation and elongation of the smooth muscle fibers. These fibers in turn compress the draining venules that allow the intracorporal pressure to rise to mean systolic pressure and cause penile rigidity. The unique geometry of the corpora leads to the erection:

- The intrasinusoidal pressure within the corpora cavernosa distends the tunica albuginea to its maximal capability.
- The midline septal fibers are tightly stretched between the dorsal and ventral corpora thus creating, in effect, an I-beam arrangement that accounts for the anteroposterior rigidity of the penis during erection.
- The relative indispensability of the paired lateral columns adds lateral stability to the penis during erection.

Detumescence can be triggered either by the cessation of sexual stimuli or by the sympathetic burst at orgasm and ejaculation. Detumescence is a reversal of the events that occur during erection: contraction of the corporeal smooth muscle and helicine arteries, decrease in arterial blood flow, and resumption of normal venous outflow; adrenergic nerve activation and release of norepinephrine from sympathetic nerve terminals; and subsequent activation of postsynaptic (α_1-adrenergic receptors are the primary mediator of this event; Lue, 2002; Rehman & Melman, 2001). Norepinephrine has generally been accepted as the principal neurotransmitter in the control of penile flaccidity. However, it has recently been demonstrated that endothelin may play an important role in the regulation of corporeal smooth-muscle tone in vivo. Therefore, as with erection, detumescence may also require the concerted efforts of several endogenous substances (cotransmission of norepinephrine and endothelin; Lue, 2002; Rehman & Melman, 2001).

Penile Erection and Flaccidity: Molecular Mechanisms

Smooth muscle contraction and relaxation are regulated by cytosolic (sarcoplasmic) free Ca^{2+}. Stimuli that induce smooth muscle contraction trigger a transient increase in cytosolic free Ca^2 from a resting level of 120 to 270 to 500 to 700 nM (M. P. Walsh, 1991). At the elevated level, Ca^2 binds to calmodulin and changes the latter's conformation to expose sites of interaction with myosin light-chain kinase. The resultant activation catalyzes phosphorylation of myosin light chains and triggers cycling of myosin cross-bridges (heads) along actin filaments and the development of force. In addition, phosphorylation of the light chain also activates myosin ATPase, which hydrolyzes ATP to provide energy for muscle contraction (Lue, 2000).

In addition to the central role of cytosolic (sarcoplasmic) free Ca^2 concentration in smooth muscle contraction, RhoA-Rho kinase acts as a Ca^2 sensitization to maintain the smooth muscle contraction (Mills, Lewis, & Wingard, 2003).

Relaxation of the muscle follows a decrease of free Ca^2 in the sarcoplasm. Calmodulin then dissociates from the myosin light-chain kinase and inactivates it. Myosin is dephosphorylated by myosin light-chain phosphatase and detaches from the actin filament, and the muscle relaxes (M. P. Walsh, 1991). Others suggest that the nitric oxide NO-cGMP inhibitory pathway in corpus cavernosum smooth muscle is not simply a reversal of excitatory signal transduction mechanisms; rather, an unidentified mechanism may contribute to relaxation by decreasing the rate of cross-bridge recruitment through phosphorylation (Chuang, Strauss, & Steers, 1998).

cAMP and cGMP are the second messengers involved in smooth muscle relaxation. They activate cAMP- and cGMP-dependent protein kinases, which in turn phosphorylate certain proteins and ion channels, resulting in (a) opening of the potassium channels and hyperpolarization; (b) sequestration of intracellular calcium by the endoplasmic reticulum; and (c) inhibition of voltage-dependent calcium channels, blocking calcium influx. The consequence is a drop in cytosolic free calcium followed by smooth muscle relaxation (Lue, 2002). The peripheral physiological erection mechanism accepted by mainstream research community is: nitric oxide (NO) released from nonadrenergic/noncholinergic (NANC) neurotransmission as the initiation event and NO released from the endothelium as the principal maintenance neurotransmitter mediating penile erection; NO diffuses into smooth muscle cells, where it activates soluble guanylyl cyclase, producing cGMP, which in turn causes the activation of cGMP-specific protein kinase, resulting in the phosphorylation and inactivation of myosin light-chain kinase, thereby causing dissociation of myosin and actin and smooth muscle relaxation (Lue, 2002).

Pathophysiology, Risk Factors, and Clinical Correlates of Erectile Dysfunction

ED, as an organogenic manifestation, is not a specific disease process but rather a symptom of certain other disease processes that result in localized or generalized vascular malfunction. Another reflection of ED associated with general disease processes, with a particular disease such as diabetes mellitus, is the effect of hyperglycemia on the cavernosal tissue on molecular markers, vascular and sinus smooth muscle dysfunction, fibrosis, and, eventually apoptosis of key cell types involved in erection. Often, more than one disease process may play a role in any one individual's ED. With the wealth of studies on molecular pathways involved in erection, understanding the physiology of erection and the pathophysiology of ED opens new options to diagnosis of the etiologies and treatment of ED in the patients suffering from this disorder, thereby eventually opening possible preventive treatments to delay or prevent the development of ED in the male, particularly those associated with certain disorders such as diabetes mellitus.

Prevalence of this disorder, as well as other sexual dysfunctions in both women and men, increases with aging (Lewis et al., 2004b). For ED, this varies from a rate of 1% to 9% in those men below 40 years of age to as high as 75% in those older than the age of 70 years. Decrease in the general health status of individual men seems to be associated with ED as well (Lewis et al., 2004b).

Despite the fact that ED is often a symptom of a physiological disease process, some still prefer a classification system for ED. A classification recommended by the International Society of Impotence Research (now the International Society of Sexual Medicine) is shown in Table 2.1 (Lizza & Rosen, 1999).

Table 2.1   Classification for Male Erectile Dysfunction

Organic

I. Vasculogenic
   A. Arteriogenic
   B. Cavernosal
   C. Mixed
II. Neurogenic
III. Anatomic
IV. Endocrinologic

Psychogenic

I. Generalized type
   A. Generalized unresponsiveness
      1. Primary lack of sexual arousability
      2. Aging-related decline in sexual arousability
   B. Generalized inhibition
      1. Chronic disorder of sexual intimacy
II. Situational type
   A. Partner related
      1. Lack of arousability in specific relationship
      2. Lack of arousability due to sexual object preference
      3. High central inhibition due to partner conflict or threat
   B. Performance related
      1. Associated with other sexual dysfunctions (e.g., rapid ejaculation)
      2. Situational performance anxiety (e.g., fear of failure)
   C. Psychological distress or adjustment related
      1. Associated with negative mood state (e.g., depression) or major life stress (e.g., death of partner)

Psychogenic

Previously, psychogenic impotence was believed to be the most common type, with 90% of impotent men thought to suffer from this condition (Masters & Johnson, 1970). However, the substantial progress in understanding the peripheral mechanisms involved in erection and erectile dysfunction reveals that most men with ED have mixed "organic and psychogenic" etiological factors (Lue, 2002). In spite of the advance in the peripheral mechanism, the key mechanisms underlying psychogenic ED have so far eluded us. Similarly, we have made only limited progress in identifying the psychological characteristics that relate to vulnerability to psychogenic ED. Some helpful attempts have been made to define the types of psychological problems that are found in psychogenic ED, for example, S. B. Levine and Althof (1991) described three levels of contributory problems: performance anxiety, antecedent life changes (such as divorce, bereavement, or vocational failure), and developmental vulnerabilities. Performance anxiety was an issue in most types of ED and was more of a "final common psychological pathway to erectile impairment than a specific explanation." What has remained unaddressed is why some men with such psychological problems develop ED and others do not. Increasingly men with ED are being diagnosed as "mixed organic and psychogenic" etiologic factors, for example, rendering the clinical usefulness of the "psychogenic" category less and less certain. So, the old belief, that 90% ED cases are psychogenic, has given way to the realization that most men with ED have a mixed condition that may be either predominantly functional or predominantly physical (Lue, 2002).

Neurogenic

Trauma to or disease of the central, spinal cord, or peripheral nerve tissue or nerve pathways can affect the function of the penile smooth muscle tissue and even provoke down regulation of key molecular messengers in the tissue itself.

The MPOA, the paraventricular nucleus, and the hippocampus have been regarded as important integration centers for sexual drive and penile erection (Sachs & Meisel, 1988). Pathologic processes in these regions, such as Parkinson's disease, stroke, encephalitis, or temporal lobe epilepsy, are often associated with ED. Parkinson's effect may be caused by the imbalance of the dopaminergic pathways (Wermuth & Stenager, 1992). Other lesions in the brain noted to be associated with ED are tumors, dementias, Alzheimer's disease, Shy-Drager syndrome, and trauma.

In the patient with a spinal cord injury, the degree of erectile function that persists depends largely on the nature, location, and extent of the spinal lesion. Reflexogenic erection is preserved in 95% of patients with complete upper cord lesions; whereas only about 25% of those with complete lower cord lesions can achieve an erection (Eardley & Kirby, 1991). It appears that sacral parasympathetic neurons are important in the preservation of reflexogenic erection. However, the thoracolumbar pathway may compensate for loss of the sacral lesion through synaptic connections (Courtois, MacDougall, & Sachs, 1993). Other disorders at the spinal level (e.g., spina bifida, disc herniation, syringomyelia, tumor, transverse myelitis, and multiple sclerosis) may affect the afferent or the efferent neural pathway in a similar manner.

Because of the close relationship between the cavernous nerves and the pelvic organs, surgery on these organs is a frequent cause of impotence. An improved understanding of the neuroanatomy of the pelvic and cavernous nerves has resulted in modified surgery for cancer of the rectum, bladder, and prostate, producing a lower incidence of iatrogenic impotence (P. C. Walsh & Donker, 1982). For example, the introduction of nerve-sparing radical prostatectomy has reduced the incidence of impotence from nearly 100% to 30% to 50% (Catalona & Bigg, 1990; Quinlan, Epstein, & Carter, 1991).

In cases of pelvic fracture, ED can result from cavernous nerve injury or vascular insufficiency, or both. In animal experiments on mature rats, alcoholism, vitamin deficiency, or diabetes may affect the cavernous nerve terminals and may result in deficiency of neurotransmitters (Lue, 2002). In diabetics, impairment of neurogenic and endothelium-dependent relaxation results in inadequate NO release (Saenz de Tejada, Goldstein, & Azadzoi, 1989).

Endocrinologic

Hypogonadism, particularly when seen in the younger male, is often accompanied by ED (Lewis et al., 2000, 2004a, 2004b). The whole debate of the existence of andropause or late onset hypogonadism (see Chapter 5, this volume) in the aging male on ED has intensified with a more rational approach suggesting that one of manifestations of low testosterone in males of any age should be referred to as testosterone deficiency syndrome, with its occurrence in the aging male as only one reflection of this disorder (Morales, Schulman, Tostain, & Wu, 2006; Tenover, 1998).

In a review of published articles from 1975 to 1992, Mulligan and Schmitt (1993) concluded: (a) testosterone enhances sexual interest; (b) testosterone increases frequency of sexual acts; and (c) testosterone increases the frequency of nocturnal erections but has little or no effect on fantasy-induced or visually induced erections. Recent research revealed that in the corpus cavernosum, androgens regulate endothelial and trabecular smooth muscle growth and metabolic function, the expression and activities of nitric oxide (NO) synthases and phosphodieslerase type 5 (PDE-5), connective tissue protein synthesis, and progenitor cell differentiation. Therefore, androgen-deficiency produces metabolic and structural and functional imbalance in the corpus cavernosum with concomitant alterations in nerve and smooth muscle responses and fibroelastic properties, resulting in poor tissue compliance and venous leakage, thus producing erectile dysfunction (Traish & Kim, 2007).

Hyperprolactinemia, whether from a pituitary adenoma or drugs, results in both reproductive and sexual dysfunction. Symptoms may include loss of libido, ED, galactorrhea, gynecomastia, and infertility. Hyperprolactinemia is associated with low circulating levels of testosterone, which appear to be secondary to inhibition of gonadotropin-releasing hormone secretion by the elevated prolactin levels (Leonard, Nickel, & Morales, 1989).

ED also may be associated with both the hyperthyroid and the hypothyroid state. Hyperthyroidism is commonly associated with diminished libido, which may be caused by the increased circulating estrogen levels, and less often with ED. In hypothyroidism, low testosterone secretion and elevated prolactin levels contribute to ED (Lue, 2002).

Diabetes mellitus, although the most common endocrinologic disorder, causes ED through vascular, neurologic, endothelial, and psychogenic complications rather than through a hormone deficiency per se (Moore & Wang, 2006).

Vasculogenic

Any lesion of the pudendal-cavernous-helicine arterial tree can decrease the perfusion pressure and arterial flow to the sinusoidal spaces, thus increasing the time to maximal erection and decreasing the rigidity of the erect penis. In the majority of patients with arteriogenic ED, the impaired penile perfusion is a component of the generalized atherosclerotic process and parallels with coronary disease (Michal & Ruzbarsky, 1980). Common risk factors associated with arterial insufficiency include hypertension, hyperlipidemia, cigarette smoking, diabetes mellitus, blunt perineal or pelvic trauma, and pelvic irradiation (Goldstein, Feldman, & Deckers, 1984; F. J. Levine, Greenfield, & Goldstein, 1990; Rosen, Greenfield, & Walker, 1990). Focal stenosis of the common penile or cavernous artery is most often seen in young patients who have sustained blunt pelvic or perineal trauma (F. J. Levine et al., 1990). Long-distance cycling is also a risk factor for vasculogenic and neurogenic ED (Anderson & Bovim, 1997; Ricchiuti, Haas, & Seftel, 1999). Failure of adequate venous occlusion has been proposed as one of the most common causes of vasculogenic impotence (Rajfer, Rosciszewski, & Mehringer, 1988). The physiologic processes resulting in veno-occlusive dysfunction (Lue, 2002) include:

- The presence or development of large venous channels draining the corpora cavernosa.
- Degenerative changes (Peyronie's disease, old age, diabetes) or traumatic injury to the tunica albuginea (penile fracture) resulting in inadequate compression of the subtunical and emissary veins.
- Structural alternation in the fibroelastic components of the trabeculae, cavernous smooth muscle, and endothelium may result in venous leak.
- Insufficient trabecular smooth muscle relaxation, causing inadequate sinusoidal expansion and insufficient compression of the subtunical venules, may occur in an anxious individual with excessive adrenergic tone or in a patient with inadequate neurotransmitter release.
- Acquired venous shunts—the result of operative correction of priapism—may cause persistent glans/cavernosum or cavernosum/spongiosum shunting.

Pathophysiology Based on a Cellular Level Classification

Another way to classify erectile dysfunction is to consider effects on different cellular compartments and types, as shown in Table 2.2.

Drug-Induced

Various classes of therapeutic drugs can cause ED as an undesired side effect and mostly with unknown mechanism. In general, drugs that interfere with central neuroendocrine or local neurovascular

Table 2.2 **Cellular Classification of Erectile Dysfunction**

Component	Deficiency	Associated Disease or Risk Factors	References
Fibroelastic tissue	Loss of compliance	Diabetes Hypercholesteremia Vascular disease Penile Injury Aging	Cerami et al. (1987) Hayashi et al. (1987) Moreland et al. (1995) Nehra et al. (1998)
Smooth muscle	Decrease in number	Patients with ED vs. normal	Saenz de Tejada et al. (1989) Mersdorf et al. (1991) Pickard et al. (1994) Sattar et al. (1996)
	Impairment in Maxi K+ channels	Diabetes mellitus	Fan et al. (1995)
	Decrease in smooth muscle relaxation	Nerve injury and cavernosal ischemia	Paick et al. (1991) Azadzoi et al. (1997)
Gap junctions	Decrease in cell membrane contact secondary to collagen deposition	Diabetes Hypercholesteremia	Persson et al. (1989) Christ et al. (1991) Lerner et al. (1993)
Endothelium	Decrease nitric oxide Prostaglandin Polypeptide endothe-lins messengers necessary for smooth muscle relaxation	Diabetes Hypertension	Saenz de Tejada & Blanco (1988) Rubanyi et al. (1989) Ignarro et al. (1990) Saenz de Tejada (1991a, 1991b) Moore & Wang (2006)

control of penile smooth muscle have a potential for causing ED (Lewis et al., 2000, 2004a, 2004b). Central neurotransmitter pathways, including 5-hydroxytryptaminergic, noradrenergic, and dopaminergic pathways involved in sexual function, may be disturbed by antipsychotics and antidepressants and some centrally acting antihypertensive drugs.

Centrally acting sympatholytics including methyldopa, clonidine (inhibition of the hypothalamic center through α2-receptor stimulation), and reserpine (depletion of the stores of catecholamines and 5-hydroxytryptamine by blocking vesicular monoamine transporters I and II) are known to cause sexual dysfunction. α-Adrenergic blocking agents such as phenoxybenzamine and phentolamine may cause ejaculatory failure or retrograde ejaculation. ß-Adrenergic blockers have also been implicated in sexual dysfunction, probably because of their central side effects, such as sedation, sleep disturbances, and depression. Thiazide diuretics have been credited with widely differing effects on potency, and spironolactone has been reported to produce erectile failure in 4% to 30% of patients and has also been associated with decreased libido, gynecomastia, and mastodynia. Major tranquilizers or antipsychotics can decrease libido, causing erectile failure and ejaculatory dysfunction. The mechanisms involved may include sedation, anticholinergic actions, a central antidopaminergic effect, α-adrenergic antagonist action, and release of prolactin.

Except for trazodone and bupropion, almost all of the four major types of antidepressants (tricyclic, heterocyclic, selective serotonin reuptake inhibitors, and monoamine oxidase inhibitors) have been reported to cause ED and ejaculatory disorders. Increased sensitivity to 5-hydroxytryptamine and adrenergic receptors in postsynaptic neurons is suspected to be the cause. The sexual side effects in patients taking minor tranquilizers may well be a result of the central sedative effects of these agents. Cigarette smoking may induce vasoconstriction and penile venous leakage because of its contractile effect on the cavernous smooth muscle (Junemann, Lue, & Luo, 1987). Alcohol in small amounts improves erection and sexual drive because of its vasodilatory effect and the suppression of anxiety; however, large amounts can cause central sedation, decreased libido, and transient ED. Chronic alcoholism may also result in liver dysfunction, decreased testosterone and increased estrogen levels, and alcoholic polyneuropathy, which may also affect penile nerves (Miller & Gold, 1988).

Cimetidine, an H_2 (histamine) receptor antagonist, has been reported to suppress the libido and produce erectile failure. It is thought to act as an antiandrogen and to increase prolactin levels (Wolfe, 1979). Other drugs known to cause ED are estrogens and drugs with antiandrogenic action, such as ketoconazole and cyproterone acetate. Finally, many of the anticancer drugs can be associated with a progressive loss of libido, peripheral neuropathy, azoospermia, and erectile failure (Lue, 2002).

Erectile Dysfunction Associated with Aging, Systemic Disease, and Other Causes

Aging induces a progressive decline in sexual function in healthy men, which includes greater latency to erection, less turgid erection, loss of forceful ejaculation, decreased ejaculatory volume, a longer refractory period, decreased frequency and duration of nocturnal erection, and a decrease in penile tactile sensitivity (Masters & Johnson, 1977; Rowland, Greenleaf, & Mas, 1989; Schiavi & Schreiner-Engel, 1988). The possible mechanisms are: (a) a heightened cavernous muscle tone, (b) hypothalamic-pituitary dysfunction, (c) a decrease in NOS activity, (d) reduced endothelium-mediated NO release from cholinergic stimulation, and (e) defect at the level of calcium-eNOS interaction (Christ, Maayani, Valcic, & Melman, 1990).

Erectile dysfunction occurs in 32% of Type 1 and 46% of Type 2 diabetic men (Vickers & Wright, 2004). Fifty percent of men with diabetes are afflicted with ED within 10 years of their diagnosis. ED may be the initial presentation in 12% of patients subsequently diagnosed with diabetes (Lewis, 2001). Between the ages of 30 to 34, ED is present in 15% of diabetics and 55% by age 60 (Smith, 1981). The Massachusetts Male Aging Study noted that diabetics have three times the prevalence of erectile dysfunction compared to nondiabetics (Feldman, Goldstein, Hatzichristou, Krane, & McKinlay, 1994). Additionally, a population-based study in Minnesota demonstrated that diabetes was associated with diminished sexual drive, ejaculatory function, and sexual satisfaction (Burke, Jacobson, & McGree, 2006).

The etiologies of erectile dysfunction in diabetic patients are multifactorial. The end-organ damage secondary to hyperglycemia, as well as the comorbidities in the patients and side effects of the various medications (i.e., antihypertensives) they consume, all contribute to their erectile dysfunction. The proposed mechanisms of ED in diabetics include: elevated advanced glycation end-products (AGE's) and increased levels of oxygen free radicals, impaired nitric oxide (NO) synthesis, decreased and impaired cyclic guanosine monophosphate-dependent kinase-1 (PKG-1), increased endothelin B receptor binding sites and ultrastructural changes, up-regulated RhoA/Rho-kinase pathway, and nitric oxide-dependent selective nitrergic nerve degeneration (Moore & Wang, 2006).

Hyperlipidemia and atherosclerosis are major contributors to ED. Hyperlipidemia is a well-known risk factor for arteriosclerosis. It enhances the deposition of lipids in the vascular lesions, causing atherosclerosis and eventual occlusion. The atherosclerotic lesions can extend to the internal pudendal or cavernous arteries to reduce inflow (Lue, 2002). In addition, the hyperlipidemia may also cause dysfunction of the cavernous smooth muscle and the endothelium. Early atherosclerotic changes in the corpus cavernosum have been demonstrated in cholesterol-fed rabbits (J. H. Kim, Klyachkin, & Svendsen, 1994). See Sidebar 2.1.

SIDEBAR 2.1

Mechanisms of Atherosclerosis and Hypercholesterolemia Induced ED

- Decreased NOS activity.
- Increased production of contractile thromboxane and prostaglandin.
- Contractile effect of oxidized low-density lipoprotein.
- Release of superoxide radicals.
- Increased production of NOS inhibitors.

Note: Based on the work of Ahn, Gomez-Coronado, and Martinez (1999); Azadzoi, Krane, and Saenz de Tejada (1999); and Azadzoi and Saenz de Tejada (1991); S. C. Kim, Kim, and Seo (1997).

Hypertension is another well-recognized risk factor for ED. However, the culprit for ED is arterial stenotic lesions instead of the increased blood pressure itself (Hsieh, Muller, & Lue, 1989). The mechanisms include: (a) the production of cyclooxygenase-derived vasoconstrictor substances, (b) reduced endothelin B-receptor–mediated NO activation, and (c) alteration in the vessel architecture, resulting in an increased wall-to-lumen ratio and reduced dilatory capacity (Lue, 2002; Taddei, Virdis, & Ghiadoni, 2000). Chronic renal failure has frequently been associated with diminished erectile function, impaired libido, and infertility (Lue, 2002). The mechanism is probably multifactorial: depressed testosterone and elevation of prolactin levels, diabetes mellitus, vascular insufficiency, multiple medications, autonomic and somatic neuropathy, and psychological stress (Nogues, Starkstein, & Davalos, 1991). After successful renal transplantation, 50% to 80% of patients returned to their pre-illness potency (Salvatierra, Fortmann, & Belzer, 1975). Patients with severe pulmonary disease often fear aggravating dyspnea during sexual intercourse. Patients with angina, heart failure, or myocardial infarction can become impotent from anxiety, depression, or arterial insufficiency. Other systemic diseases such as cirrhosis of the liver, scleroderma, chronic debilitation, and cachexia are also known to cause ED.

Other disease states associated with a higher prevalence of ED are the following: presence of cardiovascular disease, other genitourinary disease such as lower urinary tract symptoms (LUTS), psychiatric/psychological disorders (such as depression), peripheral vascular disease, coronary artery disease, or cardiac failure disorders. Other risk factors associated with a higher prevalence for ED include smoking, lower socioeconomics conditions (such as lower educational status or economic class), and obesity (Lewis et al., 2004b).

Interaction of Sexual Dysfunctions

The association of ED with other sexual disorders in the same patient is clearly known (such as the association of ED and rapid ejaculation in the same patient). In addition, there is now solid evidence that within both sexes nearly all sexual dysfunctions are closely associated with other sexual disorders in the patient and his or her partner (Fugl-Meyer & Fugl-Meyer, 2002). This pattern certainly has many implications for the management of ED and clearly suggests that multidisciplinary approaches and/or treatment plans for the couple would help greatly in achieving a greater success in treating patients.

Evaluation of the Patient with Erectile Dysfunction

Following the development of phosphodiesterase type 5 (PDE-5) inhibitors, the need to elucidate the cause of ED has greatly diminished. In fact, following a history and focused physical exam, a trial of a PDE-5 inhibitor or a vacuum device is often all that is ever needed to treat ED likely to have its etiology in a biological root. However, these therapies are not successful or a choice for all patients desiring treatment, and many of these complicated cases might benefit from a more complete evaluation into the cause of their ED.

Basic Evaluation for (Organogenic) ED

The evaluation of any patient with ED should proceed in a stepwise manner. As with all medical problems, the history of illness is important in ED. A detailed medical history is essential because many common disorders are associated with ED, including hypertension, diabetes mellitus, coronary artery disease, dyslipidemia, renal insufficiency and hypogonadism (Lobo & Nehra, 2005). Prior genitourinary, retroperitoneal, pelvic surgery, or radiation can result in ED. It is critical to conduct a complete medication review because many drugs, particularly antihypertensive and psychotropic drugs, are well known to affect erectile function, and other medications, such as nitrates, might be contraindications to oral therapy. Using a validated questionnaire such as the International Index of Erectile Function (IIEF) or the more abbreviated erectile domain of the IIEF (EDF: Questions 1 to 5 and 15) or the Sexual Health Index in Men (SHIM) can help in determining the severity of the patient's ED (see Table 2.3).

Table 2.3 **Using a Standard Validated Questionnaire for Evaluating Erectile Dysfunction Severity**

International Index of Erectile Function (IIEF; 0–5 for Each Question)

Over the past 4 weeks:

1. How often were you able to get an erection during sexual activity?
2. When you had erections with sexual stimulation, how often were your erections hard enough for penetration?
3. When you attempted sexual intercourse, how often were you able to penetrate (enter) your partner?
4. During sexual intercourse, how often were you able to maintain your erection after you had penetrated (entered) your partner?
5. During sexual intercourse, how difficult was it to maintain your erection to completion of intercourse?
6. How do you rate your confidence to get and keep an erection?

Sexual Health Index in Males (SHIM; 0–5 for Each Question)

1. How do you rate your confidence that you could get and keep an erection? (very low to very high)
2. When you had erections with sexual stimulation, how often were your erections hard enough for penetration?
3. During sexual intercourse, how often were you able to maintain your erection after you had penetrated (entered) your partner? (almost never to almost always)
4. During sexual intercourse, how difficult was it to maintain your erection to completion of intercourse?
5. When you attempted sexual intercourse, how often was it satisfactory for you? (almost never to almost always)

IIEF and SHIM Domain Scores Classify Severity of Erectile Dysfunction (ED)

Severity of ED	IIEF	SHIM
Normal erectile function	26–30	22–25
Mild ED	22–25	17–21
Mild-to-moderate ED	17–21	12–16
Moderate ED	11–16	8–11
Severe ED	10	≤7

It is also essential to perform a focused physical exam on any new patient undergoing an evaluation of ED, paying particular attention to the abdomen, genitalia, digital rectal exam, and secondary sexual characteristics (Montague, Jarow, & Roderick, 2005). The Second International Consultation on Sexual Dysfunction (2004) Committee on Sexual Dysfunction Assessment in Men recommended that serum testosterone, fasting blood glucose, fasting serum cholesterol, and a serum lipid panel should all be a part of a routine basic ED evaluation (Lobo & Nehra, 2005). Optional tests based on findings in the initial exam include tests for levels of luteinizing hormone, follicle stimulating hormone, prolactin, prostate specific antigen, complete blood count, and a thyroid function panel. Once the diagnosis of ED has been established, most clinicians will initially proceed with a trial of an oral PDE-5 inhibitor. In general, no further testing is needed to determine the exact etiology of ED prior to initiating therapy, because the initial treatment options will be the same regardless. In the setting of hypogonadal ED, it is prudent to replace testosterone or treat the rare prolactinoma prior to initiating a PDE-5 inhibitor trial.

Further Evaluation

Based on the basic evaluation, we can define patients with complex ED as (a) those with penile/pelvic/perineal trauma, (b) young men with primary ED (present since age of sexual maturity), (c) men with Peyronie's disease, (d) men who fail oral PDE-5 inhibitors or for whom PDE-5 inhibitors are contraindicated, and (e) men with a significant psychological or psychiatric component. Although technical advances in ED testing allow physicians to counsel patients on the etiology and severity of their dysfunction, significant costs and limitations are associated with each technique described. Prior to beginning any invasive testing, the physician and patient should have a thorough discussion about possible treatment options. Many patients are not interested in injection therapy or any surgical intervention, and these patients should not be subjected to needless invasive tests. If, however, the patient is motivated and an appropriate candidate for the available treatment options, then further testing can proceed in a goal-directed manner.

Psychological Evaluation

In the psychological evaluation, the interviewer should focus on not only a detailed sex-history of childhood, adolescent, and adult events resulting in erectile failure, and the central role of performance anxiety and attitude factors, but also the four following elements: (1) the impact of the couple's systemic issues on the erectile failure, (2) the male's individual psychological issues, (3) physiological impairment, and (4) the couple's sexual behavior pattern (LoPiccolo, 1999). In choice of treatment, prognosis, not diagnosis, must be the deciding factor, and psychological evaluation is critical in making prognostic evaluation for physical interventions (Mohr & Beutler, 1990).

Assessment of prognosis is made with information gathered by semi-structured interviews and symptom-focused questionnaires. Three groups of psychometric instruments are available for the evaluation of ED: (1) personality questionnaires, (2) depression inventories, and (3) questionnaires for sexual dysfunction and relationship factors (Lue, 2002). The Minnesota Multiphasic Personality Inventory (MMPI)-2 is a valuable tool for evaluating the patient's personality and its relevance to sexual dysfunction. The Beck Depression Inventory is a self-reported test for which a score exceeding 18 is considered indicative of significant clinical depression. For relationship assessment, the Short Marital Adjustment Test (for married couples) and the Dyadic Adjustment Inventory (for unmarried people) can be used to determine overall relationship quality. Specific factors examined include fidelity and level of commitment as well as sexual relations, family finances, and relationship with friends. For couples who will be undergoing sex therapy and other physical interventions, a detailed analysis of the nature of the couple's actual behavior is very useful in treatment planning.

Nocturnal Penile Tumescence Testing

Nocturnal penile tumescence (NPT) monitoring, the noninvasive investigation that monitors erections occurring during sleep, had been considered a gold standard for differentiating organic and psychogenic ED (Kaneko & Bradley, 1986). However, its use has been challenged by ongoing research. The primary assumption of NPT testing is that the presence of night erections indicates the ability to have sexually related erections for vaginal intromission. However, the critical question is, does a normal nocturnal erection equate to a normal erotic erection induced by sensory stimuli? Recent research shows some exceptions: (a) men with neurologic disease may have normal sleep erections, but peripheral neuropathy may impair processing of sensory stimuli, yielding poorly sustained erections during coitus; and (b) depression and sleep disorders adversely alter NPT without, in many cases, affecting erections while conscious (Lue, 2002).

NPT has been measured by the following methods: stamp test, snap gauges, strain gauges, nocturnal penile tumescence and rigidity (RigiScan), sleep laboratory NPT, and NPT electrobioimpedance (Lue, 2002). Despite 4 decades of clinical investigations, no universally accepted benchmarks for normal NPT have been reached. Although NPT cannot be used as a single method to distinguish psychogenic and organic ED, it still may have value for the patient without neurovascular risk factors who presents with a history suggestive of a psychogenic cause. Currently, NPT is also valuable for academic interests and for medico-legal cases.

Intracavernosal Injection Pharmaco Testing

Office intracavernosal injection (ICI) testing refers to a single intracavernosal injection of either 10 or 20 µg of a vasoactive substance like prostaglandin E1 (PGE-1) or tri-mix (phentolamine, papaverine, and PGE-1), and then an assessment of the response (Aversa, Isidori, & Caprio, 2002). A lasting quality erection confirms the presence of adequate arterial inflow and veno-occlusive function. A poor quality erection or no erection at all in response to intracavernosal injection might indicate vascular dysfunction, might be a result of insufficient pharmacologic stimulation, or might be reflective of the stress of performing the test in an office setting. Despite the simplicity of the test, it has been replaced by color duplex Doppler ultrasonography (CDDS) as an initial test following a failed PDE-5 inhibitor trial (Aversa et al., 2002).

Color Duplex Doppler Ultrasonography

Color duplex Doppler ultrasonography (CDDS) combines ICI and ultrasound evaluation (King, Lewis, & McKusick, 1994; Lewis, Parulkar, Johnson, & Miller, 1990; Quam et al., 1989). Briefly, this test involves ICI of a vasoactive drug (e.g., PGE1 or trimix) followed by duplex ultrasound assessment of both cavernosal arteries for peak systolic velocity and end diastolic velocity over a period of 20 to 30 minutes at 5-minute intervals. Normally, within the first 5 minutes after vasoactive agent injection, there should be an increase in the cavernosal artery diameter by more than 75% from its flaccid state, and the peak systolic velocity should be at least 25 to 30 cm/sec in order to exclude arterial diseases. Also, normally during the full erection phase, the intracavernous blood pressure should equal or exceed the diastolic blood pressure, making the end diastolic velocity in the penile cavernosal artery equal to or very near zero (King et al., 1994; Lewis et al., 1990; Quam et al., 1989). If the patient does not get an erection as good as he gets on his own at home, then at least one more injection should be made to ensure maximum smooth muscle relaxation, and the measurements should be repeated (Ho, Sathyanarayana, & Lewis, 1999).

CDDS can provide both anatomic detail as well as a quantitative analysis of the penile vascular system. The procedure is specific and accurate, correlates well with dynamic infusion cavernosometry and cavernosography results, and allows a diagnostic categorization of impotent patients (McMahon, 1998). However, it has several drawbacks. Different values may be obtained for the peak systolic velocities and end diastolic velocities during the same test depending on the timing of the examination, the experience of the examiner, and the position of the probe of the device on the penis. It is important to be sure that whatever type of stimulant is used, it is sufficient to overcome the anxiety and sympathetic stimulation brought on by the test itself, especially to men with psychogenic impotence (Granata, Bancroft, & Del Rio, 1995).

Dynamic Infusion Cavernosometry and Cavernosography
When the results of the vascular investigation with CDDS are abnormal, it is appropriate to consider further invasive testing with dynamic infusion cavernosometry and cavernosography (DICC), particularly when patients are candidates for penile vascular surgery. However, the use of DICC in the era of PDE-5 inhibitors and CDDS should be limited to young patients in whom surgical ligation of an identifiable venous leak is a possibility or in medico-legal cases. Because veno-occlusive dysfunction is often a multifocal problem and a result of degeneration of vascular smooth muscle rather than a site specific venous leakage, this venous occlusive test has very limited value.

Dynamic infusion cavernosometry and cavernosography is a more invasive test than CDDS. Cavernosometry involves infusion of saline into the corporal bodies while measuring cavernosal pressure. This test is made more physiologic with injection of a vasoactive substance. The key parameter is the flow to maintain a supraphysiologic cavernosal pressure of 90 mmHg. An inability to maintain this pressure with a flow of 3 mL/min or more after vasoactive injected agent is indicative of venous leakage (Mulhall, Anderson, & Parker, 2004).

Cavernosometry can be combined with cavernosography to try to identify a specific site of leakage. Typically this procedure is performed by infusing a low osmolarity contrast agent in place of saline into the cavernosal bodies at the flow to maintain rate for maximal cavernosal pressure obtained from the cavernosometry part of the evaluation. Fluoroscopy or spot films are then used to identify specific sites of leakage. The results of venous dissection and ligation or crural ligation, however, have not been successful enough over long term follow-up to support continued routine use of this procedure.

Penile Angiography
Penile arteriography is another invasive test mainly used prior to penile surgical revascularization in young men with posttraumatic or congenital arteriogenic ED with no vascular risk factors, or in studying cases of high flow priapism (King et al., 1994; McMahon, 1998).

Corpus Cavernosum Electromyography

Recently, corpus cavernosum electromyography (CC-EMG) as a method to evaluate the functional state of cavernosal smooth muscle was studied and showed significant difference between healthy men and patients with vasculogenic ED (Jiang, Frantzen, & Holsheimer, 2006a, 2006b, 2006c). However, its future role in clinical practice is unclear.

Conclusions Regarding Assessment Procedures

The advent of PDE-5 inhibitors has changed the landscape of the evaluation and treatment of ED. Health care providers in a wide variety of disciplines are now offering the basic screening evaluation and treatment options. Specialists engage in further etiological evaluation only when oral therapy is contraindicated or fails or vacuum therapy is not accepted or fails. In the case of the complicated patient, more sophisticated testing may be required from the outset. Psychological evaluation may reveal the deep intrapsychic causes of psychogenic ED or psychogenic component of mixed ED. To the organic side, CDDS is the most practical and popular diagnostic modality; additional testing with DICC or penile angiography is only rarely needed and should proceed only when surgery is being planned. Appropriate evaluation of psychological and organic risk factors is the prerequisite of successful treatment. An appropriate evaluation procedure is provided in Figure 2.4.

Figure 2.4

Algorithm for ED Evaluation and Testing

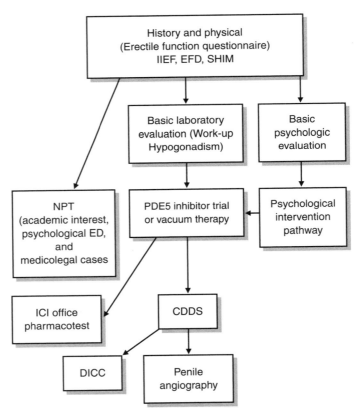

CDDS = Color duplex Doppler ultrasonography; DICC = Dynamic infusion cavernosometry and cavernosography; ED = Erectile dysfunction; EFD = Erectile function domain of IIEF; ICI = Intracavernosal injection; IIEF = International Index of Erectile Function; NPT = Nocturnal penile tumescence; PDE5 = Phosphodiesterase type 5; SHIM = Sexual Health Index in Males.

Management Paradigms for Erectile Dysfunction

Psychological Management

With two fairly effective treatments for ED with few side effects, treatment for organic ED may often entail very little diagnostic workup. However, it is imperative that health care providers initiating treatment recognize that the patient may have psychological issues that will benefit from help from a sexual therapist. A sexual function checklist may help the practitioner who is inexperienced in psychological evaluations to use patient-generated responses that suggest situational and interpersonal conflicts (Althof, Rosen, Rubio-Aurioles, Earle, & Chevret-Measson, 2006).

It may be helpful for a primary physician to seek consultation with an urologist for the management of ED. Those clinicians not trained in psychological or psychiatric management of sexual function must recognize when the patient might benefit from a multidisciplined approach involving trained sexual therapists, and either psychologists or psychiatrists.

In addition, some cases of ED are strongly psychogenic and primary management should be done by a trained sexual therapist. This is particularly relevant in those patients with ED who suffer from clinical depression as some of the medical treatments for depression have ramifications for causality to ED (Ferguson, 2001). As discussed later, combination therapy may also include use of some medical treatment along with traditional sex therapy. An excellent review of the role of evaluation and management of psychologic and interpersonal aspects for sexual disorders has been recently published (Althof et al., 2006). It is not within the scope of this chapter to detail the techniques of sexual therapy for the patient who suffers from ED, but Sidebar 2.2 outlines the scope of such interventions.

SIDEBAR 2.2

Sex Therapy Treatment Interventions for Erectile Dysfunction

- Systematic desensitization.
- Sensate focus.
- Interpersonal therapy.
- Behavioral assignments.
- Psychodynamic interventions.
- Sex education.
- Communication and sexual skills training.
- Masturbation exercises.

Note: Based on the work of Althof et al. (2006).

Risk Factor Modification

Modification of risk factors does offer some improved conditions in the corporeal cavernosal tissue, such as curtailing the use of excessive alcohol consumption, loss of weight, stopping the use of tobacco, modification of some medications (adjustments in antihypertensives or psychotropic medications), improving diabetic control, or improving exercise status (Lewis, 2004). However there is not much evidence that total relief of the condition of ED will be obtained with adjustments except perhaps in early or mild forms of ED. Certainly, incidence reports do not suggest decreasing onset of ED except in those who go from a sedentary lifestyle to more exercise-profiled lifestyle (Derby et al., 2000).

First Line Therapies for Erectile Dysfunction

The use of either oral PDE-5 agents or a vacuum device are the first line therapies for most patients presenting with ED. Oral agents are certainly more appealing to the patient than vacuum devices, but some couples who are very comfortable with their sexual interactions will prefer the vacuum device, especially since it is probably the most cost effective treatment. However, the artificial nature of the erection achieved with the vacuum device is a drawback for its use for many patients and their partners (Lewis, 2005). The use of a vacuum device might be offered to the patient as one of the primary choices for the management of ED rather than a second-line therapy unless chosen so by the patient.

Effective Oral Therapy
The most popular primary treatment option for the patient with ED is one of the three oral PDE-5 inhibitors available since 1998 (Broderick, 2005). Two of these are short acting (sildenafil and vardenafil) and one is long acting (tadalafil) based on blood peak and clearance levels. But here again basic science has shed new light by revealing fresh information. Slow release of these competing PDE-5 inhibitors from cyclic GMP receptors sites as compared to PDE-5 immediate release from cyclic GMP binding sites may account for the longer lasting effects that seem to last beyond blood clearance levels (Francis & Corbin, 2005). This would explain some of the prolonged effect for the short acting inhibitors (how long the medication is lasting in the end organ tissue) and the potential value of daily dosing. There are also competitive binding differences among the agents for other PDEs other than type 5, such as type 6 and type 11.

The oral PDE-5 treatments are highly effective for a variety of organic disease-associated ED and seem to have a continual effect over time (Porst, 2006). All show efficacy in the 70% to 80% range for most patients with ED, with the exception of those with moderate to severe diabetes mellitus and those who are post radical surgery. Response rates in these patients fall to about 20% to 30% compared to other patients suffering from ED. Rechallenging patients who claim poor response from initial trials should be done with many such patients, stressing food interactions, period of therapeutic benefit, and proper expectations for therapy. Contraindications to use are those patients on nitrate or nitrite therapy or those with retinitis pigmentosa. Recently, some ophthalmologists, who were some of the first to call attention to the association of PDE-5 inhibitors to the disorder of nonarteritic ischemic optic neuropathy (NAION), write that the only contraindication is in those patients who have suffered from unilateral blindness from this disorder (Fraunfelder, Pomeranz, & Egan, 2006). However, we suggest some caution for all patients who have suffered significant visual acuity or unilateral blindness. These latter patients should have ophthalmologic evaluation for the presence of crowded disc syndrome associated with nonarteritic ischemic optic neuropathy before being placed on PDE-5 inhibitor treatment.

It may be possible to determine whether a short-acting or long-acting PDE-5 inhibitor is preferred for the initiation of trials in any one individual, or the individual prescriber may have some preference for one of the agents. The most reliable way for the patient to determine his preference is a trial in which samples of one or both short-acting agents and the long-acting agent randomly are provided, with multiple trials (preferable 6 to 7) before the patient considers an agent ineffective. The patient can then decide which product works best for his own particular situation. If the patient obtains enough of an erection for sexual intercourse, he usually continues with this therapy unless he is bothered by one of the side effects, such as headache for all agents, or extremity pain for the long-acting agent, or cannot afford the cost of the treatment.

Vacuum Therapy

Vacuum devices, as mentioned earlier, should be considered one of the primary choices for the treatment of erectile dysfunction (Lewis, 2005). These devices can be purchased without prescription; prescription-requiring devices are preferred because they are more efficiently engineered, backed up with a technical support team, and are reimbursable in many medical insurance coverage plans. This therapy is particularly acceptable to many patients and partners who are very comfortable with their sexual interactions as a couple and whose long-term satisfaction has been documented. For many men seeking treatment for their ED as well as the physicians treating them, the vacuum device may seem rather artificial and not acceptable as a primary therapy. Such practitioner bias may be unfair to the patient's consideration of vacuum therapy as a viable choice for treatment. The patient is capable of understanding the differences of expected interventions if carefully relayed by the therapist.

Vacuum devices consist of a cylinder apparatus that fits over the penis and is connected to a manual or battery-powered vacuum pump that induces engorgement of penile tissue with blood. Preloaded (on the base of the cylinder) compression rings or bands are slipped onto the penis to trap the blood in the penis in order to produce a rigid organ capable of vaginal penetration and sexual intercourse. Usually the amount of negative pressure is limited by pop-off valves incorporated into the device. The occlusion band should generally not be in place for more than 30 minutes. There are few contraindications for use, but some patients with certain bleeding disorders or severe angulation of the penis with erection (Peyronie's disease) may not be able to use such devices. Couples who are satisfied with this low-cost solution to ED are prone to remain satisfied with this therapy over long periods of time, but the artificial nature of the erection and the coldness of the penis are drawbacks for some patients and partners (Lewis, 2005).

Second Line Therapies for Erectile Dysfunction

Intracavernosal Injection Therapy

Before effective oral therapy was available, one of the most popular therapies for erectile dysfunction was injection agents, usually containing papaverine, phentolamine, prostaglandin E-1 (PGE-1), either alone or in some combination form (Fritsche, Usta, & Hellstrom, 2005; Porst & Adaikan, 2006). Tri-mix compositions contain all three of the agents, but are usually less expensive than the two marketed PGE-1 preparations. In addition, when used in combination form, the amount of each ingredient can be lower because of the synergistic nature of these agents. When patients fail or are not satisfied with primary treatment of oral agents or vacuum devices, this therapy remains a very successful treatment for ED, but with the obvious drawback that a needle injection is required. Another drawback is that the risk of priapism is far greater with injection therapy than with other therapeutic choices. Prolonged aching penile pain associated with PGE-1 may also be a drawback for this type of therapy, especially for the FDA approved single agent products.

If a patient chooses this type of therapy or advances to this treatment after first line failure, the authors choose to evaluate the patient with the color duplex Doppler evaluation of the penile arteries with at least two injections using a tri-mix agent. This strategy allows for a more empirically based selection of dose and helps define the type and existence of the vascular deficit in the individual. An office injection with a test agent is, however performed at this juncture by some. Once the optimal dose is selected, the patient or partner is taught proper home injection technique, and warned about possible priapism and the need to seek attention if this occurs for reversal. The patient is also taught to vary the site of injection and is directed to not use more than a single injection daily. Our practice is to periodically follow the patient, at least once yearly, to check on possible corporal fibrosis and tachyphylaxsis.

Intraurethral Therapy

Another possible delivery system for second line therapy for ED is the intraurethral PGE-1 system (Fritsche et al., 2005; Porst & Adaikan, 2006). This procedure relies on intraurethral absorption of the agent from a deposited pellet into the corpus spongiosum and subsequently into the corpora cavernosal tissue via communicating vessels between the two spongy tissues. The amount of PGE-1 required by this route is 10 to 50 times the level producing results by the direct injection method. The suppositories are available in 250, 500, and 1,000 mg dose levels and it is recommended that the first dose be given in the physician's office to observe for possible dizziness episodes or priapism. Efficacy can be improved by the use of an occlusive band placed around the base of the penis at the time of delivery of the urethral suppository in order to enhance better diffusion of the product into the corpora cavernosal tissue. Overall the efficacy first reported in the published literature has not been borne out in clinical practice. However, the use of this agent as part of penile tissue rehabilitation after radical prostate surgery has suggested another potential benefit from this agent (Fenig, Robbins, Brassil, Goodwin, & McCullough, 2007).

Penile Prosthesis

One of the most satisfying treatment options for the management of ED remains the penile prosthesis, yet it is one the most invasive choices for the patient (Rajpurkar & Dhabuwala, 2003). Usually, in today's management strategies, the patient electing this therapy should have tried the more conservative therapies and have found that they have failed, or be bothered so much by their side effects that they have a strong desire for this treatment option. In addition, for some patients with severe structural damage in the corpus cavernosal tissue, this therapy may be the only solution to restore a rigid penis sufficient for penetration. The choice of a semi-rigid device or a two- or three-piece hydraulic device is a decision based on penile anatomy, intact penile sensation, and patient and surgeon preference and recommendation (Wang & Lewis, 2000). The patient should be made aware of expectations regarding the degree of erection and length of the inflated device and the risk of infection. If infection occurs, it will probably necessitate removal of the device. Overall, mechanical failure is extremely low, less than 5% over a 10- to 15-year period post implant (Lewis, 2005; Lewis & Jordan, 2002; Montague, 2007).

Vascular Surgery

For the sake of completeness, vascular surgery for ED should be mentioned. This treatment is highly selective for very specific types of ED such as pelvic trauma to the arterial supply to the corpora cavernosa in a young male or a rare congenital aberrant venous drainage system associated with the corpora cavernosa. For a more comprehensive discussion of this therapeutic choice see the major urological textbook by Lewis and Munarriz (2007).

Combination Strategies for the Management of Erectile Dysfunction

Many clinicians have described using a combination of more than one of these therapies for the management of ED, for example, combining injection therapy with psychotherapy (Wagner & Kaplan, 1993); combining an oral agent with vacuum therapy for recovery of function after radical prostatectomy (Raina, Agarwal, & Allamaneni, 2005); combining injection therapy with oral therapy as a salvage therapy for injection agent failures (McMahon, Samali, & Johnson, 1999); and oral agent failures were salvaged with the addition of injection agents (Guiterrez, Hernandez, & Mas, 2005). Using either intraurethral PGE-1 or a vacuum device in a patient who has had a penile implant and who wishes for glanular engorgement has been reported. Using injection therapy in patients who have had vascular surgery for ED and cannot obtain full rigidity on their own but were unable to get an erection by injection agent before the surgery has been reported (Lewis & Munarriz, 2007). Hormone replacement therapy in hypogonadal men enhances response to oral agents in men with ED (Porst, 2006).

Summary and Conclusions

The understanding and diagnosis of erectile dysfunction has advanced greatly over the past 20 years, with treatment options greatly expanding as a result. This chapter discussed the following:

- Great strides have been made in the understanding of penile anatomy and physiology.
- Understanding the physiological, biochemical, and molecular processes involved in erection has led to a greater understanding of organogenic ED.
- Organogenic ED is not a specific disease process but rather a symptom of other disease processes.

- Factors contributing to ED include psychogenic, neurogenic, endocrinological, and vasculogenic.
- Organogenic ED is strongly associated with diseases that affect neural, endocrinological, or vascular functioning.
- Many drugs are known to interfere with erectile functioning.
- Evaluation of ED may involve as little as a brief medical/sexual history followed by a trial of a PDE-5 inhibitor or a vacuum device.
- More detailed evaluation may involve assessment of psychological and relationship factors and clinical laboratory tests such as color duplex Doppler ultrasonography or dynamic infusion cavernosometry and cavernosography.
- Management strategies should recognize the multifactorial nature of most ED problems.
- Specific management strategies might include risk modification, oral therapies, vacuum device therapy, and when appropriate, counseling.
- Other, more invasive procedures, should be considered when first line therapies are ineffective.

References

Ahn, T. Y., Gomez-Coronado, D., & Martinez, V. (1999). Enhanced contractility of rabbit corpus cavernosum smooth muscle by oxidized low density lipoproteins. *International Journal of Impotence Research, 11,* 9–14.

Althof, S. E., Rosen, R., Rubio-Aurioles, E., Earle, C., & Chevret-Measson, M. (2006). Psychological and interpersonal aspects and their management. In H. Porst & J. Buvat (Eds.), *Standard practice in sexual medicine* (pp. 18–30). Oxford: Blackwell.

American Psychiatric Association. (2000). *Diagnostic and statistical manual of mental disorders* (4th ed., text rev.). Washington, DC: Author.

Andersen, K. V., & Bovim, G. (1997). Impotence and nerve entrapment in long distance amateur cyclists. *Acta Neurologica Scandanavia, 95,* 233–240.

Aversa, A., Isidori, A. M., & Caprio, M. (2002). Penile pharmacotesting in diagnosing male erectile dysfunction: Evidence for lack of accuracy and specificity. *International Journal of Andrology, 25,* 6–10.

Azadzoi, K. M., Krane, R. J., & Saenz de Tejada, I. (1999). Relative roles of cyclooxygenase and nitric oxide synthase pathways in ischemia-induced increased contraction of cavernosal smooth muscle. *Journal of Urology, 161,* 1324–1328.

Azadzoi, K. M., Park, K., & Andry, C. (1997). Relationship between cavernosal ischemia and corporal veno-occlusive dysfunction in an animal model. *Journal of Urology, 157,* 1011–1017.

Azadzoi, K. M., & Saenz de Tejada, I. (1991). Hypercholesterolemia impairs endothelium-dependent relaxation of rabbit corpus cavernosum smooth muscle. *Journal of Urology, 146,* 238–240.

Broderick, G. (Ed.). (2005). *Oral pharmacotherapy for male sexual dysfunction: A guide to clinical management.* Totowa, NJ: Humana Press.

Burke, F. P., Jacobson, D. F., & McGree, M. E. (2006). Diabetes and sexual dysfunction in Olmsted County, Minnesota. *Journal of Sex Medicine, 3,* 19.

Catalona, W. J., & Bigg, S. W. (1990). Nerve-sparing radical prostatectomy: Evaluation of results after 250 patients. *Journal of Urology, 143,* 538–543.

Cerami, A., Vlassara, H., & Brownlee, M. (1987). Glucose and aging. *Scientific American, 256,* 90–96.

Christ, G. J., Maayani, S., Valcic, M., & Melman, A. (1990). Pharmacologic studies of human erectile tissue: Characteristics of spontaneous contractions and alterations in alpha-adrenoceptor responsiveness with age and disease in isolated tissues. *British Journal of Pharmacology, 101,* 375–381.

Christ, G. J., Moreno, A. P., & Parker, M. E. (1991). Intercellular communication through gap junctions: A potential role in pharmacomechanical coupling and syncytial tissue contraction in vascular smooth muscle isolated from the human corpus cavernosum. *Life Science, 49,* PL195–PL200.

Chuang, A. T., Strauss, J. D., & Steers, W. D. (1998). CGMP mediates corpus cavernosum smooth muscle relaxation with altered crossbridge function. *Life Science, 63,* 185–194.

Courtois, F. J., MacDougall, J. C., & Sachs, B. D. (1993). Erectile mechanism in paraplegia. *Physiological Behavior, 53,* 721–726.

Derby, C. A., Mohr, B., Goldstein, I., Feldman, H. A., Joahannes, C. B., & McKinlay, J. B. (2000). Modifiable risk factor and erectile dysfunction: Can life-style changes modify risk? *Journal of Urology, 56,* 302–306.

Eardley, I., & Kirby, R. S. (1991). Neurogenic impotence. In R. S. Kirby, C. C. Carson, C. C Webster, & G. D. Webster (Eds.), *Impotence: Diagnosis and management of male erectile dysfunction* (pp. 227–231). Oxford: Butterworth-Heinemann.

Fan, S. F., Brink, P. R., Melman, A., & Christ, G. J. (1995). An analysis of the maxi-K^+ (KCa) channel in cultured human corporal smooth muscle cells. *Journal of Urology, 153,* 818–825.

Feldman, H. A., Goldstein, I., Hatzichristou, D. G., Krane, R. J., & McKinlay, J. B. (1994). Impotence and its medical and psychosocial correlates: Results of the Massachusetts Male Aging Study. *Journal of Urology, 151,* 54–61.

Fenig, D., Robbins, D., Brassil, D., Goodwin, B., & McCullough, A. R. (2007, March/April). 6 month interim analysis of the longitudinal effects on penile oxygen saturation from a randomized study of the nightly use of intraurethral alprostadil vs sildenafil following Nerve Sparing Radical Prostatectomy (NSRRP). *Journal of Andrology* (Suppl. 59).

Ferguson, J. M. (2001). The effects of antidepressants on sexual functioning in depressed patients: A review. *Journal of Clinical Psychiatry, 62,* 22–34.

Francis, S. H., & Corbin, J. D. (2005). Phosphodiesterase-5 inhibition: The molecular biology of erectile function and dysfunction. *Urologic Clinics of North America, 32,* 419–429.

Fraunfelder, F. W., Pomeranz, H. D., & Egan, R. A. (2006). Nonarteritic anterior optic neuropathy and sildenafil. *Archives of Ophthalmology, 124,* 733–734.

Fritsche, H. A., Usta, M. F., & Hellstrom, W. J. G. (2005). Intracavernous, transurethral, and topical therapies for erectile dysfunction in the era of oral pharmacotherapy: Salvaging first-line therapy failures with combination therapies. In G. A. Broderick (Ed.), *Oral pharmacotherapy for male sexual dysfunction: A guide to clinical management* (pp. 253–277). Totowa, NJ: Humana Press.

Fugl-Meyer, A. R., & Fugl-Meyer, K. S. (2002). Sexual disabilities are not singularities. *International Journal of Impotence Research, 14,* 487–493.

Garban, H., Vernet, D., & Freedman, A. (1995). Effect of aging on nitric oxide–mediated penile erection in rats. *American Journal of Physiology, 268,* H467–H475.

Goldstein, I., Feldman, M. I., & Deckers, P. J. (1984). Radiation-associated impotence: A clinical study of its mechanism. *Journal of the American Medical Association, 251,* 903–910.

Granata, A., Bancroft, J., & Del Rio, G. (1995). Stress and the erectile response to intracavernosal prostaglandin E_1 in men with erectile dysfunction. *Psychosomatic Medicine, 57,* 336–344.

Guiterrez, P., Hernandez, P., & Mas, M. (2005). Combining programmed intracavernous PGE1 injections and sildenafil on demand to salvage sildenafil nonresponders. *International Journal of Impotence Research, 10,* 225–231.

Hayashi, K., Takamizawa, K., & Nakamura, T. (1987). Effects of elastase on the stiffness and elastic properties of arterial walls in cholesterol-fed rabbits. *Atherosclerosis, 66,* 259–267.

Ho, L. V., Sathyanarayana, G., & Lewis, R. W. (1999). Two injection color duplex Doppler characterization of patients with successful Viagra use (Abstract No. 1043). *Journal of Urology, 161*(Suppl. 4), 270.

Hsieh, J. T., Muller, S. C., & Lue, T. F. (1989). The influence of blood flow and blood pressure on penile erection. *International Journal of Impotence Research, 1,* 35–42.

Hsu, G. L., Brock, G., & von Heyden, B. (1994). The distribution of elastic fibrous elements within the human penis. *British Journal of Urology, 73,* 566–571.

Ignarro, L. J., Bush, P. A., & Buga, G. M. (1990). Nitric oxide and cyclic GMP formation upon electrical field stimulation cause relaxation of corpus cavernosum smooth muscle. *Biochemical and Biophysics Research Communication, 170,* 843–850.

Jiang, X., Frantzen, J., & Holsheimer, J. (2006a). Corpus cavernosum electromyography in patients with penile fibrosis and patients who underwent pelvic surgery (Abstract No. 64). *Journal of Sex Medicine, 3*(34).

Jiang, X., Frantzen, J., & Holsheimer, J. (2006b). Corpus cavernosum electromyography in patients with vasculogenic erectile dysfunction (Abstract No. 65). *Journal of Sex Medicine, 3*(34).

Jiang, X., Frantzen, J., & Holsheimer, J. (2006c). Reproducibility of corpus cavernosum electromyography (Abstract No. 63). *Journal of Sex Medicine, 3*(33).

Junemann, K. P., Lue, T. F., & Luo, J. A. (1987). The effect of cigarette smoking on penile erection. *Journal of Urology, 138,* 438–441.

Kaiser, F. E., Viosca, S. P., & Morley, J. E. (1988). Impotence and aging: Clinical and hormonal factors. *Journal of American Geriatric Society, 36,* 511–519.

Kaneko, S., & Bradley, W. E. (1986). Evaluation of erectile dysfunction with continuous monitoring of penile rigidity. *Journal of Urology, 136,* 1026–1029.

Kim, J. H., Klyachkin, M. L., & Svendsen, E. (1994). Experimental hypercholesterolemia in rabbits induces cavernosal atherosclerosis with endothelial and smooth muscle cell dysfunction. *Journal of Urology, 151,* 198–205.

Kim, S. C., Kim, I. K., & Seo, K. K. (1997). Involvement of superoxide radical in the impaired endothelium-dependent relaxation of cavernous smooth muscle in hypercholesterolemic rabbits. *Urological Research, 25,* 341–346.

King, B. F., Lewis, R. W., & McKusick, M. A. (1994). Radiologic evaluation of impotence. In A. H. Bennet (Ed.), *Impotence: Principles of diagnosis and management* (pp. 7–92). Philadelphia: Saunders.

Leonard, M. P., Nickel, C. J., & Morales, A. (1989). Hyperprolactinemia and impotence: Why, when and how to investigate. *Journal of Urology, 142,* 992–994.

Lerner, S. E., Melman, A., & Christ, G. J. (1993). A review of erectile dysfunction: New insights and more questions. *Journal of Urology, 149,* 1246–1255.

Levine, F. J., Greenfield, A. J., & Goldstein, I. (1990). Arteriographically determined occlusive disease within the hypogastric-cavernous bed in impotent patients following blunt perineal and pelvic trauma. *Journal of Urology, 144,* 1147–1153.

Levine, S. B., & Althof, S. E. (1991). The pathogenesis of psychogenic erectile dysfunction. *Journal of Sex Education and Therapy, 17,* 251.

Lewis, R. W. (2001). Epidemiology of erectile dysfunction. *Urologic Clinics of North America, 28,* 209–216.

Lewis, R. W. (2004). Can weight loss improve the erectile function of obese men? (Commentary). *Nature Clinical Practice, 1*(2), 68–69.

Lewis, R. W. (2005). Sustaining the cure: Oral pharmacotherapy failure salvage with vacuum devices and penile implants. In G. A. Broderick (Ed.), *Oral pharmacotherapy for male sexual dysfunction: A guide to clinical management* (pp. 323–337). Totowa, NJ: Humana Press.

Lewis, R. W., Fugl-Meyer, K. S., Bosch, R., Fugl-Meyer, A. R., Laumann, E. O., Lizza, E., et al. (2004a). Definition, classification and epidemiology of sexual dysfunction. In T. F. Lue, R. Basson, R. Rosen, F. Giuliano, S. Khoury & F. Montrosi (Eds.), *Sexual medicine: Sexual dysfunctions in men and women* (pp. 39–72). Paris: Health Publications.

Lewis, R. W., Fugl-Meyer, K. S., Bosch, R., Fugl-Meyer, A. R., Laumann, E. O., Lizza, E., et al. (2004b). Epidemiology/risk factors of sexual dysfunction. *Journal of Sex Medicine, 1*(1), 35–39.

Lewis, R. W., Hatzichristou, D., Laumann, E. O., & McKinlay, J. (2000). Epidemiology and natural history of erectile dysfunction: Risk factors including iatrogenic and aging. In A. Jardin, G. Wagner, S. Khoury, F. Giuliano, H. Padma-Nathan, & R. Rosen (Eds.), *Erectile dysfunction* (pp. 19–51). Plymouth, England: Plymbridge Distributors.

Lewis, R. W., & Jordan, G. H. (2002). Surgery for erectile dysfunction. In P. C. Walsh (Ed.), *Campbell's Urology* (8th ed., pp. 1673–1709). Philadelphia: Saunders.

Lewis, R. W., & Munarriz, R. (2007). Vascular surgery for erectile dysfunction. In A. J. Wein, L. R. Kavoussi, A. C. Novick, A. W. Partin, & C. A. Peters (Eds.), *Campbell-Walsh Urology* (9th ed., pp. 802–817). Philadelphia: Saunders/Elsevier.

Lewis, R. W., Parulkar, B. G., Johnson, C. M., & Miller, W. E. (1990). Radiology of impotence. In B. Lytton, W. J. Catalona, L. I. Lipshultz, E. J. McGuire (Eds.), *Advances in urology* (pp. 132–153). Chicago: Mosby Year Book.

Lizza, E. F., & Rosen, R. C. (1999). Definition and classification of erectile dysfunction: Report of the nomenclature committee of the International Society of Impotence Research. *International Journal of Impotence Research, 11,* 141–143.

Lobo, J. R., & Nehra, A. (2005). Clinical evaluation of erectile dysfunction in the era of PDE-5 inhibitors. *Urological Clinics of North America, 32,* 447–455.

LoPiccolo, J. (1999). Psychological assessment of erectile dysfunction. In C. Carson, R. Kirby, & I. Goldstein (Eds.), *Textbook of erectile dysfunction* (pp. 183–193). Oxford: ISIA Medical Media.

Lue, T. F. (2000). Erectile dysfunction. *New England Journal of Medicine, 42,* 1802–1813.

Lue, T. F. (2002). Physiology of penile erection and pathophysiology of erectile dysfunction and priapism. In P. C. Walsh, A. B. Retik, & E. D. Vaughan, Jr. (Eds.), *Campbell's urology* (8th ed., pp. 1610–1696). Philadelphia: Saunders.

Masters, W. H., & Johnson, V. E. (1970). *Human sexual inadequacy* (p. 467). Boston: Little, Brown.

Masters, W. H., & Johnson, V. E. (1977). Sex after sixty-five. *Reflections, 12,* 31–43.

McMahon, C. G. (1998). Correlation of penile duplex ultrasonography, PBI, DICC and angiography in the diagnosis of impotence. *International Journal of Impotence Research, 10,* 153–158.

McMahon, C. G., Samali, R., & Johnson, H. (1999). Treatment of intracorporeal injection nonresponse with sildenafil alone or in combination with triple agent intracorporeal injection therapy. *Journal of Urology, 162,* 1992–1998.

Mersdorf, A., Goldsmith, P. C., & Diederichs, W. (1991). Ultrastructural changes in impotent penile tissue: A comparison of 65 patients. *Journal of Urology, 145,* 749–758.

Michal, V., & Ruzbarsky, V. (1980). Histological changes in the penile arterial bed with aging and diabetes. In A. W. Zorgniotti & G. Rossi (Eds.), *Vasculogenic impotence: Proceedings of the first international conference on corpus cavernosum revascularization* (pp. 113–119). Springfield, IL: Charles C Thomas.

Miller, N. S., & Gold, M. S. (1988). The human sexual response and alcohol and drugs. *Journal of Substance Abuse and Treatment, 5,* 171–177.

Mills, T. M., Lewis, R. W., & Wingard, C. J. (2003). Vasoconstriction, rhoA/rho-kinase and the erectile response. *International Journal of Impotence Research, 15*(5), 20–24.

Mohr, D. C., & Beutler, L. E. (1990). Erectile dysfunction: A review of diagnostic and treatment procedures. *Clinical Psychology Reviews, 10,* 23–150.

Montague, D. K. (2007). Prosthetic surgery for erectile dysfunction. In A. J. Wein, L. R. Kavoussi, A. C. Novick, A. W. Partin, & C. A. Peters (Eds.), *Campbell-Walsh urology* (9th ed., pp. 788–801). Philadelphia: Saunders/Elsevier.

Montague, D. K., Jarow, J. P., & Roderick, A. (2005). The management of erectile dysfunction: An AUA update. *Journal of Urology, 174,* 130–139.

Moore, C. R., & Wang, R. (2006). Pathophysiology and treatment of diabetic erectile dysfunction. *Asian Journal of Andrology, 8*(6), 675–684.

Morales, A., Schulman, C. C., Tostain, J., & Wu, F. C. W. (2006). Testosterone deficiency syndrome (TDS) need to be named appropriately: The importance of accurate terminology. *European Urology, 50,* 407–409.

Moreland, R. B., Traish, A., & McMillin, M. A. (1995). PGE1 suppresses the induction of collagen synthesis by transforming growth factor-beta 1 in human corpus cavernosum smooth muscle. *Journal of Urology, 153,* 826–834.

Mulhall, J. P., Anderson, M., & Parker, M. (2004). Congruence between veno-occlusive parameters during dynamic infusion cavernosometry: Assessing the need for cavernosography. *International Journal of Impotence Research, 16,* 146–149.

Mulligan, T., & Schmitt, B. (1993). Testosterone for erectile failure. *Journal of Internal Medicine, 8,* 517–521.

Nehra, A., Azadzoi, K. M., & Moreland, R. B. (1998). Cavernosal expandability is an erectile tissue mechanical property which predicts trabecular histology in an animal model of vasculogenic erectile dysfunction. *Journal of Urology, 159,* 2229–2236.

Nogues, M. A., Starkstein, S., & Davalos, M. (1991). Cardiovascular reflexes and pudendal evoked responses in chronic haemodialysis patients. *Functional Neurology, 6,* 359–365.

Paick, J. S., Goldsmith, P. C., & Batra, A. K. (1991). Relationship between venous incompetence and cavernous nerve injury: Ultrastructural alteration of cavernous smooth muscle in the neurotomized dog. *International Journal of Impotence Research, 3,* 185–195.

Persson, C., Diederichs, W., & Lue, T. F. (1989). Correlation of altered penile ultrastructure with clinical arterial evaluation. *Journal of Urology, 142,* 1462–1468.

Pickard, R. S., King, P., Zar, M. A., & Powell, P. H. (1994). Corpus cavernosal relaxation in impotent men. *British Journal of Urology, 74,* 485–491.

Porst, H. (2006). Oral pharmacotherapy of erectile dysfunction. In H. Porst & J. Buvat (Eds.), *Standard practice in sexual medicine* (pp. 75–93). Oxford: Blackwell.

Porst, H., & Adaikan, G. (2006). Self-injection, trans-urethral and topical therapy in erectile dysfunction. In H. Porst & J. Buvat (Eds.), *Standard practice in sexual medicine* (pp. 94–108). Oxford: Blackwell.

Quam, J. P., King, B. F., James, E. M., Lewis, R. W., Brakke, D. M., Ilstrup, D., et al. (1989). Duplex and color Doppler sonographic evaluation of vasculogenic impotence. *American Journal of Radiology, 153,* 1141–1147.

Quinlan, D. M., Epstein, J. I., & Carter, B. S. (1991). Sexual function following radical prostatectomy: Influence of preservation of neurovascular bundles. *Journal of Urology, 145,* 998–1002.

Raina, R., Agarwal, A., & Allamaneni, S. S. (2005). Sildenafil citrate and vacuum constriction device combination enhances sexual satisfaction in erectile dysfunction after radical prostatectomy. *Urology, 65,* 360–364.

Rajfer, J., Rosciszewski, A., & Mehringer, M. (1988). Prevalence of corporal venous leakage in impotent men. *Journal of Urology, 140,* 69–71.

Rajpurkar, A., & Dhabuwala, B. (2003). Comparison of satisfaction rates and erectile function in patients treated with sildenafil, intracavernous prostaglandin E1 and penile implant surgery for erectile dysfunction in urology practice. *Journal of Urology, 170,* 159–163.

Rehman, J., & Melman, A. (2001). Normal anatomy and physiology. In J. J. Mulcahy (Ed.), *Male sexual function, a guide to clinical management* (p. 46). Totowa, NJ: Humana Press.

Ricchiuti, V. S., Haas, C. A., & Seftel, A. D. (1999). Pudendal nerve injury associated with avid bicycling. *Journal of Urology, 162,* 2099–2100.

Rosen, M. P., Greenfield, A. J., & Walker, T. G. (1990). Arteriogenic impotence: Findings in 195 impotent men examined with selective internal pudendal angiography. *Radiology, 174,* 1043–1048.

Rowland, D. L., Greenleaf, W., & Mas, M. (1989). Penile and finger sensory thresholds in young, aging, and diabetic males. *Archives of Sexual Behavior, 18,* 1–12.

Rubanyi, G. M., Romero, J. C., & Vanhoutte, P. M. (1989). Flow-induced release of endothelium-derived relaxing factor. *American Journal of Physiology, 250,* H1145–H1149.

Sachs, B. D., & Meisel, R. L. (1988). The physiology of male sexual behavior. In E. Knobil, J. D. Neill, & L. L. Ewing (Eds.), *The physiology of reproduction* (pp. 1393–1423). New York: Raven Press.

Saenz de Tejada, I., & Blanco, R. (1988). Cholinergic neurotransmission in human corpus cavernosum: Pt. I. Responses of isolated tissue. *American Journal of Physiology, 254,* H459–H467.

Saenz de Tejada, I., Carson, M. P., & de las Morenas, A. (1991). Endothelin: Localization, synthesis, activity, and receptor types in human penile corpus cavernosum. *American Journal of Physiology, 261,* H1078–H1085.

Saenz de Tejada, I., Goldstein, I., & Azadzoi, K. (1989). Impaired neurogenic and endothelium-mediated relaxation of penile smooth muscle from diabetic men with impotence. *New England Journal of Medicine, 320,* 1025–1030.

Saenz de Tejada, I., Moroukian, P., & Tessier, J. (1991). Trabecular smooth muscle modulates the capacitor function of the penis: Studies on a rabbit model. *American Journal of Physiology, 260,* H1590–H1595.

Salvatierra, O., Fortmann, J. L., & Belzer, F. O. (1975). Sexual function of males before and after renal transplantation. *Urology, 5,* 64–66.

Sattar, A. A, Haot, J., Schulman, C. C., & Wespes, E. (1996). Comparison of antidesmin and antiactin staining for the computerized analysis of cavernous smooth muscle density. *British Journal of Urology, 77,* 266–270.

Schiavi, R. C., & Schreiner-Engel, P. (1988). Nocturnal penile tumescence in healthy aging men. *Journal of Gerontology, 43,* M146–M150.

Smith, A. D. (1981). Causes and classification of impotence. *Urologic Clinics of North America, 8,* 79–89.

Taddei, S., Virdis, A., & Ghiadoni, L. (2000). Vascular effects of endothelin-1 in essential hypertension: Relationship with cyclooxygenase-derived endothelium-dependent contracting factors and nitric oxide. *Journal of Cardiovascular Pharmacology, 35,* S37–S40.

Tenover, J. L. (1998). Male hormone replacement therapy including "andropause." *Endocrinology and Metabolism Clinics of North America, 27,* 969–987.

Traish, A. M., & Kim, N. N. (2007). Role of testosterone in erectile physiology and pathophysiology. *Journal of Sex Medicine, 4*(Suppl. 1), 33.

Vickers, M. A., & Wright, E. A. (2004). Erectile dysfunction in the patient with diabetes mellitus. *American Journal of Managed Care, 10,* S3–S11.

Wagner, G. (1992). Aspects of genital physiology and pathology. *Seminars in Neurology, 12,* 87–97.

Wagner, G., & Kaplan, H. S. (1993). *The new injection treatment for impotence: Medical and psychological aspects.* New York: Brunner/Mazel.

Walsh, M. P. (1991). The Ayerst award lecture: Calcium-dependent mechanisms of regulation of smooth muscle contraction. *Biochemistry and Cell Biology, 69,* 771–800.

Walsh, P. C., & Donker, P. J. (1982). Impotence following radical prostatectomy: Insight into etiology and prevention. *Journal of Urology, 128,* 492–497.

Wang, R., & Lewis, R. W. (2000). Penile implants: Types and current indications. In J. J. Mulcahy (Ed.), *Current clinical urology: Male sexual function: A guide to clinical management* (pp. 1–15). Totowa, NJ: Humana Press.

Wermuth, L., & Stenager, E. (1992). Sexual aspects of Parkinson's disease. *Seminars in Neurology, 12,* 125–127.

Wolfe, M. M. Impotence and cimetidine treatment. (1979). *New England Journal of Medicine, 300,* 94.

Premature Ejaculation

David L. Rowland and Chris G. McMahon

3
Chapter

Learning Objectives

In this chapter, we:

- Provide a brief overview of male ejaculatory response.
- Specify important dimensions of premature ejaculation.
- Indicate the definition and prevalence of premature ejaculation.
- Discuss physiological and psychological etiologies.
- Describe a range of assessment strategies.
- Discuss procedures for and relevance of counseling and sex therapy for men with premature ejaculation.
- Review the data and options for pharmacological treatment.
- Identify potential advantages of combined treatment strategies.

Premature ejaculation (PE) is a common but poorly understood male sexual dysfunction that, as new treatment options become available, is receiving increasing attention among health care professionals. Nevertheless, even as treatment strategies—whether they be primarily biomedical or primarily behavioral—show greater promise, the mechanisms through which they work remain elusive and, to a large extent, hypothetical. One of the reasons for the mystery surrounding PE is that the ejaculatory response itself is complex and not fully understood. Ejaculatory response has two distinct phases (actually three, counting the concomitant experience of orgasm); it involves cerebral, spinal, and peripheral components of the nervous system; it requires somatic and autonomic sympathetic and parasympathetic activation; it is mediated through a number of different neurotransmitters at various levels of neural functioning; and it is directly tied to a man's level of physiological and psychosexual arousal—processes that involve a multitude of biological and psychological factors of their own (Motofei & Rowland, 2005). In the following section, we provide a highly simplified description of the ejaculatory process.

Ejaculatory Response

Ejaculation represents the sequencing of two reflexes under cerebral control that typically coincide with the high point of sexual arousal (Giuliano & Clement, 2005). Unlike erection, which may occur in response to psychosexual stimulation (e.g., visual images, smells, words, sounds, nongenital touch), ejaculatory response rarely occurs in the absence of direct penile stimulation. The first reflex—emission—is a sympathetic response that closes the bladder neck (preventing urination and retrograde ejaculation) and stimulates excretion of seminal fluid (which mixes with sperm) from the prostate into the urethral tract. This first stage of ejaculation is associated with "ejaculatory inevitability" that men experience prior to actual expulsion of the seminal fluid, and serves as a partial though probably incomplete trigger for the second reflex. The second reflex—putatively involving the parasympathetic system or the somatic motor system, or both—involves the expulsion of the seminal fluid from the urethra (the outward manifestation of ejaculation), achieved through the rhythmic contractions of the bulbocavernosal and ischiocavernosal muscles (associated with anal sphincter muscle contraction). The subjective perception of these contractions, mediated through sensory neurons in the region, gives rise to the experience of orgasm, which comprises a distinct and separate loop—again a process poorly understood. Thus, ejaculation can and does occur (though rarely) without concomitant orgasm.

The mechanism that actually triggers the entire ejaculatory process is not understood. Presumably, the ejaculatory reflex is predominantly controlled by a complex interplay between central serotonergic and dopaminergic neurons with secondary involvement of cholinergic, adrenergic, nitrergic, oxytocinergic, galanergic and GABAergic neurons. The cerebral events that occur during ejaculation and the abnormalities present in men with premature ejaculation have not been clearly defined with PET and fMRI brain imaging techniques (Figure 3.1). Seminal emission and expulsion

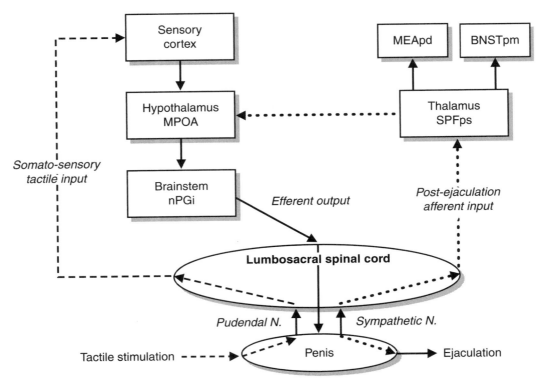

Figure 3.1

Central nervous system areas involved before, during, and after ejaculation. Somatosensory tactile input from the penis/genitals ascends to the cerebral cortex. Efferent pathways project from the hypothalamus to the sacral spinal cord and genitals. After ejaculation, information is returned from the genitals to several brain areas.

Note: BNSTpm = Posteromedial bed nucleus of stria terminalis; MEApd = Posterodorsal medial amygdala; MPOA = Medial preoptic area; nPGI = Nucleus paragigantocellularis; SPFps = Medial parvicellular subparafasicular nucleus of thalamus.

are integrated into the complex pattern of copulatory behavior by several forebrain structures including the medial preoptic area (MPOA) and the nucleus paragigantocellularis (nPGi) (Robinson & Mishkin, 1966; Yells, Hendricks, & Prendergast, 1992). Descending serotonergic pathways from the nPGI to the lumbosacral motor nuclei tonically inhibit ejaculation (Yells et al., 1992), such that disinhibition of the nPGI by the MPOA facilitates ejaculation. A population of lumbar spinothalamic neurons (LSt cells) has been identified in male rats, which constitutes an integral part of the generation of ejaculation. LSt cells send projections to the autonomic nuclei and motoneurons involved in the emission and expulsion phase, and they receive sensory projections from the pelvis

(Truitt & Coolen, 2002). Several brain areas are activated after ejaculation by ascending fibers from the spinal cord and may have a possible role in satiety and the postejaculatory refractory time.

As noted, brain or spinal serotonin has been hypothesized as one of the relevant neurotransmitters. Accordingly, various antidepressant drugs that affect the serotonergic system (e.g., tricyclics, anafranil; and SSRIs, Prozac, Zoloft) have been used fairly effectively to prolong intercourse in men who usually ejaculate very rapidly. Not surprisingly, since ejaculation is also mediated in part by the sympathetic nervous system, prescription and over-the-counter drugs that attenuate sympathetic response (and there are dozens, including some common cold remedies) may interfere with a normal ejaculatory process.

There are many possible points at which the ejaculatory process might be affected or altered. Yet, for the most part, ejaculatory disorders represent problems of timing (sooner or later than desired) rather than problems in the steps involved in ejaculation. The incidence of complete anejaculation in the absence of an obvious underlying pathophysiological or disease condition appears to be fairly rare, although its prevalence through self-report measures may be increasing.

Nomenclature, Definition, and Prevalence

PE has been known by a variety of names. The classic terminology, *ejaculatio praecox* (literally Latin for precocious ejaculation), was later replaced with "premature ejaculation," a term that was entrenched within the clinical community for decades. However, with new cultural awareness and attempts to destigmatize sexual problems, alternative nomenclatures such as "rapid" ejaculation and "early" ejaculation gained ephemeral popularity, as the term "premature" had pejorative overtones. However, neither of these alternatives successfully conveyed an important aspect of PE, namely that ejaculation occurs prior to some anticipated time. As a result, the terminology *premature ejaculation* has once again become the nomenclature of choice by most researchers and clinicians, although some still prefer to use rapid ejaculation, probably the second most common terminology in use.

Characteristics

Defining PE and diagnosing men with this condition have been the source of debate within research, medical, and clinical circles. The *DSM-IV-TR* definition of PE is probably the most commonly used reference for clinical and research investigations (*Diagnostic and Statistical Manual of Mental Disorders*, fourth edition [*DSM-IV*];

American Psychiatric Association, 1994, pp. 509–511). This definition presents a multidimensional approach to the diagnosis of PE that includes three principal components: short ejaculatory latency (i.e., "before, on, or shortly after penetration") in response to minimal stimulation, a perceived lack of control over ejaculation (i.e., "before the person wishes it"), and a negative impact of the condition on the person or relationship (i.e., "marked distress or interpersonal difficulty").

Although some researchers and clinicians emphasize one dimension over another and/or advocate using precise cut-offs in terms of ejaculatory latency (e.g., 60 or 90 seconds after vaginal penetration: Waldinger & Schweitzer, 2006), most recognize the important contribution that each of these dimensions adds to an accurate diagnosis of PE. For example, men with PE reliably take less time to reach ejaculation (on average about 1 to 2 min or less) than men without PE (on average about 7 to 9 min; Patrick et al., 2005). Using specific ejaculation latency cut-offs of 60 or 90 seconds may not necessarily improve the accuracy of a diagnosis, as the more critical dimension for PE is the *amount of stimulation that occurs intravaginally,* not simply the passage of time following vaginal intromission by the man (as is measured with latency time: Shabsigh & Rowland, 2007), as underscored by the fact that an estimated 5% to 15% of men with PE ejaculate prior to vaginal entry (ante-portal or "before the gate"). Nevertheless, the present impracticality of measuring "stimulation" will result in the continued use of some measure related to duration; most men with PE (and their partners) are more likely to recall "how long they lasted" rather than the "number of thrusts" that it took to reach ejaculation.

A second characteristic of PE is the man's perceived lack of control or ability to delay ejaculation. This measure of "self-efficacy" reliably differentiates men with PE from those without PE (Rowland, Patrick, Rothman, & Gagnon, 2007); specifically, men with PE typically report little to no ability to control the timing of their ejaculation (e.g., 1 or 2 on a 5 pt scale, where 1 = not at all, 5 = very much), contrasted with men without PE who typically report 3 to 5 on the same scale. Indeed, the central role of inadequate ejaculatory control has been borne out by two recent analyses. In the first, perceived control over ejaculation and personal distress related to ejaculation were the two most influential explanatory variables in predicting PE status (as determined by a clinician using the *DSM-IV-TR;* Rosen et al., 2007). In the second analysis, inadequate control over ejaculation was most directly responsible for the distress and relationship difficulty associated with PE (Patrick, Rowland, & Rothman, 2007).

All consensus definitions of PE include some type of negative influence on the man's life, whether described as distress, bother, upset, frustration, interpersonal difficulty, relationship difficulty, decreased enjoyment of lovemaking, and so on. Recent studies have shown that most men with PE report some type of negative impact of PE on their lives or relationships. This negative impact is as great as it is for men with ED and men with PE report their partners are adversely affected as well (Rowland et al., 2007). Such consequences typically drive men and their partners to seek treatment.

The three dimensions discussed—short latency, lack of control, and personal or interpersonal stress—can be tapped using the Premature Ejaculation Profile (PEP; see Sidebar 3.1). Response ranges typical of men with PE and men without PE are provided as well.

SIDEBAR 3.1

Items from the Premature Ejaculation Profile and Mean Responses of Men with and without PE

Item	Men with PE	Controls
Over the past month, was your control over ejaculation during sexual intercourse . . . ? (0 = very poor; 4 = very good)	0.9	3.0
Over the past month, was your satisfaction with sexual intercourse . . . ? (0 = very poor; 4 = very good)	1.9	3.3
How distressed are you by how fast you ejaculate during sexual intercourse? (4 = extremely; 0 = not at all)	2.9	0.7
To what extent does how fast you ejaculate cause difficulty in your relationship with your partner? (4 = extremely; 0 = not at all)	1.9	0.3

Source: Rowland et al., 2007.

Prevalence

Without precise criteria for diagnosing PE, determining its prevalence has been a challenge. Most community based epidemiological studies are limited by their reliance on either patient self-report of PE or inconsistent and poorly validated definitions of PE. A recent multinational community based age-ranging study of an unselected "normal" population of 500 heterosexual couples involved stopwatch timing of the intravaginal ejaculatory latency time (IELT) during sexual intercourse has provided previously lacking normative data (Waldinger et al., 2005). This study demonstrated that the distribution of the IELT was positively skewed, with a median IELT of 5.4 min (range, 0.55 to 44.1 min). The median IELT decreased with age and varied between countries. The authors regarded the 0.5 and 2.5 percentiles as acceptable standards of disease definition in this type of skewed distribution, and proposed that men with an IELT of less than 1 minute (belonging to the 0.5 percentile) have "definite" premature ejaculation, while men with IELTs between 1 and 1.5 min (between 0.5 and 2.5 percentile) have "probable" premature ejaculation (Waldinger, Zwinderman, Olivier, & Schweitzer, 2005).

In other community- or population-based studies, some 20% to 30% of men have been found to endorse the statement that they "ejaculate sooner than desired." Such endorsements, however, do not necessarily confirm a clinical diagnosis of PE; and therefore such techniques (the only ones realistic for surveys of large populations) probably overestimate the actual prevalence (Laumann, Paik, & Rosen, 1999; Patrick et al., 2005; Rowland et al., 2004).

As stricter criteria are placed on a PE classification by including additional measures, such as whether "ejaculating too early is a source of distress or bother," the prevalence is only about 15%, that is, even though 30% of men indicate that they ejaculate sooner than desired, only half are actually bothered by it. We assume, without empirical data to support it, that the other 15% have found ways to cope with their reported condition. If additional criteria are stipulated, such as whether to use a cut-off latency time to ejaculation or self-reported "no" or "very little" perceived control over the timing of ejaculation, the prevalence decreases substantially. Indeed, as might be expected, the more criteria required for a PE classification, the lower the prevalence—suggested in Table 3.1, which shows how the imposition of various and/or additional criteria may affect the prevalence rate. Because no consensus exists for specific cut-off criteria for each of the various dimensions of PE, a precise prevalence rate remains elusive. However, based on the multitude of studies that have attempted in one way or another to get a handle on the prevalence issue, most researchers in the field would agree that an estimate of 5% to 15% of men is likely. Furthermore, it appears that only a relatively small proportion of men with PE actually seek treatment, with estimates between only 10 and 50% (Shabsigh & Rowland, 2007).

Published data on impact of birth country, religion, or culture on the prevalence of premature ejaculation are rare. An increased susceptibility to premature ejaculation in men from the Indian subcontinent has been reported (Bhatia & Malik, 1991; Verma, Khaitan, & Singh, 1998). Kinsey's observation that Asian men have shorter times to ejaculation than Caucasians, who in turn have shorter times to ejaculation than African Caribbeans, has been interpreted to suggest that some races are more "sexu-

Table 3.1 **Examples of the Effect of Imposing Varying and Stricter Criteria for a Premature Ejaculation Classification[d]**

Assessment Strategy	Approximate Prevalence (%)
Self-defined by respondents (Laumann survey)	30.0
Self-defined by respondents (Internet survey)[a]	16.3
DSM-IV-based diagnosis by trained clinicians[b]	13.0
DSM-IV-based diagnosis:	
–Plus self-reported very poor/poor ejaculatory control[b]	9.3
–Plus ejaculatory latency <2 min[c]	5.6
–Plus ejaculatory latency <2 min and very poor or poor ejaculatory control	3.0–8.0

[a] "Self-Reported Premature Ejaculation and Aspects of Sexual Functioning and Satisfaction," by D. Rowland et al., 2004, *Journal of Sexual Medicine, 1*, 225–232.

[b] "Premature Ejaculation: An Observational Study of Men and Their Partners," by D. L. Patrick et al., 2005, *Journal of Sexual Medicine, 2*, 358–367.

[c] "The Psychological Burden of Premature Ejaculation," by D. L. Rowland, D. L. Patrick, M. Rothman, and D. D. Gagnon, 2007, *Journal of Urology, 177*, pp. 1065–1070.

[d] Estimated from J & J clinical trials.

ally restrained" than others (Kinsey, Pomeroy, & Martin, 1948; Rushton & Bogaert, 1998). A recent study reported a preponderance of men from Middle Eastern and Asian backgrounds presenting for treatment of PE that exceeded the representation of these ethnic groups in the local population (Richardson & Goldmeier, 2005; Richardson, Wood, & Goldmeier, 2006).

Lifelong versus Acquired

In a study of 1,326 consecutive men with PE, lifelong premature ejaculation was present in 736 men (74.4%) and acquired premature ejaculation was present in 253 men (25.6%; McMahon, 2002). Men with PE appear younger than those without, and after adjusting for concomitant erectile dysfunction, the risk of PE significantly decreased with aging (Fasolo, Mirone, Gentile, Parazzini, & Ricci, 2005). Higher levels of education, divorce and the presence of social phobia appear to increase the risk of PE (Fasolo et al., 2005; Tignol, Martin-Guehl, Aouizerate, Grabot, & Auriacombe, 2006). A decreased risk of PE has been reported in men with treated diabetes, and no association was found with hypertension, cardiac disease, hypercholesterolemia, and peripheral or central neuropathy. Men with self-reported PE have a lower frequency of sexual intercourse, higher levels of intercourse related anxiety and note greater impairment in intercourse satisfaction, sexual relationship satisfaction compared to men without PE (Perelman, McCullough, & Bull, 2004). The extent to which their condition affects their overall quality of life is still unresolved (Perelman et al., 2004; Rowland et al., 2007).

Etiology of Premature Ejaculation

Preliminary Considerations

The causes of sexual problems in men vary, but generally they might be attributed to one of three sources: physiological, psychological, and relational. The etiological factors identified herein represent *potential* causes for problems or "risk factors," that is, while they may increase the likelihood of a sexual dysfunction, they do not determine it. These sources represent overlapping domains used for the sake of convenience; they do not represent mutually exclusive etiologies. A distressful relationship between the man and his partner may impact his psychological well-being, which in turn has the potential to influence his physiological response. Conversely, a man with a clear medical etiology responsible for ejaculating rapidly may lose confidence and begin to avoid sexual intimacy, a situation that typically impacts the dyadic relationship. Furthermore, the factors responsible for precipitating or predisposing a sexual problem may be quite different from those that eventually end up maintaining it. For example, the inability to delay ejaculation due to medication or to a novel situation where sexual excitement is particularly high may result in anxiety and diminished self-confidence surrounding future sexual encounters, factors that may eventually come to maintain the problem. Finally, there is a great deal of variation in how each of these sources (physiological, psychological, or relational) might affect any given individual. For most instances involving premature ejaculation, clear etiologies simply do not exist. In the following sections, a number of common risks, predisposing and maintaining factors for PE—some of which are more hypothetical than empirically based—are discussed (see Table 3.2).

As noted previously, clinicians may specify whether PE has been a lifelong condition, or is one that has been acquired, and whether it is situational or global. Making such distinctions does not necessarily reveal an etiology and practitioners should avoid the trap of assuming, for example, that lifelong PE is necessarily genetic, or that acquired PE is necessarily the product of sexual experiences. However, these distinctions can provide guideposts that help establish a line of inquiry for an accurate diagnosis (see section on Diagnosis).

Table 3.2 **Selected Putative Risk and/or Maintaining Factors for Premature Ejaculation**

Physiological

  –Chronic neurological disease

  –Pelvic/spinal surgery or trauma

  –Urinary tract disease or lower urinary problems

  –Various medications

Psychological

  –Anxiety (general or specific)

  –Lack of attention to somatic cues

  –Situations causing hyperarousal (e.g., novelty)

Relationship

  –Hostility/anger

  –Control/dominance

  –Partner dysfunction

Physiological versus Pathophysiological

In establishing etiology, the term *physiological* (sometimes also called organic or organogenic) is often not well defined. First, it is essential to distinguish factors that are truly physiological from those that are pathophysiological. Physiological refers to those factors that are biologically inherent to the system, perhaps "hardwired" through genetic and normal maturational processes. Pathophysiological refers to those factors that occur through disruption of the normal physiological processes, through disease, trauma, surgery, medication and so on.

For most men with PE, no obvious pathophysiology exists; thus to indicate that PE is a pathophysiological condition ignores the fact that for the majority of men with PE, no underlying problem in structural or functional anatomy, physiology, or biochemistry can be identified. When PE does have a pathophysiological origin, it is usually fairly easy to identify and is likely to surface during a medical history and exam. For example, among the conditions commonly associated with PE are problems in the lower urinary tract such as prostatitis and urethritis; and endocrine problems, particularly hyperthyroidism. Sometimes, however, the site of the pathophysiology may be far removed from the pelvic or genital area: cerebrovascular accidents have sometimes been linked to PE. Specific medications may sometimes induce PE, though not necessarily with any reliability. For example, use of L-dopa, pimozide (an antipsychotic used to control tics), amphetamine, heroin, and OTC drugs that mimic sympathetic activation have on occasion been associated with PE.

Two additional factors, though not necessarily pathophysiological, deserve mention: age, and erectile dysfunction. For years it had been assumed that PE was more prevalent among young men, and indeed, when erectile function is controlled, using cross-sectional analysis over age groups, the prevalence of PE does appear to decrease. However, the long-time supposition that rapid ejaculation is attenuated with age, although logically sound, has not been adequately tested in longitudinal studies, and therefore no firm conclusions can be drawn. Given that penile sensitivity decreases substantially with age (Rowland, 1998), however, a tendency toward increased ejaculatory latencies with aging is not implausible and may account for the slight increase in the prevalence of inhibited ejaculation in older men.

A sizable portion of men with PE, approximately 40% to 50%, report problems with erectile function (Kaplan, Kohl, Pomeroy, Offit, & Hogan, 1974). The relationship between PE and ED is not well characterized, but it may be bidirectional. For some men, the onset of ED may result in rapid ejaculation before erection is lost, that is, PE is secondary to the ED. In other men, the ED and PE may be concomitant in that both are manifestations of an underlying (and as yet undefined) pathophysiology.

Inherent Physiological Factors
More difficult to identify are inherent physiological factors that account for variation in ejaculatory latency and thus might play a role in PE. Researchers, for example, have noted that (a) ejaculatory latencies across men take the shape of a skewed distribution, and (b) men with PE consistently lie at the low end (left side) of the continuum, presumably, the result of innate or "hardwired" properties of their ejaculatory reflex. Although data supporting this idea are minimal, it is plausible to assume that, as with most biobehavioral responses (e.g., eating, emotion), inherent differences in response tendencies exist and that, for the specific biobehavioral response of ejaculation, men do possess predispositions to respond with shorter or longer latencies. However, the actual inherent physiological properties that differentiate men with PE from men with more typical latencies are unknown. Is it in the sensory receptor and afferent system? Is it something about the way the spinal cord and brain process and respond? Is it due to a hyperexcitable response (efferent) system? Although several studies have identified higher penile sensitivity in some men with PE, this difference is probably not critical, as men with low sensitivity may just as well exhibit premature ejaculation (Paick, Jeong, & Park, 1998; Rowland, 1998). If not the hypersensitivity of the sensory system, then perhaps the response system in PE men is more easily triggered.

Several studies have demonstrated shorter latencies and stronger bulbocavernous EMG (electromyographic) and ERP (event related potentials) responses in men with rapid ejaculation. Furthermore, because SSRI antidepressants inhibit ejaculation, a role for serotonergic involvement in the ejaculatory response has been suggested, that is, perhaps the serotonergic thresholds are lower or more easily exceeded in men with PE. While each of these factors may contribute to short ejaculatory latencies, it is more likely that ejaculatory response and latency are influenced by interacting inherent biological and situational- and contextually driven central (cognitive-affective-arousal) processes (Motofei & Rowland, 2005).

Finally, men with PE may exhibit an anomalous sympathetic nervous system response during sexual arousal. Specifically, as indicated previously, parasympathetic dominance early in the sexual response cycle is normally necessary to initiate and sustain erection, with concomitant or subsequent sympathetic activation responsible in part for mediating ejaculation. In men with PE, this typical progression from parasympathetic to sympathetic control may be disrupted, such that sympathetic activation prevails earlier in the response cycle (e.g., due to anxiety or negative affect), which in turn might interfere with parasympathetically controlled erectile tumescence. At the same time, this earlier sympathetic dominance may trigger ejaculation prematurely, perhaps even before the man reaches maximum genital or subjective arousal (Kaplan et al., 1974; Rowland, Tai, & Brummett, 2007; Williams, 1984). Evidence supporting this position has been offered through studies showing that during papaverine-induced erections, PE men showed less suppression of sympathetically mediated skin potentials than controls (Ertekin, Colakoglu, & Altay, 1995), suggesting greater sympathetic activation than normal during the earlier phases of sexual response, and from higher heart rates—a sign of sympathetic activation—in PE men than controls during sexual arousal (Rowland, Tai, & Brummet, 2007).

Psychological Risk Factors

In some respects, it is not possible to separate psychological factors from physiological factors because all psychological processes are rooted in underlying biological functions. Thus, anxiety—an often deployed construct to explain dysfunctional sexual response by sex therapists—has both an experiential (psychological) and an underlying physiological component.

As might be expected, the relationships among psychological risk or predisposing factors and PE are more tenuous (though no less important) than pathophysiological factors, and more likely to impact the entire sexual response cycle rather than just specific components. Furthermore, some or all of these psychological factors may be interconnected, such that no one factor can truly be understood without recognizing its interaction with other psychological dimensions. Indeed, although factors such as early developmental psychosexual experiences, hyperarousal, anxiety, and lack of attentiveness to somatic cues may appear to be independent and unrelated, they may in fact represent individual pieces to a common pathway that results in rapid and uncontrollable ejaculation. In this respect, the approach to psychological factors needs to be more holistic than the approach to identifying relationships between pathophysiological factors and PE, which typically follows a more linear cause-and-effect pathway.

Psychosexual Experiences

Early sexual experiences may shape a man's expectations regarding both his own and his partner's sexual enjoyment and performance. A learning/shaping (or lack thereof) component has long been assumed a factor in the development of PE (Masters & Johnson, 1970). Nevertheless, the connection—while plausible—remains more hypothetical than empirical.

Nevertheless, sexual experience may play an important role in learning to delay or control the timing of ejaculation. For a reason as yet unexplained, men with PE typically have a lower frequency of intercourse than functional counterparts. This lower frequency suggests two possible mechanisms that might add to an endpoint of rapid ejaculation: longer intervals between sex, thereby resulting in greater excitement (or hyperarousal?) when it does occur; and fewer opportunities to learn how to delay the ejaculatory response. This latter point is relevant in that one therapeutic approach to premature ejaculation directs patients to attend more to somatic feedback so they become more attuned to the premonitory signals of impending ejaculation. In doing so, they can learn to adjust their behavior and cognitions so as to attenuate their level of arousal.

Anxiety and Sympathetic Activation

Many sexual problems that are psychological in nature stem from the self- and other-evaluative component of sexual response (hence the common reference to sexual "performance"). Anxiety stemming from the man's lack of confidence to perform adequately, to appear and feel attractive (body image), to satisfy his partner sexually, to experience an overall sense of self-efficacy, and—despite new age efforts to downplay the idea—to measure up against the competition is likely to impact most men at some point in their lives (Zilbergeld, 1993). This anxiety often generates a number of maladaptive responses, such as the man's setting unrealistic expectations or focusing attention on his own sexual response (i.e., self-monitoring) at the cost of ignoring important erotic cues from the partner. Such problems may arise from various cultural expectations and stereotypes linked to the male gender role. Although these issues tend to surface at the beginning of a new relationship, they may also emerge when the ongoing balance in a relationship is changed or disrupted. These issues may be embedded in the relationship itself (and therefore might also be viewed as "relationship" risk factors), but they may also be the consequence of factors that impact the relationship in indirect ways.

With respect to PE, anxiety by itself is not likely to be the major precipitating or causal factor; nevertheless, negative affect is higher in men with PE (Rowland, Tai, & Slob, 2003) and this factor may exacerbate an existing propensity toward rapid ejaculation. For example, if men with PE are prone to earlier and higher sympathetic activation during sexual arousal, anxiety, which itself may be associated with elevated sympathetic tone, may compound an existing tendency toward rapid ejaculation. Although evidence for this interaction is yet circumstantial, this theoretical framework helps link the phenomenological experiences of men with PE to their physiological responding.

Problems Surrounding Subjective Sexual Arousal

Perhaps more a symptom than an actual risk factor, subjective sexual arousal may play a role in some sexual dysfunctions. Men with PE often report hyperarousibility during psychosexual stimulation and recent findings do suggest that such men may underestimate their physiological/genital arousal (Rowland & Cooper, 2005). For these reasons, Kaplan (1989) has posited that men with PE lack awareness of their level of arousal and their preorgasmic sensations. In this respect, some argue that disorders of ejaculation may be more a problem of arousal than a problem with the ejaculatory process per se. Since a man's sexual arousal level is driven by any number of factors, including sexual interest, partner stimulation and attraction, context, anticipation, and so on, it might be viewed as a proxy for a number of other psychological and relationship factors.

Relationship Factors

Relationship factors influencing sexual function are the most difficult to pinpoint and describe in brief terminologies or phrases. Nevertheless, the lack of an adequate/appropriate nosology should not be misconstrued as a lack of importance because many of the dysfunction-precipitating and/or maintaining factors mentioned earlier involve a relationship component. Furthermore, because the quality of the sexual relationship often hinges on the overall quality of the marital/partner relationship, these two elements are often interdependent (Rosen et al., 2004; Schnarch, 2000).

Sexual dynamics most likely to contribute to an etiology of rapid ejaculation include a female partner who has a sexual aversion, exhibits sexual avoidance, or is concerned about sexual pain. Such partner issues may lead men to ejaculate rapidly, although the PE in this case is actually secondary to the partner's dysfunction. Treatment would therefore focus on the partner's problem and the overall relationship rather than the man's ejaculatory response.

More often than not, partners of men with PE share in the distress of the patient and experience sexual dissatisfaction as a result of the man's problem. For this reason, female partners of men with PE are often motivated to encourage their men to seek treatment (Moreira, 2005). As with other sexual dysfunctions, probably more important than any single relationship factor is the overall quality of the relationship itself. Thus, preceding sex therapy with couples therapy for those with significant relationship issues tends to result in better outcomes for the sex therapy (Althof, 2005; Carey, 1998; Rowland, Cooper, & Slob, 1998). Conversely, sex therapy in nondistressed couples often leads to improved dyadic functioning.

Assessment of Premature Ejaculation

Ideally, evaluation of a sexual problem involves an in-depth analysis of the specific problem, its severity, etiology, and contributing/maintaining factors. In practice, evaluation procedures vary widely, depending on the door through which the man enters the health system when seeking help. In the primary care physician's office, where economic factors (third-party reimbursement) may restrict the investment of time, and lack of expertise about nonmedical factors involved in sexual problems may limit the scope of the conversation, the evaluation may be cursory and limited. In contrast, psychiatrists and behavioral/mental health clinicians, whose qualifications increase the likelihood for third partner reimbursement for delving into psychological and interpersonal issues, may undertake a thorough evaluation that extends through multiple sessions. Such evaluations typically include a complete medical and psychological history, the use of standardized assessment instruments, and a psychosexual history that includes the man's sexual partner.

Organization of the Evaluation

Reduced to its simplest elements, a sexual assessment should identify (a) the nature and severity of the sexual dysfunction, (b) medical/biological, psychological, and/or relationship factors that cause or contribute to the problem or that might diminish the effects of any particular treatment strategy, and (c) the goals, needs, and preferences of the patient and partner regarding treatment options (see Table 3.3). The means by which each of these is achieved—through face-to-face interview, physical examination,

Table 3.3   Goals of the Evaluation Procedure

Defining and specifying the sexual dysfunction, including severity

Eliminating other factors in the sexual response cycle

Potential medical/physiological, psychological, relationship contributors

Biomedical assessment

Psychosexual history and function

Relationship function

Patient's and partner's goals for treatment

Developing a treatment strategy

Costs and benefits of treatment options

Patient's and partner's preferences for treatment

symptom assessment scales, laboratory tests, or some combination thereof—may be driven by a number of factors, such as the specific orientation of the health provider and the resources and time available to the patient. For the behavioral or mental health clinician who encounters a male client with sexual dysfunction, the assessment process should entail referral to a physician for a physical examination, who then might determine whether further referral to a medical specialist (urologist, endocrinologist) is warranted or beneficial. In order to optimize outcomes, medical specialists should refer any patient with a sexual dysfunction who enters the health care system through the "medical" door to a sex therapist for at least a brief assessment of general psychosocial and relationship functioning.

The Evaluation Process: Identification of the Problem and Quantifying Severity

The first step in the process requires identifying and confirming the specific sexual problem. Carefully worded questions (see Table 3.4) can usually narrow the problem to premature ejaculation quite rapidly, although optimally each question should be augmented with further questioning that affirms the presence and type of the dysfunction.

Once the problem is identified, quantification of its severity is important, for example, the frequency of occurrence of the dysfunctional response and the degree to which the response is impaired. For PE, parameters such as the estimated latency to ejaculation following vaginal penetration and the ability to delay (or control) ejaculation provide measures of impairment. The level of distress, bother, or dissatisfaction regarding sexual response and function is critically important to assess as well. A

Table 3.4 Typical Questions for Identifying a Sexual Dysfunction*

Initial Question	Sample Elaborations
Do you have sexual interests, desire, thoughts, fantasies?	Masturbation frequency?
	Initiator of intercourse?
	Interest or attraction to partner?
Do you have difficulty getting or keeping an erection?	Frequency of coital impairment?
	Loss of erection before ejaculating?
	Degree of erection (none, some, etc.)
Do you ejaculate or come before you wish?	Ejaculate before intercourse begins?
	Within 1 or 2 minutes after penetration?
	Able to delay/postpone ejaculation?
	Ejaculate for fear of losing erection?
Do you take longer than you wish to reach orgasm?	Ever ejaculate, for example, during masturbation?
	Ratio of orgasms to attempts?
	Duration of intercourse?
Do you have pain during intercourse?	Before, during, or after?

*These items are meant only as starters that help narrow the problem to a specific domain. A full assessment would include a complete psychosexual history and evaluation (see text for further discussion).

number of standardized assessment tools are available to assist clinicians with these tasks (Rosen et al., 2004).

The Evaluation Process: Identifying Etiological Factors

The second step of the evaluation process typically accounts for most of the variation across clinicians and health care providers. No matter how extensive or limited this step of the process might be, because sexual dysfunction may sometimes serve as a marker for other health problems, a physical examination is generally recommended.

The primary care physician may well end the evaluation at this point and simply move on to a discussion of treatment options. In contrast, health care specialists (e.g., urologist, sex therapist) are likely to carry out further evaluation in the biological, psychological, and relationship domains, with bias toward those domains consistent with their clinical training. Although the traditional need to differentiate psychogenic from organogenic etiologies is often less critical with the introduction of effective biomedical interventions (that can alleviate specific dysfunctions of any origin), knowing whether the problem has a strong biological, psychological, or relationship component may assist in determining the most effective treatment therapy.

Biomedical Assessment

Medical assessments for PE are typically limited, unless a pathophysiological cause is suspected. In addition to the physical examination, a family/medical history, including the use of prescription and over-the-counter medications, nutritional supplements, and recreational substances (tobacco, alcohol, cocaine, etc.) is typical. Beyond this, however, no broad consensus exists regarding what procedures are likely to yield information most helpful to the treatment process. Clearly, for men exhibiting hypoactive sexual desire disorder, a basic endocrine analysis for testosterone and prolactin is indicated. For men with comorbid ED, laboratory tests for comorbidities (e.g., diabetes mellitus, hyperlipidemia) and psychiatric assessment for mood disorders can help determine whether the dysfunction is secondary to another disease or condition. More extensive evaluation is usually not essential (Rosen et al., 2004).

Psychological and Psychosexual History

In men, sexual functioning and psychological health are often interrelated. Indeed the two are bidirectional in nature in that each has the potential to affect the other. In carrying out a psychosexual and general psychological evaluation, the clinician is better able to understand whether psychological (and relationship) factors are causal to physiological sexual dysfunction, including whether they sustain or exacerbate the dysfunction. Whether considering cause or effect or the mutual and reciprocal flow between the two, one of the immediate goals of psychological evaluation is to determine which factor is primary, and thus where treatment should be focused.

At the individual psychological level, besides assessment for major or minor psychological disorders (depression, anxiety), the psychosexual history is perhaps the most critical element of the overall assessment process. The sexual history may be taken verbally, may make use of a script, and/or may involve any number of standardized assessment instruments available for this process (see Rosen et al., 2004). In general, however, the evaluation should include information about current and past sexual functioning, as well as the history (onset and duration) and specificity of the problem (e.g., with a particular partner; only during coitus and not during masturbation). Information about the patient's understanding of and education about the problem, psychosocial factors surrounding the problem (anxiety, etc.), specific cultural expectations, child and adolescent sexual histories and experiences, and family-of-origin attitudes and practices often reveals important factors related to the sexual problem that will suggest specific treatment strategies. Clinicians, of course, need to tread lightly when dealing with private and sensitive matters related to sexuality and should take steps to ensure that the patient does not feel stigmatized, judged, or embarrassed.

Relationship Assessment

Finally, the potential for a relationship contribution to the PE warrants investigation. A relationship history that includes major events such as extramarital activity, divorce, separation, pregnancies, and deaths should be noted, and any current relationship concerns or distress should be discussed (see Pridal & LoPiccolo, 2000). Standardized assessment instruments such as the DAS (Spanier, 1976) and GRISS (Rust & Golombok, 1986) may be helpful in drawing out such concerns because patients may be reluctant to appear critical of their partner's sexual, emotional, and behavioral interactions. Initially, the patient and partner may be assessed separately to avoid attributions of fault or blame, to identify potential partner dysfunctions and counterproductive attitudes, and to obtain each person's individual perspective (including distress) about the problem and its severity.

The Evaluation Process: Defining the Desired Outcome of the Patient and Partner

In the transition step between evaluation and treatment, an important intermediate step lies in defining the relevant outcomes. Although the patient's and partner's involvement is essential to this process, men sometimes focus heavily on genital issues at the cost of neglecting more subtle, but no less important, psychological and interpersonal issues. Although clinicians would agree that treatment of the physical symptoms is crucial (e.g., prolongation of ejaculation latency, obtaining an erection sufficient for intercourse), most would also note that improved genital performance in the absence of improved sexual satisfaction and a better sexual relationship is meaningless (Rowland & Burnett, 2000). These latter outcomes, though not always easily quantified, typically correlate well with overall patient satisfaction with treatment (Hawton, 1998).

Although these three outcomes—improved genital response, increased sexual satisfaction, and improved sexual relationship—are themselves interrelated, each may need to be addressed individually in the course of the therapeutic process. That is, in many situations alleviation of the symptoms may improve the man's sexual satisfaction and the overall sexual relationship; however, in others the change in interpersonal dynamics that results from the dysfunction (e.g., avoidance of intimacy, or a partner's anger and distress) may not easily be reversed by merely "fixing" the genital dysfunction. In such cases, a number of psychological and interpersonal issues may need to be addressed, at least if increased sexual satisfaction and an improved sexual relationship are viewed as important outcomes.

Treatment of Premature Ejaculation

Before beginning treatment, the practitioner should understand (a) the specific sexual problem; (b) the severity of the problem and the degree of functional impairment it causes; (c) at least broadly, if not in detail, the biological, psychological, and relationship factors that contribute to or maintain the problem; and (d) the specific treatment goals of the man and his partner. These four elements converge to suggest an appropriate strategy that may utilize one, some, or all of the therapeutic tools available to the health care provider. Thus, oral medications and other biomedical treatments, bibliotherapy, individual sex therapy and counseling, and couples' marital and/or sex therapy represent a range of options that may eventually constitute an effective treatment plan. Important to this approach, however, is not only the notion that each strategy can address a specific dimension of the problem, but that even when the etiology lies primarily within one domain (e.g., psychological anxiety), the use of auxiliary strategies (e.g., oral medications) may be helpful to achieving the larger goals of the patient and his partner. Finally, it is important for both clinician and patient to recognize, early in the therapeutic process, the importance of and need for periodic follow-up.

Counseling Strategies

Cognitive-behavioral factors are likely involved in PE, and therefore health care providers should be aware of and sensitive to such factors in the treatment of this disorder. Indeed, despite the fact that cognitive-behavioral therapy for PE has been criticized by some as lacking long-term efficacy, long-term success rates for PE treatment have simply not been adequately investigated, and the reasons for purported failures remain largely unknown. For example, it is not known whether relapse occurs because cognitive-behavioral techniques become less effective with continued use or because couples merely cease using them once the novelty has worn off. Furthermore, cognitive-behavioral techniques are specific to the problem, are neither harmful nor painful, and impart no negative side effects. Once learned and incorporated into lovemaking, these techniques become personally integrated such that PE men will always have access to the tools that enable them to control their ejaculatory response. On the negative side, cognitive-behavioral techniques typically require significant cooperation of the partner; entail greater effort, expense, and time on the part of the client; and tend to have less well documented efficacy (lower "level of evidence"; Rowland et al., 1998).

The severity of the PE may suggest varied treatment approaches that combine oral medications and stimulus reduction creams (applied to the penis) with either brief or more extended cognitive-behavioral counseling. As with ED, these pharmacological strategies can assist the man in redeveloping self-confidence and self-efficacy, and afford the man the opportunity to develop and use cognitive-behavioral strategies as his response latency approximates a more typical pattern. These strategies may be acquired through bibliotherapy, but the patient and his partner can also benefit from a counselor who can educate them about the sexual response cycle, facilitate communication about sexual issues, and give permission regarding an expanded repertoire of behaviors for greater sexual satisfaction. As examples, the clinician might encourage the couple to enjoy a second intercourse after one involving a short ejaculation latency to take advantage of the decreased sexual arousal most men experience during the refractory period. Or the couple could be encouraged to vary their intercourse-related behaviors to attenuate the patient's level of sexual arousal for the purpose of keeping it below the level of ejaculatory inevitability.

Standard behavioral strategies for the treatment of PE include the start-"frenulum squeeze" and start-pause techniques introduced several decades ago by Masters and Johnson (1970) and Kaplan (1989). In addition, the couple could be encouraged to experiment with the partner (e.g., female) superior or lateral positions as these typically provide men with a greater sense of ejaculatory control. Couples could also be advised to engage in mutual masturbation and then oral sex prior to coitus (depending on the acceptability of the sexual behaviors to the couple). Other suggestions include slowing down during intercourse, breathing deeply, having shallower penile penetration, or moving the pelvis in a circular motion. Excellent resources for both men (Zilbergeld, 1993) and women (Heiman & LoPiccolo, 1988) could be made available to assist the couple in dealing with the problem.

Relevant cognitive strategies include the man's increased attention to his somatic sensations so he might better monitor his level of physical arousal, and the use of sensate focus which permits enjoyment of physical sensations without necessarily generating sexual arousal (Carey, 1998). This latter procedure also de-emphasizes the focus on intercourse and orgasm within the sexual relationship and may help reduce the man's performance anxiety that, because it presumably operates through sympathetic pathways, may serve to prime the ejaculatory response prematurely. Ideally, as the man and his partner gain a greater sense of self-efficacy, reliance on oral medications or anesthetizing creams could be reduced.

Important to any treatment plan is the substitution of counterproductive behaviors and beliefs with positive therapeutic strategies. Thus, strong emphasis on latency to ejaculation or on using distracting stimuli (at the cost of ignoring relevant body cues) can actually increase PE symptoms. As important, deliberate strategies to achieve relapse prevention, particularly by predicting the likelihood of occasional setbacks and preparing couples appropriately, and by using increased spacing between sessions as progress is noted, are typical (McCarthy, 2004). Depending on the level of PE severity, these goals may be achieved in just a couple sessions or, if significant relationship issues and partner dysfunction exist, it may take as many as 10 to 20. By itself, cognitive-behavioral treatment has a fairly high initial success rate although, for reasons as yet undetermined, this drops off to about 50% or less by about a year post treatment. Combined with oral medications, long-term success rates are likely to increase, assuming couples continue to practice their newly acquired strategies and adhere to treatment procedures.

Pharmacological Treatment

Pharmacological modulation of ejaculatory response represents a fairly recent development in the treatment of PE and a significant departure from an exclusive psychosexual model of treatment—specifically, the introduction of the selective serotonin reuptake inhibitors (SSRIs) has largely changed the model for treatment. Selective serotonin reuptake inhibitors encompass five compounds—citalopram, fluoxetine, fluvoxamine, paroxetine and sertraline—with a similar pharmacological mechanism of action. Although the methodology of the initial drug treatment studies was rather poor, later double-blind and placebo-controlled studies replicated the genuine effect of clomipramine and SSRIs to delay ejaculation.

Daily Treatment with SSRIs
Daily treatment can be performed with paroxetine 20 to 40 mg, clomipramine 10 to 50 mg, sertraline 50 to 100 mg, and fluoxetine 20 to 40 mg. Paroxetine appears to exert the strongest ejaculation delay, increasing intravaginal ejaculatory latency time (IELT) approximately 8.8 fold over baseline (Waldinger, 2003). Ejaculation delay usually occurs within 5 to 10 days but may occur earlier. Adverse effects are usually minor, start in the first week of treatment, gradually disappear within 2 to 3 weeks and

include fatigue, yawning, mild nausea, loose stools or perspiration. Diminished libido or mild erectile dysfunction is infrequently reported. Significant agitation is reported by a small number of patients and treatment with SSRIs should be avoided in men with a history of bipolar depression.

On-Demand Treatment with SSRIs

Administration of clomipramine, paroxetine, sertraline, or fluoxetine 4 to 6 hours before intercourse is efficacious and well tolerated but is associated with less ejaculatory delay than daily treatment. Daily administration of an SSRI is associated with superior fold increases in IELT compared to on-demand administration due to greatly enhanced 5-HT neurotransmission resulting from several adaptive processes that may include presynaptic 5-HT1a and 5-HT1b/1d receptor desensitization (Waldinger, Berendsen, Blok, Olivier, & Holstege, 1998). On-demand treatment may be combined with either an initial trial of daily treatment or concomitant low-dose daily treatment (S. W. Kim & Paick, 1999; McMahon & Touma, 1999; Strassberg, de Gouveia Brazao, Rowland, Tan, & Slob, 1999).

On-Demand Treatment with Dapoxetine

A number of rapid-acting short half-life SSRIs are under investigation as on-demand treatments for PE. Dapoxetine is the first compound specifically developed for the treatment of PE. Dapoxetine is a potent selective serotonin re-uptake inhibitor, structurally similar to fluoxetine (Sorbera, Castaner, & Castaner, 2004). Dapoxetine binds to 5-HT, norepinephrine (NE), and dopamine (DA) re-uptake transporters and inhibits uptake in the following rank order of potency: 5-HT > NE > DA (Gengo et al., 2005). The pharmacokinetic profile of dapoxetine—rapid-acting and fairly short half life—suggests that it may eventually be a good candidate for on-demand treatment of PE (Dresser, Modi, Staehr, & Mulhall, 2005).

Preliminary data suggest that dapoxetine (Johnson & Johnson) administered 1 to 2 hours prior to planned intercourse, is effective and well tolerated, superior to placebo, and increases IELT two- to threefold over baseline in a dose-dependent fashion (Hellstrom, Gittelman, & Althof, 2004). In randomized, double-blind, placebo-controlled, multicenter, clinical trials involving 2,614 men with a mean baseline IELT $\leq$ 2 min, dapoxetine (30 mg or 60 mg) was more effective than a placebo for all study endpoints (Pryor et al., 2006). Intravaginal ejaculatory latency time (IELT) increased from 0.91 min at baseline to 2.78 and 3.32 min at study end with dapoxetine (30 mg and 60 mg, respectively). Mean patient rating of control-over-ejaculation as fair, good, or very good increased from 2.8% at baseline to 51.8% and 58.4% at study end with dapoxetine (30 mg and 60 mg, respectively). Treatment-related side effects (nausea, diarrhea, headache, dizziness) were uncommon and dose dependent, and were responsible for study discontinuation in 4% (30 mg) and 10% (60 mg) of subjects.

On-Demand Treatment with Tramadol

The efficacy of on-demand tramadol in the treatment of PE was recently reported (Safarinejad & Hosseini, 2006). Tramadol is a centrally acting synthetic opioid analgesic with an unclear mode of action that is thought to include binding of parent and M1 metabolite to İ-opioid receptors and weak inhibition of re-uptake of norepinephrine and serotonin (Frink, Hennies, Englberger, Haurand, & Wilffert, 1996). Serotonin syndrome has been reported as an adverse effect of tramadol alone or in combination with SSRI class drugs (Garrett, 2004; Mittino, Mula, & Monaco, 2004). In this double-blind, placebo-controlled study, the on-demand use of 50 mg tramadol, taken 2 hours prior to intercourse, exerted a clinically relevant ejaculation delay in men with premature ejaculation with a 12.7 fold increase in IELT (Safarinejad & Hosseini, 2006). Additional flexible dose studies and long-term follow-up studies to evaluate the risk of opioid addiction are required.

Anesthetic Topical Ointments

The use of topical local anesthetics such as lidocaine and/or prilocaine as a cream, gel, or spray is well established and is moderately effective in retarding ejaculation. A recent study reported that a metered-dose aerosol spray containing a mixture of lidocaine and prilocaine produced in 2.4 fold increase in baseline IELT and significant improvements in ejaculatory control and both patient and partner sexual quality-of-life (Dinsmore et al., 2007). Topical ointments may be associated with significant penile hypoanesthesia and possible transvaginal absorption, resulting in vaginal numbness and female anorgasmia unless a condom is used (Berkovitch, Keresteci, & Koren, 1995; Busato & Galindo, 2004; Xin, Choi, Lee, & Choi, 1997).

Phosphodiesterase Inhibitors

Medications that inhibit phosphodiesterase type-5 isoenzyme (PDE-5), sildenafil, tadalafil, and vardenafil, are effective treatments for erectile dysfunction. Several authors have reported their experience with PDE-5 inhibitors alone or in combination with SSRIs as a treatment for PE (Abdel-Hamid, El Naggar, & El Gilany, 2001; Atan et al., 2006; Chen, Mabjeesh, Matzkin, & Greenstein, 2003; Chia, 2002; Erenpreiss & Zalkalns, 2002; Li, Zhang, Cheng, & Zhang, 2003; Linn, Ginesin, Hardak, & Mertyk, 2002; Lozano, 2003; Mattos & Lucon, 2005; McMahon, Stuckey, & Andersen, 2005; Salonia et al., 2002; Sommer, Klotz, & Mathers, 2005; Tang, Ma, Zhao, Liu, & Chen, 2004; Zhang et al., 2005). A recent systematic review of 14 studies published in peer reviewed journals or the proceedings of major international and regional scientific meetings on the phosphodiesterase type 5 inhibitor (PDE-5i) drug treatment of premature ejaculation examined the role of nitric oxide (NO) as a neurotransmitter involved in the central and peripheral control of ejaculation, the methodology of PDE-5i drug treatment studies for PE, the adherence of methodology to the contemporary consensus of ideal PE drug trial design, the impact of methodology on treatment outcomes and the role of PDE-5i drugs in the treatment of PE (McMahon, McMahon, Leow, & Winestock, 2006). These studies comprise a total of 1,102 subjects suffering PE treated with sildenafil (Abdel-Hamid et al., 2001; Atan et al., 2006; Li et al., 2003; Lozano, 2003; McMahon et al., 2005; Tang et al., 2004), tadalafil (Mattos & Lucon, 2005), or vardenafil (Sommer et al., 2005), either as monotherapy or in combination with SSRI drugs (Abdel-Hamid et al., 2001; Chia, 2002; Colpi et al., 2004; Erenpreiss & Zalkalns, 2002; Lozano, 2003; Mattos & Lucon, 2005; Salonia et al., 2002; Sommer et al., 2005; Zhang et al., 2005), clomipramine (Abdel-Hamid et al., 2001), or topical anesthetics (Atan et al., 2006; Erenpreiss & Zalkalns, 2002).

Most of these studies support a role for PDE-5i's in the treatment of PE and speculate multiple mechanisms including a central effect involving increased NO and reduced sympathetic tone, smooth muscle dilatation of the vas deferens and seminal vesicles, which may oppose sympathetic vasoconstriction and delay ejaculation, reduced performance anxiety due to better erections, and down-regulation of the erectile threshold to a lower level of arousal so that increased levels of arousal are required to achieve the ejaculation threshold.

The small number of publications and the lack of sufficient data preclude any meta-analysis of results. However, examination of the methodology of these studies, the adherence of methodology to the contemporary consensus of ideal clinical trial design (McMahon et al., 2004), and the impact of study methodology on treatment outcomes fails to provide any robust empirical evidence to support a role of PDE-5 inhibitors in the treatment of PE with the exception of men with PE and comorbid erectile dysfunction. Of the 14 studies reviewed, only one fulfilled these criteria and this study failed to confirm any significant treatment effect on IELT (McMahon et al., 2005).

Caution should be exercised in interpreting PDE-5i and on-demand SSRI treatment data in inadequately designed studies and their results must be regarded as preliminary. The extremely broad range of IELT fold-increases reported with sildenafil (2.7 to 15.0, mean 6.6), combined sildenafil and on-demand sertraline (3.3 to 10.0, mean 6.9), combined sildenafil and on-demand paroxetine (6.6 to 14.9, mean 10.7) in this systematic review is testament to the unreliability of inadequate study design. In contrast to these findings, the range of placebo IELT fold-increases was relatively narrow (IELT-range 1.2 to 1.6, mean 1.4) and was identical with the mean 1.4 IELT fold-increase reported in a meta-analysis of other PE drug studies (Waldinger, Zwinderman, Schweitzer, & Olivier, 2004).

Pharmacological Treatment of Premature Ejaculation and Comorbid Erectile Dysfunction

Recent evidence suggests that PDE-5i's alone or in combination with a SSRI may have a role in the management of PE in men with comorbid erectile dysfunction. In 45 men with PE and comorbid erectile dysfunction treated with flexible doses of sildenafil (50 to 100 mg) for periods of 1 to 3 months, Li et al. reported improved erectile function in 40 men (89%) and reduced severity of PE in 27 men (60%) (Li et al., 2003). Improved erectile function was reported by all of the 27 men with reduced severity of PE, of whom 81.5% described themselves as satisfied or very satisfied. Contrary to these findings, only 1 of the 18 men (5.6%) who did not obtain improvement of PE reported treatment satisfaction. Furthermore, in a group of 37 men with primary or acquired PE with mild erectile dysfunction, Sommer et al. reported a 9.7 fold IELT increase and normalization of erectile function (IIEF EF 26.9) with vardenafil treatment as opposed to lesser 4.4 fold IELT increase with on-demand sertraline (Sommer et al., 2005).

The high level of correlation between improved erectile function with sildenafil and reduced severity of PE reported by Li et al., and the superior IELT fold-increase observed with vardenafil reported by Sommer et al. indicates that PDE-5i related reduced PE severity is due to improved erectile function (Sommer et al., 2005). The IELT fold-increase observed by Sommer et al. with on-demand sertraline (4.4) is less than that reported in reviewed studies on men with normal erectile function (mean 5.57, range 3.0 to 8.5; Abdel-Hamid et al., 2001; Chia, 2002; Lozano, 2003; Zhang et al., 2005), suggesting that men with PE and comorbid erectile dysfunction are less responsive to the administration of only on-demand SSRIs and are best managed with a PDE-5i alone or in combination with an SSRI. Furthermore, the report that addition of sertraline to the sildenafil treatment of men with erectile dysfunction with comorbid PE was associated with a lesser IELT fold-increase (3.3) and lower levels of treatment satisfaction than that seen in men with lifelong PE and normal erectile function treated with on-demand sertraline suggests that this group of men is less responsive to pharmacotherapy (Chia, 2002).

The proposed mechanism of action of PDE-5i's as monotherapy or in combination with an SSRI in the treatment of acquired PE in men with comorbid erectile dysfunction includes the ability to maintain an erection following ejaculation, reduction of the erectile refractory period (Aversa et al., 2000; McMahon et al.,

2005; Mondaini et al., 2003) and thus reliance on a second and more controlled ejaculation during a subsequent episode of intercourse, a reduction in performance anxiety due to better erections, or reduction of the erectile threshold to a lower level of arousal so that increased levels of arousal are required to achieve the ejaculation threshold.

Surgery

Several authors have reported the use of surgically induced penile hypo-anesthesia via selective dorsal nerve neurotomy or hyaluronic acid gel glans penis augmentation in the treatment of lifelong premature ejaculation that is unresponsive to behavioral and/or pharmacological treatment (J. J. Kim, Kwak, Jeon, Cheon, & Moon, 2004). The role of surgery in the management of PE remains unclear until the results of further studies have been reported.

Summary and Conclusions

Although its etiology is yet far from being understood, premature ejaculation is responsive to both psychobehavioral therapy and pharmacological approaches:

Pharmacotherapy

- Gets the ejaculatory problem under control very rapidly.
- Increases self-confidence and self efficacy for the man.
- Increase partner's sexual satisfaction.

Counseling

- Improves couple's communication about sexual issues.
- Encourages a fuller repertoire of behaviors that enhance sexual satisfaction.
- Offers long term strategies for controlling ejaculation independent of drugs.
- Increases likelihood of adherence to treatment procedures (drug and counseling techniques).

Psychobehavioral therapy offers the advantages of being specific to the problem, of actively engaging the partner in the treatment process, of imparting no adverse effects, and of enabling the man to rely on techniques and strategies that are forever at his disposal. On the downside, couples are often reluctant to bear the time and expense to learn and assimilate these procedures into their lovemaking.

Pharmacological strategies offer the advantages of being reliably effective, of providing rapid relief from the condition, and of costing little. On the downside, this approach often requires planning for intercourse (for on-demand use of the agents), imparts negative side effects, may not be effective for all men with PE, and treats the problem but does not cure it, as withdrawal from the chemical agent typically leads to relapse.

Longer term follow up indicates problems with both psychobehavioral and pharmacological approaches. The former is associated with decreased efficacy after one or more years; the latter with about half the men eventually abandoning treatment due to any number of various reasons, including diminished satisfaction with the treatment and avoidance of adverse effects.

Recent attempts have been made to integrate the use of psychobehavioral and pharmacological approaches (e.g., Althof, 2005; Perelman, 2006), relying on the benefits of each to assist the man and his partner to manage the problem. For example, pharmacological treatment can provide the means for rapidly developing a sense of self-efficacy, regaining confidence, and addressing problems of partner satisfaction. Psychobehavioral counseling can assist the couple in developing further techniques that reduce the man's reliance on chemical agents and engages the partner with the treatment process. Such an approach is likely to improve overall and long term efficacy and therefore makes "therapeutic" sense; however, empirical data demonstrating the superiority of a combined approach over the exclusive use of one or the other has yet to be produced. Nevertheless, a strong and thorough assessment process that identifies important parameters of the dysfunction (e.g., has the relationship suffered significantly because of the problem: see Althof, 2005) can assist in developing a treatment strategy that maximizes overall sexual satisfaction and treatment satisfaction for the couple.

References

Abdel-Hamid, I. A., El Naggar, E. A., & El Gilany, A. H. (2001). Assessment of as needed use of pharmacotherapy and the pause-squeeze technique in premature ejaculation. *International Journal of Impotence Research, 13*(1), 41–45.

Althof, S. E. (2005). Psychological treatment strategies for rapid ejaculation: Rationale, practical aspects, and outcome. *World Journal of Urology, 23,* 89–92.

American Psychiatric Association. (1994). *Diagnostic and statistical manual of mental disorders* (4th ed.). Washington, DC: Author.

Atan, A., Basar, M. M., Tuncel, A., Ferhat, M., Agras, K., & Tekdogan, U. (2006). Comparison of efficacy of sildenafil-only, sildenafil plus topical EMLA cream, and topical EMLA-cream-only in treatment of premature ejaculation. *Urology, 67*(2), 388–391.

Aversa, A., Mazzilli, F., Rossi, T., Delfino, M., Isidori, A. M., & Fabbri, A. (2000). Effects of sildenafil (Viagra) administration on seminal parameters and post-ejaculatory refractory time in normal males. *Human Reproduction, 15*(1), 131–134.

Berkovitch, M., Keresteci, A. G., & Koren, G. (1995). Efficacy of prilocaine-lidocaine cream in the treatment of premature ejaculation. *Journal of Urology, 154*(4), 1360–1361.

Bhatia, M. S., & Malik, S. C. (1991). Dhat syndrome: A useful diagnostic entity in Indian culture. *British Journal of Psychiatry, 159,* 691–695.

Busato, W., & Galindo, C. C. (2004). Topical anaesthetic use for treating premature ejaculation: A double-blind, randomized, placebo-controlled study. *BJU International, 93*(7), 1018–1021.

Carey, M. P. (1998). Cognitive-behavioral treatment of sexual dysfunction. In V. E. Caballo (Ed.), *International handbook of cognitive and behavioural treatments for psychological disorders* (pp. 251–280). Kidlington, Oxford: Pergamon Press.

Chen, J., Mabjeesh, N. J., Matzkin, H., & Greenstein, A. (2003). Efficacy of sildenafil as adjuvant therapy to selective serotonin reuptake inhibitor in alleviating premature ejaculation. *Urology, 61*(1), 197–200.

Chia, S. (2002). Management of premature ejaculation: A comparison of treatment outcome in patients with and without erectile dysfunction. *International Journal of Andrology, 25*(5), 301–305.

Colpi, G., Weidner, W., Jungwirth, A., Pomerol, J., Papp, G., Hargreave, T., et al. (2004). EAU guidelines on ejaculatory dysfunction. *European Urology, 46*(5), 555–558.

Dinsmore, W. W., Hackett, G., Goldmeier, D., Waldinger, M., Dean, J., Wright, P., et al. (2007). Topical eutectic mixture for premature ejaculation (TEMPE): A novel aerosol-delivery form of lidocaine-prilocaine for treating premature ejaculation. *BJU International, 99*(2), 369–375.

Dresser, M., Modi, N. B., Staehr, P., & Mulhall, J. P. (2005). The effect of food on the pharmacokinetics of dapoxetine, a new on-demand treatment for premature ejaculation (Abstract 37). *Journal of Sexual Medicine, 3*(Suppl. 1), 25.

Erenpreiss, J., & Zalkalns, J. (2002). Premature ejaculation: Comparison of patroxetine alone, paroxetine plus local lidocaine and paroxetine plus sildenafil (Abstract No. PS-7). *International Journal of Impotence Research, 14*(Suppl. 4), S33, 4.

Ertekin, C., Colakoglu, Z., & Altay, B. (1995). Hand and genital sympathetic skin potentials in flaccid and erectile penile states in normal potent men and patients with premature ejaculation. *Journal of Urology, 153,* 76–79.

Fasolo, C. B., Mirone, V., Gentile, V., Parazzini, F., & Ricci, E. (2005). Premature ejaculation: Prevalence and associated conditions in a sample of 12, 558 men attending the Andrology Prevention Week 2001—A study of the Italian Society of Andrology (SIA). *Journal of Sexual Medicine, 2*(3), 376–382.

Frink, M. C., Hennies, H. H., Englberger, W., Haurand, M., & Wilffert, B. (1996). Influence of tramadol on neurotransmitter systems of the rat brain. *Arzneimittelforschung, 46*(11), 1029–1036.

Garrett, P. M. (2004). Tramadol overdose and serotonin syndrome manifesting as acute right heart dysfunction. *Anaesthesia and Intensive Care, 32*(4), 575–577.

Gengo, R. J., Giuliano, F., McKenna, K. E., Lovenberg, T., & Gupta, S. K. (2005). Monoaminergic transporter binding and inhibition profile of dapoxetine: A medication for the treatment of premature ejaculation (Abstract No. 878). *Journal of Urology, 173*(4), 230.

Giuliano, F., & Clement, P. (2005). Neuroanatomy and physiology of ejaculation. *Annual Review of Sex Research, 16,* 190–216.

Hawton, K. (1998). Integration of treatments for male erectile dysfunction. *Lancet, 351,* 7–8.

Heiman, J. R., & LoPiccolo, J. (1988). *Becoming orgasmic: A sexual and personal growth program for women* (Rev. ed.). New York: Prentice Hall.

Hellstrom, W. J., Gittelman, M., & Althof, S. (2004). Dapoxetine HCl for the treatment of premature ejaculation: A phase II, randomised, double-blind, placebo controlled study. *Journal of Sexual Medicine, 1*(Suppl. 1), 59–97.

Kaplan, H. S. (1989). *Premature ejaculation: How to overcome premature ejaculation.* New York: Brunner/Mazel.

Kaplan, H. S., Kohl, R. N., Pomeroy, W. B., Offit, A. K., & Hogan, B. (1974). Group treatment of premature ejaculation. *Archives of Sexual Behavior, 3*(5), 443–452.

Kim, J. J., Kwak, T. I., Jeon, B. G., Cheon, J., & Moon, D. G. (2004). Effects of glans penis augmentation using hyaluronic acid gel for premature ejaculation. *International Journal of Impotence Research, 16*(6), 547–551.

Kim, S. W., & Paick, J. S. (1999). Short-term analysis of the effects of as needed use of sertraline at 5 PM for the treatment of premature ejaculation. *Urology, 54*(3), 544–547.

Laumann, E. O., Paik, A., & Rosen, R. C. (1999). Sexual dysfunction in the United States: Prevalence and predictors. *Journal of the American Medical Association, 281*(6), 537–544.

Li, X., Zhang, S. X., Cheng, H. M., & Zhang, W. D. (2003). [Clinical study of sildenafil in the treatment of premature ejaculation complicated by erectile dysfunction]. *Zhonghua Nan Ke Xue, 9*(4), 266–269.

Linn, R., Ginesin, Y., Hardak, S., & Mertyk, S. (2002). Treatment of sildenfil as part of the treatment in premature ejaculation (Abstract No. P-168). *International Journal of Impotence Research, 14*(Suppl. 4), S39.

Lozano, A. F. (2003). Premature ejaculation: Pharmacological treatment three years after (Abstract No. MP-2-6). *International Journal of Impotence Research, 15*(Suppl. 6), S11.

Masters, W. H., & Johnson, V. E. (1970). *Human sexual inadequacy.* Boston: Little, Brown.

Mattos, R. M., & Lucon, A. M. (2005). Tadalafil and slow-release fluoxetine in premature ejaculation: A prospective study (Abstract No. 880). *Journal of Urology, 173*(4), 239.

McCarthy, B. (2004). Cognitive-behavioral strategies and techniques in the treatment of early ejaculation. In S. R. Leiblum, & R. D. Rosen (Eds.), *Principles and practice of sex therapy: Update for the 1990s* (pp. 141–167). New York: Guilford Press.

McMahon, C. G. (2002). Long term results of treatment of premature ejaculation with selective serotonin re-uptake inhibitors. *International Journal of Impotence Research, 14*(Suppl. 3), S19.

McMahon, C. G., Abdo, C., Incrocci, L., Perelman, M., Rowland, D., Stuckey, B., et al. (2004). Disorders of orgasm and ejaculation in men. In T. F. Lue, R. Basson, R. Rosen, F. Giuliano, S. Khoury, & F. Montsorsi (Eds.), *Sexual medicine: Sexual dysfunctions in men and women* (pp. 409–468). Paris: Health Publications.

McMahon, C. G., McMahon, C. N., Leow, L. J., & Winestock, C. G. (2006). Efficacy of type-5 phosphodiesterase inhibitors in the drug treatment of premature ejaculation: A systematic review. *BJU International, 98*(2), 259–272.

McMahon, C. G., Stuckey, B., & Andersen, M. L. (2005). Efficacy of viagra: Sildenafil citrate in men with premature ejaculation. *Journal of Sexual Medicine, 2*(3), 368.

McMahon, C. G., & Touma, K. (1999). Treatment of premature ejaculation with paroxetine hydrochloride as needed: 2 single-blind placebo controlled crossover studies. *Journal of Urology, 161*(6), 1826–1830.

Mittino, D., Mula, M., & Monaco, F. (2004). Serotonin syndrome associated with tramadol-sertraline coadministration. *Clinical Neuropharmacology, 27*(3), 150–151.

Mondaini, N., Ponchietti, R., Muir, G. H., Montorsi, F., Di Loro, F., Lombardi, G., et al. (2003). Sildenafil does not improve sexual function in men without erectile dysfunction but does reduce the postorgasmic refractory time. *International Journal of Impotence Research, 5*(3), 225–228.

Moreira, E. D., Jr. (2005). Help-seeking behaviour for sexual problems: The global study of sexual attitudes and behaviors. *International Journal of Clinical Practice, 59*, 6–16.

Motofei, I., & Rowland, D. L. (2005). The neurophysiology of ejaculation: Developing perspectives. *BJU International, 96*, 1333–1338.

Paick, J. S., Jeong, H., & Park, M. S. (1998). Penile sensitivity in men with early ejaculation. *International Journal of Impotence Research, 10*, 247–250.

Patrick, D. L., Althof, S. E., Pryor, J. L., Rosen, R., Rowland, D. L., Ho, K. F., et al. (2005). Premature ejaculation: An observational study of men and their partners. *Journal of Sexual Medicine, 2*, 358–367.

Patrick, D. L., Rowland, D. L., & Rothman, M. (2007). Interrelationships among measures of premature ejaculation: The central role of perceived control. *Journal of Sexual Medicine, 4*(3), 780–788.

Perelman, M. A. (2006). A new combination treatment for premature ejaculation: A sex therapist's perspective. *Journal of Sexual Medicine, 3*(6), 1004–1012.

Perelman, M. A., McCullough, A. R., & Bull, S. (2004). The impact of self-reported premature ejaculation on other aspects of sexual function. *Journal of Sexual Medicine, 1*(Suppl.1), 59–98.

Pridal, C. G., & LoPiccolo, J. (2000). Multi-element treatment of desire disorders: Integration of cognitive, behavioral, and systemic therapy. In S. R. Lieblum & R. C. Rosen (Eds.), *Principles and practice of sex therapy* (3rd ed., pp. 205–241). New York: Guilford Press.

Pryor, J. L., Althof, S. E., Steidle, C., Rosen, R. C., Hellstrom, W. J., Shabsigh, R., et al. (2006). Efficacy and tolerability of dapoxetine in treatment of premature ejaculation: An integrated analysis of two double-blind, randomised controlled trials. *Lancet, 368*(9539), 929–937.

Richardson, D., & Goldmeier, D. (2005). Premature ejaculation: Does country of origin tell us anything about etiology? *Journal of Sexual Medicine, 2*(4), 508–512.

Richardson, D., Wood, K., & Goldmeier, D. (2006). A qualitative pilot study of Islamic men with lifelong premature (rapid) ejaculation. *Journal of Sexual Medicine, 3*(2), 337–343.

Robinson, B. W., & Mishkin, M. (1966). Ejaculation evoked by stimulation of the preoptic area in monkeys. *Physiology and Behavior, 1*, 269–272.

Rosen, R. C., Hatzichristou, D., Broderick, G., Clayton, A., Cuzin, B., Derogatis, L., et al. (2004). Clinical evaluation and symptom scales: Sexual dysfunction assessment in men. In T. F. Lue, R. Basson, R. Rosen, F. Giuliano, S. Khoury, & F. Montsorsi (Eds.), *Sexual medicine: Sexual dysfunctions in men and women* (pp. 173–220). Paris: Health Publications.

Rosen, R. C., McMahon, C. G., Niederberger, C., Broderick, G. A., Jamieson, C., & Gagnon, D. D. (2007). Correlates to the clinical diagnosis of premature ejaculation: Results from a large observational study of men and their partners. *Journal of Urology, 177,* 1059–1064.

Rowland, D. L. (1998). Penile sensitivity in men: An overview of recent findings. *Urology, 52,* 1101–1105.

Rowland, D. L., & Burnett, A. (2000). Pharmacotherapy in the treatment of male sexual dysfunction. *Journal of Sex Research, 37,* 226–243.

Rowland, D. L., & Cooper, S. E. (2005). Behavioral and psychological models in ejaculatory function research. *Current Science Inc., 2,* 29–34.

Rowland, D. L., Cooper, S. E., & Slob, A. K. (1998). Treatment of premature ejaculation: Psychological and biological strategies. *Drugs of Today, 34,* 879–899.

Rowland, D. L., Patrick, D. L., Rothman, M., & Gagnon, D. D. (2007). The psychological burden of premature ejaculation. *Journal of Urology, 177,* 1065–1070.

Rowland, D. L., Perelman, M., Althof, S., Barada, J., McCullough, A. R., Bull, S., et al. (2004). Self-reported premature ejaculation and aspects of sexual functioning, and satisfaction. *Journal of Sexual Medicine, 1,* 225–232.

Rowland, D. L., Tai, W., & Brummett, K. (2007). Interactive processes in ejaculatory disorders: Psychophysiological considerations. In E. Janssen (Ed.), *The psychophysiology of sex* (pp. 227–243). Bloomington: Indiana University Press.

Rowland, D. L., Tai, W., & Slob, A. K. (2003). An exploration of emotional response to erotic stimulation in men with premature ejaculation: Effects of treatment with clomipramine. *Archives of Sexual Behavior, 32,* 145–154.

Rushton, J. P., & Bogaert, A. F. (1998). Race versus social class differences in sexual behaviour: A follow up test of the r/K dimension. *Journal of Research in Personality, 22,* 259–272.

Rust, J., & Golombok, S. (1986). *The Golombok Rust Inventory of Sexual Satisfaction.* Odessa, FL: Psychological Assessment Resources.

Safarinejad, M. R., & Hosseini, S. Y. (2006). Safety and efficacy of tramadol in the treatment of premature ejaculation: A double-blind, placebo-controlled, fixed-dose, randomized study. *Journal of Clinical Psychopharmacology, 26*(1), 27–31.

Salonia, A., Maga, T., Colombo, R., Scattoni, V., Briganto, A., Cestari, A., et al. (2002). A prospective study comparing paroxetine alone versus paroxetine plus sildenafil in patients with premature ejaculation. *Journal of Urology, 168*(6), 2486–2489.

Schnarch, D. M. (2000). Desire problems: A systemic perspective. In S. R. Lieblum & R. C. Rosen (Eds.), *Principles and practice of sex therapy* (3rd ed., pp. 17–56). New York: Guilford Press.

Shabsigh, R., & Rowland, D. (2007). The DSM-IV-TR as an appropriate diagnostic for premature ejaculation. *Journal of Sexual Medicine, 4,* 1468–1478.

Sommer, F., Klotz, T., & Mathers, M. J. (2005). Treatment of premature ejaculation: A comparative vardenafil and SSRI crossover study (Abstract No. 741). *Journal of Urology, 173*(4), 202.

Sorbera, L. A., Castaner, J., & Castaner, R. M. (2004). Dapoxetine hydrochloride. *Drugs of the Future, 29,* 1201–1205.

Spanier, G. B. (1976). Measuring dyadic adjustment: New scales for assessing the quality of marriage and similar dyads. *Journal of Marriage and Family, 38,* 15–28.

Strassberg, D. S., de Gouveia Brazao, C. A., Rowland, D. L., Tan, P., & Slob, A. K. (1999). Clomipramine in the treatment of rapid (premature) ejaculation. *Journal of Sex and Marital Therapy, 25*(2), 89–101.

Tang, W., Ma, L., Zhao, L., Liu, Y., & Chen, Z. (2004). [Clinical efficacy of Viagra with behavior therapy against premature ejaculation.] *Zhonghua Nan Ke Xue, 10*(5), 366–367, 370.

Tignol, J., Martin-Guehl, C., Aouizerate, B., Grabot, D., & Auriacombe, M. (2006). Social phobia and premature ejaculation: A case-control study. *Depression and Anxiety, 23*(3), 153–157.

Truitt, W. A., & Coolen, L. M. (2002). Identification of a potential ejaculation generator in the spinal cord. *Science, 297*(5586), 1566–1569.

Verma, K. K., Khaitan, B. K., & Singh, O. P. (1998). The frequency of sexual dysfunctions in patients attending a sex therapy clinic in north India. *Archives of Sexual Behavior, 27*(3), 309–314.

Waldinger, M. (2003). Towards evidence based drug treatment research on premature ejaculation: A critical evaluation of methodology. *International Journal of Impotence Research, 15*(5), 309–313.

Waldinger, M. D., Berendsen, H. H., Blok, B. F., Olivier, B., & Holstege, G. (1998). Premature ejaculation and serotonergic antidepressants-induced delayed ejaculation: The involvement of the serotonergic system. *Behavior and Brain Research, 92*(2), 111–118.

Waldinger, M. D., Quinn, P., Dilleen, M., Mundyat, R., Schweitzer, D. H., & Boolell, M. (2005). A multinational population survey of intravaginal ejaculation latency time. *Journal of Sexual Medicine, 2,* 492–497.

Waldinger, M. D., & Schweitzer, D. H. (2006). Changing paradigms from a historical DSM-III and DSM-IV view toward an evidence-based definition of premature ejaculation: Pt. I. Validity of DSM-IV-TR. *Journal of Sexual Medicine, 3,* 682–692.

Waldinger, M. D., Zwinderman, A. H., Olivier, B., & Schweitzer, D. H. (2005). Proposal for a definition of lifelong premature ejaculation based on epidemiological stopwatch data. *Journal of Sexual Medicine, 2*(4), 498–507.

Waldinger, M. D., Zwinderman, A. H., Schweitzer, D. H., & Olivier, B. (2004). Relevance of methodological design for the interpretation of efficacy of drug treatment of premature ejaculation: A systematic review and meta-analysis. *International Journal of Impotence Research, 16*(4), 369–381.

Williams, W. (1984). Secondary premature ejaculation. *Australian and New Zealand Journal of Psychiatry, 18*(4), 333–340.

Xin, Z. C., Choi, Y. D., Lee, S. H., & Choi, H. K. (1997). Efficacy of a topical agent SS-cream in the treatment of premature ejaculation: Preliminary clinical studies. *Yonsei Medical Journal, 38*(2), 91–95.

Yells, D. P., Hendricks, S. E., & Prendergast, M. A. (1992). Lesions of the nucleus paragigantocellularis: Effects on mating behavior in male rats. *Brain Research, 596*(1/2), 73–79.

Zhang, X. S., Wang, Y. X., Huang, X. Y., Leng, J., Li, Z., & Han, Y. F. (2005). [Comparison between sildenafil plus sertraline and sertraline alone in the treatment of premature ejaculation.] *Zhonghua Nan Ke Xue, 11*(7), 520–522, 525.

Zilbergeld, B. (1993). *The new male sexuality.* New York: Bantam Books.

Retarded and Inhibited Ejaculation

Michael A. Perelman and
David L. Rowland

4

Chapter

Learning Objectives

In this chapter, we:

- Review the nomenclature/classifications for inhibited or retarded ejaculation.
- Refine, describe, and review the prevalence of this dysfunction.
- Discuss organogenic and psychogenic etiologies for retarded ejaculation.
- Describe diagnostic and evaluative procedures.
- Identify treatment procedures, including strategies for dealing with resistance to treatment and various partner issues.
- Review treatment efficacy.
- Summarize the major issues and points.

Retarded ejaculation (RE) is probably the least common, least studied, and least understood of the male sexual dysfunctions. This dysfunction typically results in a lack of sexual fulfillment for both the man and his partner. Men whose sexual relationships are disrupted because of their inability to ejaculate and reach orgasm experience a number of psychological consequences including anxiety, distress, and a lack of confidence. Such negative effects are likely to be compounded when procreation is among the couple's goals of sexual intercourse.

Within the framework of the sexual response cycle, orgasm/ejaculation in men is both a biological (reproductive) and psychological (reward) endpoint. Arousability and arousal—distinct but interrelated constructs—are precursors to this endpoint. Arousability and/or sexual libido is a psychological construct used to explain variability in the intensity and/or desire for a sexual response. Arousability might best be conceptualized as the organism's readiness to respond. This state of readiness depends on both internal (hormonally "primed" diencephalic brain structures) and external (appropriate partner and situation) stimulus conditions. Sexual arousal or excitement—the organism's actual response to the stimulus conditions—represents both a subjective/cerebral state of autonomic activation and peripheral physiological responses (e.g., erection) that prepares the man for sexual activity. During sexual activity, increasing levels of sexual arousal reach a threshold that triggers the ejaculatory response, which then typically terminates the sexual episode for the male. The subjective (brain) perception of urethral distension and bladder neck closure of the emission phase of ejaculation is associated with the sensation experienced as "ejaculatory inevitability." The perception of the striated muscle contractions and resulting semen expelled during ejaculation, mediated through sensory neurons in the pelvic region, gives rise to the experience of orgasm. Given the recursive interactions among the components of the sexual response cycle as well as the high level of psychophysiological integration required for a coordinated response, it is not surprising that sexual response, important as it is to procreation, is sensitive to a myriad of physiological and psychological factors.

Definition and Descriptive Characteristics

RE is one of the diminished ejaculatory disorders (DED), which is a subset of male orgasmic disorders (MOD). MOD is a spectrum of disorders perceived by the individual as a deviation from the "normal" pattern of response (Perelman, McMahon, & Barada, 2004). As a broadly defined category, MOD includes premature ejaculation (PE) as well as DED.

DED is a collective term for an alteration of ejaculation and/or orgasm that includes:

- Retarded or inhibited ejaculation.
- Complete inability to ejaculate or anejaculation.
- Retrograde ejaculation.
- Diminished seminal volume, force, and sensation.
- Anorgasmia.
- Painful ejaculation.

- Partially retarded ejaculation.
- Orgasmic anesthesia.

At the extremes are anejaculation (time) and retrograde ejaculation (direction), but more commonly encountered is inhibited or retarded ejaculation (RE). Partially retarded ejaculation (PRE) is sometimes observed in men who attempt to control ejaculation by suppressing the muscular contractions associated with ejaculation. These men experience diminished pleasure and sensation as semen is released during emission, and the ejaculatory sensations are dulled through overcontrol of striated muscle. PRE is sometimes observed in men with PE as they first attempt to consciously delay their orgasm. A final disorder, anorgasmia, refers to a perceived absence of the orgasm experience, independent of whether or not any or all of the physiologic concomitants of ejaculation have taken place.

Retarded ejaculation, delayed ejaculation, inadequate ejaculation, inhibited ejaculation, idiopathic anejaculation, primary impotentia ejaculations, and psychogenic anejaculation have all been used synonymously to describe a delay or absence of male orgasmic response. Similar to the term *premature ejaculation*, the most commonly used term—*retarded ejaculation*—is sometimes avoided because of its pejorative associations. The abbreviation EjD has been suggested as a less stigmatized term, encompassing all disorders of ejaculation (Perelman et al., 2004).

The *DSM-IV-TR* defines RE as the persistent or recurrent delay in, or absence of, orgasm after a normal sexual excitement phase during sexual activity that the clinician, taking into account the person's age, judges to be adequate in focus, intensity, and duration. The disturbance causes marked distress or interpersonal difficulty; it should not be better accounted for by another Axis I (clinical) disorder or caused exclusively by the direct physiologic effects of a substance or a general medical condition (*Diagnostic and Statistical Manual of Mental Disorders*, fourth edition, text revision [*DSM-IV-TR*]; American Psychiatric Association, 2000). Similarly, the World Health Organization 2nd Consultation on Sexual Dysfunction defines RE as the persistent or recurrent difficulty, delay in, or absence of attaining orgasm after sufficient sexual stimulation, which causes personal distress (McMahon, Meston, Abdol, et al., 2004).

There are no clear criteria as to when a man actually meets the conditions for RE because operationalized criteria do not exist. Given that most sexually functional men ejaculate within about 7 to 10 minutes following intromission (Patrick et al., 2005), a clinician might assume that men with latencies beyond 25 or 30 min (21 to 23 min represents about two standard deviations above the mean) who report distress or men who simply cease sexual activity due to exhaustion or irritation qualify for this diagnosis. Such symptoms, together with the fact that a man and/or his partner decide to seek help for the problem, are usually sufficient for an RE diagnosis.

Failure of ejaculation can be a lifelong primary event (e.g., congenital anorgasmia) or an acquired or secondary problem. It can be global and happen in every sexual encounter or it may be intermittent or situational. Normative descriptive data from large samples of RE men have not been available, but a recent analysis identified 25% of a clinical sample suffering from primary RE, with the remainder reporting a secondary problem (Perelman, 2004). While coital anorgasmia is frequently the treatment driver (especially for extremely religious individuals referred for fertility problems), heterosexual men also seek treatment when distressed by their inability to achieve orgasm in response to manual, oral, or vaginal stimulation by their partner. Data available on homosexual men are limited, but distress/frustration associated with not being able to ejaculate by any desired/chosen mode of stimulation remains fairly constant across all men, regardless of sexual orientation (Perelman, 2006c).

Many men with secondary RE can masturbate to orgasm, whereas others, for multiple reasons, will or cannot. Loss of masturbatory capacity secondary to emotional or physical trauma is also seen. Approximately 75% of one clinical sample (Perelman, 2004) could reach orgasm through masturbation, while the remainder either would not or could not. Interestingly, correlational evidence suggests that masturbatory frequency and style may be predisposing factors for RE, since a substantial portion of men who present with coital RE report high levels of activity with an idiosyncratic masturbatory style (Perelman, 2005b; Rowland, van Diest, Incrocci, & Slob, 2005).

Similar to men with other types of sexual dysfunction, men with RE indicate high levels of relationship distress, sexual dissatisfaction, anxiety about their sexual performance, and general health issues—significantly higher than sexually functional men. In addition, along with other sexually dysfunctional counterparts, men with RE typically report lower frequencies of coital activity (Rowland et al., 2005). A distinguishing characteristic of men with RE—and one that has implications for treatment—is that they usually have little or no difficulty attaining or keeping their erections—in fact, they are often able to maintain erections for prolonged periods of time. But despite this, they report low levels of subjective sexual arousal, at least compared with sexually functional men (Rowland, Keeney, & Slob, 2004).

Prevalence

The prevalence of ejaculatory disorders is unclear, partly because of the dearth of normative data for defining the duration of "normal" ejaculatory latency, particularly regarding the right "tail" of the distribution (i.e., beyond the mean latency to orgasm). Furthermore, larger epidemiologic studies have not subdivided various types of DED, further limiting our knowledge of the prevalence of RE. In general, RE is reported at low rates in the literature, rarely exceeding 3% (Laumann, Paik, & Rosen, 1999; Perelman et al., 2004; Simons & Carey, 2001). Since the beginning of sex therapy, RE was seen as a clinical rarity, with Masters and Johnson (1970) initially reporting only 17 cases. Apfelbaum (2000) reported 34 cases and Kaplan (1995) fewer than 50 cases in their respective practices. However, based on clinical experiences, some urologists and sex therapists are reporting an increasing prevalence of RE (Perelman, 2003a; Perelman et al., 2004; Simons & Carey, 2001). The prevalence of RE appears to be moderately and positively related to age, which is not surprising in view of the fact that ejaculatory function as a whole tends to diminish as men age.

Etiology

In some instances, a somatic condition may account for RE, and indeed, any procedure or disease that disrupts sympathetic or somatic innervation to the genital region has the potential to affect ejaculatory function and orgasm. Thus, spinal cord injury, multiple sclerosis, pelvic-region surgery, severe diabetes, and medications that inhibit α-adrenergic innervation of the ejaculatory system have been associated with RE (Master & Turek, 2001; Vale, 1999; Witt & Grantmyre, 1993). Nevertheless, a sizable portion of men with RE exhibits no clear somatic factors that account for the disorder. These men neither ejaculate nor experience orgasm in response to varying forms of sexual stimulation. Men whose problem cannot be linked to a specific somatic or pathophysiological etiology are frequently assumed, though perhaps in error, to have a psychogenic etiology. Just as a pathophysiological etiology should not be assumed without a thorough medical investigation, a psychogenic etiology should not be assumed without an appropriate psychosexual history. Of course, psychogenic and organogenic etiologies are neither independent nor mutually exclusive classifications—not only do the categories themselves overlap (e.g., is a problem of diminished sympathetic arousal a psychogenic or organogenic classification?), but the causes of sexual dysfunctions often include a mix of factors involving both domains. In fact, recent studies suggest that RE is unlikely to result from a single set of causal factors (see Table 4.1).

Table 4.1 **Common Etiological and Risk Factors for Retarded or Inhibited Ejaculation**

Biological	
–Physiological(hypothesized)	Diminished penile sensitivity.
	Inherently sluggish or muted response system and/or high ejaculatory threshold.
–Pathophysiological	Iatrogenic, including medication.
	Pelvic surgery or trauma (e.g., spinal cord injury, prostatectomy, resection of prostate, etc.).
	Neuropathy (e.g., diabetes, other diseases affecting neural functioning).
	Endocrine (hypogonadism, hypothyroidism).
	Age-related.
Psychological	Religious beliefs and orthodoxy.
	Strong autosexual orientation.
	Diminished sexual desire.
	Inadequate sexual arousal/excitement.
	Sexual performance anxiety.
Relational	Disparity between fantasy and partner.
	Partner sexual dysfunction.

Note: Factors within and across categories may reciprocate or interact to exacerbate the problem.

Organogenic

The precise mechanism of ejaculation is much less firmly established than the physiology of erection, and for this reason, the physiology of ejaculatory disorders is less understood than that of erectile dysfunction (ED). For conceptual convenience, normal ejaculation is identified by its two seamless phases, emission and expulsion, with each representing distinct events regulated by separate neural pathways (Giuliano & Clement, 2005). After a variable period of sensory stimulation and psychosexual arousal, a rapid, involuntary sequence of events ensues (Masters & Johnson, 1966; Motofei & Rowland, 2005). The emission phase, under the control of the sympathetic nervous system, begins with closure of the bladder neck to prevent urinary contamination followed by deposition of semen from the seminal vesicles and prostate into the posterior urethra. A sensation experienced as "ejaculatory inevitability" arises from the urethral distension, which, in turn, stimulates rhythmic contractions of the bulbocavernous and ischiocavernous muscles responsible for semen expulsion—a process under probable parasympathetic control (Motofei & Rowland, 2005).

The ejaculatory reflex is mediated through the spinal control center, sometimes also referred to as the spinal ejaculation generator, spinal pattern generator, or spinal pacemaker. A combination of sensory input from the pudendal nerve (dorsal nerve of the penis) and descending cerebral pathways activates the spinal ejaculation generator, which coordinates the sympathetic, parasympathetic, and motor outflow needed to induce emission and expulsion (Motofei & Rowland, 2005; Perelman et al., 2004). As with other spinal reflex processes (e.g., urination), cerebral control is presumed to supersede spinal control of the ejaculatory response.

To understand organogenic causes of ejaculatory dysfunction, it is essential to distinguish factors that are physiological from those that are pathophysiological. *Physiological* refers to those that are biologically inherent to the system, perhaps "hardwired" through genetic and normal maturational processes. *Pathophysiological* refers to those factors that occur through disruption of the normal physiological processes, through disease, trauma, surgery, medication, and so on. Pathophysiological causes of RE are far more readily identifiable; they generally surface during a medical history and examination, and they typically stem from fairly predictable sources: anomalous anatomic, neuropathic, endocrine, and medication (iatrogenic; see Table 4.1). For example, surgical therapy for prostatic obstruction is likely to disrupt bladder neck competence during emission. Pathologic lesions of the sympathetic innervation of the coordinated ejaculatory reflex may have variable effects on the quality of ejaculation or orgasm. All types of RE show an age-related increases in prevalence, and there is also concomitant increased severity with lower urinary tract symptoms independent of age (Blanker et al., 2001; Rosen et al., 2003). Commonly used medications, particularly antidepressants, may centrally inhibit or delay ejaculation as well. Classes of pharmacological agents known to inhibit ejaculation are listed in Table 4.2.

More difficult to identify are inherent physiological factors that account for variation in ejaculatory latency and thus might play a role in RE (particularly primary anorgasmia). Low penile sensitivity, most often associated with aging (Paick, Jeong, & Park, 1998; Rowland, 1998), may exacerbate difficulty with reaching orgasm, but it is unlikely to be a primary cause. Alternatively, variability in the sensitivity of the ejaculatory reflex may be a factor, as several studies have demonstrated shorter latencies and stronger bulbocavernous EMG (electromyographic) and ERP (event-related potentials) responses in men with rapid ejaculation—perhaps men with RE exhibit long-latency and weaker EMG and ERP patterns, respectively. More likely, how-

Table 4.2 **Common Classes of Drugs that May Delay or Inhibit Ejaculation**

Class	Examples
Analgesics	Opioids, including methadone
Antidepressants	SSRIs, MAOIs, tricyclics
Antihypertensives	α and ß blockers, sympathetic inhibitors
Antipsychotics	Phenothiazines, select thioxanthenes
Anxiolytic/tranquilizers	Benzodiazepines
Hypnotics/sedatives	Barbiturates, alcohol
Muscle relaxants	GABA ß receptor agonists
Other	Marijuana
	Tobacco
	Amylnitrate

Note: For a more comprehensive list, see Perelman, McMahon, and Barada (2004).

ever, ejaculatory response and latency are influenced by central (cognitive-affective-arousal) processes than dominated by the simple hardwiring of the spinal reflex components (Motofei & Rowland, 2005).

Psychogenic

Multiple psychosocial explanations have been offered for RE, with unconscious aggression, unexpressed anger, and malingering as themes recurring in the psychoanalytic literature. In addition, fear of pregnancy often emerges, as professional referral has often been tied to the female partner's wish to conceive. Masters and Johnson (1970) were the first to suggest an association between RE and religious orthodoxy, positing that certain beliefs may inhibit normal ejaculatory response or limit the sexual experience necessary for developing the knowledge to learn to ejaculate. Consistent with this notion, a recent report of a clinical sample of 75 RE men (Perelman, 2004) noted about 35% scored high on religious orthodoxy. Some of these men tended to have limited sexual knowledge and had masturbated minimally or not at all. Others, similar to their more secular counterparts, masturbated for years, but with guilt and anxiety about "spilling seed" which in turn resulted in RE (Perelman, 2001b).

Although religious orthodoxy may play a role in RE for some men, the majority do not fall into this category. A number of relevant behavioral, psychological and relationship factors appear to contribute to difficulty reaching orgasm for these men. For example, men with RE sometimes indicate greater arousal and enjoyment from masturbation than from intercourse. This "autosexual" orientation may involve an idiosyncratic and vigorous masturbation style—carried out with high frequency—with which the vagina is unable to compete. Apfelbaum (2000) labels this as a desire disorder when masturbation is preferred to "partnered sex." Sank (1998) has described a similar "traumatic masturbatory syndrome." Perelman (2005b) noted the problematic conditioning effect of idiosyncratic masturbation, which could not be easily duplicated by a partner's hand, mouth, or vagina. Specifically, many men with RE engage in self-stimulation that is striking in the speed, pressure, duration, and intensity necessary to produce an orgasm, and dissimilar to what they experience with a partner. Almost universally, these men failed to communicate their preferences to either their doctor or their partners because of shame, embarrassment, or ignorance. Thus, they may predispose themselves to difficulty with a partner and experience secondary RE. Consistent with this idea, recent evidence indicates that, unlike sexually functional men or men with other sexual dysfunctions, men with RE report *better* erections during masturbation than during foreplay or intercourse (Rowland et al., 2005).

Disparity between the reality of sex with the partner and the sexual fantasy (whether or not unconventional) used during masturbation is another potential cause of RE (Perelman, 1994, 2001c). This disparity takes many forms, such as partner attractiveness and body type (Rowland et al., 2004), sexual orientation, and the specific sex activity performed. In summary, high-frequency idiosyncratic masturbation, combined with fantasy/partner disparity, may well predispose men to experiencing problems with arousal and ejaculation.

These patterns suggest that RE men, rather than withholding ejaculation as had been suggested by earlier psychoanalytic interpretations, may lack sufficient levels of physical and/or psychosexual arousal during coitus to achieve orgasm. That is, their arousal response to their partner cannot match their response to self-stimulation, self-generated fantasy, and/or pornography. In this respect, RE may be viewed more as a problem of psychosexual and physical arousal than a problem of the ejaculatory response. Support for this idea has been provided by several observations. First, psychophysiological investigation of men with RE has demonstrated that although these men attain erectile responses comparable to sexually functional controls or men with premature ejaculation during visual and penile psychosexual stimulation, they report far lower levels of subjective sexual arousal (Rowland et al., 2004, 2005). Apfelbaum (2000) has suggested that the couple interprets the man's strong erectile response as erroneous evidence that he is ready for sex and capable of achieving orgasm. Second, it has been posited that inadequate arousal may be responsible for increased anecdotal clinical reports of RE for men using oral medications for the treatment for ED (Perelman, 2001a).

Urologists had received a few early complaints of RE secondary to successful penile prosthesis surgery and intracavernosal injections, but PDE-5-inhibitors (i.e., phosphodiesterase type 5 inhibitors) such as Viagra brought much larger numbers of patients to physicians' offices. While most men using PDE-5 inhibitors experienced restored erections and coitus with ejaculation, others experienced erection without adequate psycho-emotional arousal. They did not experience sufficient erotic stimulation before and during coitus to reach orgasm, confusing their erect state as an indication of sexual arousal when it primarily indicated vasocongestive success (Perelman, 2001b).

Finally, the evaluative/performance aspect of sex with a partner often creates sexual performance anxiety for the man, a factor that may contribute to RE. Such anxiety typically stems from the man's lack of confidence to perform adequately, to appear and feel attractive (body image), to satisfy his partner sexually, to experience an overall sense of self-efficacy, and—despite new age efforts to downplay the idea—to measure up against the competition (Althof, Leiblum, Chevret-Measson et al., 2004; Zilbergeld, 1993). The impact of this anxiety on men's sexual response varies depending on the individual and the situation. But in some men, it may interfere with the ability to respond adequately and it may, as a result, generate a number of maladaptive responses (e.g., setting unrealistic expectations). With respect to inhibited or retarded ejaculation, anxiety surrounding the inability to ejaculate may draw the man's attention away from erotic cues that normally serve to enhance arousal. Apfelbaum (2000), for example, has emphasized the need to remove the "demand" (and thus anxiety-producing) characteristics of the situation, noting that men with RE may be overly conscientious about pleasing their partner. This ejaculatory performance anxiety interferes with the erotic sensations of genital stimulation, resulting in levels of sexual excitement and arousal that are insufficient for climax (although more than adequate to maintain their erections).

An Integrated Biopsychosocial Approach

Comprehending the factors that account for variation in latency to ejaculation following vaginal intromission is key to understanding any MOD. As with many biobehavioral responses, variation in ejaculatory latency is undoubtedly under the control of both biological and psychological-behavioral factors. One way of conceptualizing the interaction of these systems has been proposed by those who study evolutionary psychology (Gaulin & McBurney, 2004). The ejaculatory latency range for each individual may be biologically set or predisposed (e.g., via genetics), but the actual timing or moment of ejaculation within that range depends on a variety of contextual, psychological-behavioral, and relationship-partner variables (Perelman, 2006a). Such thinking is clearly supported by the fact that ejaculatory latency in men with ejaculatory disorders (either premature or retarded ejaculation) is often quite different during coitus than during masturbation (Rowland, Strassberg, de Gouveia Brazao, & Slob, 2000).

The most useful approach to understanding biobehavioral responses is that of integrating—rather than isolating—the biological and psychological-behavioral components, with the goal of identifying those organismic elements—peripheral and/or central—that contribute to and explain variation in the response. Undoubtedly, some components of the ejaculatory response that influence latency, particularly in nonhumans, are hardwired and not easily modified, with individual differences accounted for by gene-regulated processes (membrane receptors; biodynamics of neurotransmitter synthesis, activation, modulation, and degradation; androgenic and estrogenic hormones, etc.). All such genetic predispositions are likely to impact the typical speed and ease of ejaculation for any particular organism. At the same time, however, some components are "softwired," that is, they are influenced by the past experiences and present contexts in which the response is occurring. In the human, most such processes are central and/or cerebral and, although no less biological in nature than the hardwired system, allow for flexibility as the organism responds to the demands of the particular situation. These underlying biological processes give rise to subjective experiences that are then identified and studied as psychological-behavioral constructs that carry both descriptive (naming) and explanatory meaning for men and women. Thus, emotion, anxiety, motivation, arousal, and learning represent constructs—all underlain by biological events—used by biopsychosocial scientists and clinicians to help explain variation in the intensity, speed, frequency, latency, and duration of a response. Retarded ejaculation, then, is best understood as an endpoint or response that represents the interaction of biological, psychological, and relationship factors over the course of a man's life cycle.

Evaluation

Diagnostic evaluation of ejaculatory dysfunction focuses on finding potential physical and specific psychological/learned causes of the disorder (see Table 4.3).

The sexual tipping point® (STP) model (see Figure 4.1; Perelman, 2006b) offers a clinically useful heuristic for evaluating the role of both organic and psychosocial factors in determining the

Table 4.3 **Typical Steps in the Evaluation of Retarded Ejaculation**

Step	Goal	Information/Procedure
Medical history and exam	Pathophysiological etiology	Physical exam, review of illness, surgeries, medications, injuries, drug use, and so on
Current sexual patterns	Psychosocial precipitators/maintainers	Coital and masturbatory practices including foreplay, frequency, opportunity; assessment of desire, arousal, orgasm; sexual fantasy; use of contraception (condoms, etc.); thoughts and feelings (e.g., intrusive antisexual thoughts, anxiety)
Dysfunction history	Development of the problem	Lifelong or acquired; onset, duration, situation, exacerbation, self-management; motivation for change
General sexual history	Psychosocial predisposing factors	Family and religious attitudes, early and past sexual experiences, sexual knowledge, influencing cultural beliefs
Relationship factors	Relationship precipitators/maintainers	General relationship quality and stability; partner assessment; sexual fantasies and perceive partner attractiveness; partner dysfunction
General life stressors	General precipitators	Major life transitions: job-related, financial, relationship, family (deaths, illnesses)

etiology of sexual dysfunction (SD) generally, and RE in particular. The STP is the threshold for an expression of a sexual response for any individual, a threshold that may be inhibited or facilitated across and within sexual experiences due to a mix of psychogenic and organic factors. The specific threshold for the sexual response is determined by these multiple factors for any given moment or circumstance, with certain factors dominating and others receding in importance. For instance, every man, whether experiencing a "normal" ejaculatory latency, or premature or retarded ejaculation, has a multidimensional predetermined "ejaculatory tipping point" (Perelman, 2006a). Appropriate assessment requires an appreciation of the interdependent influence of all these factors on the endpoint dysfunction for a particular individual, at a particular moment in time.

The Multifactorial Etiology of RE

The Sexual Tipping Point™: The characteristic threshold for an expression of sexual response for any individual that may vary within and between any given sexual experience.

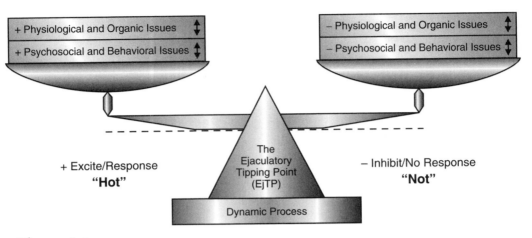

Figure 4.1

Ejaculatory Tipping Point

Source: Michael A. Perelman, PhD © 2006.

Medical History

A genitourinary examination and medical history may identify physical anomalies associated with ejaculatory dysfunction. In addition, concomitant or contributory neurologic, endocrinologic, or erectile disorders can be identified and addressed. Particular attention should be given to identifying reversible urethral, prostatic, epididymal, and testicular infections.

While recognizing the likelihood of ejaculatory variability and appreciating other potential organic components, clinicians can also note relevant psychosocial determinants, which typically emerge from the focused sex history. Particularly with secondary RE, adverse pharmaceutical side effects—most commonly from serotonin-based prescriptions—should be ruled out.

A focused psychosexual evaluation is critical to any diagnosis, whether the etiology is primarily pathophysiological or one with no obvious somatic etiology. Evaluation begins by differentiating this sexual dysfunction from other sexual problems (e.g., terminating intercourse due to pain) and reviewing the conditions under which the man is able to ejaculate (e.g., during sleep, with masturbation, with the partner's hand or mouth stimulation, or in specific coital positions). Domains related to the psychological and relationship issues commonly associated with RE (identified in the previous section) require investigation. Thus, the developmental course of the problem—including predisposing issues of religiosity—and variables that improve or worsen performance, particularly those related to psychosexual arousal, should be noted. Perceived partner attractiveness, the use of fantasy during sex, anxiety surrounding performance, and coital and masturbatory patterns all require exploration. Consistent with the discussion of etiology, patients presenting to a health care professional with symptoms of RE should be asked about their frequency and manner (technique) of masturbation.

If orgasmic attainment had been possible previously, the clinician should review the life events/circumstances temporally related to orgasmic cessation—events in question might include the use of pharmaceuticals, illness, or life stressors and other psychological factors previously highlighted in the section on etiology. Generally, a complete psychosexual history and evaluation should identify predisposing, precipitating, and maintaining factors for the dysfunction.

Since many men attempt their own remedies, the patient's previous approaches to improving ejaculatory response should be investigated, including the use of herbal or folk therapies, prior treatments, and home remedies (e.g., using particular cognitive or behavioral strategies). Information regarding the partners' perception of the problem and their satisfaction with the overall relationship is often helpful. Once this body of knowledge is complete, an appropriate treatment plan, developed in conjunction with the couple, can be implemented.

Treatment

Treatment strategies for RE have typically been based on the etiologies previously described, and most benefit from cooperation of the sexual partner. Successful treatment approaches typically begin by recognizing the importance of de-stigmatizing the dysfunction, providing appropriate sex-response education to the couple, and defusing dyadic tension that might have evolved in response to the dysfunction. For example, discussion of a potential biologic predisposition is often helpful in reducing patient and partner anxiety and mutual recriminations, while simultaneously assisting the formation of a therapeutic alliance with the health care professional (Perelman, 2004).

Masters and Johnson (1970) were among the first to advocate specific exercises as part of the treatment for RE, utilizing a progressive behavioral shaping methodology. They prescribed partner-assisted manual stimulation that simulated the patient's own techniques (including vibrator use) to the point of ejaculatory

inevitability, at which point the couple would switch to intercourse. Most current sex therapy approaches to RE continue to
emphasize the importance of masturbation in the treatment of RE;
however, much of the focus now is on masturbatory retraining, integrated into sex therapy (Kaplan, 1995; Perelman, 2004). Indeed,
masturbation serves as a type of dress rehearsal for sex with a
partner. By informing the patient that his difficulty is merely a reflection of "not rehearsing the part he intended to play," the stigma
associated with this problem can be minimized and cooperation of
both the patient and his partner in the therapeutic process can be
readily engaged (Perelman, 2004).

Masturbation retraining is only a means to an end, and the
true goal of most current therapeutic techniques for RE (either
primary or secondary) is not merely to provide more intense stimulation, but rather to induce higher levels of psychosexual arousal
so the man can attain orgasm within the framework of a satisfying
partnered experience. A number of strategies have been utilized
to achieve the endpoint of increased arousal and satisfaction.

Men with primary anorgasmia, like their female counterparts,
typically need help determining their sexual arousal preferences
through self-exploration and then in communicating that knowledge to their partner. Masturbation training may use a modification
of the model described by Barbach (1974) for women, although the
use of vibrators, sometimes recommended by urologists, is rarely
necessary (Perelman, 2007). Progressing from neutral sensations to
the ability to identify and experience pleasurable sensations is encouraged whether or not ejaculation should occur.

Typically, self-stimulation techniques incorporating fantasy
can be used to achieve incremental increases in a cascading arousal
pattern that eventually enables orgasm. Fantasy can serve the purpose of increasing arousal and blocking inhibiting (often critical)
thoughts that might otherwise interfere. Once the man's ejaculatory
ability is established through masturbation, the same skill set can be
incorporated into partnered sex. Although some cultures and religions forbid masturbation, temporary religious dispensation is sometimes available, especially when procreation is a goal of treatment.

An important component in the treatment of any type of RE is
the removal of the demand (and thus anxiety-producing) characteristics of the situation (Apfelbaum, 2000). Ejaculatory performance
anxiety can interfere with the erotic sensations of genital stimulation and may result in levels of sexual excitement insufficient
for climax (although they may be more than adequate to maintain
an erection). To reduce anxiety, treatment may include recognition
of RE men's overeagerness to please their partners, validation of
(though not necessarily encouragement of) the man's autosexual
orientation, removal of stigmas suggesting hostility or withholding
toward their partner, and general anxiety reduction techniques such
as relaxation and desensitization. By normalizing the anorgasmia,

therapy can then proceed to the exploration of factors that increase the man's arousal (similar to treatment of anorgasmia in women). Finally, like a previously anorgasmic woman, the man is taught to effectively communicate his preferences to his partner so that both their needs are incorporated into the sexual experience.

Management of Resistance

Therapy for secondary RE follows a strategy similar to that of primary anorgasmia. Successful treatment may require a temporary elimination of masturbation and orgasmic release only to the desired activity, coitus, in order to heighten the man's arousal when sex does occur. However, a therapeutic dictum to temporarily discontinue masturbation is usually met with resistance by the patient; the therapist may be questioned about the length of suspension, its potential benefit and necessity. This "suspension" strategy, which may extend from 14 to 60 days, is likely to be frustrating for the patient and thus will require the strong support and encouragement of the practitioner.

The therapeutic benefit of temporarily discontinuing self-stimulation cannot be overestimated. Like any therapeutic intervention, this recommendation must be balanced with maintenance of a therapeutic rapport and alliance with the patient(s). Sometimes the issue of masturbation interruption must be compromised and negotiated. One man felt such a treatment approach required more patience than he could provide. His frequent masturbation ejaculations reduced his high levels of anxiety and provided a useful and not uncommon soporific effect for him. In this case, the man's treatment plan was adjusted so he could continue to masturbate, but with reduced frequency from daily to every other day while also agreeing to use his nonpreferred hand ("switch hands" technique), with which he had never ejaculated ("it feels like a stranger"). He was able to learn to masturbate in this manner after several attempts, which then allowed for an easier transition to manual stimulation to orgasm by his partner. Thus, a man who continues to masturbate can be encouraged to alter the style of masturbation to approximate (in terms of speed, pressure, and technique) the stimulation likely to be experienced through manual, oral, or vaginal stimulation by his partner (Perelman, 2006c).

In addition to suspending masturbation, the patient should be encouraged to use fantasy and bodily movements during coitus that help approximate the thoughts and sensations previously experienced in masturbation. This process is facilitated and resistance minimized when the man's partner is supported by the practitioner and understands that the alteration in coital style is part of a series of steps designed to reach a long term goal of coital harmony and satisfaction for them both.

Partner Issues

The partner needs to collaborate in the therapeutic process, finding ways to pleasure the man that not only enhance his arousal, but that also can be incorporated into the couple's lovemaking. Resistance to this process from the partner may be mitigated by providing the partner a similar opportunity. Because fantasy plays an important role in arousal, sexual fantasies may have to be realigned (i.e., through stimulus fading) so that ideations experienced during masturbation better match those occurring during intercourse with the partner. The attractiveness and seductive/arousing capacity of the partner might be increased to reduce the disparity between the man's fantasy and the actuality of coitus with his partner. Significant disparity tends to characterize more severe and recalcitrant RE and relationship problems, with a consequent poorer treatment prognosis (Perelman, 2003b).

While there are a number of other partner related issues that may impact men's ejaculatory interest and capacity, two require special attention: conception and anger/resentment. When one or both of these issues are involved, the practitioner is challenged to identify a strategy that allows the couple to experience coital ejaculation while maintaining a therapeutic rapport with both partners. Although the pressure of her biological clock is often the initial treatment driver, the female partner—sometimes the man as well—may meet any potential intrusion on their plan to conceive (with or without high technology reproductive medical assistance) with strong resistance. If a man with RE is able to experience a coital ejaculation with contraception (including condoms) but not able/willing to do so "unprotected," then issues surrounding conception and parenthood undoubtedly play a primary role in the RE. While a diagnosis of RE is technically incorrect for such an individual, struggling with the couple over diagnostic labels would be a greater therapeutic error. In such instances, the practitioner must find an acceptable way to refocus the treatment, at least temporarily, on the underlying issues responsible for the man's ambivalence in order for treatment to succeed overall. This may require individual sessions with the man and occasionally with the partner as well.

Whether related to conception, a man's anger (expressed/ unexpressed) toward his partner may be an important mediating factor that should be addressed through individual and/or conjoint consultation. Anger can act as a powerful anti-aphrodisiac. While some men avoid sexual contact entirely when angry at a partner, others may attempt intercourse, finding themselves only moderately aroused and unable to maintain an erection/and or reach orgasm. Under such circumstances, treatment requires balancing the needs of both the man and his partner who now may be subjected to a new found anger by the man with RE. While encouraging the man's assertiveness, the practitioner must also remain responsive to the impact of this change on the partner and the resulting alteration in the equilibrium of the relationship.

Additionally, interventions used in treatment may be experienced by the female partner as mechanistic (e.g., using a stepwise program) and insensitive to her current sexual needs and/or long term goals (both sexual and otherwise) for the relationship. In particular, many women respond negatively to the accurate impression that, at least initially, the man is essentially masturbating himself with her various body parts, as opposed to engaging in the connected lovemaking that she may prefer. This response is exacerbated for the female partner when her partner needs actual pornography/erotica rather than mere fantasy to distract himself from negative thoughts and emotions that might interfere with sexual functioning. The practitioner must help the partner accept postponement of her needs until the patient has progressed to a level of functionality, which then allows for encouragement and development of a greater sensitivity and sharing between them. The therapeutic challenge is to facilitate the rapport between the partners, while maintaining a therapeutic alliance with both partners and simultaneously optimizing his response to her manual, oral, and vaginal stimulation. Later, once the man is able to reach orgasm, he would be encouraged to support his partner's desire for more spontaneous and connected lovemaking.

Alternatives to Therapy

This discussion has concentrated on the use of counseling methods because no United States Food and Drug Administration (FDA) approved treatments are currently available to treat RE. However, a number of pharmacological agents have been used to facilitate orgasm in patients taking SSRI antidepressants, drugs known to delay or completely inhibit ejaculatory response. Specifically, the anti-serotonergic agent cyproheptadine and the dopamine agonist amantadine have been used with moderate success in this population of patients (McMahon, Abdo, Incrocci, et al., 2004). But the fact that no large scale, well controlled studies have been carried out on these and other ejaculatory-facilitating agents in men with noniatrogenic RE suggests a high ratio of adverse effects to potential efficacy. Furthermore, a lack of efficacy in men with RE may result, in part, from the potentially strong psychological and relational contributions to this dysfunction. Nevertheless, as research continues to uncover greater understanding of the ejaculatory process, the likelihood of finding pro-ejaculatory agents increases. As with both PE and ED, if and when safe and effective pharmacological treatment becomes available for RE, treatment for this dysfunction will likely undergo a major paradigm shift. Although, due to the multifaceted etiology of this disorder, like other sexual dysfunctions, the greatest efficacy for the majority of cases is likely to result from a combination treatment approach. In the future, practitioners could easily apply the STP model to conceptualize a combination treatment where sex coaching and sexual pharmaceuticals are integrated into a more satisfactory efficacious treatment where physiology, psychology, and culture are all addressed (Perelman, 2005a).

Treatment Efficacy

While anecdotally viewed by urologists as a difficult-to-treat sexual dysfunction, some sex therapists have reported good success rates, in the neighborhood of 70% to 80% (Masters & Johnson, 1970; Perelman, 2004). This disparity probably reflects clinically different treatment populations as well as the lack of an easily identified or single etiology for RE. Additionally, confidence in such reports is limited by the few studies that have been conducted, their uncontrolled designs (including lack of placebo groups), the lack of standardized treatment formats, and again the heterogeneous samples that include men with varying biological and psychological etiologies.

Finally, the treatment of RE often consumes more of a practitioner's time than the treatment of other sexual dysfunctions such as erectile dysfunction. Therefore, the general medical or mental health practitioner may choose to treat or may refer to a sex therapist colleague, depending on comfort, preference and availability. Assuming new drugs are developed to increase the ease and speed of ejaculatory latency, combination drug and sex therapy protocols that address the multifactorial etiology of RE are likely to ensure an optimal response while minimizing relapse potential.

Summary and Conclusions

There is ample evidence that despite its low prevalence retarded or inhibited ejaculation results in considerable distress, anxiety, and lack of sexual confidence for those suffering from it:

- RE may result from organogenic and psychogenic factors, or both.
- Organogenic factors can be identified through a medical history and physical exam.
- Identification of psychogenic factors requires a comprehensive psychosexual evaluation.
- Treatment is best accomplished with the cooperation of the sexual partner.
- Treatment may involve masturbatory retraining, alignment of fantasies with actual partner characteristics and behaviors, increased psychosexual arousal, and reduction of sexual anxiety.

- Patient resistance and partners issues need to be addressed as part of the therapeutic process.
- Several pharmacological agents have been used for RE, but their efficacy is limited.
- Treatment success for psychogenically derived RE tends to be high.

Furthermore, men with partners often experience impairment of both the sexual and nonsexual aspects of their relationships, with such negative effects compounded when procreation is a consideration. Although consensus is emerging, a precise definition for RE remains ambiguous due to the variability and paucity of data regarding normal coital ejaculatory latency times. In addition, the extent to which phenomenological variables such as ejaculatory control, overall distress, and sexual dissatisfaction should be operationalized and included as part of the definition is yet undecided by the clinical/medical community. The etiology of RE is presumed to include varying degrees of both biogenic and psychogenic components that vary over time both between and within individuals. While specific pathophysiology can sometimes be identified, further clarification of the biogenic components of this dysfunction will require greater understanding of the physiological mechanisms underlying ejaculation. Yet, the most useful strategies for understanding RE will integrate rather than isolate the various biological and psychosocial aspects of this dysfunction. Finally, although the level of evidence based evaluation and treatment protocols for this disorder is lower than for that of other sexual dysfunctions, recent reports suggest that the more psychogenic the etiology, the greater the treatment efficacy. As with erectile dysfunction and premature ejaculation, if efficacious oral pharmaceuticals are eventually developed to treat this condition, the treatment algorithm is likely to undergo significant alteration. Even then, however, the most effective treatments are likely to result from a combination treatment that integrates sex coaching with pharmacotherapy.

References

Althof, S. E., Leiblum, S. R., Chevret-Measson, M., Hartmann, U., Levine, S. B., McCabe, M., et al. (2004). Psychological and interpersonal dimensions of sexual function and dysfunction. In T. F. Lue, R. Basson, R. Rosen, F. Giuliano, S. Khoury, & F. Montorsi (Eds.), *Sexual medicine: Sexual dysfunctions in men and women* (pp. 73–116). Paris: 2nd International Consultation on Sexual Dysfunctions.

American Psychiatric Association. (2000). *Diagnostic and statistical manual of mental disorders* (4th ed., text rev.). Washington, DC: Author.

Apfelbaum, B. (2000). Retarded ejaculation: A much-misunderstood syndrome. In S. R. Leiblum & R. C. Rosen (Eds.), *Principles and practice of sex therapy* (2nd ed., pp. 205–241). New York: Guilford Press.

Barbach, L. G. (1974). *For yourself: A guide to female orgasmic response.* New York: Doubleday.

Blanker, M. H., Bosch, J. L., Broeneveld, F. P., Bohnen, A. M., Prins, A., Thomas, S., et al. (2001). Erectile and ejaculatory dysfunction in a community-based sample of men 50 to 78 years old: Prevalence, concern, and relation to sexual activity. *Urology, 57,* 763–768.

Gaulin, S. J. C., & McBurney, D. H. (2004). *Evolutionary psychology* (2nd ed.). Upper Saddle River, NJ: Pearson Prentice Hall.

Giuliano, F., & Clement, P. (2005). Neuroanatomy and physiology of ejaculation. *Annual Review of Sex Research, 16,* 190–216.

Kaplan, H. (1995). *The evaluation of sexual disorders: Psychologic and medical aspects.* New York: Brunner/Mazel.

Laumann, E. O., Paik, A., & Rosen, R. C. (1999). Sexual dysfunction in the United States: Prevalence and predictors. *Journal of the American Medical Association, 281,* 537–544.

Master, V. A., & Turek, P. J. (2001). Ejaculatory physiology and dysfunctions. *Urologic Clinics of North America, 28,* 363–375.

Masters, W. H., & Johnson, V. E. (1966). *Human sexual response.* Boston: Little, Brown.

Masters, W. H., & Johnson, V. E. (1970). *Human sexual inadequacy.* Boston: Little, Brown.

McMahon, C. G., Abdo, C., Incrocci, L., Perelman, M., Rowland, D., Waldinger, M., et al. (2004). Disorders of orgasm and ejaculation in men. *Journal of Sexual Medicine, 1,* 58–65.

McMahon, C. G., Meston, C., Abdo, C., Incrocci, L., Perelman, M., Rowland, D., et al. (2004). Disorders of orgasm and ejaculation in men. In T. F. Lue, R. Basson, R. Rosen, F. Giuliano, S. Khoury, & F. Montorsi (Eds.), *Sexual medicine: Sexual dysfunction in men and women* (pp. 409–468). Plymouth, England: Health Publications.

Motofei, I. G., & Rowland, D. (2005). Neurophysiology of the ejaculatory process: Developing perspectives. *BJU International, 96,* 1333–1338.

Paick, J. S., Jeong, H., & Park, M. S. (1998). Penile sensitivity in men with early ejaculation. *International Journal of Impotence Research, 10,* 247–250.

Patrick, D. L., Althof, S. E., Pryor, J. L., Rosen, R., Rowland, D. L., Ho, K. F., et al. (2005). Premature ejaculation: An observational study of men and their partners. *Journal of Sexual Medicine, 2,* 358–367.

Perelman, M. (1994). Masturbation revisited. *Contemporary Urology, 6*(11), 68–70.

Perelman, M. (2001a). The impact of the new sexual pharmaceuticals on sex therapy. *Current Psychiatry Reports, 3,* 195–201.

Perelman, M. (2001b). Integrating sildenafil and sex therapy: Unconsummated marriage secondary to ED & RE. *Journal of Sex Education and Therapy, 26*(1), 13–21.

Perelman, M. (2001c). Sildenafil, sex therapy, and retarded ejaculation. *Journal of Sex Education and Therapy, 26,* 13–21.

Perelman, M. (2003a). Regarding ejaculation: Delayed and otherwise [Letter to the editor]. *Journal of Andrology, 24*(4), 496.

Perelman, M. (2003b). Sex coaching for physicians: Combination treatment for patient and partner. *International Journal of Impotence Research, 15*(Suppl. 5), S67–S74.

Perelman, M. (2004). Retarded ejaculation. In J. Mulhall (Ed.), *Current sexual health reports, 2004* (pp. 1, 3, 95–101). Philadelphia: Current Science.

Perelman, M. (2005a). Combination therapy: Integration of sex therapy and pharmacotherapy. In R. Balon & R. Seagraves (Eds.), *Handbook of sexual dysfunction* (pp. 13–41). New York: Marcel Dekker.

Perelman, M. (2005b). Idiosyncratic masturbation patterns: A key unexplored variable in the treatment of retarded ejaculation by the practicing urologist. *Journal of Urology, 173*(Suppl. 4), S340.

Perelman, M. (2006a). A new combination treatment for premature ejaculation: A sex therapist's perspective. *Journal of Sexual Medicine, 3*(6), 1004–1012.

Perelman, M. (2006b). The sexual tipping point: A model to conceptualize etiology, diagnosis, and combination treatment of female and male sexual dysfunction. *Journal of Sexual Medicine, 3*(Suppl. 1), 52.

Perelman, M. (2006c). Unveiling retarded ejaculation (Abstract No. 1337). *Journal of Urology, 175*(4, Suppl. 430).

Perelman, M. (2007). Editorial comment. *Urology, 69*(3), 555–556.

Perelman, M., McMahon, C., & Barada, J. (2004). Evaluation and treatment of ejaculatory disorders. In T. F. Lue (Ed.), *Atlas of male sexual dysfunction* (pp. 127–157). Philadelphia: Current Medicine LLC.

Rosen, R., Altwein, J., Boyle, P., Kirby, R. S., Lukacs, B., Meuleman, E., et al. (2003). Lower urinary tract symptoms and male sexual dysfunction: The multinational survey of the aging male (MSAM-7). *European Urology, 44,* 637–649.

Rowland, D. L. (1998). Penile sensitivity in men: An overview of recent findings. *Urology, 52,* 1101–1105.

Rowland, D. L., Strassberg D., de Gouveia Brazao, C. A., & Slob, A. K. (2000). Ejaculatory latency and control in men with premature ejaculation: A detailed analysis across sexual activities using multiple sources of information. *Journal of Psychosomatic Research, 48,* 69–77.

Rowland, D. L., Keeney, C., & Slob, A. K. (2004). Sexual response in men with inhibited or retarded ejaculation. *International Journal of Impotence Research, 16*(3), 270–274.

Rowland, D., van Diest, S., Incrocci, L., & Slob, A. K. (2005). Psychosexual factors that differentiate men with inhibited ejaculation from men with no dysfunction or another sexual dysfunction. *Journal of Sexual Medicine, 2*(3), 383–389.

Sank, L. I. (1998). Traumatic masturbatory syndrome. *Journal of Sex and Marital Therapy, 24*(1), 37–42.

Simons, J., & Carey, M. P. (2001). Prevalence of sexual dysfunctions: Results from a decade of research. *Archives of Sexual Behavior, 30*(2), 177–219.

Vale, J. (1999). Ejaculatory dysfunction. *BJU International, 83,* 557–563.

Witt, M. A., & Grantmyre, J. E. (1993). Ejaculatory failure. *World Journal of Urology, 11,* 89–95.

Zilbergeld, B. (1993). *The new male sexuality.* New York: Bantam Books.

Androgens and Endocrine Function in Aging Men: Effects on Sexual and General Health

Louis Gooren

5

Chapter

Learning Objectives

In this chapter, we discuss:

- Aspects of male aging.
- The role of declining testosterone on sexual functioning in aging men.
- The wider role of testosterone on general health in men.
- Diagnostic strategies for sexual problems that encompass a broad biopsychosocial approach.
- Diagnostic strategies for androgen deficiency.
- Treatment approaches in dealing with androgen and other hormone deficiencies related to aging.

Sexuality and Aging in Men: An Introduction

Aging is a powerful predictor of sexual dysfunction. Age-related changes in sexual behavior in men, with attention to possible contributing factors to individual variability, have been systematically reviewed (Schiavi & Rehman, 1995; Schiavi, Schreiner-Engel, Mandeli, Schanzer, & Cohen, 1990). In this review, we pay special attention to the intertwined issues of aging, health and illness, and sexual functioning, concluding that aging is associated with decreases in sexual desire, arousal, and activity, even when the effects of illness, medication, and psychopathology are minimized or eliminated as confounding variables (Schiavi & Rehman, 1995).

We observe wide variability in the level of sexual activity in older men, but it remains unclear which factors contribute to individual variability in sexual responses at different age levels. A proportion of subjects in the oldest age group remained sexually active and continued to have regular intercourse in the presence of a marked decrement in erectile capacity, as measured by nocturnal penile tumescence (Schiavi & Rehman, 1995). These sexually active individuals differed from inactive counterparts in the higher value they attributed to sexuality in their lives (Schiavi & Rehman, 1995; Schiavi et al., 1990). The two groups differed in the frequency and range of past sexual behaviors, in their motivation and ability to experiment and develop compensatory sexual strategies, and in the supportive attitudes of partners. Self-reported sexual satisfaction and the self-perception of "not being sexually dysfunctional" further characterized the sexually active group. Schiavi recommended further investigation of the psychological and interpersonal dimensions in older individuals in order to clarify their role in the process of "successful" sexual aging.

Physiological Aspects of Male Aging

Although aging is characterized by significant physiological (neural, endocrinological, cardiovascular), psychological, and relationship changes, this chapter focuses on one aspect of aging in men: the role of testosterone (T) in male sexual functioning and in general health in older men. While testosterone has been known to play a key role in sexual functioning, the past 2 decades have convincingly shown that its biological role extends far beyond simply maintaining sexual function. For example, testosterone has potent effects on muscle and bone; on bone the effects may be androgenic in nature or come about through its aromatization to estradiol. Furthermore, testosterone deficiency is associated with the emergence of the so-called metabolic syndrome and its sequelae, diabetes mellitus type 2 and cardiovascular disease (Handelsman & Liu, 2005; Schultheiss, Jonas, & Musitelli, 2002; Smith, Betancourt, & Sun, 2005). This new information is important regarding decisions to treat older men with testosterone deficiency, particularly insofar as the metabolic syndrome, and its associated diseases diabetes and cardiovascular disease, are also factors in the development of erectile failure (Crawford, Liu, Kean, Bleasel, & Handelsman, 2003; Harman, Naftolin, Brinton, & Judelson, 2005). As a result of these discoveries, in the not too distant future, adequate testosterone levels may be an important consideration in the assessment of health of older men.

The Biology of Aging

Aging can be viewed as a time-related functional decline of health into the frailty of old age, with an ever-increasing vulnerability to disease and eventually to death. Changes related to aging occur in every human, given sufficient time to live. As characterized by Lunenfeld (2002), probably all we can do about aging is to: "prevent the preventable and delay the inevitable."

Among the many processes of aging, endocrine changes are relatively easy to identify and quantify, given the current reliable and sensitive methods for determining hormone levels in men. The question has been raised whether a counterpart to menopause (i.e., an andropause) exists in the male. Levels of testosterone do, indeed, show an age-related decline, but the characteristics of this decline are so fundamentally different from the menopause that drawing a parallel generates more confusion than clarity. In men, testosterone production is affected in a slowly progressive way as part of the normal aging process. Testosterone decline is rarely manifested in men under 50 years of age but usually becomes quantitatively significant in men over 60. However, this age-related decline of testosterone shows considerable inter-individual variation: some men in their eighties still have normal testosterone levels. So, unlike the menopause, the age-related decline in testosterone does not present itself in an all-or-none fashion; whereas the majority of women are able to retrospectively identify their age of menopause, men are unable to pinpoint the start of their decline of testosterone.

The age-related decline of testosterone in men thus calls for terminology distinct from that describing female menopause. When scientific investigation first produced evidence of an age-related decline of testosterone, terms such as *male menopause, male climacteric,* or *andropause* were introduced. But for the reasons cited, partial androgen decline in the aging male (PADAM or ADAM) is a better description, although now the terminology *late onset hypogonadism* (LOH) appears to be taking precedence (Nieschlag et al., 2005b).

Testosterone deficiency in LOH is usually less profound and less manifest than in other hypogonadal states, but it is nevertheless clinically significant and deserves the attention of the medical profession. Questions as to who will benefit from testosterone treatment are therefore timely and important and deserve research and clinical attention. However, the notion of an andropause or male menopause—or LOH—has been viewed with some skepticism by the medical profession (Handelsman & Liu, 2005). This concept all too readily lends itself to opportunistic exploitation by anti-aging entrepreneurs, usually working outside the public health sector, who tout "rejuvenation cures." The history of this field, which includes people like Voronoff and Lespinasse and, surprisingly, even such reputable scientists as Brown-Sequard and Steinach, is not a proud one (Schultheiss et al., 2002). The fear is that those who peddle the indiscriminate use of androgens, growth hormone, melatonin, and adrenal androgens for rejuvenation will perpetuate this quackery (Handelsman & Liu, 2005). Only well-designed studies investigating the endocrinology of aging, with clear clinical objectives and proper terminology, can ensure that history does not repeat itself.

Neuroendocrine Mechanisms of Aging

Most hormone deficiencies associated with aging are based on neuroendocrine mechanisms, through changes in the brain structures that produce hormones that stimulate the further release of hormones from the pituitary gland (Smith et al., 2005). One of the best-known examples of the age-related decline of hormone production is the menopause. Originally believed to result from "exhaustion of the ovary," it is becoming clear that neuroendocrine mechanisms orchestrate the loss of reproductive capacity in women. Its sequels can be alleviated by the administration of estrogens, the end products of ovarian hormone production, though this clinical practice has stirred some controversy (Harman et al., 2005). As with menopause in women, the decline of testosterone and growth hormone is also largely explained by neuroendocrine mechanisms, all leading to a diminished stimulation of the pituitary to produce stimulatory hormones of the peripheral endocrine glands (e.g., gonads and adrenal glands). But in addition to neuroendocrine mechanisms, local testicular factors also play a role in the decline of testosterone production in older men.

As indicated, endocrine changes are relatively easy to identify and quantify with reliable, sensitive and highly specific methods for determining hormone levels. However, it is not only the reproductive hormones that decline with aging; numerous other endocrine systems are affected. The production of the sleep-related pineal hormone melatonin declines with aging. Adrenal androgens start to decline in both sexes from the age of 30 years (adrenopause), becoming very low at and beyond age 80 years. In contrast with adrenal androgens, the main adrenal hormone cortisol does not decline with aging, raising the question of whether the imbalance between the catabolic cortisol and anabolic testosterone contributes to the sarcopenia (the loss of skeletal muscle mass) of old age (Crawford et al., 2003). Growth hormone secretion also undergoes an age-related decline (somatopause). While insulin levels do not generally fall with aging, sensitivity to the biological action of insulin decreases considerably. Changes in calcium,

water, and electrolyte metabolism, and thyroid function all characterize aging; and some of these changes are clinically relevant. Hypothyroidism or hyperthyroidism may be associated with forms of
senile dementia, a diagnosis that can often be overlooked and can
also affect sexuality in elderly men. Asthenia and muscle weakness
may find their cause in disturbances of the electrolytes or androgen
and growth hormone physiology. Therefore, the relationship between aging and hormonal changes is a two-way street: aging affects the endocrine system but endocrine dysfunction may also
mimic and aggravate symptoms of the aging process.

The attraction of identifying hormonal factors in the aging
process is that they lend themselves to relatively easy correction.
Admittedly, it would be simple-minded to interpret all age-related
changes of hormones as deficiencies awaiting correction (Lamberts, Romijn, & Wiersinga, 2003). Substantial research still needs
to be done to ascertain whether the replacement of age-related reductions in hormone production is meaningful and, even more so,
whether it is safe. Hormones such as estrogens, androgens, and
growth hormone are potential factors in the development and
growth of tumors that occur in old age, so benefits and risks need
to be carefully balanced.

This chapter focuses primarily on the age-related decline of
testosterone, for which the terminology late onset hypogonadism
(LOH) has been recommended by the International Study of the
Aging Male (ISSAM), the International Society of Andrology
(ISA), and the European Association of Urology (EAU) to replace
the previous terminologies such as andropause, androgen deficiency of the aging male (ADAM), and partial androgen deficiency
of the aging male (PADAM; Nieschlag et al., 2005c).

LOH is a clinical and biochemical syndrome associated with
advancing age and characterized by typical symptoms and a deficiency in serum testosterone levels. It may result in significant
detriment to a high quality of life and adversely affect the function of multiple organ systems. Since many aging men have questions about growth hormone, adrenal androgens, and melatonin,
the role of these hormones will be addressed as well.

Quantitative Aspects of the Decline of Androgen Levels with Aging

With respect to endocrinological correlates, a decline in gonadal
function and a decrease in bioavailable testosterone are associated
with aging. But levels of testosterone usually remain above a
threshold shown to be critical in younger men. Even though hormonal factors appear to play no significant role as a determinant
of individual differences in sexual behavior in healthy aging
men (Schiavi, Schreiner-Engel, White, & Mandeli, 1991), the
threshold for hormonally activated spontaneous sleep erections

may be elevated (Schiavi, White, Mandeli, & Schreiner-Engel, 1993), a finding confirmed in a more recent study (Gray et al., 2005).

Several studies document the androgen decline with aging (for a review, see Kaufman & Vermeulen, 2005). Longitudinal studies (Araujo et al., 2004; Moffat et al., 2002; Morley et al., 1997) have documented a statistical decline of plasma testosterone of approximately 30% in healthy men between the ages of 25 to 75. Testosterone is largely bound to carrier proteins: a good 60% to sex hormone-binding globulin (SHBG) and 30% to 40% to albumin. Only 1% to 2% is circulating free, nonbound, and only this fraction can enter the target organs so testosterone can exert its biological effects. The unbound testosterone is called the *free testosterone fraction*. The binding of testosterone to albumin is much less strong than to SHBG. The free testosterone plus the fraction bound to albumin are called the bioavailable testosterone fraction. Since plasma levels of SHBG increase with aging, even more testosterone is bound to SHBG, with levels of free and bioavailable testosterone decreasing by about 50%. Studies in twins have shown that genetic factors account for 63% of the variability of plasma testosterone levels, and for 30% of the variability of SHBG levels (Meikle, Bishop, Stringham, & West, 1986).

Systemic diseases that increase with age, particularly diseases related to the metabolic syndrome such as cardiovascular disease and diabetes mellitus type 2, contribute to declining plasma levels of testosterone (Handelsman, 1994). While it now has been shown, beyond doubt, that plasma testosterone, and in particular bioavailable and free testosterone, decline with aging, it remains uncertain what percentage of men becomes actually testosterone deficient with aging in the sense that they suffer the clinical consequences from testosterone deficiency and thus would benefit from testosterone replacement. A study of 300 healthy men between the ages of 20 to 100 years (Vermeulen, 2001) that defined the reference range of total plasma testosterone between 11 and 40 nmol/l, found one man with subnormal testosterone in the age group between 20 to 40 years, but more than 20% above the age of 60 years. However, 15% of men above the age of 80 years still had testosterone values above 20 nmol/l. It follows that only a certain proportion of men have lower-than-normal testosterone levels in old age.

Several problems occur in diagnosing testosterone deficiency. For one, it is difficult to rely solely on clinical symptoms, particularly in elderly men. In adult men who have previously been eugonadal, symptoms of testosterone deficiency emerge only gradually and insidiously. So, only the physical signs of long-standing testosterone deficiency will be clinically recognized. Further, stringent criteria for diagnosing testosterone deficiency have not been formulated, neither in the young nor in the elderly male population. In the elderly population, testosterone deficiency is difficult to identify since symptoms of aging mimic symptoms of testosterone deficiency. Other criteria for testosterone deficiency may need to be established in aging men.

Testosterone has a number of physiological functions in the male. In adulthood, it is responsible for maintenance of reproductive capacity and of secondary sex characteristics; it has positive effects on mood and libido; it has anabolic effects on bone and muscle; and it affects fat distribution and the cardiovascular system. Threshold plasma values of testosterone for each of these functions are becoming established. Several studies (Bhasin et al., 2001; Kelleher, Conway, & Handelsman, 2004) analyzing the dose response relationships between plasma testosterone and biological effects have shown that low-to-midnormal plasma levels of testosterone suffice for most biological actions of testosterone. Another consideration is whether threshold values change over the life cycle. Theoretically, in old age, androgen levels may suffice for some but not all androgen-related functions. Yet with regard to the anabolic actions of testosterone, elderly men are as responsive as young men (Bhasin et al., 2001). Male sexual functioning in younger adults can be maintained with lower-than-normal values (Buena et al., 1993; Gooren, 1987) of testosterone, but the threshold required for sexual behavior may increase with aging (Schiavi & Rehman, 1995). This contrast was recently confirmed in a laboratory study showing that libido and erectile function require higher testosterone levels in older compared to younger men (Gray et al., 2005), but it has also been apparent from clinical observations (Steidle et al., 2003) and suggested by a meta-analysis of studies on the topic (Jain, Rademaker, & McVary, 2000).

Correlations between Androgen and Symptoms of Male Aging

Before addressing the impact of LOH specifically on sexual functioning, we review several age-related physical and mental changes. While most nonendocrinologists associate testosterone only with sexual functioning, recent insights show convincingly that testosterone has a wide impact on male physical and mental functioning far beyond sexual functioning. In other words, testosterone deficiency profoundly affects general health. This relationship is of particular relevance since the quality of health is associated with sexual functioning (Lewis et al., 2004).

Body Composition

Body composition is seriously affected by the aging process (for reviews see Isidori et al., 2005; Kaufman & Vermeulen, 2005;

Makhsida, Shah, Yan, Fisch, & Shabsigh, 2005; Moretti et al., 2005). Aging is almost universally accompanied by an increase in abdominal fat mass and a decrease of muscle mass. Androgens have a substantial impact on muscle mass and on fat distribution, and therefore the relationship between these signs of aging and testosterone levels has been assessed.

Increase in Fat Mass
Several studies have convincingly documented an inverse correlation between abdominal fat mass and free testosterone levels that is independent of age. This finding has clinical relevance: the amount of visceral fat is strongly associated with an increased risk of cardiovascular disease, impaired glucose tolerance, and noninsulin dependent diabetes mellitus (the dysmetabolic syndrome, or just metabolic syndrome). Whether the abdominal and, more specifically, visceral obesity is the consequence of the low testosterone or vice versa is not yet clear. What is clear, however, is that visceral obesity leads to decreased testosterone, mainly via a decrease in SHBG levels. As significant, however, there are also indications that low testosterone levels induce accumulation of visceral fat and the development of the metabolic syndrome.

Decline in Muscle Mass and Strength
An impressive decline in muscle mass occurs with age (26 lb or 12 kg between age 20 and 70 yrs). This loss of muscle mass is a major contributor to the age-associated decline in muscle strength and fatigue. Maximal muscle strength is correlated with muscle mass, independent of age. Loss of muscle mass is related to the occurrence of falls and fractures, and the consequent limitations of independent living. The correlation between testosterone levels and muscle mass appears stronger than the correlation with muscle strength.

Bone Mineral Density
An exponential increase in bone fracture rate (Isidori et al., 2005; Kaufman & Vermeulen, 2005; Vanderschueren et al., 2004) occurs with aging, an effect related to a decrease of bone mineral density (BMD). In view of the significance of sex steroids in the maintenance of BMD at all ages, the question whether the partial androgen deficiency in aging men plays an important role in the decrease of BMD is pertinent. A pivotal role of androgens in the decrease of BMD has, however, been difficult to establish. Not all scientific findings agree. Indeed, some studies find a significant, though weak, correlation between androgen levels and bone mineral density at some but not all bone sites. Others are unable to establish a correlation. Several large-scale studies of several hundred elderly men have demonstrated that bone density in the radius, spine,

and hip are correlated with levels of bioavailable testosterone. The correlation with levels of bioavailable estradiol was much more prominent, probably pointing to the significance of estrogens in men, also in old age.

Cardiovascular Function

Premenopausal women suffer significantly less from cardiovascular disease than men, and traditionally it has been thought that the relationship between sex steroids and cardiovascular disease was predominantly determined by the relatively beneficial effects of estrogens and by the detrimental effects of androgens on lipid (cholesterol) profiles (for reviews, see Liu, Death, & Handelsman, 2003; Shabsigh, Katz, Yan, & Makhsida, 2005; Wu & von Eckardstein, 2003). Nevertheless, the vast majority of cross-sectional studies in men do not agree with this assumption; they show a positive correlation between free testosterone levels and HDL-C, and negative correlations with fibrinogen, plasminogen activator inhibitor-1, and insulin levels, as well as with coronary heart disease, although not with cardiovascular mortality.

Research shows effects of sex steroids on biological systems other than lipids. Fat distribution, endocrine/paracrine factors produced by the vascular wall (such as endothelins, nitric oxide), blood platelets, and coagulation must also be considered in the analysis of the relationship between sex steroids and cardiovascular disease. In fact, reviews of the topic emphasize the fact that short-term studies actually have shown a benefit to the cardiovascular system (Liu et al., 2003; Shabsigh et al., 2005) and that the therapeutic use of testosterone in men need not be restricted by concerns regarding cardiovascular side effects (Wu & von Eckardstein, 2003).

Cognitive and Emotional Factors

Testosterone may influence performance on cognitive tasks (for a review, see Cherrier, 2005; Janowsky, 2006; Lessov-Schlaggar et al., 2005), supported by the finding that testosterone administration to older men enhances performance on measures of spatial cognition. The correlation between testosterone levels and cognitive performance such as spatial abilities or mathematical reasoning has been confirmed in western and nonwestern cohorts of healthy males.

Testosterone has also been associated with general mood elevating effects. Some studies have found associations between lowered testosterone levels and depressive symptoms. Depression is not rare in aging men and impairs their quality of life (Carnahan & Perry, 2004), so the effects of declining androgen on mood and on specific aspects of cognitive functioning in aging are worthy of investigation.

Impact of Androgens on Sexual Functioning with Age

Aging is the most robust factor predicting erectile difficulties, that is, aging per se is associated with a deterioration of the biological functions mediating erectile function: hormonal, vascular, and neural. This aging effect is often aggravated by intercurrent disease in old age, such as diabetes mellitus, cardiovascular disease, and the use of medical drugs. This section addresses the role of testosterone, which, as indicated previously, is only one of several elements that may explain sexual dysfunction with aging.

Erectile response in mammals is centrally and peripherally regulated by androgens. Severe hypogonadism in men usually results in loss of libido or desire, and loss of potency or erectile ability. The insight into the more precise mechanisms of action of androgens on sexual functions is of rather recent date. Studies in the 1980s showed that androgens exert effects particularly on libido and on sleep-related erections; yet erections in response to erotic stimuli, somewhat surprisingly, were relatively androgen-independent (Bancroft, 1984; Bancroft & Wu, 1983). Later studies modified this view somewhat, showing that penile responses to erotic stimuli with regard to the duration of response, maximal degree of rigidity, and speed of detumescence were related to circulating androgens (Carani, Granata, Bancroft, & Marrama, 1995; Granata, Rochira, Lerchl, Marrama, & Carani, 1997). In addition, hypogonadal patients (with a wide age range) that showed erectile response required androgen levels only at or below the low end of reference (normal) values of testosterone (Bhasin et al., 2001; Buena et al., 1993; Gooren, 1987). The previous considerations—the relative androgen-independence of erections in response to erotic stimuli and the relatively low androgen levels required—were reason to believe that testosterone would not be a useful treatment for men with erectile difficulties whose testosterone levels were only marginally low.

An even more important element that minimized the potential importance of testosterone as a treatment option was the advent of other successful treatments for erectile dysfunction (ED), for example, first the use of penile intracorporal smooth muscle relaxants (papaverine, prostaglandinE1) and later the PDE-5-inhibitors (e.g., sildenafil) in 1998.

A number of recent developments shed new light on the role of testosterone treatment for ED in aging men:

- The recent insight that, in contrast with results obtained in younger men (Bhasin et al., 2001; Buena et al., 1993; Gooren, 1987), elderly men might require higher levels of testosterone for normal sexual functioning (Gray et al., 2005; Seftel, Mack, Secrest, & Smith, 2004). Recent reviews on the effects of testosterone administration to elderly men on libido and erectile potency are quite encouraging (Jain et al., 2000; Morley & Perry, 2003).

- Several studies now indicate that the administration of PDE-5-inhibitors is not always sufficient to restore erectile potency in men (Aversa, Isidori, Spera, Lenzi, & Fabbri, 2003; Kalinchenko, Kozlov, Gontcharov, & Katsiya, 2003; Park, Ku, Kim, & Paick, 2005; Shabsigh, 2004) and that administration of testosterone improves the therapeutic response to PDE-5-inhibitors considerably (Aversa et al., 2003; Kalinchenko et al., 2003; Shabsigh, 2004).

- Testosterone probably has profound effects on tissues of the penis involved in erection, and testosterone deficiency impairs the anatomical and physiological substrate of erectile capacity, reversible after androgen replacement. Although these data come mainly from animal experimentation, studies support their relevance for the human as well. Specifically, androgen receptors are found in the human corpus cavernous (Schultheiss et al., 2003). Morelli et al. (2004) has shown that the synthesis of phosphodiesterase 5 in the corpus cavernosum is up-regulated by androgens. Aversa et al. (2003) demonstrated that the arterial inflow into the penis is improved by androgen administration. In one review paper, Lewis and Mills (2004) remarked that data on testosterone effects on the human penis are still limited, yet found it reasonable to extrapolate from animal dependency of androgens for molecular activity in the penile tissue to humans.

This set of findings provides compelling evidence for a reexamination of the merits of testosterone administration to aging men with ED, particularly in view of the conclusion that the beneficial effects of PDE-5 inhibitors (e.g., sildenafil) are optimally expressed only in a eugonadal environment. Obviously, the past and present experience (Greenstein et al., 2005; Guay, Jacobson, Perez, Hodge, & Velasquez, 2003; Mulhall, Valenzuela, Aviv, & Parker, 2004) indicate that testosterone replacement alone may not suffice to restore erectile potency. Since ED is strongly age-related, it is evident that, inherent in the process of aging, etiology is multifactorial, and combinations of drugs and other therapies might be needed to restore it. Clinical judgment guides the type of treatment that should be tried first, PDE-5 inhibitors or testosterone; nevertheless, insufficient success with one type of treatment might require addition of the other.

Diagnosis: General Issues

A Context for Diagnosis

As with any man having erectile difficulties, the approach to the diagnosis and treatment of an aging male should be comprehensive. The scientific disciplines that research and treat sexual problems vary strongly in theoretical approaches and research methods, and it is an understatement to say that no one discipline has successfully encompassed both biological and psychological variables into a workable model of human sexuality. Practitioners in these different disciplines often speak different professional languages and may not always have a good sense of concepts and treatment strategies of other disciplines. As a result, almost inevitably, patients undergo a biased diagnostic and therapeutic process.

Nevertheless, it is difficult to find a more powerful example of a psychosomatic relationship than the human sexual response (Bancroft, 1984, 2002). The biologic characteristics of an essentially sexual experience include changes in the genitalia, in particular, erection of the penis and tumescence and lubrication of the vagina, heightened awareness of pleasurable erotic sensations, and changes in our subjective state called sexual excitement— processes involving neurophysiological arousal. Of equal importance, this arousal is linked with cognitive processes attending to the sexual meaning of what is happening, with focus on external events or internal processes such as imagery. Through this cognitive component, the whole range of social and interpersonal influences impinges on sexuality (Bancroft, 2002). The psychosomatic nature of sexual response relies on communication and (positive and negative) feedback between different parts of the system, put simply: between the pelvic organs and the brain. Dysfunctions in one area, by nature of the psychosomatic circle, will not be inconsequential to the other area.

The Need for a Comprehensive Diagnostic Process

Sexual difficulties in aging men can only be meaningfully interpreted when both areas of the psychosomatic response are thoroughly investigated and addressed in treatment. This is not an easy task. A complaint of erectile impotence or low sexual desire should serve as an introduction to acquire a wider understanding of an individual's interaction of somatic and psychic processes as components of the psychosomatic circle. Naturally, the ways in which individuals and couples present their complaints of sexual problems often obscure the interaction between psychic and somatic processes. A patient has only limited possibilities to express to a clinician his or her perceived sexual dysfunction or dissatisfaction.

Common clinical dysfunctions affecting the sexual response cycle in aging men include erectile dysfunction, premature ejaculation, and delayed ejaculation. Another condition, particularly common in aging couples, is that of sexual withdrawal, a marked decrease in the frequency of sexual activity in the absence of a primary sexual disorder (such as erectile failure or anorgasmia).

Traditionally, the major focus in the medical diagnostic work-up for aging men has been on erectile function. One of the priorities in diagnosing erectile failure has traditionally been the differential diagnosis between psychogenic or somatogenic origin of the problem. Newer insights convincingly demonstrate the fallacy dichotomizing erectile dysfunction into such categories (Sakheim, Barlow, Abrahamson, & Beck, 1987). Recent studies carried out in connection with the introduction of the PDE-5 inhibitors (e.g., sildenafil) report that somatogenic problems from neurological, vascular, and hormonal abnormalities are involved in a considerable percentage of cases of erectile failure, although such data may be biased due to selective referrals for inclusion in these studies. Such research conceptually suffers from the flaw of attempting to categorize the patients into discrete, nonoverlapping categories of organic or psychogenic erectile failure. Indeed, the most powerful predictor of erectile dysfunction is age, and the majority of these cases involve both organic and psychogenic factors. This fact is often not fully appreciated by practitioners: when the practitioner finds a clear psychological cause of the erection problem, it is often assumed that there is no need to conduct any organic evaluation, and vice versa.

Finally, men often view their sex organs and their functions as a piece of machinery so in cases of failure they seek a mechanical solution to their problem. They have expectations that if erectile difficulties can be remedied, their problems will be solved. They may, for example, overlook the fact that sexual problems may be either the cause of, or consequence of, dysfunctional or unsatisfactory relationships. Often, it is difficult to determine which is the cause and which is the effect: a nonintimate and nonloving relationship, or sexual desire and/or performance problems for which the partner is blamed and subsequently leads to partner avoidance and antipathy.

Factors for Consideration in the Diagnosis of Sexual Problems in Aging Men

Although this chapter focuses heavily on the relationship between testosterone and sexual problems in aging men, before assuming that endocrine factors are causal, the practitioner should consider exploration of a number of other dimensions of sexual response.

Assessment of Male Sexual Dysfunction

The essential components of sexual function assessment in the male always include: erectile response (onset, duration, progression, severity of the problem, nocturnal/morning erections, self-stimulatory and visual erotic induced erections), sexual desire, ejaculation, orgasm, sexually related genital pain disorders, deficient sexual stimulation, and partner sexual function, if available (Althof et al., 2005). Often, a dysfunction in one phase of function may precipitate a dysfunction in another. For instance, men with erectile dysfunction may report a loss of sexual desire that may become a vicious circle of dysfunction. Whenever possible, the temporal association or causal relationship between the symptoms should be assessed.

Clinical Features of Sexual Dysfunction

Sexual dysfunction is typically influenced by a variety of predisposing, precipitating, maintaining, and contextual factors as listed in Sidebar 5.1 (Hawton & Catalan, 1986). No data currently suggest that any one factor is more important than another. Predisposing factors include somatic factors (hormonal dysfunctions, malformations or deformities of the body and the genitalia). Early life experiences, such as difficulties in bonding, parental neglect or abuse, sex-negative upbringing, and sexual and physical abuse may be relevant, although usually these surface prior to elder years. Predisposing factors are often associated with a greater prevalence of sexual dysfunctions and emotional difficulties in adult life, though variance exists: some persons with an adverse life history do remarkably well, others with few negative predisposing factors appear more affected.

SIDEBAR 5.1

Factors Influencing Sexual Dysfunction

Predisposing Factors

- Somatic factors (hormonal dysfunctions, malformation of genitalia and the body).
- Early life history (abuse, bonding difficulties, parental neglect, negative sexual upbringing).

Precipitating Factors

- May include various life occurrences such as but not limited to infidelity or unsatisfying sexual experiences.
- Repetition may play a role in the impact of various life events.

Maintaining Factors

- Disharmony in the relationship.
- Inadequate sexual information.

- Performance anxiety.
- Feelings of guilt/incapacity to let go.
- Insufficient sexual stimulation.
- Psychiatric disorders.
- Loss of sexual attraction.
- Fear of intimacy.
- Impaired self-image.
- Poor communication/lack of privacy.

Contextual Factors

- Can include environmental constraints.
- May be affected by the relationship with one's partner (i.e., presence of resentment or anger toward partner).

Precipitating factors trigger sexual problems and tend to be highly variable across subjects because different people attribute different meanings to occurrences in a relationship, or in life in general. Infidelity, for instance, may for one person be a point of no return, for another a forgivable mistake. An important issue is how an individual's personal or internal resources, including his ability to cope, enable him to deal with precipitating factors. An initial precipitating event may be problematic and distressing, but it need not necessarily lead to a diagnosable long-term dysfunction. Over time however, repetition of such events may cause lasting damage and result in sexual dysfunction, such as might occur with repeatedly unsatisfying sexual experiences.

Maintaining factors need to be identified. Disharmony in the relationship, inadequate sexual information, performance anxiety, feelings of guilt and inhibition, insufficient sexual stimulation, psychiatric disorders, loss of sexual attraction, fear of intimacy, impaired self-image, poor communication, and lack of privacy may prolong and exacerbate problems, irrespective of the original predisposing or precipitating conditions. Contextual factors may also interfere with or interrupt sexual activity, such as environmental constraints or anger/resentment toward a partner. Each of the above factors may adversely affect the individual's and the couples' ability to sustain an active and satisfying sexual life. Such factors may be interrelated and feed one another, thus aggravating the situation. When these factors have become chronic they become resistant to therapeutic interventions and may lead to strong sexual avoidance or arousal inhibition.

Psychological and Interpersonal Factors
The practitioner should assess the patient's psychological state (Althof et al., 2005). Are there symptoms of anxiety or depression (particularly common among older men, though often not

recognized as such by them), what is the nature of past and present partner relationships, are there stressors that impede enjoyment of sex, have there been traumatic experiences? An all-important question is the identification of patient needs and expectations, which may be influenced by cultural, social, ethnic, and religious perspectives. Efforts should be made to involve the patient's partner early in the diagnostic and therapeutic process, although this may not always be possible or practical. In fact, at times the patient may prefer to be seen alone. Discrepancies in information between the patient and partner may point to problems in communication or provide clues for therapeutic interventions. The desirability of partner participation may be influenced by cultural, social, and societal factors.

Depression and Sexual Function

Sexuality is an expression of vitality and it does not come as a surprise that depression impacts on sexual functioning (Seidman, 2003), particularly in aging men: aging and depression are known covariates. The relationship between sexual response and depression may be bidirectional in that sexual dysfunction is a factor in depressive moods and, vice versa, depressive moods lead to sexual dysfunction. Depression as a clinical entity is not rare, yet many clinicians fail to recognize it and many patients are unable to differentiate between an appropriate psychological response of sadness and depression. Organic diseases impacting on general health (cardiac, pulmonary, renal and liver diseases, but also the aging process) are quite frequently associated with depression. Mood disorders may cause and maintain sexual dysfunction, and men with sexual dysfunction exhibit both higher levels of acute depressive symptoms and a markedly higher lifetime prevalence of affective disorders. Sexual difficulties related to depression are sometimes difficult to treat; in many instances, the treatment itself (e.g., antidepressant medication) may exacerbate the sexual problem (Gitlin, 2003).

Hypoactive Sexual Desire Disorder

Even though testosterone deficiency has been related to low sexual desire in men, most complaints of hypoactive sexual desire disorder (HSDD) in men are not due to low testosterone (Meuleman & van Lankveld, 2005). Clinical experience teaches that four dynamics are generally associated with psychological HSDD. These include: depression, anger and relationship discord, same-sex attractions, and sexual arousal patterns that are not available within the present relationship, such as paraphilias. Addressing these factors may lead to an improvement, but same-sex attraction and unconventional sexual aspirations (as in paraphilias) are often resistant to improvement.

Diagnosis of Late Onset Hypogonadism

Screening

It is difficult to make a fair assessment of the infirmity associated with the aging process. Part of it will be due to natural aging and part to emerging disease processes, which are increasingly present with aging. Natural aging and emerging diseases affect individuals in varying degrees. Age-related hormone deficiencies do not affect all men to the same degree, and some men will have normal hormone levels until very old age. Furthermore, other conditions affecting erectile response such as hypertension and diabetes mellitus range from mild to severe. Therefore, it would be useful to have tools that provide a "grip" on signs and symptoms of aging. Such an instrument would also allow assessment of the successes of interventions in these populations.

Developing rating scales is a difficult venture, and the validation of questionnaires is an arduous process. Translation into other languages requires new validation in that language to test whether questions are understood and interpreted linguistically and culturally in the same way as in the original language. One useful instrument is the Aging Males' Symptoms (AMS) rating scale (Daig et al., 2003; Heinemann et al., 2003). This rating scale measures somatic, sexual, and psychological aspects of an aging man's life. Originally developed in the German language, it has now been validated for English (Heinemann et al., 2003) and other European languages (Myon, Martin, Taieb, & Heinemann, 2005; Valenti et al., 2005). Validation in other languages and in other geographical areas is still needed. As an adjunctive procedure, a scale developed by Morley et al. (2000) tests whether certain symptoms are more likely to be present in aging men with declining levels of bioavailable testosterone.

Biochemical Diagnosis

Laboratory reference values for testosterone and free testosterone show a wider range than those for most other hormones (for instance, thyroid hormones), making it difficult to establish whether measured values of testosterone in patients are normal or abnormal. Is a patient whose plasma levels of testosterone fall from the upper to the lower range of normal testosterone levels—a drop of as much as 50%—testosterone deficient? Levels may well remain within the reference range but may be inappropriately low for that particular individual. Interestingly, in thyroid pathophysiology, plasma thyroid stimulating hormone (TSH) proves to be a better criterion of thyroid hyper/hypofunction than plasma thyroid itself (T4 or T3). But whether this strategy applies to testosterone is uncertain, that is, whether plasma luteinizing hormone (LH) is a more reliable indicator of male hypogonadism in the elderly man than plasma testosterone. With aging, LH pulse frequency and amplitude are reduced. Several studies have found that LH levels are elevated in response to the decline of testosterone levels with aging, but less so than observed in younger men with similarly decreased testosterone levels (Kaufman & Vermeulen, 2005). This difference may be due to an age-related shift in the setpoint of the negative feedback of testosterone on the hypothalamic pituitary unit, resulting in an enhanced negative feedback action that consequently leads to a relatively lower LH output in response to lowered circulating levels of testosterone.

The previous discussion points out the many unresolved questions regarding the verification of deficiencies in the biological action of androgens in old age and regarding exactly which plasma testosterone levels conclusively represent androgen deficiency. Consequently, until these important questions are resolved, the practitioner must take a pragmatic approach so aging, androgen-deficient men can still benefit from replacement therapy. However, the broader question regarding the criteria for LOH has received serious attention in the past years (Black, Day, & Morales, 2004; Nieschlag et al., 2005b). For example, Vermeulen (2001) argues there is no generally accepted cut off value of plasma testosterone for defining androgen deficiency, and in the absence of convincing evidence for an altered androgen requirement in elderly men, he considers the normal range of free T levels in young males also valid for elderly men. Furthermore, the age associated decline in testosterone, and even more so in free testosterone, has both a testicular (decreased Leydig cell number) and central origin, the latter being characterized by a decrease in the orderliness and amplitude of LH pulses in elderly men. However, many elderly men have normal LH levels, and therefore elevated LH levels are unlikely to be a requirement for the diagnosis of hypogonadism in elderly men.

Another variable that might be significant to assess the androgen status in old age is plasma levels of SHBG. Vermeulen, Verdonck, and Kaufman (1998) demonstrated that the free testosterone value, calculated by total testosterone/SHBG (according to a second degree equation following the mass action law) as determined by immunoassay, appears to be a rapid, simple, and reliable indicator of bioavailable and free testosterone, comparable to testosterone values obtained by equilibrium dialysis. An easy-to-use calculator of free and bioavailable testosterone can be found on www.issam.ch/ or www.him-link.com.

In any case, without a clear set of criteria for testosterone deficiency, determination of values of testosterone and SHBG might provide a reasonable index of the androgen status of an aging person. To avoid a false diagnosis of hypogonadism, sampling of testosterone should preferably take place before 11 a.m. to control for its diurnal rhythm. Though less apparent in elderly men, the diurnal rhythm of testosterone is usually not absent. The consequences of diagnosing lower-than-normal values by inappropriate sampling of testosterone have significant implications for treatment recommendations. If indeed plasma testosterone values and the calculated ratio of bioavailable/free testosterone are so low that testosterone replacement is considered, the measurement should be repeated several weeks later. For example, the stress of a common cold may temporarily depress testosterone secretion. Otherwise, serial measurements of testosterone in elderly men are fairly stable (Tancredi, Reginster, Luyckx, & Legros, 2005; Vermeulen & Verdonck, 1992).

For measurement of total testosterone, commercial radioimmunoassay and nonradioactive immunoassays kits, as well as automated platform immunoassays that mostly use chemiluminescence detection, are widely available and provide fairly accurate measurements between 10 to 35 nmol/L. Below 10 nmol/L, accuracy is considerably less. But reference values vary significantly from laboratory to laboratory, and from measurement method to method. Consequently, it is advisable that every laboratory establishes its own "normal range" of testosterone in men (Matsumoto & Bremner, 2004; Wang, Catlin, et al., 2004).

As mentioned, in the absence of a reliable, clinically useful biological parameter of androgen action, the above laboratory criteria of hypogonadism in aging men are somewhat arbitrary but at least provide some initial guidance. Algorithms have been developed to guide the clinician in the interpretation of the results of laboratory measurements of testosterone and SHBG (see Figure 5.1).

Different countries have different health economies and therefore different guidelines apply regarding reimbursements of laboratory measurements. In fact, measurement of SHBG is helpful only at the low end of reference values of testosterone. If values are clearly in the normal range, additional measurement of SHBG is redundant. A total testosterone value below 6.5 nmol/L is sufficient evidence of hypogonadism, whereas a value above 13.0 nmol/L rules out hypogonadism in adult males. This strategy has led to significant time and cost savings (Gheorghiu, Moshyk, Lepage, Ahnadi, & Grant, 2005).

Treatment of Late Onset Hypogonadism

Suitable Testosterone Preparations

If some men may benefit from androgen supplements, are suitable testosterone preparations, such as those listed in Table 5.1,

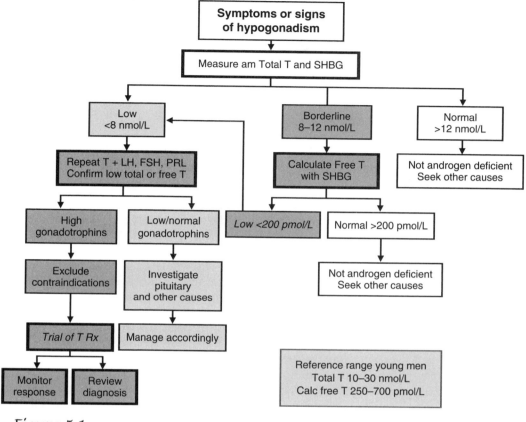

Figure 5.1

Algorithm for the Management of Suspected Symptomatic Hypogonadism in an Older Man

available to treat them? The androgen deficiency of the aging male is only partial, and consequently only partial substitution is required.

Parenteral Testosterone Preparations
Conventional parenteral (systemically injected) testosterone preparations are far from ideal, even for young hypogonadal men. Plasma testosterone levels fluctuate strongly following administration. The most widely used pharmaceutical forms for parenteral administration are the intramuscular administered hydrophobic long chain testosterone-esters in oily depot, enanthate and the cypionate, at a dose of 200 to 250 mg/2 weeks. They yield transient supraphysiological levels the first 2 to 3 days after injection, followed by a steady decline to subphysiological levels just prior to the next injection (Schurmeyer & Nieschlag, 1984). These fluctuations

Table 5.1   **Testosterone-Related Treatments**

Parenteral testosterone undecanoate (systemically injected)

Oral testosterone undecanoate

Transbuccal administration of testosterone (avoiding intestinal absorption in favor of oral absorption)

Transdermal delivery of testosterone through injection (in genital or nongenital skin)

Transdermal patches

Testosterone gel

in testosterone levels are experienced by some patients as unpleasant and are accompanied by changes in energy, libido, and mood. The transient supraphysiological levels might increase the frequency of side-effects.

Parenteral testosterone undecanoate (TU) is a new treatment modality for androgen replacement therapy. Several studies have documented its use in hypogonadal men (Harle, Basaria, & Dobs, 2005; Schubert et al., 2004). In short, after two loading doses of 1,000 mg TU at 0 and 6 weeks, repeated injections at 12-week intervals are sufficient to maintain testosterone levels in the reference range of eugonadal men. This preparation may be less suitable for initiating testosterone treatment of aging men (Nieschlag et al., 2005a), as the long duration of action might constitute a problem in case a prostate malignancy is diagnosed. Experienced urologists, however, have reasoned that the delay between diagnosing prostate cancer and its commencing treatment is usually much longer than 12 weeks, without an adverse effect on the outcome (Schurmeyer & Nieschlag, 1984). In addition, current recommendations advocate initial follow-up at 3-month intervals for the first year, which fits well with the schedule of TU injections. In the unlikely situation that a tumor is discovered, treatment would be discontinued and use of an antiandrogen considered. After the first uneventful year of androgen administration, it seems reasonable to administer long-acting testosterone preparations to elderly men (Nieschlag et al., 2005a).

Oral Testosterone Undecanoate

Testosterone undecanoate (TU) is dissolved in oil and encapsulated in soft gelatin. Of the 40 mg capsules, 60% (25 mg) is testosterone. After ingestion, its route of absorption from the gastrointestinal tract is shifted from the portal vein to the thoracic duct (Gooren & Bunck, 2004). For its adequate absorption from the gastrointestinal tract, oral TU is taken with a meal that contains dietary fat (Bagchus, Hust, Maris, Schnabel, & Houwing, 2003). Without dietary fat, the resorption and the resulting serum levels of testosterone are minimal (Bagchus et al., 2003). Maximum serum levels are reached 2 to 6 hr after ingestion. To increase shelf life, the preparation has recently been reformulated and the oil in the capsule is now castor oil. Recent studies show dose proportionality between serum testosterone levels and the dose range of 20 to 80 mg (Gooren & Bunck, 2004). With a dose of 120 to 240 mg per day, over 80% of hypogonadal men showed plasma testosterone levels in the normal range over 24 hr (Gooren & Bunck, 2004).

TU, also on the basis of its flexible dosing, is probably best suited to supplement the reduced, but still present, endogenous testicular testosterone production in the aging male with lower than normal, but not deeply hypogonadal levels, of testosterone (Gooren & Bunck, 2004). Long-term use has been proven safe as demonstrated in a 10-year observation (Gooren, 1994).

Transbuccal Testosterone Administration

Transbuccal administration of testosterone provides a means of oral administration of testosterone. The resorption of testosterone through the oral mucosa avoids intestinal absorption and subsequent hepatic inactivation of testosterone. Two studies have assessed the efficacy of transbuccal administration of testosterone (Dobs, Matsumoto, Wang, & Kipnes, 2004; Wang, Swerdloff, et al., 2004). Both have found that administration of 30 mg of testosterone formulated as a bioadhesive buccal tablet twice daily generated plasma testosterone and DHT levels in the normal range in hypogonadal men (Dobs et al., 2004; Wang, Swerdloff, et al., 2004). Gum irritation was noted in approximately 3% of men.

Transdermal Delivery

Testosterone can be delivered to the circulation through the intact skin, both genital and nongenital (Gooren & Bunck, 2004). Transdermal administration (through either patches or gel) delivers testosterone at a controlled rate into the systemic circulation, avoiding hepatic first pass and reproducing the diurnal rhythm of testosterone secretion, without the peak.

Transdermal scrotal patches were first designed to deliver testosterone through the scrotal skin, where the permeability is five times greater than for other skin sites. It required weekly scrotal shaving and was difficult for some patients to apply and maintain in position for 24 hr. Transdermal scrotal testosterone administration is associated with high levels of DHT as a result of high concentrations of 5α-reductase in the scrotal skin (Gooren & Bunck, 2004). The patch may be irritating and use is not feasible if the scrotal surface is not adequate. To overcome these limitations, nonscrotal skin patches that have a reservoir containing testosterone with a permeation-enhancing vehicle and gelling agents have been developed (Dobs et al., 2004). Improvements have been reported in sexual function, libido, energy level, and mood (Dobs et al., 2004). The most common adverse effects are local skin reactions: 50% of men participating in a clinical trial reported transient, mild to moderate erythema (abnormal redness of the skin from capillary congestion) at some time during therapy. However, most reactions were associated with application of the patch over a bony prominence or on parts of the body that could have been subject to prolonged pressure during sleep or sitting.

Transdermal testosterone gel is also used for replacement therapy. Testosterone gel is hydro-alcoholic, 1% (10 mg testosterone per gram gel) and administered between 5 and 10 g of gel a day, amounting to 50 and 100 mg testosterone (Ebert, Jockenhovel, Morales, & Shabsigh, 2005; Gooren & Bunck, 2004). The pharmacokinetics of testosterone gel have been extensively studied. Serum testosterone levels rise two- to threefold 2 hr after application and four- to fivefold after 24 hr. Thereafter, serum testosterone remained in the upper range of normal and returned to baseline within 4 days after termination of application of testosterone gel. Mean DHT levels followed the same pattern as testosterone and were at or above the normal adult male range. Serum estradiol levels rose and followed the same pattern as testosterone. The application of the testosterone gel at one site or four sites did not have a substantial impact on the pharmacokinetic profile (Wang, Cunningham, et al., 2004). Later studies showed that 9% to 14% of the testosterone administered is bioavailable. Steady state testosterone levels are achieved 48 to 72 hr after the first application, and serum testosterone and free testosterone are similar on days 30, 90, and 180 after starting the administration. The formulation of the testosterone gel allows easy dose adjustments (50 to 75 to 100 mg; Meikle, Matthias, & Hoffman, 2004).

The clinical efficacy of transdermal testosterone gel on various androgen dependent target organ systems has been well documented (Wang, Cunningham, et al., 2004). The safety profile showed that prostate specific antigen (PSA) levels rose in proportion to the increase of testosterone levels but did not exceed normal values. Skin irritation was noted in 5.5% of patients in the study (Dobs et al., 1999; Wang, Cunningham, et al., 2004). Remarkably, washing the site 10 min after application did not affect pharmacokinetic profiles (Rolf, Knie, Lemmnitz, & Nieschlag, 2002). Transfer from one person to another was found to be insignificant: no increase of serum testosterone was found after intense rubbing of skins with persons whose endogenous testosterone levels had been suppressed (Rolf et al., 2002). Recently, a new formulation of testosterone gel has been introduced (McNicholas & Ong, 2006; Nieschlag et al., 2005a), which claims to have a better absorption from the skin but this claim has not been confirmed in later studies.

Adrenal Androgens

While it is now well documented that serum levels of adrenal androgens strongly decline with aging, it has not been definitively established whether this decline has any (patho)physiological significance. Theoretically, it could be a meaningful mechanism of adaptation to aging. Strong correlations have been established between the declining levels of adrenal androgens and ailments of aging, but whether these statistical associations are causally and pathophysiologically interrelated remains to be established. One way of establishing a relationship between the two is through intervention studies. Suppressing or elevating levels of adrenal androgens and monitoring the subsequent biological effects could help determine whether the age-related decline in adrenal androgens is a cause for concern. Thus far, the effects in laboratory animals have been impressive; adrenal androgens have been associated with beneficial effects on processes such as atherosclerosis, type 2 diabetes, obesity, immune function/cancer prevention, and brain function. However, laboratory animals such as rats and rabbits do not physiologically produce adrenal androgens in the quantities that humans do.

So far, studies in humans are limited and inconclusive. Some have found correlations between circulating levels of adrenal androgens and age-related ailments, others have not. Intervention designs have also been used, with one study reporting a positive effect on well-being (Cameron & Braunstein, 2005). In related research, the effects of DHEA replacement in men and women with complete adrenal insufficiency, who are devoid of adrenal androgens, appear overall convincing (Arlt et al., 1999), and a positive effect on self-esteem and possibly well-being was found in men whose own adrenal androgen production was almost absent (Hunt et al., 2000). This finding argues in favor of an independent effect of DHEA on the brain (relative to testosterone), since these men were not testosterone-deficient. Others that might benefit from DHEA administration are those receiving glucocorticoid treatment and whose ACTH levels, and therefore both cortisol and adrenal androgens, are suppressed (Cameron & Braunstein, 2005).

A consequence of the conversion of DHEA to androgens and estrogens is that the effects of DHEA administration are not necessarily harmless. DHEA may influence hormone-sensitive diseases such as breast or prostate cancer. So far there are no reports of any side effects from self-administration of DHEA, which occurs on a massive scale since DHEA is sold over the counter as a health product. Well-designed studies investigating the effects of deficiency of adrenal androgens and the results of replacement therapy in humans are required to resolve the long-term effect of levels of adrenal androgens (Cameron & Braunstein, 2005).

Growth Hormone

Signs associated with aging show a striking similarity with features observed in adults who are growth hormone (GH) deficient, and therefore speculation has arisen that some of the features of aging might be ascribed to the age-related decline in GH and therefore could be remedied with GH (Harman & Blackman, 2004; Toogood, 2004).

The interrelationship between sleep and the somatotropic axis (which involves GH) is well documented. This relationship is relevant since most aging subjects experience a deterioration of their sleep. During aging, slow wave sleep and GH decline concurrently, raising the possibility that the age-related decline of GH is also a reflection of age-related alterations in sleep-wake patterns.

Unlike the diagnosis of androgen deficiency, it is much more difficult to establish GH-deficiency in adulthood. The pulsatile nature of GH secretion and the large number of factors determining circulating levels of GH complicate the matter considerably in that a single measurement of GH does not provide meaningful information. A single measurement of insulin-like growth factor (IGF)-1 is a reasonable first indicator of GH status. In subjects over 40 years, an IGF-1 value of 15 nmol/L or higher excludes a deficiency of GH. The problem lies among patients with values below this level. Surprisingly, some patients with proven GH deficiency (on the basis of extensive testing such as insulin-hypoglycaemia, GHRH, and L-dopa stimulation tests) still have normal IGF-1 levels. Another useful index of GH status is IGF-binding protein-3. For now, the combination of signs and symptoms potentially attributable to GH deficiency and an IGF-1 level and IGF-binding protein-3 in the lowest tertile provide a reasonable first indication of (relative) GH deficiency (Giordano et al., 2005). To confirm the diagnosis, provocation testing with growth-hormone-releasing hormone in combination with arginine or synthetic growth hormone releasing substance (GHS) is highly desirable (Giordano et al., 2005). The starting dose of GH administration is not well established but a dose of 0.05 to 0.1 U/kg subcutaneously seems reasonable. Once on GH administration, individual dose titration is done on the basis of the IGF-1 levels resulting from GH administration and the occurrence of side effects. The aim is to produce IGF-1 levels in the normal or slightly above normal range (0 to 1 standard deviation above mean levels of IGF-1; Harman & Blackman, 2004). Second, if side effects occur (flu-like symptoms, gynecomastia, myalgia, arthralgia, carpal tunnel syndrome, edema, or impairment of glucose homeostasis), GH dosage is reduced in steps of 25%. Contra-indications against GH use include type I diabetes, active (or a history of) cancer, intracranial hypertension, diabetic retinopathy or carpal tunnel syndrome, and severe cardiac insufficiency. It seems there is a place for GH administration in aging subjects at this point in time, if only to gather information about groups that might benefit from its supplementation. In view of the narrow dose limits and potential side effects, treatment should be reserved for patients with proven GH deficiency; it is not advisable at present to administer GH to aging patients outside the framework of a clinical trial that provides intensive guidance and safeguards to patients (Harman & Blackman, 2004; Toogood, 2004), particularly since the increase of rIGF-1 following GH administration could accelerate the development of neoplasia (abnormal cell growth). Studies have found that high normal IGF-1 levels are associated with significant increased risks of prostate and colon cancer (Toogood, 2004).

Melatonin

Melatonin is a hormone produced in the pineal gland, synthesized from the amino acid tryptophan (derived from serotonin) by the enzyme 5-hydroxyindole-O-methyltransferase. Normally, production of melatonin by the pineal gland is inhibited by light and permitted by darkness. Melatonin and the pineal gland play a role in regulating sleep-wake cycles and, more generally, circadian rhythms. Residents of nursing homes or others who are not exposed to daylight may experience sleeping problems on the basis of a disturbed light/dark cycle with an associated impaired melatonin rhythm (Buscemi et al., 2006). Beta-blockers decrease nocturnal melatonin release and might affect sleep negatively.

Melatonin has become available as a medication and a dietary supplement. Because it does not have to be prescribed, few clinical trials have been conducted to determine its effectiveness in treating sleep disorders. Whether melatonin has some use against insomnia, jet lag, and other types of misalignments in circadian rhythms is still debated. A recent meta-analysis found that that melatonin is not helpful in treating sleep disorders or improving symptoms of jet lag (Buscemi et al., 2006), but it was nevertheless found to be safe, at least in the short term. In contrast, other studies report more favorable effects (Kunz, Mahlberg, Muller, Tilmann, & Bes, 2004; Zhdanova et al., 2001).

Melatonin is practically nontoxic and exhibits almost no side effects, except for the occurrence of somnolence in most of the population at higher doses and sensations of chilliness due to its effects on thermogenesis. Individuals who experience orthostatic intolerance (symptoms related to standing or sitting upright) may experience a worsening of symptoms when taking melatonin. Exogenous melatonin normally does not affect the endogenous melatonin profile in the short or medium term.

Integrated Treatment for Sexual Problems in Aging Men

With respect to sexual dysfunction, somatic treatments alone are often insufficient in helping aging men embark or resume a satisfying sex life (Althof et al., 2005). As indicated above, it is an exigency of the nature of human sexuality that an integrated approach with concurrent or stepwise combinations of psychological and medical interventions be implemented. Medical treatments are often directed narrowly at a specific problem, including a sexual dysfunction, and fail to address the larger biopsychosocial context. Modern medical therapies, especially for erectile dysfunction, are a step forward and they are efficacious (50% to 90%) depending on the clinical population. Yet, approximately 50% of individuals discontinue treatment since the wider context of the patient's erotic and sexual functioning has not been addressed in diagnosis and treatment. Ideally, a physician treating aging men, including those with sexual difficulties, should recognize and advocate for more specialized psychological intervention when it is appropriate.

Summary and Conclusions

There is no more powerful an example of a biopsychosocial phenomenon than human sexual response. The contributions that biology, psychology, and psychosocial factors make to sexual functioning may be differentiated, but they are inseparable parts of the whole. The reality of the scientific study of sex and of the professions that offer help to people with sexual problems is that integrated treatment approaches are often lacking.

This contribution has focused on the role of testosterone in male human sexuality, particularly in older men. However, recent insights now show that testosterone affects more than simply on sexual and reproductive functions. Normal levels of testosterone are required for the health of bones and muscles; and testosterone deficiency is associated with an increased risk of cardiovascular disease and diabetes type 2, both of which have profound impacts on erectile function.

Testosterone levels decline in elderly men, particularly in obese men with related ailments, and in some of these men, a state of clinical testosterone deficiency will develop. Although no solid guidelines have been established to ascertain testosterone deficiency in elderly men, the best strategy is likely to take into account both clinical symptoms and laboratory measurements. Men who are clearly testosterone deficient will benefit from testosterone treatment, showing improvement not just in sexual health but also in general health. Although many physicians associate testosterone administration with elderly men who have an increased risk of prostate cancer, guidelines have been developed for responsible testosterone treatment of elderly men.

In this contribution, the following points have been addressed:

- Human sexuality is a biopsychosocial phenomenon.
- Recent insights show that the role of testosterone is much wider than on sexual and reproductive functions.
- Testosterone affects the health of bones and muscles and the onset of cardiovascular disease and diabetes type 2, ailments that impact erectile function.
- Testosterone deficiency may be complicated to diagnose for various reasons.
- Men who are truly testosterone deficient may benefit in both sexual and general health from testosterone treatment.
- Guidelines have been developed for responsible testosterone treatment of elderly men.

References

Althof, S. E., Leiblum, S. R., Chevret-Measson, M., Hartmann, U., Levine, S. B., McCabe, M., et al. (2005). Psychological and interpersonal dimensions of sexual function and dysfunction. *Journal of Sexual Medicine, 2,* 793–800.

Araujo, A. B., O'Donnell, A. B., Brambilla, D. J., Simpson, W. B., Longcope, C., Matsumoto, A., et al. (2004). Prevalence and incidence of androgen deficiency in middle-aged and older men: Estimates from the Massachusetts Male Aging Study. *Journal of Clinical Endocrinology and Metabolism, 89,* 5920–5926.

Arlt, W., Callies, F., van Vlijmen, J. C., Koehler, I., Reincke, M., Bidlingmaier, M., et al. (1999). Dehydroepiandrosterone replacement in women with adrenal insufficiency. *New England Journal of Medicine, 341,* 1013–1020.

Aversa, A., Isidori, A. M., Spera, G., Lenzi, A., & Fabbri, A. (2003). Androgens improve cavernous vasodilation and response to sildenafil in patients with erectile dysfunction. *Clinical Endocrinology, 58,* 632–638.

Bagchus, W. M., Hust, R., Maris, F., Schnabel, P. G., & Houwing, N. S. (2003). Important effect of food on the bioavailability of oral testosterone undecanoate. *Pharmacotherapy, 23,* 319–325.

Bancroft, J. (1984). Hormones and human sexual behavior. *Journal of Sex and Marital Therapy, 10,* 3–21.

Bancroft, J. (2002). Biological factors in human sexuality. *Journal of Sex Research, 39,* 15–21.

Bancroft, J., & Wu, F. C. (1983). Changes in erectile responsiveness during androgen replacement therapy. *Archives of Sexual Behavior, 12,* 59–66.

Bhasin, S., Woodhouse, L., Casaburi, R., Singh, A. B., Bhasin, D., Berman, N., et al. (2001). Testosterone dose-response relationships in healthy young men. *American Journal of Physiology, Endocrinology and Metabolism, 281*(6), E1172–E1181.

Black, A. M., Day, A. G., & Morales, A. (2004). The reliability of clinical and biochemical assessment in symptomatic late-onset hypogonadism: Can a case be made for a 3-month therapeutic trial? *BJU International, 94,* 1066–1070.

Buena, F., Swerdloff, R. S., Steiner, B. S., Lutchmansingh, P., Peterson, M. A., Pandian, M. R., et al. (1993). Sexual function does not change when serum testosterone levels are pharmacologically varied within the normal male range. *Fertility and Sterility, 59,* 1118–1123.

Buscemi, N., Vandermeer, B., Hooton, N., Pandya, R., Tjosvold, L., Hartling, L., et al. (2006). Efficacy and safety of exogenous melatonin for secondary sleep disorders and sleep disorders accompanying sleep restriction: Meta-analysis. *BMJ, 332*(7538), 385–393.

Cameron, D. R., & Braunstein, G. D. (2005). The use of dehydroepiandrosterone therapy in clinical practice. *Treatments in Endocrinology, 4,* 95–114.

Carani, C., Granata, A. R., Bancroft, J., & Marrama, P. (1995). The effects of testosterone replacement on nocturnal penile tumescence and rigidity and erectile response to visual erotic stimuli in hypogonadal men. *Psychoneurodocrinology, 20,* 743–753.

Carnahan, R. M., & Perry, P. J. (2004). Depression in aging men: The role of testosterone. *Drugs and Aging, 21,* 361–376.

Cherrier, M. M. (2005). Androgens and cognitive function. *Journal of Endocrinological Investigation, 28,* 65–75.

Crawford, B. A., Liu, P. Y., Kean, M. T., Bleasel, J. F., & Handelsman, D. J. (2003). Randomized placebo-controlled trial of androgen effects on muscle and bone in men requiring long-term systemic glucocorticoid treatment. *Journal of Clinical Endocrinology and Metabolism, 88,* 3167–3176.

Daig, I., Heinemann, L. A., Kim, S., Leungwattanakij, S., Badia, X., Myon, E., et al. (2003). The Aging Males' Symptoms (AMS) scale: Review of its methodological characteristics. *Health and Quality of Life Outcomes, 1,* 77.

Dobs, A. S., Matsumoto, A. M., Wang, C., & Kipnes, M. S. (2004). Short-term pharmacokinetic comparison of a novel testosterone buccal system and a testosterone gel in testosterone deficient men. *Current Medical Research and Opinion, 20,* 729–738.

Dobs, A. S., Meikle, A. W., Arver, S., Sanders, S. W., Caramelli, K. E., & Mazer, N. A. (1999). Pharmacokinetics, efficacy, and safety of a permeation-enhanced testosterone transdermal system in comparison with bi-weekly injections of testosterone enanthate for the treatment of hypogonadal men. *Journal of Clinical Endocrinology and Metabolism, 84,* 3469–3478.

Ebert, T., Jockenhovel, F., Morales, A., & Shabsigh, R. (2005). The current status of therapy for symptomatic late-onset hypogonadism with transdermal testosterone gel. *European Urolology, 47,* 137–146.

Gheorghiu, I., Moshyk, A., Lepage, R., Ahnadi, C. E., & Grant, A. M. (2005). When is bioavailable testosterone a redundant test in the diagnosis of hypogonadism in men? *Clinical Biochemistry, 38,* 813–818.

Giordano, R., Aimaretti, G., Lanfranco, F., Bo, M., Baldi, M., Broglio, F., et al. (2005). Testing pituitary function in aging individuals. *Endocrinology and Metabolism Clinics of North America, 34,* viii–ix 895–906.

Gitlin, M. (2003). Sexual dysfunction with psychotropic drugs. *Expert Opinion on Pharmacotherapy, 4,* 2259–2269.

Gooren, L. J. (1987). Androgen levels and sex functions in testosterone-treated hypogonadal men. *Archives of Sexual Behavior, 16,* 463–473.

Gooren, L. J. (1994). A ten-year safety study of the oral androgen testosterone undecanoate. *Journal of Andrology, 15,* 212–215.

Gooren, L. J., & Bunck, M. C. (2004). Androgen replacement therapy: Present and future. *Drugs, 64,* 1861–1891.

Granata, A. R., Rochira, V., Lerchl, A., Marrama, P., & Carani, C. (1997). Relationship between sleep-related erections and testosterone levels in men. *Journal of Andrology, 18,* 522–527.

Gray, P. B., Singh, A. B., Woodhouse, L. J., Storer, T. W., Casaburi, R., Dzekov, J., et al. (2005). Dose-dependent effects of testosterone on sexual function, mood, and visuospatial cognition in older men. *Journal of Clinical Endocrinology and Metabolism, 90,* 3838–3846.

Greenstein, A., Mabjeesh, N. J., Sofer, M., Kaver, I., Matzkin, H., & Chen, J. (2005). Does sildenafil combined with testosterone gel improve erectile dysfunction in hypogonadal men in whom testosterone supplement therapy alone failed? *Journal of Urology, 173,* 530–532.

Guay, A. T., Jacobson, J., Perez, J. B., Hodge, M. B., & Velasquez, E. (2003). Clomiphene increases free testosterone levels in men with both secondary hypogonadism and erectile dysfunction: Who does and does not benefit? *International Journal of Impotence Research, 15,* 156–165.

Handelsman, D. J. (1994). Testicular dysfunction in systemic disease. *Endocrinology and Metabolism Clinics of North America, 23,* 839–856.

Handelsman, D. J., & Liu, P. Y. (2005). Andropause: Invention, prevention, rejuvenation. *Trends in Endocrinology and Metabolism, 16,* 39–45.

Harle, L., Basaria, S., & Dobs, A. S. (2005). Nebido: A long-acting injectable testosterone for the treatment of male hypogonadism. *Expert Opinion on Pharmacotherapy, 6,* 1751–1759.

Harman, S. M., & Blackman, M. R. (2004). Use of growth hormone for prevention or treatment of effects of aging. *Journals of Gerontology, 59A,* 652–658.

Harman, S. M., Naftolin, F., Brinton, E. A., & Judelson, D. R. (2005). Is the estrogen controversy over? Deconstructing the Women's Health Initiative Study: A critical evaluation of the evidence. *Annals of the New York Academy of Sciences, 1052,* 43–56.

Hawton, K., & Catalan, J. (1986). Prognostic factors in sex therapy. *Behaviour Research and Therapy, 24,* 377–385.

Heinemann, L. A., Saad, F., Zimmermann, T., Novak, A., Myon, E., Badia, X., et al. (2003). The Aging Males' Symptoms (AMS) scale: Update and compilation of international versions. *Health and Quality of Life Outcomes, 1,* 15.

Hunt, P. J., Gurnell, E. M., Huppert, F. A., Richards, C., Prevost, A. T., Wass, J. A., et al. (2000). Improvement in mood and fatigue after dehydroepiandrosterone replacement in Addison's disease in a randomized, double blind trial. *Journal of Clinical Endocrinology and Metabolism, 85,* 4650–4656.

Isidori, A. M., Giannetta, E., Greco, E. A., Gianfrilli, D., Bonifacio, V., Isidori, A., et al. (2005). Effects of testosterone on body composition, bone metabolism and serum lipid profile in middle-aged men: A meta-analysis. *Clinical Endocrinology (Oxford), 63,* 280–293.

Jain, P., Rademaker, A. W., & McVary, K. T. (2000). Testosterone supplementation for erectile dysfunction: Results of a meta-analysis. *Journal of Urology, 164,* 371–375.

Janowsky, J. S. (2006). The role of androgens in cognition and brain aging in men. *Neuroscience, 138,* 1015–1020.

Kalinchenko, S. Y., Kozlov, G. I., Gontcharov, N. P., & Katsiya, G. V. (2003). Oral testosterone undecanoate reverses erectile dysfunction associated with diabetes mellitus in patients failing on sildenafil citrate therapy alone. *Aging Male, 6,* 94–99.

Kaufman, J. M., & Vermeulen, A. (2005). The decline of androgen levels in elderly men and its clinical and therapeutic implications. *Endocrine Reviews, 26,* 833–876.

Kelleher, S., Conway, A. J., & Handelsman, D. J. (2004). Blood testosterone threshold for androgen deficiency symptoms. *Journal of Clinical Endocrinology and Metabolism, 89,* 3813–3817.

Kunz, D., Mahlberg, R., Muller, C., Tilmann, A., & Bes, F. (2004). Melatonin in patients with reduced REM sleep duration: Two randomized controlled trials. *Journal of Clinical Endocrinology and Metabolism, 89*(1), 128–134.

Lamberts, S. W., Romijn, J. A., & Wiersinga, W. M. (2003). The future endocrine patient: Reflections on the future of clinical endocrinology. *European Journal of Endocrinology, 149*(3), 169–175.

Lessov-Schlaggar, C. N., Reed, T., Swan, G. E., Krasnow, R. E., DeCarli, C., Marcus, R., et al. (2005). Association of sex steroid hormones with brain morphology and cognition in healthy elderly men. *Neurology, 65,* 1591–1596.

Lewis, R. W., Fugl-Meyer, K. S., Bosch, R., Fugl-Meyer, A. R., Laumann, E. O., Lizza, E., et al. (2004). Epidemiology/risk factors of sexual dysfunction. *Journal of Sexual Medicine, 1,* 35–39.

Lewis, R. W., & Mills, T. M. (2004). Effect of androgens on penile tissue. *Endocrine, 23,* 101–105.

Liu, P. Y., Death, A. K., & Handelsman, D. J. (2003). Androgens and cardiovascular disease. *Endocrinology Review, 24,* 313–340.

Lunenfeld, B. (2002). The aging male. *Aging Male, 5,* 73.

Makhsida, N., Shah, J., Yan, G., Fisch, H., & Shabsigh, R. (2005). Hypogonadism and metabolic syndrome: Implications for testosterone therapy. *Journal of Urology, 174,* 827–834.

Matsumoto, A. M., & Bremner, W. J. (2004). Serum testosterone assays: Accuracy matters. *Journal of Clinical Endocrinology and Metabolism, 89,* 520–524.

McNicholas, T., & Ong, T. (2006). Review of Testim gel. *Expert Opinion on Pharmacotherapy, 7,* 477–484.

Meikle, A. W., Bishop, D. T., Stringham, J. D., & West, D. W. (1986). Quantitating genetic and nongenetic factors that determine plasma sex steroid variation in normal male twins. *Metabolism, 35,* 1090–1095.

Meikle, A. W., Matthias, D., & Hoffman, A. R. (2004). Transdermal testosterone gel: Pharmacokinetics, efficacy of dosing and application site in hypogonadal men. *BJU International, 93,* 789–795.

Meuleman, E. J., & van Lankveld, J. J. (2005). Hypoactive sexual desire disorder: An underestimated condition in men. *BJU International, 95,* 291–296.

Moffat, S. D., Zonderman, A. B., Metter, E. J., Blackman, M. R., Harman, S. M., & Resnick, S. M. (2002). Longitudinal assessment of serum free testosterone concentration predicts memory performance and cognitive status in elderly men. *Journal of Clinical Endocrinology and Metabolism, 87,* 5001–5007.

Morelli, A., Filippi, S., Mancina, R., Luconi, M., Vignozzi, L., Marini, M., et al. (2004). Androgens regulate phosphodiesterase type 5 expression and functional activity in corpora cavernosa. *Endocrinology, 145,* 2253–2263.

Moretti, C., Frajese, G. V., Guccione, L., Wannenes, F., De Martino, M. U., Fabbri, A., et al. (2005). Androgens and body composition in the aging male. *Journal of Endocrinological Investigation, 28,* 56–64.

Morley, J. E., Charlton, E., Patrick, P., Kaiser, F. E., Cadeau, P., McCready, D., et al. (2000). Validation of a screening questionnaire for androgen deficiency in aging males. *Metabolism, 49,* 1239–1242.

Morley, J. E., Kaiser, F. E., Perry, H. M., III, Patrick, P., Morley, P. M., Stauber, P. M., et al. (1997). Longitudinal changes in testosterone, luteinizing hormone, and follicle-stimulating hormone in healthy older men. *Metabolism, 46,* 410–413.

Morley, J. E., & Perry, H. M., III. (2003). Androgen treatment of male hypogonadism in older males. *Journal of Steroid Biochemistry and Molecular Biology, 85,* 367–373.

Mulhall, J. P., Valenzuela, R., Aviv, N., & Parker, M. (2004). Effect of testosterone supplementation on sexual function in hypogonadal men with erectile dysfunction. *Urology, 63,* 348–352, discussion 352–353.

Myon, E., Martin, N., Taieb, C., & Heinemann, L. A. (2005). Experiences with the French Aging Males' Symptoms (AMS) scale. *Aging Male, 8,* 184–189.

Nieschlag, E., Swerdloff, R., Behre, H. M., Gooren, L. J., Kaufman, J. M., Legros, J. J., et al. (2005a). Investigation, treatment and monitoring of late-onset hypogonadism in males. *Aging Male, 8,* 56–58.

Nieschlag, E., Swerdloff, R., Behre, H. M., Gooren, L. J., Kaufman, J. M., Legros, J. J., et al. (2005b). Investigation, treatment and monitoring of late-onset hypogonadism in males: ISA, ISSAM, and EAU recommendations. *European Urology, 48,* 1–4.

Nieschlag, E., Swerdloff, R., Behre, H. M., Gooren, L. J., Kaufman, J. M., Legros, J. J., et al. (2005c). Investigation, treatment and monitoring of late-onset hypogonadism in males: ISA, ISSAM, and EAU recommendations. *International Journal of Andrology, 28,* 125–127.

Park, K., Ku, J. H., Kim, S. W., & Paick, J. S. (2005). Risk factors in predicting a poor response to sildenafil citrate in elderly men with erectile dysfunction. *BJU International, 95,* 366–370.

Rolf, C., Knie, U., Lemmnitz, G., & Nieschlag, E. (2002). Interpersonal testosterone transfer after topical application of a newly developed testosterone gel preparation. *Clinical Endocrinology (Oxford), 56,* 637–641.

Sakheim, D. K., Barlow, D. H., Abrahamson, D. J., & Beck, J. G. (1987). Distinguishing between organogenic and psychogenic erectile dysfunction. *Behaviour Research and Therapy, 25,* 379–390.

Schiavi, R. C., & Rehman, J. (1995). Sexuality and aging. *Urological Clinics of North America, 22,* 711–726.

Schiavi, R. C., Schreiner-Engel, P., Mandeli, J., Schanzer, H., & Cohen, E. (1990). Healthy aging and male sexual function. *American Journal of Psychiatry, 147,* 766–771.

Schiavi, R. C., Schreiner-Engel, P., White, D., & Mandeli, J. (1991). The relationship between pituitary-gonadal function and sexual behavior in healthy aging men. *Psychosomatic Medicine, 53,* 363–374.

Schiavi, R. C., White, D., Mandeli, J., & Schreiner-Engel, P. (1993). Hormones and nocturnal penile tumescence in healthy aging men. *Archives of Sexual Behavior, 22,* 207–215.

Schubert, M., Minnemann, T., Hubler, D., Rouskova, D., Christoph, A., Oettel, M., et al. (2004). Intramuscular testosterone undecanoate: Pharmacokinetic aspects of a novel testosterone formulation during long-term treatment of men

with hypogonadism. *Journal of Clinical Endocrinology and Metabolism, 89,* 5429–5434.

Schultheiss, D., Badalyan, R., Pilatz, A., Gabouev, A. I., Schlote, N., Wefer, J., et al. (2003). Androgen and estrogen receptors in the human corpus cavernosum penis: Immunohistochemical and cell culture results. *World Journal of Urology, 21,* 320–324.

Schultheiss, D., Jonas, U., & Musitelli, S. (2002). Some historical reflections on the ageing male. *World Journal of Urology, 20,* 40–44.

Schurmeyer, T., & Nieschlag, E. (1984). Comparative pharmacokinetics of testosterone enanthate and testosterone cyclohexanecarboxylate as assessed by serum and salivary testosterone levels in normal men. *International Journal of Andrology, 7,* 181–187.

Seftel, A. D., Mack, R. J., Secrest, A. R., & Smith, T. M. (2004). Restorative increases in serum testosterone levels are significantly correlated to improvements in sexual functioning. *Journal of Andrology, 25,* 963–972.

Seidman, S. N. (2003). The aging male: Androgens, erectile dysfunction, and depression. *Journal of Clinical Psychiatry, 64*(Suppl. 10), 31–37.

Shabsigh, R. (2004). Testosterone therapy in erectile dysfunction. *Aging Male, 7,* 312–318.

Shabsigh, R., Katz, M., Yan, G., & Makhsida, N. (2005). Cardiovascular issues in hypogonadism and testosterone therapy. *American Journal of Cardiology, 96,* M67–M72.

Smith, R. G., Betancourt, L., & Sun, Y. (2005). Molecular endocrinology and physiology of the aging central nervous system. *Endocrine Reviews, 26,* 203–250.

Steidle, C., Schwartz, S., Jacoby, K., Sebree, T., Smith, T., & Bachand, R. (2003). AA2500 testosterone gel normalizes androgen levels in aging males with improvements in body composition and sexual function. *Journal of Clinical Endocrinology and Metabolism, 88,* 2673–2681.

Tancredi, A., Reginster, J. Y., Luyckx, F., & Legros, J. J. (2005). No major month to month variation in free testosterone levels in aging males: Minor impact on the biological diagnosis of "andropause." *Psychoneuroendocrinology, 30,* 638–646.

Toogood, A. A. (2004). The somatopause: An indication for growth hormone therapy? *Treatments in Endocrinology, 3,* 201–209.

Valenti, G., Gontero, P., Sacco, M., Fontana, F., Strollo, F., Castellucci, A., et al. (2005). Harmonized Italian version of the Aging Males' Symptoms scale. *Aging Male, 8,* 180–183.

Vanderschueren, D., Vandenput, L., Boonen, S., Lindberg, M. K., Bouillon, R., & Ohlsson, C. (2004). Androgens and bone. *Endocrinology Review, 25,* 389–425.

Vermeulen, A. (2001). Androgen replacement therapy in the aging male: A critical evaluation. *Journal of Clinical Endocrinology and Metabolism, 86,* 2380–2390.

Vermeulen, A., & Verdonck, G. (1992). Representativeness of a single point plasma testosterone level for the long term hormonal milieu in men. *Journal of Clinical Endocrinology and Metabolism, 74,* 939–942.

Vermeulen, A., Verdonck, L., & Kaufman, J. M. (1998). A critical evaluation of simple methods for the estimation of free testosterone in serum. *Journal of Clinical Endocrinology and Metabolism, 84,* 3666–3672.

Wang, C., Catlin, D. H., Demers, L. M., Starcevic, B., & Swerdloff, R. S. (2004). Measurement of total serum testosterone in adult men: Comparison of current laboratory methods versus liquid chromatography-tandem mass spectrometry. *Journal of Clinical Endocrinology and Metabolism, 89,* 534–543.

Wang, C., Cunningham, G., Dobs, A., Iranmanesh, A., Matsumoto, A. M., Snyder, P. J., et al. (2004). Long-term testosterone gel (AndroGel) treatment maintains beneficial effects on sexual function and mood, lean and fat mass, and bone mineral ensity in hypogonadal men. *Journal of Clinical Endocrinology and Metabolism, 89,* 2085–2098.

Wang, C., Swerdloff, R., Kipnes, M., Matsumoto, A. M., Dobs, A. S., Cunningham, G., et al. (2004). New testosterone buccal system (Striant) delivers physiological testosterone levels: Pharmacokinetics study in hypogonadal men. *Journal of Clinical Endocrinology and Metabolism, 89,* 3821–3829.

Wu, F. C., & von Eckardstein, A. (2003). Androgens and coronary artery disease. *Endocrinology Review, 24,* 183–217.

Zhdanova, I. V., Wurtman, R. J., Regan, M. M., Taylor, J. A., Shi, J. P., & Leclair, O. U. (2001). Melatonin treatment for age-related insomnia. *Journal of Clinical Endocrinology and Metabolism, 86*(10), 4727–4730.

Problems with Sexual Interest and Desire in Women

Jacques van Lankveld

$$6$$

Chapter

Learning Objectives

In this chapter, we discuss:

- The nature of female sexual desire and the problem of low desire, including contemporary linear and circular models of sexual desire that stress, respectively, incentive motivation, and life-phase dependence of sexual desire.
- The physiology and pathophysiology of sexual desire, and specifically, the role of androgens and prolactin.
- The epidemiology of sexual desire problems and select psychological, sexual, and relational correlates of low sexual desire.
- Etiological factors in sexual desire problems, specifically the role of affective disorders and treatment with antidepressants, and sexual victimization history.
- A number of diagnostic instruments for the assessment of female sexual desire and desire disorder.
- The psychological treatment of female sexual desire problems and the results of therapy outcome research. The most common treatment is sensate focus therapy as described by Masters and Johnson (1970). More recently, cognitive interventions have been added to the sensate focus format. Systems-based approaches to female sexual desire problems have been described, but empirical support is scarce.
- Pharmacological therapy for female sexual desire disorder, specifically androgen replacement therapy for women with

low androgen levels, either with androgens alone or combined with estrogen.

Definitions and Classifications

Although female problems with sexual interest and desire encompass both too low and too high sexual desire, this chapter focuses on low or reduced sexual desire. Too high sexual desire is associated with sexual compulsiveness or uninhibited expression of sexual behavior and is covered in Chapter 19 in this volume.

Sexual desire and interest deal with the individual experience of wanting to become or to continue being sexual. Sexual desire may include erotic fantasies and thoughts and may be expressed as the initiative to engage in self-directed or other-directed sexual behavior (for a discussion of operational definitions of sexual desire, see Heiman, 2001). Definitions of sexual problems, dysfunctions, or disorders inevitably evoke scientific debate regarding the position of designated sexual phenomena within or outside the range of what is considered "normal," "healthy," or "desirable." Because the expression of sexual behavior itself cannot be assumed to possess any survival value for individual members of a species, it could be completely left out of the behavioral repertoire without incurring a penalty. "For the individual engaged in it, sexual behavior has no finality or purpose other than its own execution" (Agmo, 1999, p. 129). Therefore, absent or low sexual interest is not intrinsically pathological. In fact, following the "dual-control model of the sexual response" (Bancroft & Janssen, 2000), for the majority of individuals who experience it, inhibition of sexual interest or response might occur "as an appropriate or at least understandable reaction to certain circumstances, which in today's world may include states of fatigue or depression or the presence of adverse circumstances in the woman's sexual relationship or situation in life. These may appropriately be regarded as manifestations or even symptoms of a problematic state, but not necessarily evidence of malfunction of the sexual response system" (Bancroft, Loftus, & Long, 2003, p. 194).

In the *DSM-IV-TR* classification system, the condition of low or reduced sexual desire, when clinically relevant, is referred to as hypoactive sexual desire disorder (HSDD), and it can be diagnosed in both women and men. The description of HSDD in *DSM-IV-TR* is as follows: "Persistent or recurrent deficiency (or absence) of sexual fantasies and desire for sexual activity. This disturbance causes marked distress or interpersonal difficulty" (American Psychiatric Association, 2000, p. 541).

The terminology *hypoactive sexual desire* implies that sexual desire possesses an intrinsically activating or motivating quality that acts independently of other aspects of sexual functioning. This stance is proliferated through well-known twentieth-century models of the sexual response cycle. Theorists like Kaplan (1979) and Lief (1977) introduced sexual desire as a construct distinct from sexual arousal and orgasm. The sexual desire construct complemented Masters and Johnson's (1966) model of the sexual response cycle that described subsequent phases of sexual arousal, plateau, orgasm, and resolution, but which lacked a specific sexual desire dimension. These models thus postulated the independent existence of (the conscious experience of) a motivational force to be or become sexual. This force was seen as preceding and driving sexual approach behavior and, in a subsequent phase of the sexual response cycle, inducing physiological and psychological arousal. In these models, the individual first experiences spontaneous desire to become sexual, before erotic stimulation has in fact commenced. This desire is supposed to be internal in origin and is marked by the emergence into awareness of sexual thoughts and fantasies. Kaplan's model postulates that anxiety, and even more so anger, are important maintaining factors in hypoactive sexual desire. In a study by Beck and Bozman (1995), anxiety impaired sexual desire but did not affect genital arousal, providing partial support for Kaplan's hypothesis.

Kaplan's model describes a linear process, progressing from desire, through arousal, to orgasm and resolution, in which each later phase builds on a preceding phase. Desire is thus considered to be a prerequisite for the occurrence of normal arousal and orgasm. Basson (2000, 2005; Basson et al., 2004) presented a circular extension to these models and differentiated between newly formed and long-term relationships. In Basson's view, the sexual response of women in new relationships can well be described by a linear sequence, and the woman can experience her sexual motivation as a need stemming from within. However, this is not descriptive of the sexual motivation of women in relationships of longer duration. That state could be more accurately described as a state of sexual neutrality and receptivity. Women then may decide to engage in erotic stimulation as a result of widely varying sexual and nonsexual motives or needs that include, among others, the wish to please or pacify a partner, to feel strong or desirable, to chase away boredom, to distract oneself from negative preoccupations, to continue a longstanding habit, or to satisfy a felt obligation. Physiological and psychological sexual arousal then develops in response to adequate sexual stimulation. In the final step, the experience of satisfactory sexual arousal reinforces the exhibited approach behavior. In sum, according to Basson's (2000) model, sexual desire can be spontaneous or responsive, depending on the state of the relationship. When it is responsive, the sexual system is activated as a first step, after which sexual interest and desire emerge, thereby leading to further sexual action, and this may be the primary mode of inducing sexual desire in women. Specifically, community and other studies (Avis et al., 2005; Beck, Bozman, & Qualtrough, 1991; Cawood & Bancroft, 1996) have found that only a minority of premenopausal women report having frequent spontaneous sexual desire, or that an inherent sexual desire is the main reason for having sex. Hill and Preston (1996) have found empirical support for the existence of nonerotic dispositional motives for engaging in sexual interaction, such as the desire for feeling valued by one's partner, obtaining relief from stress, and enhancing one's feelings of personal power. They have also found several gender differences in these motives. Whereas women more strongly endorsed the desire to express their partner's value by engaging in sex with him, men more strongly endorsed the desire to experience relief from stress by having sex and by the desire to experience the power of their sexual partner.

Basson's (2000) model and earlier linear models were criticized for retaining the concept of "need" or "urge" as a primal motivational force (Both & Everaerd, 2002), the objection being that "sexual urge" is viewed as being "possessed" by the individual at some level. In Basson's view, women have less of it than men, who are endowed with higher physiological levels of testosterone. According to Both and Everaerd, the urge concept does not explain the phenomenon of sexual desire because it is not self-evident and thus, in its turn, needs to be explained.

Incentive-motivation models (Bindra, 1974; Both & Everaerd, 2002; Everaerd & Laan, 1995; Singer & Toates, 1987) have provided yet another perspective of female sexual motivation. Incentive-motivation models, believed to apply across human and other species, do not assume the existence of intrinsic motivation that resides somewhere in the brain. Motivation "is an emerging property that will come about when all conditions are fulfilled" (Everaerd, Laan, & Spiering, 2000, pp. 76–77). Considering the fact that individuals who are in good physical health are not continuously sexually active, sexually aroused, or motivated to have sex, it seems warranted to assume that, although biological factors are prerequisite to the presence of a sexual system that awaits proper sexual stimulation, other—psychological or contextual—factors modulate sexual desire. The requirements for sexual motivation to emerge are: (a) an internal disposition (the sexual response system), (b) the presence of sexual stimuli (or mental representations of these stimuli) that the sexual system requires for its activation, (c) and rules for the access to sexual partners (Singer & Toates, 1987, p. 494). Some would claim that desire is always responsive, even though it may be experienced as a spontaneous event, and consequently, there is no need to assume the separate existence of a construct such as "sex drive" or "urge" to understand women's sexual desire in long-term relationships. Specifically, based on their laboratory research (e.g., Janssen, Everaerd, Spiering, & Janssen, 2000; Laan, Everaerd, van-Bellen, & Hanewald, 1994; Spiering, Everaerd, & Janssen, 2003), both and Everaerd (2002) postulate that an efferent response such as relaxation of genital smooth muscle tissue is automatically activated by sexual stimuli that are encoded in the sexual system. The capacity of an incentive stimulus to activate the sexual system, or the palatability of such stimulus, however, is *not* based on any intrinsic qualities of a stimulus, but rather is moderated by the organism's hormonal state, its state of deprivation, and its prior learning (conditioning) process (Pfaus, Kippin, & Coria-Avila, 1996; Singer & Toates, 1987, p. 492). The automatic responses to sexually palatable stimuli are elicited at an unconscious, preattentive level. Conscious awareness of sexual arousal and desire is only experienced when feedback information from the active sexual response system exceeds the threshold of perception. At that point, when the individual becomes aware of those sexual feelings, a strategic decision needs to be made, weighing the pros and cons of proceeding with the ongoing sexual encounter. This model, in sum, assumes that female sexual desire is always responsive and emerges as an action tendency when external or internal sexual stimuli engage the sexual system and when the state of activation of this system reaches awareness.

Extending this model further, the variability in levels of sexual desire will, at least to some extent, be governed by the same mechanisms as those known in the domain of human sexual arousal. Consequently, a number of interfering cognitive processes may also impair sexual desire: ruminative, worrisome ideation (Barlow, 1986; van den Hout & Barlow, 2000), low outcome expectancy (Bach, Brown, & Barlow, 1999), displaced focus of attention (Meston, 2006), general insufficient attentional capacity (Elliott & O'Donohue, 1997; Salemink & van Lankveld, 2006), and low propensity for sexual excitation and high propensity for sexual inhibition (Bancroft & Janssen, 2000; Carpenter, 2002).

In the following sections, the physiological aspects of female sexual desire that constitute and constrain the sexual response system are first discussed. Then, the epidemiology of low sexual desire and the risk factors for the impairment of sexual desire, the procedures and instruments for assessment of low sexual desire, and, finally, the approaches to effective treatment are discussed.

Physiological Aspects of Female Sexual Arousal

Although the physiology and neurobiology of sexual arousal and motivation in women is still under researched, animal research and the limited number of available studies in humans suggest a pivotal role in female sexual functioning for certain endogenous hormones and neurotransmitters. Here we discuss the roles of testosterone and other androgens and of prolactin. These hormones represent only a fragment of the physiological factors contributing to female sexual desire. Interested readers are referred to scholarly reviews (e.g., Apperloo, van der Stege, Hoek, & Weijmar Schultz, 2003; Bancroft, 2005).

Testosterone

The frequent administration in clinical practice of androgen replacement therapy for low female sexual desire suggests that low sexual desire is caused by an androgen deficit. The evidence for this causal inference, however, is limited. Androgens in women are produced by the ovaries and the adrenal glands and are metabolized in other tissues from precursors (e.g., pregnenolone). Free testosterone in the bloodstream and dihydrotestosterone, formed from testosterone in peripheral tissues after 5-alpha-reductase, are the biologically active androgens because only they can bind to androgen receptors in target tissues (e.g., in the brain, the gonads, bone tissue). The production of androgens in women decreases with age. This decrease is independent of the menopausal transition (Apperloo et al., 2003), when a sharp drop in estrogen production occurs. In fact, in the transitory stage and in menopause, androgen production may even increase. As lower estrogen levels cause concomitant decreases in sex hormone binding globulin (SHBG) production, the decrease in androgen binding to SHBG may result in higher levels of bio-available testosterone. Oral contraceptive use may also increase levels of sex hormone binding globulin, thereby reducing free testosterone levels. Some women are particularly sensitive to these effects (Basson, 2006).

Low androgen levels in the woman may be caused by congenital conditions (e.g., Turner syndrome) or by various medical conditions, including adrenal disease, bilateral oophorectomy, and ovarian failure after chemotherapy or radiotherapy in the pelvic area (thus causing premature menopause). Low sexual desire and difficulties with attaining orgasm are common in women with disease-related or iatrogenic low androgen levels (Apperloo et al., 2003). Furthermore, in samples of women with androgen insufficiency, due to natural or oophorectomy-induced menopause or adrenal dysfunction, androgen replacement therapy consistently improves female sexual desire (e.g., Arlt et al., 1999; see for a review: Apperloo et al., 2003).

The study of sexual functioning under low androgen conditions in women suffering from major disease might introduce confounding factors, such as the effect of the disease on individual psychological well-being and on the dynamics of the partner relationship. However, the association of androgen level and sexual desire in healthy women has also been studied using paradigms that circumvent such confounds.

The fluctuation of sexual desire and sexual activity over the menstrual cycle in naturally cycling premenopausal women offers such a window on the androgen-desire association. In a study of 21 heterosexual premenopausal women with regular menstrual cycles, the ovulatory peak in free testosterone was associated with an increase in sexual interest and sexual behavior—both intercourse and masturbation—around the time of ovulation (van Goozen, Wiegant, Endert, & Helmond, 1997). Woman initiated sexual interaction with the partner more frequently in the pre-ovulatory period and around ovulation, whereas male initiative predominated during the period directly following menstruation. Between ovulation and menstruation, both partners were equally likely to initiate sexual contact. Although estradiol (estrogen) levels are also elevated around ovulation, a strong causal link between estrogen level and sexual desire is not likely, as the peak in the frequency of woman-initiated sexual intercourse during the late-menstrual phase cannot be caused by high estrogen level. This study has thus far not been replicated.

Cross-sectional investigations of healthy women in larger samples more likely to uncover associations between androgen level and sexual functioning independent of the variability associated with the menstrual cycle offer yet another paradigm for studying the relationship between testosterone and sexual desire. In one study of 99 healthy, nonobese, premenopausal women, no association was found between these two variables (van Anders & Hampson, 2005). In this study, testosterone samples were taken in the first 7 days of the menstrual cycle, and when potential influences of body-mass index, age and depressive mood were statistically removed, no association was apparent. In a community study conducted in Australia, serum levels of total and free testosterone, androstenedione, or dehydroepiandrosterone sulfate (DHEAS) did not predict sexual desire or arousal levels in 1,021 unmedicated (without oral contraception) women between 18 and 75 years (Davis, Davison, Donath, & Bell, 2005). Although this study found that very low levels of DHEAS were associated with low sexual responsiveness, most women with low DHEAS levels did not report impaired sexual function.

Relying on yet another paradigm used in a number of studies, the androgen levels of healthy premenopausal women with and without low sexual desire have been compared. For example, 15 women with lifelong "absence of sexual drive" were assessed on several endocrine parameters and on sexual desire measured with a detailed diary. Women with reduced sexual desire had lower free testosterone than control women, but other endocrine parameters were not different (Riley & Riley, 2000). In a small ($n = 20$) study carried out in Turkey, women with low sexual desire (measured with the Female Sexual Function Inventory: FSFI) were compared with healthy, age-matched controls (Turna et al., 2005). Among these women were both pre- and postmenopausal subgroups; the premenopausal women had regular menstrual cycles and all post-menopausal women were on estrogen replacement therapy. Compared with controls, women with low sexual desire had lower total testosterone, free testosterone, and dehydroepiandrosterone sulfate (DHEAS). As in the observational studies in community samples, however, comparisons between groups of sexually functional and dysfunctional women, cannot determine the causal direction of the association.

Finally, pharmacological studies using androgen supplementation in healthy women could provide an experimental window on the dose-response relationship between supraphysiological androgen levels and sexual desire or other aspects of sexual functioning. Until now, no direct tests of the effect of increased androgen on "spontaneous" sexual desire have been conducted. However, a number of studies investigated the effect of supra-physiological androgen levels on subjective sexual arousal, and sexual arousal might have a strong connection to responsive sexual desire (Basson, 2000; Both & Everaerd, 2002). Results have been inconsistent. Tuiten and colleagues (2000) administered a single dose of 0.5 mg sublingual testosterone undecanoate or placebo to 16 healthy, sexually functional women. Although total testosterone returned to baseline within 90 min, participants experienced increased "sexual lust" while watching erotic film segments up to 4 hr following drug intake. In this study, sexual lust was self-reported after each film segment. In contrast, Apperloo et al. (2006) found no androgen effect on subjective sexual arousal when they compared a single vaginal dose of testosterone propionate (2 mg) with placebo in a randomized, double-blind, crossover study design of 10 healthy premenopausal women. Although markedly elevated levels of androgens occurred, no effects were found on the genital or subjective sexual response. Sexual lust and subjective sexual arousal in these studies, however, were not measured independently from active visual erotic stimulation, and may therefore not represent an adequate analog of sexual desire and motivation.

These studies might be summarized in the following way:

- Female androgen insufficiency due to surgical and natural menopause appears to reliably decrease sexual desire and interest, a condition that can be reversed with exogenous androgen.
- Many healthy, pre- and postmenopausal women with low sexual desire have lower androgen levels than healthy control women, but sexual interest and desire are not strongly associated with elevated testosterone around ovulation.

- Variability in androgen level does not predict sexual desire in the population at large, and supraphysiological androgen levels pharmacologically induced in healthy women do not consistently increase "spontaneous" sexual desire.
- Androgen effects on sexual arousal have been equivocal.
- Although no clinically applicable thresholds have been reported yet, extremely low androgen in women is strongly associated with low sexual desire, but in normal, healthy women, normal and drug-induced variability in androgen appears unrelated to sexual desire.

Prolactin

Prolactin has been thought to exert negative feedback control on sexual motivation (Kruger, Haake, Hartmann, Schedlowski, & Exton, 2002). Prolactin is a peptide hormone that is produced by lactotrophs in the posterolateral anterior pituitary gland. The release of prolactin is under inhibitory dopaminergic control of the hypothalamus and has been shown to regulate lactation. The release of prolactin is tonically inhibited by dopamine that activates dopamine D_2 receptors in the pituitary. Prolactin regulates its own release in a short-loop negative feedback process by stimulating hypothalamic dopamine neurons. Prolactin receptors have been located in the brain in several structures associated with sexual behavior, including the hippocampus, cortex, hypothalamus, and amygdala (for a review, see Andrews, 2005).

Animal research and a small number of human studies consistently reveal that increased prolactin levels in the bloodstream inhibit both appetitive and consummatory aspects of sexual behavior (Hulter & Lundberg, 1994; Kadioglu et al., 2005). Weizman and colleagues (1983) noticed that many male and female uremic patients maintained on chronic hemodialysis reported sexual dysfunction, specifically low sexual desire and sexual activity. The men and women had significantly higher serum prolactin levels than those with normal sexual function. In some patients, treatment with bromocriptine reduced serum prolactin levels to a normal level and sexual dysfunction subsequently disappeared.

Hyperprolactinemia, that is, chronically increased prolactin production, is common during pregnancy and the lactation period, but it can also result from pituitary tumors, adrenal and kidney disease, and other medical conditions. Although pregnancy-, lactation-, and disease-related chronic increases in prolactin level can thus reduce sexual desire, low sexual desire is not always associated with chronically elevated prolactin. When groups of otherwise healthy women with normal and clinically relevant low sexual desire have been compared, their prolactin was not found to differ (Schreiner-Engel, Schiavi, White, & Ghizzani, 1989; Stuart, Hammond, & Pett, 1986).

Postorgasmic release of prolactin has been found to temporarily suppress sexual arousability in women and men (Krüger et al., 2002). Prolactin levels were not affected by a nonsexual film, or by the first minutes of exposure to erotic film. However, when participants reached orgasm through masturbation or coitus, prolactin markedly increased and remained elevated up to 60 min after orgasm. No correlation was found between prolactin level and level of physical effort required to reach orgasm, and prolactin was unaffected when masturbation did not lead to orgasm.

Epidemiology and Risk Factors

As for other sexual dysfunctions, the epidemiological study of problematic sexual desire has shown widely varying percentages of women in the general population, depending on the diagnostic criteria, survey method, and sampling strategies. Across different countries and ethnic groups, 5% to 46% of women report low sexual desire (Laumann et al., 2005; Mercer et al., 2003; Simons & Carey, 2001). Many studies reporting higher prevalence rates were based on postmenopausal women. When the co-occurrence of low sexual desire and distress were both used as criteria—thereby matching the diagnostic requirements for a *DSM* classification—lower percentages were found. In a recent community study (Leiblum, Koochaki, Rodenberg, Barton, & Rosen, 2006) of 952 women in a U.S. national probability sample, premenopausal (20 to 49 years), surgically postmenopausal (20 to 49 years), naturally postmenopausal (50 to 70 years), and surgically postmenopausal (50 to 70 years) were compared, using the Short Form-36 (SF-36) to measure overall health status, the Profile of Female Sexual Function (PFSF) to measure sexual desire, and the Personal Distress Scale (PDS) to assess the distress associated with low level of sexual desire. The prevalence of women that suffered from hypoactive sexual desire disorder (HSDD), that is, including low desire as well as high distress, varied from 9% in naturally postmenopausal women to 26% in surgically menopausal women between 20 and 49 years of age. Approximately 14% of premenopausal women and of surgically menopausal women between 50 and 70 years reported HSDD.

In addition to the disease-related and iatrogenic biological factors discussed previously, cross-sectional studies have suggested a considerable number of psychological risk factors for low sexual desire in women, including:

- Female androgen insufficiency due to surgical and natural menopause.
- Chronic renal failure, especially when maintained on chronic hemodialysis.
- Hyperprolactinemia caused by pituitary tumors, adrenal or kidney disease.
- Pregnancy and lactation.
- Longer relationship duration.
- Marital problems.
- Low partner attractiveness.
- Affective disorders and treatment with antidepressants.
- Psychotic disorders.
- Other sexual dysfunctions of the woman or her partner.
- Negative sexual attitudes, including religious morality.
- Perceived personal stress.
- History of sexual abuse.

This list is by no means exhaustive. Several of these risk factors are predicted from the female sexual desire models of Basson (2000) and Both and Everaerd (2002).

Longer relationship duration is predicted to lower spontaneous emergence of sexual desire (Basson, 2000). This hypothesis was supported by survey results from student samples (e.g., Klusmann, 2002) and general population studies. Not being married and starting a new relationship are both positively related to feelings of sexual desire, as documented by the multiethnic U.S. Study of Women's Health Across the Nation (SWAN; Avis et al., 2005). In a Croatian community study in which inhibited sexual desire was defined as having no sexual thoughts, fantasies, or dreams, the likelihood of inhibited sexual desire was found to increase independently with both age and length of relationship (Stulhofer et al., 2005). In another study on students, the decrease of sexual desire occurring with increasing length of relationship was specific to women and did not apply to men.

Marital Problems and Low Partner Attractiveness

Responsive desire will be more difficult to experience when discord between partners exists for prolonged periods, as they reduce the expectancy of reward contingent upon sexual interaction (Basson, 2000; Both & Everaerd, 2002). Many studies have documented an association between female sexual desire and relationship quality variables. Despite large differences in study designs and operational definitions of *sexual interest*, most studies revealed an association between positive relationship quality and more frequent sexual desire in the woman or lower discrepancy of sexual desire between partners. The experiences of marital satisfaction (Dennerstein, Koochaki, Barton, & Graziottin, 2006; Trudel, Boulos, & Matte, 1993; Trudel, Landry, & Larose, 1997), marital happiness (Donnelly, 1993), and intimacy between partners (McCabe, 1997), as well as better partner communication (Brezsnyak & Whisman, 2004; Stulhofer et al., 2005) have been associated with reports of more frequent sexual desire and smaller discrepancy of sexual desire between partners.

Other Sexual Dysfunctions

Responsive desire in the context of sexual interaction with a partner is not reinforced when the woman's sexual arousal, genital lubrication, or orgasm are diminished due to sexual dysfunction, either of herself or of her partner. This suggests that cross-sectional studies will demonstrate correlations of low sexual desire with decreased functioning on other aspects of the sexual response, of both the woman and her partner. Several studies have supported this hypothesis. Of 475 women with a primary diagnosis of hypoactive sexual desire disorder (HSDD), 41% had at least one other sexual dysfunction (K. B. Segraves & Segraves, 1991). Sexual inactivity, reflecting low sexual interest of the woman, her partner, or both, was indeed a good predictor of women's distress about their sexual relationship, but not about their own sexuality (Bancroft et al., 2003).

Other research supports these general relationships. Nobre, Pinto-Gouveia, and Gomes (2006) found high correlations between problems with female sexual desire, sexual arousal, and orgasm in a sample of 47 Portuguese women. In a community study of 2,467 European women between 20 and 70 years, sexual desire, sexual arousal, orgasm, and sexual pleasure were all highly correlated (Dennerstein et al., 2006). Similar results were found in a U.S. community study (Leiblum et al., 2006) where women with HSDD were more likely than controls to experience problems with sexual arousal, sexual pleasure, and with orgasm, regardless of age or hormonal status. This last study also provided further support for the notion of the responsive nature of sexual motivation, as proposed in some models of female sexual desire (Basson, 2000; Both & Everaerd, 2002). The findings of Leiblum et al. (2006) differentiated between (perceived) spontaneous and responsive sexual desire. Women with normal and with low sexual desire differed in all four groups (lower versus higher age, premenopausal versus [surgically] postmenopausal) with respect to the frequency of woman-initiated sexual interaction, in the sense that women with HSDD reported lower frequency of self-initiated interaction. However, with respect to partner-initiated sexual interaction, this difference was found only in the older group and was independent of the cause (natural or surgical) of postmenopausal status. This implies that, in younger women, the frequency of partner-initiated sexual contact does not depend on the woman's level of sexual desire, or her hormonal status. In contrast, it depends more on her level of responsiveness to sexual initiatives of her partner, independent of her hormonal status.

Sexual Attitudes, Including Religious Morality

In the aforementioned SWAN study, over 3,000 women between 42 and 52 years were dichotomized into two groups, those experiencing strong sexual desire (at least once a week) and those who did so infrequently or not at all (Avis et al., 2005). Sexual desire was independent of both menopause and the women's perceived physical health. In contrast, sexual desire was strongly associated with how important the women considered sex in their personal lives. Compared with women who considered sex quite important or extremely important, those who found it moderately important were 87% less likely to report frequent feelings of sexual desire (odds ratio = 3.09). Moreover, women with negative attitudes toward aging and with higher levels of perceived stress were more likely to report experiencing low sexual desire. Thus, while the influence of sexual attitudes on sexual desire has been both consistent and strong, an inhibitory influence of religious morals on sexual desire has been less consistent. For example, Stulhofer et al. (2005), in a Croatian community study, found that women with strong religious morals were more likely to report sexual desire problems; and Hartmann, Heiser, Ruffer-Hesse, and Kloth (2002) found conventional morals to be typical in women with low sexual desire. Yet, a Swedish study of a national representative sample of women found no significant association between sexual desire problems and religiosity (Öberg, Fugl-Meyer, & Fugl-Meyer, 2004). These findings seem to reflect cultural differences regarding the impact of religiosity on the lives of women.

In a recent multivariate study of 1,011 adolescents comprised of equal groups of African American and Caucasian men and women in the southeastern United States, the relative impact of educational (parental), religious, demographic, school-related, and peer-related variables, and level of exposure to sex in the media was assessed on sexual intentions and on two types of self-reported sexual behavior using multiple linear regression modeling (L'Engle, Brown, & Kenneavy, 2006). When the effects of age, gender, race, and socioeconomic status were controlled, religious variables explained only between 0% and 2% of the variance in intentions to become sexual over the next year, and on sexual behavior. In contrast, exposure to sex in the mass media explained 13% of the adolescents' sexual intentions and somewhat less than 10% of their self-reported sexual behavior. Parents' sexual beliefs and sexual behavior in the peer group had still larger effects on all outcome variables in this study. Thus, the impact of attitudes and moral values on the level of sexual desire and the development of problematic low desire presents a complex picture that warrants careful clinical assessment in women who present with problems of low sexual desire.

Affective Disorders and Treatment with Antidepressants

Although comorbid and previous psychopathology had been studied in women and men with sexual dysfunctions (Derogatis, Meyer, & King, 1981; Faulk, 1973), it was only after the inclusion of inhibited sexual desire in the psychiatric classification system (*DSM-III*, 1980) that psychopathology in people with this condition was investigated. Following up on many clinical observations, Mathew and Weinman (1982) and Schreiner-Engel and Schiavi (1986) were among the first to compare women with low sexual desire to matched controls on dimensions of psychopathology. These researchers found elevated lifetime prevalence of major and intermittent depressive disorders and premenstrual syndrome in women with low sexual desire. The onset of the desire problem typically coincided with the presence of the first depressive episode or was preceded by it. Several studies, including large population studies, later replicated the strong association of depressed mood and low sexual desire. For instance, in a factor-analytic study of 682 women between 45 and 65 years in the United Kindgom who were neither on estrogen therapy nor hysterectomized, a "sexual problems" factor that included dissatisfaction with the sexual relationship, loss of sexual interest, and vaginal dryness was strongly related to depression (Hunter, Battersby, & Whitehead, 1986). In a computer-assisted population survey of Brazilian women, lack of sexual interest was significantly associated with diagnosed depression (odds ratio = 1.68; Moreira Jr., Glasser, Santos, & Gingell, 2005). In a German study, mood instability, low and fragile self-regulation and self-esteem, cognitive rumination and anxiety were higher among women with HSDD than sexually functional women (Hartmann et al., 2002).

Not only depression in itself, but also its commonly practiced treatment with antidepressants, especially the selective serotonin reuptake inhibitors (SSRI), has been reported to impair sexual functioning in general, and sexual desire in particular. Although many premarketing studies on side effects of antidepressant medication failed to find high rates of sexual dysfunction (low sexual desire or other types) due to the open-ended nature of the relevant questions (Landen, Hogberg, & Thase, 2005), most antidepressants interfere with female sexual functioning, with the possible exceptions of bupropion and nefazodone (for a review, see Ferguson,

2001). While the effect of SSRIs on depression may be equal, their inhibiting effects on sexual desire may differ substantially, as has been found with reboxetine versus paroxetine (Baldwin, Bridgman, & Buis, 2006). Lowering the dose, change of medication, or the use of temporary drug holidays are possible approaches to antidepressant-induced decreases of sexual desire in clinically depressed women. For example, changing to bupropion, which is a dopamine reuptake inhibitor, can successfully treat SSRI-induced hypoactive sexual desire disorder (Clayton et al., 2004). But such approaches are not always effective. Kennedy et al. (2006) found no differential effect of bupropion versus paroxetine on sexual function in clinically depressed women. And in a study on nondepressed premenopausal women with clinically low sexual desire, bupropion did not significantly enhance sexual desire when compared with placebo (R. T. Segraves, Clayton, Croft, Wolf, & Warnock, 2004). However, this latter study suffered from a substantial dropout rate caused by a lack of treatment efficacy. A recent multivariate study on depressed women found that treatment with SSRI had an effect only on orgasm, and not on sexual desire (Cyranowski, Frank, Cherry, Houck, & Kupfer, 2004).

In sum, contradictory findings surround the issue of the differential effect of various antidepressants on sexual desire in women with clinical depression. While inhibition of sexual desire (and of orgasmic capacity) has consistently been reported for virtually all antidepressant medications, current research does not warrant favoring some medications over others.

Other Psychiatric Conditions

Based on outpatient samples, sexual desire disorder is more prevalent in those with schizophrenia ($n = 100$) and affective psychosis ($n = 58$) than in those with dermatological problems ($n = 30$; Kockott & Pfeiffer, 1996). Patients on neuroleptic medication in this study were mainly affected, but type and dosage were not found to moderate the sexual disorder. In an Italian study, women with schizophrenia reported hyposexuality more often than women with schizo-affective or bipolar disorders (Raja & Azzoni, 2003). In contrast with the above relationships, low sexual desire has not been associated with drug or alcohol use (Johnson, Phelps, & Cottler, 2004).

Sexual Abuse History

Childhood sexual abuse has been found to disrupt adult sexual functioning in both clinical and population samples (Najman, Dunne, Purdie, Boyle, & Coxeter, 2005; Sarwer & Durlak, 1996; for reviews see Leonard & Follette, 2002; Rumstein-McKean & Hunsley, 2001), although research on college students has generally failed to find associations between childhood sexual abuse and aspects of adult sexual functioning, including sexual desire (Fromuth, 1986).

In a study among 728 Moroccan women, women who were sexually abused during childhood reported more depressive symptoms than nonabused women and increased prevalence of sexual problems, but no difference with respect to sexual desire was revealed (McHichi Alami & Kadri, 2004).

In some women sexually abused as children, elevated sexual desire has been reported. For example, Bergmark, Avall-Lundqvist, Dickman, Steineck, and Henningsohn (2005) reported a higher likelihood of experiencing sexual desire more than once a week in women with a history of sexual abuse compared with women with no abuse, and even higher likelihood when women with a history of sexual abuse also were also affected with cervical cancer. Obviously, sexual abuse is characterized by many different parameters (age of abuse, frequency of abuse, type of abuse, etc.) and therefore its effects on sexual desire are not likely to be uniform.

Because a history of sexual abuse may lead to episodes of depression and posttraumatic stress disorder in adult life (e.g., Cheasty, Clare, & Collins, 1998), careful evaluation of both traumatic life events and comorbid mental disorder is required. A history of sexual abuse, however, does not necessarily preclude effective treatment of a sexual dysfunction (Sarwer & Durlak, 1997).

General

Many of the risk factors leading to or maintaining low sexual desire are intercorrelated and might reflect transdiagnostic mechanisms and processes that are involved in different nosological entities or fields of study. A necessary next step in the study of the correlates of problems with sexual desire is to disentangle these intercorrelated factors and to assess their relative contributions, alone or in interaction with other factors. Cross-sectional studies with a multivariate design constitute a first phase in this process and several recent examples have been published. Speer et al. (2005) conducted a cross-sectional study of 55 female breast cancer survivors with low sexual desire and found that neither type of cancer treatment nor hormone levels were related to sexual functioning. Although the low sexual desire was alleviated, depression and having traditional role preferences had strong associations with low sexual desire, suggesting that any number of factors may at any given time affect a woman's level of sexual desire.

Assessment and Measurements

The first and most important instrument for the assessment and clarification of the complaint of low female sexual desire is the sexual history interview. Interview formats to assess sexual desire and interest typically contain questions or statements concerning self-perceived sexual motivation, the frequency of erotic thoughts and fantasies, the frequency of initiatives to engage in self-directed or partner-directed sexual acts, and the willingness to respond positively to sexual initiatives of appropriate partners. Medical screening and endocrinological testing appear warranted only when the woman reports lifelong and generalized low sexual desire (Heiman & Meston, 1997).

In the interview, questions may be asked such as:

- How long have you had these concerns with respect to your sexual desire/interest?
- Currently would you feel some interest in sex from something that was potentially erotic to you, for example, a picture, book, movie, dancing?
- Especially in longer-term relationships, women often start out a sexual experience without any feeling of sexual desire. However, they can respond to their partner or to other sexual stimuli. So I need to ask you about the circumstances when you consider being sexual, or when your partner is instigating. Can you describe the circumstances?
- Can you, in time, respond to the sexual touching and stimuli and then feel some desire to continue?

See Basson et al. (2004, p. 864) for additional information on this procedure.

Against the background of the "responsive" model of female sexual desire, the practitioner needs to focus the sexual history taking and the broader clinical interview on those aspects of the client's functioning that might provide or, in contrast, withhold the rewards that constitute the necessary incentives motivating her to engage in sexual activity. This includes other aspects of sexual functioning such as deficient sexual arousal or lubrication during sexual stimulation, problems with having an orgasm, or the occurrence of pain during sex. It also includes poor skills for erotic stimulation of her partner or herself, as well as sexual dysfunction of the partner. It further includes the woman's perceived physical and psychological well-being and the rewards or punishment that might be attached to the partner relationship in the broadest sense. The focus should be on reward and punishment as perceived by the client and not so much on whether they are objectively delivered.

Several assessment instruments, in both self-report and structured interview formats, are available to assess sexual desire and to compare the level of desire/interest with normative populations (for reviews, see Daker-White, 2002; Meston & Derogatis,

2002). We review three instruments developed specifically to assess aspects of female sexual desire, followed by four instruments designed to cover a broader range of symptoms and dimensions of female sexual dysfunction (see Table 6.1 for overview). In the latter four instruments, level of sexual desire and interest and problems in this domain are assessed in conjunction with other relevant domains, thus yielding a more comprehensive profile of sexual functioning. This enables the clinician to gauge the strength of the client's sexual desire in the context of her functioning with regard to sexual arousal, her orgasmic capacity, the occurrence of pain during sex, and her overall sexual satisfaction.

The Sexual Interest and Desire Inventory—Female (SIDI-F; Clayton et al., 2006; Sills et al., 2005) is a 13-item instrument, purporting to assess symptom severity in women with HSDD. Administered by clinicians with expertise in female sexual dysfunction, it is not available as a self-report questionnaire. Clayton et al. (2006) found good internal consistency, discriminant validity, and diagnostic specificity because women with a clinical diagnosis of HSDD had lower SIDI-F scores than sexually functional women as well as women with only orgasmic disorder. Convergent validity was shown to be satisfactory by a high correlation between SIDI-F scores and, among others, scores on the Female

Table 6.1 **Instruments for Assessment of Sexual Desire and Overall Sexual Functioning**

Instrument	References
Specific to aspects of female sexual desire	
Sexual Interest and Desire Inventory—Female (SIDI-F)	Clayton et al. (2006); Sills et al. (2005)
Hurlbert Index of Sexual Desire (HISD)	Apt & Hurlbert (1992)
Sexual Desire Inventory (SDI)	Spector, Carey, & Steinberg (1996)
Comprehensive profile of sexual functioning	
Derogatis Interview for Sexual Functioning (DISF/DISF-SR)	Derogatis (1997)
Brief Index of Sexual Functioning for Women (BISF-W)	Taylor, Rosen, & Leiblum (1994)
Female Sexual Function Index (FSFI)	Rosen et al. (2000)
Sexual Function Questionnaire (SFQ)	Quirk et al. (2002)

Sexual Function Index (FSFI; Rosen et al., 2000; see later discussion). Divergent validity was demonstrated by a small-size correlation with a modified Marital Adjustment Scale (MAS; Locke & Wallace, 1959), measuring general (nonsexual) satisfaction with the relationship. Clayton et al. (2006) collected provisional normative data on small samples of women with HSDD ($N = 31$), female orgasmic disorder ($N = 24$), and sexually functional women ($N = 35$).

The Hurlbert Index of Sexual Desire (HISD; Apt & Hurlbert, 1992) is a 25-item self-report questionnaire using a Likert-type rating scale. The HISD has excellent test-retest reliability, and internal consistency, as well as construct, discriminant, and concurrent validity. It contains items such as "it is hard for me to fantasize about sexual things" and "my desire for sex should be stronger." Normative data are not available.

The Sexual Desire Inventory (SDI; Spector, Carey, & Steinberg, 1996) measures both interactional and solitary aspects of sexual desire. This 14-item scale assesses sexual desire as an experiential construct that is separate from overt behavior. It thus reflects Beach's (1956) model of sexuality that distinguishes between a motivational and a consummatory phase. Factor analyses have demonstrated the underlying existence of two related but distinct features: dyadic (partner-related) desire and solitary desire. Sufficient internal consistency and discriminant validity has been shown in student samples. The SDI does not presume actual sexual experience in completers. Normative data are not available.

The Derogatis Interview for Sexual Functioning (DISF/DISF-SR; Derogatis, 1997) is a 25-item semi-structured interview for multidimensional assessment of sexual functioning in men and women. It takes approximately 15 min to administer. A self-report version, the DISF-SR, is also available. Items represent five domains of sexual functioning: sexual cognition/fantasy, sexual arousal, sexual behavior/experience, orgasm, and sexual drive/relationship. A total score summarizes level of sexual functioning across the five domains. Norms were developed in studies on healthy community samples of men and women (ages between 19 and 64). Currently, no norms are available with respect to the DISF/DISF-SR scores for women with sexual dysfunction. Test-retest, internal consistency, and interrater reliabilities were satisfactory.

The Brief Index of Sexual Functioning for Women (BISF-W; J. F. Taylor, Rosen, & Leiblum, 1994) was designed to measure female sexual functioning and sexual satisfaction. It is a self-report questionnaire with 22 items that takes 15 to 20 min to complete. J. F. Taylor et al. (1994) conducted satisfactory tests of its test-retest reliability, internal consistency (at least for the sexual desire subdomain), and concurrent validity. With the use of a scoring algorithm (Mazer, Leiblum, & Rosen, 2000), an overall score for quality of female sexual functioning can be calculated, as well as seven subdomain scores for sexual desire, arousal, frequency of sexual activity, receptivity/initiation of sexual interaction, pleasure/orgasm, relationship satisfaction, and problems affecting sexual function. Normative scores for total scale and subdomains were derived from healthy (ages between 20 and 55 years), surgically menopausal, sexually-active women in the same age range who expressed problems with sexual functioning (Mazer et al., 2000). The discriminant validity of the BISF-W between sexually functional and dysfunctional women was found reliable with the exception of the sexual desire domain. In general, it proved to be sensitive to change during treatment with transdermal testosterone in oophorectomized women with sexual desire problems, as the total score showed significant correlations with changes assessed in a diary format with daily telephone contact (Shifren et al., 2000). However, the sexual thoughts/sexual desire subdomain was not found to be sensitive to treatment changes in this study.

The Female Sexual Function Index (FSFI; Rosen et al., 2000) is a brief, 19-item self-report instrument for the measurement of female sexual function, requiring about 15 min to complete. The FSFI consists of five domains of female sexual functioning; domain scores may be added to obtain a global score for overall female sexual functioning. The sexual desire domain contains only two items and is therefore limited in its reflection of the different aspects of sexual desire and interest. The FSFI discriminates between samples of healthy women between 21 and 68 years and age-matched women with sexual arousal disorder on all domains and the overall domain score. Internal consistency and test-retest reliabilities were acceptable. Divergent validity was investigated by examining correlations between FSFI and the Locke-Wallace MAS (1959). The association of the sexual desire FSFI subscale with marital adjustment was small ($r = .19$ in the full sample), indicating sufficient dissociation of both measures. Meston (2003) compared FSFI scores of women with orgasmic disorder, women with HSDD, and healthy control women. Internal consistency and discriminant validity for the existence of female sexual dysfunction were again demonstrated, as both dysfunction groups had different scores compared with healthy controls, although the design of the study did not allow comparison of women with HSDD and with orgasmic disorder. In a subsequent validation study (Wiegel, Meston, & Rosen, 2005), the psychometric qualities of the instrument were replicated, although the study in part consisted of the same participant samples as the previously reported studies on the FSFI. Again, the FSFI scores did not enable satisfactory discrimination of the HSDD groups from women with other types of sexual dysfunction, although they allowed distinction between women with HSDD and healthy controls. The discriminant power of the FSFI between various types of female sexual dysfunction, including women with HSDD, thus remains to be demonstrated. Norms are available for female sexual arousal disorder (FSAD) patients and controls at item and domain levels, and for the full-scale score.

The Sexual Function Questionnaire (SFQ; Quirk et al., 2002) is a 31-item self-report instrument with seven subdomains measuring sexual desire, sensations of physical arousal, physical arousal and lubrication, enjoyment, orgasm, pain, and partner relationship. The original study found good internal consistency, satisfactory discriminant validity, and satisfactory sensitivity to changes in sexual function during pharmacological treatment, but widely varying test-retest reliability scores across subscales. In a follow-up study, data from five clinical trials of medication for female sexual dysfunction and two general population surveys were aggregated and amounted to 1,160 completers of the SFQ, including 201 nonsymptomatic women. The sexual desire subscale score reliably distinguished between women with and without a diagnosis of HSDD, including women with arousal disorder, orgasmic disorder, dyspareunia, and healthy control women (Quirk, Haughie, & Symonds, 2005). Norms were developed to indicate low, intermediate, and high probability of sexual dysfunction with regard to sexual desire, lubrication, subjective sexual arousal, orgasm, and sexual pain.

In sum, a number of interview and paper-and-pencil instruments are available to support and qualify the clinical assessment of female sexual desire problems. Future research is necessary to compare the various instruments with regard to the feasibility of administration, their reliability across time and assessors, and—critically—their performance in clinical decision analysis. Ideal instruments would reliably screen women with sexual desire problems from general population groups and clinical subpopulations (e.g., women with chronic disease, natural and surgically menopausal women, women using hormonal contraception), and would be sensitive to changes in sexual desire as a result of treatment. Currently, the use of at least two different instruments is recommended for clinical applications when assessing a client: for instance, an instrument that specifically measures sexual desire together with a broad-spectrum measurement instrument that can assess multiple dimensions of female sexual function.

Treatment

Sexual desire problems in women may be treated with pharmacological therapy, psychological therapy, or a combination of both approaches (e.g., Dow & Gallagher, 1989). Compared with other sexual problems, sexual desire problems have traditionally been considered to be more difficult to treat (see for reviews, Beck, 1995 and Heiman, 2001), and many speculative explanations for these difficulties have been put forward. As the understanding of the nature and etiology of sexual desire problems has increased, the reasons for the therapy-resistant nature of many sexual desire problems have become clearer.

One such reason may derive from the conceptualization of sexual desire as an intrinsic driving force, one that occupies a position early in the linear sequence of the sexual response. Replacement of this linear model with a more circular-responsive model may be useful as a treatment tool. Although sexual desire may exist as a spontaneous intrinsic factor in some episodes during the lives of women (e.g., in dating situations, or in the early phase of a relationship, see Basson, 2000), in many other conditions, and especially in long relationships, sexual desire may best be regarded as a responsive phenomenon that results from a large array of sexual and nonsexual factors. Sexual desire will emerge when all necessary conditions for its emergence are fulfilled (Both & Everaerd, 2002; Singer & Toates, 1987). This thinking implies that low sexual desire might also be approached as the consequence of problematic functioning in other domains of sexuality, of the partner relationship, or of the physical and psychological condition of the female client or her partner.

Consistent with this "responsive" model of female sexual desire, treatment would focus on helping the client to increase the rewards and incentives necessary to experience stronger motivation to engage in sexual activity. Again, this includes other aspects of sexual functioning, such as her sexual arousal response and lubrication during sexual stimulation, the ability to experience orgasm, or the reduction of pain during sex. Treatment might also help to improve her partner's or her own skills for erotic stimulation and to relieve sexual dysfunction of the partner. Treatment might further aim at increasing the rewards and reducing punishment that the woman experiences within nonsexual domains of her partner relationship.

This view of problems of sexual desire might explain why some therapeutic approaches, reviewed in subsequent paragraphs, were found to be successful even though they addressed other aspects of sexual and relational functioning than desire itself. These efficacious treatments addressed one or more of the "low reward" aspects of the woman's individual sexual and nonsexual functioning or of her partner relationship.

A number of descriptions of the treatment of low female sexual desire are found in the clinical literature. Here we focus on a small number of treatment programs that have been subjected to empirical testing and found beneficial. For the most part, the treatment administered in these studies matches the sensate focus approach described by Masters and Johnson

(1970). In this approach, the rationale of treatment is first explained, then sexual education is given, and a temporary ban on intercourse is discussed with the client and her partner. The partners follow a program of exercises, including mutual nongenital and genital pleasuring, communication exercises, and exercises aimed at reducing performance demand and the anxiety resulting from it. In some formats, cognitive interventions have been added to the treatment (Hurlbert, White, Powell, & Apt, 1993). Methodological factors have made it difficult to interpret the results of some studies; these have included the use of heterogeneous samples, including patients with HSDD as well as with other sexual dysfunction types, or the reporting of lumped analyses of outcomes in which the results for various diagnostic groups were indistinguishable.

Sex and Cognitive-Behavioral Therapy Strategies

Early studies of treatment outcomes of generic Masters and Johnson type sex therapy for couples with low sexual desire (Schover & LoPiccolo, 1982) reported significant positive changes after treatment regarding marital adjustment, overall sexual satisfaction, frequency of intercourse and masturbation, and patterns of initiation of sexual activity that could be ascribed to the efficacy of treatment. Later, Hawton, Catalan, and Fagg (1991) followed up with 60 consecutive couples with female low sexual desire as their primary complaint that received Masters and Johnson therapy consisting of 12 sessions on average and delivered by sole therapists, most of whom were female. Although a quarter of the couples dropped out before completion, an intent-to-treat analysis of all couples ($N = 60$) indicated that 57% had a favorable outcome as rated by the therapist. In those couples completing treatment, 84% had a positive outcome. Positive outcomes were predicted by stronger motivation of the male partner before starting treatment whereas poor outcome was related to a younger age of the couple, especially the male partner, and a shorter problem duration. Unexpectedly, general satisfaction with the relationship before treatment start, except for a history of previous separations, was not related to outcome, nor was current or lifetime psychopathology. The findings of this study should be considered with caution because its internal validity is unclear due to the absence of experimental control conditions and of independent assessment of outcome.

Another clinical study investigated 39 women with HSDD and compared group therapy alone with group therapy combined with orgasm consistency training (Hurlbert, 1993). Women who also received orgasm consistency training reported more improvement with respect to sexual arousal and sexual assertiveness at posttreatment and at two follow-up evaluations. This group also reported more sexual satisfaction at a 6-month follow-up. Be-

cause this study did not examine the effect of treatment on perceived level of sexual desire, a second study of 57 women with
HSDD was conducted (Hurlbert et al., 1993). Participants were
randomly allocated to one of three groups: a women-only group,
a couples-only group, or a waiting-list group. Both active treatments included the orgasm consistency training that included an
introduction to the technique of directed masturbation, sensate
focus exercises, techniques to increase the male partner's ejaculatory self-control, an instruction to the couple to allow the woman
to orgasm first during sexual interaction before the male partner
climaxes and before intercourse is initiated (the "ladies come first"
rule), and the coital alignment technique to ensure direct clitoral
stimulation by the penis during intercourse. Compared with the
waiting list group, women in both treatment groups reported improved sexual desire at posttreatment. Women in the couples-
only group reported higher frequency of sexual fantasy following
treatment, and at follow-up the couples-only treatment format
was superior to the women-only format on outcome measures of
sexual compatibility between partners, sexual self-esteem, sexual
desire, fantasy, and sexual satisfaction.

Two other studies of interest have demonstrated improved
sexual desire resulting from sex therapy. McCabe (2001) reported
an outcome study of a 10-session cognitive-behavioral treatment
of male and female sexual dysfunction, in which 54 women with
various sexual dysfunctions were included. Treatment consisted
of Masters and Johnson (1970) type sex therapy and cognitive interventions for overcoming cognitions and behaviors that impeded sexual performance and enjoyment of sexual activities. Of
54 women completing the treatment, the percentage with lack of
sexual interest decreased from 80% at pretreatment to 54% after
treatment, with the largest gains related to female anorgasmia.

And finally, in a randomized, controlled clinical trial of
cognitive-behavioral therapy for female HSDD, treatment was administered as two-hour group sessions of couple sex therapy during
12 weeks (Trudel et al., 2001). Group interventions included sex
education, couple sexual intimacy enhancing exercises, sensate
focus, communication skills training, emotional communication
skills training, sexual fantasy training, cognitive restructuring, and
various homework assignments, including manual reading. Assessments were carried out on 74 couples that met six study criteria for
HSDD and that were not diagnosed as having concurrent psychopathology—especially depressive disorder—at pretreatment, posttreatment, and follow-up at 3 and 12 months after treatment. At
posttreatment, improvement in the treated group was superior to
waiting list. Furthermore, of the treated women, only 26% still met
all criteria for HSDD at posttreatment, as compared with 100% at
pretreatment. However, this percentage gradually increased to 36%
at the 3-month follow-up but stabilized thereafter at the 12-month

follow-up. This global result was supported by positive changes on various questionnaire measures of sexual functioning, including pleasure with sexual activities and decreased frequency of negative thoughts during sex.

In summary, various types of sex therapy, most based on key elements of Masters and Johnson techniques, have demonstrated gains in sexual functioning, including sexual interest and desire. More effective treatments appear to include a combination of sex therapy and cognitive-behavioral strategies, deal with couples rather than women only, and typically involve techniques that address elements of sexual functioning that extend beyond just sexual desire. However, the limited amount of data prevent strong conclusions regarding the effectiveness of some procedures, techniques, or formats over others; broad based rather than narrowly focused approaches appear to have the most efficacy.

Relationship Therapy for Female Low Sexual Desire

Some treatment approaches focus on improving key aspects of the relationship such as intimacy and partner communication rather than simply on improving low sexual desire (e.g., Gehring, 2003; Russell, 1990; Schnarch, 1991; Zimmer, 1987), but research on the efficacy of these treatments is lacking. Treatments typically build on systemic notions of partner communication and use interventions to enhance communication on emotional and non-emotional issues, as well as interventions to break the recurrent circular patterns of fighting and blaming. McCarthy (1999) describes a relapse prevention strategy that builds on a "use it or lose it" rationale for couples who are vulnerable to sexual desire difficulties and also implements a behavioral strategy to challenge existing avoidance tendencies. In this regard, the therapist encourages both partners to agree that if 2 weeks go by without sexual contact, the partner who usually has the higher level of sexual desire is responsible to initiate a sexual date within a week. If this partner fails to do so, the partner who usually has the lower level of sexual desire is then responsible for initiating a pleasuring or erotic contact within the next week. If neither partner meets their respective responsibilities, they must schedule an appointment with the therapist. This strategy is consistent with incentive-motivation models, although it has not been empirically tested.

Other treatment studies suggest that relationship therapy may be helpful in dealing with low sexual desire. Zimmer (1987) compared couples with unspecified female dysfunction that received sex therapy and relaxation training with couples that received a combination of sex therapy and marital therapy. Larger treatment gains were observed for couples also receiving marital therapy. MacPhee, Johnson, and van der Veer (1995) compared couples having female low sexual desire who received emotionally focused couples therapy (EFT) with waiting list couples and couples without female HSDD. Although differences between waiting list and treatment were small, treated women showed improvement on one measure of sexual desire as well as a decrease in depressive symptoms.

Summarizing, a limited number of clinical studies have shown that treatment with sensate focus therapy of couples in which the female partner suffers from low sexual desire can be beneficial. However, several of these studies were methodologically weak and their results should be treated with caution. Orgasm consistency training (Hurlbert, 1993) and cognitive-behavioral treatment (Trudel et al., 2001) are promising approaches that should be scrutinized more in order to establish their robustness. The incentive-motivation model of (responsive) sexual desire also predicts higher levels of sexual desire when marital discord is relieved by systemic or other partner relationship oriented therapies. However, these treatment types, although abundant in the literature, are currently under-researched, and few empirical data are available to support their application.

Pharmacological Treatment of Female Low Sexual Desire

Hormonal Therapies

A number of clinical studies were conducted comparing androgen substitution to placebo in women with reduced androgen levels, either due to menopause induced by oophorectomy or by natural menopause (see for a review: Apperloo, van der Stege, Hoek, & Weijmar Schultz, 2003). In some studies, androgen administration alone was compared with a combination of androgen and estrogen administration. In all, higher scores for sexual desire, arousal, and sexual thoughts and fantasies were found in women treated with androgens, although frequency of intercourse and orgasm was not affected. Higher scores on sexual desire and interest were found for combination treatments of androgens and estrogen. For example, in a study comparing daily use of tibolone, a steroid agent with tissue-specific estrogenic, androgenic, and progestagenic effects (2.5 mg/day) with placebo in 38 healthy, naturally postmenopausal women (< 65 years), women receiving tibolone had higher frequency of sexual fantasies, higher sexual arousability, including sexual thoughts, higher sensitivity to sexual stimuli, and stronger feelings of sexual attraction (Laan, van Lunsen & Everaerd, 2001); the mean frequency of perceived desire for sex was marginally higher in the tibolone condition. More recently, healthy naturally postmenopausal women with HSDD were treated with estrogens alone or the combination of esterified estrogens and methyltestosterone in a double-blind randomized trial (Lobo, Rosen, Yang, Block, & van der Hoop, 2003), with the combined treatment resulting in improved sexual interest/desire as measured by one scale (Sexual Interest Questionnaire), but not by another (BISF-W), although directional differences were consistent across scales.

In a review of the field, Apperloo et al. (2003) conclude that it is advisable to start androgen substitution only in women with normal estrogen levels (see also Bachmann et al., 2002). Consistent with this recommendation, the North American Menopause Society (2005) explicitly recommends the use of exogenous testosterone with concomitant estrogen therapy for women after spontaneous or surgically induced menopause. Transdermal applications are favored to avoid effects on liver function that might occur with oral administration. However, androgen therapy is contraindicated in women with breast cancer or uterine cancer or in women with cardiovascular or liver disease. Concerns regarding long-term androgen use pertain to a potential increase in insulin resistance and increased risk of the metabolic syndrome or of exacerbating this syndrome if it already exists (see Basson, 2000).

Treatment of Comorbid Psychopathology and Antidepressant-Induced Sexual Desire Problems

Currently, no studies are known that investigate the beneficial effect on female sexual desire of psychological or combined psychological and pharmacological treatment of major depression (Schreiner-Engel & Schiavi, 1986). Somewhat more evidence is available with regard to treatment of antidepressant-induced sexual dysfunction, including female low sexual desire. A review of 15 randomized controlled trials that included 393 women compared management strategies for antidepressant-induced sexual dysfunction (M. J. Taylor, Rudkin, & Hawton, 2005). Despite limited evidence, a trend favoring treatment with bupropion was discerned. When antidepressant treatment was augmented with bupropion, increased sexual desire generally ensued (Clayton et al., 2004; but see DeBattista, Solvason, Poirier, Kendrick, & Loraas, 2005; Masand, Ashton, Gupta, & Frank, 2001). A number of reviews also mention potential advantages of moclobemide, nefazodone, and reboxetine over other antidepressants in reducing the potential iatrogenic effects on sexual desire, although the paucity of studies and inferior methodologies limit the strength of conclusions (Baldwin, 2004; Ferguson, 2001).

Combined Psychological and Pharmacological Treatment of Low Sexual Desire in Women

Several studies have addressed general female "sexual unresponsiveness" using a balanced factorial design that included both psychological and pharmacological approaches (Carney, Bancroft, & Mathews, 1978; Dow & Gallagher, 1989; Mathews, Whitehead, & Kellett, 1983). In general, participants have been women with various sexual dysfunctions, with exclusion of women with vaginismus, and treatment consisted of Masters and Johnson type sex therapy as well as administration of sublingual testosterone (10 mg/day for 3 months), compared with placebo or diazepam (10 mg/day). All studies reported significant positive changes after treatment, including a less impaired sexual relationship, and increased interest and arousal of the female partner ascribed to the androgen treatment. Gains were generally maintained at follow-up. The results of testosterone (at least in the dosage used) have been mixed. Whereas Carney et al. (1978) found testosterone superior to diazepam on behavioral and attitudinal measures, Mathews et al. (1983) found no effect of testosterone compared with placebo. Dow and Gallagher (1989) randomly allocated 30 couples with general sexual unresponsiveness of the female partner to testosterone plus sexual counseling; placebo plus the same form of counseling; or testosterone alone. Both counseling groups showed greater improvement on measures of sexual adjustment and attitude change than the women who received only testosterone. However, all groups received some form of treatment and all female participants reported increases in the frequency of sexual desire. Testosterone alone was not superior to either of the other treatments on any outcome measure.

Summary and Conclusions

Although the field of sexual desire in women has been underresearched, several general conclusions may be drawn from studies investigating these sexual problems:

- Circular-responsive models of sexual desire seem better at characterizing sexual desire in women than the more traditional linear models first proposed by Kaplan and Lief. Specifically, incentive-motivation and life-phase dependence of sexual desire may explain research findings on sexual desire that contradict the older linear model of sexual desire.
- In understanding the physiology and pathophysiology of sexual desire in women, androgens and prolactin are important in explaining variation in sexual desire in women across the menstrual cycle, the sexual response, and across the life span.
- Epidemiological data of sexual desire problems are scarce and inconsistent with regard to psychological, sexual, and relational correlates of low sexual desire.
- Regarding the etiology of sexual desire problems, such factors as relationship variables, affective disorders, and treatment

with antidepressants, and sexual victimization history are potential risk factors.

- Several diagnostic instruments for the assessment of female sexual desire and desire disorder are available in the English language.

- The most common psychological treatment of female sexual desire problems is sensate focus therapy as described by Masters and Johnson (1970). More recently, cognitive interventions have been added to the sensate focus format. Therapy outcome research in this field is scarce but suggests favorable outcomes.

- The systems-based approach—one involving relationship therapy—to the treatment of female sexual desire problems has been described in a number of reports but few have yet been empirically validated.

- Pharmacological therapy for female sexual desire disorder, specifically androgen replacement therapy for women with low androgen levels, either with androgens alone or combined with estrogen, appears to yield positive outcomes, but evidence is yet meager.

References

Agmo, A. (1999). Sexual motivation: An inquiry into events determining the occurrence of sexual behavior. *Behavioral Brain Research, 105*(1), 129–150.

American Psychiatric Association. (2000). *Diagnostic and statistical manual of mental disorders* (4th ed., text rev.). Washington, DC: Author.

Andrews, Z. B. (2005). Neuroendocrine regulation of prolactin secretion during late pregnancy: Easing the transition into lactation. *Journal of Neuroendocrinology, 17*(7), 466–473.

Apperloo, M. J., Midden, M., van der Stege, J., Wouda, J., Hoek, A., & Weijmar Schultz, W. (2006). Vaginal application of testosterone: A study on pharmacokinetics and the sexual response in healthy volunteers. *Journal of Sexual Medicine, 3*(3), 541–549.

Apperloo, M. J., van der Stege, J. G., Hoek, A., & Weijmar Schultz, W. C. M. (2003). In the mood for sex: The value of androgens. *Journal of Sex and Marital Therapy, 29*(2), 87–102.

Apt, C. V., & Hurlbert, D. F. (1992). Motherhood and female sexuality beyond one year postpartum: A study of military wives. *Journal of Sex Education and Therapy, 18*(2), 104–114.

Arlt, W., Callies, F., van Vlijmen, J. C., Koehler, I., Reincke, M., Bidlingmaier, M., et al. (1999). Dehydroepiandrosterone replacement in women with adrenal insufficiency. *New England Journal of Medicine, 341*(14), 1013–1020.

Avis, N. E., Zhao, X., Johannes, C. B., Ory, M., Brockwell, S., & Greendale, G. A. (2005). Correlates of sexual function among multi-ethnic middle-aged women: Results from the Study of Women's Health Across the Nation (SWAN). *Menopause, 12*(4), 385–398.

Bach, A. K., Brown, T. A., & Barlow, D. H. (1999). The effects of false negative feedback on efficacy expectancies and sexual arousal in sexually functional males. *Behavior Therapy, 30*, 79–95.

Bachmann, G., Bancroft, J., Braunstein, G., Burger, H., Davis, S., Dennerstein, L., et al. (2002). Female androgen insufficiency: The Princeton consensus statement on definition, classification, and assessment. *Fertility and Sterility, 77*(4), 660–665.

Baldwin, D. S. (2004). Sexual dysfunction associated with antidepressant drugs. *Expert Opinion on Drug Safety, 3*(5), 457–470.

Baldwin, D. S., Bridgman, K., & Buis, C. (2006). Resolution of sexual dysfunction during double-blind treatment of major depression with reboxetine or paroxetine. *Journal of Psychopharmacology, 20*(1), 91–96.

Bancroft, J. (2005). The endocrinology of sexual arousal. *Journal of Endocrinology, 186*(3), 411–427.

Bancroft, J., & Janssen, E. (2000). The dual control model of male sexual response: A theoretical approach to centrally mediated erectile dysfunction. *Neuroscience and Biobehavioral Reviews, 24*(5), 571–579.

Bancroft, J., Loftus, J., & Long, J. S. (2003). Distress about sex: A national survey of women in heterosexual relationships. *Archives of Sexual Behavior, 32*(3), 193–208.

Barlow, D. H. (1986). Causes of sexual dysfunction: The role of anxiety and cognitive interference. *Journal of Consulting and Clinical Psychology, 54*, 140–148.

Basson, R. (2000). The female sexual response: A different model. *Journal of Sex and Marital Therapy, 26*, 51–65.

Basson, R. (2005). Female hypoactive sexual desire disorder. In R. Balon & R. T. Segraves (Eds.), *Handbook of sexual dysfunction* (pp. 43–66). Boca Raton, FL: Taylor & Francis.

Basson, R. (2006). Clinical practice: Sexual desire and arousal disorders in women. *New England Journal of Medicine, 354*(14), 1497–1506.

Basson, R., Weijmar Schultz, W. C. M., Binik, Y. M., Brotto, L. A., Eschenbach, D. A., Laan, E., et al. (2004). Women's sexual desire and arousal disorders and sexual pain. In T. F. Lue, R. Basson, R. Rosen, F. Giuliano, S. Khoury, & F. Montorsi (Eds.), *Sexual medicine: Sexual dysfunctions in men and women.* 2nd International Consultation on Sexual Dysfunctions, Paris.

Beach, F. (1956). Characteristics of masculine sex drive. In M. R. Jones (Ed.), *Nebraska Symposium on Motivation* (Vol. 4, pp. 1–32). Lincoln: University of Nebraska Press.

Beck, J. G. (1995). Hypoactive sexual desire disorder: An overview. *Journal of Consulting and Clinical Psychology, 63*(6), 919–927.

Beck, J. G., & Bozman, A. W. (1995). Gender differences in sexual desire: The effects of anger and anxiety. *Archives of Sexual Behavior, 24*(6), 595–612.

Beck, J. G., Bozman, A. W., & Qualtrough, T. (1991). The experience of sexual desire: Psychological correlates in a college sample. *Journal of Sex Research, 28*(3), 443–456.

Bergmark, K., Avall-Lundqvist, E., Dickman, P. W., Steineck, G., & Henningsohn, L. (2005). Synergy between sexual abuse and cervical cancer in causing sexual dysfunction. *Journal of Sex and Marital Therapy, 31*(5), 361–383.

Bindra, D. (1974). A motivational view of learning, performance, and behavior modification. *Psychological Review, 81*, 199–213.

Both, S., & Everaerd, W. (2002). Comment on "The female sexual response: A different model." *Journal of Sex and Marital Therapy, 28*(1), 11–15.

Brezsnyak, M., & Whisman, M. A. (2004). Sexual desire and relationship functioning: The effects of marital satisfaction and power. *Journal of Sex and Marital Therapy, 30*(3), 199–217.

Carney, A., Bancroft, J., & Mathews, A. (1978). Combination of hormonal and psychological treatment for female sexual unresponsiveness: A comparative study. *British Journal of Psychiatry, 133*, 339–346.

Carpenter, D. L. (2002). The dual control model: Gender, sexual problems, and the prevalence of sexual excitation and inhibition profiles. *Dissertation Abstracts International, Section B: Sciences and Engineering, 63*(5-B), 2575.

Cawood, E. H., & Bancroft, J. (1996). Steroid hormones, the menopause, sexuality and well-being of women. *Psychological Medicine, 26*(5), 925–936.

Cheasty, M., Clare, A. W., & Collins, C. (1998). Relation between sexual abuse in childhood and adult depression: Case-control study. *British Medical Journal, 316*(7126), 198–201.

Clayton, A. H., Segraves, R. T., Leiblum, S., Basson, R., Pyke, R., Cotton, D., et al. (2006). Reliability and validity of the Sexual Interest and Desire Inventory-Female (SIDI-F), a scale designed to measure severity of female hypoactive sexual desire disorder. *Journal of Sex and Marital Therapy, 32*(2), 115–135.

Clayton, A. H., Warnock, J. K., Kornstein, S. G., Pinkerton, R., Sheldon-Keller, A., & McGarvey, E. L. (2004). A placebo-controlled trial of bupropion SR as an antidote for selective serotonin reuptake inhibitor-induced sexual dysfunction. *Journal of Clinical Psychiatry, 65*(1), 62–67.

Cyranowski, J. M., Frank, E., Cherry, C., Houck, P., & Kupfer, D. J. (2004). Prospective assessment of sexual function in women treated for recurrent major depression. *Journal of Psychiatric Research, 38*(3), 267–273.

Daker-White, G. (2002). Reliable and valid self-report outcome measures in sexual (dys)function: A systematic review. *Archives of Sexual Behavior, 31*(2), 197–209.

Davis, S. R., Davison, S. L., Donath, S., & Bell, R. J. (2005). Circulating androgen levels and self-reported sexual function in women. *Journal of the American Medical Association, 294*(1), 91–96.

DeBattista, C., Solvason, B., Poirier, J., Kendrick, E., & Loraas, E. (2005). A placebo-controlled, randomized, double-blind study of adjunctive bupropion sustained release in the treatment of SSRI-induced sexual dysfunction. *Journal of Clinical Psychiatry, 66*(7), 844–848.

Dennerstein, L., Koochaki, P., Barton, I., & Graziottin, A. (2006). Hypoactive sexual desire disorder in menopausal women: A survey of Western European women. *Journal of Sexual Medicine, 3*(2), 212–222.

Derogatis, L. R. (1997). The Derogatis Interview for Sexual Functioning (DISF/DISF-SR): An introductory report. *Journal of Sex and Marital Therapy, 23*(4), 291–304.

Derogatis, L. R., Meyer, J. K., & King, K. M. (1981). Psychopathology in individuals with sexual dysfunction. *American Journal of Psychiatry, 138*(6), 757–763.

Donnelly, D. A. (1993). Sexually inactive marriages. *Journal of Sex Research, 30*(2), 171–179.

Dow, M. G., & Gallagher, J. (1989). A controlled study of combined hormonal and psychological treatment for sexual unresponsiveness in women. *British Journal of Clinical Psychology, 28,* 201–212.

Elliott, A. N., & O'Donohue, W. T. (1997). The effects of anxiety and distraction on sexual arousal in a nonclinical sample of heterosexual women. *Archives of Sexual Behavior, 26*(6), 607–624.

Everaerd, W., & Laan, E. (1995). Desire for passion: Energetics of sexual response. *Journal of Sex and Marital Therapy, 21*(4), 255–263.

Everaerd, W., Laan, E. T. M., & Spiering, M. (2000). Male sexuality. In L. T. Szuchman & F. Muscarella (Eds.), *Psychological perspectives on human sexuality* (pp. 60–101). Hoboken, NJ: Wiley.

Faulk, M. (1973). "Frigidity": A critical review. *Archives of Sexual Behavior, 2*(3), 257–266.

Ferguson, J. M. (2001). The effects of antidepressants on sexual functioning in depressed patients: A review. *Journal of Clinical Psychiatry, 62*(Suppl. 3), 22–34.

Fromuth, M. E. (1986). The relationship of childhood sexual abuse with later psychological and sexual adjustment in a sample of college women. *Child Abuse and Neglect, 10*(1), 5–15.

Gehring, D. (2003). Couple therapy for low sexual desire: A systemic approach. *Journal of Sex and Marital Therapy, 29*(1), 25–38.

Hartmann, U., Heiser, K., Ruffer-Hesse, C., & Kloth, G. (2002). Female sexual desire disorders: Subtypes, classification, personality factors and new directions for treatment. *World Journal of Urology, 20*(2), 79–88.

Hawton, K., Catalan, J., & Fagg, J. (1991). Low sexual desire: Sex therapy results and prognostic factors. *Behaviour Research and Therapy, 29*(3), 217–224.

Heiman, J. R. (2001). Sexual desire in human relationships. In W. Everaerd, E. Laan, & S. Both (Eds.), *Sexual appetite, desire and motivation: Energetics of the sexual system* (pp. 117–132). Amsterdam: Royal Dutch Academy of Science.

Heiman, J. R., & Meston, C. M. (1997). Evaluating sexual dysfunction in women. *Clinical Obstetrics and Gynecology, 40*(3), 616–629.

Hill, C. A., & Preston, L. K. (1996). Individual differences in the experience of sexual motivation: Theory and measurement of dispositional sexual motives. *Journal of Sex Research, 33*(1), 27–45.

Hulter, B., & Lundberg, P. O. (1994). Sexual function in women with hypothalamo-pituitary disorders. *Archives of Sexual Behavior, 23*(2), 171–183.

Hunter, M., Battersby, R., & Whitehead, M. (1986). Relationships between psychological symptoms, somatic complaints and menopausal status. *Maturitas, 8*(3), 217–228.

Hurlbert, D. F. (1993). A comparative study using orgasm consistency training in the treatment of women reporting hypoactive sexual desire. *Journal of Sex and Marital Therapy, 19*(1), 41–55.

Hurlbert, D. F., White, L. C., Powell, R. D., & Apt, C. (1993). Orgasm consistency training in the treatment of women reporting hypoactive sexual desire: An outcome comparison of women-only groups and couples-only groups. *Journal of Behavior Therapy and Experimental Psychiatry, 24*(1), 3–13.

Janssen, E., Everaerd, W., Spiering, M., & Janssen, J. (2000). Automatic processes and the appraisal of sexual stimuli: Toward an information processing model of sexual arousal. *Journal of Sex Research, 37*(1), 8–23.

Johnson, S. D., Phelps, D. L., & Cottler, L. B. (2004). The association of sexual dysfunction and substance use among a community epidemiological sample. *Archives of Sexual Behavior, 33*(1), 55–63.

Kadioglu, P., Yalin, A. S., Tiryakioglu, O., Gazioglu, N., Oral, G., Sanli, O., et al. (2005). Sexual dysfunction in women with hyperprolactinemia: A pilot study report. *Journal of Urology, 174*(5), 1921–1925.

Kaplan, H. S. (1979). *Disorders of sexual desire.* New York: Brunner/Mazel.

Kennedy, S. H., Fulton, K. A., Bagby, R. M., Greene, A. L., Cohen, N. L., & Rafi-Tari, S. (2006). Sexual function during bupropion or paroxetine treatment of major depressive disorder. *Canadian Journal of Psychiatry, 51*(4), 234–242.

Klusmann, D. (2002). Sexual motivation and the duration of partnership. *Archives of Sexual Behavior, 31*(3), 275–287.

Kockott, G., & Pfeiffer, W. (1996). Sexual disorders in nonacute psychiatric outpatients. *Comprehensive Psychiatry, 37*(1), 56–61.

Kruger, T. H., Haake, P., Hartmann, U., Schedlowski, M., & Exton, M. S. (2002). Orgasm-induced prolactin secretion: Feedback control of sexual drive? *Neuroscience and Biobehavioral Reviews, 26*(1), 31–44.

Laan, E., Everaerd, W., van-Bellen, G., & Hanewald, G. (1994). Women's sexual and emotional responses to male- and female-produced erotica. *Archives of Sexual Behavior, 23*(2), 153–169.

Laan, E., van Lunsen, R. H., & Everaerd, W. (2001). The effects of tibolone on vaginal blood flow, sexual desire and arousability in postmenopausal women. *Climacteric, 4*(1), 28–41.

Landen, M., Hogberg, P., & Thase, M. E. (2005). Incidence of sexual side effects in refractory depression during treatment with citalopram or paroxetine. *Journal of Clinical Psychiatry, 66*(1), 100–106.

Laumann, E. O., Nicolosi, A., Glasser, D. B., Paik, A., Gingell, C., Moreira, E., et al. (2005). Sexual problems among women and men aged 40–80 yrs: Prevalence and correlates identified in the Global Study of Sexual Attitudes and Behaviors. *International Journal of Impotence Research, 17*(1), 39–57.

Leiblum, S. R., Koochaki, P. E., Rodenberg, C. A., Barton, I. P., & Rosen, R. C. (2006). Hypoactive sexual desire disorder in postmenopausal women: US results from the Women's International Study of Health and Sexuality (WISHeS). *Menopause, 13*(1), 46–56.

L'Engle, K. L., Brown, J. D., & Kenneavy, K. (2006). The mass media are an important context for adolescents' sexual behavior. *Journal of Adolescent Health, 38*(3), 186–192.

Leonard, L. M., & Follette, V. M. (2002). Sexual functioning in women reporting a history of child sexual abuse: Review of the empirical literature and clinical implications. *Annual Review of Sex Research, 13,* 346–388.

Lief, H. I. (1977). Inhibited sexual desire. *Medical Aspects of Human Sexuality, 7,* 94–95.

Lobo, R. A., Rosen, R. C., Yang, H. M., Block, B., & van der Hoop, R. G. (2003). Comparative effects of oral esterified estrogens with and without methyltestosterone on endocrine profiles and dimensions of sexual function in postmenopausal women with hypoactive sexual desire. *Fertility and Sterility, 79*(6), 1341–1352.

Locke, H. J., & Wallace, K. M. (1959). Short marital-adjustment and prediction tests: Their reliability and validity. *Marriage and Family Living, 21,* 251–255.

MacPhee, D. C., Johnson, S. M., & van der Veer, M. M. (1995). Low sexual desire in women: The effects of marital therapy. *Journal of Sex and Marital Therapy, 21*(3), 159–182.

Masand, P. S., Ashton, A. K., Gupta, S., & Frank, B. (2001). Sustained-release bupropion for selective serotonin reuptake inhibitor-induced sexual dysfunction: A randomized, double-blind, placebo-controlled, parallel-group study. *American Journal of Psychiatry, 158*(5), 805–807.

Masters, W. H., & Johnson, V. E. (1966). *Human sexual response.* Oxford, England: Little, Brown.

Masters, W. H., & Johnson, V. E. (1970). *Human sexual inadequacy.* Boston: Little, Brown.

Mathew, R. J., & Weinman, M. L. (1982). Sexual dysfunctions in depression. *Archives of Sexual Behavior, 11*(4), 323–328.

Mathews, A., Whitehead, A., & Kellett, J. (1983). Psychological and hormonal factors in the treatment of female sexual dysfunction. *Psychological Medicine, 13*(1), 83–92.

Mazer, N. A., Leiblum, S. R., & Rosen, R. C. (2000). The brief index of sexual functioning for women (BISF-W): A new scoring algorithm and comparison of normative and surgically menopausal populations. *Menopause, 7*(5), 350–363.

McCabe, M. P. (1997). Intimacy and quality of life among sexually dysfunctional men and women. *Journal of Sex and Marital Therapy, 23*(4), 276–290.

McCabe, M. P. (2001). Evaluation of a cognitive behavior therapy program for people with sexual dysfunction. *Journal of Sex and Marital Therapy, 27*(3), 259–271.

McCarthy, B. W. (1999). Relapse prevention strategies and techniques for inhibited sexual desire. *Journal of Sex and Marital Therapy, 25*(4), 297–303.

McHichi Alami, K., & Kadri, N. (2004). Moroccan women with a history of child sexual abuse and its long-term repercussions: A population-based epidemiological study. *Archives of Womens Mental Health, 7*(4), 237–242.

Mercer, C. H., Fenton, K. A., Johnson, A. M., Wellings, K., Macdowall, W., McManus, S., et al. (2003). Sexual function problems and help seeking behaviour in Britain: National probability sample survey. *BMJ, 327*(7412), 426–427.

Meston, C. M. (2003). Validation of the Female Sexual Function Index (FSFI) in women with female orgasmic disorder and in women with hypoactive sexual desire disorder. *Journal of Sex and Marital Therapy, 29,* 39–46.

Meston, C. M. (2006). The effects of state and trait self-focused attention on sexual arousal in sexually functional and dysfunctional women. *Behaviour Research and Therapy, 44*(4), 515–532.

Meston, C. M., & Derogatis, L. R. (2002). Validated instruments for assessing female sexual function. *Journal of Sex and Marital Therapy, 28*(Suppl. 1), 155–164.

Moreira, E. D., Jr., Glasser, D., Santos, D. B., & Gingell, C. (2005). Prevalence of sexual problems and related help-seeking behaviors among mature adults in Brazil: Data from the global study of sexual attitudes and behaviors. *Sao Paulo Medical Journal, 123*(5), 234–241.

Najman, J. M., Dunne, M. P., Purdie, D. M., Boyle, F. M., & Coxeter, P. D. (2005). Sexual abuse in childhood and sexual dysfunction in adulthood: An Australian population-based study. *Archives of Sexual Behavior, 34*(5), 517–526.

Nobre, P. J., Pinto-Gouveia, J., & Gomes, F. A. (2006). Prevalence and comorbidity of sexual dysfunctions in a Portuguese clinical sample. *Journal of Sex and Marital Therapy, 32*(2), 173–182.

North American Menopause Society. (2005). The role of testosterone therapy in postmenopausal women: Position statement of The North American Menopause Society. *Menopause, 12*(5), 496–511.

Öberg, K., Fugl-Meyer, A. R., & Fugl-Meyer, K. S. (2004). On categorization and quantification of women's sexual dysfunctions: An epidemiological approach. *International Journal of Impotence Research, 16*(3), 261–269.

Pfaus, J. G., Kippin, T. E., & Coria-Avila, G. (1996). What can animal models tell us about human sexual response? *Annual Review of Sex Research, 14*, 1–63.

Quirk, F. H., Haughie, S., & Symonds, T. (2005). The use of the Sexual Function Questionnaire as a screening tool for women with sexual dysfunction. *Journal of Sexual Medicine, 2*(4), 469–477.

Quirk, F. H., Heiman, J. R., Rosen, R. C., Laan, E., Smith, M. D., & Boolell, M. (2002). Development of a sexual function questionnaire for clinical trials of female sexual dysfunction. *Journal of Womens Health and Gender Based Medicine, 11*(3), 277–289.

Raja, M., & Azzoni, A. (2003). Sexual behavior and sexual problems among patients with severe chronic psychoses. *European Psychiatry, 18*(2), 70–76.

Riley, A., & Riley, E. (2000). Controlled studies on women presenting with sexual drive disorder: I. Endocrine status. *Journal of Sex and Marital Therapy, 26*(3), 269–283.

Rosen, R., Brown, C., Heiman, J., Leiblum, S., Meston, C., Shabsigh, R., et al. (2000). The Female Sexual Function Index (FSFI): A multidimensional self-report instrument for the assessment of female sexual function. *Journal of Sex and Marital Therapy, 26*(2), 191–208.

Rumstein-McKean, O., & Hunsley, J. (2001). Interpersonal and family functioning of female survivors of childhood sexual abuse. *Clinical Psychology Review, 21*(3), 471–490.

Russell, L. (1990). Sex and couples therapy: A method of treatment to enhance physical and emotional intimacy. *Journal of Sex and Marital Therapy, 16*(2), 111–120.

Salemink, E., & van Lankveld, J. J. (2006). The effects of increasing neutral distraction on sexual responding in women with and without sexual problems. *Archives of Sexual Behavior, 35*(2), 179–190.

Sarwer, D. B., & Durlak, J. A. (1996). Childhood sexual abuse as a predictor of adult female sexual dysfunction: A study of couples seeking sex therapy. *Child Abuse and Neglect, 20*(10), 963–972.

Sarwer, D. B., & Durlak, J. A. (1997). A field trial of the effectiveness of behavioral treatment for sexual dysfunctions. *Journal of Sex and Marital Therapy, 23*(2), 87–97.

Schnarch, D. M. (1991). *Constructing the sexual crucible: An integration of sexual and marital therapy.* New York: Norton.

Schover, L. R., & LoPiccolo, J. (1982). Treatment effectiveness for dysfunctions of sexual desire. *Journal of Sex and Marital Therapy, 8*(3), 179–197.

Schreiner-Engel, P., & Schiavi, R. C. (1986). Lifetime psychopathology in individuals with low sexual desire. *Journal of Nervous and Mental Diseases, 174*(11), 646–651.

Schreiner-Engel, P., Schiavi, R. C., White, D., & Ghizzani, A. (1989). Low sexual desire in women: The role of reproductive hormones. *Hormones and Behavior, 23*(2), 221–234.

Segraves, K. B., & Segraves, R. T. (1991). Hypoactive sexual desire disorder: Prevalence and comorbidity in 906 subjects. *Journal of Sex and Marital Therapy, 17*(1), 55–58.

Segraves, R. T., Clayton, A., Croft, H., Wolf, A., & Warnock, J. (2004). Bupropion sustained release for the treatment of hypoactive sexual desire disorder in premenopausal women. *Journal of Clinical Psychopharmacology, 24*(3), 339–342.

Shifren, J. L., Braunstein, G. D., Simon, J. A., Casson, P. R., Buster, J. E., Redmond, G. P., et al. (2000). Transdermal testosterone treatment in women with impaired sexual function after oophorectomy. *New England Journal of Medicine, 343*(10), 682–688.

Sills, T., Wunderlich, G., Pyke, R., Segraves, R. T., Leiblum, S., Clayton, A., et al. (2005). The Sexual Interest and Desire Inventory-Female (SIDI-F): Item response analyses of data from women diagnosed with hypoactive sexual desire disorder. *Journal of Sexual Medicine, 2*(6), 801–818.

Simons, J. S., & Carey, M. P. (2001). Prevalence of sexual dysfunctions: Results from a decade of research. *Archives of Sexual Behavior, 30*(2), 177–219.

Singer, B., & Toates, F. M. (1987). Sexual motivation. *Journal of Sex Research, 23*(4), 481–501.

Spector, I. P., Carey, M. P., & Steinberg, L. (1996). The sexual desire inventory: Development, factor structure, and evidence of reliability. *Journal of Sex and Marital Therapy, 22*(3), 175–190.

Speer, J. J., Hillenberg, B., Sugrue, D. P., Blacker, C., Kresge, C. L., Decker, V. B., et al. (2005). Study of sexual functioning determinants in breast cancer survivors. *Breast Journal, 11*(6), 440–447.

Spiering, M., Everaerd, W., & Janssen, E. (2003). Priming the sexual system: Implicit versus explicit activation. *Journal of Sex Research, 40*(2), 134–145.

Stuart, F. M., Hammond, D. C., & Pett, M. A. (1986). Psychological characteristics of women with inhibited sexual desire. *Journal of Sex and Marital Therapy, 12*(2), 108–115.

Stulhofer, A., Gregurovic, M., Pikic, A., & Galic, I. (2005). Sexual problems of urban women in Croatia: Prevalence and correlates in a community sample. *Croatian Medical Journal, 46*(1), 45–51.

Taylor, J. F., Rosen, R. C., & Leiblum, S. R. (1994). Self-report assessment of female sexual function: Psychometric evaluation of the Brief Index of Sexual Functioning for Women. *Archives of Sexual Behavior, 23*(6), 627–643.

Taylor, M. J., Rudkin, L., & Hawton, K. (2005). Strategies for managing antidepressant-induced sexual dysfunction: Systematic review of randomised controlled trials. *Journal of Affective Disorders, 88*(3), 241–254.

Trudel, G., Boulos, L., & Matte, B. (1993). Dyadic adjustment in couples with hypoactive sexual desire. *Journal of Sex Education and Therapy, 19*(1), 31–36.

Trudel, G., Landry, L., & Larose, Y. (1997). Low sexual desire: The role of anxiety, depression and marital adjustment. *Sexual and Marital Therapy, 12*(1), 95–99.

Trudel, G., Marchand, A., Ravart, M., Aubin, S., Turgeon, L., & Fortier, P. (2001). The effect of a cognitive-behavioral group treatment program on hypoactive sexual desire in women. *Sexual and Relationship Therapy, 16*(2), 145–164.

Tuiten, A., Van Honk, J., Koppeschaar, H., Bernaards, C., Thijssen, J., & Verbaten, R. (2000). Time course of effects of testosterone administration on sexual arousal in women. *Archives of General Psychiatry, 57*(2), 149–153.

Turna, B., Apaydin, E., Semerci, B., Altay, B., Cikili, N., & Nazli, O. (2005). Women with low libido: Correlation of decreased androgen levels with female sexual function index. *International Journal of Impotence Research, 17*(2), 148–153.

van Anders, S. M., & Hampson, E. (2005). Waist-to-hip ratio is positively associated with bioavailable testosterone but negatively associated with sexual desire in healthy premenopausal women. *Psychosomatic Medicine, 67*(2), 246–250.

van den Hout, M. A., & Barlow, D. (2000). Attention, arousal and expectancies in anxiety and sexual disorders. *Journal of Affective Disorders, 61,* 241–256.

van Goozen, S. H. M., Wiegant, V. M., Endert, E., & Helmond, F. A. (1997). Psychoendocrinological assessment of the menstrual cycle: The relationship between hormones, sexuality, and mood. *Archives of Sexual Behavior, 26*(4), 359–382.

Weizman, R., Weizman, A., Levi, J., Gura, V., Zevin, D., Maoz, B., et al. (1983). Sexual dysfunction associated with hyperprolactinemia in males and females undergoing hemodialysis. *Psychosomatic Medicine, 45*(3), 259–269.

Wiegel, M., Meston, C., & Rosen, R. (2005). The Female Sexual Function Index (FSFI): Cross-validation and development of clinical cutoff scores. *Journal of Sex and Marital Therapy, 31*(1), 1–20.

Zimmer, D. (1987). Does marital therapy enhance the effectiveness of treatment for sexual dysfunction? *Journal of Sex and Marital Therapy, 13*(3), 193–209.

Problems with Arousal and Orgasm in Women

Cindy M. Meston, Brooke N. Seal,
and Lisa Dawn Hamilton

7

Chapter

Learning Objectives

In this chapter, we:

- Provide definitions and epidemiological data.
- Describe biological and psychosocial etiological risk factors that contribute to arousal and orgasm disorders in women.
- Provide an extensive assessment that addresses the biopsychosocial nature of arousal and orgasm difficulties.
- Recommend pharmacological and psychological treatments.

Definitions and Epidemiology

Arousal and orgasm are intimately linked as important components in healthy female sexual function. Disorders of arousal and orgasm are quite common, with prevalence rates estimated at 25% of sexually active women reporting difficulties in each domain. The classification of female sexual dysfunction has undergone change over the past 50 years (for a review, see Leiblum, 2006). And while definitions have recently been revised (Sidebar 7.1), they will continue to evolve as new research and data emerge (Leiblum, 2006).

Defining Sexual Arousal Disorders (FSAD) in Women

The *DSM-IV-TR* definition of FSAD is limited to physiological sexual response only.

The following three subtypes of FSAD have been recommended:

1. Subjective sexual arousal disorder.
2. Genital sexual arousal disorder.
3. Combined genital and subjective sexual arousal disorder.

A new arousal disorder, persistent sexual arousal disorder (PSAD), has been suggested.

Sexual Arousal Disorders

The most widely used definition for female sexual arousal disorder (FSAD) within psychological/psychiatric settings is that of the *DSM-IV-TR* (American Psychiatric Association, 2000), which states that FSAD is a persistent or recurrent inability to attain or to maintain until completion of sexual activity an adequate lubrication or swelling response of sexual excitement that causes marked distress or interpersonal difficulty. A panel of 13 experts in female sexual dysfunction selected from five countries convened to review the existing definitions of women's sexual dysfunction. With regard to women's arousal concerns, the committee criticized the *DSM-IV-TR* definition because it was based exclusively on a physiological response. An underlying assumption of this definition is that physiological and subjective experiences of sexual arousal are synchronous in women when, in fact, research indicates they are often desynchronous. In the publication that resulted from this conference, the committee suggested that the following three subtypes of FSAD better describe women's sexual arousal concerns than did existing definitions (Basson et al., 2003):

1. *Subjective sexual arousal disorder*, which refers to the absence of or markedly diminished feelings of sexual arousal (sexual excitement and sexual pleasure) from any type of sexual stimulation. Vaginal lubrication or other signs of physical response still occur.

2. *Genital sexual arousal disorder*, which is often seen in women with autonomic nerve damage and in some estrogen deficient women and refers to absent or impaired genital sexual arousal (e.g., minimal vulval swelling or vaginal lubrication from any type of sexual stimulation and reduced sexual

sensations from caressing genitalia). Subjective sexual excitement still occurs from nongenital sexual stimuli.

3. *Combined genital and subjective arousal disorder,* which is the most common clinical presentation and is usually comorbid with lack of sexual interest.

The committee also recommended a provisional definition of a new disorder, persistent sexual arousal disorder (PSAD), which includes a spontaneous, intrusive, and unwanted genital arousal (e.g., tingling, throbbing, pulsating) in the absence of sexual interest and desire. Awareness of subjective arousal is typically but not invariably unpleasant, and the arousal is unrelieved by orgasm and persists for hours or days (Basson et al., 2003; Leiblum, Brown, Wan, & Rawlinson, 2005). This disorder was previously considered extremely rare, but now is increasingly reported by clinicians (Basson, Leiblum, et al., 2004).

Epidemiological research indicates that between 8% to 15% of all women and 21% to 31% of sexually active women experience lubrication difficulties (for a review, see Lewis et al., 2004). Approximately 21% of these women report distress about their sexuality (Bancroft, Loftus, & Long, 2003) and 44% would like to receive help for their disorder (Dunn, Croft, & Hackett, 1998). To date, prevalence rates of PSAD have not been established.

Female Orgasmic Disorder

Female orgasmic disorder (FOD) is defined in the *DSM-IV-TR* as follows: "persistent or recurrent delay in, or absence of, orgasm following a normal sexual excitement phase" (American Psychiatric Association, 2000, p. 549). The diagnosis of FOD is made only when there is no dysfunction in the preceding phases of sexual response; so, women who experience difficulties in the excitement phase of sexual response would not be diagnosed with FOD (see Sidebar 7.2). "Women exhibit wide variability in the type or intensity of stimulation that triggers orgasm. The diagnosis of FOD should be based on the clinician's judgment that the woman's orgasmic capacity is less than would be reasonable for her age, sexual experience, and the adequacy of sexual stimulation she receives" (American Psychiatric Association, 2000, p. 549). According to the *DSM-IV-TR* criteria, in order to be diagnosed with FOD, the patient must have "marked distress or interpersonal difficulty" as a result of the orgasmic difficulties. FOD diagnoses should specify the nature of the onset (lifelong versus acquired), the context in which the problem occurs (generalized versus specific), and the associated etiological factors (psychological or combined). Lifelong FOD is often referred to in the literature as primary anorgasmia and acquired FOD as secondary anorgasmia. A woman who can achieve orgasm through masturbation or through manual stimulation with a partner but not from intercourse alone would not meet American Psychiatric Association criteria for a diagnosis of FOD.

SIDEBAR 7.2

Defining Female Orgasmic Disorder (FOD)

FOD is only diagnosed when all preceding phases of sexual response are functional and when the woman is distressed by the lack of orgasm.

Primary anorgasmia is diagnosed in women who have never had an orgasm, while secondary anorgasmia is acquired after previously being orgasmic.

The definition of orgasm itself has proven difficult in part because the neural changes that underlie it are not well understood (Meston, Hull, Levin, & Sipski, 2004). An article cataloging definitions of orgasm included more than 25 comprehensive definitions written by different authors (Mah & Binik, 2001). The following definition of female orgasm was derived by the committee on female orgasm, presented at the International Consultation on Urological Diseases in Official Relationship with the World Health Organization (WHO), Paris, 2003:

> *An orgasm in the human female is a variable, transient peak sensation of intense pleasure, creating an altered state of consciousness, usually accompanied by involuntary, rhythmic contractions of the pelvic, striated circumvaginal musculature often with concomitant uterine and anal contractions and myotonia that resolves the sexually induced vasocongestion (sometimes only partially), usually with an induction of well-being and contentment. (Meston et al., 2004, p. 785)*

According to the National Social and Health Life Survey (NSHLS), orgasm difficulties are the second most frequently reported sexual problems for women (Laumann, Gagnon, Michael, & Michaels, 1994). The women who completed the NSHLS were a random sample of 1,749 American women, and 24% reported orgasm difficulties over the past year. Further studies of healthy women recruited in clinic settings reported similar percentages of women with orgasmic difficulties or anorgasmia (e.g., Read, King, & Watson, 1997).

Etiologic Factors

Biological factors such as an endocrine deficiency or other organic problems may be the sole cause of the development of FSAD. More often, biological factors contributing to FSAD arise in conjunction with or as a result of psychological factors, and therefore it is nearly impossible to separate conditions due to organic causes from those due to psychological causes (Leiblum, 2006). To date, etiological explanations for PSAD have not been well established. FOD is usually psychologically based.

For expediency, biological factors have been categorized into endocrine, autonomic nervous system, and medical/cardiovascular. Endocrine factors include sex steroids, peptide hormones, and general endocrine conditions. Autonomic factors refer to the relative contributions of the sympathetic and parasympathetic nervous systems. Medical and cardiovascular factors include those that are endocrine-related, cardiovascular, mobility/physical, and drug related. Table 7.1 lists organic factors that affect sexual arousal in women.

Endocrine Factors

Sex Steroids

It is difficult to separate the effects of the various sex steroids (estrogens, androgens, and progestins) on female sexual arousal and orgasm because they are all structurally related and derived from one another. However, researchers have been able to make edu-

Table 7.1   Organic Factors Related to Sexual Arousal in Women

Estrogens are critical for vaginal functioning; postmenopausal women experience the most difficulties due to reduced estrogen.

Androgens are believed to be related to arousal and orgasm, but the nature of the relationship is still unclear.

PDE-5 Inhibitors increase genital arousal in women, but not subjective arousal.

An optimal level of sympathetic nervous system arousal appears necessary for sexual arousal in women.

Medical factors that interfere with arousal and orgasm include endocrine and cardiovascular problems and use of antidepressants and antipsychotics.

Aside from using antidepressants, women with Persistent Sexual Arousal Disorder (PSAD) report low levels of medical problems.

cated assumptions about which hormones are active for specific purposes. Estrogens in the peripheral nervous system are critical for the maintenance of vaginal tissue function and structure (Traish & Kim, 2006), and estrogen deficiency has been linked to various vaginal problems, including reduced or delayed lubrication, reduced vaginal blood flow, and increased dyspareunia (e.g., Sarrel, 2000). Estrogens are not related to the ability to experience orgasm, as demonstrated through studies of estrogen treatment on postmenopausal and oophorectomized women (for a review, see Meston et al., 2004).

Most research on the effects of estrogen on sexual function has been done in women who are postmenopausal or who have undergone ovarian removal (oophorectomy). In postmenopausal women, the reduction in estrogen levels occurring when the menstrual cycle ends is associated with increased pH in the vagina, a reduction or delayed onset of lubrication in response to sexual stimulation, and structural changes to the vagina and vulva. These structural changes can include thinning and reduction of elasticity of the vaginal wall, changes to the vaginal epithelium, and loss of collagen in the vulva (Bachmann, Ebert, & Burd, 1999). In turn, these changes can lead to arousal difficulties, due to a reduction in tissue sensitivity and impaired vaginal lubrication. In a study of postmenopausal women, Sarrel (1990) found that women treated with estradiol experienced fewer problems with vaginal dryness and pain than counterparts with less estradiol. Furthermore, oophorectomized and postmenopausal women who received estrogen replacement therapy showed increased lubrication, increased vulvar and vaginal blood flow, decreased pain with intercourse, and a reduction in vaginal pH (e.g., Patel, Brown, & Bachmann, 2006).

In premenopausal women, androgens are secreted from both the adrenal glands and the ovaries. Dehydroepiandrosterone (DHEA) and androstenedione are precursors to testosterone, and all three hormones are involved in desire and motivation for sexual activity. Some speculate that androgens are also involved in female sexual arousal and orgasm, although the mechanisms are not well understood (Traish, Kim, Min, Munarriz, & Goldstein, 2002). One study found a positive correlation between testosterone and genital arousal over the menstrual cycle in healthy, premenopausal women (Schreiner-Engel, Schiavi, Smith, & White, 1981), and more directly, administration of testosterone to premenopausal women increases genital arousal (Tuiten et al., 2002). However, androgens also affect sexual arousal indirectly because they moderate mood, energy, sexual desire, and overall well-being (Traish & Kim, 2006).

Postmenopausal women with low levels of testosterone and DHEA tend to have difficulties with orgasm (Guay & Davis, 2002).

Decreased testosterone has been anecdotally related to a reduction in intensity of orgasm, but this information is based on a population of patients taking anti-epilepsy drugs (S. Duncan, Blacklaw, Beastall, & Brodie, 1997), and on postmenopausal women (Guay & Sparks, 2006). As women age, even before menopause, levels of testosterone, DHEA, and DHEA-S decline significantly and reliably (e.g., Labrie, Belanger, Cusan, Gomez, & Candas, 1997; Zumoff, Strain, Miller, & Rosner, 1995). To date, no studies have shown a definitive relationship between the decline in these hormones and changes in sexual arousal or orgasm (Guay et al., 2004). Of the few studies directly assessing the effect of DHEA on sexual arousal, administration of exogenous DHEA resulted in increased genital arousal in postmenopausal women (Hackbert & Heiman, 2002) but had no influence on genital or subjective arousal in premenopausal women (Meston & Heiman, 2002).

Clinically assessed androgen insufficiency in pre- and postmenopausal women is associated with general difficulties in sexual functioning, including sexual arousal. Sexual symptoms of androgen insufficiency include reductions in desire and motivation for sexual activity, sexual arousability, vaginal lubrication, and orgasmic capabilities (Guay & Davis, 2002). The etiology of androgen insufficiency is often rooted in a specific medical problem or its treatment, such as cancer treatments, oophorectomy, natural menopause, adrenal problems, hypopituitarism, Addison's disease, and use of estrogen, progesterone, antiandrogens, or corticosteroids (Bachmann et al., 2002).

Oxytocin

Research on animals has shown a strong relationship between oxytocin and muscle contractions similar to those in human orgasm. In humans, this link is less certain due to difficulties measuring oxytocin during sexual activity, or in the central nervous system given that central oxytocin does not cross the blood brain barrier. Measured in blood plasma, oxytocin has been positively correlated with the intensity of smooth muscle contractions during orgasm (Anderson-Hunt & Dennerstein, 1995) and, as it changes across the menstrual cycle, with vaginal lubrication (Salonia et al., 2005). To our knowledge, no studies have examined the effects of oxytocin deficiency on arousal or orgasmic ability in women.

General Endocrine Factors

Although the influence of steroid hormones on sexual arousal and orgasm is not fully understood in women, an appropriate balance of androgens, estrogens, and progestins appears critical (for a review, see Meston et al., 2004). Gonadal steroid hormones are believed to increase sensitivity and arousability to sexual stimuli, acting in the brain to increase attention to sexually related incentives, emotions, and potential rewards (Guay & Davis, 2002) and on vaginal tissues to make genital arousal and orgasm possible (Scepkowski, Georgescu, & Pfaus, 2006). Hormones control much of the female arousal response both directly and through control of various neurotransmitters, which influence arousal components (Basson, Weijmar Shultz, et al., 2004). Although alteration in hormone balance may lead to problems in arousal and orgasm, they rarely are the cause of such problems in premenopausal women (Traish & Kim, 2006).

Nitric Oxide

Nitric oxide, released from the autonomic nervous system into the genital area, plays an important role in vaginal vasocongestion. In animals, the administration of a phosphodiesterase type 5 (PDE-5) inhibitor (e.g., sildenafil), which indirectly increases nitric oxide in vaginal tissues, greatly enhances clitoral and vaginal blood flow resulting from stimulation of the pelvic nerve (e.g., Angulo, Cuevas, Cuevas, Bischoff, & Saenz de Tejada, 2003). Several placebo controlled studies of sildenafil and other nitric oxide agonists have been conducted on women with and without arousal problems. Self-report studies have shown improvement in measures of arousal and orgasm in premenopausal women with FSAD (Caruso, Intelisano, Lupo, & Agnello, 2001) and increased arousal and genital sensation in postmenopausal women with FSAD (J. R. Berman, Berman, Toler, Gill, & Haughie, 2003). Studies using physiological measures of arousal have found increased vaginal pulse amplitude (VPA, a measure of genital arousal) in women with FSAD who received the nitric oxide precursor, L-arginine, combined with yohimbine (Meston & Worcel, 2002) and in healthy premenopausal women who received sildenafil (Laan et al., 2002). However, in one study of postmenopausal women with genital arousal disorder, only those women with the most severely reduced levels of vaginal vasocongestion responded to treatment with a PDE-5 inhibitor (Basson & Brotto, 2003). Although there appear to be improvements in physiological arousal in response to nitric oxide agonists, none of the studies has shown a significant improvement in women's subjective sexual arousal.

Autonomic Nervous System

Sympathetic and parasympathetic nervous systems (SNS and PNS) each play an important role in genital arousal and orgasm in women, but the relationship between the two systems is not well understood. Norepinephrine (NE) is the key neurotransmitter involved in SNS communication, and when measured after exposure to a sexually arousing film, plasma NE is higher than pre-film levels (Exton et al., 2000). Acetylcholine is the main neurotransmitter involved in PNS (cholinergic) communication, but because it is also involved in SNS communication, it is difficult to isolate the contribution of the PNS in genital arousal and orgasm. However, both adrenergic (NE) and cholinergic (Ach) systems are important contributors to normal arousal and orgasm.

The SNS contribution to genital arousal has been demonstrated in animal models, in women with spinal cord injuries (SCI), and in humans through drug manipulations and exercise-induced activation of the SNS. In animal models, stimulation of both PNS fibers and SNS fibers triggers contractions in uterine and cervical smooth muscle (Kim, Min, Huang, Goldstein, & Traish, 2002; Sato, Hotta, Nakayama, & Suzuki, 1996). However, stimulation of the pelvic nerve (part of the PNS) causes increased uterine blood flow, while stimulation of the hypogastric nerve (SNS) causes decreased uterine blood flow (Sato et al., 1996). Women with spinal cord injuries in areas that give rise to efferent (outgoing) SNS fibers provide excellent models for studying the contributions of the SNS to sexual arousal. Specifically, women with injuries between T10 and T12 levels in the spinal cord, an area of sympathetic nerves that project to the genital region, show a lack of lubrication in reflex and psychogenic arousal conditions (Berard, 1989).

Evidence for the role of SNS involvement in genital arousal has also been demonstrated through laboratory manipulations designed to increase SNS activity. Anxiety-evoking films, thought to increase SNS activity, increase vaginal blood volume (VBV) during subsequent erotic films in functional and dysfunctional women (e.g., Palace & Gorzalka, 1990). But more recent research has shown a curvilinear relationship between acute anxiety and VBV response, with the optimal arousal response occurring at a moderate level of anxiety (Bradford & Meston, 2006).

Similarly, several studies on the effects of exercise (e.g., Meston & Gorzalka, 1995, 1996) and ephedrine (Meston & Heiman, 1998) on sexual arousal support the notion of an optimal level of SNS arousal necessary for adequate genital arousal. Interference with normal SNS activity, through stress for example, can influence a woman's ability to become aroused. In women with orgasm disorders, this optimal level of SNS arousal may be disrupted; for example, women with orgasm difficulties respond to increased SNS activity with a reduction in physiological sexual response (Meston & Gorzalka, 1996).

Medical and Cardiovascular Factors

Endocrine-Related

Many medical treatments and/or conditions that interfere with endocrine function can alter the female sexual arousal and orgasm. Hyperprolactinemia, a condition in which abnormally high amounts of prolactin are secreted, interferes with sexual arousal and orgasm; subjective measures of sexual functioning as measured by the Female Sexual Functioning Index (FSFI; Rosen et al., 2000) are lower in women with hyperprolactinemia compared to control women, and FSFI arousal and orgasm domain scores are negatively correlated with prolactin levels (Kadioglu et al., 2005). High levels of prolactin inhibit gonadotropin releasing hormone (GnRH; Sauder, Frager, Case, Kelch, & Marshall, 1984) that, in turn, inhibits hormone release further down the hypothalamic-pituitary-gonadal (HPG) axis.

Other endocrine-related disorders may also affect women's sexual response. Women with diabetes mellitus show various sexual problems, including sexual arousal dysfunction, reduced vaginal lubrication, and inability to reach orgasm (Salonia, Briganti, Rigatti, & Montorsi, 2006). The mechanisms by which the insulin abnormalities associated with diabetes affect the rest of the endocrine system are not known. Bilateral oopherectomy, which results in a reduction of estrogen and testosterone secretion, also causes problems with arousal through mechanisms discussed in the previous section on endocrine factors. Finally, women who have undergone hysterectomy often have long-term difficulties attaining orgasm and vaginal lubrication (Jensen et al., 2004).

Cardiovascular Disease

A connection between coronary artery disease and erectile dysfunction has been well established in men (for a review, see Russell, Khandheria, & Nehra, 2004), but less is known about the effects of cardiovascular disease on women's sexual functioning. One comprehensive study showed that women with coronary artery disease reported clinically significant problems with arousal, lubrication, and orgasm compared to healthy controls (Salonia, Briganti, & Montorsi, 2002 as cited in Salonia et al., 2006). Women with hypertension have a general impairment of physiological response and, because normal blood flow to the genitals is restricted, problems in attaining adequate genital arousal. Hypertensive women have been shown to have reduced lubrication, reduced frequency of orgasms, and greater difficulty attaining orgasm (L. E. Duncan et al., 2001). Regarding women with PSAD, an Internet survey reported that medical problems (diabetes, stroke, hypothyroidism, seizure disorders, myocardial infarctions, angina pectoris) occurred in less than 10% of women believing they had PSAD (Leiblum et al., 2005).

Physical/Mobility Related

Any ailment that impinges on a patient's ability to move or to feel sensation can interfere with sexual arousal. Both multiple sclerosis (MS) and spinal cord injuries (SCI) have been linked to difficulties in attaining orgasm, although both arousal and orgasm are possible in these women (e.g., Salonia et al., 2006; Sipski, Alexander, &

Rosen, 1995b). SCI and control women respond differently to erotic visual stimuli. Control women show both increased genital and subjective arousal to erotic visual stimuli whereas women with SCI show only increased subjective arousal. Only when tactile clitoral stimulation is applied do SCI women respond with an increase in genital arousal. Tactile stimulation alone (without erotic visual stimuli) in women with SCI does not increase subjective sexual arousal because the neurological pathway mediating this response via the brain is interrupted by the injury (Sipski, Alexander, & Rosen, 1995a). Women with SCI at T6 and below have been able to achieve orgasm 52% of the time in a laboratory study, compared to 100% of healthy controls (Sipski et al., 1995b). Women with SCI in the sacral region—thus interfering with the sacral reflex arc—show the most difficulty attaining orgasm (Sipski, Alexander, & Rosen, 2001). Data from human and animal studies have led to the suggestion that the vagus nerve connection between the cervix of the uterus and the brain is key in maintaining SCI patient's ability to experience orgasm (Whipple, Gerdes, & Komisaruk, 1996).

Drug-Related

Some antidepressants, especially ones that increase serotonin such as the SSRIs, have an inhibitory influence on libido and orgasmic functioning (Rosen, Lane, & Menza, 1999). Patients using the antidepressants buproprion, moclobemide, and nefazodone are less likely to report orgasm difficulties than patients using SSRIs. The latter increases levels of norepinephrine and serotonin, while the former two increase the levels of NE and dopamine (DA), in addition to serotonin. The increase in NE and DA seems to reduce the interference in arousal and orgasm caused by increased serotonin (Meston et al., 2004). Consistent with this, mirtazapine, an SSRI with noradrenergic effects, has also been shown to reduce the orgasmic difficulties experienced by depressed patients (Boyarsky, Haque, Rouleau, & Hirschfeld, 1999). Of the SSRIs, paroxetine has the strongest inhibiting effect on orgasm (Bobes et al., 2002; Montejo-Gonzalez et al., 1997), possibly due to its stronger effect on the serotonin transporter and lack of effect on the dopamine transporter (Rosen et al., 1999). In an Internet survey of women who met at least one criterion for PSAD, 48% of respondents answered the question about "use of antidepressants," and all of these respondents answered affirmatively regarding their use (Leiblum et al., 2005).

Several antipsychotic drugs have also been shown to inhibit or delay orgasm in women. Trifluoperazine, fluphenazine, and thiorizdazine interfere with orgasm (Ghadirian, Choinard, & Annable, 1982; Shen & Sata, 1990) whereas haloperidol and clozapine do not (Hummer et al., 1999). Antipsychotics may cause orgasmic difficulties either directly by blocking dopamine receptors or indirectly by increasing prolactin levels or causing sedation (Meston et al., 2004). Compared with controls, women taking anti-epileptic or antiseizure drugs report less satisfying orgasms, but the mechanism through which the benzodiazepines and other anti-seizure medications affect orgasmic experience is not known.

Psychological Factors, Sexual Arousal, and Orgasm

Psychological factors also play an important role in women's sexual arousal and orgasm. Among these broadly classified factors are relationship issues, cognitive and affective factors, and cultural and societal factors.

Relationship Issues

Higher orgasm frequency and level of arousal have been linked to marital satisfaction (Hurlbert, Apt, Hurlbert, & Pierce, 2000), while problems with arousal and orgasm have been linked to marital difficulties and relationship dissatisfaction (e.g., Laumann, Paik, & Rosen, 1999). Couples reporting sexual difficulties, compared to nonclinical control couples, have less satisfaction in their relationships (e.g., Chesney, Blakeney, Cole, & Chan, 1981), an increased number of disagreements (Chesney et al., 1981), more communication and conflict resolution problems (e.g., Chesney et al., 1981; Ernst, Földényi, & Angst, 1993), and more sexual communication problems (e.g., Chesney et al., 1981), including discomfort discussing sexual activities related to their particular sexual difficulty (Kelly, Strassberg, & Kircher, 1990). Within their relationship interactions, they also display less playfulness and spontaneity (Metz & Lutz, 1990), less closeness, intimacy, and feelings of mutual love, and more aversive feelings and thoughts regarding their interactions (Birnbaum, Glaubman, & Mikulincer, 2001). Warmth, caring, and affection within the relationship have also been linked to increased sexual arousal (Persky et al., 1982), while conflict and hostility have been linked to lower orgasmic responses (Swieczkowski & Walker, 1978). However, overall sexual satisfaction for women is determined more by closeness with one's partner than by the number of orgasms or sexual arousal (Hurlbert, Apt, & Rabehl, 1993).

Cognitive and Affective Factors

Depression and Anxiety

There is a strong relationship between depression and impaired sexual arousal and orgasm (e.g., Kennedy, Dickens, Eisfeld, & Bagby, 1999; Leiblum et al., 2005). High levels of anxiety have also been reported among sexually dysfunctional women (see Norton & Jehu, 1984 for a review), and high levels of sexual difficulties have been reported among women with anxiety disorders (e.g., Bodinger et al., 2002). The specific type of anxiety disorder may play an important role; for instance, women with obsessive-compulsive disorder have more difficulties with orgasm than women with generalized anxiety disorder (Aksaray, Yelken, Kaptanoglu, Oflu, & Ozaltin, 2001).

Findings on anxiety and sexual response in laboratory studies show mixed results. Anxiety-inducing stimuli prior to erotic visual stimulation have been shown to increase *physiological* sexual response in sexually functional women (e.g., Laan, Everaerd, van Aanhold, & Rebel, 1993) and dysfunctional women (e.g., Palace & Gorzalka, 1992), but such stimuli may increase, decrease, or not affect *subjective* sexual arousal (for a review, see Meston & Bradford, in press). The variable findings regarding the effects of anxiety-inducing stimuli on subjective arousal may be attributable to different definitions of anxiety across studies. State anxiety (an acute emotional response that can be easily manipulated), but not trait anxiety (a relatively stable measure that reflects one's dispositional tendency to experience state anxiety), is negatively linked to subjective sexual arousal in response to erotic stimuli (Bradford & Meston, 2006). In terms of genital arousal, as noted earlier, the relationship between state anxiety and physiological sexual arousal is curvilinear, such that moderate levels of state anxiety facilitated, and high levels of state anxiety impaired, vaginal arousal.

Based on an Internet survey of women who met at least one criterion for PSAD, stress and anxiety were the most common triggers of PSAD symptoms, reported by approximately 46% and 34% of women, respectively. Furthermore, approximately 62% of all women described themselves as worriers, 68% reported that they "carried a lot of stress in their body," 31% reported having anxiety or panic attacks, and 22% reported having obsessive thoughts or behaviors (Leiblum et al., 2005).

Cognitive Distraction and Self-Focused Attention
Barlow's model of sexual functioning implicates cognitive interference in the cause and maintenance of sexual difficulties through a shift of attention from erotic cues to internal negative self-evaluative cues (Barlow, 1986). Consistent with this model are findings showing that cognitive distraction can impair the sexual response in women (e.g., Koukounas & McCabe, 1997), as well as studies linking "trait private self-consciousness" (i.e., tendency to focus on internal bodily sensations) with enhanced sexual functioning (Meston, 2006) and "state self-focused attention" (i.e., instructed focus on oneself) to impaired physiological sexual arousal response in sexually functional (Meston, 2006)

women. However, in response to erotic stimuli among sexually dysfunctional women who were made to self-focus on their appearance, subjective sexual response was found to be unchanged (Meston, 2006) or enhanced (Seal & Meston, 2007), suggesting that the way a woman feels about her body and body image may be important factors in understanding sexual arousal (e.g., Wiederman, 2000).

Women experience a variety of concerns during sexual activity, including worries about pleasing their partner, their ability to reach orgasm, becoming pregnant, contracting sexually transmitted infections, and losing their partner because of sexual problems. Women who experience orgasmic disorder have particularly strong anxieties related to intercourse (Birnbaum, 2003) and tend to blame themselves rather then external factors for their difficulty (Loos, Bridges, & Critelli, 1987).

Personality Characteristics

Women with sexual dysfunctions have higher extraversion (Anderson & Cyranowski, 1994) and neuroticism scores (e.g., Costa, Fagan, Piedmont, Ponticas, & Wise, 1992; Hartmann, Keiser, Ruffer-Hesse, & Kloth, 2002). Neuroticism has also been linked to lower sexual satisfaction among women (Costa et al., 1992) and to poorer sexual adjustment among college-aged women (Meston, Trapnell, & Gorzalka, 1993). Women diagnosed with mixed sexual difficulties (desire, arousal, and orgasm) are often characterized by lower extraversion and lower openness to experience than women without sexual difficulties (Hartman et al., 2002). Compared to women without a personality disorder, women diagnosed with histrionic personality disorder exhibit more orgasmic dysfunction, despite having higher sexual esteem (Apt & Hurlbert, 1994). In contrast, general openness and sensation seeking have been linked to increased sexual functioning and arousability, respectively (Apt & Hurlbert, 1992; Costa et al., 1992).

Sexual Abuse

Sexual abuse in childhood and/or adulthood can result in negative affect during physiological arousal (L. A. Berman, Berman, Bruck, Pawar, & Goldstein, 2001) and reduced feelings during sexual activity (Herman & Hirschman, 1977). As noted earlier, in sexually healthy women, physiological sexual arousal is enhanced with SNS activation (via exercise; Meston & Gorzalka, 1995). In contrast, in women with a history of childhood sexual abuse, physiological arousal is not enhanced with SNS activation and, in fact, may be impaired (Rellini & Meston, 2006). This difference may reflect disruptions in endocrine function—in particular the hypothalamus-pituitary-adrenal axis—known to exist in women with a history of childhood sexual abuse and comorbid posttraumatic stress disorder (Rellini & Meston, 2006). Sexual arousal difficulties following sexual abuse may also be related to a misinterpretation of physical sensations, such as heart rate and lubrication, with women associating these sensations during sexual activity with similar negative traumatic responses experienced during the early sexual abuse experience (Rellini, 2006).

Cultural and Societal Factors

Research suggests cultural differences in sexual functioning (e.g., Brotto, Chik, Ryder, Gorzalka, & Seal, 2005), sexual satisfaction (e.g., Fugl-Meyer & Fugl-Meyer, 1999), knowledge about and attitudes toward sexuality (e.g., Meston, Trapnell, & Gorzalka, 1996), and sexual experiences such as age of first intercourse and rates of masturbation (e.g., Tang, Lai, & Chung, 1997). In a study of over 3,000 women from a variety of ethnic groups, Cain et al. (2003) found less frequent physical pleasure reported by Hispanic, Chinese, and Japanese women than Caucasian women, and less frequent sexual arousal reported among all ethnic groups, including African American women, than among Caucasian women.

Aging

An abundance of research shows a decline in normal female sexual functioning with age, including decreased frequency of orgasm (e.g., Adams & Turner, 1985) and impaired sexual arousal (e.g., Cain et al., 2003). While this decline may be partly related to menopause, pre- and peri-menopausal women aged 42 to 52 years do not differ in their experience of physical pleasure and arousal (Cain et al., 2003), suggesting that other factors are involved, such as an age-related decrease in sexual communication (Deeks & McCabe, 2001) and in the relative importance of sex (e.g., Bergstrom-Walan & Neilsen, 1990).

In summary, the following points regarding the role of psychological factors in sexual arousal and orgasm in women can be made:

- Difficulties with orgasm and/or arousal have been linked to sexual and nonsexual difficulties within the relationship.
- A strong relationship exists between depression and impaired sexual arousal and/or orgasm.
- State, but not trait, anxiety may be linked to decreased subjective sexual arousal.
- Based on findings from an Internet survey, stress and anxiety are reported by a large portion of women experiencing PSAD symptoms.
- There is a curvilinear relationship between state anxiety and physiological sexual arousal, such that moderate levels of

state anxiety facilitate arousal the most, and high levels impair arousal.

- Factors that cause cognitive distraction during sexual activity, such as body image concerns, may play a role in the cause and maintenance of sexual difficulties.

- Personality factors may be linked to sexual response (neuroticism, lower extraversion, and lower openness are linked to decreased sexual functioning).

- Sexual abuse can result in orgasm and arousal difficulties and may be related to misinterpretation of the physical sensations during sexual activity.

- Research shows substantial cultural differences across sexuality measures.

- Age-related decline in sexual arousal and frequency of orgasm in women may be partially attributable to factors such as menopause and changes in sexual communication.

Assessment

The presenting problem of the woman should first be ascertained in a clinic interview. She should be asked to describe her difficulty in her own words. To provide a more comprehensive structured assessment, the questions in Table 7.2, which expand on Basson, Weijmar Shultz, et al. (2004), Brandenburg and Schwenkhagen (2006), and Perelman (2006), may be used.

Self-reported information from the woman collected through interviews, questionnaires, and sexual behavior logs are suitable methods to assess and monitor changes in female sexual dysfunction (Rosen, 2002). Techniques may include logs of objective ratings of sexual response, such as orgasm and lubrication, and questionnaires assessing sexual functioning (e.g., The Female Sexual Function Index [FSFI]: Rosen et al., 2000; The Brief Index of Sexual Functioning for Women [BISF-W]: Taylor, Rosen, & Leiblum, 1994), sexual satisfaction (e.g., The Sexual Satisfaction Scale [SSS-W]: Meston & Trapnell, 2005), and sexual beliefs (e.g., The Derogatis Interview for Sexual Functioning, Sexual Beliefs Subscale: Derogatis, 1997). Some of these reliably differentiate women with FSAD, FOD, and no dysfunction (e.g., SSS-W: Meston & Trapnell, 2005; FSFI: Meston, 2003) and are sensitive to change over time (e.g., BISF-W: Shifren et al., 2000).

As outlined in Table 7.3, the practitioner should also assess relationship and sexual history, psychosocial history, and medical history. Questionnaires measuring relationship functioning include:

Table 7.2   **Assessing the Presenting Problem**

Criteria	Questions
Degree of distress	What do these symptoms mean for her?
	What has her reaction been?
Onset of problem	Has the problem been lifelong or was it acquired?
	If acquired:
	–What is her belief about the causes of the change? (e.g., major life stresses, change in medication use)
	–What has the progression been since the onset?
Context of problem	Is the problem situational or generalized?
	How has it been with other partners?
	How is it when she is alone?
	Does she experience this difficulty all the time or only under specific circumstances?
Frequency	Out of 10 times engaging in intercourse, how often does she experience this difficulty?
	How has this changed over time?
Other sexual problems	Are there any other sexual problems present?
	Does her partner have sexual dysfunction?
Nonsexual factors	What are the cognitive and emotional factors involved?
	What are the woman's and her partner's responses to her sexual difficulty?
	What does the partner think the cause of the problem is?
Prior treatment	Have any prior treatments been attempted?
	If yes, what was the outcome?
Arousal questions	Mental excitement—How is it when she is alone (e.g., reading erotica) versus when she is stimulating her partner versus when her partner stimulates her?
	Does she experience genital sensations (e.g., tingling, swelling, pulsing) and to what degree?
	Is her genital lubrication completely absent, inadequate, or does it disappear?
Orgasm questions	Is orgasm absent, delayed, or of reduced intensity?
	What is her frequency of masturbation?
	How often does she experience sexual fantasy?

Table 7.3   **Assessment of Patient History**

Sexual and Relationship History	
Sexual history	Ask participant to describe her first sexual experiences.
	What was her family's attitude toward sex?
	Is there any history of sexual violence or trauma?
Relationships	What is the nature and duration of current and past relationships (sexual and in general)?
Psychosocial History	
Children	Does the woman have children?
	If yes, how many and what are their ages?
Work/finance	How does the woman feel about her job if she has one?
	Are there any stresses surrounding her finances?
Other stressors	Are there any other stressors or factors that would influence her sexual functioning?
Mental health	Measurements of mental health in the patient and her partner may be helpful (e.g., The Beck Depression Inventory: Beck, Ward, Mendelson, Mock, & Erbaugh, 1961).
	What religious, societal, family of origin, cultural values, beliefs, or restrictions may be affecting sexual functioning?
Medical History (Information Needed about Historical and Current Medical Factors)	
Illness	Cervical or breast cancer
	Diabetes
	Prolactinemia
	Multiple Sclerosis
	Spinal cord injury
	Brain injury
	Cardiovascular disease
Medications and treatments	Antidepressants
	Psychotropic drugs
	Anti-epileptics
	Radiation
	Chemotherapy
	Antihypertensives
Emotional factors	Depression
	Anxiety and stress
	Childhood sexual abuse

The Dyadic Adjustment Scale (Spanier, 1976), The Relationship Beliefs Scale (Fletcher & Kininmonth, 1992), and the Locke Wallace Marital Adjustment Scale (Locke & Wallace, 1959).

A full physical exam is also recommended for all complaints of sexual function (for details, see Stewart, 2006). In addition to ruling out or identifying various medical factors, the exam serves to educate women about their anatomy, and what is normal or problematic.

Pelvic Exam

A pelvic exam is recommended for women who have been diagnosed with FSAD or FOD. However, unless the woman has specifically complained of pain during sexual arousal or intercourse or is post menopausal, usually no organic problems are associated with these sexual disorders. For women with a subjective arousal disorder or FOD, a pelvic exam can help educate them about their genitals, and information discounting the existence of organic problems may help alleviate concerns for many patients (Stewart, 2006). For women with genital arousal disorder, the exam may be able to reveal an estrogen deficiency, pH imbalance, or structural or organic problem such as vaginal atrophy (e.g., Patel et al., 2006).

Genital Arousal

Vaginal blood volume (VBV), genital engorgement, genital lubrication, and sexual sensations such as throbbing and tingling are important components of physical sexual arousal in women. Women with subjective sexual arousal disorder have VBV and vaginal pulse amplitude (VPA) responses similar to controls; so, assessment of these measures would not be useful for diagnosing subjective FSAD as part of a routine exam. For women who have genital arousal disorder, where there is a possibility of a vascular genital problem, assessment of genital response could be informative. Genital arousal is most commonly assessed in research studies using vaginal photoplethysmography to determine VPA and, less commonly, VBV. This methodology for assessing genital response is not as effective for clinical assessment, however, because of the wide variance in VPA response among women—making it difficult to establish a "normal response"—and because vaginal photoplethysmography is not readily available outside of research settings. On the other hand, the use of VPA measurements can be useful for within-person assessment, for example, before and after treatment or to gauge changes in response to various components of sexual stimuli (Prause & Janssen, 2006). Genital arousal can also be measured through fMRI of the genital area. Although

MRI machines are now more readily available, the high cost remains an obstacle (Maravilla, 2006). Doppler ultrasound is a relatively new tool for assessing VBV. This technology is useful because it is not affected by movement, so participants can masturbate during the procedure, allowing examination of orgasmic response in addition to arousal (Garcia Nader, Maitland, Munarriz, & Goldstein, 2006).

Hormone Assays

If a hormonal problem is suspected, practitioners can request assays for prolactin, total testosterone, free testosterone, sex hormone binding globulin (SHBG), DHEA, estrogens, and cortisol to ensure that all levels are within a reasonable range. Androgens should be measured during peak times in the morning on days 8 to 18 of the menstrual cycle. A limiting factor in diagnosis is a lack of norms for androgen levels in women, mainly due to a lack of sensitivity of most assays at the low end of the scale.

Treatment

General Psychological Treatments

Education, communication training, and cognitive behavioral techniques such as sensate focus and systematic desensitization have been successful in treating female sexual dysfunctions (see Sidebar 7.3). Sensate focus, introduced by Masters and Johnson in the 1970s, is a cognitive behavioral technique in which couples learn to focus on the pleasurable sensations brought about by touching, and to decrease the focus on goal directed sex (e.g., orgasm). Couples are first instructed to explore their partner's nonsexual body regions without the potential for sexual activity, gradually moving to the next phase in which the female guides her partner in genital stimulation and sexual positions that enhance her arousal. Intercourse is incorporated only in the final stages when both partners feel comfortable. The effectiveness of sensate focus by itself on sexual dysfunction has not been examined in randomized, controlled research. Results from studies using sensate focus as well as treatment techniques such as increasing sexual skills, lowering sexual and performance anxiety, and addressing cognitions and behaviors have shown success among women with FOD and/or FSAD (McCabe, 2001), with the percentage of women who experienced FOD and FSAD dropping from 66.7% and 33.3% pretreatment to 11.1% and 14.8%, respectively, posttreatment.

SIDEBAR 7.3

Psychological Approaches to Sexual Arousal and Orgasm Disorders

Education and communication training are useful components of treatment for orgasm and/or arousal difficulties.

Sensate focus is a cognitive-behavioral technique used to treat both orgasm and arousal difficulties.

Systematic desensitization, involving relaxation and working through a hierarchy of anxiety-provoking stimuli, decreases anxiety surrounding sexual activity and may improve some aspects of sexual functioning.

Systematic desensitization involves deep relaxation exercises that enable the woman to replace fear responses with relaxation responses. A succession of anxiety-provoking stimuli is developed by the woman and the therapist to represent increasingly threatening sexual situations. For example, a hierarchy can be developed ranging from the least anxiety-provoking stimuli of lying naked next to one's partner to the most anxiety-provoking stimuli of experiencing an orgasm following a partner's request. The woman's task is to approach each set of stimuli on her hierarchy and experience fearful to relaxed responses, resulting in a net decrease of anxiety. She moves up her hierarchy gradually, tackling items of increasing intensity over time. After the woman can successfully imagine each anxiety-provoking item from her hierarchy without anxiety, she engages in the actual activities of each item on her hierarchy until her anxiety is decreased.

Outcome studies for sensate focus and systematic desensitization show that these techniques can improve some aspects of sexual functioning, although the most reliable improvement is a decrease in sexual anxiety. No well-controlled studies have shown a clinically significant increase in orgasmic function after sensate focus or systematic desensitization training alone. Meston et al. (2004) have recommended that these techniques be used to treat FOD only when concurrent sexual anxiety problems exist.

Treatments Specific to FSAD/PSAD

Pharmacological Treatments

Currently no medications have been approved by the U.S. Food and Drug Administration for the treatment of FSAD. However, several placebo-controlled studies suggest that selective PDE-5 inhibitors (e.g., sildenafil or Viagra™) may be an effective treatment for difficulties stemming from perceptions of physical sensations and physiological aspects of FSAD. Findings indicate a variety of positive effects. These include improved genital sensation, vaginal lubrication, satisfaction with intercourse, clitoral sensitivity, and overall sexual experience among postmenopausal women with FSAD (J. R. Berman et al., 2003); increased subjective sexual arousal, perception of genital arousal, and reduced latency to orgasm among postmenopausal women with FSAD and FOD who had low physiological sexual arousal responses to erotic stimuli (Basson & Brotto, 2003); increased self-reported sexual arousal, orgasm, sexual fantasy, intercourse, and enjoyment of sexual activity among premenopausal women with FSAD and FOD (Caruso et al., 2001); and improved vaginal engorgement among sexually functional premenopausal women (Laan et al., 2002). The combined administration of the nitric oxide-precursor L-arginine and the alpha 2-blocker yohimbine in postmenopausal women with FSAD also improves genital arousal compared to placebo, despite no specific effect on subjective arousal (Meston & Worcel, 2002).

In a study comparing sustained-release bupropion to placebo in premenopausal women with hypoactive sexual desire disorder (HSDD), bupropion had no effect on desire but did improve self-reported sexual arousal, ability to attain orgasm, and sexual satisfaction, suggesting that this drug may be helpful in some women suffering from arousal and/or orgasm difficulties (Segraves, Clayton, Croft, Wolf, & Warnock, 2004).

Drugs that act as vasodilators also appear to improve sexual response in women. For example, increases in self-reported vaginal lubrication and pleasurable sensations in the vagina, along with trends toward increased VPA, have also been found with oral phentolamine in postmenopausal women with FSAD. Compared with placebo, vaginally applied phentolamine increases physiological and subjective sexual arousal among postmenopausal women using hormone replacement therapy (Rubio-Aurioles et al., 2002). In an uncontrolled study, topical alprostadil cream increased labial and clitoral engorgement among women with FSAD and FOD assessed with Doppler ultrasonography (Becher, Bechara, & Casabe, 2001), but later research found no effect beyond placebo in women with FSAD, assessed with vaginal photoplethysmography and self-report questionnaires (Islam et al., 2001; Padma-Nathan et al., 2003).

The dopaminergic agonist apomorphine increases subjective sexual arousal in premenopausal women with FSAD and hypoactive sexual desire disorder (HSDD; Caruso et al., 2004), and tibolone, a Selective Estrogen Receptor Modulator (SERM), improves genital response and frequency of arousability and sexual fantasies in postmenopausal women (Laan, van Lunsen, & Everaerd, 2001).

Testosterone may increase genital arousal in healthy pre-menopausal women (Tuiten et al., 2002). Clinical trials have shown improvement in sexual interest, desire, activity, and satisfaction following testosterone administration. As noted earlier, DHEA has no significant impact on premenopausal women (Meston & Heiman, 2002) but appears to impart positive effects for post-menopausal and older (over 70) women, including increased subjective sexual arousal (Hackbert & Heiman, 2002), physical sexual excitement, sexual activity, and sexual satisfaction (Baulieu et al., 2000). Treatment of sexual dysfunction with hormone therapy is inappropriate for premenopausal women who have ovulatory cycles, as evidence of effectiveness and safety is currently lacking (Davis, 2006).

Other Treatment
The FDA approved the EROS clitoral therapy device (CTD; Urometrics, St. Paul, MN, United States) for use in women with FSAD following a noncontrolled study showing that the device, which increases vasocongestion through suction, increased vaginal lubrication, sensation, orgasm, and overall sexual satisfaction (Billups et al., 2001).

Based on an Internet survey of 103 women experiencing at least one symptom of PSAD, orgasms were reported to provide some relief in almost half of all women, eliminating symptoms in approximately 13% of women. However, a mean of 5.2 orgasms were necessary to quell the feelings of genital arousal, and many women viewed the process as either painful or physically distressing. Other activities reported to provide relief of symptoms included taking medication (52%), distraction (39%), intercourse (36%), physical exercise (25%), and using cold compresses (13%; Leiblum et al., 2005).

Treatments Specific to FOD

Pharmacological Treatments
So far, no pharmacological treatments for FOD have been found more effective than placebo (for a review, see Meston et al., 2004). If the patient is taking SSRIs and the orgasmic difficulties coincide with the onset of the drug treatment, practitioners may recommend a change in prescription to an antidepressant that also affects DA and NE. These include bupropion, nefazodone, and moclobemide. Mirtazapine also improves orgasmic abilities compared to other antidepressants, but one study reported a 50% drop out rate due to side effects such as drowsiness (Boyarski et al., 1999).

Nonpharmacological Treatments
Directed masturbation (DM) uses cognitive-behavioral therapy to educate a woman about her body and the sensations she is

able to elicit while manually stimulating herself. First, a woman engages in a visual exploration of her body, using a mirror and educational material depicting female genital anatomy. Following visual and manual identification of the sensitive genital areas that elicit pleasure, the woman is instructed to apply targeted manual stimulation to these regions. Allowing a woman to explore her body on her own is beneficial because it eliminates several factors that may be barriers to orgasm, including anxiety that may be associated with the presence of a partner. Once a woman is able to attain orgasm with masturbation, her partner may become involved in the DM sessions. Women experiencing FOD have successfully been treated using DM in a variety of therapy settings with success rates as high as 100% in one study (for a review of studies demonstrating the efficacy of DM, see Meston et al., 2004; for a detailed guide to DM, refer to Heiman & LoPicollo, 1988).

Kegel exercises have been included as part of the treatment regimen for FOD but studies that have looked solely at the effect of Kegel exercises on orgasmic ability have found no substantial improvement (Table 7.4; Chambless et al., 1984).

Summary and Conclusions

The most efficacious treatments for FSAD are the EROS clitoral device; behavioral and cognitive techniques, including sensate focus, systematic desensitization, and anxiety reduction; and communication training and education. While no pharmacologic medications have been approved by the FDA for the treatment of FSAD, several hormonal and nonhormonal agents have shown benefit over placebo. There is no specific therapy for PSAD. For FOD, the most effective treatment seems to be directed masturbation, which involves educating the woman and her partner about her body, and increasing the familiarity and comfort level of a woman with her body. No pharmacological agents have been found to directly increase orgasmic ability.

In summary:

- No pharmacological treatments for FOD are available, but a woman taking SSRIs may change to antidepressant medication that also targets dopamine and norepinephrine.
- Directed masturbation can help a woman learn about her body and is beneficial for increasing orgasmic ability.
- Kegel exercises help strengthen pelvic floor muscles, which can aid in orgasm, but research evidence is lacking.

Table 7.4 **Major Diagnostic Points and Treatment Options**

Disorder	Diagnostic Points
FSAD	Subjective, genital, or combined?
FOD	Lifelong or acquired?
	Completely absent, diminished intensity, and/or marked delay?
Both	Assess degree of distress
	Assess other factors possibly involved:
	–Relationship factors
	–Emotional factors (depression, sexual abuse)
	–Health/medical factors
	–Medication use (e.g., SSRIs)
	–Age
	–Menopause
	–Endocrine factors

Disorder	Treatment Options
FSAD	Pharmacological treatments (none currently approved by FDA):
	–Selective phosphodiesterase type 5 inhibitors (post and premenopausal women; genital and subjective sensations, orgasm, and physiological aspects)
	–Nitric oxide-precursor L-arginine (postmenopausal women; physiological arousal)
	–Alpha blocker yohimbine (postmenopausal women; physiological arousal)
	–Buproprion sustained release (premenopausal women; subjective arousal, ability to attain orgasm)
	–Oral phentolamine (postmenopausal women; genital and subjective sensations and physiological aspects)
	–Dopaminergic agonist apomorphine (premenopausal women; subjective reports of arousal)
	–Selective Estrogen Receptor Modulator Tibolone (postmenopausal women; subjective and physiological aspects)
	–Testosterone
	–DHEA (postmenopausal women; subjective arousal)
	Note: It is suggested that treatment of hormone therapy is inappropriate for premenopausal women who have ovulatory cycles, as evidence of effectiveness and safety data are currently lacking (Davis, 2006).
FOD	Directed masturbation (DM):
	–Visual exploration of own body with mirror
	–Manual identification of sensitive areas that elicit pleasure

Table 7.4 *(Continued)*

Disorder	Treatment Options
	−Manual stimulation by patient
	−Once orgasm is attained, involve partner in DM sessions
	−Refer to *Becoming Orgasmic: A Sexual and Personal Growth Program for Women* by Heiman & LoPicollo, 1988
	Kegel exercises
Both	Education:
	−Existence of difficulties
	−Information about genitals
	Relationship counseling (e.g., to increase communication about sexuality)
	Treatment of underlying problems (e.g., medical factors, emotional difficulties)
	Hormone treatment if hormonal problem is suspected
	Sensate focus:
	−Decrease goal-directed sex (e.g., attainment of orgasm)
	−Focus on pleasurable sensations
	−Explore partner's nonsexual body
	−Gradually move to sexual exploration and intercourse when both partners comfortable
	Systematic desensitization (if sexual anxiety is present):
	−Relaxation techniques
	−Create and work through fear/anxiety hierarchy
	EROS clitoral therapy device (FDA approved)
	−Increases vaginal lubrication, sensation, orgasm, and overall sexual satisfaction

References

Adams, C. G., & Turner, B. F. (1985). Reported change in sexuality from young adulthood to old age. *Journal of Sex Research, 21,* 126–141.

Aksaray, G., Yelken, B., Kaptanoglu, C., Oflu, S., & Ozaltin, M. (2001). Sexuality in women with obsessive compulsive disorder. *Journal of Sex and Marital Therapy, 27,* 273–277.

American Psychiatric Association. (2000). *Diagnostic and statistical manual of mental disorders* (4th ed., text rev.). Washington, DC: Author.

Anderson, B. L., & Cyranowski, J. M. (1994). Women's sexual self schema. *Journal of Personality and Social Psychology, 67,* 1079–1100.

Anderson-Hunt, M., & Dennerstein, L. (1995). Oxytocin and female sexuality. *Gynecologic and Obstetric Investigation, 40,* 217–221.

Angulo, J., Cuevas, P., Cuevas, B., Bischoff, E., & Saenz de Tejada, I. (2003). Vardenafil enhances clitoral and vaginal blood flow responses to pelvic nerve stimulation in female dogs. *International Journal of Impotence Research, 15,* 137–141.

Apt, C., & Hurlbert, D. F. (1992). The female sensation seeker and marital sexuality. *Journal of Sex and Marital Therapy, 19,* 315–324.

Apt, C., & Hurlbert, D. F. (1994). The sexual attitudes, behavior, and relationships of women with histrionic personality disorder. *Journal of Sex and Marital Therapy, 20,* 125–133.

Bachmann, G., Bancroft, J., Braunstein, G., Burger, H., Davis, S., & Dennerstein, L. (2002). Female androgen insufficiency: The Princeton consensus statement on definition, classification, and assessment. *Fertility and Sterility, 77,* 660–665.

Bachmann, G. A., Ebert, G. A., & Burd, I. D. (1999). Vulvovaginal complaints. In R. A. Lobo (Ed.), *Treatment of the postmenopausal woman: Basic and clinical aspects* (pp. 195–201). Baltimore: Lippincott, Williams & Wilkins.

Bancroft, J., Loftus, J., & Long, J. (2003). Distress about sex: A national survey of women in heterosexual relationships. *Archives of Sexual Behavior, 32,* 193–208.

Barlow, D. H. (1986). Causes of sexual dysfunction: The role of anxiety and cognitive interference. *Journal of Consulting and Clinical Psychology, 54,* 140–148.

Basson, R., & Brotto, L. A. (2003). Sexual psychophysiology and effects of sildenafil citrate in oestrogenised women with acquired genital arousal disorder and impaired orgasm: A randomized controlled trial. *British Journal of Obstetrics and Gynaecology, 110,* 1014–1024.

Basson, R., Leiblum, S., Brotto, L., Derogatis, L., Fourcroy, J., Fugl-Meyer, K., et al. (2003). Definitions of women's sexual dysfunction reconsidered: Advocating expansion and revision. *Journal of Psychosomatic Obstetrics and Gynecology, 24,* 221–229.

Basson, R., Leiblum, S., Brotto, L., Derogatis, L., Fourcroy, J., Fugl-Meyer, K., et al. (2004). Revised definitions of women's sexual dysfunctions. *Journal of Sexual Medicine, 1,* 40–48.

Basson, R., Weijmar Shultz, W. C. M., Binik, Y. M., Brotto, L. A., Eschenbach, D. A., Laan, E., et al. (2004). Women's sexual desire and arousal disorders and sexual pain. In T. F. Lue, R. Basson, R. Rosen, F. Giuliano, & F. Montorsi (Eds.), *Sexual medicine: Sexual dysfunctions in men and women* (pp. 39–72). Paris: Health Publications.

Baulieu, E. E., Thomas, G., Legrain, S., Lahlou, N., Roger, M., Debuire, B., et al. (2000). Dehydroepiandrosterone (DHEA), DHEA sulfate, and aging: Contribution of the DHEAge study to a sociobiomedical issue. *Proceedings of the National Academy of Sciences of the United States of America, 97,* 4279–4284.

Becher, E. G., Bechara, A., & Casabe, A. (2001). Clitoral hemodynamic changes after a topical application of alprostadil. *Journal of Sex and Marital Therapy, 27,* 405–410.

Beck, A. T., Ward, C. H., Mendelson, M., Mock, J., & Erbaugh, J. (1961). An inventory for measuring depression. *Archives of General Psychiatry, 4,* 561–571.

Berard, E. J. J. (1989). The sexuality of spinal cord injured women: Physiology and pathophysiology—A review. *Paraplegia, 27,* 99–112.

Bergstrom-Walan, M., & Neilsen, H. (1990). Sexual expression among 60–80 year old men and women: A sample from Stockholm, Sweden. *Journal of Sex Research, 27,* 289–295.

Berman, J. R., Berman, L. A., Toler, S. M., Gill, J., & Haughie, S. (2003). Safety and efficacy of sildenafil citrate for the treatment of female sexual arousal disorder: A double-blind, placebo controlled study. *Journal of Urology, 170,* 2333–2338.

Berman, L. A., Berman, J. R., Bruck, D., Pawar, R. V., & Goldstein, I. (2001). Pharmacotherapy or psychotherapy? Effective treatment for FSD to unresolved childhood sexual abuse. *Journal of Sex and Marital Therapy, 27,* 421–425.

Billups, K. L., Berman, L., Berman, J., Metz, M. E., Glennon, M. E., & Goldstein, I. (2001). A new non-pharmacological vacuum therapy for female sexual dysfunction. *Journal of Sex and Marital Therapy, 27,* 435–441.

Birnbaum, G., Glaubman, H., & Mikulincer, M. (2001). Women's experience of heterosexual intercourse: Scale construction, factor structure, and relations to orgasmic disorder. *Journal of Sex Research, 38,* 191–204.

Birnbaum, G. E. (2003). The meaning of heterosexual intercourse among women with female orgasmic disorder. *Archives of Sexual Behavior, 32,* 61–71.

Bobes, J., Gonzalez, M. P., Bascaran, M. T., Clayton, A., Garcia, M., Rico-Villade Moros, F., et al. (2002). Evaluating changes in sexual functioning in depressed patients: Sensitivity to change of the CSFQ. *Journal of Sex and Marital Therapy, 28,* 93–103.

Bodinger, L., Hermesh, H., Aizenberg, D., Valevski, A., Marom, S., Shiloh, R., et al. (2002). Sexual function and behavior in social phobia. *Journal of Clinical Psychiatry, 63,* 874–879.

Boyarsky, B. K., Haque, W., Rouleau, M. R., & Hirschfeld, R. M. A. (1999). Sexual functioning in depressed outpatients taking mirtazapine. *Depression and Anxiety, 9,* 175–179.

Bradford, A., & Meston, C. M. (2006). The impact of anxiety on sexual arousal in women. *Behavior Research and Therapy, 44,* 1067–1077.

Brandenburg, U., & Schwenkhagen, A. (2006). Sexual history. In I. Goldstein, C. M. Meston, S. R. Davis, & A. M. Traish (Eds.), *Women's sexual function and dysfunction: Study, diagnosis, and treatment* (pp. 343–346). New York: Taylor & Francis.

Brotto, L. A., Chik, H. M., Ryder, A. G., Gorzalka, B. B., & Seal, B. N. (2005). Acculturation and sexual function in Asian women. *Archives of Sexual Behavior, 34,* 613–626.

Cain, V. S., Johannes, C. B., Avis, N. E., Mohr, B., Schocken, M., Skurnick, J., et al. (2003). Sexual functioning and practices in a multi-ethnic study of midlife women: Baseline results from SWAN. *Journal of Sex Research, 40,* 266–276.

Caruso, S., Agnello, C., Intelisano, G., Farina, M., Di Mari, L., & Cianci, A. (2004). Placebo-controlled study on efficacy and safety of daily apomorphine SL intake in premenopausal women affected by hypoactive sexual desire disorder and sexual arousal disorder. *Urology, 63,* 955–959.

Caruso, S., Intelisano, G., Lupo, L., & Agnello, C. (2001). Premenopausal women affected by sexual arousal disorder treated with sildenafil: A double-blind, cross-over, placebo-controlled study. *British Journal of Obstetrics and Gynaecology, 108,* 623–628.

Chambless, D. L., Stern, D., Sultan, F. E., Williams, A. J., Goldstein, A. J., Lineberger, M. H., et al. (1984). The pubococcygeus and female orgasm: A correlational study with normal subjects. *Archives of Sexual Behavior, 11,* 479–490.

Chesney, A. P., Blakeney, P. E., Cole, C. M., & Chan, F. A. (1981). A comparison of couples who have sought sex therapy with couples who have not. *Journal of Sex and Marital Therapy, 7,* 131–140.

Costa, P. T., Fagan, P. J., Piedmont, R. L., Ponticas, Y., & Wise, T. N. (1992). The five-factor model of personality and sexual functioning in outpatient men and women. *Psychiatric Medicine, 10,* 199–215.

Davis, S. R. (2006). Available therapies and outcome results in premenopausal women. In I. Goldstein, C. M. Meston, S. R. Davis, & A. M. Traish (Eds.), *Women's sexual function and dysfunction: Study, diagnosis, and treatment* (pp. 539–548). New York: Taylor & Francis.

Deeks, A. A., & McCabe, M. P. (2001). Sexual function and the menopausal woman: The importance of age and partners' sexual functioning. *Journal of Sex Research, 38,* 219–225.

Derogatis, L. R. (1997). The Derogatis Interview for Sexual Functioning (DISF/DISF-SR): An introductory report. *Journal of Sex and Marital Therapy, 23,* 291–304.

Duncan, L. E., Lewis, C., Smith, C. E., Jenkins, P., Nichols, M., & Pearson, T. A. (2001). Sex, drugs, and hypertension: A methodological approach for studying a sensitive subject. *International Journal of Impotence Research, 13,* 31–40.

Duncan, S., Blacklaw, J., Beastall, G. H., & Brodie, M. J. (1997). Sexual function in women with epilepsy. *Epilepsia, 38,* 1074–1081.

Dunn, K. M., Croft, P. R., & Hackett, G. I. (1998). Sexual problems: A study of the prevalence and need for health care in the general population. *Family Practice, 15,* 519–524.

Ernst, C., Földényi, M., & Angst, J. (1993). The Zurich study: XXI. Sexual dysfunctions and disturbances in young adults: Data of a longitudinal epidemiological study. *European Archives of Psychiatry and Clinical Neuroscience, 243,* 179–188.

Exton, N. G., Truong, T. C., Exton, M. S., Wingenfeld, S. A., Leygraf, N., Saller, B., et al. (2000). Neuroendocrine response to film-induced sexual arousal in men and women. *Psychoneuroendocrinology, 25,* 187–199.

Fletcher, G. J. O., & Kininmonth, L. A. (1992). Measuring relationship beliefs: An individual differences scale. *Journal of Research in Personality, 26,* 371–397.

Fugl-Meyer, A. R., & Fugl-Meyer, K. S. (1999). Sexual disabilities, problems and satisfaction in 18- to 74-year-old Swedes. *Scandinavian Journal of Sexology, 2,* 79–105.

Garcia Nader, S., Maitland, S. R., Munarriz, R., & Goldstein, I. (2006). Blood flow: Duplex Doppler ultrasound. In I. Goldstein, C. M. Meston, S. R. Davis, & A. M. Traish (Eds.), *Women's sexual function and dysfunction: Study, diagnosis, and treatment* (pp. 383–390). New York: Taylor & Francis.

Ghadirian, A. M., Choinard, G., & Annable, L. (1982). Sexual dysfunction and plasma prolactin levels in neuroleptic-treated schizophrenic outpatients. *Journal of Nervous and Mental Diseases, 170,* 463–467.

Guay, A., & Davis, S. R. (2002). Testosterone insufficiency in women: Fact or fiction? *World Journal of Urology, 20,* 106–110.

Guay, A., Jacobson, J., Munarriz, R., Traish, A., Talakoub, L., Quirk, F., et al. (2004). Serum androgen levels in health premenopausal women with and without sexual dysfunction: Part B: Reduced serum androgen levels in healthy premenopausal women with complaints of sexual dysfunction. *International Journal of Impotence Research, 16,* 121–129.

Guay, A. T., & Sparks, R. (2006). Pathophysiology of sex steroids in women. In I. Goldstein, C. M. Meston, S. R. Davis, & A. M. Traish (Eds.), *Women's sexual function and dysfunction: Study, diagnosis, and treatment* (pp. 218–227). New York: Taylor & Francis.

Hackbert, L., & Heiman, J. R. (2002). Acute dehydroepiandosterone (DHEA) effects on sexual arousal in postmenopausal women. *Journal of Women's Health and Gender-Based Medicine, 11,* 155–162.

Hartmann, U., Keiser, K., Ruffer-Hesse, C., & Kloth, G. (2002). Female sexual desire disorders: Subtypes, classification, personality factors and new directions for treatment. *World Journal of Urology, 20,* 79–88.

Heiman, J. R., & LoPiccolo, J. (1988). *Becoming orgasmic: A sexual and personal growth program for women* (Rev. and exp. ed.). New York: Prentice-Hall.

Herman, J. R., & Hirschman, L. (1977). Father-daughter incest. *Signs, 2,* 735–756.

Hummer, M., Kemmler, G., Kurz, M., Kurtzthaler, I., Oberbauer, H., & Fleischhacker, W. W. (1999). Sexual disturbances during clozapine and haloperidol treatment for schizophrenia. *American Journal of Psychiatry, 156,* 463–467.

Hurlbert, D. F., Apt, C., Hurlbert, M. K., & Pierce, A. P. (2000). Sexual compatibility and the sexual desire-motivation relation in females with hypoactive sexual desire disorder. *Behavior Modification, 24,* 325–347.

Hurlbert, D. F., Apt, C., & Rabehl, S. M. (1993). Key variables to understanding female sexual satisfaction: An examination of women in nondistressed marriages. *Journal of Sex and Marital Therapy, 19,* 154–165.

Islam, A., Mitchel, J., Rosen, R., Phillips, N., Ayers, C., Ferguson, D., et al. (2001). Topical alprostadil in the treatment of female sexual arousal disorder: A pilot study. *Journal of Sex and Marital Therapy, 27,* 531–540.

Jensen, P. T., Groenvold, M., Klee, M. C., Thranov, I., Petersen, M. A., & Machin, D. (2004). Early-stage cervical carcinoma, radical hysterectomy, and sexual function: A longitudinal study. *Cancer, 100,* 97–106.

Kadioglu, P., Yalin, A. S., Tiryakioglu, O., Gazioglu, N., Oral, G., Sanli, O., et al. (2005). Sexual dysfunction in women with hyperprolactinemia: A pilot study report. *Journal of Urology, 174,* 1921–1925.

Kelly, M. P., Strassberg, D. S., & Kircher, J. R. (1990). Attitudinal and experiential correlates of anorgasmia. *Archives of Sexual Behavior, 19,* 165–177.

Kennedy, S. H., Dickens, S. E., Eisfeld, B. S., & Bagby, R. M. (1999). Sexual dysfunction before antidepressant therapy in major depression. *Journal of Affective Disorders, 56,* 201–208.

Kim, N. N., Min, K., Huang, Y., Goldstein, I., & Traish, A. M. (2002). Biochemical and functional characterization of alpha-adrenergic receptors in the rabbit vagina. *Life Sciences, 71,* 2909–2920.

Koukounas, E., & McCabe, M. (1997). Sexual and emotional variables influencing sexual response to erotica. *Behaviour Research and Therapy, 35,* 221–230.

Laan, E., Everaerd, W., van Aanold, M. T., & Rebel, M. (1993). Performance demand and sexual arousal in women. *Behaviour Research and Therapy, 31,* 25–35.

Laan, E., van Lunsen, R. H., & Everaerd, W. (2001). The effects of tibolone on vaginal blood flow, sexual desire and arousability in postmenopausal women. *Climacteric, 4,* 28–41.

Laan, E., van Lunsen, R. H., Everaerd, W., Riley, A., Scott, E., & Boolell, M. (2002). The enhancement of vaginal vasocongestion by sildenafil in healthy premenopausal women. *Journal of Women's Health and Gender-Based Medicine, 11,* 357–365.

Labrie, F., Belanger, A., Cusan, L., Gomez, J.-L., & Candas, B. (1997). Marked decline in serum concentrations of adrenal C19 sex steroid precursors and conjugated androgen metabolites during aging. *Journal of Clinical Endocrinology and Metabolism, 82,* 396–402.

Laumann, E. O., Gagnon, J. H., Michael, R. T., & Michaels, S. (1994). *The social organization of sexuality: Sexual practices in the United States* (pp. 368–374). Chicago: University of Chicago Press.

Laumann, E. O., Paik, A., & Rosen, R. C. (1999). Sexual dysfunction in the United States: Prevalence and predictors. *Journal of American Medical Association, 281,* 537–544.

Leiblum, S., Brown, C., Wan, J., & Rawlinson, L. (2005). Persistent sexual arousal syndrome: A descriptive study. *Journal of Sexual Medicine, 2,* 331–337.

Leiblum, S. R. (2006). Classification and diagnosis of female sexual disorders. In I. Goldstein, C. M. Meston, S. R. Davis, & A. M. Traish (Eds.), *Women's sexual function and dysfunction: Study, diagnosis, and treatment* (pp. 323–330). New York: Taylor & Francis.

Lewis, R. W., Fugl-Meyer, K. S., Bosch, R., Fugl-Meyer, A. R., Laumann, E. O., Lizza, E., et al. (2004). Definitions, classification, and epidemiology of sexual dysfunction. In T. F. Lue, R. Basson, R. Rosen, F. Giuliano, S. Khoury, & F. Montorsi (Eds.), *Sexual medicine: Sexual dysfunctions in men and women* (pp. 39–72). Paris: Health Publications.

Locke, H. J., & Wallace, K. M. (1959). Short marital adjustment and prediction tests: Their reliability and validity. *Marriage and Family Living, 21,* 251–255.

Loos, V. E., Bridges, C. F., & Critelli, J. W. (1987). Weiner's attribution theory and female orgasmic consistency. *Journal of Sex Research, 23,* 348–361.

Mah, K., & Binik, Y. M. (2001). The nature of human orgasm: A critical review of major trends. *Clinical Psychology Review, 21,* 823–856.

Maravilla, K. R. (2006). Blood flow: Magnetic resonance imaging and brain imaging for evaluating sexual arousal in women. In I. Goldstein, C. M. Meston, S. R. Davis, & A. M. Traish (Eds.), *Women's sexual function and dysfunction: Study, diagnosis, and treatment* (pp. 368–382). New York: Taylor & Francis.

McCabe, M. (2001). Evaluation of a cognitive behavior therapy program for people with sexual dysfunction. *Journal of Sex and Marital Therapy, 27,* 259–271.

Meston, C. M. (2003). Validation of the Female Sexual Function Index (FSFI) in women with female orgasmic disorder and in women with hypoactive sexual desire disorder. *Journal of Sex and Marital Therapy, 29,* 39–46.

Meston, C. M. (2006). The effects of state and trait self-focused attention on sexual arousal in sexually functional and dysfunctional women. *Behaviour Research and Therapy, 44,* 515–532.

Meston, C. M., & Bradford, A. (in press). Autonomic nervous system influences: The role of the sympathetic nervous system in female sexual arousal. In *The psychophysiology of sexual desire, arousal, and behavior.* Bloomington, IN: Indiana University Press.

Meston, C. M., & Gorzalka, B. B. (1995). The effects of sympathetic activation following acute exercise on physiological and subjective sexual arousal in women. *Behaviour Research and Therapy, 33,* 651–664.

Meston, C. M., & Gorzalka, B. B. (1996). Differential effects of sympathetic activation on sexual arousal in sexually dysfunctional and functional women. *Journal of Abnormal Psychology, 105,* 582–591.

Meston, C. M., & Heiman, J. R. (1998). Ephedrine-activated physiological sexual arousal in women. *Archives of General Psychiatry, 55,* 652–656.

Meston, C. M., & Heiman, J. R. (2002). Acute dehydroepiandrosterone effects on sexual arousal in premenopausal women. *Journal of Sex and Marital Therapy, 28,* 53–60.

Meston, C. M., Hull, E., Levin, R. J., & Sipski, M. (2004). Women's orgasm. In T. F. Lue, R. Basson, R. Rosen, F. Giuliano, S. Khoury, & F. Montorsi (Eds.), *Sexual medicine: Sexual dysfunctions in men and women* (pp. 783–849). Paris: Health Publications.

Meston, C. M., & Trapnell, P. (2005). Development and validation of a five-factor sexual satisfaction and distress scale for women: The Sexual Satisfaction Scale for Women (SSS-W). *Journal of Sexual Medicine, 2,* 66–81.

Meston, C. M., Trapnell, P. D., & Gorzalka, B. B. (1993, June). *Sex and the five factor model of personality.* Paper presented at the annual meeting of the International Academy of Sex Research, Pacific Grove, CA.

Meston, C. M., Trapnell, P. D., & Gorzalka, B. B. (1996). Ethnic and gender differences in sexuality: Variations in sexual behavior between Asian and non-Asian university students. *Archives of Sexual Behavior, 25,* 33–72.

Meston, C. M., & Worcel, M. (2002). The effects of yohimbine plus L-arginine glutamate on sexual arousal in postmenopausal women with sexual arousal disorder. *Archives of Sexual Behavior, 31,* 323–332.

Metz, M. E., & Lutz, G. (1990). Dyadic playfulness differences between sexual and marital therapy couples. *Journal of Psychology and Human Sexuality, 3,* 169–182.

Montejo-Gonzalez, A. L., Llorca, G., Izquierdo, J. A., Ledesma, A., Bousono, M., Calcedo, A., et al. (1997). SSRI-induced sexual dysfunction: Fluoxetine, paroxetine, sertraline, and fluvoxamine in a prospective, multicenter, and descriptive clinical study of 344 patients. *Journal of Sex and Marital Therapy, 23,* 176–194.

Norton, G. R., & Jehu, D. (1984). The role of anxiety in sexual dysfunctions: A review. *Archives of Sexual Behavior, 13,* 165–183.

Padma-Nathan, H., Brown, C., Fendl, J., Salem, S., Yeager, J., & Haring, R. (2003). Efficacy and safety of topical alprostadil cream for the treatment of female sexual arousal disorder (FSAD): A double-blind, multicenter, randomized, and placebo-controlled clinical trial. *Journal of Sex and Marital Therapy, 29,* 329–344.

Palace, E. M., & Gorzalka, B. B. (1990). The enhancing effects of anxiety on arousal in sexually dysfunctional and function women. *Journal of Abnormal Psychology, 99,* 403–411.

Palace, E. M., & Gorzalka, B. B. (1992). Differential patterns of arousal in sexually functional and dysfunctional women: Physiological and subjective components of sexual response. *Archives of Sexual Behavior, 21,* 135–159.

Patel, M., Brown, C. S., & Bachmann, G. (2006). Sexual function in the menopause and perimenopause. In I. Goldstein, C. M. Meston, S. R. Davis, & A. M. Traish (Eds.), *Women's sexual function and dysfunction: Study, diagnosis, and treatment* (pp. 251–262). New York: Taylor & Francis.

Perelman, M. A. (2006). Psychosocial history. In I. Goldstein, C. M. Meston, S. R. Davis, & A. M. Traish (Eds.), *Women's sexual function and dysfunction: Study, diagnosis, and treatment* (pp. 336–342). New York: Taylor & Francis.

Persky, H., Charney, N., Strauss, D., Miller, W. R., O'Brien, C. P., & Lief, H. I. (1982). The relationship of sexual adjustment and related sexual behaviors and attitudes to marital adjustment. *American Journal of Family Therapy, 10,* 38–49.

Prause, N., & Janssen, E. (2006). Blood flow: Vaginal photoplethysmopgraphy. In I. Goldstein, C. M. Meston, S. R. Davis, & A. M. Traish (Eds.), *Women's sexual function and dysfunction: Study, diagnosis, and treatment* (pp. 359–367). New York: Taylor & Francis.

Read, S., King, M., & Watson, J. (1997). Sexual dysfunction in primary medical care: Prevalence, characteristics and detection by the general practitioner. *Journal of Public Health and Medicine, 19,* 387–391.

Rellini, A. H. (2006). Sexual abuse. In I. Goldstein, C. M. Meston, S. R. Davis, & A. M. Traish (Eds.), *Women's sexual function and dysfunction: Study, diagnosis, and treatment* (pp. 98–101). New York: Taylor & Francis.

Rellini, A. H., & Meston, C. M. (2006). Psychophysiological sexual arousal in women with a history of childhood sexual abuse. *Journal of Sex and Marital Therapy, 32,* 5–22.

Rosen, R. C. (2002). Assessment of female sexual dysfunction: Review of validated methods. *Fertility and Sterility, 77*(Suppl. 4), 89–93.

Rosen, R. C., Brown, C., Heiman, J. R., Leiblum, S., Meston, C. M., Shabsigh, R., et al. (2000). The Female Sexual Function Index (FSFI): A multidimensional self-report instrument for the assessment of female sexual function. *Journal of Sex and Marital Therapy, 26,* 191–208.

Rosen, R. C., Lane, R. M., & Menza, M. (1999). Effects of SSRIs on sexual function: A critical review. *Journal of Clinical Psychopharmacology, 19,* 67–85.

Rubio-Aurioles, E., Lopez, M., Lipezker, M., Lara, C., Ramirez, A., Rampazzo, C., et al. (2002). Phentolamine mesylate in postmenopausal women with female sexual arousal disorder: A psychophysiological study. *Journal of Sex and Marital Therapy, 28*(Suppl. 1), 205–215.

Russell, S. T., Khandheria, B. K., & Nehra, A. (2004). Erectile dysfunction and cardiovascular disease. *Mayo Clinic Proceedings, 79,* 782–794.

Salonia, A., Briganti, A., Rigatti, R., & Montorsi, F. (2006). Medical conditions associated with female sexual dysfunctions. In I. Goldstein, C. M. Meston, S. R. Davis, & A. M. Traish (Eds.), *Women's sexual function and dysfunction: Study, diagnosis and treatment* (pp. 263–275). New York: Taylor & Francis.

Salonia, A., Nappi, R. E., Pontillo, M., Daverioc, R., Smeraldid, A., Brigantia, A., et al. (2005). Menstrual cycle-related changes in plasma oxytocin are relevant to normal sexual function in healthy women. *Hormones and Behavior, 47,* 164–169.

Sarrel, P. (1990). Sexuality and menopause. *Obstetrics and Gynecology, 75,* 26S–32S.

Sarrel, P. (2000). Effects of hormone replacement therapy on sexual psychophysiology and behavior in postmenopause. *Journal of Women's Health and Gender-Based Medicine, 9*(Suppl. 1), 25–32.

Sato, Y., Hotta, H., Nakayama, H., & Suzuki, H. (1996). Sympathetic and parasympathetic regulation of the uterine blood flow and contraction in the rat. *Journal of the Autonomic Nervous System, 59,* 151–158.

Sauder, S. E., Frager, M., Case, G. D., Kelch, R. P., & Marshall, J. C. (1984). Abnormal patterns of pulsatile luteinizing hormone secretion in women with hyperprolactinemia and amenorrhea: Responses to bromocriptine. *Journal of Clinical Endocrinology and Metabolism, 59,* 941–948.

Scepkowski, L. A., Georgescu, M., & Pfaus, J. G. (2006). Neuroendocrine factors in sexual desire and motivation. In I. Goldstein, C. M. Meston, S. R. Davis, & A. M. Traish (Eds.), *Women's sexual function and dysfunction: Study, diagnosis and treatment* (pp. 159–167). New York: Taylor & Francis.

Schreiner-Engel, P., Schiavi, R. C., Smith, H., & White, D. (1981). Sexual arousability and the menstrual cycle. *Psychosomatic Medicine, 43,* 199–214.

Seal, B. N., & Meston, C. M. (2007). The impact of body awareness on sexual arousal in women with sexual dysfunction. *Journal of Sexual Medicine, 4,* 990–1000.

Segraves, R. T., Clayton, A., Croft, H., Wolf, A., & Warnock, J. (2004). Bupropion sustained release for the treatment of hypoactive sexual desire disorder in premenopausal women. *Journal of Clinical Psychopharmacology, 24,* 339–342.

Shen, W. W., & Sata, L. S. (1990). Inhibited female orgasm resulting from psychotropic drugs: A five year, updated, clinical review. *Journal of Reproductive Medicine, 35,* 11–16.

Shifren, J. L., Braunstein, G. D., Simon, J. A., Casson, P. R., Buster, J. E., Redmond, G., et al. (2000). Transdermal testosterone treatment in women with impaired sexual function after oophorectomy. *New England Journal of Medicine, 343,* 682–688.

Sipski, M. L., Alexander, C. J., & Rosen, R. C. (1995a). Orgasm in women with spinal cord injuries: A laboratory-based assessment. *Archives of Physical Medicine and Rehabilitation, 76,* 1097–1102.

Sipski, M. L., Alexander, C. J., & Rosen, R. C. (1995b). Physiological parameters associated with psychogenic sexual arousal in women with complete spinal cord injuries. *Archives of Physical Medicine and Rehabilitation, 76,* 811–818.

Sipski, M. L., Alexander, C. J., & Rosen, R. C. (2001). Sexual arousal and orgasm in women: Effects of spinal cord injury. *Annals of Neurology, 49,* 35–44.

Spanier, G. B. (1976). Measuring dyadic adjustment: New scales for assessing the quality of marriage and similar dyads. *Journal of Marriage and the Family, 38,* 15–28.

Stewart, E. G. (2006). Physical examination and female sexual dysfunction. In I. Goldstein, C. M. Meston, S. R. Davis, & A. M. Traish (Eds.), *Women's sexual function and dysfunction: Study, diagnosis and treatment* (pp. 347–355). New York: Taylor & Francis.

Swieczkowski, J. B., & Walker, C. E. (1978). Sexual behavior correlates of female orgasm and marital happiness. *Journal of Nervous and Mental Disorders, 166,* 335–342.

Tang, C. S., Lai, F. D., & Chung, T. K. H. (1997). Assessment of sexual functioning for Chinese college students. *Archives of Sexual Behavior, 26,* 79–90.

Taylor, J. F., Rosen, R. C., & Leiblum, S. R. (1994). Self-report assessment of female sexual function: Psychometric evaluation of the Brief Index of Sexual Function for Women. *Archives of Sexual Behavior, 23,* 627–643.

Traish, A. M., & Kim, N. N. (2006). Modulation of female genital sexual arousal by sex steroid hormones. In I. Goldstein, C. M. Meston, S. R. Davis, & A. M. Traish (Eds.), *Women's sexual function and dysfunction: Study, diagnosis and treatment* (pp. 181–193). New York: Taylor & Francis.

Traish, A. M., Kim, N. N., Min, K., Munarriz, R., & Goldstein, I. (2002). Role of androgens in female genital sexual arousal: Receptor expression, structure, and function. *Fertility and Sterility, 77*(Suppl. 4), 11–18.

Tuiten, A., van Honk, J., Verbaten, R., Laan, E., Everaerd, W., & Stam, H. (2002). Can sublingual testosterone increase subjective and physiological measures of laboratory-induced sexual arousal. *Archives of General Psychiatry, 59,* 465–466.

Whipple, B., Gerdes, C. A., & Komisaruk, B. R. (1996). Sexual response to self-stimulation in women with complete spinal cord injury. *Journal of Sex Research, 33,* 231–240.

Wiederman, M. W. (2000). Women's body image self-consciousness during physical intimacy with a partner. *Journal of Sex Research, 37,* 60–68.

Zumoff, B., Strain, G. W., Miller, L. K., & Rosner, W. (1995). Twenty four hour mean plasma testosterone concentration declines with age in normal premenopausal women. *Journal of Clinical Endocrinology and Metabolism, 80,* 1429–1430.

Female Genital Pain and Its Treatment

Melissa A. Farmer, Tuuli Kukkonen,
and Yitzchak M. Binik

Learning Objectives

In this chapter, we:

- Examine issues and controversies surrounding traditional definitions of genital pain, as well as empirically supported alternative conceptualizations of dyspareunia and vaginismus.

- Describe research on the course, development and prevalence of genital pain.

- Discuss biomedical, genetic, and psychological risk factors associated with female genital pain.

- Assess genital pain from a multidisciplinary perspective, including biomedical, psychosocial and pain-focused assessment and measurement, as well as the impact of genital pain on relationships and patient self-perception.

- Provide an overview of research on the treatment of superficial pain, deep pain and vaginismus, with a comment on therapeutic strategies for managing genital pain.

Consider the following case study that introduces a patient who is experiencing genital pain:

Case Study 8.1

Charlene is a 24-year-old woman who complains of genital pain during sexual intercourse and when wearing tight jeans. She experienced no pain with her previous sexual partners. The pain began suddenly 7 months ago as a diffuse ache; however, she currently reports a sharp, cutting pain "inside the vagina" with occasional spasms at the introitus when attempting intercourse. This provoked pain worsens during ovulation and gradually lessens over the month. Charlene believes she has pain because "my vagina is too tight." A gynecological examination reveals pain only at the vulvar vestibule. When asked about whether she has had yeast infections, Charlene laughs and pauses, "This year?" She currently avoids any sexual activity with her boyfriend of 1 year, for fear he will want to have sexual intercourse with penetration. Although she used to see herself as a sexual person, she currently experiences minimal sexual desire, rarely masturbates, and complains of a complete lack of lubrication. Charlene becomes extremely distressed every time her boyfriend demands to know why she isn't attracted to him anymore.

The woman described might receive a wide range of diagnoses depending on whom she consulted. A family doctor might prescribe a low dose tricyclic antidepressant with a follow-up appointment in 3 months. A sex therapist may suspect a sexual pain disorder and recommend sex and/or couples therapy. A gynecologist might diagnose her with vulvar vestibulitis and prescribe topical lidocaine cream. A psychologist might see her as an anxious, somaticizing woman with ambivalent attitudes toward sexuality and recommend psychotherapy. Finally, a physiotherapist would likely discover increased pelvic floor hypertonicity and decreased pelvic floor muscle stability and commence treatment to improve muscle relaxation and normalize muscle tone. While each of these professionals can see part of the problem, none of them is viewing the whole picture, and is thus unlikely to alleviate all of her pain.

The study of dyspareunia and vaginismus has been complicated by inconsistent diagnoses, ambiguous etiology, and controversy regarding the type, quality, and significance of genital pain (Binik, 2005). The vague terms, dyspareunia and vaginismus, encompass multiple pain conditions of varying etiologies. Indeed, even trained professionals may not be able to reliably differentiate between the two conditions, let alone provide differential diagnoses (Reissing, Binik, Khalifé, Cohen, & Amsel, 2004; but see Bergeron, Binik, Khalifé, Pagidas, Glazer, Meana, et al., 2001). When faced with a woman experiencing genital pain, what should one do? In our clinical experience, the optimal treatment of genital pain is accomplished through a multidisciplinary approach in which psychologists, sex and couple therapists, physicians, and pelvic floor specialists work together.

Our conceptualizations of genital pain have changed dramatically over the past century, from the early belief that the pain was a psychogenic confabulation of hysterical women to the present day view that genital pain, like all other pains, is the result of a complex synthesis of psychological, physical, social, cultural, and contextual factors. Traditional diagnostic categories do not capture the diverse presentations of genital pain and dismiss the presence of genital pain in nonsexual situations such as gynecological examinations or tampon insertion. Indeed, our clinical experiences have led us to endorse some controversial interpretations of genital pain: we believe that vaginismus and dyspareunia lie on a continuum of a variety of dimensions, including pain, physical pathology, fear, avoidance, and muscle tension, and that specific diagnoses may not be mutually exclusive.

Definitions

The mention of pain associated with sexual intercourse dates back over 3,500 years to the Ramesseum papyri of ancient Egypt where dyspareunia appears to have been linked with abnormal menstruation (Barns, 1956; Costa, Talens, & Colorado Vicente, 1971). Early accounts of vaginismus can be found in a text from the mid-1500s by Trotula of Salerno, a female physician, who described in her work a tightening of the vulva. Numerous descriptions of dyspareunia and vaginismus exist in gynecological texts from the nineteenth and twentieth centuries, but Sims (1861) gave a classic description of vaginismus involving vaginal spasms and contractions and Barnes (1874) coined the term dyspareunia to refer to painful conditions interfering with intercourse.

Barnes stressed that the etiology of dyspareunia was physiologically based. However, it was the influential psychoanalytic movement of the twentieth century that shifted the view of "sexual" pain to the realm of psychogenic dysfunction. Within this context, dyspareunia and vaginismus first appeared in the *Diagnostic and Statistical Manual of Mental Disorders*, second edition (*DSM-II*, American Psychiatric Association, 1968) under the category of genitourinary disorders within the psychosomatic diseases section. In the *DSM-II*, vaginismus and dyspareunia were grouped with other diseases thought to have a psychosomatic basis such as various skin conditions, musculoskeletal disorders, and respiratory illnesses. In an attempt to incorporate empirical research into standardized diagnostic classifications, the committees for the *DSM-III* and *DSM-III-R* initiated field trials to determine the reliability and validity of psychiatric diagnoses (American Psychiatric Association, 1980, 1987). Although no empirical research was conducted on the sexual dysfunctions, dyspareunia and vaginismus were transferred from the psychosomatic category to that of sexual dysfunction, where they have remained for the *DSM-IV* and *DSM-IV-TR* (American Psychiatric Association, 1994, 2000). Currently, the *DSM-IV-TR* distinguishes dyspareunia and vaginismus subtypes into lifelong versus acquired and generalized versus situational. The *DSM-IV-TR* definition of dyspareunia is as follows:

A. *Recurrent or persistent genital pain associated with sexual intercourse in either a male or a female.*

B. *The disturbance causes marked distress or interpersonal difficulty.*

C. *The disturbance is not caused exclusively by vaginismus or lack of lubrication, is not better accounted for by another Axis I disorder (except another Sexual Dysfunction) and is not due exclusively to the direct physiological effects of a substance (e.g., a drug of abuse, a medication) or a general medical condition. (p. 556)*

Numerous problems arise with this definition: (a) genital pain can occur in a variety of situations and is rarely exclusive to sexual intercourse, (b) it is plausible that a lack of lubrication results from painful sexual experience but the expectation of pain may be causally related to the lack of lubrication, (c) vaginismus cannot be reliably differentiated from dyspareunia, (d) genital pain is the only pain in the *DSM-IV-TR* that is classified according to the activity with which it interferes; all other pains are listed under the category of pain disorders.

Equally problematic is the *DSM-IV-TR* definition of vaginismus:

A. *Recurrent or persistent involuntary spasm of the musculature of the outer third of the vagina that interferes with sexual intercourse.*

B. *The disturbance causes marked distress or interpersonal difficulty.*

C. *The disturbance is not better accounted for by another Axis I disorder (e.g., Somatization Disorder) and is not due exclusively to the direct physiological effects of a general medical condition. (p. 558)*

Recent evidence suggests that the main criterion of vaginal spasm is not a reliable indicator of vaginismus, nor does it differentiate this condition from dyspareunia.

Much like the *DSM-IV-TR*, the *International Classification of Diseases*, tenth edition (*ICD-10*; World Health Organization, 1992) classifies dyspareunia and vaginismus under sexual dysfunctions not caused by organic disorders or disease. What distinguishes the

ICD-10 from the *DSM-IV-TR*, however, is that these disorders are also found in the category of *pain and other conditions associated with female genital organs and the menstrual cycle*. Under this heading, dyspareunia and vaginismus are presumed to have physiological causes, whereas within the sexual dysfunctions category their etiology is presumed to be psychogenic.

These traditional definitions have remained unchallenged for many years. However, such categorical classifications do not capture the complexity and variations of genital pain experienced by women. The International Consensus Conference on Female Sexual Disorders proposed the addition of "noncoital" genital pain in order to validate and classify pain that occurs beyond the context of vaginal penetrative intercourse (Basson, Leiblum, et al., 2004). The consensus document concluded that etiology be considered in the diagnosis of genital pain, including four etiological variations: organic, psychogenic, mixed organic/psychogenic, and unknown. These amendments are promising steps toward revising how we think about genital pain. However, more dramatic modifications of how these disorders are conceptualized and diagnosed are needed.

The rationale for the *DSM-IV-R* categories of dypareunia and vaginismus, as well as their differentiation, lacks empirical evidence. The diagnosis of vaginismus is most often indicated based on patient self-report rather than on any physical examination for vaginal spasms or physiological abnormalities. For instance, Reissing and colleagues (2004) demonstrated that the main *DSM-IV-R* diagnostic criterion for vaginismus—muscle spasm—did not reliably differentiate among women suffering from vaginismus, from dyspareunia, or matched healthy controls (see also Basson, Weijman Shultz, et al., 2004; van Lankveld, Brewaeys, ter Kuile, & Weijenborg, 1995). Instead, reported pain, fear of pain, and behavioral avoidance may be more useful than muscle spasm as diagnostic indicators of vaginismus. Along the same lines, Rosenbaum (2005) highlights the overlap between dyspareunia and vaginismus, suggesting that the lack of anxiety and physical withdrawal during a physical examination leads health professionals to diagnose women as having dyspareunia rather than vaginismus. None of these diagnostic factors are based on the presenting problems of genital pain.

Meana and colleagues (1997) have argued for a pain-based approach to clinically differentiate subtypes of genital pain using the International Association for the Study of Pain (IASP) *Classification of Chronic Pain*. The IASP diagnostic criteria classify pain according to five major axes: region affected, systems involved, temporal characteristics, patient's statement of intensity and duration, and etiology. Within this framework, we can differentiate between different types of dyspareunia. For example, a woman who experiences a deep throbbing pain in her uterus during thrusting would not be classified as having the same problem as a woman who experiences a sharp cutting and burning sensation at the vulvar vestibule upon penetration.

An example of the successful integration of the pain perspective into the diagnosis of genital pain was the 2003 decision by the International Society for the Study of Vulvovaginal Disease to update the classification of vulvar pain, or vulvodynia. The revised classification of vulvodynia included vulvar pain related to a specific disorder and vulvodynia that could be generalized, localized, provoked, or unprovoked; it also specified that the pain could be sexual and nonsexual (Moyal-Barracco & Lynch, 2004). By focusing on the pain aspect of these disorders, the new classification expanded the understanding and treatment of these disorders. Research also suggests that while dyspareunia and vaginismus have been considered as separate entities in the past, conceptualizing them as existing on a continuum might be more useful (Reissing et al., 2004).

Course, Development, and Prevalence of Pain

Much controversy surrounds the course and prevalence of dyspareunia and vaginismus. Whereas some research suggests that younger women are more likely to experience genital pain or that pain during intercourse decreases with age, other research indicates that the prevalence of genital pain remains constant with age (Hayes & Dennerstein, 2005; Laumann, Gagnon, Michael, & Michaels, 1994). No longitudinal studies, however, have evaluated the temporal development of these disorders.

Prevalence research mirrors the inconsistencies regarding the course and development of genital pain, and both types of research are limited by the following factors:

- Reliance on convenience samples of participants.
- An inclusion criterion of currently engaging in sexual activity.
- Devoting only one yes or no survey question to pain during intercourse.
- Neglect of potential confounding variables such as relationship issues or hormone levels.
- Overgeneralization of results from one subtype of dyspareunia, vulvar vestibulitis syndrome (VVS).
- Difficulty of eliciting candid responses given the sensitive and personal nature of the topic.
- Response biases concerning differing survey methods (e.g., personal interview, mail survey, telephone survey).

With these limitations in mind, current estimates of pain during sexual intercourse range from 12% to 39% for sexually active premenopausal women (Harlow, Wise, & Stewart, 2001; Hayes & Dennerstein, 2005; Johnson, Phelps, & Cottler, 2004; Laumann, Gagnon, Michaci, & Michaels, 1999; Oberg, Fugl-Meyer, & Fugl-Meyer, 2004; Talakoub et al., 2002). One Swedish study that differentiated vaginismus from dyspareunia reported a prevalence of 5% for women who experience vaginismus with distress and 28% for women who report dyspareunia with distress (Oberg et al., 2004). Studies on pain during intercourse from North America, however, have found lower prevalence rates for dyspareunia, ranging from 12% to 19% (Harlow & Stewart, 2003; Harlow et al., 2001; Johnson et al., 2004; Laumann et al., 1999; Talakoub et al., 2002). Prevalence rates may be higher in specific populations: in perimenopausal oncology patients, rates for dyspareunic pain may reach up to 65% (Amsterdam, Carter, & Krychman, 2006). Currently, there is no population-based work on vaginismus, but in clinical settings approximately 12% to 17% of women who consult have vaginismus (Hirst, Baggaley, & Watson, 1996; Spector & Carey, 1990).

Little knowledge of prevalence across different age groups exists. The National Health and Social Life Survey study by Laumann et al. (1999) reports pain during intercourse in 21% of 18- to 29-year-olds, 15% of 30- to 39-year-olds, 13% of 40- to 49-year-olds, and 8% of 50- to 59-year-olds. Although our specific knowledge of prevalence is poor, dyspareunia and vaginismus affect a significant portion of women.

One alternative approach for population prevalence studies which could possibly generate more in depth information involves taking a "pain approach." Harlow and colleagues (2001, 2003) studied the pain itself rather than the clinical categories of dyspareunia and vaginismus, assessing symptoms of four types of lower genital tract discomfort: onset and frequency, whether symptoms were provoked or spontaneous, whether they caused discomfort or prevented intercourse, and how participants sought treatment. Their results identified various subgroups of women who experience genital pain, with an overall lifetime incidence estimate of 16%. Examining genital pain in this way leads to a better understanding of its etiology and thus suggests more suitable treatment and prevention strategies.

Risk Factors

Multiple population factors have been associated with genital pain in women. One study found that women with a college education were at lower risk of experiencing pain during intercourse than high school graduates (Laumann et al., 1999) whereas another has found that those without a high school diploma were less likely to report painful intercourse (Johnson et al., 2004). Caucasian women are at greater risk for genital pain than African American women (Laumann et al., 1999). When examining age, current marital status, or educational attainment, however, Harlow and Stewart (2003) did not find differences in lifetime prevalence of vulvar discomfort and pain symptoms. What they did find was that pain is less common in women who began using tampons at age 14 or later compared to those who started earlier. Furthermore, they found that Hispanic women were at greater risk for unexplained chronic vulvar pain than Caucasian and African American women.

A variety of biomedical risk factors have been implicated in the development of genital pain. However, these risk factors are largely correlational and rely on retrospective self-report, with a heavy bias toward specific populations of women. Frequent or recurrent vulvar and/or vaginal infections have been reported in a subset of women with dyspareunia (Pukall, Binik, Khalifé, Amsel, & Abbott, 2002). The concurrence of dyspareunia and vaginal atrophy suggests that estrogen may indirectly influence genital pain (Willhite & O'Connell, 2001). Oral contraceptives, pregnancy, and the peri-ovulatory phase of the menstrual cycle have been associated with increased genital pain. For example, Bohm-Starke, Johannesson, Hilliges, Rylander and Torebjörk (2004) demonstrated that in a small group of healthy, pain-free women using estrogenic oral contraceptives, a reduction in vestibular mechanical pain thresholds was observed when compared to healthy, pain-free women using other forms of contraception. Similar to the relationship between hormones and genital pain in premenopausal women, reduced estrogen levels following the menopause are linked with vaginal atrophy, vaginal dryness, and dyspareunia (Sarrel, 2000).

In addition to gynecological conditions and hormonal fluctuations, past abdominal or pelvic surgeries or physical trauma to the genitals may provoke tissue damage and ultimately lead to abnormal peripheral pain transmission. Tissue damage may also result from the experience of sexual abuse or assault during childhood or adulthood (Emmert & Köhler, 1998). Dyspareunia has also been reported in women who have received radiotherapy for cervical, ovarian, and endometrial cancer (e.g., Thranov & Klee, 1994). Retrospective self-reports further suggest that genital pain can typically start at any time, including at the onset of menstruation and sexual activity, after childbirth, following pain-free intercourse, and postmenopausally (reviewed in Meana & Binik, 1994). Two factors associated with early vulvar genital pain onset are an avoidance of or pain with tampon use and having regular sexual intercourse before the age of 16 (Berglund, Nigaard, & Rylander, 2002).

Yet another factor linked with both vaginismus and dyspareunia is vaginal spasms or contractions—phenomena referred to as pelvic floor hypertonicity (Reissing et al., 2004; Weijmar Schultz et al., 1996). Pelvic floor hypertonicity may contribute to the maintenance of genital pain by exacerbating pressure on sensitive genital tissue and muscle. In addition to hypertonicity, weak pelvic muscles and a lack of control over pelvic floor musculature can play a role in the maintenance of genital pain.

Finally, growing evidence implicates a genetic predisposition in the development of genital pain in some women. Both Goetsch (1991) and Bergeron, Binik, Khalifé, and Pagidas (1997) report that between one-quarter and one-third of women interviewed had female relatives who also experienced dyspareunia, suggesting a possible genetic vulnerability. Emerging support for genetic polymorphisms in women with VVS supports this evidence (e.g., Foster, Sazenski, & Stodgell, 2004; Gerber, Bongiovanni, Ledger, & Witkin, 2003).

To date, there is little consistent support for a set of psychological risk factors for genital pain; however, the small literature points to a variety of factors including depression, anxiety, catastrophizing, hypervigilance, and less positive sexual attitudes. Evidence of clinical levels of psychopathology in women with dyspareunia and vaginismus is poor; however, these women report greater sadness and anxiety as compared to healthy control women, and this higher negative mood can play a role in the initiation and/or maintenance of pain (Basson, Weijmar Schultz, et al., 2004). It is unclear whether anxiety and depression are risk factors for developing genital pain or whether painful sexual experiences predispose the development of negative mood, given that sexual problems are often part of the clinical diagnosis of depression. Additionally, women who continue to seek treatment likely do so because they are distressed, and thus the correlation between genital pain and negative mood may be attributable to the selection bias of women who end up in gynecologists' offices or research settings.

Correlational evidence indicates that women with genital pain endorse less positive sexual attitudes (Reissing, Binik, Khalifé, Cohen, & Amsel, 2003). Factors loosely associated with genital pain include conservative sexual values, self-reported religiosity, religious participation, adherence to more conservative religious traditions, negative sexual attitudes, and lack of sexual experience (Bassett, Smith, Newell, & Richards, 1999; Davidson, Moore, & Ullstrup, 2004; Laumann et al., 1994; Lefkowitz, Gillen, Shearer, & Boone, 2004). No research has, however, causally linked any of these factors with dyspareunia and vaginismus.

Two psychological variables linked with dyspareunia are catastrophizing and hypervigilance. Specifically, compared to healthy women, women suffering from VVS report significantly higher distress in relation to the pain intensity and have a greater tendency to catastrophize about their genital pain (Pukall et al., 2002). The catastrophizing, however, appears to be specific to genital pain and is not generalizable to other physical pains in women with VVS (see Assessment section). In addition to catastrophizing, women with VVS exhibit hypervigilance toward their genital pain (Payne, Binik, Amsel, & Khalifé, 2005): they scored higher on pain interference during a Stroop task than healthy controls and higher on the Pain Vigilance Awareness Questionnaire for recurrent pain. These findings indicate that women with VVS may have an implicit and explicit attentional bias toward genital pain. Table 8.1 provides a biomedical and psychosocial risk analysis for factors that alone or in combination may indicate an elevated risk for genital pain.

Assessment

The assessment of genital pain requires a multidisciplinary collaboration among health professionals, psychologists, gynecologists, and pelvic floor specialists in order to formulate practical and successful treatment options. The failure to refer a patient for both biomedical and psychosocial assessments may result in a limited understanding of the pain problem and may prevent a patient from obtaining the treatment(s) best suited to her unique pain experience. Table 8.2 provides a snapshot of appropriate referrals for common complaints of women with genital pain.

Table 8.1   **Risk Analysis for Genital Pain**

Categories of Risk (check all that apply)

History	Behavior	Psychological	Physical Trauma	Hormonal
☐ Previous infection ☐ Current infection ☐ Female relatives with genital pain	☐ Avoidance of tampons ☐ Tampon use before age 14 ☐ Sex before age of 16 ☐ Pelvic floor hypertonus	☐ Negative mood ☐ Catastrophizing ☐ Hypervigilance ☐ Negative attitudes toward sex	☐ Abdominal or pelvic surgery ☐ Injury ☐ Radiotherapy	☐ Vaginal atrophy ☐ Hormone therapy ☐ Pregnancy ☐ Oral contraceptive use ☐ Peri-ovulatory phase

Note: Risk categories are based solely on correlational, retrospective research and should be interpreted with caution.

Table 8.2 **A Referral Guide for the Concurrent Multidisciplinary Assessment of Genital Pain**

Complaints	Psychology	Gynecology	Pelvic Floor Specialist
Does patient feel helpless regarding the genital pain?	X		
Does patient report high levels of anxiety regarding the pain?	X		
Has patient had great difficulty in undergoing a gynecological exam, or does she refuse to do so?	X		
Does patient have comorbid psychological disorders?	X		
Has patient reported comorbid sexual dysfunction and/or reduced sexual satisfaction?	X		
Is patient primarily concerned with relational factors?	X		
Does patient complain of frequent vaginal infections?		X	
Has pain corresponded with hormonal shifts (i.e., menstrual cycle, pregnancy, menopause, oral contraceptives)?		X	
Indicators			
Does patient experience pain spontaneously?		X	
Does patient report a history of genital trauma or injury, including tissue damage from surgery or radiotherapy?		X	
Does patient feel tension in the pelvic region or tightening of the pelvic muscles with attempted penetration?			X
Does patient report coexisting bladder control problems?			X
Does patient report a history of childhood sexual abuse or sexual assault?	X	X	
Does patient report pain before genital contact occurs during sexual activity?	X		X

Sources of Referral

Biomedical Assessment and Measurement

Considering the numerous and varied risk factors for developing genital pain, a multidisciplinary assessment is essential. In its current form, the biomedical approach focuses on surgical, pharmacological, and physiotherapeutic interventions aimed at correcting and treating disease states (see Table 8.2).

Gynecological Examination

A gynecological examination is important for an accurate diagnosis of dyspareunia and vaginismus. A gynecologist will provide results of physical examinations and, ideally, tissue cultures to clarify whether the pain is related to a medical condition or a previous gynecological procedure such as hysterectomy, radical cystectomy, perineal surgeries, and procedures following ovarian cancer (Tunuguntla & Gousse, 2006; Zippe, Nandipati, Agarwal, & Raina, 2005). In the case of women with suspected vaginismus, the problem is evaluating whether they can manage the distress associated with a gynecological assessment and, if so, convincing them to undergo the experience.

Pain Behavior

The gynecological examination may provide a unique window into a woman's genital pain experience. Difficulties may occur in gynecological assessments because women with dyspareunia or vaginismus are practically assured a painful experience. During the examination, diverse pain behaviors communicate anxiety; these behaviors include grimacing, vocalizations, crying, leg crossing, lifting of the buttocks, backing up on the examination table, rocking of the head or torso, or other guarding behavior. Some women with dyspareunia and many with vaginismus may be too fearful to undergo a proper physical examination (Kaneko, 2001).

Some gynecologists diagnose such women with vaginismus solely by virtue of their fear response. For instance, a 23-year-old reported intense anxiety about any form of vaginal penetration and had to be coaxed to the gynecological table. During the examination, she fearfully slammed her knees together and twisted her body away from the gynecologist. After multiple attempts by the gynecologist to help her relax, it became clear that she could not endure a physical examination.

Sensory Testing

Mounting evidence indicates sensory abnormalities in women with dyspareunia, so sensory testing may be incorporated into physical examination. Women with VVS have lower vestibular and labial tactile and pain thresholds, and their pain severity is positively associated with hyperalgesic responses to heat, pressure, and punctuate pressures (Bohm-Starke et al., 2004; Granot,

Friedman, Yarnitsky, & Zimmer, 2002; Lowenstein et al., 2004; Pukall et al., 2002). Similarly, women with vulvodynia have shown higher pressure pain sensitivity at the vulva, thumb, deltoid, and shin (Giesecke et al., 2004). Reduced pain thresholds at the vulva reflect the clinical phenomenon of vulvar pain, but when additional sensory differences are measurable elsewhere in the body, the mechanism underlying altered sensory thresholds may reflect abnormalities in central pain processing (Pukall, Strigo, Binik, Amsel, Khalifé, & Bushnell, 2005).

Systematic sensory testing may be conducted with one of the recently developed spring-loaded pressure devices designed specifically to measure genital pain threshold, such as the vulvalgesiometer (Pukall, Binik, & Khalifé, 2004), the vulvodolorimeter (Giesecke et al., 2004), or similar springed pressure devices (Lowenstein et al., 2004). For instance, the vulvalgesiometer exerts standardized amounts of pressure to vulvar sites with a cotton swab tip; its use has successfully distinguished women with VVS from age- and oral contraceptive-matched control women (Pukall et al., 2004). Although there is no standardized procedure for the physiological assessment of vaginismus, the techniques established for dyspareunia (e.g., cotton swab and vulvalgesiometer tests) can also indicate pain thresholds in women with vaginismus.

Pelvic Floor Examination

A comprehensive evaluation of the pelvic floor musculature by an experienced pelvic floor physiotherapist or gynecologist can provide insight into the maintaining factors of vaginismus and dyspareunia. However, a sensitivity and understanding of the woman's fear and anxiety is crucial to help guide her through this difficult experience (Rosenbaum, 2005). During a typical examination, the vagina and perineum are gently examined for tenderness. An internal vaginal and, if indicated, anal examination allows the physiotherapist to determine the tension, tone, strength, and motion of the pelvic musculature. Recent research has indicated high reliability between different physiotherapists blind to patient condition in distinguishing women with VVS from healthy pain-free controls, suggesting that such examination can provide valuable information in the assessment of genital pain (Reissing, Brown, Lord, Binik, & Khalifé, 2005).

Psychosocial Assessment

The specialists involved in psychosocial assessment of genital pain (mental health professionals, pain specialists, psychiatrists, sex therapists) must obtain a comprehensive picture of how a woman's personality, cognitive vulnerabilities, relationship history, and personal and social situations shape her responses to her pain. Psychological factors, including the role of anxiety and fear, reliance on maladaptive coping strategies, personal illness perceptions, impact on sexual relationships, and comorbid sexual dysfunction may play prominent roles in the development and maintenance of genital pain. The psychosocial assessment may also help to assure the woman that her pain is real and to build a therapeutic alliance.

Assessment of Pain

Assessments of pain include information about the location of the pain (superficial versus deep), pain onset in relation to vaginal penetration, and pain duration. Pain reported shortly before vaginal contact is indicative of a strong fear component, like that seen in women with vaginismus. In contrast, unprovoked pain may indicate the presence of vulvodynia. Pain duration indicates whether the pain solely interferes with sexual activity or whether it impacts other domains of daily living, such as sitting for prolonged periods, walking, standing, riding a bicycle, or wearing tight clothing. According to one study, approximately 68% of women with dyspareunia experience genital pain in nonsexual contexts (Danielsson, Sjöberg, & Wikman, 2000). Events temporally connected to pain onset, such as genital injury or oral contraceptive use, should be noted. Factors that increase (e.g., stress, anxiety, fatigue) and decrease pain (e.g., relaxation, medication, partner support) may guide treatment options. Keeping a pain diary may help a woman to independently monitor and identify pain symptoms and intensity, pain quality, activity level, emotional state, coping strategies, and circumstances preceding the onset of pain, as well as those that decrease the pain.

Pain intensity is easily assessed with the widely used Visual Analog Scale (VAS) of 0 to 10, where 0 describes absence of pain and 10 the worst pain imaginable. Additionally, the McGill Pain Questionnaire (MPQ; Melzack, 1975), a commonly used measure of sensory, affective, and evaluative dimensions of physical pain, may be modified to address genital pain. Descriptors of the quality of pain, such as burning, sharp, aching, or throbbing, may have important implications for diagnosis and in outlining potential causes of genital pain. Over 85% of women with VVS, for example, describe their genital pain as hot, burning, scalding, searing, sharp, or cutting (Bergeron et al., 2001).

Mood Disruptions

Primary to the assessment of genital pain is eliciting the woman's descriptions of pain quality, intensity, and frequency and how these factors relate to her emotional experience of the pain. The clinician should inquire about the impact of mood on the genital pain. Does pain increase during times of stress or fatigue? Has the patient noticed a reduction of pain when she feels relaxed? Such clues can inform the clinician about the contribution of anxiety or fear in amplifying and maintaining the pain. Women may have varying levels of insight into how their pain relates to their emotions, and this assessment can show the client the link between anxiety and the pain experience.

Fear of and anxiety about painful vaginal penetration are important emotional responses of women with vaginismus and dyspareunia. In Kaneko's sample (2001), up to 47% of women with vaginismus showed fear and 67% of women with dyspareunia felt disgust toward sexual intercourse. Negative emotional states may amplify or exacerbate pain through the physiological consequences of negative affect (e.g., pain enhanced by muscle tension) and/or the cognitive processes associated with fear, anxiety, and depression. Conversely, distraction may reduce the awareness of physical pain by directing attention away from it. Although the mechanisms of the affective processing of pain are poorly understood, a cognitive orientation toward pain-related information may influence how attention is preferentially directed toward descriptors relevant to genital pain in VVS women (i.e., burning, throbbing, ache, cutting). This "hypervigilance" toward pain is mediated by self-reported anxiety and fear of pain (Payne et al., 2005). Importantly, negative emotion may influence the subjective sensory experience of pain. Indeed, negative emotional states have been correlated with reduced pain tolerance and increased self-reported pain severity (Carter et al., 2002). In short, the emotional experience of pain can enhance (or reduce) coexisting cognitive processes. As one patient put it, "I wait for the pain to come. My whole body waits for the pain."

Elevated state and trait anxiety commonly distinguish women with VVS from healthy controls (Granot et al., 2002; Nunns & Mandal, 1997; Nylanderlundqvist & Bergdahl, 2003; Payne et al., 2005). Anxiety is thought to increase fear about sexual penetration (Tugrul & Kabakci, 1997) and drive behaviors such as the avoidance of sexual activity or of gynecological examinations (Pukall, Reissing, Binik, Khalifé, & Abbott, 2000). Avoidance of pain-related situations is anxiety-reducing in the short term, but it may reinforce the woman's fear of potentially painful stimuli, exacerbate pelvic muscle tension, and augment hypervigilance toward pain. A cyclical relationship between negative affect from performance anxiety, increased attention to threat cues such as pain, comorbid sexual dysfunction, and sexual avoidance may maintain anxiety-related coping responses (van den Hout & Barlow, 2000).

Coping Strategies

Assessment of coping strategies can indicate how a woman reacts to her pain and how her reactions may alleviate or perpetuate the experience of pain. Coping strategies consist of any cognitive or behavioral response that results from pain, with the aim of modifying how one acclimates to the experience of pain (Keefe, Dunsmore, & Burnett, 1992). Adaptive coping strategies increase the feeling of control over pain, which enhances an individual's ability to function in daily life (Haythornthwaite, Menefee, Heinberg, & Clark, 1998). Common coping strategies include avoidance, cognitive reappraisal, expression of emotion, problem-focused coping, seeking social support, and medical visits. To date, no empirical research has shown a relationship between positive coping strategies and decreased genital pain.

A maladaptive coping response expressed by some women with dyspareunic pain is catastrophizing (Pukall et al., 2002). Catastrophizing describes an attentional bias that preferentially orients an individual to pain-related information through both cognitive and affective components (Jones, Rollman, White, Hill, & Brooke, 2003) and correlates positively with perceived pain and disability in chronic pain populations (Martin et al., 1996; Sullivan, Bishop, & Pivik, 1995). In addition to increasing the perception of pain, catastrophizing may also reflect a perceived lack of control over pain, as characterized by Sullivan and colleagues' (2001) description of catastrophizing as a combination of magnification, rumination, and helplessness. Catastrophizing may also facilitate social support and thus may have an adaptive coping dimension (Sullivan et al., 2001). The Pain Catastrophizing Scale (PCS: Sullivan et al., 1995) is a valid and reliable self-report measure that can be used to evaluate dimensions of catastrophizing. A construct that parallels catastrophizing—harm avoidance—is overrepresented in populations with dyspareunia (Danielsson, Eisemann, Sjöberg, & Wikman, 2001). Harm avoidance consists of a pessimistic and apprehensive evaluation of current and future outcomes, sometimes leading to "passively avoidant" behavior. Assessment of unhelpful coping strategies is particularly important for psychotherapeutic interventions because these strategies may change as genital pain worsens (Graziottin & Brotto, 2004).

Impact on Interpersonal Relationships

Interpersonal conflict resulting from genital pain often depends on the type of intimate relationship involved. Whereas vaginal spasm may not be problematic when a woman occasionally dates, experiencing this pain in the context of a primary intimate relationship may take on a very different meaning. An assessment of recent and current relationships may help to account for the level of psychological distress a woman experiences. Length and type of relationships, partners with whom pain has been experienced, concomitant sexual dysfunction in the partner (e.g., erectile dysfunction), and relationship satisfaction may provide insight into factors that contribute to and maintain the pain.

Pain experienced during a "relationship" activity such as sexual intercourse naturally has relationship consequences. The impact of pain on intimate relationships involves a woman's own pain perception, the perception of her sexual partner(s), and the resulting interpersonal context. Linking the origin of pain to psychological and interpersonal problems may implicitly target the relationship as a fundamental part of the pain problem. In contrast, a woman who believes her pain has a physiological cause may view the relationship as a source of support rather than pain, with the expression of pain becoming a shared experience. Indeed, as marital adjustment increases, dyspareunic pain is reduced (Meana, Binik, Khalifé, & Cohen, 1998). Because soliciting social support to manage psychological distress may underlie some forms of coping with pain—as exemplified by the communal coping model of catastrophizing—a supportive relationship may meet these interpersonal goals (Sullivan et al., 2001). Interestingly, this pattern of spousal solicitousness differs from that found in chronic pain research, where a spouse's solicitous responding is positively correlated with self-reported pain severity when marital adjustment is high (see Leonard, Cano, & Johansen, 2006).

Interpersonal support may relieve some of the sexual difficulties faced by these couples. For instance, a 22-year-old woman presented with deep vaginal pain during intercourse. She had recently begun taking a progestin-only oral contraceptive, but the precise cause of the pain was unclear. In order to manage the pain, she and her fiancée had developed a variety of alternative sexual positions that emphasized clitoral stimulation and shallow thrusting. As a result of creativity and partner support, the couple's sexual intimacy was not compromised despite the presence of vaginal pain.

Impact on Sexual Relationships
The sexual relationship is impacted by comorbid sexual dysfunctions (Danielsson et al., 2000; Jantos & White, 1997; Nunns & Mandal, 1997; Reissing et al., 2003; van Lankveld, Weijenborg, & ter Kuile, 1996). Although genital pain interferes with penetrative sexual intercourse, there is no evidence that genital pain per se adversely impacts the female sexual response cycle (e.g., desire, arousal, orgasm). However, negative appraisals of sexual stimuli may limit the level of attainable sexual arousal (Wouda, Hartman, Bakker, Bakker, van de Wiel, & Weijmar Schultz, 1998). Blunted sexual desire, difficulties with arousal and vaginal lubrication, and anorgasmia are typical sexual problems that arise with the expectation of painful sexual activity. In some instances, pain and arousal states may interact. Such was the case with a 33-year-old woman who began to experience a deep vaginal pain during sexual intercourse with her husband. Continued pain with sexual intercourse was soon followed by a drop in sexual arousal that she

described as the inability to get "turned on." The lack of arousal and the anticipation of discomfort further exacerbated her pain with vaginal penetration and in turn maintained the genital pain.

Useful psychometric measures to assess sexual functioning include the Female Sexual Functioning Index (FSFI; Rosen et al., 2000), which inquires about pain during and after sex, as well as pain intensity, and the Golombok Rust Inventory of Sexual Satisfaction (GRISS; Rust & Golombok, 1986), which includes a vaginismus subscale. These are well-validated, reliable self-report measures. Although no strict cutoff scores exist for vaginismus or dyspareunia, the mean FSFI score for the pain domain is 2.02, and 3.7 for women with vulvodynia (Masheb, Lozano-Blanco, Kohorn, Minkin, & Kerns, 2004; Weigel, Meston, & Rosen, 2005).

Closely linked with sexual dysfunction is how a woman's sexual self-concept is influenced by genital pain. Although little evidence exists on the qualitative aspects of dyspareunia or vaginismus, a recent qualitative analysis has explored the detrimental impact of vulvodynia on a small sample of women (Kaler, 2006). Pain not only prevented these women from engaging in vaginal-penile intercourse—a behavior that implicitly defines normative heterosexuality and a woman's relationship to intimate partners—but it also produced in them feelings of inadequacy and the sense that they were not "real" women.

Dominant themes in a woman's psychological history, including a history of physical or sexual abuse, sexual interferences (e.g., attempted sexual abuse), or other traumatic events, may influence a woman's experience of pain and should be addressed respectfully (Rellini & Meston, 2004). For instance, an increased self-report of sexual abuse has been linked with vaginismus (Reissing et al., 2003). However, research does not consistently support an increased prevalence of sexual abuse in women with dyspareunia (Meana et al., 1997).

Illness Perceptions of the Patient

In an attempt to understand the cause of their pain, many women have sought health care from multiple medical professionals. A recent study on vaginismus found that 69% of the sample had previously sought treatment from a variety of health professionals including physicians, psychologists, physical therapists and alternative healers (van Lankveld et al., 2006). Similarly, the typical woman with dyspareunia has consulted health professionals for an average of 13 months before receiving a correct diagnosis (Gates & Galask, 2001). She has probably been told that the pain is "all in her head."

An individual's cognitive and emotional experience of a health threat such as pain can be conceptualized as an illness perception (Schiaffino & Cea, 1995). The cognitive dimension of a pain-related illness perception integrates beliefs about the identity (e.g., symptoms, diagnosis), duration, consequences (e.g., severity and impact on functioning), etiology (biological and/or psychological), and ability to control pain. In contrast, the emotional dimension of illness perceptions pertains to positive and negative affective responses related to the pain experience. By helping to explain how an illness is perceived, illness perceptions provide insight into how an individual chooses to act based on this experience.

The illness perceptions of women with vaginismus and dyspareunia may be disproportionately based on symptoms, diagnosis, and consequences of pain, thereby leading to hypervigilance of physical symptoms (i.e., identity) and the psychological effects of those symptoms (i.e., consequences). Distorted beliefs about pain may lead to negative affective responses and less adaptive health behaviors in attempts to cope with the pain. Maladaptive coping responses may result from chronic pain duration, serious consequences of the pain, strong illness identity, or a preoccupation with pain symptoms. For instance, Meana, Binik, Khalifé, and Cohen (1999) demonstrated that women who attributed their dyspareunic pain to psychological causes—such as anxiety, relationship difficulties, a history of sexual victimization, or poor sexual skills—reported greater pain ratings, distress, sexual aversion, and interpersonal conflict. In contrast, adaptive responses result from perceived pain controllability (Heijmans & de Ridder, 1998; Lacroix, 1991; Scharloo et al., 1998). Illness perceptions may therefore contribute to the maintenance of genital pain independent of the factors that originally evoked the pain.

For instance, illness perceptions played a prominent role in a 32-year-old patient who presented with superficial vaginal pain following a pregnancy. She desperately wanted to have another child but could not tolerate the pain of vaginal intercourse. She had tried estrogen preparations, topical lidocaine, and even capsaicin, but she did not want to pursue systemic treatments while attempting to conceive. The patient described constant anxiety about her pain—was there a physical problem that would prevent her from conceiving? Why couldn't anyone cure her pain? Was it cancer? Her persistent focus on her symptoms of pain and her fear about not being able to have another child had transformed her situation-specific pain problem into a daily preoccupation.

Treatment

Few randomized controlled outcome studies have been conducted for either the biomedical or psychosocial treatment of vaginismus or dyspareunia. The sparse evidence from randomized controlled treatments is paralleled by a large body of uncontrolled evidence. Figure 8.1 summarizes the range of treatment strategies in rela-

Figure 8.1

Multidisciplinary Assessment and Treatment Strategies for Genital Pain

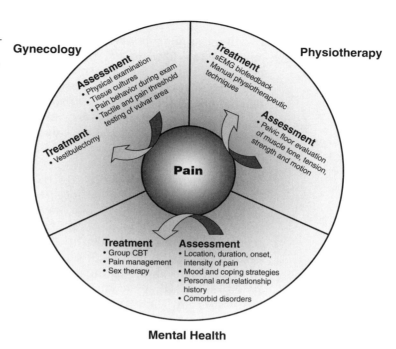

Gynecology

Assessment
• Physical examination
• Tissue cultures
• Pain behavior during exam
• Tactile and pain threshold testing of vulvar area

Treatment
• Vestibulectomy

Physiotherapy

Treatment
• sEMG biofeedback
• Manual physiotherapeutic techniques

Assessment
• Pelvic floor evaluation of muscle tone, tension, strength and motion

Pain

Treatment
• Group CBT
• Pain management
• Sex therapy

Assessment
• Location, duration, onset, intensity of pain
• Mood and coping strategies
• Personal and relationship history
• Comorbid disorders

Mental Health

tion to psychological, gynecological/sensory, and physiotherapeutic assessment of genital pain. In order to better understand the existing evidence, treatments are presented by pain condition.

Superficial Pain

Treatment studies for VVS dominate the literature; however, only a handful have evaluated controlled treatment of VVS. To date, vestibulectomy (the excision of painful vestibular tissue) has produced the greatest reductions in VVS pain. It is unclear why this surgery reduces or resolves vulvar pain in some women; however, hypotheses have focused on the interruption of abnormal peripheral pain transmission through the excision of painful vulvar tissue. Two randomized controlled trials provide empirical support for the efficacy of surgery in the reduction of VVS pain. Weijmar Schultz and colleagues (1996) initiated a randomized comparison of perineoplasty followed by behavioral therapy ($n = 7$) versus behavioral therapy only ($n = 7$) for the treatment of VVS. The behavioral therapy included components of psychoeducation, sex therapy, and physiotherapy and lasted on average 11.3 to 16.9 months. Both treatments were equally effective in reducing complaints of pain, and the investigators discontinued the randomized portion of the study due to ethical concerns about assigning surgery for a condition that could be treated equally well with behavioral treatment. When additional participants were allowed to

self-select their treatment, no outcome differences emerged between the surgery-behavioral therapy ($n = 6$) and behavioral therapy only ($n = 28$) groups. This study, however, lacked statistical
power due to small group sizes and limited outcome measures.
The primary outcome measure was self-reported, using a 1 (pain
had completely resolved) to 5 (pain had worsened) scale.

In an effort to extend and improve on these initial results,
Bergeron and colleagues (2001) found additional support for surgery in a randomized uncontrolled study comparing vestibulectomy, sEMG (surface electromyography) biofeedback, and group
cognitive behavioral therapy (GCBT) in the treatment of VVS.
During a 6-week baseline period, participants refrained from any
form of treatment for their pain, including use of potentially aller-
genic topical applications. All groups reported an improvement in
pain from baseline to follow-up. Using analysis by treatment received, the vestibulectomy group showed the greatest reductions
in genital pain after treatment and at a 6-month follow-up compared to sEMG biofeedback and GCBT groups. Specifically,
vestibulectomy yielded a 70% improvement in a vestibular pain
index and a 52.5% reduction in pain intensity during sexual intercourse. Similar to Weijmar Schultz et al.'s study (1996), the
cognitive behavioral therapy component produced a 39% reduction in dyspareunic pain, or the equivalent of 2.7 points improvement in pain on a Likert scale of 0 to 10 (Bergeron et al., 2001).
An intent-to-treat analysis reinforced these differences at posttreatment, but 6-month follow-up analyses indicated greater reductions in pain in the vestibulectomy group compared to the
sEMG biofeedback group, but not the GCBT group. Among the
limitations of this study were that the investigators were not blind
to treatment conditions and that seven women randomized to the
vestibulectomy group declined participation before treatment.

Consistent with previous retrospective data indicating the efficacy of vestibulectomy in reducing genital pain (Haefner, 2000),
at a 3-year follow-up, Bergeron and colleagues found that the
vestibulectomy group maintained the posttreatment reductions in
pain (unpublished data). Based on a standardized measurement
of vulvar pain threshold, the surgery group remained superior to
both biofeedback and GCBT. However, the surgery and GCBT
groups reported comparable reductions in self-reported pain during intercourse after 3 years, suggesting that psychotherapy
yielded long-term benefits that became apparent only over time.
These results reinforce the importance of selecting appropriate
outcome measures in future treatment trials.

In contrast to the promising results of surgery, biofeedback,
and GCBT, a double-blind placebo controlled trial of the efficacy of
cromolyn 4% cream for VVS yielded no significant difference between the cromolyn and placebo cream, regardless of concurrent
level of sexual activity (Nyirjesy et al., 2001). Based on a popular

theory that VVS is the result of chronic vaginal inflammation, the authors reasoned that cromolyn's mechanism of action—blocking histamine release from sensitized mast cells—could counter the increased numbers of mast cells shown in a previous retrospective uncontrolled histological study of vulvar tissue biopsies of women with VVS (Chaim, Meriwether, Gonik, Qureshi, & Sobel, 1996). Yet, contrary to this hypothesis, 54% of the cromolyn group and 38% of the placebo group reported at least a 50% reduction in a composite score of symptoms and clinical signs of VVS. The extraordinary placebo response may be attributable to potential confounds such as poor reliability of subjective self-reports of pain, inclusion of potentially treatment-resistant participants, and a lack of statistical power. Well-designed empirical evaluations have not yet been conducted on other topical preparations in the treatment of genital pain, although case reports have supported topical treatments such as corticosteroids, antifungals, lidocaine, and capsaicin as effective treatments for the reduction or relief of VVS pain (Bornstein, Livnat, Stolar, & Abramovici, 2000; Murina, Tassan, Roberti, & Bianco, 2001; Steinberg, Oyama, Rejba, Kellogg-Spadt, & Whitmore, 2005; Zolnoun, Hartmann, & Steege, 2003).

A randomized controlled study was also conducted to examine the effect of fluconazole (an antifungal commonly used to treat vulvovaginal candidiasis, or VVC) on the reduction of pain in women with both VVS and coincident VVC versus women without VVC (Bornstein et al., 2000). Due to increased self-reports of yeast infections in women with VVS (Pukall et al., 2002), recurrent VVC may trigger and/or maintain a chronic inflammation response, which ultimately produces VVS. Women taking 150 mg of fluconazole weekly with a low oxalate diet ($n = 20$) were compared to women with a low oxalate diet only ($n = 20$). No treatment differences were reported after a 3-month follow-up, although women with coexisting VVC were more likely to report dissatisfaction with treatment response. The lack of a true placebo control, ambiguity regarding the assessment of diet adherence, and the use of a dichotomous outcome variable to assess treatment success were weaknesses that may contribute to the null findings.

Clearly, there exists a wide gulf between the handful of empirically supported treatments and the variety of treatments most commonly administered by health practitioners. Based on a cross-sectional survey of physicians, case reports and clinical experience have led physicians to prescribe a gamut of empirically unsupported treatments, including tricyclic antidepressants, gabapentin, topical preparations (estrogen, corticosteroids, lidocaine), and botulinium toxin for generalized and localized vulvar pain (Updike & Wiesenfeld, 2005). Responding physicians further indicated that the most efficacious treatment—vestibulectomy—was typically a strategy of last resort, and only half of the physicians reported that they would consent to performing the surgery.

These diverse treatment approaches likely reflect presumed mechanisms of the pain; however, the lack of empirical support for them underlines the need for randomized controlled trials to assess and guide medical practice.

Deep Pain

Other forms of gynecological surgery such as hysterectomy may also reduce abdominal and vaginal pain and yield improvement in sexual functioning (Flory, Bissonnette, Amsel, & Binik, 2006; Krychman, 2005; Kuppermann et al., 2004). Nevertheless, the pain-relieving mechanisms of gynecological surgery for deep pain are poorly understood (see Flory, Bissonnette, & Binik, 2005).

Three randomized controlled trials have found that subtotal versus total hysterectomy produced comparable but clinically significant reductions in genital pain (Flory et al., 2006; Thakar, Ayers, Clarkson, Stanton, & Manyonda, 2002; Zobbe et al., 2004). The effects of hysterectomy on participants' superficial pain were variable. Although these studies suggest that hysterectomy helps with deep pain, they were limited by poor trial recruitment, the reliance on self-reported dichotomous measures of vaginal or pelvic pain, samples biased by attrition, and lack of information on location and quality of pain.

In a randomized controlled trial comparing hysterectomy and alternate medical treatments, Kuppermann and colleagues (2004) monitored changes in generalized pelvic pain and pelvic pain interference with sex. The hysterectomy group consisted of women receiving vaginal or abdominal surgery, and the medical treatment group received any combination of the following: oral contraceptives, prostaglandin synthetase inhibitors, oral or intramuscular progestogens, intermittent estrogen-progestin treatment, or other treatments chosen at the discretion of the treating physician. All women had unsuccessfully tried medroxyprogesterone and reported a median of 4 years of abnormal uterine bleeding or anemia with heavy menstrual bleeding. A mean of 81% of all women reported pelvic pain and 32% reported pelvic problems that interfered with sex. Using an intent-to-treat analysis, the hysterectomy group reported reduced pelvic problem interference with sex compared to the medical treatment group at 6-month follow-up. However at 2-year follow-up, the medical treatment group evidenced improvements in pelvic problem interference with sex that rivaled hysterectomy group outcomes. Notably, additional analyses indicated that 53% of women in the medical treatment group received hysterectomies between 6-month and 2-year follow-ups. These women reported benefits comparable to the hysterectomy group, although the authors did not provide specific change scores for pelvic pain interference with sex for the subgroup. Study limitations include small group sizes and potentially confounding within-group variations in treatment. For instance, a lack of standardized treatment approaches in the medical treatment group introduced the potential for time and hormone-related confounds that can influence genital pain. The use of intent-to-treat analysis in women in the medical treatment group who ultimately obtained hysterectomies may also confound the results.

To date, information on the efficacy of psychosocial interventions in the treatment of deep pain is lacking (but see Peters, van Dorst, Jellis, van Zuuren, Hermans, & Trimbos, 1991).

Vaginismus

Sex therapists have traditionally been taught that vaginismus can be resolved with Masters and Johnson-type sex therapy using vaginal dilation exercises (Leiblum, 2000). However, evidence supporting this intervention is weak (Heiman & Meston, 1998; Reissing, Binik, & Khalifé, 1999). The first randomized controlled trial of GCBT for vaginismus indicates that 14% of participants in the treatment conditions (group therapy and bibliotherapy, both including vaginal dilation exercises) were able to achieve at least one penile-vaginal intercourse immediately following treatment versus 0% of the wait list control group (van Lankveld et al., 2006). Furthermore, the percentage of women achieving successful penile-vaginal intercourse for the treatment conditions increased at both 3- and 12-month follow up, with 21% and 15% of the GCBT and bibliotherapy groups achieving penetration at 12 months, respectively. It is important to note, however, that "successful" penile-vaginal intercourse was quantified as a single completed act of penetration. Many women who successfully achieved penetrative intercourse at the end of the study did not report continued penile-vaginal intercourse. The study was also limited by the lack of partner participation in GCBT, which could enhance treatment effects beyond those attained by individual participation.

Therapeutic Mechanisms and Strategies

Sex Therapy

Sex therapy as a treatment for genital pain conditions lacks empirical support, and yet sex therapy may complement and enhance other medical and therapeutic interventions. The primary tools of a sex therapist include sexual psychoeducation, directed masturbation, exploration of sexual fantasies, enhancement of body image, relaxation training, sensate focus and sexual assertiveness training. Currently, no controlled treatment outcome studies on sex therapy exist for dyspareunia or vaginismus. Randomized studies have incorporated elements of sex therapy into larger cognitive-behavioral or pain management frameworks (Bergeron et al., 2001; van Lankveld et al., 2006; Weijmar Schultz et al., 1996); however, the therapeutic impact of the approaches cannot be easily teased apart. A handful of uncontrolled studies that have included women with vaginismus or dyspareunia in their samples of mixed sexual dysfunction suggest a lack of treatment effects from sex-therapy based psychotherapy (Clement & Schmidt, 1983; Hartman & Daly, 1983; Mathews et al., 1976; O'Gorman, 1978). This research has been limited by small sample sizes, design inconsistencies, and a failure to control for a variety of confounding variables, such as therapist factors, treatment adherence, no-treatment controls, or placebo controls.

Pain Management

The goal of biopsychosocially based pain management is not to fully resolve pain, but to manage pain and reduce distress. A pain management approach in psychotherapy provides biopsychosocial education about genital pain as a pain condition; incorporates pain diaries to help a woman parallel her pain intensity with specific thoughts, feelings, behaviors, and sexual contexts; enhances useful coping skills; and addresses reasons for the avoidance of sexual activity. Typical interventions include a strong emphasis on restoring and enhancing sexual functioning. In principle this is a powerful approach because it allows a woman to learn to understand her pain, increase her self-efficacy, reduce her perception of pain, decrease her level of psychological distress, and improve sexual functioning. When sufficient pain relief is not attained, the pain management approach can be combined with other medical, surgical, or psychosocial therapies.

Overview of Treatments

Each of the existing treatment trials assumes unique mechanisms of pain, and because such mechanisms are rarely known, the current biomedical and psychosocial interventions for genital pain are at best of hit-and-miss efficacy. For superficial dyspareunia, surgery has produced the most consistent reductions in pain, although biofeedback and GCBT are also associated with improvement. However, the mechanism through which vestibulectomy reduces VVS pain is unknown, and data on treatments for non-VVS pain are sorely lacking.

Evidence suggests that deep dyspareunia may be reduced with both subtotal and total hysterectomy. Additional controlled research is needed to further explore the treatments for deep pain, using large samples and extensive follow-up periods. This research should also provide comparisons across a variety of gynecological procedures, including total abdominal hysterectomy, vaginal hysterectomy, laparoscopic-assisted vaginal hysterectomy, laparoscopic supracervical hysterectomy, radical hysterectomy, endometrial ablation, and myomectomy/myolysis.

The only empirically supported treatment for vaginismus to date is GCBT with elements of sex therapy, but long-term research is still needed to evaluate which treatments produce lasting improvements. Finally, sex therapy and pain management approaches may help manage the psychological response to genital pain and are useful directions for future work.

Summary and Conclusions

Our goal has been to emphasize the multidimensional nature of dyspareunia and vaginismus. Traditional definitions classify dyspareunia and vaginismus as separate entities and highlight their interference with sexual intercourse. However, these disorders are not inherently sexual and may be more usefully conceptualized on a continuum of multiple dimensions of physical pathology, pain, fear, avoidance, and muscle tension. Based on this biopsychosocial conceptualization, promising avenues for future research on dyspareunia and vaginismus include:

- Diagnostic studies confirming the value of a multidimensional conceptualization.
- Risk factor and prospective longitudinal research on younger populations to resolve the ambiguities of past correlational research.
- The pursuit of animal models to complement and extend clinical findings.
- Genetic vulnerability research to enhance knowledge of different subtypes of dyspareunia that may be linked with chronic inflammation.
- Studies on coping styles to understand the role of catastrophizing, hypervigilance, and mood in the development and maintenance of dyspareunia and vaginismus.
- Multidisciplinary randomized controlled trials to provide precise treatment regimens.

In sum, genital pain disorders are multidimensional pain conditions that require multidisciplinary approaches to assessment, treatment, and research. An approach to genital pain management in which psychologists, physicians, and pelvic floor specialists collaborate may produce optimal pain reduction for women suffering from dyspareunia and vaginismus. Our experience has convinced us that knowledge from the literature, including but not limited to psychology, pain, sexology, genetics, and gynecology, can inform and direct clinically useful advancements in the study and treatment of genital pain.

References

American Psychiatric Association. (1968). *Diagnostic and statistical manual of mental disorders* (2nd ed.). Washington, DC: Author.

American Psychiatric Association. (1980). *Diagnostic and statistical manual of mental disorders* (3rd ed.). Washington, DC: Author.

American Psychiatric Association. (1987). *Diagnostic and statistical manual of mental disorders* (3rd ed., rev.). Washington, DC: Author.

American Psychiatric Association. (1994). *Diagnostic and statistical manual of mental disorders* (4th ed.). Washington, DC: Author.

American Psychiatric Association. (2000). *Diagnostic and statistical manual of mental disorders* (4th ed., text rev.). Washington, DC: Author.

Amsterdam, A., Carter, J., & Krychman, M. (2006). Prevalence of psychiatric illness in women in an oncology sexual health population: A retrospective pilot study. *Journal of Sexual Medicine, 3,* 292–295.

Barnes, R. A. (1874). *Clinical history of the medical and surgical diseases of women.* Philadelphia: Lea & Febiger.

Barns, J. W. B. (Ed.). (1956). *Five ramasseum papyri.* Oxford: Oxford University Press.

Bassett, R. L., Smith, H. L., Newell, R. J., & Richards, A. H. (1999). Thou shalt not like sex: Taking another look at religiousness and sexual attitudes. *Journal of Psychology and Christianity, 18,* 205–216.

Basson, R., Leiblum, S., Brotto, L., Derogatis, L., Fourcroy, J., Fugl-Meyer, K., et al. (2004). Revised definitions of women's sexual dysfunction. *Journal of Sexual Medicine, 1,* 40–48.

Basson, R., Weijmar Schultz, W. C. M., Binik, Y. M., Brotto, L. A., Eschenbach, D. A., Laan, E., et al. (2004). Women's sexual desire and arousal disorders and sexual pain. In T. F. Lue, R. Basson, R. Rosen, F. Giuliano, S. Khoury, & F., Montorsi (Eds.), *Sexual medicine: Sexual dysfunctions in men and women.* Paris, France: Health Publications.

Bergeron, S., Binik, Y. M., Khalifé, S., & Pagidas, K. (1997). Vulvar vestibulitis syndrome: A critical review. *Clinical Journal of Pain, 13,* 27–42.

Bergeron, S., Binik, Y. M., Khalifé, S., Pagidas, K., Glazer, H. I., Meana, M., et al. (2001). A randomized comparison of group cognitive-behavioral therapy, surface electromyographic biofeedback, and vestibulectomy in the treatment of dyspareunia resulting from vulvar vestibulitis. *Pain, 91,* 297–306.

Berglund, A. L., Nigaard, L., & Rylander, E. (2002). Vulvar pain, sexual behavior and genital infections in a young population: A pilot study. *Acta Obstetrica Gynecologia Scandinavica, 81,* 738–742.

Binik, Y. M. (2005). Dyspareunia looks sexy on first but how much pain will it take for it to score? A reply to my critics concerning the DSM classification of dyspareunia as a sexual dysfunction. *Archives of Sexual Behavior, 34,* 63–67.

Bohm-Starke, N., Johannesson, U., Hilliges, M., Rylander, E., & Torebjörk, E. (2004). Decreased mechanical pain threshold in the vestibular mucosa of women using oral contraceptives. *Journal of Reproductive Medicine, 49,* 888–892.

Bornstein, J., Livnat, G., Stolar, Z., & Abramovici, H. (2000). Pure versus complicated vulvar vestibulitis: A randomized trial of fluconazole treatment. *Gynecologic and Obstetric Investigation, 50,* 194–197.

Carter, L. E., McNeil, D. W., Vowles, K. E., Sorrell, J. T., Turk, C. L., Ries, B. J., et al. (2002). Effects of emotion on pain reports, tolerance, and physiology. *Pain Research and Management, 7,* 21–30.

Chaim, W., Meriwether, C., Gonik, B., Qureshi, F., & Sobel, J. D. (1996). Vulvar vestibulitis subjects undergoing surgical intervention: A descriptive analysis and histopathological correlates. *European Journal of Obstetrics, Gynecology, and Reproductive Biology, 68,* 165–168.

Clement, U., & Schmidt, G. (1983). The outcome of couple therapy for sexual dysfunctions using three different formats. *Journal of Sex and Marital Therapy, 9,* 67–78.

Costa Talens, P., & Colorado Vicente, M. J. (1971). Un problema ginecologico en el papiro ramesseum, I. V. *Medica Espanola, 66,* 274.

Danielsson, I., Eisemann, M., Sjöberg, I., & Wikman, M. (2001). Vulvar vestibulitis: A multi-factorial condition. *British Journal of Obstetrics and Gynaecology, 108*, 456–461.

Danielsson, I., Sjöberg, I., & Wikman, M. (2000). Vulvar vestibulitis: Medical, psychosexual and psychological aspects, a case-control study. *Acta Obstetricia et Gynecologica Scandinavica, 79*, 872–878.

Davidson, J. K., Moore, N. B., & Ullstrup, K. M. (2004). Religiosity and sexual responsibility: Relationships of choice. *American Journal of Health Behavior, 28*, 335–346.

Emmert, C., & Köhler, U. (1998). Data about 154 children and adolescents reporting sexual assault. *Archives of Gynecology and Obstetrics, 261*, 61–70.

Flory, N., Bissonnette, F., Amsel, R. T., & Binik, Y. M. (2006). The psychosocial outcomes of total and subtotal hysterectomy: A randomized controlled trial. *Journal of Sexual Medicine, 3*, 483–491.

Flory, N., Bissonnette, F., & Binik, Y. M. (2005). Psychosocial effects of hysterectomy: Literature review. *Journal of Psychosomatic Research, 59*, 117–129.

Foster, D. C., Sazenski, T. M., & Stodgell, C. J. (2004). Impact of genetic variation in interleukin-1 receptor antagonist and melanocortin-1 receptor genes on vulvar vestibulitis syndrome. *Journal of Reproductive Medicine, 49*, 503–509.

Gates, E. A., & Galask, R. P. (2001). Psychological and sexual functioning in women with vulvar vestibulitis. *Journal of Psychosomatic Obstetrics and Gynecology, 22*, 221–228.

Gerber, S., Bongiovanni, A. M., Ledger, W. J., & Witkin, S. S. (2003). Interleukin-1beta gene polymorphism in women with vulvar vestibulitis syndrome. *European Journal of Obstetrics and Gynecology and Reproductive Biology, 107*, 74–77.

Giesecke, J., Reed, B. D., Haefner, H. K., Giesecke, T., Clauw, D. J., & Gracely, R. H. (2004). Quantitative sensory testing in vulvodynia patients and increased peripheral pressure pain sensitivity. *Obstetrics and Gynecology, 104*, 126–133.

Goetsch, M. F. (1991). Vulvar vestibulitis: Prevalence and historic features in a general gynecologic practice population. *American Journal of Obstetrics and Gynecology, 164*, 1614–1616.

Granot, M., Friedman, M., Yarnitsky, D., & Zimmer, E. Z. (2002). Enhancement of the perception of systemic pain in women with vulvar vestibulitis. *British Journal of Obstetrics and Gynecology, 109*, 863–866.

Graziottin, A., & Brotto, L. (2004). Vulvar vestibulitis syndrome: A clinical approach. *Journal of Sex and Marital Therapy, 30*, 125–139.

Haefner, H. K. (2000). Critique of new gynecological surgical procedures: Surgery for vulvar vestibulitis. *Clinical Obstetrics and Gynecology, 43*, 689–700.

Harlow, B. L., & Stewart, E. G. (2003). A population-based assessment of chronic unexplained vulvar pain: Have we underestimated the prevalence of vulvodynia? *Journal of the American Medical Women's Association, 58*, 82–88.

Harlow, B. L., Wise, L. A., & Stewart, E. G. (2001). Prevalence and predictors of chronic lower genital tract discomfort. *American Journal of Obstetrics and Gynecology, 185*, 545–550.

Hartman, L. M., & Daly, E. M. (1983). Relationship factors in the treatment of sexual dysfunction. *Behaviour Research and Therapy, 21*, 153–160.

Hayes, R., & Dennerstein, L. (2005). The impact of aging on sexual function and sexual dysfunction in women: A review of population-based studies. *Journal of Sexual Medicine, 2*, 317–330.

Haythornthwaite, J. A., Menefee, L. A., Heinberg, L. J., & Clark, M. R. (1998). Pain coping strategies predict perceived control over pain. *Pain, 77*, 33–39.

Heijmans, M., & de Ridder, D. (1998). Assessing illness representations of chronic illness: Explorations of their disease-specific nature. *Journal of Behavioral Medicine, 21*, 485–503.

Heiman, J. R., & Meston, C. M. (1998). Empirically validated treatments for sexual dysfunction. In K. S. Dobson & K. D. Craig (Eds.), *Empirically supported therapies: Best practice in professional psychology* (pp. 259–303). New York: Sage.

Hirst, J. F., Baggaley, M. R., & Watson, J. P. (1996). A four year survey of an inner city psychosexual problems clinic. *Sexual and Marital Therapy, 11*, 19–36.

Jantos, M., & White, G. (1997). The vestibulitis syndrome: Medical and psychosexual assessment of a cohort of patients. *Journal of Reproductive Medicine, 42*, 145–152.

Johnson, S. D., Phelps, D. L., & Cottler, L. B. (2004). The association of sexual dysfunction and substance use among a community epidemiological sample. *Archives of Sexual Behavior, 33*, 55–63.

Jones, D. A., Rollman, G. B., White, K. P., Hill, M. L., & Brooke, R. I. (2003). The relationship between cognitive appraisal, affect, and catastrophizing in patients with chronic pain. *Journal of Pain, 4*, 267–277.

Kaler, A. (2006). Unreal women: Sex, gender, identity and the lived experience of vulvar pain. *Feminist Review, 82*, 50–75.

Kaneko, K. (2001). Penetration disorder: Dyspareunia exists on the extension of vaginismus. *Journal of Sex and Marital Therapy, 27*, 153–155.

Keefe, F. J., Dunsmore, J., & Burnett, R. (1992). Behavioral and cognitive-behavioral approaches to chronic pain: Recent advances and future directions. *Journal of Consulting and Clinical Psychology, 60*, 528–536.

Krychman, M. (2005). Survey of the literature: Sexual functioning after total compared with supracervical hysterectomy: A randomized trial. *Journal of Sexual Medicine, 2,* 871–874.

Kuppermann, M., Varner, R. E., Summitt, R. L., Jr., Learman, L. A., Ireland, C., Vittinghoff, E., et al. (2004). Effect of hysterectomy versus medical treatment on health-related quality of life and sexual functioning: The medicine or surgery (Ms) randomized trial. *Journal of the American Medical Association, 291,* 1447–1455.

Lacroix, J. M. (1991). Assessing illness schemata in patient populations. In J. A. Skelton & R. T. Croyle (Eds.), *Mental representation in health and illness* (pp. 193–219). New York: Springer Verlag.

Laumann, E. O., Gagnon, J. H., Michael, R. T., & Michaels, S. (1994). *The social organization of sexuality: Sexual practices in the United States.* Chicago: University of Chicago Press.

Laumann, E. O., Gagnon, J. H., Michaci, R. T., & Michaels, S. (1999). Sexual dysfunction in the United States: Prevalence and predictors. *Journal of the American Medical Association, 281,* 537–544.

Lefkowitz, E. S., Gillen, M. M., Shearer, C. L., & Boone, T. L. (2004). Religiosity, sexual behaviors, and sexual attitudes during emerging adulthood. *Journal of Sex Research, 41,* 150–159.

Leiblum, S. R. (2000). Vaginismus: A most perplexing problem. In S. R. Leiblum & R. Rosen (Eds.), *Principles and practice of sex therapy* (2nd ed., pp. 181–204). New York: Guilford Press.

Leonard, M. T., Cano, A., & Johansen, A. B. (2006). Chronic pain in a couples context: A review and integration of theoretical models and empirical evidence. *Journal of Pain, 7,* 377–390.

Lowenstein, L., Vardi, Y., Deutsch, M., Friedman, M., Gruenwald, I., Granot, M., et al. (2004). Vulvar vestibulitis severity—Assessment by sensory and pain testing modalities. *Pain, 107,* 47–53.

Martin, M. Y., Bradley, L. A., Alexander, R. W., Alarcon, G. S., Triana-Alexander, M., Aaron, L. A., et al. (1996). Coping strategies predict disability in patients with primary fibromyalgia. *Pain, 68,* 45–53.

Masheb, R. M., Lozano-Blanco, C., Kohorn, E. I., Minkin, M. J., & Kerns, R. D. (2004). Assessing sexual function and dyspareunia with the Female Sexual Function Index (FSFI) in women with vulvodynia. *Journal of Sex and Marital Therapy, 30,* 315–324.

Mathews, A., Bancroft, J., Whitehead, A., Hackmann, A., Julier, D., Bancroft, J., et al. (1976). The behavioral treatment of sexual inadequacy: A comparative study. *Behaviour Research and Therapy, 14,* 427–436.

Meana, M., Binik, I., Khalifé, S., & Cohen, D. (1998). Affect and marital adjustment in women's rating of dyspareunic pain. *Canadian Journal of Psychiatry, 43,* 381–385.

Meana, M., & Binik, Y. M. (1994). Painful coitus: A review of female dyspareunia. *Journal of Nervous and Mental Diseases, 182,* 264–272.

Meana, M., Binik, Y. M., Khalifé, S., & Cohen, D. R. (1997). Dyspareunia: Pain symptomatology, biopsychosocial correlates and classification. *Journal of Nervous and Mental Diseases, 185,* 561–569.

Meana, M., Binik, Y. M., Khalifé, S., & Cohen, D. R. (1999). Psychosocial correlates of pain attributions in women with dyspareunia. *Psychosomatics, 40,* 497–502.

Melzack, R. (1975). The McGill Pain Questionnaire: Major properties and scoring methods. *Pain, 1,* 277–299.

Moyal-Barracco, M., & Lynch, P. J. (2004). 2003 ISSVD terminology and classification of vulvodynia: A historical perspective. *Journal of Reproductive Medicine, 932,* 772–777.

Murina, F., Tassan, P., Roberti, P., & Bianco, V. (2001). Treatment of vulvar vestibulitis with submucous infiltrations of methylprednisolone and lidocaine: An alternative approach. *Journal of Reproductive Medicine, 46,* 713–716.

Nunns, D., & Mandal, D. (1997). Psychological and psychosexual aspects of vulvar vestibulitis. *Genitourinary Medicine, 73,* 541–544.

Nyirjesy, P., Sobel, J. D., Weitz, M. V., Leaman, D. J., Small, M. J., & Gelone, S. P. (2001). Cromolyn cream for recalcitrant idiopathic vulvar vestibulitis: Results of a placebo controlled study. *Sexually Transmitted Infections, 77,* 53–57.

Nylanderlundqvist, E., & Bergdahl, J. (2003). Vulvar vestibulitis: Evidence of depression and state anxiety in patients and partners. *Acta Dermato-Venereologica, 83,* 369–373.

Oberg, K., Fugl-Meyer, A. R., & Fugl-Meyer, K. S. (2004). On the categorization and quantification of women's sexual dysfunction: An epidemiological approach. *International Journal Impotence Research, 16,* 261–269.

O'Gorman, E. C. (1978). The treatment of frigidity: A comparative study of group and individual desensitization. *British Journal of Psychiatry, 132,* 580–584.

Payne, K. A., Binik, Y. M., Amsel, R., & Khalifé, S. (2005). When sex hurts, anxiety and fear orient attention towards pain. *European Journal of Pain, 9,* 427–436.

Peters, A., van Dorst, E., Jellis, B., van Zuuren, E., Hermans, J., & Trimbos, J. (1991). A randomized clinical trial to compare two different approaches in women with chronic pelvic pain. *Obstetrics and Gynecology, 77,* 740–744.

Pukall, C. F., Binik, Y. M., & Khalifé, S. (2004). A new instrument for pain assessment in vulvar vestbulitis syndrome. *Journal of Sex and Marital Therapy, 30,* 69–78.

Pukall, C. F., Binik, Y. M., Khalifé, S., Amsel, R., & Abbott, F. V. (2002). Vestibular tactile and pain thresholds in women with vulvar vestibulitis syndrome. *Pain, 96,* 163–175.

Pukall, C. F., Reissing, E. D., Binik, Y. M., Khalifé, S., & Abbott, F. V. (2000). New clinical and research perspectives on sexual pain disorders. *Journal of Sex Education and Therapy, 25,* 36–44.

Pukall, C. F., Strigo, I. A., Binik, Y. M., Amsel, R., Khalifé, S., & Bushnell, M. C. (2005). Neural correlates of painful genital touch in women with vulvar vestibulitis syndrome. *Pain, 115,* 118–127.

Reissing, E. D., Binik, Y. M., & Khalifé, S. (1999). Does vaginismus exist? A critical review of the literature. *Journal of Nervous and Mental Diseases, 187,* 261–274.

Reissing, E. D., Binik, Y. M., Khalifé, S., Cohen, D., & Amsel, R. (2003). Etiological correlates of vaginismus: Sexual and physical abuse, sexual knowledge, sexual self-schema, and relationship adjustment. *Journal of Sex and Marital Therapy, 29,* 47–59.

Reissing, E. D., Binik, Y. M., Khalifé, S., Cohen, D., & Amsel, R. (2004). Vaginal spasm, pain and behavior: An empirical investigation of the diagnosis of vaginismus. *Archives of Sexual Behavior, 33,* 5–17.

Reissing, E. D., Brown, C. L., Lord, M. J., Binik, Y. M., & Khalifé, S. (2005). Pelvic floor functioning in women with vulvar vestibulitis syndrome. *Journal of Psychosomatic Obstetrics and Gynecology, 26,* 107–113.

Rellini, A., & Meston, C. M. (2004). Sexual abuse and female sexual dysfunction: Clinical implications. *Urodinamica, 14,* 80–83.

Rosen, R., Brown, C., Heiman, J., Leiblum, S., Meston, C., Shabsigh, R., et al. (2000). The Female Sexual Function Index (FSFI): A multidimensional self-report instrument for the assessment of female sexual function. *Journal of Sex and Marital Therapy, 26,* 191–208.

Rosenbaum, T. Y. (2005). Physiotherapy treatment of sexual pain disorders. *Journal of Sex and Marital Therapy, 31,* 329–340.

Rust, J., & Golombok, S. (1986). The GRISS: A psychometric instrument for the assessment of sexual dysfunction. *Archives of Sexual Behavior, 15,* 157–165.

Sarrel, P. M. (2000). Effects of hormone replacement therapy on sexual psychophysiology and behavior in postmenopause. *Journal of Women's Health and Gender-Based Medicine, 9,* S25–S32.

Scharloo, M., Kaptein, A. A., Weinman, J., Hazes, J. M., Willems, L. N. A., Bergman, W., et al. (1998). Illness perceptions, coping and functioning in patients with rheumatoid arthritis, chronic obstructive pulmonary disease and psoriasis. *Journal of Psychosomatic Research, 44,* 573–585.

Schiaffino, K., & Cea, C. D. (1995). Assessing chronic illness representations: The implicit models of illness questionnaire. *Journal of Behavioral Medicine, 18,* 531–548.

Sims, M. J. (1861). On vaginismus. *Transactions of the Obstetrical Society of London, 3,* 356–367.

Spector, I. P., & Carey, M. P. (1990). Incidence and prevalence of the sexual dysfunctions: A critical review of the empirical literature. *Archives of Sexual Behavior, 19,* 389–408.

Steinberg, A. C., Oyama, I. A., Rejba, A. E., Kellogg-Spadt, S., & Whitmore, K. E. (2005). Capsaicin for the treatment of vulvar vestibulitis. *American Journal of Obstetrics and Gynecology, 192,* 1549–1553.

Sullivan, M. J., Thorn, B., Haythornthwaite, J. A., Keefe, F., Martin, M., Bradley, L. A., et al. (2001). Theoretical perspectives on the relation between catastrophizing and pain. *Clinical Journal of Pain, 17,* 52–64.

Sullivan, M. J. L., Bishop, S. R., & Pivik, J. (1995). The Pain Catastrophizing Scale: Development and validation. *Psychological Assessment, 7,* 524–532.

Talakoub, L., Munarriz, R., Hoag, L., Gioia, M., Flaherty, E., & Goldstein, I. (2002). Epidemiological characteristics of 250 women with sexual dysfunction who presented for initial evaluation. *Journal of Sex and Marital Therapy, 28,* 217–224.

Thakar, R., Ayers, S., Clarkson, P., Stanton, S., & Manyonda, I. (2002). Outcomes after total versus subtotal abdominal hysterectomy. *New England Journal of Medicine, 347,* 1318–1325.

Thranov, I., & Klee, M. (1994). Sexuality among gynaecologic cancer patients: A cross-sectional study. *Gynecologic Oncology, 52,* 14–19.

Tugrul, C., & Kabakci, E. (1997). Vaginismus and its correlates. *Sexual and Marital Therapy, 12,* 23–34.

Tunuguntla, H. S. G. R., & Gousse, A. E. (2006). Female sexual dysfunction following vaginal surgery: A review. *Journal of Urology, 175,* 439–446.

Updike, G. M., & Wiesenfeld, C. M. (2005). Insight into the treatment of vulvar pain: A survey of clinicians. *American Journal of Obstetrics and Gynecology, 193,* 1404–1409.

van den Hout, M., & Barlow, D. (2000). Attention, arousal, and expectancies in anxiety and sexual disorders. *Journal of Affective Disorders, 61,* 241–256.

van Lankveld, J. J. D. M., Brewaeys, A. M., ter Kuile, M. M., & Weijenborg, P. T. (1995). Difficulties in the differential diagnosis of vaginismus, dyspareunia, and mixed sexual pain disorder. *Journal of Psychosomatic Obstetrics & Gynaecology, 16,* 201–209.

van Lankveld, J. J. D. M., ter Kuile, M. M., de Groot, E., Melles, R., Nefs, J., & Zandbergen, M. (2006). Cognitive-behavioral therapy for women with lifelong vaginismus: A randomized waiting-list controlled trial of efficacy. *Journal of Consulting and Clinical Psychology, 74,* 168–178.

van Lankveld, J. J. D. M., Weijenborg, P. T. M., & ter Kuile, M. M. (1996). Psychologic profiles of and sexual function in women with vulvar vestibulitis and their partners. *Obstetrics and Gynecology, 88,* 65–70.

Weijmar Schultz, W. C. M., Gianotten, W. L., van der Meijden, W. I., van de Miel, H. B. M., Blindeman, B., Chadha, S., et al. (1996). Behavioral approach with or without surgical intervention for vulvar vestibulitis syndrome: A prospective randomized and non-randomized study. *Journal of Pscyhosomatic Obstetrics and Gynecology, 17,* 143–148.

Wiegel, M., Meston, C. M., & Rosen, R. (2005). The Female Sexual Function Index (FSFI): Cross-validation and development of clinical cutoff scores. *Journal of Sex and Marital Therapy, 31,* 1–20.

Willhite, L. A., & O'Connell, M. B. (2001). Urogenital atrophy: Prevention and treatment. *Pharmacotherapy, 21,* 464–480.

World Health Organization. (1992). *Manual of the international statistical classification of diseases, injuries, and causes of death* (10th ed.). Geneva, Switzerland: Author.

Wouda, J. C., Hartman, P. M., Bakker, R. M., Bakker, J. O., van de Wiel, H. B. M., & Weijmar Schultz, W. C. M. (1998). Vaginal plethysmography in women with dyspareunia. *Journal of Sex Research, 35,* 141–147.

Zippe, C. D., Nandipati, K. C., Agarwal, A., & Raina, R. (2005). Female sexual dysfunction after pelvic surgery: The impact of surgical modifications. *BJU International, 96,* 959–963.

Zobbe, V., Gimbel, H., Andersen, B. M., Filtenborg, T., Jakobsen, K., Sorensen, C., et al. (2004). Sexuality after total vs. subtotal hysterectomy. *Acta Obstetrica et Gynecological Scandinavica, 83,* 191–196.

Zolnoun, D. A., Hartmann, K. E., & Steege, J. F. (2003). Overnight 5% lidocaine ointment for treatment of vulvar vestibulitis. *Obstetrics and Gynecology, 102,* 84–87.

Menopause, Aging, and Sexual Response in Women

Lori A. Brotto and Mijal Luria

9

Chapter

Learning Objectives

In this chapter, we:

- Define menopause and discuss specific hormonal alterations in estrogens, progesterone, and androgens.
- Describe hormonal effects on general and sexual functioning.
- Review the literature on sexuality during the menopausal transition with a specific focus on population-based epidemiological studies.
- Discuss effects of age on sexuality and attempt to separate effects of age from effects of menopause.
- Describe the psychophysiological aspects of sexuality during menopause.
- Describe the relationships among mood, culture, and sexuality during the menopause.
- Review major sexual difficulties and disorders that women experience during the menopause.
- Describe evidence-based psychological and pharmacological (including hormonal) treatments for sexual difficulties during the menopause.

With an increasing life expectancy currently at 80.1 years for Caucasian women (U.S. Centers for Disease Control,

251

2006), the average woman will spend a significant portion of her life in the postreproductive (i.e., postmenopausal) phase. As such, quality-of-life factors in the postmenopausal phase, with sexual health being one integral component, are important to identify and understand so that effective and timely interventions may be given. Indeed, data collected on women aged 40 to 80 from 29 different countries suggest that subjective sexual well-being remains important into old age, and the predictors of it are relatively constant from region to region around the world (Laumann et al., 2006). Moreover, older and postmenopausal women are becoming increasingly vocal about having resources available to address their sexual health questions and concerns.

In this chapter, we outline some of the major menopause-related aspects of sexuality, making a careful effort to distinguish effects due to menopause, per se, from effects linked to aging. The role of psychosocial factors and the role of hormones, both in causing menopause-related sexual problems and in ameliorating them, are discussed.

In previous decades, the number of older and/or postmenopausal women participating in research studies was comparatively small. For example, only 61 women older than 40 participated in Masters and Johnson's research program of nearly 700 individuals (Masters & Johnson, 1966), and in Kinsey's two volumes (1948, 1953), only three pages were devoted to sexuality in older individuals. In contrast, a number of recent large-scale studies have focused exclusively on the sexuality of older women, such as the Global Study of Sexual Attitudes and Behaviors of 27,500 men and women aged 40 to 80 from 29 different countries (Laumann et al., 2005). With several additional longitudinal studies currently underway, our current state of knowledge about menopausal effects on sexuality is becomingly increasingly comprehensive.

What Is Menopause?

The term *menopause* was introduced in 1821 by the French physician Gardanne. Because Gardanne emphasized that this was a condition worthy of medical attention, the term became popular in medical texts. The term originates from the Greek roots of "month" and "cessation" and is often used interchangeably with the term *climacteric* although the latter is not specific to women and refers to the biological changes occurring in both men and women during the transition from middle to older age.

According to the Stages of Reproductive Aging Workshop (STRAW) in July 2001, menopause is "the anchor point that is defined after 12 months of amenorrhea (lack of menses), following the final menstrual period, which reflects a near complete but natural decrease in ovarian hormone secretion" (Soules et al., 2001). The final menstrual period can only be diagnosed retrospectively, and occurs at a median age of 51.4 years. The term *perimenopause* was described by the World Health Organization in 1996 as "the period immediately prior to the menopause and the first year after the final menstrual period." Perimenopause captures both early and late stages of transition, described in further detail at STRAW (see Figure 9.1).

A woman is considered to have entered the early transition if she has either skipped a menstrual period or has noted an increase in irregularity of her cycles by more than 7 days. Between 3 and 11 months of amenorrhea, a woman is said to be in the late transition. Although previously believed to be a time of progressively declining hormonal production, the menopausal transition is marked by wide fluctuations in reproductive hormones and intermittent negative symptomatology (N. Santoro, 2005).

In the natural (i.e., not induced by surgical removal of the ovaries) early menopausal transition, a decline in the ovarian follicular pool interferes with the hormonal feedback loop to the hypothalamus in the brain. This results in increased levels of follicle stimulating hormone (FSH) that has the dual effect of shortening ovulatory cycles and increasing estradiol levels (Prior, 1998). In the late menopausal transition, cycles become irregular and there are dramatic swings in estradiol levels. Levels of estradiol eventually decline and are undetectable after the final menstrual period. This dwindling has significant effects on the

Stages:	−5	−4	−3	−2	−1	**0** ▼	+1	+2
Terminology:	**Reproductive**			**Menopausal Transition**			**Postmenopause**	
	Early	Peak	Late	Early	Late*		Early*	Late
				Perimenopause				
Duration of stage:	Variable			Variable		ⓐ 1 yr.	ⓑ 4 yrs.	Until demise
Menstrual cycles:	Variable to regular	Regular		Variable cycle length (>7 days different from normal)	≥2 skipped cycles and an interval of amenorrhea	Amen x 12 mos.	None	
Endocrine:	Normal FSH		↑ FSH	↑ FSH			↑ FSH	

*Stages most likely to be characterized by vasomotor symptoms.   ↑ = elevated

Figure 9.1

The STRAW Staging System

Source: "Executive Summary: Stages of Reproductive Aging Workshop (STRAW)," by M. R. Soules et al., 2001, *Fertility and Sterility, 76,* pp. 874–878. Reprinted with permission.

reproductive tract and surrounding tissues; there is reduced genital vasocongestion and overall less blood flow, which translate into an increased risk of sexual complaints. Vaginal dryness is a major factor contributing to the symptom of dyspareunia (i.e., painful intercourse) in menopausal women, discussed in detail later (see also Chapter 8, this volume).

In summary, whereas the menopause signifies a distinct event in a woman's life, the perimenopausal transition can span some years and is characterized by numerous hormonal fluctuations. Recent advances in delineating the different phases of menopause have been helpful in capturing menopause-related changes in sexuality. The specific hormonal changes and their effects on sexuality are discussed in turn.

Hormonal Alterations with Menopause and Their Effects

Estrogens

Menopausal symptoms can be linked to specific changes in the steroid hormones: estrogens, progestogens, and androgens. The hormone of interest, estradiol, belongs to the class of hormones known as estrogens. Postmenopausal women have only small amounts of circulating estradiol, and at these levels this hormone does not appear to have broad general effects. Instead, estradiol is synthesized in a number of peripheral sites from adrenal and ovarian prohormones where it acts primarily at the local level (Simpson et al., 2005). The major estrogen in blood serum of postmenopausal women is estrone, considerably weaker than estradiol and not measured by clinically available assays.

Symptoms characteristic of the perimenopausal period are hot flushes, breast tenderness, breast enlargement and fibrocystic breast problems, increased premenstrual syndrome, and migraine headaches. Because estrogens modulate central alpha$_2$-adrenergic receptors, estrogen decline during menopause has been linked to an elevated sympathetic nervous system activation, which plays a role in the initiation of hot flushes. Blood plasma levels of 3-methoxy-4-hydroxyphenylglycol (MHPG), the main metabolite of norepinephrine, are significantly higher in symptomatic than in asymptomatic postmenopausal women and, further, this metabolite increases significantly during hot flushes. There is no correlation, though, between hot flush occurrence and plasma, urinary, or vaginal levels of estrogen; nor are there differences in plasma levels between symptomatic and asymptomatic women (R. R. Freedman, 2005).

In the peripheral and central nervous system, estrogens influence nerve transmission (Berman & Goldstein, 2001) and sensory perception (Marks, 1990). In the urogenital system, estradiol acts on estrogen receptors found in the vagina, vulva, urethra, and neck of the bladder (as well as in the breast; M. A. Freedman, 2000; McCoy, 2001) and is required for normal blood flow to these tissues to thicken and moisten the vaginal epithelium. Consequently, urogynecological symptoms such as an increased prevalence of urinary tract infections are more likely with low estrogen levels (Stenberg, Heimer, & Ulmsten, 1995). Other urogenital changes that may directly affect sexual function are a thinning of the vaginal mucosal epithelium, atrophy of vaginal wall smooth muscle, and vaginal dryness (Dennerstein, Dudley, Hopper, & Burger, 1997). Estrogens also have a role in regulating vaginal and clitoral nitric oxide synthase expression, the enzyme responsible for the production of nitric oxide, a primary mediator of the physiological sexual (genital) response. As nitric oxide synthase levels decrease, smooth muscle relaxation and genital blood flow decrease as well.

In summary, whereas estrogen levels in menopause have not been reliably linked to hot flush occurrence, they are related to urogenital symptoms such as vaginal dryness. The decline in estrogen is also related to the less frequent symptom of breast tenderness, which is experienced positively by women undergoing these changes.

Androgens

The term *androgen* is generally applied to the class of steroids produced by the gonads and the adrenals in both sexes, which produce masculinizing effects. These include testosterone, dehydroepiandrosterone (DHEA), and dehydroepiandrosterone sulphate (DHEAS). Androstenedione (A_4) and 5α-dihydrotestosterone (DHT) are prohormones that can be converted into either testosterone or estrogen in peripheral tissues. Of the androgenic steroids, testosterone and DHT have the most potent biological activity. In premenopausal women, approximately 25% of androgen biosynthesis takes place in the ovaries, 25% in the adrenal gland, and the remainder in peripheral tissue sites (Bachmann et al., 2002). The biologically active androgen in women is testosterone, which circulates through the body in a form that is bound tightly to sex hormone binding globulin (SHBG) and to some extent albumin. The fraction of testosterone that remains unbound is considered "bioavailable," that is, available for biological action rather than being inertly bound to another molecule (Nappi et al., 2005). Androgen levels peak when women are in their 20s and drop gradually with age, so that women in their 40s have approximately half the circulating total testosterone as women in their 20s (Graziottin & Leiblum, 2005). In addition, intracellular production of testosterone declines. In contrast to the sharp decline in circulating estrogens during natural menopause, testosterone levels decline in the few years before menopause, with no consistent decline during or after menopause (Bancroft, 2002). Androgens are known to act on multiple tissue and receptor sites, including the central nervous system pathways in the hypothalamus and limbic system, and important peripheral sites such as bone, breast, pilosebaceous unit (hair and follicle), skeletal muscle, adipose, and genital tissues (Bachmann et al., 2002).

The role of androgens in maintaining overall health, mood, and sexual function during and after menopause has been the subject of research for more than 50 years; but the consequences of declining androgen levels are still unclear. The most common changes associated with low androgen in women include loss of pubic and axillary hair, increased vasomotor flushing and insomnia, loss of bone and muscle mass, replacement of muscle with adipose tissue, increased prevalence of depression and headaches, and diminution in quality of life. In 2002, a consensus conference on androgens agreed that androgen insufficiency in women with adequate estrogen levels could lead to a diminished sense of well-being, blunted energy, persisting unexplained fatigue, and decreased sexual desire and receptivity (Bachmann et al., 2002). The conferees noted, however, that these are nonspecific symptoms characteristic of a wide variety of medical and psychological states—including depression and relationship conflict—and that a lack of sufficient epidemiological data and limitations in current laboratory assays prevent linking these psychological changes directly to androgens (Bachmann et al., 2002). Recent guidelines from the Endocrine Society recommend against making a diagnosis of "androgen insufficiency" because of the lack of a well-defined clinical syndrome and of normative data on testosterone levels across the life span that can be used to define the disorder (Wierman et al., 2006).

Testosterone is considered by some to be the hormone of sexual desire and motivation in women (Myers, Dixen, Morrissette, Carmichael, & Davidson, 1990). Changes in sexual function thought to be related to low androgens include: a decline in sexual motivation, fantasy, and enjoyment; diminished sexual arousal; and decreased vaginal vasocongestion in response to erotic stimuli (as reviewed in Bachmann, 2002). This research, however, is limited by the finding that in larger studies no correlation has been found between testosterone levels and sexuality in women. In the longitudinal Melbourne Midlife Women's Health Project, androgen levels did not correlate with any aspect of sexual functioning in women going through menopausal transition (Dennerstein, Randolph, Taffe, Dudley, & Burger, 2002). However, this research is limited by the fact that current standard assays are designed to measure testosterone in the male range or to identify hyperandrogenic states in women (Basson, 2005; Davis, Guay, Shifren, &

Mazer, 2004). Given the decline in androgen levels that takes place with age, such assays are unreliable for providing an index of androgen activity in older women. Moreover, the intracellular production of testosterone is not measured in standard assays that assess blood serum levels. The field of intracrinology, to be discussed later, proposes a new method that could more accurately capture androgen activity in women and that, in turn, may have implications for understanding the relationship between androgens and sexuality in women. In addition to problems with androgen assays, women respond with great variability to natural androgens. For example, the sexuality of adolescent females seems to be affected to a larger extent by peer group interactions and psychosocial issues than by their androgen levels (Hutchinson, 1995). The oral contraceptive pill also has inconsistent effects on sexual interest (Caruso et al., 2004; Guida et al., 2005). The pill increases the concentration of SHBG, thereby decreasing the amount of circulating bioavailable testosterone (Panzer et al., 2006).

In summary, a number of androgens are synthesized in women and the period with the greatest amount of decline in androgens is prior to menopause, with no consistent change following menopause. Whereas androgens have been correlated with medical and psychological symptoms, data are insufficient to suggest a direct link between them. Moreover, the link between androgens and sexual desire in menopausal women is equivocal and is limited by the sensitivity of standard androgen assays.

Progesterone

Progesterone is secreted by the corpus luteum of the ovaries each month after ovulation. Ovulatory disturbances, and therefore low progesterone levels, are typical of the perimenopause. After menopause progesterone is no longer produced. The primary actions of progestogens, the class of steroids to which progesterone belongs, have been studied mostly in the uterus, where it functions as an anti-estrogen by decreasing the number of nuclear estrogen receptors (Whitehead, Townsend, Pryse-Davies, Ryder, & King, 1981). Progesterone receptors are found in many of the same brain areas as estrogen receptors, including the hypothalamus and the limbic system, the latter of which plays an important role in regulating emotions and mood. Progesterone has been linked with depression, has potent anesthetic properties, and dampens brain excitability. However, the role of progesterone in mood has received far less attention than that of the estrogens.

Data on the effects of progesterone on human sexual behavior are scarce. In nonhumans, progesterone is related to proceptive behaviors, a form of sexual solicitation in rodents (Crews, 2005; Giraldi et al., 2004). Some human research, however, has linked progestogens to negative effects on sexual desire

(Sherwin, 1999). Unfortunately, compared to research on estrogens and androgens, far less is known about progesterone's role in sexuality in the menopausal woman; thus, firm conclusions cannot be drawn.

Menopause and Sexuality

For decades, researchers have attempted to define the sexual changes taking place with menopause: decreased number and intensity of orgasmic contractions, decreased sexual desire (Bachman & Leiblum, 2004), difficulty achieving orgasm, decreased genital sensations, and vaginal atrophy leading to dyspareunia (Berman & Goldstein, 2001). The number of population-based longitudinal studies exploring this topic has surged. In the Melbourne Women's Midlife Health Project initiated in 1991 in Australia, a representative sample of women from the general population was recruited via random digit dialing, and these women were followed yearly for health experiences and risk factors during the menopausal transition. Annual samples of estradiol, serum testosterone, SHBG, and DHEA-S were collected, along with a number of physical measurements at 2-year intervals. Women also completed questionnaires exploring stress, lifestyle factors, general somatic complaints, menopausal symptoms, health behaviors, medical status, menstrual diaries, and sexuality. In their 9-year review, Guthrie and colleagues found a number of significant hormonal changes such as a 60% reduction in estradiol and a 43% decline in SHBG, but minimal change in testosterone (Guthrie, Dennerstein, Taffe, Lehert, & Burger, 2004). Three-quarters of the women experienced bothersome menopausal symptoms such as hot flushes at some point during the transition, and most of these women consulted a physician about the complaints. Women who reported premenstrual psychological and physical complaints were more likely to report distressing effects of menopause. Although a slight decline in mood occurred in the first 2 years after the final menstrual period, mood, along with overall well-being, improved after this point. Correlates of changes in well-being included changes in marital status, work satisfaction, daily hassles, and life events—many of which were not *directly* associated with the menopause (Guthrie et al., 2004).

The overall proportion of women with sexual problems significantly increased from 42% to 88% from early to late menopausal transition (Guthrie et al., 2004). Moreover, sexual symptoms were significantly correlated with estradiol but not with testosterone levels. Most of the variance in sexual behavior could be accounted for by a woman's previous behavior, a change in the status of her partner (divorced, deceased, or new partner), and feelings toward that partner. Overall, although a decline in estradiol was directly associated with an increase in vasomotor symptoms, vaginal dryness, and dyspareunia, aging and partner-related factors had a greater effect than estradiol on sexuality (Guthrie et al., 2004). In the Michigan Bone Health Study, 660 Caucasian women were recruited between the ages of 24 and 44 in 1992 and followed yearly over the ensuing 10 years. The investigators assessed the prevalence of certain menopausal and sexual symptoms, as well the "level of bother" associated with those symptoms (Ford, Sowers, Crutchfield, Wilson, & Jannausch, 2005). Whereas 28% of the sample reported sexual problems at baseline, 46% reported problems 9 years later—a figure half that of the Australian longitudinal data. Variables that predicted the degree of "bother" from sexual symptoms included: increasing age, higher Body Mass Index, increasing FSH, being postmenopausal, being in the middle (as opposed to the lower) quartile for testosterone levels (a somewhat surprising finding), having more children, and smoking (Ford et al., 2005). Use of hormonal therapy was more likely to be associated with "bother from sexual symptoms," perhaps reflecting the fact that women with bothersome symptoms are more likely to seek hormonal remedies.

The Study of Women's Health Across the Nation (SWAN), another large-scale, population-based project that controlled for the effects of ethnicity, recruited 16,065 postbaby-boomer premenopausal or perimenopausal women aged 40 to 55 from seven U.S. cities, with a subset of this group ($n = 3,302$) followed longitudinally (Avis et al., 2005). The authors explored ethnic group differences in sociodemographic, health-related, psychosocial, menopausal, and sexuality-related variables, with specific analyses between Japanese, Chinese, non-Hispanic White, Hispanic, and African American subgroups. Among women who were currently sexually active (76% of the total sample), the majority reported experiencing sexual desire at least once per week (59%), and many reported feeling sexually aroused in all sexual encounters (70%), with neither variable being associated with menopausal status (Avis et al., 2005). Women of Chinese or Japanese descent were less likely to report sexual desire than the other ethnicities, and desire was most strongly influenced by the belief that sexual activity is important. Hispanic women were least likely to report physical pleasure during sexual activity, and this was linked to the Machismo emphasis in Hispanic culture of greater pleasure in the male partner. Emotional satisfaction was not influenced by ethnicity, but was influenced (negatively) by vaginal dryness, depression, and relationship deterioration. Sexual arousal was lowest among Hispanic and African American women and was associated with negative attitudes to aging, higher perceived stress, relationship deterioration, and relationship abuse. Menopausal status was associated with pain during intercourse but not with frequency of intercourse. Although pain is normally explained by the decline of estrogen, data from this study found that psychosocial factors such as attitudes toward aging, relationship happiness, believing that sex is important, perceived stress, and depression were more predictive of pain than estrogen levels. In fact, reports of pain were 40% higher in perimenopausal than in premenopausal women, and were somewhat higher than in other population-based studies. Overall, the significant ethnic group differences in sexuality suggest that sexual behavior in women has a strong cultural component, even after controlling for other possible explanatory variables (Avis et al., 2005).

Researchers have also attempted to correlate menopausal changes in testosterone with sexual function. Neither serum testosterone levels nor the Free Androgen Index correlated with sexual function among women in the SWAN study (A. Santoro et al., 2005). Another community-based study of 1,021 Australian women also failed to correlate serum androgen levels with sexual response measures (Davis, Davison, Donath, & Bell, 2005). A different longitudinal 5-year study of women undergoing natural menopause found no correlation between free testosterone and sexual satisfaction at year 1 or year 5; however, no attempt was made to document menopausal status (Gerber, Johnson, Bunn, & O'Brien, 2005). Bilateral ovarian removal, also known as bilateral salpingo-oophorectomy (BSO), includes removal of the ovaries and fallopian tubes and results in a dramatic decline in estrogen and androgen, but, in a recent study of perimenopausal women undergoing elective hysterectomy with and without BSO, no correlation between ovarian removal and reduced sexual function was found (Aziz, Brannstrom, Bergquist, & Silfverstolpe, 2005). Collectively, this research suggests minimal, if any, relationship between androgen levels and sexual response among menopausal women.

The contribution of surgical, as opposed to natural, menopause has been studied in women from different countries in the Women's International Study of Health and Sexuality (WISHES), which recruited 4,517 women from France, Germany Italy, the United Kingdom, and the United States (Dennerstein, Koochaki, Barton, & Graziottin, 2006). In this study, age-matched groups of women who had either received hysterectomy plus BSO or undergone no surgery were compared. Of the 1,356 women with a current sexual partner, those who had had a surgical menopause had significantly lower desire, with 16% of younger women (versus 7% of nonsurgical younger women), and 12% of older women (versus 9% of nonsurgical older women) meeting criteria for a sexual desire disorder (Dennerstein et al., 2006). Women with low desire also reported more frequent negative emotions and a lower frequency of sexual intercourse; and the loss of desire was strongly associated with arousal, orgasm, and pleasure complaints. The use of hormonal therapy, while improving complaints of vaginal dryness, did not alleviate women's com-

Menopause, Aging, and Sexual Response in Women **261**

plaints of distress. Although not assessed in this study, the more deleterious effects of BSO seen in younger women may be mediated by psychosocial factors such as beliefs about early menopause and loss of fertility.

In conclusion, these population-based studies suggest that although menopause is an important predictor of sexual function among naturally menopausal women, psychosocial aspects of menopause may be more robust predictors of change in sexual function than biological predictors. In fact, testosterone levels do not seem to correlate with any measure of sexual response or satisfaction among women throughout the menopausal transition. However, the radical change in hormonal status that comes with BSO may be especially deleterious for sexual function—particularly for younger women—and the woman's interpretation of the early menopause must be taken into account. The implications of these findings for assessment of menopausal sexuality are outlined in Table 9.1.

Table 9.1 **Assessment Guidelines for Sexuality in Menopausal and Older Women Based on a Review of the Literature on Effects of Menopause and Aging on Women's Sexuality**

Suggested Assessment Guideline	Based on Publication
Assess sexual response and behavior prior to menopause (retrospectively)	Guthrie et al. (2004)
Assess degree of bother from menopausal and sexual symptoms	Ford et al. (2005)
If hormonal measurements are taken, note that estradiol, but not testosterone, may be correlated with sexual response. Postmenopausal estrogens are usually not detected in available assays.	Guthrie et al. (2004); Ford et al. (2005); Santoro et al. (2005); Davis et al. (2005); Gerber et al. (2005); Aziz et al. (2005)
Assess the influence of culture and ethnicity in sexual changes—noting that there may be cross-cultural differences even among English-speaking women	Adekunle et al. (2000); Avis et al. (2005); Lock (1998); Nicolosi et al. (2006)
Assess beliefs about aging and sexuality	Avis et al. (2005); DeLamater & Sill (2005); Laumann et al. (2005); Nicolosi et al. (2006)
Assess mood and current/past stressors including domestic violence and childhood sexual abuse	Guthrie et al. (2004); Freeman et al. (2006)
Assess type and intensity of sexual stimuli employed	Laan & van Lunsen (1997); van Lunsen & Laan (2004)
Assess aspects of the relationship including: feelings for partner, expectations about the future of the relationship, and partner's sexual function	Dennerstein et al. (2003); Laumann et al. (2005)

Age and Sexuality

Coinciding with the menopausal transition is advancing age, and Kinsey identified age as the most important factor to understanding human sexuality. Thus, when exploring the effects of menopause on sexual response, we must consider age-related changes that may account for the observed effects. Even when other risk factors are absent, advancing age constitutes a risk factor for various health issues such as vascular dysfunction and the need for medications (Camacho & Reyes-Ortiz, 2005). In general, older women report that their physicians do not inquire about sexual health as frequently as is done with younger women, despite women's willingness to discuss sexuality if it were raised (Nusbaum, Singh, & Pyles, 2004). We must also consider age-related differences in the experience of distress from sexual symptoms, given that a recent review of population-based studies exploring sexuality after menopause found that although sexual problems were more common in older women, the younger cohort was more distressed by these changes (Dennerstein, Alexander, & Kotz, 2003).

In the American Association of Retired Persons Modern Maturity Sexuality Survey, 1,384 women and men older than 45 were mailed questionnaires that assessed age-related factors (e.g., biological, psychological, and relational factors) associated with low sexual desire (DeLamater & Sill, 2005). Although age was strongly associated with a decline in desire ($r = .51$), a subset of older women (22%) reported very high levels of desire. High blood pressure was linked to low sexual desire whereas a diagnosis of diabetes, arthritis, or depression was not. In contrast, the factors found to be associated with higher desire in older aged women were the belief that sexual activity is important for quality of life, disagreeing with the belief that "sex is only for younger people," and having a partner. These psychological variables accounted for 59% of the explained variance in desire and were overall more predictive of sexual desire than any biological factor (DeLamater & Sill, 2005).

The Global Study of Sexual Attitudes and Behaviors (GSSAB) conducted with 27,500 men and women across 29 countries focused exclusively on 40- to 80-year-old individuals, although the study did not control for menopausal status (Laumann et al., 2005). A subsample of women that was currently sexually active showed lower sexual desire with increasing age, and this was associated with the belief that aging reduces sexual desire. Among the different sexual complaints, low sexual desire was the most common, and, even in a subsample analysis of just the five Anglophone countries, the prevalence of this complaint ranged from 11% to 35% (Nicolosi et al., 2006). Whereas lubrication complaints increased from the 40 to 49 to the 50 to 59 age groups, no significant differences were found between the youngest and the oldest age cohorts. Pain with intercourse among this group of 40- to 80-year-old women was the least common sexual complaint among Anglophone women, ranging from 5% to 11% (Nicolosi et al., 2006), although dyspareunia associated with vaginal atrophy tends to affect approximately 40% of older women (Stenberg et al., 1995).

In summary, available data suggest that age is significantly associated with a decline of sexual desire in women, and that this may be mediated, at least in part, by certain cognitive beliefs that sexuality declines with age.

Effects of Age versus Effects of Menopause

Given the confounding effects of aging and menopause in menopause-associated sexual complaints, researchers have attempted to separate these contributors via statistical techniques. In the Melbourne Women's Midlife Health Project, sexual function was compared across women currently in the menopausal transition, an age-matched premenopausal group, and an age-matched postmenopausal group. Sexual responsivity (a composite measure of desire and lubrication) was independently affected by both menopause and aging (Guthrie et al., 2004). Specifically, estradiol levels were related negatively to dyspareunia and positively to sexual responsivity; however, the estradiol effect was less predictive than prior level of sexual function, change in partner status, and overall feelings for the partner—factors influenced more by aging per se (Dennerstein, Lehert, & Burger, 2005). In fact, psychosocial factors related to attitudes and partner status may be more predictive of sexual function than any biological or hormonal variable (Dennerstein & Hayes, 2005).

In a more recent study of 1,525 British women who were followed longitudinally from age 47 to 54, independent effects of menopause and aging on sexual functioning were also found (Mishra & Kuh, 2006). In addition, even after controlling for effects of vaginal dryness, psychological symptoms and life stressors were associated with a self-reported decline in sex life.

Combining the research on the effects of menopause and on the effects of aging suggests that these variables may share some of the variance in explaining sexual changes in older women; however, both contribute unique effects. Sexual complaints increase as women move through menopausal transition, with the most common complaint being loss of sexual desire. Beliefs about aging and sexuality strongly predict sexual difficulties in women, whereas testosterone levels do not. Cross-cultural effects are also apparent: East Asian women report low sexual desire more frequently and Hispanic women report less sexual arousal and genital pleasure.

Finally, surgical menopause appears to be more deleterious to sexual function for younger rather than older women. Implications of these findings in the assessment of sexuality in menopausal women are considered in Table 9.1.

Physiological Aspects of Sexual Response in Menopausal Women

With advances in sexual psychophysiology, researchers have been able to explore whether impairments in the physiological aspects of sexual responding (e.g., vaginal lubrication) may underlie sexual complaints with menopause. This research has implications for treatment of menopause-related sexual complaints, given that medications that increase genital physiological responding may be helpful for some postmenopausal women (Basson & Brotto, 2003; Berman, Berman, Toler, Gill, Haughie, & Sildenafil Study Group, 2003). Masters and Johnson concluded that "there seems to be no physiologic reason why the frequency of sexual expression found satisfactory for the younger woman should not be carried over into the postmenopausal years" (Masters & Johnson, 1966). It has been hypothesized, however, that with the menopausal reduction in estradiol, women may be prone to vasculogenic sexual dysfunction detectable with vaginal physiological measures. In two studies of postmenopausal women without sexual complaints, no physiological differences in vaginal response during arousal were found between premenopausal and postmenopausal women (Brotto & Gorzalka, 2002; Laan & van Lunsen, 1997). However, in the absence of an arousing sexual stimulus, postmenopausal women did show lower vaginal pulse amplitude, suggestive of reduced estrogen levels (Laan & van Lunsen, 1997). Thus, in the absence of adequate arousal, postmenopausal women may be more likely to experience genital sexual symptoms than premenopausal women. Moreover, in a separate study comparing age-matched postmenopausal women with and without sexual arousal disorder, no differences in physiological response were found (van Lunsen & Laan, 2004), suggesting that arousal complaints after menopause are unrelated to the ability to become genitally responsive in the majority of women. Instead, contextual and relationship variables related to insufficient stimulation may play a causal role in these sexual complaints. In addition, the correlation between genital vasocongestion, measured via vaginal photoplethysmography, and subjective sexual arousal is highly variable in women (Rosen & Beck, 1988).

In sum, these findings suggest that methods of increasing genital vasocongestion via medications may not necessarily improve sexual function among postmenopausal women with sexual arousal disorder (e.g., Basson, McInnes, Smith, Hodgson, & Koppiker, 2002) and that, instead, enhancing the types and intensities of stimuli during sexual activity might be a more efficacious first-line strategy.

Mood Changes with Menopause

Fluctuations in estradiol levels during perimenopause have been linked to irritability, tearfulness, anxiety, depressed/labile mood, lack of motivation/energy, poor concentration, and interrupted sleep (Prior, 1998). Given the complex interplay between neurotransmitters and steroid hormones, it is not surprising that menopause may be associated with mood fluctuations. Each system (neurotransmitters and hormones) appears to modulate the other, and changes in one system may have a dramatic effect on the other (Steiner, Dunn, & Born, 2003). The extent to which the transition to menopause may lead to a specific increase in the occurrence of mood disturbances has been a point of controversy (Soares, Joffe, & Steiner, 2004). Recent longitudinal data suggest that the transition to menopause and its changing hormonal milieu are strongly associated with the onset of depressed mood among women with no history of depression (Freeman, Sammel, Lin, & Nelson, 2006).

Sexual symptoms acquired during menopause may be associated with changes in mood. The aging process and menopause may lead to significant alterations in a woman's body image that may evoke feelings of loss or sadness over lost youth and beauty. The Melbourne Women's Midlife Health Project found that menopausal women with negative mood were more likely to have negative mood prior to menopause, experience bothersome menopausal symptoms, have poor self-rated health, have negative feelings for partner, smoke, not exercise, and report many daily hassles and high stress (Guthrie et al., 2004). By amplifying the effects of such psychosocial variables, the menopausal transition may exert additional effects on mood, which then impacts sexual function.

Other forms of stress found to influence menopausal effects on sexuality are childhood sexual abuse and domestic violence. In an Australian sample, 28.5% of the women had experienced some form of domestic violence during their lifetime, and a high proportion had experienced childhood sexual abuse (Guthrie et al., 2004). Those women with a history of childhood sexual abuse were more likely to have different feelings for a partner and shorter current relationships. They also reported a lower frequency of current sexual activities.

Taken together, some of the effects of menopause on sexual function may be mediated by mood and stress. This conclusion has obvious implications for the clinical setting (see Table 9.1) where postmenopausal women with sexual complaints may also have significant changes in mood and affect. It also suggests that one appropriate treatment target among menopausal women with sexual complaints is to improve their mood and to reduce their current stressors.

Cultural Aspects of Menopause and Sexuality

Data from the GSSAB and SWAN projects suggest cross-cultural and ethnicity effects on menopausal sexuality. Research on menopause of women from non-Western countries strongly suggests that the health and well-being of menopausal women is influenced by social, cultural, and economic factors. For example, the frequency of vasomotor menopausal symptoms varies widely cross-culturally from 0% of Mayan women in Mexico (Beyene, 1986), to 18% of Chinese factory workers in Hong Kong (Tang, 1994), to 70% of North American women (McKinlay & Jefferys, 1974), and to 80% of Dutch women (Dennerstein, 1996). Popular culture suggests that menopause signals the start of a decline in health due to lowered estrogen levels. However, anthropological data suggest that menopause is not a universally recognized phenomenon. Instead, perhaps a more accurate way of considering the influence of culture is to consider it as "a continuous feedback relationship [with biology] of ongoing exchange, in which both are subject to variation" (Lock, 1998, p. 410). For example, in Japanese the word for menopause, *konenki*, refers to the change of life (Lock, 1994), and three different Japanese terms can be used to describe hot flushes. For women, the concept of *konenki* is individually interpreted and may or may not include the cessation of menses.

Lock (1998), a Canadian anthropologist, studied the construct of menopause in depth in Japan and compared it with North American experiences of menopause. The Japanese women were recruited from a rural area, a blue-collar working area, and a suburb where women are "professional housewives." Japanese women did not consider the end of menstruation to be a significant marker of middle age, and in comparison with North American women, very few associated it with distressing symptoms. When given a checklist of general body symptoms, women from Canada and the United States reported significantly more symptoms than Japanese women—with the exception of diarrhea/constipation, likely attributed to a higher rice diet in Japanese women. The rate of reporting multiple symptoms and chronic health problems was significantly lower among the Japanese women (28%) compared to the Canadian (45%) and American (53%) women. Lock attributed the lower rates in part to the fact that rural Japanese women were too busy to experience distress with menopause, and that any discomfort associated with it was considered of minor importance. Moreover, the "professional housewife" is idealized and considered to be the standard by which all women are measured.

In another study affording insight into cross-cultural differences, 676 Nigerian postmenopausal women were interviewed to obtain their perceptions of the menopause. Treatment-seeking and the use of hormonal therapies were both very low among Nigerian women, perhaps stemming from the belief that doctors are too busy treating life-threatening conditions, and that symptoms of menopause are considered a normal physiological process not requiring medical attention (Adekunle, Fawole, & Okunlola, 2000). This contrasts with the GSSAB subsample analysis of Anglophone women that found that most women with a sexual complaint sought treatment or support (Nicolosi et al., 2006). Most women from the Nigerian sample were happy to experience menopause. Although 70% of the women stated that the menopause affected their sexuality, a statement primarily influenced by the cultural belief that "menopause ends sex lives," only a small subgroup indicated that their relationship with their husbands was affected. Dyspareunia was given by only 2% of women as the reason why intercourse stopped. When asked about their feelings about themselves following menopause, many noted that menopause gave them "an increased sense of maturity," "peace of mind," "increased access to worship," and "a sense of fulfillment as a woman"—all suggesting a positive outlook on menopause.

Thus, data based on different cultural groups suggest that negative symptoms of menopause are not universal and, instead, may be the product of a cultural construction. Given that attitudes toward aging and menopause can significantly predict sexual function, specific attitudes shown by other cultures may protect against menopause-associated sexual complaints. Moreover, attitudes and perceptions about menopause and aging are important to assess when considering menopausal symptoms and sexuality.

Classification, Diagnosis, and Treatment

This chapter has thus far focused on sexual symptoms and complaints; however, some women may meet the criteria for an acquired sexual *dysfunction* with menopause. Criteria for sexual desire, arousal, orgasm, and pain disorders have been reviewed in prior chapters, so this section focuses on menopausal considerations when making a sexual dysfunction diagnosis. It is important to place such sexual concerns in the context of other contributing factors in the menopausal woman's life and to carefully assess the level of distress. Given the multidimensional nature of women's sexuality and the wide variety of changes that take place during menopause, a helpful approach for conceptualizing sexual changes with menopause is to assess the roles of predisposing, precipitating, and maintaining (perpetuating) factors (Graziottin & Leiblum, 2005). *Predisposing factors* increase an individual's vulnerability for a sexual complaint later on in life and, with respect to menopause, may include:

- Preexisting medical or endocrine disease.
- Surgery.
- Drug treatments affecting hormones or the menstrual cycle.
- Longstanding and underlying psychological factors related to body image, personality, or relationship views.
- Psychiatric disorders.
- Past sexual experiences.
- Issues related to culture, religion, and social support.

Precipitating factors are events more directly linked, chronologically, to the acquired sexual complaints with menopause. These include:

- Menopause itself and the hormonal, anatomical, and psychological factors associated with it.
- Current use of medications or alcohol.
- Changes in psychosexual status such as relationship changes.
- Larger contextual life changes such as major stressors, economic difficulties, or medical/psychological treatments.

Maintaining (perpetuating) factors are those responsible for the persistence of the sexual complaint, despite the completion of menopause. These factors include:

- The continuing aging process and all the biological and psychological consequences therein.
- Contextual factors such as ongoing relationship discord or lack of privacy or time (Graziottin & Leiblum, 2005).

Thus, with such a variety of contributing factors exerting effects at different times, the practitioner should perform a detailed biopsychosocial evaluation when determining if sexual complaints in a menopausal woman meet the criteria for a sexual dysfunction.

By using a structured diagnostic method that consists of validated questionnaires and a structured face-to-face interview, trained interviewers can make reliable and valid diagnoses of postmenopausal women with sexual dysfunction comparable to those of sexual health experts (Utian et al., 2005). However, clinical wisdom suggests that diagnoses of sexual dysfunction should not rely on self-report instruments alone, and that the face-to-face interview is the gold-standard for determining if a sexual complaint is a sexual dysfunction.

The definitions of women's sexual dysfunction have been reconceptualized (Basson et al., 2003) as a result of extensive review of the empirical literature combined with the clinical expertise of international experts in the area of women's sexual health (see Table 9.2). Drawing from a model of sexual desire that may be more pertinent for mature women in established relationships, "Women's sexual interest/desire disorder" has been redefined to emphasize the role of responsive desire as opposed to hormone-driven spontaneous desire (Basson, 2002). Moreover, this newer model emphasizes reasons/motivations/incentives that might move a woman from sexually "neutral" status to deciding to be sexual with her partner. With the menopausal decline in hormones, teaching women to identify such incentives for being sexual, and normalizing the lack of spontaneous desire, may be a powerfully therapeutic tool.

Sexual Arousal Disorder has been subtyped into two categories: (1) women experiencing difficulties only in the subjective aspects of sexual arousal, termed "Subjective Sexual Arousal Disorder," and (2) women experiencing arousal complaints focused only on genital excitement, termed "Genital Sexual Arousal Disorder" (Basson et al., 2003). While prevalence rates for these subtypes do not yet exist, some estrogen-deficient women may experience the genital subtype of an arousal disorder and therefore might be candidates for local topical estrogen or a vasoactive medication such as sildenafil (Barentsen, van de Weijer, & Schram, 1997). Women with the combined subtypes of Sexual Arousal Disorder are likely the most common presentation (Basson et al., 2003). In such women, psychoeducation into the factors that promote subjective sexual arousal, such as limiting distracting stimuli and increasing the frequency of effective sexual stimuli, should be emphasized.

Among postmenopausal women with acquired Orgasmic Disorder, an arousal disorder should first be ruled out. Although not uncommon in the clinical setting, the prevalence of an acquired orgasmic disorder with menopause is unknown but may be related to hormonal factors.

The slightly revised definition of dyspareunia recognizes that intercourse may be either complete or attempted but incomplete (Basson et al., 2003). New onset vestibulodynia (previously vulvar vestibulitis syndrome), the most frequent cause of dyspareunia in young women, is less common in menopausal women, and painful intercourse instead has been linked most often to reduced estrogen levels leading to vaginal dryness and loss of lubrication. When assessing dyspareunia in menopausal women, the

Table 9.2 **New Definitions of Women's Sexual Dysfunction and Implications for Assessment of Sexual Symptoms in the Menopausal Woman**

Sexual Dysfunction	Definition	Assessment and Treatment Points for Menopausal Women
Sexual Interest/Desire Disorder	Absent or diminished feelings of sexual interest or desire, absent sexual thoughts or fantasies and a lack of responsive desire. Motivations (here defined as reasons/incentives) for attempting to become sexually aroused are scarce or absent. The lack of interest is considered to be beyond a normative lessening with life cycle and relationship duration.	Encourage patient to consider reasons/incentives for sexual activity that may motivate her to initiate or be receptive to a partner. Normalize the absence of spontaneous sexual desire. Emphasize the role of responsive desire that follows arousal in contributing to her sexual satisfaction.
Subjective Sexual Arousal Disorder	Absence of or markedly diminished feelings of sexual arousal (sexual excitement and sexual pleasure) from any type of sexual stimulation. Vaginal lubrication or other signs of physical response still occur.	Limit distractions. Challenge distorted thoughts that may impede arousal. Improve body image. Vary the type and intensity of sexual stimuli. Improve context such as addressing feelings about partner.
Genital Sexual Arousal Disorder	Complaints of absent or impaired genital sexual arousal. Self-report may include minimal vulval swelling or vaginal lubrication from any type of sexual stimulation and reduced sexual sensations from caressing genitalia. Subjective sexual excitement still occurs from nongenital sexual stimuli.	Vary the type and intensity of sexual stimuli. Local estrogen therapy.
Combined Genital and Subjective Arousal Disorder	Absence of or markedly diminished feelings of sexual arousal (sexual excitement and sexual pleasure) from any type of sexual stimulation, as well as complaints of absent or impaired genital sexual arousal (vulval swelling, lubrication).	A combination of techniques used for subjective and genital sexual arousal disorders.
Women's Orgasmic Disorder	Despite the self-report of high sexual arousal/excitement, there is either lack of orgasm, markedly diminished intensity of orgasmic sensations, or marked delay of orgasm from any kind of stimulation.	Ensure adequate sexual stimulation (see previous points for arousal disorder). Ensure consistent focus on the arousal and responsive desire.

Table 9.2   *(Continued)*

Sexual Dysfunction	Definition	Assessment and Treatment Points for Menopausal Women
		Address interpersonal factors that may be leading to dissatisfaction.
		Consider medical, surgical, and hormonal contributors to anorgasmia.
Dyspareunia	Persistent or recurrent pain with attempted or complete vaginal entry and/or penile vaginal intercourse.	Is intercourse attempted or completed?
		Careful inquiry and detailed genital pelvic examination to establish the contribution from altered tissue health (e.g., vaginal atrophy, vestibulitis) and/or anatomical changes (e.g., stenosis, prolapse).
		Consider whether the use of topical lubricants ameliorates the dysparuenia.
		Assess presence of a partner and other nonintercourse penetrative sexual activities.

Source: "Definitions of Women's Sexual Dysfunction Reconsidered: Advocating Expansion and Revision," by R. Basson et al., 2003, *Journal of Psychosomatic Obstetrics and Gynaecology, 24,* 221–229.

practitioner should determine if intercourse has stopped due to pain or if a lubricant ameliorates the dyspareunia. Moreover, a careful genital examination to rule out other pathologies such as lichen sclerosis is necessary.

In summary, a biopsychosocial approach that explores the predisposing, precipitating, and perpetuating factors associated with sexual difficulties in menopause is essential. This is best performed through an in-depth interview and may be facilitated with validated questionnaires. In making a diagnosis of sexual dysfunction in the menopausal woman, the revised definitions of women's sexual dysfunctions, which normalize the lack of spontaneous sexual desire in mature women, may be more applicable to women in long-term relationships than the traditional definitions of sexual dysfunction provided in the *DSM-IV-TR* (American Psychiatric Association, 2000).

Psychosocial Treatment Approaches to Sexual Difficulties during Menopause

Based on Basson's (2002) model emphasizing responsive sexual desire and on the literature documenting the importance of psychosocial factors in accounting for sexual difficulties during menopause, specific treatment strategies may follow (see Table 9.2 for an abbreviated version). The lack of spontaneous sexual desire, which women may refer to as the absence of "butter-flies," should be "normalized" through the use of psychoeducation about the typical decline in testosterone levels accounting for this change. But women should then be encouraged to consider reasons, or incentives, for being sexually active. These may include: to exchange love with a partner, to feel emotional close-ness, to feel happier or a sense of relief, to provide physical pleasure to a partner or to herself, to satisfy a belief that this is a normal act, and so on. In other words, women should be encouraged to consider why they might seek sexual activity, despite not experiencing any intrinsic sexual desire to do so. Following this, a woman should be encouraged to optimize the types of stimuli that will arouse her, and to ensure a healthy context during which sexual activity with her partner may take place. Education about different types of sexual stimulation should be offered, and reluctance or embarrassment should be carefully explored and normalized throughout. Exploration of the context also involves an assessment of attitudes and attraction toward her partner, and methods of enhancing these may proceed. As indicated in Table 9.2, for women who also experience difficulties with genital arousal, a combination of these approaches together with a local topical estrogen preparation may be an effective first-line treatment. For women with Orgasmic Disorder, behavioral techniques that teach the woman to focus on sexual stimulation while minimizing distractions may be helpful. Attention to relational factors (in particular feelings of attraction toward the partner) may be important to explore.

Hormonal Treatments of Menopausal and Sexual Symptoms

We now shift to reviewing hormone therapies for menopausal and age-related sexual symptoms. Hormone therapies for symptomatic menopausal women are estrogen-alone therapy, estrogen and progestin therapy, androgens preparations, and tibolone. Systemic estrogen-alone (without progestin) is recommended only for women without a uterus, given the increased risk of endometrial cancer if used "unopposed." Androgen supplementation has recently been approved by the European Medicines Agency (EMEA) but is currently not approved by the U.S. Food and Drug Administration (FDA). Although evidence supports its effectiveness (Sarrel, 2006), long-term use lacks safety data. Tibolone has been used in Europe for 20 years but is neither approved for use by the FDA nor available in the United States (although it is currently under regulatory review in the United States). The decision to institute any hormonal therapy must be individualized and the patient adequately informed about risks and benefits. Various hormone regimens for the treatment of menopausal and sexual symptoms are briefly reviewed next.

Estrogens

For women complaining of generalized menopausal symptoms, estrogen therapy (with or without progesterone) can be delivered systemically in three ways: oral tablets, transdermal patch, and transdermal gel. If the complaint is localized to the vagina, estrogen may be delivered locally in the form of vaginal cream, a ring, or a tablet. Currently, no justification exists for systemic (i.e., oral) estrogen or estrogen/progestin therapy in asymptomatic postmenopausal women. However, newly menopausal women with symptoms might experience relief from these climacteric symptoms following systemic estrogen therapy (Davis et al., 2004).

The Women's Health Initiative (WHI) was a large randomized trial of 16,608 minimally symptomatic postmenopausal women of mean age 63, randomized to either estrogen plus progestin (.625 mg conjugated equine estrogen plus 2.5 mg medroxyprogesterone acetate) or to a placebo. In a separate study, 10,739 postmenopausal women without a uterus were randomized to either estrogen alone or placebo conditions. A series of publications based on data collected in these trials began in July 2002, following its early discontinuation due to significant adverse events. Women in the estrogen plus progestin study experienced a small and nonclinically meaningful benefit in terms of sleep disturbance, physical functioning, and improved vasomotor symptoms (Rossouw et al., 2002). No significant effects were found on general health, vitality, mental health, depressive symptoms, or sexual satisfaction (Hays et al., 2003). Unfortunately, the WHI study did not include sexual function as a study endpoint and the assessment tool that was used was inadequate.

Estrogen-alone therapy was not found to increase the risk of breast cancer in postmenopausal women (Stefanick et al., 2006). An increased risk of venous thromboembolism in the initial years, including deep vein thrombosis and pulmonary embolism, was found. These negative effects dramatically impacted the willingness of women and their treatment providers to consider estrogen therapy (Morabia & Costanza, 2006). Moreover, researchers saw no significant improvements in the areas of general health, physical functioning, pain, vitality, role functioning, mental health, depressive symptoms, cognitive function, or sexual satisfaction from the estrogen therapy (Brunner et al., 2005).

Vaginal estrogen preparations are effective for restoring the vaginal epithelium, relieving vaginal atrophy, increasing vaginal blood flow (Semmens & Wagner, 1982), and improving vaginal lubrication and reducing dyspareunia (Sarrel, 2000). In general, the risk of endometrial stimulation with estrogen preparations is low and depends on the dose and type of estrogen used (Davis et al., 2004).

Estrogen restores clitoral vibration and pressure thresholds (Sarrel, 1990). A subgroup of women with sexual arousal and orgasmic complaints initially responded to estrogen therapy but subsequently reverted to their initial problems, especially when the presenting problem was loss of libido (Sarrel, 2000). Transdermal estradiol, instead, restored sexual desire in women treated for vaginal dryness and dyspareunia, suggesting that some women may benefit from the local effects of estrogen in the vagina to improve loss of sexual desire (i.e., motivation; Sarrel, 1990).

For women who cannot take estrogen therapy, over-the-counter lubricants are helpful (Bachmann & Leiblum, 2004). Moreover, there is a "use it or lose it" phenomenon such that, although not fully understood, sexually active postmenopausal women are less likely to experience vaginal atrophy, and sexual stimulation or greater sexual frequency can improve vaginal lubrication. This finding has obvious therapeutic implications in that sexual activity may be normalized and even encouraged in the older years among women with negative attitudes toward sex and aging.

In summary, although locally applied estrogen may improve vaginal symptoms, the findings from the WHI showing that systemic (oral) estrogen for minimally symptomatic women may lead to some adverse events and have led to extreme caution when considering estrogen treatment. However, estrogen may lead to an improvement in desire and arousal symptoms. For women who cannot tolerate estrogen, over-the-counter lubricants and more frequent sexual activity have both been found to ease sexual complaints during menopause.

Androgens

Although no androgen therapies are currently approved by the FDA for female sexual difficulties, they have been used in clinical practice for some time and have been aggressively studied in randomized controlled testing over the past several years. Products approved for men and used "off-label" for women include oral testosterone, topical ointment or gel, intramuscular injections and implants, and oral DHEA. Some different androgen therapies are considered here.

TESTOSTERONE   Studies performed in the 1980s and 1990s involved administration of high pharmacological doses of testosterone with untoward masculinizing side effects. More recently, lower doses of testosterone, achieving levels that are more typically physiological for younger premenopausal women, have been tested for efficacy in improving postmenopausal women's sexual response and, in particular, sexual desire. In a recent study, women with distressing Hypoactive Sexual Desire Disorder (HSDD) after BSO who were using transdermal estrogen were recruited to a 24-week, double-blind, placebo controlled trial. Sixty-one women were randomized to either a transdermal placebo or testosterone (300 μg/day) matrix patch (Davis et al., 2006). The testosterone-treated group experienced greater sexual desire, as well as greater arousal and orgasm, decreased sexual concerns, greater responsiveness, and better self-image. Compared to placebo, the testosterone group experienced a significantly greater decrease in sexual distress, with a trend toward improved frequency of satisfactory sexual events. Adverse events occurred with similar frequency in both groups, and no serious risks were observed. A virtually identical trial (24 weeks, double-blind, randomized, placebo controlled) with a larger sample ($n = 318$) found that the 300 μg/day testosterone patch, but not the 450 μg/day patch, increased sexual desire and frequency of satisfying sexual activity in women with HSDD following surgical menopause (Braunstein et al., 2005). In three recent randomized controlled trials, testosterone benefited postmenopausal women's sexual desire as well as other aspects of female sexual response (Buster et al., 2005; Shifren et al., 2006; Simon et al., 2005).

Although together these five randomized trials suggest that testosterone treatment benefits estrogenized postmenopausal women with HSDD, for purposes of regulatory agency approval, the number of trials is too limited, particularly with respect to those extending beyond 24 weeks. As such, the testosterone patch (Intrinsa™, marketed by Procter & Gamble in Europe) did not receive regulatory approval by the FDA in December 2004, and more controlled trials exploring efficacy and long-term safety of testosterone for women are necessary. Moreover, there is need for assessment of testosterone therapy concomitant with systemic long-term estrogen treatment.

DEHYDROEPIANDROSTERONE   Dehydroepiandrosterone (DHEA) is the first androgen in the biosynthetic pathway and is thus considered both an androgen and estrogen precursor. DHEA was classified in 1994 by the FDA as a dietary supplement and is available over-the-counter in the United States and other countries. DHEA therapy has been investigated in various populations and under various conditions, with inconsistencies across studies (Cameron & Braunstein, 2005). For example, whereas no effect of 50 mg/day oral DHEA was found when given to older women for a period of 3 months (Morales, Nolan, Nelson, & Yen, 1994), a positive effect on both subjective and psychophysiological sexual arousal from 300 mg DHEA was found when given acutely (Hackbert &

Heiman, 2002). The positive effects of DHEA might thus depend on the duration of use and the age of participant, given that another report found that chronic administration of 50 mg/day DHEA for 1 year positively influenced sexual attitudes, libido, sexual activity (intercourse or masturbation), and satisfaction only in women older than 70 (Baulieu et al., 2000).

Tibolone   Tibolone is a synthetic steroid having estrogenic and weak progestogenic and androgenic effects. Tibolone decreases SHBG levels and therefore free testosterone, and DHEA-S levels increase (Kenemans, Speroff, & Tibolone Consensus Group, 2005). Because it lacks regulatory agency approval in the United States, much of the research on tibolone comes from Europe. In one double-blind, multicenter study, 437 postmenopausal women without sexual dysfunction were randomized to either tibolone or 17 beta-estradiol (2 mg) plus norethisterone acetate, and then measured on different aspects of self-reported sexual function over 30 days. Compared to the estrogen group, tibolone resulted in higher scores in all sexual domains (Nathorst-Boos & Hammar, 1997). Another small randomized, double-blind, crossover study in 38 postmenopausal women with no diagnosed sexual dysfunction compared tibolone (2.5 mg/day) for 3 months to a placebo on measures of vaginal blood flow, sexual desire and arousability, and climacteric symptoms (Laan, van Lunsen, & Everaerd, 2001). Tibolone significantly increased vaginal blood flow in response to erotic fantasy; it also increased sexual desire, frequency of arousability, and sexual fantasies compared to placebo. More recent studies on tibolone are not placebo controlled, not double-blinded, or limited in sample size (Uygur, Yesildaglar, & Erkaya, 2005). Therefore, whether tibolone consistently improves aspects of postmenopausal sexual response is still unknown.

In summary, although no FDA-approved androgen products are available to treat women's sexual concerns, several recent placebo-controlled trials support the beneficial effect of testosterone for sexual desire in estrogen-treated postmenopausal women. Unfortunately, neither long-term safety data nor data on women not concurrently receiving estrogen have been generated. Support for other androgens, including tibolone and DHEA, is limited, and conclusions are hindered by the absence of well-controlled trials.

Natural Herbal Remedies

Despite intense interest among women seeking care for climacteric and sexual symptoms, few randomized controlled studies have explored the efficacy of natural products for the treatment of sexual complaints in postmenopausal woman. A review of 200 articles on this topic revealed the greatest support for phytoestrogens, which occur in highest concentration in soy products (Seidl & Stewart, 1998). St. John's Wort extract has also been found to significantly improve sexual well-being among menopausal women compared to a placebo group (Grube, Walper, & Wheatley, 1999). Unfortunately, few studies have tested an herbal product in post-menopausal women *with sexual dysfunction.* One study involved the administration of "Herbal vX," a combination of Muira Puama and Ginkgo Biloba, which significantly improved sexual desire, intercourse, fantasies, orgasm, and sexual satisfaction (Waynberg & Brewer, 2000). However, the lack of a double-blind control group prevents an unbiased conclusion. More recently, "ArginMax," a proprietary blend of herbal extracts including L-arginine, was tested in a double-blind placebo-controlled trial and found to enhance sexual desire in postmenopausal women and to reduce vaginal dryness in perimenopausal women (Ito, Polan, Whipple, & Trant, 2006).

Future Directions

Recently, large-scale population based studies of women's sexuality during menopause, some with a longitudinal component, have allowed researchers to explore the relative effects of biological and psychosocial aspects of menopause and aging. Moreover, such research may eventually identify protective factors that buffer against a deterioration of sexual response. Regarding hormones—in particular testosterone—and menopausal sexuality, more research using improved methodologies is needed before conclusions can be drawn. First, the development of more accurate methods of assessing androgen levels in postmenopausal women is needed. Current assays are not reliable for measuring androgens in the postmenopausal range and therefore they provide an index of testosterone that may not be accurate. As mass spectrometry methods become available, more accurate measurement of androgen activity may be possible; however, intracellular production of testosterone still cannot be assessed even with this technique.

A second area needing further exploration is the apparent lack of correlation between testosterone and postmenopausal women's sexual responses. This may be due to the fact that until recently, androgen assays have measured testosterone in blood serum. However, a good proportion of testosterone may be derived from *inside the cell* from precursor steroids and never diffuse into the blood stream, thus preventing its assessment with traditional assay procedures. With the postmenopausal ovarian decline in androgen and estrogen production, or with an abrupt absence of ovarian hormones from surgical menopause, all estrogen and most androgen is derived through intracellular production of DHEA, DHEA-S, or A_4 in tissues such as the bone and brain. After exerting androgenic effects, testosterone synthesized intracellularly is broken down into metabolites that then spill into the blood stream. By measuring only testosterone in blood serum, the intracellular production of testosterone is not captured, and only 10% of its metabolite spills into the serum to be measured (Labrie et al., 2003). Endocrinologists argue that one particular androgen metabolite, ADT-G, may be the best candidate to measure, given that it differs significantly between older and younger women (Labrie, 2006). Using mass spectrometry, androgen metabolites such as ADT-G can be measured in blood serum and may provide a more accurate measure of total androgen activity. We await research on the relationship between these androgen metabolites and various indices of sexual response in postmenopausal women in the growing field known as intracrinology—the study of the local formation of sex steroids (Labrie et al., 2005). The measurement of androgen metabolites might replace the current clinical practice of measuring serum androgen in the future and thus provide a more reliable measure in the clinical setting.

Finally, the search for an effective and safe testosterone preparation needs to continue. The recent FDA decision to not approve the Intrinsa™ patch was tied to recent legal issues arising from the negative side effects of other medications, the fact that the pharmaceutical sponsor, Procter & Gamble, rather than an independent contractor, carried out the majority of randomized trials, and the absence of long-term safety data of testosterone or testosterone plus estrogen, especially in light of the WHI findings. Data on long-term use (beyond 24 weeks), information on potential metabolic and masculinizing side effects, and the effects of this preparation in specific subgroups of women, such as those with a history of breast cancer, are greatly needed.

Summary and Conclusions

Menopausal sexuality is an important research area that will continue to guide assessment and treatment. The large number of recent population-based studies will help the understanding of sexual symptoms women report as they transition through and complete menopause, and will help clinicians identify factors that predict those who might experience such sexual symptoms. A multidisciplinary approach is required when dealing with menopausal sexuality, given that aging and menopause are confounded and that biological/hormonal changes coincide with psychological/social changes. In addition, attitudes toward menopause/aging and partner-related factors emerge as the strongest predictors of sexual problems related to menopause and aging, thereby highlighting the importance of these variables. More research exploring psychoeducational interventions for menopausal women experiencing sexual complaints is needed, particularly to counter the current climate of aggressive randomized-controlled trials of hormone treatment and the more general "medicalization" of women's sexuality. Practitoners can look forward to the next decade of research on menopausal sexuality as new psychological and medical treatment strategies are developed, to be used both alone and in combination, that will guide the assessment and treatment of menopausal and postmenopausal women.

References

Adekunle, A. O., Fawole, A. O., & Okunlola, M. A. (2000). Perceptions and attitudes of Nigerian women about the menopause. *Journal of Obstetrics and Gynaecology, 20,* 525–529.

Avis, N. E., Zhao, X., Johannes, C. B., Ory, M., Brockwell, S., & Greendale, G. A. (2005). Correlates of sexual function among multi-ethnic middle-aged women: Results from the Study of Women's Health Across the Nation (SWAN). *Menopause, 12,* 385–398.

Aziz, A., Brannstrom, M., Bergquist, C., & Silfverstolpe, G. (2005). Perimenapausal androgen decline after oophorectomy does not influence sexuality or psychological well-being. *Fertility and Sterility, 83,* 854–859.

Bachmann, G., Bancroft, J., Braunstein, G., Burger, H., Davis, S., Dennerstein, L., et al. (2002). Female androgen insufficiency: The Princeton consensus statement on definition, classification, and assessment. *Fertility and Sterility, 77,* 660–665.

Bachmann, G. A. (2002). The hypoandrogenic woman: Pathophysiologic overview. *Fertility and Sterility, 77*(Suppl. 4), S72–S76.

Bachmann, G. A., & Leiblum, S. R. (2004). The impact of hormones on menopausal sexuality: A literature review. *Menopause, 11,* 120–130.

Bancroft, J. (2002). Biological factors in human sexuality. *Journal of Sex Research, 39,* 15–21.

Barentsen, R., van de Weijer, P. H., & Schram, J. H. (1997). Continuous low dose estradiol released from a vaginal ring versus estriol vaginal cream for urogenital atrophy. *European Journal of Obstetrics and Gynecology, 71,* 73–80.

Basson, R. (2002). Women's sexual desire: Disordered or misunderstood? *Journal of Sex and Marital Therapy, 28,* 17–28.

Basson, R. (2005). Women's sexual dysfunction: Revised and expanded definitions. *Canadian Medical Association Journal, 172,* 1327–1333.

Basson, R., & Brotto, L. A. (2003). Sexual psychophysiology and effects of sildenafil citrate in oestrogenised women with acquired genital arousal disorder and impaired orgasm: A randomised controlled trial. *British Journal of Obstetrics and Gynaecology, 110,* 1014–1024.

Basson, R., Leiblum, S., Brotto, L., Derogatis, L., Fourcroy, J., Fugl-Meyer, K., et al. (2003). Definitions of women's sexual dysfunction reconsidered: Advocating expansion and revision *Journal of Psychosomatic Obstetrics and Gynaecology, 24,* 221–229.

Basson, R., McInnes, R., Smith, M. D., Hodgson, G., & Koppiker, N. (2002). Efficacy and safety of sildenafil citrate in women with sexual dysfunction associated with female sexual arousal disorder. *Journal of Women's Health and Gender-Based Medicine, 11,* 367–377.

Baulieu, E. E., Thomas, G., Legrain, S., Lahlou, N., Roger, M., Debuire, B., et al. (2000). Dehydroepiandrosterone (DHEA), DHEA sulfate, and aging: Contribution of the DHEAge Study to a sociobiomedical issue. *Proceedings of the National Academy of Sciences, 97,* 4279–4284.

Berman, J. R., Berman, L. A., Toler, S. M., Gill, J., Haughie, S., & Sildenafil Study Group. (2003). Safety and efficacy of sildenafil citrate for the treatment of female sexual arousal disorder: A double-blind, placebo controlled study. *Journal of Urology, 170,* 2333–2338.

Berman, J. R., & Goldstein, I. (2001). Female sexual dysfunction. *Urologic Clinics of North America, 28,* 405–416.

Beyene, Y. (1986). Cultural significance and physiological manifestations of menopause: A biocultural analysis. *Culture and Medical Psychiatry, 10,* 47–71.

Braunstein, G. D., Sundwall, D. A., Katz, M., Shifren, J. L., Buster, J. E., Simon, J. A., et al. (2005). Safety and efficacy of a testosterone patch for the treatment of hypoactive sexual desire disorder in surgically menopausal women: A randomized, placebo-controlled trial. *Archives of Internal Medicine, 165,* 1582–1589.

Brotto, L. A., & Gorzalka, B. B. (2002). Genital and subjective sexual arousal in postmenopausal women: Influence of laboratory-induced hyperventilation. *Journal of Sex and Marital Therapy, 28,* 39–53.

Brunner, R. L., Gass, M., Aragaki, A., Hays, J., Granek, I., Woods, N., et al. (2005). Effects of conjugated equine estrogen on health-related quality of life in postmenopausal women with hysterectomy: Results from the Women's Health Initiative Randomized Clinical Trial; Women's Health Initiative Investigators. *Archives of Internal Medicine, 165,* 1976–1986.

Buster, J. E., Kingsberg, S. A., Aguirre, O., Brown, C., Breaux, J. G., Buch, A., et al. (2005). Testosterone patch for low sexual desire in surgically menopausal women: A randomized trial. *Obstetrics and Gynaecology, 105*(5), 944–952.

Camacho, M. E., & Reyes-Ortiz, C. A. (2005). Sexual dysfunction in the elderly: Age or disease? *International Journal of Impotence Research, 17*(Suppl. 1), S52–S56.

Cameron, D. R., & Braunstein, G. D. (2005). The use of Dehydroepiandrosterone therapy in clinical practice. *Treatments in Endocrinology, 4,* 95–114.

Caruso, S., Agnello, C., Intelisano, G., Farina, M., Di Mari, L., & Cianci, A. (2004). Sexual behavior of women taking low-dose oral contraceptive containing 15 microg ethinylestradiol/60 microg gestodene. *Contraception, 69,* 237–240.

Crews, D. (2005). Evolution of neuroendocrine mechanisms that regulate sexual behavior. *Trends in Endocrinology and Metabolism, 16,* 354–361.

Davis, S. R., Davison, S. L., Donath, S., & Bell, R. J. (2005). Circulating androgen levels in self-reported sexual function in women. *Journal of the American Medical Association, 294,* 91–96.

Davis, S. R., Guay, A. T., Shifren, J. L., & Mazer, N. A. (2004). Endocrine aspects of female sexual dysfunction. *Journal of Sexual Medicine, 1,* 82–86.

Davis, S. R., van der Mooren, M. J., van Lunsen, R. H., Lopes, P., Ribot, J., Rees, M., et al. (2006). Efficacy and safety of a testosterone patch for the treatment of hypoactive sexual desire disorder in surgically menopausal women: A randomized, placebo-controlled trial. *Menopause, 13,* 387–396.

DeLamater, J. D., & Sill, M. (2005). Sexual desire in later life. *Journal of Sex Research, 42,* 138–149.

Dennerstein, L. (1996). Well-being, symptoms and menopausal transition. *Maturitas, 23,* 147–157.

Dennerstein, L., Alexander, J. L., & Kotz, K. (2003). The menopause and sexual functioning: A review of the population-based studies. *Annual Review of Sex Research, 14,* 64–82.

Dennerstein, L., Dudley, E. C., Hopper, J. L., & Burger, H. (1997). Sexuality, hormones and the menopausal transition. *Maturitas, 26,* 83–93.

Dennerstein, L., & Hayes, R. D. (2005). Confronting the challenges: Epidemiological study of female sexual dysfunction and the menopause. *Journal of Sexual Medicine, 2*(Suppl. 3), 118–132.

Dennerstein, L., Koochaki, P., Barton, I., & Graziottin, A. (2006). Hypoactive sexual desire disorder in menopausal women: A survey of Western European women. *Journal of Sexual Medicine, 3,* 212–222.

Dennerstein, L., Lehert, P., & Burger, H. (2005). The relative effects of hormones and relationship factors on sexual function of women through the natural menopausal transition. *Fertility and Sterility, 84,* 174–180.

Dennerstein, L., Randolph, J., Taffe, J., Dudley, E., & Burger, H. (2002). Hormones, mood, sexuality, and the menopausal transition. *Fertility and Sterility, 77*(Suppl. 4), S42–S48.

Ford, K., Sowers, M., Crutchfield, M., Wilson, A., & Jannausch, M. (2005). A longitudinal study of the predictors of prevalence and severity of symptoms commonly associated with menopause. *Menopause, 12,* 308–317.

Freedman, M. A. (2000). Sexuality and the menopausal woman. *Contemporary Obstetrics and Gynecology, 45*(3), S4–S18.

Freedman, R. R. (2005). Hot flashes: Behavioral treatments, mechanisms, and relation to sleep. *American Journal of Medicine, 118,* 124–130.

Freeman, E. W., Sammel, M. D., Lin, H., & Nelson, D. B. (2006). Associations of hormones and menopausal status with depressed mood in women with no history of depression. *Archives of General Psychiatry, 63,* 375–382.

Gerber, J. R., Johnson, J. V., Bunn, J. Y., & O'Brien, S. L. (2005). A longitudinal study of the effects of free testosterone and other psychosocial variables on sexual function during the natural traverse of menopause. *Fertility and Sterility, 83,* 643–648.

Giraldi, A., Marson, L., Nappi, R., Pfaus, J., Traish, A. M., Vardi, Y., et al. (2004). Physiology of female sexual function: Animal models. *Journal of Sexual Medicine, 1,* 237–253.

Graziottin, A., & Leiblum, S. R. (2005). Biological and psychosocial pathophysiology of female sexual dysfunction during the menopausal transition. *Journal of Sexual Medicine, 2*(Suppl. 3), 133–145.

Grube, B., Walper, A., & Wheatley, D. (1999). St. John's Wort extract: Efficacy for menopausal symptoms of psychological origin. *Advances and Therapeutics, 16,* 177–186.

Guida, M., Di Spiezio Sardo, A., Bramante, S., Sparice, S., Acunzo, G., Tommaselli, G., et al. (2005). Effects of two types of hormonal contraception: Oral versus intravaginal: On the sexual life of women and their partners. *Human Reproduction, 20,* 1100–1106.

Guthrie, J. R., Dennerstein, L., Taffe, J. R., Lehert, P., & Burger, H. G. (2004). The menopausal transition: A 9-year prospective population-based study; The Melbourne Women's Midlife Health Project. *Climacteric, 7,* 375–389.

Hackbert, L., & Heiman, J. R. (2002). Acute dehydroepiandrosterone (DHEA) effects on sexual arousal in postmenopausal women. *Journal of Women's Health and Gender-Based Medicine, 11,* 155–162.

Hays, J., Ockene, J. K., Brunner, R. L., Kotchen, J. M., Manson, J. E., Patterson, R. E., et al. (2003). Effects of estrogen plus progestin on health-related quality of life; Women's Health Initiative Investigators. *New England Journal of Medicine, 348,* 1839–1854.

Hutchinson, K. A. (1995). Androgens and sexuality. *American Journal of Medicine, 98*(Suppl. 1), S111–S115.

Ito, T. Y., Polan, M. L., Whipple, B., & Trant, A. S. (2006). The enhancement of female sexual function with ArginMax, a nutritional supplement, among women differing in menopausal status. *Journal of Sex and Marital Therapy, 32,* 369–378.

Kenemans, P., Speroff, L., & International Tibolone Consensus Group. (2005). Tibolone: Clinical recommendations and practical guidelines: A report of the International Tibolone Consensus Group. *Maturitas, 51*(1), 21–28.

Kinsey, A. C., Pomeroy, W. B., & Martin, C. E. (1948). *Sexual behavior in the human male.* Philadelphia: Saunders.

Kinsey, A. C., Pomeroy, W. B., Martin, C. E., & Gebhard, P. H. (1953). *Sexual behavior in the human female.* Philadelphia: Saunders.

Laan, E., van Lunsen, R. H., & Everaerd, W. (2001). The effects of tibolone on vaginal blood flow, sexual desire, and arousability in postmenopausal women. *Climacteric, 4,* 28–41.

Laan, E., & van Lunsen, R. H. W. (1997). Hormones and sexuality in postmenopausal women: A psychophysiological study. *Journal of Psychosomatic Obstetrics and Gynaecology, 18,* 126–133.

Labrie, F. (2006). Is DHEA a hormone? *Journal of Endocrinology, 184,* 427–433.

Labrie, F., Luu-The, V., Belanger, A., Lin, S. X., Simard, J., Pelletier, G., et al. (2005). Is dehydroepiandrosterone a hormone? *Endocrinology, 187,* 169–196.

Labrie, F., Luu-The, V., Labrie, C., Belanger, A., Simard, J., Lin, S. X., et al. (2003). Endocrine

and intracrine sources of androgens in women: Inhibition of breast cancer and other roles of androgens and their precursor dehydroepiandrosterone. *Endocrine Reviews, 24,* 152–182.

Laumann, E. O., Nicolosi, A., Glasser, D. B., Paik, A., Gingell, C., Moreira, E., et al. (2005). Sexual problems among women and men aged 40–80: Prevalence and correlates identified in the Global Study of Sexual Attitudes and Behaviors. *International Journal of Impotence Research, 17,* 39–57.

Laumann, E. O., Paik, A., Glasser, D. B., Kang, J., Wang, T., Levinson, B., et al. (2006). A cross-national study of subjective well-being among older women and men: Findings from the Global Study of Sexual Attitudes and Behaviors. *Archives of Sexual Behavior, 35,* 145–161.

Lock, M. (1994). Menopause in cultural context. *Experimental Gerontology, 29,* 307–317.

Lock, M. (1998). Menopause: Lessons from Anthropology. *Psychosomatic Medicine, 60,* 410–419.

Marks, L. E. (1990). Sensory perception and ovarian secretions. In F. Naftolein, A. H. DeCherney, J. N. Gutmann, & P. M. Sarrel (Eds.), *Ovarian secretions and cardiovascular and neurological function* (pp. 223–238). New York: Raven Press.

Masters, W. H., & Johnson, V. E. (1966). *Human sexual response.* Boston: Little, Brown.

McCoy, N. L. (2001). Female sexuality during aging. In P. R. Hof & C. V. Mobbs (Eds.), *Functional neurobiology of aging* (pp. 769–779). New York: Academic Press.

McKinlay, S. M., & Jefferys, M. (1974). The menopausal syndrome. *British Journal of Preventive and Social Medicine, 28,* 108–115.

Mishra, G., & Kuh, D. (2006). Sexual functioning through menopause: The perceptions of women in a British cohort. *Menopause, 13,* 880–890.

Morabia, A., & Costanza, M. (2006). Recent reversal of trends in hormone therapy use in a European population. *Menopause, 13,* 111–115.

Morales, A. J., Nolan, J. J., Nelson, J. C., & Yen, S. S. (1994). Effects of replacement dose of dehydroepiandrosterone in men and women of advancing age. *Journal of Clinical Endocrinology and Metabolism, 78,* 1360–1367.

Myers, L. S., Dixen, J., Morrissette, D., Carmichael, M., & Davidson, J. M. (1990). Effects of estrogen, androgen, and progestin on sexual psychophysiology and behavior in postmenopausal women. *Journal of Clinical Endocrinology and Metabolism, 70,* 1124–1131.

Nappi, R., Salonia, A., Traish, A. M., van Lunsen, R. H., Vardi, Y., Kodiglu, A., et al. (2005). Clinical biologic pathophysiologies of women's sexual dysfunction. *Journal of Sexual Medicine, 2,* 4–25.

Nathorst-Boos, J., & Hammar, M. (1997). Effect on sexual life—A comparison between tibolone and a continuous estradiol-norethisterone acetate regimen. *Maturitas, 26*, 15–20.

Nicolosi, A., Laumann, E. O., Glasser, D. B., Brock, G., King, R., & Gingell, C. (2006). Sexual activity, sexual disorders and associated help-seeking behavior among mature adults in five Anglophone countries from the Global Survey of Sexual Attitudes and Behaviors (GSSAB). *Journal of Sex and Marital Therapy, 32*, 331–342.

Nusbaum, M. R., Singh, A. R., & Pyles, A. A. (2004). Sexual healthcare needs of women aged 65 and older. *Journal of the American Geriatric Society, 52*, 117–122.

Panzer, C., Wise, S., Fantini, G., Kang, D., Munarriz, R., Guay, A., et al. (2006). Impact of oral contraceptives on sex hormone-binding globulin and androgen levels: A retrospective study in women with sexual dysfunction. *Journal of Sexual Medicine, 3*, 104–113.

Prior, J. C. (1998). Perimenopause: The complex endocrinology of the menopausal transition. *Endocrinology Reviews, 19*, 397–428.

Rosen, R., & Beck, J. G. (1988). *Patterns of sexual arousal: Psychophysiological processes and clinical applications.* New York: Guilford Press.

Rossouw, J. E., Anderson, G. L., Prentice, R. L., LaCroix, A. Z., Kooperberg, C., Stefanick, M. L., et al. (2002). Risks and benefits of estrogen plus progestin in healthy postmenopausal women: Principal results from the Women's Health Initiative randomized controlled trial; Writing Group for the Women's Health Initiative Investigators. *Journal of the American Medical Association, 17*, 321–333.

Santoro, A., Torrens, J., Crawford, S., Allsworth, J. E., Finkelstein, J. S., Gold, E. B., et al. (2005). Correlates of circulating androgens in mid-life women: The study of women's health across the nation. *Journal of Endocrinology and Metabolism, 90*, 4970–4972.

Santoro, N. (2005). The menopausal transition. *American Journal of Medicine, 118*(Suppl. 2), 8–13.

Sarrel, P. M. (1990). Sexuality and menopause. *Obstetrics and Gynaecology, 75*, S26–S30.

Sarrel, P. M. (2000). Effects of hormone replacement therapy on sexual psychophysiology and behaviour in postmenopause. *Journal of Women's Health and Gender Based Medicine, 9*(Suppl. 1), 25–32.

Sarrel, P. M. (2006). Testosterone therapy for postmenopausal decline in sexual desire: Implications of a new study. *Menopause, 13*, 328–330.

Seidl, M. M., & Stewart, D. E. (1998). Alternative treatments for menopausal symptoms: Systematic review of scientific and lay literature. *Canadian Family Physician, 44*, 1299–1308.

Semmens, J. P., & Wagner, G. (1982). Estrogen deprivation and vaginal function in postmenopausal women. *Journal of the American Medical Association, 248*, 445–448.

Sherwin, B. B. (1999). Progestogens used in menopause: Side effects, mood and quality of life. *Journal of Reproductive Medicine, 44*, 227–232.

Shifren, J. L., Davis, S. R., Moreau, M., Waldbaum, A., Bouchard, C., Derogatis, L., et al. (2006). Testosterone patch for the treatment of hypoactive sexual desire disorder in naturally menopausal women: Results of the INTIMATE NM1 study. *Menopause, 14*, 770–779.

Simon, J., Braunstein, G., Nachtigall, L., Utian, W., Katz, M., Miller, S., et al. (2005). Testosterone patch increases sexual activity and desire in surgically menopausal women with hypoactive sexual desire disorder. *Journal of Clinical Endocrinology and Metabolism, 90*, 5226–5233.

Simpson, E. R., Misso, M., Hewitt, K. N., Hill, R. A., Boon, W. C., Jones, M. E., et al. (2005). Estrogen: The good, the bad, and the unexpected. *Endocrinology Review, 26*, 322–330.

Soares, C. N., Joffe, H., & Steiner, M. (2004). Menopause and mood. *Clinical Obstetrics and Gynecology, 47*, 576–591.

Soules, M. R., Sherman, S., Parrott, E., Rebar, R., Santoro, N., Utian, W., et al. (2001). Executive summary: Stages of reproductive aging workshop (STRAW). *Fertility and Sterility, 76*, 874–878.

Stefanick, M. L., Anderson, G. L., Margolis, K. L., Hendrix, S. L., Rodabough, R. J., Paskett, E. D., et al. (2006). Effects of conjugated equine estrogens on breast cancer and mammography screening in postmenopausal women with hysterectomy. *Journal of the American Medical Association, 295*, 1647–1657.

Steiner, M., Dunn, E., & Born, L. (2003). Hormones and mood: From menarche to menopause and beyond. *Journal of Affective Disorders, 74*, 67–83.

Stenberg, A., Heimer, G., & Ulmsten, U. (1995). The prevalence of urogenital symptoms in postmenopausal women. *Maturitas, 22*, S1–S47.

Tang, G. W. (1994). The climacteric of Chinese factory workers. *Maturitas, 19*(3), 177–182.

U.S. Centers for Disease Control. (2006). *United States Life Tables, 2003, 54*(14), 1–40. Retrieved July 1, 2006, from www.cdc.gov/nchs/data/nvsr/nvsr54/nvsr54_14.pdf.

U.S. Food and Drug Administration. (1994). *Dietary Supplement Health and Education Act 1994.* Public Law 103–141.

Utian, W. H., MacLean, D. B., Symonds, T., Symons, J., Somayaji, V., & Sisson, M. (2005). A methodology study to validate a structured diagnostic method used to diagnose female sexual dysfunction and its subtypes in postmenopausal women. *Journal of Sex and Marital Therapy, 31,* 271–283.

Uygur, D., Yesildaglar, N., & Erkaya, S. (2005). Effect on sexual life: A comparison between tibolone and continuous combined conjugated equine estrogens and medroxyprogesterone acetate. *Gynecology and Endocrinology, 20,* 209–212.

van Lunsen, R. H., & Laan, E. (2004). Genital vascular responsiveness and sexual feelings in midlife women: Psychophysiologic, brain, and genital imaging studies. *Menopause, 11*(6, Pt. 2), 741–748.

Waynberg, J., & Brewer, S. (2000). Effects of Herbal vX on libido and sexual activity in pre-

menopausal and postmenopausal women. *Advances and Therapeutics, 17,* 255–262.

Whitehead, M. I., Townsend, P. T., Pryse-Davies, J., Ryder, T. A., & King, R. J. (1981). Effects of estrogens and progestins on the biochemistry and morphology of the postmenopausal endometrium. *New England Journal of Medicine, 305,* 1599–1605.

Wierman, M., Basson, R., Davis, S., Khosla, S., Miller, K. K., Rosner, W., et al. (2006). Androgen therapy in women: An Endocrine Society Practice Guidelines. *Journal of Clinical Endocrinology and Metabolism, 91,* 3697–3710.

Disease and Sexuality

Luca Incrocci and Woet L. Gianotten

10
Chapter

Learning Objectives

In this chapter, we discuss:

- Relationships among various types of cancer and sexual functioning in men and women.
- A variety of other disease states that impact sexual functioning, including traumatic spinal cord and brain injury, stroke, and various other chronic diseases that impact sexual functioning in men and women.
- Issues regarding prognosis, treatment, and recovery of sexual function.

Cancer and Sexual Function

In this section, we summarize our approach by noting that the quality of life in general and sexual functioning in particular are becoming increasingly important to cancer patients.

Patients should be offered sexual counseling and informed about the availability of effective treatments for erectile dysfunction, such as oral drugs, intracavernosal injections, and vacuum devices. Because cancer affects both the quality of life and sexual function, the challenge for the oncologist is to address this issue with compassion.

Despite the decrease in overall cancer mortality rates in developed countries, cancer remains a major public health problem, with the lifetime probability of developing cancer higher in men (46%) than in women (38%). Although all patients and their physicians at cancer treatment centers are strongly focused on survival, younger patients tend to be more emotionally distressed by cancer because it is more disruptive of their lifestyle. However, younger patients are also more likely to respond to and improve with counseling under these circumstances.

Sexual dysfunction is one of the more common consequences of cancer treatment. The life-threatening nature of cancer might lead to the assumption that sexual activity is not important to patients and their partners, but this view has not been supported. Nevertheless, men in particular are often reluctant to seek professional help for mental and physical health problems, including sexual problems, due most probably to cultural norms of masculinity that conflict with help-seeking behavior (Addis & Mahalik, 2003). This attitude may, however, be changing, as specific sexual problems such as erectile dysfunction (ED) become more normalized with the introduction of new pharmacological treatments and increased media attention.

Because cancer affects both the quantity and quality of life, the challenge for the clinician is to address both components with compassion. Evaluating sexual functioning in an oncology population is different from evaluating it in a healthy population because of its specific medical, psychological, and social factors. In busy oncology clinics where outpatient visits must include educating patients about their disease, prognosis, and treatment, physicians and nurses often do not have the time to assess quality of life issues, including those surrounding sexual functioning (Schover, 1999).

In this chapter, we present an overview of changes in sexual functioning following the treatment of various forms of cancer and give suggestions for treating the resulting sexual problems.

Prostate Cancer

Among men, the most common cancer affects the prostate and occurs more often in the older population (Jemal et al., 2006). In recent years, the number of patients diagnosed with prostate cancer (PCa) has increased dramatically, the result of the widespread use of prostate specific antigen (PSA) testing and the possibility for cure with early detection. Standard treatments for PCa include radical prostatectomy, external-beam radiotherapy (EBRT), brachytherapy, hormonal therapy, or observation. The choice of treatment is determined by tumor staging, the patient's age and comorbidity, and the urologist's and patient's preferences. The patient's quality of life, including sexual functioning, also plays a significant role in the decision-making process.

Men may remain interested in sex and eroticism well into old age (Mulligan & Moss, 1991). In general, being treated for cancer—any type, not just PCa—is detrimental to the patient's sexual life. In such patients, sexual activity may drop from two times weekly to once a month (Schover, Evans, & von Eschenbach, 1987).

Evaluating Erectile Dysfunction

The fastest and most practical way to evaluate ED in an oncology clinic is by using a questionnaire. A variety of questionnaires for ED evaluation have been reported in the literature, with queries on sexual functioning often limited to a few separate items or ones incorporated into a more general questionnaire on the side effects of cancer treatment. The International Index of Erectile Function (IIEF: Rosen et al., 1997) is an instrument commonly used to assess ED; it has been translated into many languages and validated in many countries, therefore offering the possibility of making comparisons across studies. One limitation of this instrument is that it has not been developed specifically with cancer patients in mind. As with any assessment of this type, a measure of pretreatment erectile functioning is helpful in assessing the impact of both the cancer and the cancer treatment on erectile functioning.

Definition of Potency

The National Institutes of Health (NIH) Consensus on ED defined impotence as the consistent inability to attain and maintain a penile erection sufficient to permit satisfactory sexual intercourse (NIH Consensus Development Panel on Impotence, 1993). Due to the focus on intercourse, this definition is relevant only when a willing partner is involved. Therefore, the use of the more general terminology *sexual activity* over *sexual intercourse* may be more appropriate, as this term encompasses both intercourse and masturbation. The rigidity of erections as well as the frequency of spontaneous daytime or morning/night erections should also be taken into consideration when assessing potency. And because psychological and relationship factors typically play a role in post-treatment ED, they too may need to be considered.

Erectile Dysfunction after Treatment of Prostate Cancer

In general, many comorbidities have an impact on erectile functioning (see Figure 10.1). With respect to cancer, the clinical stage,

Figure 10.1

**Schematic of
the Male
Genitalia and
Innervation**

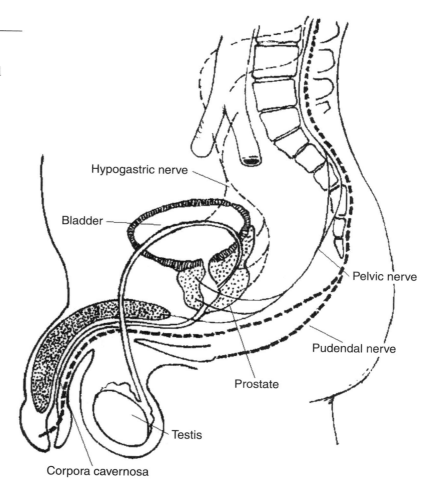

Hypogastric nerve

Bladder

Pelvic nerve

Pudendal nerve

Prostate

Testis

Corpora cavernosa

grade, and location of the cancerous tumor are important factors in predicting the likelihood of developing postoperative ED (Mc-Cullough, 2001). After bilateral nerve-sparing prostatectomy, erectile response may be impaired due to trauma to the neurovascular bundles, resulting in a loss of normal nerve tissue connections to the penile bodies (Kendirci, Beijma, & Hellstrom, 2006).

Venous leakage may be another pathophysiologic cause of postsurgery ED (Kendirci et al., 2006), and as early as the 1980s, it had been suggested that postradiation ED in prostate patients was attributable to vascular damage. This suggestion was recently confirmed by Zelefsky and Eid (1998) who evaluated 98 patients who became impotent after EBRT or prostatectomy. Specifically, in this study, the penis was scanned with Duplex ultrasound before and after intracavernosal injection of prostaglandins to assess penile response capacity. Among EBRT patients, 63% had arterio-genic dysfunction (peak penile blood flow rates less than 25 cm/sec), 32% had cavernosal dysfunction (abnormal cavernosal distensibility with a normal penile peak blood flow); and only 3% had neurogenic dysfunction. Such data suggest that the predominant etiology of radiation-induced impotence was arteriogenic.

Recent research also indicates a strong effect of both radiation dose and the volume of the penile bulb that has been radiated on posttreatment ED (Fisch, Pickett, Weinberg, & Roach, 2001). Figure 10.2 illustrates the relation of the penile bodies with the radiation fields. Specifically, patients receiving 70 Gray or more to 70% of the bulb of the penis were at very high risk of developing radiation-induced ED. Furthermore, the time elapsed between EBRT treatment and ED evaluation appears to be an important consideration, as studies indicate that the clinician should allow at least 18 to 24 months to lapse after treatment, the approximate time frame during which erectile problems are likely to peak and stabilize.

Figure 10.2

Example of an Anterior-Posterior Conformal Radiation Field for Prostate Cancer. Relation of the Penile Bodies with the Radiation Field

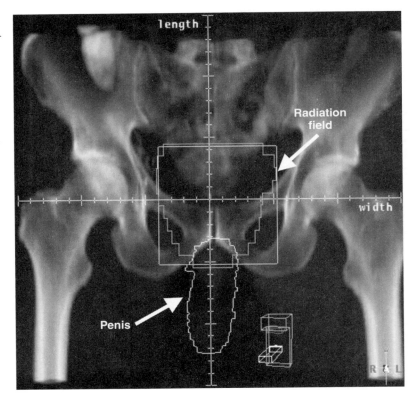

Erectile Dysfunction after Radical Prostatectomy

Based on the clinical literature, the reported incidence of ED following radical prostatectomy varies tremendously (Kendirci et al., 2006). In a large study with more than 1,200 patients assessed 18 months after surgery, ED was self-reported by 60% (Stanford et al., 2000). In a more recent evaluation, at 60 months, 28% of these men reported erections firm enough for intercourse, suggesting a 70% rate of erectile problems (Penson et al., 2005). A Scandinavian study reported an 80% rate of ED following surgery (Steineck et al., 2002). The overall incidence of sexual dysfunction following bilateral nerve-sparing prostatectomy is further affected by age. For example, 61% of men 39 to 54 years reported erections firm enough for intercourse after surgery compared to only 44% in patients 60 to 64 years (Penson et al., 2005).

Erectile Dysfunction after Radiotherapy

Until the 1970s, surgery was the primary treatment for PCa, as this type of cancer was considered resistant to radiotherapy. As radiotherapy became more accepted, the incidence of resulting ED became clearer, up to 41% of the patients treated with EBRT (Incrocci, Slob, & Levendag, 2002). In the 1980s, radiotherapy was delivered using modern megavolt energies; post-EBRT ED using this method typically ranged from 11% to 73%. The 1990s were characterized by the more refined technique of three-dimensional conformal radiotherapy (3DCRT). The use of more fields and shaped blocks, a computer planning system, and three-dimensional treatment plans resulted in smaller treatment volumes and therefore reduced toxicity. However, only a few prospective studies from the 1990s have dealt specifically with sexual functioning after radiation therapy. In these studies, ED varied from 7% to 72% (Incrocci, Slob, et al., 2002). Brachytherapy, or interstitial radiotherapy, was introduced not only to limit the detrimental effects of radiation on bowel and urinary function, but also to help preserve sexual function. Rates of ED after brachytherapy have ranged from 0 to 61%, with higher rates (89%) when brachytherapy is combined with EBRT (Incrocci, Slob, et al., 2002).

Therapy for Erectile Dysfunction after PCa Treatment

Prior to the introduction of sildenafil (Viagra™), only three treatment options for ED were available to prostate cancer patients: intracavernosal injections (ICI) of a vasoactive drug, vacuum devices, and penile implants, all three with or without concomitant sexual counseling. With the availability of sildenafil and later tadalafil (Cialis™) and vardenafil (Levitra™), the original options for therapy have been losing popularity. The three oral medications are now commonly used for ED resulting from the treatment of prostate cancer. These medications are selective inhibitors of cyclic guanosine monophosphate (cGMP) specific phosphodi-esterase type 5 (PDE-5), and hence they inhibit the degradation of cGMP in the cavernosal smooth-muscle cells, thereby restoring erectile response to sexual stimulation in patients with ED of different etiologies.

Sildenafil has been reported effective in 71% of the patients, in 50% after a unilateral procedure, and in 15% if the neurovascular bundles had not been spared (Zippe et al., 2000). Seventy-one percent of patients complaining of ED following bilateral nerve-sparing surgery responded to vardenafil 20mg (Brock et al., 2003); 52% could achieve successful intercourse with tadalafil 20mg (Montorsi et al., 2004). Not surprisingly, age is likely to play a role in the effect of PDE5 inhibitors in restoring erectile capacity. Zagaja, Mhoon, Aikens, and Brendler (2000) showed 80% response rate to sildenafil in men younger than 55 years and 40% in men older than 55 years after bilateral nerve-sparing prostatectomy.

Other treatments for ED have also been used after radical prostatectomy. Although less popular, ICI and vacuum devices have reasonable efficacy; even after nonnerve sparing procedures, 60% seem to respond to these therapies (Kendirci et al., 2006). Placement of a penile prosthesis, considered only when all other therapies have failed, provides a definitive solution for ED but carries the risks related to any surgical procedure, such as anesthesia, bleeding, and infection. This procedure is therefore indicated only for a small number of selected patients.

The efficacy of sildenafil after EBRT in open-label studies has reportedly been as high as 90%. However, in the only double-blind, randomized trial published so far, compared with placebo, 100 mg sildenafil significantly improved erections in 60 patients, with 55% having successful intercourse (Incrocci, Koper, Hop, & Slob, 2001). Similar results have been reported with 20mg tadalafil, with 48% of patients reporting successful intercourse (Incrocci, Slagter, Slob, & Hop, 2006). Side effects of these drugs have been mild or moderate and decrease over time.

A summary of key issues related to cancer and ED are provided in Sidebar 10.1.

SIDEBAR 10.1

Erectile Dysfunction and Prostate Cancer

The definition of (im)potence advocated by the NIH should be used, and ED evaluation should be standardized by using prospectively validated questionnaires on quality of life and sexual functioning.

As of now, conclusive data on radiotherapy techniques, field sizes, energy used, and their specific influence on ED are not yet available.

The etiology of postsurgery ED is more likely neurogenic, while postradiotherapy ED is more likely vascular.

Although the radiation dose received by the penile bodies and bulb appears important in the etiology of ED, nerve injury cannot be excluded.

A multifactorial etiology has to be considered, taking into account comorbidity, use of medications, and pretreatment level of erectile function.

Ejaculatory and Other Sexual Dysfunctions

Ejaculatory dysfunction, particularly a decrease in volume or an absence of semen, has been associated with prostate cancer treatment (Arai et al., 2000). After PCa treatment, a lack of ejaculation or a diminished sperm volume has been reported in up to 100% of the patients (Arai et al., 2000). Dissatisfaction with sex life, decreased libido, and decreased sexual desire are also commonly reported among these patients (Incrocci, Slob, et al., 2002).

Hematological Cancer

Hematological malignancies such as leukemia and lymphomas affect mostly young adults; indeed, such individuals often feel healthy at the time the disease is discovered (Wise, 1983). Van Tulder, Aaronson, and Bruning (1994) reported on the quality of life of patients in complete remission after treatment for Hodgkin's disease. Patients had received radiotherapy; prior to that some had also received chemotherapy. The responses of 42 male patients (27 to 77 years) were compared with an age-matched control group consisting of 51 healthy male visitors to the hospital. Questions related to sexual functioning dealt with interest in sex, frequency of sexual activity, dissatisfaction with frequency of sex, and overall satisfaction with the quality of the sexual relationship. Patients showed lower levels of sexual functioning.

Oral drugs are effective in about 50% of the patients complaining of ED after treatment of PCa on all items when compared with controls (Table 10.1). Results consistent with this pattern in Hodgkin's disease patients (22% to 37% sexual dysfunction) have also been reported by Yellen, Cella, and Bonomi (1993).

In a study of patients having a variety of hematological cancers, including non-Hodgkin's and Hodgkin's lymphomas, multiple myeloma, and acute myeloid leukemia, Howell, Radford, Smets, and Shalet (2000) reported on 66 patients on items about their interest in sex, frequency of sex, enjoyment of intercourse and masturbation, and presence of morning erections. Leydig cell dysfunction, assessed by testosterone and luteinizing hormone (LH) blood levels, was also assessed. Thirty patients had normal

Table 10.1 **Sexual Function in Male Patients Treated for Hodgkin's Disease and in Controls**

	Patients (%) (N = 42)	Controls (%)* (N = 51)
Little/no interest in sex	25	10*
Sexual activity once/week	50	73*
Dissatisfaction with frequency of sex	29	16*
Dissatisfaction with quality of sex	12	5*

*$p = .01$.

testosterone; 36 had low testosterone (T). Of the 30 with normal testosterone, 87% were sexually active versus 69% of those with low T, although this difference was not statistically significant. Patients with normal T reported sexual activity 3.2 times/week compared with 1.8 times/week for those with low T. However, sexual interest and erectile function were similar in both groups. Because the low T did not interfere with erectile function, the authors recommended that androgen replacement therapy was critical to improved quality of sex life in the majority of patients following treatment for hematological malignancies.

ED is a well-recognized complication of high-dose chemotherapy followed by hemopoietic stem cell transplantation (HSCT), procedures sometimes used in the treatment of hematological cancer. Although such ED is likely to be multifactorial in origin, the most common cause of ED in patients having this type of cancer/treatment is cavernosal arterial insufficiency and primary hypogonadism. A recent study, for example, has shown cavernosal arterial insufficiency as a significant factor for ED after treatment with melphalan, total body irradiation, and autologous HSCT (Chatterjee, Kottaridis, Lees, Ralph, & Goldstone, 2000). Doppler studies of penile arteries show subnormal blood flow in all patients, and the low testosterone levels were indicative of Leydig cell insufficiency (Chatterjee et al., 2000). Leydig cell insufficiency with diminished androgen levels has been recognized as a cause of diminished libido and the absence of nocturnal erections (Chatterjee et al., 2000; Howell et al., 2000).

Treatment of ED after Treatment of Hematological Cancer

The combination of testosterone and sildenafil has been an effective treatment for ED in patients after bone marrow transplantation. Sildenafil alone is less effective because these patients have diminished libido. Furthermore, testosterone can improve energy and drive and can alleviate generalized symptoms of depression and fatigue often present in these patients (Chatterjee, Kottaridis, McGarrigle, & Linch, 2002).

Penile Cancer

Carcinoma of the penis is a rare malignancy, comprising less than 1% of all male cancers in Western countries. The conventional treatment for this cancer is partial or total penile amputation, or radiation. Radiation therapy provides good results in superficially infiltrating tumors, although it may have both cosmetic and functional results, often resulting in psychosexual dysfunction (Windhal, Skeppner, Andersson, & Fugl-Meyer, 2004). Opjordsmoen, Wahere, Aass, and Fossa (1994) reported on the sexual function of 30 patients (28 to 75, mean 57 years) after different treatment modalities for low stage penile carcinoma. Using a global score for overall sexual functioning based on sexual interest, ability, enjoyment and satisfaction, identity, and frequency of intercourse, they reported that penectomy patients had lower scores than either radiation or local surgery patients. Patients who had undergone only partial penectomy were also dissatisfied and, interestingly, did not function sexually substantially better than patients after total penectomy (Opjordsmoen et al., 1994). Based on such results, radiotherapy, laser beam therapy, and local incision might provide the better options for penile cancer when preserving sexual function is important. Regarding the use of laser beam therapy, for example, Windhal and associates (2004), in a retrospective analysis, reported on 67 patients treated from 1986 to 2000 with laser beam therapy. Of these, 58 were still living, and 46% of them agreed to participate in the interview. Eighty-seven percent of the participating patients reported being sexually active; 72% had no ED, though 22% had a decrease in sexual function (but 6% indicated improved sexual function); and 50% were satisfied with their sexual life. Thus, it appears that most patients with penile carcinoma can still enjoy a sexual life if laser treatment is used; more invasive procedures such as surgery or radiotherapy reduce this likelihood (Opjordsmoen et al., 1994).

Bladder Cancer

The optimal treatment for patients with invasive bladder cancer is radical cystectomy or radiotherapy. The choice depends on the patient's age, condition, and comorbidities. Although the general opinion is that survival following cystectomy is greater than that following radiotherapy, no randomized trials have been performed to confirm this opinion. Radical cystectomy is associated with changes in the patient's physiological and the psychological well-being; in contrast, radiotherapy preserves the bladder, but bladder function is likely to be altered following the treatment. Either treatment modality is associated with a high percentage of sexual dysfunction (Little & Howard, 1998).

In a retrospective study of 18 patients (56 to 75, median 70 years old) treated with EBRT, 13 (72%) recalled being sexually active and having good erections before treatment (Little & Howard, 1998). Of these, only 6 patients (56%) were active after treatment; 3 had ED and 4 reported a decrease in the quality of their erections. Eight of 17 patients reported that their sexual life had worsened after EBRT. In a more recent and controlled study, higher percentages of ED were reported in 62 irradiated patients (median age 77 years) than in a control group of healthy men (Fokdal, Hoyer, Meldgaard, & von der Maase, 2004). Sixty-five percent of both the patients and the controls were not sexually active at the time of the study; 87% of the patients had ED, but only 52% of the men in the control group (Fokdal et al., 2004).

Cystectomy and bladder substitution also have significant effects of sexual function. These procedures resulted in ED in 84% of the patients; 63% reported abnormal orgasm and 48% diminished sexual drive (Månsson et al., 2000). In another study, Bjerre, Johansen, and Steven (1998) reported on 76 patients, 27 of whom underwent an ileal conduit diversion and 49 a bladder substitution. Preoperatively 82% had normal erections, whereas postoperatively, only 9% did. Postoperatively, 38% achieved normal orgasm and 26% were sexually active with intercourse. Of the nonsexually active men, 77% had ED, 29% decreased libido, 13% had partner refusal, and 20% felt less sexually attractive. There was no statistically significant difference between those treated through ileal conduit diversion versus those treated with bladder substitution. In either case, the effects of the treatment for bladder cancer on sexual functioning were found to be quite severe.

Rectal Cancer

Colorectal surgeons are becoming more aware of the details of the surgical anatomy of the rectum and pelvic structures, and as such, have made significant progress in their attempts to spare sexual and other functions. In the past, ED after proctectomy had been attributed to the presence of a stoma or the fear of cancer. Rates of ED after surgery for rectal cancer vary from 0 to 73% and ejaculation disorders have been reported in up to 59% (Table 10.2);

Table 10.2 **Sexual Dysfunction after Surgery for Rectal Cancer**

Author	N	Impotence (%)	Ejaculation Disorders (%)
Danzi et al. (1983)	25	27	19
Kinn & Ohman (1986)	10	33	50
Santangelo et al. (1987)	25	32	24
Cunsolo et al. (1990)	22	18	59
Maas et al. (1998)	30	11	38
Nesbakken et al. (2000)	24	25	8
Pocard et al. (2002)	13	0	8
Bonnel et al. (2002)			
–With preoperative radiation	15	73	18
–Without preoperative radiation	24	27	8

however, the studies generating these data included only small numbers of patients.

The main cause of sexual dysfunction after proctectomy appears to be injury to the autonomic nerves in the pelvis and along the distal aorta. Dysfunction is more common after abdominoperineal resection than after low anterior resection. In 1992, total mesorectal excision (TME) was introduced for the treatment of rectal cancer, a procedure that preserves autonomic nerves.

Radiation therapy is an important part of the multimodality treatment of locally advanced rectal carcinomas. Although multimodality treatment produces better results, the side effects are also increased. Nesbakken and colleagues (Nesbakken, Nygaard, Bull-Njaa, Carlsen, & Eri, 2000) prospectively assessed sexual functioning in patients undergoing a total or partial TME procedure without previous radiotherapy. A visual analogue scale assessing libido, sexual activity, potency, and ejaculation was administered before and 6 months after surgery. Six of 24 men reported a decrease in erectile function, one was fully impotent, and 2 reported retrograde ejaculation. Pocard and associates (2002) reported on 20 patients, of these 13 were males (42 to 76, mean 57.5 years). Of the 13 men, 9 (69%) were sexually active both pre- and postoperatively. One reported retrograde ejaculation. After 3 months, 4 patients reported less rigid erections but these normalized at 1 year after surgery. The authors concluded that TME and autonomic nerve preservation spares sexual functioning in patients with rectal cancer, at least in the patients without preoperative radiotherapy (Pocard et al., 2002).

The specific effect of radiotherapy on ED in rectal cancer patients has been addressed by Bonnel et al. (2002) who reported on

42 patients, 15 of whom had received preoperative radiotherapy. No difference in erectile capacity was seen across groups, but ejaculation difficulties were higher in the radiotherapy group (2 out of 11 patients as compared to 2 of 24 patients). These authors concluded that sexual dysfunction may be due to a direct effect of radiotherapy or to the more difficult surgical procedure to visualize the autonomic nerves in the irradiated area (Bonnel et al., 2002). Specifically, the inferior hypogastric plexus is responsible for erection and the superior hypogastric plexus for ejaculation, mediated by the sympathetic system, and these systems are likely to be compromised during surgery. However, a multicenter study has shown that even with a careful nerve-preservation technique, men reported impotence or were permanently unable to ejaculate (38%; Maas et al., 1998).

Standardization of intraoperative techniques together with knowledge of pelvic neuroanatomy is fundamental for preserving quality of life and sexual function as much as possible in patients with rectal cancer. As a result, patients should be informed preoperatively about the possibility of becoming impotent after surgery for rectal cancer.

Testicular Cancer

Germ cell tumors of the testis are relatively rare and account for about 1% of all male cancers, although the reported incidence appears to be increasing over the last 2 decades (Che et al., 2002; Huyghe, Matsuda, & Thonneau, 2003). Testicular malignancies can be classified histopathologically into seminomas, nonseminomas, and combined tumors. Following a diagnostic orchiectomy (removal of the testes), most seminomas are treated by radiotherapy to the para-aortic lymph nodes and most nonseminomas by chemotherapy, in case of metastases. About one third of the nonseminoma patients undergo retroperitoneal lymph nodes dissection (RPLND) that can affect ejaculatory function. The long-term survival for early disease detection approaches 100%. Since most patients undergo treatment during the most sexually active period of their life, the impact of therapy on the quality of life in general, and on sexual functioning, fertility, and body image in particular, is very important. Self-report measures of sexual function conducted soon after treatment indicate high levels of dysfunction that tend to improve over time, in general 3 to 6 months after treatment (van Basten, Koops Schraffoedt, et al., 1997). Limited research data on sexual functioning are available in long-term survivors of testicular seminoma treated with orchiectomy and radiotherapy.

Following radiotherapy, deterioration in sexual functioning has been reported in between 1% and 25% of the patients treated for testicular cancer (Caffo & Amichetti, 1999; Incrocci, Hop, Wijnmaalen, & Slob, 2002; Jonker-Pool et al., 1997; Schover, Gonzales, & von Eschenbach, 1986; Tinkler, Howard, & Kerr, 1992). Tinkler et al. (1992) reported on 237 patients after orchiectomy and abdominal radiotherapy and compared these data with 402 age-matched controls. On almost all parameters studied, including erection, ejaculation, and libido, patients scored lower than controls (reduction in orgasm, in libido, and in interest in sex). Caffo and Amichetti (1999) evaluated toxicity and quality of life of 143 patients treated for early stage testicular cancer. Twenty-three percent reported decreased libido, 27% had problems reaching orgasm, and 38% had ejaculation disturbances. A decrease in sexual desire, orgasm, and volume of semen was negatively correlated with age (Schover et al., 1986). Jonker-Pool et al. (1997) reported on three groups of patients with testicular cancer after one of three conditions: radiotherapy, wait and see, or chemotherapy. Radiotherapy patients reported decreased libido in 22% compared to 12% in the wait-and-see group and 30% in the chemotherapy group. Decrease (or absence) of ejaculate was reported in 15%, 7%, and 21% in the three groups, respectively; decreased orgasm in 15%, 12%, and 30%, respectively (Jonker-Pool et al., 1997). Although the differences were not statistically significant, the radiotherapy group exhibited higher ejaculation and orgasm disturbances than the wait-and-see group. Similar results have been reported by Arai, Kawakita, Okada, and Yoshida (1997).

Nazareth, Lewin, and King (2001) have published an excellent review on sexual function in patients after treatment for testicular cancer. Although some findings were difficult to interpret since they were based on uncontrolled samples, nonvalidated questionnaires, or patients who had received a variety of treatments, the authors concluded that, in general, treatment of testicular cancer is highly likely to result in sexual dysfunction. Significantly more ED occurred in patients treated for testicular cancer than in healthy controls, and sexual drive (sexual desire and frequency of sexual intercourse) was significantly reduced (Nazareth et al., 2001). Ejaculatory function worsened in all studies where a nonnerve-sparing RPLND was performed. In studies without control procedures, sexual dysfunction reached even higher levels (Nazareth et al., 2001).

Of these dysfunctional outcomes, the effect on ejaculation is perhaps most readily explained. Ejaculation is achieved by neural impulses conducted via the sympathetic trunk, postganglionic nerve fibers, and hypogastric nerves, all of which are closely connected with the retroperitoneal lymph nodes. During RPLND, performed in case of residual tumor mass after chemotherapy, these nerves are difficult to recognize and might be damaged, resulting in decreased semen volume or dry ejaculation. Sympathetic-induced contraction of the internal bladder sphincter prevents passage of semen into the bladder. As a result of careful anatomical studies, the technique of the RPLND has now been modified to include a nerve sparing procedure so that antegrade ejaculation is now maintained in 80% to 100% of patients (van Basten, Koops Schraffoedt, et al., 1997).

Polychemotherapy induces loss of libido, decreased arousal, decreased erectile function in patients with testicular cancer (van Basten, Jonker-Pool, et al., 1997). Chemotherapy has a major effect on the hormonal, vascular, and nervous systems, all important for normal sexual functioning. In more than half of testicular cancer survivors, Leydig cell dysfunction occurs, as indicated by low plasma testosterone and elevated luteinizing hormone levels (van Basten, Jonker-Pool, et al., 1997). Decreased amount of semen is also reported significantly more often by chemotherapy-treated patients than those simply under observation, possibly caused by lower testosterone levels.

Given the potential deforming effects of treatment for testicular removal, several studies have addressed issues of body image following treatment of testicular cancer (Gritz et al., 1989; Incrocci, Hop, et al., 2002; Tinkler et al., 1992). More than half of testicular cancer patients reported that their body image had changed after treatment (orchiectomy and radiotherapy; Incrocci, Bosch, & Slob, 1999). Yet, only about half of the patients reported being informed by their urologist about the availability of testicular implants (Gritz et al., 1989; Incrocci, Hop, et al., 2002). As expected, body image has been reported to improve after implantation of a testicular prosthesis (Adshead, Khoubehi, Wood, & Rustin, 2001; Gritz et al., 1989; Incrocci et al., 1999; Lynch & Pryor, 1992).

In conclusion, controlled studies indicate that sexual dysfunction persists for about 2 years posttreatment in testicular cancer patients and may be due to a combination of biological and psychological factors. However, before concluding that sexual dysfunction is a frequent and serious outcome of treatment of testicular cancer, more evidence is needed from controlled studies that include greater numbers of patients.

Gynecological Cancer

Gynecological cancer is the third most common female cancer. Sexual dysfunction after treatment of cervical cancer has been described in several studies, though comparisons across studies are difficult because of the different methods used to assess, analyze, and report sexual function and because of the heterogeneous patient population (different diagnoses, stages, and treatment modalities). The surgical approach to early stage cervical cancer consists of radical hysterectomy and bilateral lymph node dissection, with or without oophorectomy. Radiotherapy consists of EBRT followed by intracavitary radiation. Whether the patient undergoes primary surgery or radiotherapy depends on a variety of factors, including tumor characteristics, comorbidity, and patient's and specialist's preference. In general, patients with advanced cervical cancer are treated by a combination of chemo- and radiotherapy. Autonomic nerve damage plays a crucial role in the etiology of sexual dysfunction in women after radical hysterectomy. Surgical preservation of these nerves should preserve vaginal orgasm, though clitoral orgasm should also be present after hysterectomy. Oophorectomy can reduce sexual interest, arousal, and orgasm as a result of the ensuing hormonal deficit (estrogen, progesterone, and androgen).

In a retrospective comparison of treatment modalities (Frumovitz et al., 2005) 5 to 7 years after initial treatment, cervical cancer survivors treated with radiotherapy reported worse sexual functioning than patients treated with surgery. Sexual desire did not differ across groups, but irradiated women had more difficulty becoming sexually aroused, attaining vaginal lubrication, reaching orgasm, and achieving sexual satisfaction. Jensen et al. (2003) conducted a longitudinal study after radiotherapy for cervical cancer: 85% of the women had low or no sexual interest, 35% had a lack of lubrication, half had dyspareunia, and 30% were dissatisfied with their sexual life. Reduced vaginal dimension was reported in 50% and almost half of the women could not complete sexual intercourse. Interestingly, the same percentage (60) of the women who were sexually active before treatment remained active after treatment, although with decreased frequency (Jensen et al., 2003). Sexual functioning improves the first year after hysterectomy; in contrast after radiotherapy chronic fibrotic changes in pelvic tissues can worsen up to 2 years after treatment, and vagina lubrication may be diminished (Jensen et al., 2003).

The use of vaginal dilators or performing sexual intercourse frequently and soon after radiotherapy is strongly advised to maintain the length, width and elasticity of the vaginal canal. The use of lubricants is also strongly advised to alleviate problems and discomfort associated with vaginal dryness.

Breast Cancer

Breast cancer is the most common cancer in women today. The diagnosis and subsequent treatment of breast cancer greatly impact psychosexual functioning and intimacy within the sexual relationship (Henson, 2002). Ganz, Desmond, Meyerowitz, and Wyatt (1998) performed one of the most extensive studies on sexual functioning in breast cancer survivors. One to 5 years after diagnosis, in about 70% of the women, the breast may become smaller, painful, and fibrotic; about half of the women were less interested in sex and about 30% of treated women reported a decrease in their sexual activity. Though a variety of dysfunctions were reported, 70% of survivors were still sexually active (Ganz et al., 1998). As a result of chemotherapy or hormonal treatment, patients may complain about decreased vaginal lubrication, vaginal atrophy, and dyspareunia. The etiology for the sexual problems in these women seemed to be multifactorial, and the long-term impact of breast cancer treatment on the sexual quality of life depended on the patient's age at diagnosis as well as several aspects of treatment. Specifically, and as might be expected, younger women have greater difficulties adjusting, and patients who have undergone chemo- or radiotherapy (as opposed to surgery) have significant fatigue that may influence sexual interest and activity. Premature menopause and estrogen deficiency typically cause a decrease in vaginal lubrication, and vaginal atrophy can cause dyspareunia. Although women may avoid their breast because of the physical disfigurement, the specific type of breast surgery (breast sparing or mastectomy) does not seem predictive of overall sexual health after surgery (Ganz et al., 1998). Finally, radiation-induced dermatitis may also affect sexual desire.

Broader Issues Surrounding Cancer and Sexuality

Sexual dysfunction in cancer patients may result from a variety of biological, psychological, and social factors (Dobkin & Bradley, 1991). Biological factors such as anatomic alterations (rectum amputation, penile amputation), physiological changes (hormonal status), and the secondary effect of medical intervention may preclude normal sexual functioning even when sexual desire is intact. The patient's physical status is related to both the stage of the disease and the type of medical intervention. Side effects of the treatment such as nausea, vomiting, fatigue, and hair loss, together with disfiguring surgery, can result in impaired sexual functioning.

Negative emotional states such as anxiety, depression, and anger may contribute to the disruption of sexual activity. Disturbances of body image can contribute to the development of sexual dysfunction, orchiectomy being one such example. Other important psychological factors associated with sexual dysfunction in cancer patients are financial difficulties and occupational changes—stressors often related to the general effects of any serious illness.

Patients and their physicians at a cancer center are strongly focused on their survival. However, younger patients are more emotionally distressed by the cancer since the illness is more disruptive of their lifestyle; yet younger patients are more likely to improve with counseling (Schover et al., 1987). In a program of sexual rehabilitation in 308 men and 76 women (mean ages of 55 and 41 years respectively), Schover et al. (1987) showed that being treated for cancer was clearly detrimental to patients' frequency of sexual activity. In that study, sexual activity dropped from two times weekly to once a month during treatment. Furthermore, all sexual dysfunctions increased in such patients, although sexual problems did not increase in spouses. The stability of sexual function in husbands and wives of cancer patients suggests that the sexual problems developing after cancer treatment in the patients are caused as much by the emotional and medical impact of the illness as by the stress in the couple's relationship.

Evaluating sexual functioning in an oncology population is different from evaluating it in a healthy population because of its specific medical, psychological, and social factors. In oncology clinics where outpatient visits must include educating patients about their disease, prognosis, and treatment, physicians and nurses often do not have the time for assessing quality of life issues (Schover, 1999); a topic such as sexuality may simply take too much time in the clinic when life and death issues are being confronted. Furthermore, discomfort among both health care providers and patients in discussing matters about sexuality is typical, particularly when age and gender differences exist (i.e., young doctor treating an older patient). Different religious and ethnic backgrounds can also add to the difficulty of discussing highly personal issues regarding sexuality.

Given the complexity of the task, a multidisciplinary team with expertise in medical, psychological, and sexological issues is often needed for a holistic approach to the treatment of cancer patients. Even without such resources, however, it is possible to assess patients' overall quality of life, including their social support network, reaction to the cancer, past and current mood or anxiety disorders, and sexuality within the framework of a 30 to 45 min interview (Schover, 1999). A large number of existing instruments are available to assess quality of life in cancer patients, and some of these tap sexual symptoms as well, although the information on this topic might be limited (Cella, 1996).

As research in the area of cancer and sexuality continues, specific research design issues need to be addressed. For example, data collection on sexual parameters should be taken both before and long after treatment, and the use of control procedures and groups should be incorporated whenever possible. At the same time, however, in designing such research, the health care provider needs to be sensitive to the burden placed on the cancer patient; for this reason, questionnaires requiring 15 min or less to complete, followed by an interview, are most likely to ensure compliance.

In the large majority of cancer patients, a brief counseling format appears to be adequate for dealing with many of the patients' issues. In a review of almost 400 patients who consulted a psychologist in a cancer center for sexual rehabilitation, 73% needed to be seen only once or twice (Schover, 1999). Unfortunately, however, in many cancer treatment centers, even this limited access to counseling services may not be available. Furthermore, physicians themselves are often not prepared to address issues of sexuality during routine health care and in patients with cancer—few have had any significant formal sexuality education in their medical school and residency program. And for reasons not always clear, despite its obvious value to the patient, sexual counseling has not become a routine part of oncology care in most hospitals.

In conclusion, a number of general recommendations emerge from our understanding of the way in which the treatment of cancer is likely to affect sexual functioning. These recommendations are summarized in Sidebar 10.2.

SIDEBAR 10.2

Summary Points for Dealing with Sexual Problems in Cancer Patients

Sexual counseling should be routinely provided in an oncology clinic, for example, by having a physician or oncology nurse specialist to assess quality of life, including sexuality.

Patients should be provided with information about the impact of cancer treatment on sexuality. Patients and their partners are often uninformed about the sexual physiology and anatomy and may need to be counseled on the effects of specific cancers and their treatments on sexual response, for example, regarding the effects that radiotherapy for PCa has on ejaculation.

Counseling regarding the safety and any risk factors related to sexual activity during radiation therapy is important. For example, men irradiated for PCa sometimes believe that cancer can be spread by sexual contact or that ejaculation may be harmful to the partner.

Open sexual communication between partners should be encouraged. Often couples have not discussed issues about their sexuality for years, yet the introduction of changes in the couple's sex life necessitates communication about such issues.

The changes in sexual function occurring after cancer treatment may disrupt the sexual relationship and may require adaptation to the new situation, for example, in case of painful orgasm after brachytherapy.

Chronic Disease

Chronic diseases are often accompanied by problems with sexual functioning and intimacy. There are two important reasons to address the fact that such diseases affect sexual functioning. First, patients often want relief from these sexual problems even though only a small percentage may actually seek help, probably due to the embarrassment or shame surrounding sexual issues. Second, good sexual functioning and intimacy within a relationship are often important to a person's overall quality of life. Apart from these, sexual expression has several additional health benefits. A healthy sex life may decrease muscular and emotional tension, increase the pain threshold in women, reduce physical stress, improve sleep, and reduce emotional stress within the relationship (Gianotten, Whipple, & Owens, 2007). In addition, sex may be used to console, to gain affirmation as a man or a woman, and to cope with overwhelming emotions. So sexuality in patients with chronic disease or physical handicaps deserves consideration.

The subfield of sexology dealing with disease and handicap is sometimes referred to as "medical sexology." Whereas the field of sexology in general typically focuses on improving the quality of sexual functioning, medical sexology often focuses attention on simple "sexual survival," regaining intimacy, and restructuring the meaning of sex. For most patients with chronic and debilitating diseases, the health care provider must face a wide range of potential causes, contributory factors, and maintaining factors that underlie sexual and intimacy problems. Some are physiological, some disease-related psychological, some person-related psychological, some partner-related, and some social. Detailed characteristics of each of these etiological domains are:

- *Physiological factors* include: fatigue; impaired movements or positions; adverse effects of medication either directly influencing sexual function or indirectly (for instance, via increase in weight or decrease in saliva); hormonal changes; changed body sensations (anesthesia, paresthesia, itching, skin irritation); changes in the sexual response; anatomical changes (especially in the genital area); pain; and cerebrally caused depression.

- *Psychological factors broadly related to being ill or having a handicap* include: a sense of failing to be normal; changed priorities; changed meaning of life; preoccupation with disease or symptoms; loss of control; fear of failing as sexual partner; fear of contagiousness; disturbing heavy emotions (fear, shame, guilt, anger); avoidance behavior; reexperiencing past sexual or medical trauma; maimed appearance (disfigurement); and sadness due to lost fertility.

- *Psychological factors belonging to this specific person* include: a rigid coping style; low enduring capacity; lack of self-confidence; disturbed physical self-respect; disturbed male or female identity ("I am not a real man or woman"); unable to accept enjoying life and having positive emotions; limited or limiting sexual habits.

- *Partner related factors* include: disturbed partner relationship; communication problems; power struggle; partner reacting negatively; changed roles; mutual mistrust; and other changed relationship dynamics.

- *Social factors* include: social isolation; not having or being able to find a partner; situational handicaps; lack of intimacy in aloneness; and other social restrictions (e.g., living in assisted care facility).

The Connection between Cause and Treatment

For decades, ED in diabetic men has provided the classic example of the contention between psychological versus somatic (i.e., disease) etiologies. Even with a proven neuropathy and angiopathy, some diabetic men with ED have benefited from relationship therapy or from having a new partner, such that they were then able to have good erectile response. This, of course, does not suggest that somatic pathophysiology does not play an important role in sexual dysfunction in persons with disease, but it does illustrate the fact that nonsomatic factors can play an important role as well. If, because of his diabetes, a man's erectile system begins to deteriorate at age 30, and 90% of erectile function is lost by age 50, this man has experienced a 20-year period of gradual decline. Yet, with only 10% erectile function left, a stimulating partner, pleasure in nongenital excitement, noncoital fun, creativity, less demand for an erection, and appropriate kinds of stimulation may partially overcome the 90% damage, with the possibility of occasional erections adequate for intercourse. In contrast, other men may still have 90% erectile function left, but with vulnerable male pride, a passive partner, little creativity, and multiple experiences of performance failure, the actual 10% loss of function may be sufficient to end his sex life entirely. This paradox has led us to develop a treatment model for sexual problems associated with disease called the *balance model*.

In this model, sexual function is the net sum of the total amount of inhibitions on one side of the balance, and the total amount of stimulation on the other side. Inhibitory factors include such things as neural damage, vascular damage, adverse effects of medication, fatigue, performance failure, pain, too much responsibility, fear, stress, shame, feelings of guilt, and so on. These inhibiting factors form the range of primary and ancillary causes as well as maintaining factors. Stimulation factors include such things as an active partner, adequate foreplay, visual stimulation (especially for men), use of vibrators and other assisting devices, erotica, massage, the right environment and adequate time, the use and sharing of fantasy, and so on. When the total "weight" of inhibitions is greater than the total weight of stimulation, sexual response will diminish, whereas when stimulation exceeds inhibition, sexual response will occur and/or be enhanced. In using this model as a part of a treatment program, charts illustrating the full range of inhibitions (both the irreversible ones and those that may change) and the full range of potentially available stimuli can be used effectively with patients. Then, the patient can decide how to construct his or her own treatment process, which may follow one or more of the four tracks indicated next. Patients typically begin with the first two tracks:

1. Diminish inhibitions (for instance, reduce fatigue, deal with performance failure, reduce pain with painkillers, reduce spasm with a spasmolytic or hot bath, deal with partner and relationship stress).

2. Increase the level of stimulation (broaden the range of satisfying sexual scenarios).

3. Should these first two adaptations not have the desired effect, then symptomatic treatment might be considered (for instance, a lubricant or vacuum therapy).

4. When symptomatic treatment fails, the patient's focus might be redirected. Is it possible, for example, to give sexuality and intimacy another meaning whereby the failing function is replaced by other satisfying ways to have a satisfactory release of tension or to have intimate contact?

In medical sexology, where significant damage is frequently caused by trauma or disease, the health care provider may have to use the fourth track with some regularity. In the next sections of this chapter, we consider in some detail eight diseases or handicaps that have significant consequences for sexuality. For each condition, we provide some basic information about the disease, about how sexuality is likely to be influenced, and about relevant treatment strategies.

Spinal Cord Injury

The spinal cord carries messages from the body to the brain (e.g., being caressed, the experience of orgasm, or having a full bladder) and from the brain to the body (e.g., coital hip and buttock movements, muscle tension). In patients with spinal cord injury (SCI), connections between the higher and lower levels of the neural pathways are interrupted and the functions are stopped. Neither a caress, nor an orgasm, nor a full bladder is experienced, and voluntary coital movements are impossible.

Most SCIs are caused by accidents, but some are caused by spinal cord disease (tumor, infarct, or infection) or surgery. The interruption may be complete (= 60%) or partial (incomplete SCI). The incidence in the western world is 1 to 3 per 100,000 persons per year and the prevalence, 22 to 75 per 100,000 persons; not surprisingly, SCIs (75% or higher) are more common among males (Wyndaele & Wyndaele, 2006). The level at which the spinal cord is injured is a critically important variable in predicting sexual dysfunctions. The higher the level, the more parts of the neural system are disconnected from the brain. In about 30% of SCIs, the disconnection is at a cervical (shoulder/neck) level, thereby causing damage to the function of the arms/hands. In case of a high level (at or above Thoracic 6) lesion, there is danger of autonomic dysreflexia resulting in excessively high blood pressure during sexual activity or mechano- or electro-forced ejaculation. Typically, after any spinal cord injury, an extended period of rehabilitation is needed. Following rehabilitation, some survivors may be able to function well in the community while others may need continuous care.

Sexual Capacity

Sexual function is determined partly by voluntary control from the brain and partly by reflexes under the control of two centers in the spinal cord. One reflex center is situated at level T12-L2 (thoracic/lumbar) and the other at level S2-S4 (sacral). In case of a complete SCI, we could expect the following clinical pictures:

- *SCI above T11:* Psychogenic erection and lubrication would not be possible in these patients although reflex erection and lubrication would be. Because of the disruption of brain influence over the reflex response, a reflex erection could not be negatively influenced (inhibited) by a psychological (brain) process (e.g., the experience of performance failure). Thus, in these patients a sexually stimulating striptease act will not result in erection, whereas an unattractive health care provider cleaning the penis will. Even with complete SCI, some men continue to have nocturnal erections (Tay, Juma, & Joseph, 1996), and ejaculation is in principle possible if there is sufficient stimulation.

- *SCI between T11-L2:* For these patients, psychogenic erection and lubrication depend on the amount of damage. Reflex erection and reflex lubrication are possible. Since the first part of male ejaculation (transport from epididymis, seminal vesicles, and prostate gland into the prostate lumen) originates at this level, this process will be disrupted. The second part (contraction of pelvic floor and expulsion of semen) remains intact.

- *SCI between L2-S2 (i.e., between both centers):* Erection and lubrication would be expected from psychogenic and from genital (reflex) stimulation. Ejaculation would be possible as well.

- *SCI between S2-S4:* In these patients, psychogenic erection and psychogenic lubrication would be possible, while reflex erection and reflex lubrication would not be possible. For ejaculation, transport from epididymis, seminal vesicles, and prostate gland is intact, but the second phase of ejaculation (originating from this S2-S4 level) is impossible. As a result, semen will not be expelled, but it will dribble out of the penis.

Other Components of Sexual Response: Orgasm and Sexual Desire

Orgasm is experienced in the brain and for this there needs to be a viable neural pathway to the brain. Although it is not clearly understood, some men and women with a complete SCI apparently can experience orgasm. At least in women, the experience of orgasm via the traditional neural pathway through the spinal cord may bypass the spinal cord and travel to the brain via the vagal nerve (Komisaruk et al., 2004).

Although sexual desire is not influenced directly by SCI, many SCI-related effects can influence desire. For instance changes in mobility (wheelchair), disturbed passage of stool and urine (sometimes with incontinence during sex), pain, muscular spasm, and disturbed fertility in men may all affect a person's desire for and interest in sex.

In general, SCI imposes a major change on people, forcing them to reframe the meaning of life and of sexuality. For a small portion of SCI survivors, this life change may actually result in a better sex life.

Relevant Treatment Aspects

Technically, nearly all pro-sexological strategies and devices can be of value in SCI patients. For those with ED, PDE-5 inhibitors, vacuum devices, intracavernosal injection, and vibrators may be used. For ejaculation (especially for purposes of reproduction), normal vibrators may be used, or the special SCI-vibrator with adapted amplitude (FertiCare®) may be considered. If these fail, rectal electro-stimulation may be attempted, but this treatment is usually carried out in a tertiary care setting. No matter the method, the health care provider should convey an important additional message: "We do not know exactly what will work or how your body will react, so just try!" Both vibratory stimulation and orgasm may sometimes result in a (several hour) period of diminished spasticity and better bladder function. Some men may benefit from the use of a ring vibrator around the base of the penile shaft, which can help them maintain erection during intercourse.

Spina Bifida

Spina bifida is a defect of the neural tube and spinal cord caused by incomplete closure of the neural tube during intrauterine (fetal) development. The defect may occur at several locations in the spinal cord, with lumbar and sacral areas having the greatest implications for sexual functioning. At these levels, no hydrocephalus develops and thus no cerebral damage and mental impairment occurs. The defect can be mild, with the skin closed and only minor deficits (spina bifida occulta), moderate with meningeal tissue protruding, or extensive with part of the spinal cord protruding, with that portion of the cord being more dysfunctional. The symptoms are diminished or absent sensation, muscular weakness or paralysis, and reduced control over bladder and bowels. After birth, part of the damage may be surgically repaired, with varying degrees of success depending on the severity of the defect. Many spina bifida patients require a wheelchair. The origin of the disease is multifactorial, and includes such factors as heredity, folic acid deficiency, and antiepileptic medication during early intrauterine life. Spina bifida has a worldwide incidence of 150 per 100,000 births, with racial and geographical variations. In the United States, the incidence is 70 per 100,000 births, with 100 for Caucasians and 25 for African Americans. In the developed world, the numbers are decreasing because of peri-conceptional folate supplements, prenatal counseling, and selective abortion.

Sexual Capacity

Diminished sensation, diminished control over bladder and bowels, and diminished muscular function (with both weakness and spasm) influence sexual response. On a purely functional level, the sexual consequences are somewhat comparable to the situation of the patient with SCI, but the clinical picture is less predictable. However, there are important differences with respect to the personal experiences of spinal bifida patients versus SCI patients. Because the person with spina bifida began life with this ailment, he or she has both disadvantages and advantages relative to the SCI patient. The physical impairment can be a handicap in developing social contacts and in the experimenting phases toward healthy sexuality. Never having had or never expecting a normal sex life can decrease the sense of the (sexual) self. An additional burden for girls may be the early onset of puberty (1.5 years ahead of other girls). Furthermore, a higher than expected percentage of spina bifida children (especially girls) have been sexually abused, similar to the pattern for all children with physical or mental impairments. In contrast to the SCI patient, the spina bifida patient does not have the handicap of knowing "how good sex has been," so he or she is more accustomed to a less perfect situation and is usually better at adapting and finding creative solutions to sexual problems.

Relevant Treatment Aspects

Next to dealing with actual sexual functioning (as is the case in the SCI patient), issues of sexual development may need attention in the spina bifida patient. When an individual has never had sex and thus has not had the opportunity to develop a "sexual identity," "habilitation" rather than "rehabilitation" of sexual identity and development of sexual knowledge and experience take precedence. Patients with severe handicaps have often become so accustomed to genital observation, touching, and manipulation (for instance for catheterization) that it becomes difficult for them to consider their bodies as sexual and sensual. Patients with mild handicaps, on the other hand, have the problem that their physical disturbance (for instance, incontinence and impaired sexual function) cannot be seen from the outside, which makes it more difficult to communicate such matters to a partner toward the beginning of a sexual encounter or of a relationship.

Stroke-Cerebrovascular Accident

The origin of sexual desire and sexual fantasies lies within the brain. The brain serves as the repository for good and the bad sexual memories; it is where incoming stimuli are processed as being exciting or inhibiting, where impulses are regulated, and where orgasm and satisfaction are experienced. Since the brain serves as the origin, control center, and terminus of sexual function, damage to the brain has a major impact on sexuality.

In stroke (CVA), brain damage is caused by a lack of blood flow to the brain and consequent oxygen deprivation to cells, with subsequent dying of brain tissue and loss of vital functions. In 80% of victims, stroke is caused by an infarct ("white stroke"), usually as a result of arteriosclerosis. In 20%, it is caused by bleeding ("red stroke"), usually as a result of hypertension and weakened vascular walls. In a small percentage, the bleeding is caused by a congenital weak spot in the arterial wall (aneurysm). Depending on the localization and the amount of damage, the patient may develop various combinations of neurological impairment, cognitive defects, behavioral changes, psychological disturbances, and sexual impairment. Frequently noted are:

- Paralysis or muscular weakness and numbness, usually on one side of the body (hemiplegia).
- Damage to the speech center with loss of speech (aphasia, which is more common in males).
- Loss of balance and coordination (with urinary incontinence).
- Childish behavior and emotional incontinence.
- Apathy but also coercing behavior.
- Depression as a direct result of cerebral damage and as a result of the more complicated life.

The incidence of stroke in the western world is 135 to 235 per 100,000 persons per year and the prevalence 800 to 1,100 per 100,000 persons. The rate for stroke in men is 20% higher than that in women, and the majority (75% to 83%) occur in persons over the age of 64 years. Thirty-three percent of victims die within 1 year, with an average survival period of 4 years.

Sexual Capacity

A considerable portion of stroke patients had preexistent sexual problems caused by the same vascular damage that caused the stroke. Usually after a stroke, all sexual expression is diminished for both the patient and partner. Sexual desire, intercourse, erection, lubrication, orgasm, and sexual satisfaction all decrease. Stroke regularly causes premature ejaculation, probably as a result of diminished control over sexual response. After a stroke, partners (and patients) often express fear that sexual activity might result in another stroke, but in the 80% of strokes caused by an infarct, this fear is unfounded. Speech and communication problems in male patients can reduce sexual desire in partners because for many of them appropriate communication is important for sexual intimacy. Female stroke survivors usually have more trouble with loss of attractiveness (disfigurement) and male stroke survivors more with the loss of autonomy; both conditions negatively influence sexual self-respect. Sexuality is also indirectly impaired by physical complaints like pain, muscular spasms, and urinary incontinence, and by behavioral changes like loss of control, impulsivity, and diminished control of sexual impulses.

Relevant Treatment Aspects

Few direct sexological interventions have been described for these patients, but much can be gained by listening to the sexual concerns and worries of the patients. Depending on the vascular situation, PDE-5 inhibitors (e.g., sildenafil) may sometimes be used for erectile dysfunction. Usually, however, they are not prescribed until at least 6 months following the event. When premature ejaculation is caused by the stroke, an SSRI may be considered.

Traumatic Brain Injury

Traumatic or acquired brain injury (TBI) is the result of non-stroke damage to brain tissue. Usually caused by fall, traffic accident, or violence, it may also result from temporary oxygen loss due to cardiac failure or drowning. Depending on the extent of the brain damage, symptoms can vary from mild to very severe. The more severe cases are characterized by various combinations of complaints in five different areas: (1) neurological (disturbed function of sensation, muscles, bowel and bladder, and coordination); (2) cognitive (memory, attention, speech, understanding, problem solving, perception); (3) psychiatric (psychosis, post traumatic stress syndrome, anxiety disorder, mood disorder); (4) emotional/behavioral (apathy, irritability, mood swings, outbursts of anger, loss of decorum, egocentrism, emotional disinhibition or numbing); and (5) hormonal due to posttraumatic hypopituitarism. One year after TBI, 36% of patients still had disturbed pituitary function with the gonadotropic axis affected in 21% (Schneider et al., 2006).

In the United States, the incidence of TBI is 200 per 100,000 persons per year, with the majority of cases being children and young men. The average age is 30 years, and two thirds are male. In the United States, there are 100 admissions per 100,000 persons for nonfatal TBI, of which 20% will retain severe symptoms.

Sexual Capacity

The sexual consequences of TBI can be enormous. In young patients, the physical and emotional effects cause additional insecurity and set them behind in the development of sexuality and relationships. During puberty, sexual impulses are often uncontrolled in both boys and girls. For those who have already had sexual experience, TBI may change sexual functioning in three different ways: a complete loss of sexual desire, development of sexual dysfunctions, or the expression of deviant sexual behavior. Due to changes in neurological function and personality, emotional and sensual flexibility are lost. The majority of partners report that their "old lover and mate" has disappeared and has been replaced by someone with harsh physical and emotional lovemaking. After TBI, half of all relationships end up in divorce or separation (Wood & Yordakul, 1997).

Relevant Treatment Aspects

Especially for young people with TBI and disturbed impulse control, measures to prevent unwanted pregnancy, sexual abuse, and sexually transmitted diseases (STDs) should be incorporated into the care. When sexual desire is lost completely, a hormonal imbalance might be explored, and if found, eventually remedied with hormone replacement. When a sexual dysfunction develops, the health care provider needs to attend strongly to the partner relationship. In case the TBI patient exhibits insufficient control over sexual behavior, medication may be used to diminish the danger of sexual abuse toward others or injury to oneself. Here the health care provider faces the additional complication that TBI patients tend not to react in the typical way to antipsychotic medication. An alternative medication strategy is therefore to use the impulse reducing properties of some SSRIs. Aloni and Katz (2003) have developed an extensive treatment program for sexual difficulties after TBI that includes surrogate therapy as part of the intervention program for single TBI survivors.

Cerebral Palsy

Cerebral palsy (CP) refers to a group of neurological disorders appearing in infancy or early childhood that permanently affect body movement and muscle coordination but that do not worsen over time. Although CP affects muscle movement, it is not caused by a muscular problem, but rather by abnormalities in parts of the brain that control muscle movements. The majority of CP cases (75%) develop during pregnancy (e.g., intrauterine bleeding, developmental failure), 5% during delivery (birth trauma), and 15% in the first years of life (infection, physical trauma, or child abuse). The most common symptoms are lack of muscle coordination when trying to use them (ataxia); stiff muscles and exaggerated reflexes (spasticity); unbalanced gait; and too stiff or too floppy muscle tonus. CP can be combined with other disorders (of hearing, eyesight, epilepsy, and difficulties with talking, eating, and drinking). CP is nonprogressive, but the muscular dysfunction causes secondary orthopedic deformities especially in spine, hips, and lower extremities. An important part of medical care is limited to treatment and prevention of complications. The amount of handicap shows a wide range, with 35% to 40% having only difficulties in higher-level skills and 17% having very limited self-mobility, even with assistive technology. CP has an incidence of 200 per 100,000 live births with approximately 60% developing mental retardation. Although obstetric care has improved greatly over the past decades, the CP rate has not decreased due to the survival of very premature babies who have an increased risk to develop CP.

Sexual Capacity

In both girls and boys with CP, puberty begins earlier and ends later than in age-matched controls. When the physical aspects of sexual expression are disturbed, it is mainly due to muscular spasm (including pelvic floor), limited positions (cannot spread the legs), lack of self-reliance (cannot enter a partner's bed without help), or limited motor function (cannot hold a vibrator in his hand). Disturbed motor skills of the mouth can cause inarticulate speech and dribbling saliva, complicating interpersonal contact. CP youngsters do feel sufficient attraction, but have difficulty when it comes to getting a partner. With reduced mobility, there are few moments of privacy and few partners available. However, when the CP patient is mobile, making contact is not a problem, but CP patients are frequently disappointed because able-bodied partners do not continue the contact. CP patients have less experience with all levels of sexual contact from kissing to intercourse (Wiegerink, Roebroeck, Donkervoort, Stam, & Cohen-Kettenis, 2006).

Relevant Treatment Aspects

Some CP patients need anticholinergic medication prior to sexual activity when urinary incontinence during sex is a complication. Others may require spasmolytic medication to prevent muscular spasms during sex. Or they might benefit from dietary advice and small tools to prevent fecal incontinence. When masturbation is complicated due to diminished hand function, sexual aids in the form of a sleeve vibrator or shaft vibrator may suffice. Severely incapacitated patients who cannot establish a relationship can benefit from specialized sex workers (experienced with physically handicapped patients). Many have been helped by a no-intervention strategy in their transition years when they move from a dependent situation (with overly protective parents and for many, overly involved rehabilitation professionals) toward a more independent situation where they take control of their own decision making.

Multiple Sclerosis

Multiple sclerosis (MS) destroys the nerves of the central nervous system (CNS), that is, in both the spinal cord and the brain. Myelin, the insulation covering the nerve fibers, is slowly damaged, resulting in multiple patches of scarred hard tissue plaques and creating short circuits in neural networks. Axons, the long filaments that carry electric impulses away from a nerve cell, are destroyed, thus playing a major role in permanent MS disability. The symptoms, severity, and course of MS vary widely depending partly on the sites of the plaques and the extent of the demyelination. The disease process starts long before the first symptoms are shown and in many patients it takes years before the diagnosis is confirmed. The causes of the disease are unknown, and it can neither be prevented nor cured, but the disease is not fatal. There are two main clinical pictures in MS: relapsing-remitting and chronic-progressive.

In the relapsing-remitting type, remissions (in which symptoms disappear or improve) are followed by attacks (relapses or exacerbations). About 20% of patients with relapsing-remitting MS experience little or no progression after a first attack for long periods of time; although by 25 years most patients have converted to a progressive phase. In the chronic-progressive type, symptoms continue to worsen slowly without remission. About 20% of patients with MS (usually those whose first symptoms occur after age 45) have the chronic-progressive form without first developing relapsing-remitting MS. Chronic-progressive MS generally follows a downhill course, but its severity varies widely. Nearly all patients fall into the chronic progressive type within 25 years. Early symptoms are: eye problems (in half of the patients) with double and hazy vision, fatigue, muscle weakness and spasticity, and bladder disturbances. In later stages, speech and swallowing difficulties, loss of bowel and bladder control, and sexual dysfunctions may occur. Cerebral involvement causes cognitive impairment, emotional mood swings (frequently) depression, and sometimes psychosis. Incidence and prevalence depend on geographical latitude (with higher MS-rates in more Nordic countries) and sex (with women accounting for 65% to 70% of all cases). The prevalence per 100,000 persons varies from 69 in Italy to 135 in Norway, and the incidence per 100,000 persons per year varies from 2.3 in Italy to 8.7 in Norway.

Sexual Capacity

As could be expected, MS is accompanied by a range of sexual disturbances. Desire is indirectly diminished by fatigue and depression; erection and lubrication are directly influenced by the damaged nerves. The same goes for orgasm. The somatosensory function of the dorsal nerve of the clitoris and penis is damaged, causing orgasm to be absent or difficult (Yang, Bowen, Kraft, Uchio, & Kromm, 2000, 2001). Urine loss (and sometimes fecal loss) during sex, depression, muscular spasm, and pain are additional complicating factors. The proportion of patients with sexual dysfunction is over 70%, and symptoms of sexual dysfunction increase in significance and number over time in patients. Changes in sexual function appear to be associated with bladder dysfunction (Zorzon et al., 2001).

Relevant Treatment Aspects

Handling fatigue and the risk of incontinence during sex are important aspects of dealing with desire problems. For MS patients, sexual activity is better in a cool environment since warmth aggravates symptoms (the Uthoff phenomenon). To treat erectile problems, PDE-5 inhibitors generally produce positive results (Fowler et al., 2005). Orgasm problems present a bigger challenge. As long as some neural connection to the orgasm center in the spinal cord still exists, maximum stimulation can be attempted to "charge" the center. Because vibrators surpass penis, finger, or tongue capacity, their use may be helpful. For MS patients, reaching orgasm can actually reduce muscular spasms, an effect that may last for several hours. In some countries, cannabis (marijuana) has been used to diminish a variety of MS symptoms including pain and muscular and bladder dysfunction. Positive side effects of cannabis are improved sexual function and increased sexual pleasure.

Additional attention needs to be directed toward the MS patient's partner. In many couples where the woman has MS, the male partner may become a caretaker with little or no sex life, causing stress for him and feelings of guilt for her. Good sexological care should address the partner's physical and sexual needs without disturbing the patient's body. Most patients accommodate such needs, especially when the health benefits of sexual expression are introduced (Gianotten et al., 2007).

Parkinson's Disease

Parkinson's disease (PD) is a chronic and progressive disorder of the central nervous system. The best-known symptoms are

tremors (shaking), muscle rigidity (stiffness), and slowed movement. Other symptoms are urinary incontinence, constipation,
and an oily skin. PD is frequently accompanied by depression. In
the advanced stages, cognitive function and language become impaired. PD is caused by disrupted dopamine action (and production) in the brain cells. Besides PD itself, a person may exhibit the
full range of symptoms (called parkinsonism) due to non-Parkin-
son's cause, for instance, drugs, head trauma, or intoxication. In
PD, the symptoms are treated by various medication regimes usually including L-dopa or dopaminergic drugs. PD is mainly a disease of the elderly, with only a minor percentage (4%) of patients
under the age of 50. In the United States the prevalence of PD is
250 cases per 100,000 persons with an annual incidence of 19 per
100,000 males and 9.9 per 100,000 females. In Europe the male-
female ratio is approximately 1.0.

Sexuality Capacity

For the majority of untreated patients, low dopamine levels in the
brain are accompanied by low sexual desire. Depression adds
further to this low interest in sex. For partners, usually the patient's appearance and change in flexibility diminishes their sexual
desire as well. The motor and movement disturbance can hamper
masturbation and coital movements. When sexually excited, PD
patients may experience increased muscular spasms that may
continue 30 to 60 min after orgasm. Dopaminergic medication
can have several sexual side effects. One is heightened sexual desire, which while pleasant in some instances may approach levels
of hypersexuality in the estimation of both the partner and patient. In addition, dopaminergic medication may result in premature ejaculation in the male patient.

Relevant Treatment Aspects

In PD cases, the relationship and the partner require significant
attention from the health care provider, especially in the case of
hypersexuality. Hypersexuality can also be cause for reducing the
medication. The majority of PD patients with ED can be easily
treated by PDE-5 inhibitors, with the additional benefit that depression is likely to subside. Premature ejaculation may be treated
with topical anesthetics.

Diabetes Mellitus

Diabetes mellitus (DM) is a cluster of different metabolic disorders. The main sign is an excessively high level of blood sugar

(hyperglycemia); the higher the levels and the longer they exist, the more harm is done to both blood vessels (angiopathy) and nerves (neuropathy). For sexology, there are two important types of DM, neither of which can be cured, but both of which may be treated (at least partially) with a combination of lifestyle, diet, medication, and the eventual use of insulin. Type 1 DM usually starts at a young age and is caused by destruction of the insulin-producing cells in the pancreas. Insulin supplement is absolutely essential to treating this condition. Type 2 DM was formerly called late-onset diabetes because it was not found in young children. However, an important impetus to DM Type 2 is central obesity (fat in the belly area), which is becoming epidemic in many modern societies due to too much food intake and insufficient physical activity. Now increasingly, children and young adolescents are developing this disease. Serious long-term complications of DM are cardiovascular disease including stroke, chronic renal failure, eye damage with blindness, and amputation of lower limbs. In the Western world, 5% to 10% of diabetes patients are Type 1, the rest are Type 2. The worldwide prevalence is 2.6 per 100,000 people, but in the United States it has reached 6.9 per 100,000 persons. In all probability, the prevalence is higher because many DM people are unaware of their condition. The incidence is probably somewhere between 200 and 600 per 100,000 persons per year.

Sexual Capacity

DM slowly destroys both the endothelial cells of the vessels that supply and regulate the genital organs and the endothelial cells in the erectile tissue itself, causing erectile and lubrication difficulties. In addition, DM can destroy the nerves supplying the genitals, causing decreased sensation and difficulty reaching orgasm. Autonomic neuropathy may damage the nerve responsible for closing the sphincter between prostate and bladder, causing retrograde ejaculation in 1% to 14% of DM men (Ertekin, 1998). The longer the blood sugar levels are high or unstable, the more damage is done and so sexual dysfunctions tend to keep pace with other diabetic complications (of kidney, eye, and extremities). Enzlin et al. (2002) showed that Type 1 patients with diabetic complications have higher rates of sexual dysfunctions compared to Type 1 patients without complications (for male desire problems 19% versus 4%; for erectile dysfunction 31% versus 6%; for male orgasm problems 31% versus 2% and for all male dysfunctions 40.5% versus 6%). In Italy, erectile problems were found in 51% of 1,383 Type 1 males and in 37% of 8,373 Type 2 males (Fedele et al., 2000). Comparing Type 1 female patients with and without diabetic complications, Enzlin et al. (2002) found for female desire no difference, for lubrication problems 19% versus 9%, and for female orgasm dysfunction also 19% versus 9%. Comparing male and female Type 1 patients, Enzlin et al. (2002) also found a clear difference in how each gender reacts to the disease. In men, the sexual dysfunctions are related primarily to somatic factors whereas in women they are more likely related to depression. In women with Type 1 DM, 25% scored in the range of a clinical depression (versus 7% in male with Type 1 DM).

Relevant Treatment Aspects

The treatment of erectile and lubrication problems depends strongly on residual circulatory and neural capacity, and also on the management of the blood sugar. Blood sugar management is assessed through the HbA1C level. When the HbA1C is below 9.0%, sildenafil has been effective in 63% of men, but when the HbA1C level is above 9.0%, sildenafil is effective only in 44% (Guay, 2003). When the patient has difficulty reaching ejaculation or orgasm due to neuropathy, the use of a strong vibrator is recommended.

Summary and Conclusions

In this chapter, we have discussed a limited number of diseases, some of their etiologies and causes, and a variety of treatment considerations that are likely to help solve the sexual problems of patients with various diseases. In our introduction, we stressed the importance of addressing issues of sexuality in all patients, including those with diseases and physical handicaps. Sexuality is critically important for the great majority of people, even when they are faced with significant handicaps due to their disease condition. For many health care professionals, the complexity of the medical condition and its impact on sexual functioning is neither clear nor appreciated. Furthermore, the entire topic of sexual care is difficult to broach for many medical professionals.

We have also underscored the benefits to patients when sexuality and intimacy are included in the health care process. We would like to conclude with one final benefit: When the topic of sexuality is incorporated into the discussion and the treatment of disease with the patient, the working relationship between the health care provider and the patient is usually greatly improved. Patients perceive the medical professional as having greater concern and warmth. Such empathy is warranted toward those who are undergoing significant suffering or life changes because of their disease or condition.

In the meantime, the field of medicine needs to invest in the development of subspecialties such as oncosexology and rehabilitation sexology. To function well in these areas, sexology professionals need to be able to handle loss, mourning, progressive diseases, and the prospect of death. In addition, their skills should include dealing with complicated organic disturbances that involve pain, disfigured bodies, and hormone deficiencies. In order to make progress in the field of disease and sexuality, not only will new technical and pharmacological aids need to be developed, but new strategies and approaches toward establishing or reestablishing sexual meaning and intimacy within relationships will need to be tested and tried.

Summary points for dealing with sexual problems in patients with cancer and chronic disease:

- Sexual dysfunction is one of the more common consequences of cancer treatment.
- Regarding erectile dysfunction after treatment of prostate cancer, a multifactorial etiology has to be considered.
- Before concluding that sexual dysfunction is frequent after treatment of testicular cancer, more evidence is needed from controlled studies using more patients.
- The most common sexual sequelae of treatment of gynecological cancer are dyspareunia, vaginal dryness, decrease of sexual interest, and dissatisfaction with sexual life.
- Sexual counseling should routinely be provided in an oncology clinic.
- Sexuality is critically important for the great majority of people, even when they are faced with significant handicaps due to their disease condition.
- When the topic of sexuality is incorporated into the treatment of disease with the patient, the working relationship between the health care provider and the patient is greatly improved.

Appendix I: Cancer and Noncancer Related Factors Influencing Sexual Function

Cancer Related Factors

Treatment
  –Surgery
  –Chemotherapy
  –Radiotherapy
  –Combination of above

Psychological factors
    –Anxiety
    –Depression
    –Body image

Noncancer Related Factors

Age

Comorbidity
    –Diabetes Mellitus
    –Cardiovascular disease
    –Neurologic disease

Medication

Appendix II: Cancer Treatment and Its Effects on Sexual Functioning

Surgery

Male

Erectile dysfunction	Prostatectomy, cystectomy, rectal amputation
Ejaculatory dysfunction	Retro-peritoneal lymph node dissection, rectal amputation
Decreased libido	Orchiectomy
Altered body image	Orchiectomy, colostomy, urostomy

Female

Dyspareunia	Hysterectomy, cystectomy, rectal amputation
Vaginal shortness	Hysterectomy
Altered body image	Mastectomy, colostomy, urostomy

Chemotherapy, Hormonal Treatment

Male

Erectile dysfunction	Testicular cancer, prostate cancer, lymphomas, leukemia, rectal cancer
Azoo/oligospermia	Testicular cancer, lymphomas, leukemia
Decreased libido	Prostate, testicular cancer, lymphomas, leukemia
Altered body image	Testicular cancer, lymphomas, leukemia

Female

Premature menopause	Gynecological cancer, lymphomas, leukemia, breast cancer
Amenorrhea	Gynecological cancer, lymphomas, leukemia, breast cancer

| Dyspareunia | Gynecological cancer, lymphomas, leukemia, breast cancer |
| Altered body image | Gynecological cancer, lymphomas, leukemia, breast cancer |

Radiotherapy

Male

| Erectile dysfunction | Prostate cancer, bladder cancer, rectal cancer |
| Ejaculation dysfunction | Prostate cancer, rectal cancer |

Female

Premature menopause	Gynecological cancer, lymphomas, leukemia
Amenorrhea	Gynecological cancer, lymphomas, leukemia
Dyspareunia	Gynecological cancer, bladder cancer, lymphomas, leukemia
Vaginal dryness	Gynecological cancer, rectal cancer
Vaginal stenosis	Gynecological cancer, rectal cancer

References

Addis, M. E., & Mahalik, J. R. (2003). Men, masculinity, and the context of help-seeking. *American Psychologist, 58,* 5–14.

Adshead, J., Khoubehi, B., Wood, J., & Rustin, G. (2001). Testicular implants and patient satisfaction: A questionnaire-based study of men after orchidectomy for testicular cancer. *BJU International, 88,* 559–562.

Aloni, R., & Katz, S. (2003). *Sexual difficulties after traumatic brain injury and ways to deal with it.* Springfield: Charles C Thomas.

Arai, Y., Aoki, Y., Okubo, K., Maeda, H., Terada, N., Matsuta, Y., et al. (2000). Impact of interventional therapy for benign prostatic hyperplasia on quality of life and sexual function: A prospective study. *Journal of Urology, 164,* 1206–1211.

Arai, Y., Kawakita, M., Okada, Y., & Yoshida, O. (1997). Sexuality and fertility in long-term survivors of testicular cancer. *Journal of Clinical Oncology, 15,* 1444–1448.

Bjerre, B., Johansen, C., & Steven, K. (1998). Sexological problems after cystectomy: Bladder substitution compared with ileal conduit diversion. *Scandinavian Journal of Urology and Nephrology, 32,* 187–193.

Bonnel, C., Parc, Y. R., Pocard, M., Dehni, N., Caplin, S., Parc, R., et al. (2002). Effects of preoperative radiotherapy for primary resectable rectal adenocarcinoma on male sexual and urinary function. *Diseases of the Colon and Rectum, 45,* 934–939.

Brock, G., Nehra, A., Lipschultz, L. I., Karlin, G. S., Gleave, M., Seger, M., et al. (2003). Safety and efficacy of vardenafil for the treatment of men with erectile dysfunction after radical retropubic prostatectomy. *Journal of Urology, 170,* 1278–1283.

Caffo, O., & Amichetti, M. (1999). Evaluation of sexual life after orchidectomy followed by radiotherapy for early-stage seminoma of the testis. *BJU International, 83,* 462–468.

Cella, D. F. (1996). Quality of life outcomes: Measurement and validation. *Oncology, 10,* 233–246.

Chatterjee, R., Kottaridis, P. D., Lees, W. R., Ralph, D. J., & Goldstone, A. H. (2000). Cavernosal arterial insufficiency and erectile dysfunction in recipients of high-dose chemotherapy and total body irradiation for multiple meyloma. *Lancet, 355,* 1335–1336.

Chatterjee, R., Kottaridis, P. K., McGarrigle, H. H., & Linch, D. C. (2002). Management of erectile dysfunction by combination therapy with testosterone and sildenafil in recipients of high-dose therapy for hematological malignancies. *Bone Marrow Transplantation, 29,* 607–610.

Che, M., Tamboli, P., Ro, J., Park, D. S., Ro, J. S., Amato, R. J., et al. (2002). Bilateral testicular germ cell tumours: Twenty-year experience at M. D. Anderson Cancer Center. *Cancer, 95,* 1228–1233.

Cunsolo, A., Bragaglia, R. B., Manara, G., Poggioli, G., & Gozzetti, G. (1990). Urogenital dysfunction after abdominoperineal resection for carcinoma of the rectum. *Diseases of the Colon and Rectum, 3,* 918–922.

Danzi, M., Ferulano, G. P., Abate, S., & Califano, G. (1993). Male sexual function after abdominoperineal resection for rectal cancer. *Diseases of the Colon and Rectum, 26,* 665–668.

Dobkin, P. L., & Bradley, I. (1991). Assessment of sexual dysfunction in oncology patients: Review, critique, and suggestions. *Journal of Psychological Oncology, 9,* 43–74.

Enzlin, P., Mathieu, C., van den Bruel, A., Bosteels, J., Vanderschueren, D., & Demyttenaere, K. (2002). Sexual dysfunction in women with type 1 diabetes: A controlled study. *Diabetes Care, 25,* 672–677.

Ertekin, C. (1998). Diabetes mellitus and sexual dysfunction. *Scandinavian Journal of Sexology, 1,* 3–21.

Fedele, D., Bortolotti, A., Coscelli, C., Santeusanio, F., Chatenoud, L., Colli, E., et al. (2000). Erectile dysfunction in type 1 and type 2 diabetics in Italy: On behalf of Gruppo Italiano Studio Deficit Erettile nei Diabetici. *International Journal of Epidemiology, 29,* 524–531.

Fisch, B. M., Pickett, B., Weinberg, V., & Roach, M. (2001). Dose of radiation received by the bulb of the penis correlates with risk of impotence after three-dimensional conformal radiotherapy for prostate cancer. *Urology, 57,* 955–959.

Fokdal, L., Hoyer, M., Meldgaard, P., & von der Maase, H. (2004). Long-term bladder, colorectal, and sexual functions after radical radiotherapy for urinary bladder cancer. *Radiotherapy and Oncology: Journal of the European Society for Therapeutic Radiology and Oncology, 17,* 139–145.

Fowler, C. J., Miller, J. R., Sharief, M. K., Hussain, I. F., Stecher, V. J., & Sweeney, M. (2005). A double blind, randomised study of sildenafil citrate for erectile dysfunction in men with multiple sclerosis. *Journal of Neurology, Neurosurgery, and Psychiatry, 76,* 700–705.

Frumovitz, M., Sun, C. C., Schover, L. R., Munsell, M. F., Jhingran, A., Wharton, J. T., et al. (2005). Quality of life and sexual functioning in cervical cancer survivors. *Journal of Clinical Oncology, 30,* 7428–7436.

Ganz, P., Desmond, K., Meyerowitz, B. E., & Wyatt, G. E. (1998). Life with breast cancer: Understanding women's health-related quality of life and sexual functioning. *Journal of Clinical Oncology, 16,* 501–514.

Gianotten, W. L., Whipple, B., & Owens, A. F. (2007). Sexual activity is a cornerstone of quality of life: An Update of "The health benefits of sexual expression." In J. Kuriansky (Series Ed.) & M. S. Tepper, & A. F. Owens (Vol. Eds.), *Sex, love and psychology: sexual health: Vol. 1. Psychological foundations* (pp. 28–42). Westport, CT: Praeger.

Gritz, E. R., Wellisch, D. K., Wang, H. J., Siau, J., Landsverk, J. A., & Cosgrove, M. D. (1989). Long-term effects of testicular cancer on sexual functioning in married couples. *Cancer, 64,* 1560–1567.

Guay, A. T. (2003). Optimizing response to phosphodiesterase therapy: Impact of risk factor management. *Journal of Andrology, 24,* S59–S62.

Henson, H. K. (2002). Breast cancer and sexuality. *Sexuality and Disability, 20,* 261–275.

Howell, S. J., Radford, J. A., Smets, E. M. A., & Shalet, S. M. (2000). Fatigue, sexual function and mood following treatment for hematological malignancy: The impact of mild Leydig cell dysfunction. *British Journal of Cancer, 82,* 789–793.

Huyghe, E., Matsuda, T., & Thonneau, P. (2003). Increasing incidence of testicular cancer worldwide: A review. *Journal of Urology, 170,* 5–11.

Incrocci, L., Bosch, J. L. H. R., & Slob, A. K. (1999). Testicular prostheses: Body image and sexual functioning. *BJU International, 84,* 1043–1045.

Incrocci, L., Hop, W. C. J., Wijnmaalen, A., & Slob, A. K. (2002). Treatment outcome, body image, and sexual functioning after orchiectomy and radiotherapy for stage I-II testicular seminoma. *International Journal of Radiation Oncology, Biology, Physics, 53,* 1165–1173.

Incrocci, L., Koper, P. C. M., Hop, W. C. J., & Slob, A. K. (2001). Sildenafil citrate (Viagra) and erectile dysfunction following external-beam radiotherapy for prostate cancer: A randomized, double-blind, placebo-controlled, cross-over study. *International Journal of Radiation Oncology, Biology, Physics, 51,* 1190–1195.

Incrocci, L., Slagter, C., Slob, A. K., & Hop, W. C. J. (2006). A randomized, double-blind, placebo-controlled, cross-over study to assess the efficacy of tadalafil (Cialis®) in the treatment of erectile dysfunction following three-dimensional conformal external-beam radiotherapy for prostatic carcinoma. *International Journal of Radiation Oncology, Biology, Physics, 51,* 1190–1195.

Incrocci, L., Slob, A. K., & Levendag, P. C. (2002). Sexual (dys)function after radiotherapy for prostate cancer: A review. *International Journal of Radiation Oncology, Biology, Physics, 52,* 681–693.

Jemal, A., Siegel, R., Ward, E., Murray, T., Xu, J., Smigal, C., et al. (2006). Cancer statistics, 2006. *CA: A Cancer Journal for Clinicians, 56,* 106–130.

Jensen, P. T., Groenvold, M., Klee, M. C., Thranov, I., Petersen M. A., & Machin, D. (2003). Longitudinal study of sexual function and vaginal changes after radiotherapy for cervical cancer. *International Journal of Radiation Oncology, Biology, Physics, 56,* 937–949.

Jonker-Pool, G., van Basten, J. P., Hoekstra, H. J., van Driel, M. F., Sleijfer, D. T., Koops, H. S., et al. (1997). Sexual functioning after treatment for testicular cancer. *Cancer, 80,* 454–464.

Kendirci, M., Beijma, J., & Hellstrom, W. J. G. (2006). Update on erectile dysfunction in prostate cancer patients. *Current Opinion in Urology, 16,* 186–195.

Kinn, A. C., & Ohman, U. (1986). Bladder and sexual function after surgery for rectal cancer. *Diseases of the Colon and Rectum, 29,* 43–48.

Komisaruk, B. R., Whipple, B., Crawford, A., Liu, W. C., Kalnin, A., & Mosier, K. (2004). Brain activation during vaginocervical self-stimulation and orgasm in women with complete spinal cord injury: FMRI evidence of mediation by the vagus nerves. *Brain Research, 1024,* 77–88.

Little, F. A., & Howard, G. C. W. (1998). Sexual function following radical radiotherapy for bladder cancer. *Radiotherapy and Oncology: Journal of the European Society for Therapeutic Radiology and Oncology, 49,* 157–161.

Lynch, M. J., & Pryor, J. P. (1992). Testicular prostheses: The patient's perception. *British Journal of Urology, 70,* 420–422.

Maas, C. P., Moriya, Y., Steup, W. H., Kiebert, G. M., Kranenbarg, W. M., & van de Velde, C. J. (1998). Radical and nerve-preserving surgery for rectal cancer in the Netherlands: A prospective study on morbidity and functional outcome. *British Journal of Surgery, 85,* 92–97.

Månsson, A., Caruso, A., Capovilla, E., Colleen, S., Bassi, P., Pagano, F., et al. (2000). Quality of life after radical cystectomy and orthotopic bladder substitution: A comparison between Italian and Swedish men. *BJU International, 85,* 26–31.

McCullough, A. R. (2001). Prevention and management of erectile dysfunction following radical prostatectomy. *Urologic Clinics of North America, 28,* 613–627.

Montorsi, F., Verheyden, B., Meuleman, E., Junemann, K. P., Moncada, I., Valiquette, L., et al. (2004). Long-term safety and tolerability of tadalafil in the treatment of erectile dysfunction. *European Urology, 45,* 339–344.

Mulligan, T., & Moss, C. R. (1991). Sexuality and aging in male veterans: A cross-sectional study of interest, ability, and activity. *Archives of Sexual Behavior, 20,* 17–25.

Nazareth, I., Lewin, J., & King, M. (2001). Sexual dysfunction after treatment for testicular cancer: A systematic review. *Journal of Psychosomatic Research, 51,* 735–743.

Nesbakken, A., Nygaard, K., Bull-Njaa, T., Carlsen, E., & Eri, L. M. (2000). Bladder and sexual dysfunction after mesorectal excision for rectal cancer. *British Journal of Surgery, 87,* 206–210.

NIH Consensus Conference. (1993). Impotence: NIH Consensus Development Panel on Impotence. *Journal of the American Medical Association, 270,* 83–90.

Opjordsmoen, S., Wahere, H., Aass, N., & Fossa, S. D. (1994). Sexuality in patients treated for penile cancer: Patients' experience and doctors' judgment. *British Journal of Urology, 73,* 554–560.

Penson, D. F., McLerran, D., Feng, Z., Li, L., Albertsen, P. C., Gilliland, F. D., et al. (2005). 5-year urinary and sexual outcomes after radical prostatectomy: Results from the prostate cancer outcomes study. *Journal of Urology, 173,* 1701–1705.

Pocard, M., Zinzindohoue, F., Haab, F., Caplin, S., Parc, R., & Tiret, E. (2002). A prospective study of sexual and urinary function before and after total mesorectal excision with autonomic nerve preservation for rectal cancer. *Surgery, 131,* 368–372.

Rosen, R. C., Riley, A., Wagner, G., Osterloh, I. H., Kirkpatrick, J., & Mishra, A. (1997). The International Index of Erectile Function (IIEF). A multidimensional scale for assessment of erectile dysfunction. *Urology, 49,* 822–830.

Santangelo, M. L., Romano, G., & Sassaroli, C. (1987). Sexual function after resection for rectal cancer. *American Journal of Surgery, 154,* 502–504.

Schneider, H. J., Schneider, M., Saller, B., Petersenn, S., Uhr, M., Husemann, B., et al. (2006). Prevalence of anterior pituitary insufficiency 3 and 12 months after traumatic brain injury. *European Journal of Endocrinology, 154,* 259–265.

Schover, L. R. (1999). Counseling cancer patients about changes in sexual function. *Oncology, 11,* 1585–1590.

Schover, L. R., Evans, R. B., & von Eschenbach, A. C. (1987). Sexual rehabilitation in a cancer center: Diagnosis and outcome in 384 consultations. *Archives of Sexual Behavior, 16,* 445–446.

Schover, L. R., Gonzales, M., & von Eschenbach, A. C. (1986). Sexual and marital relationships after radiotherapy for seminoma. *Urology, 27,* 117–123.

Stanford, J. L., Feng, Z., Hamilton, A. S., Gilliland, F. D., Stephenson, R. A., Eley, J. W., et al. (2000). Urinary and sexual function after radical prostatectomy for clinically localized prostate cancer: The Prostate Cancer Outcomes Study. *Journal of the American Medical Association, 283,* 354–360.

Steineck, G., Helgason, F., Adolfsson, J., Dickman, P. W., Johansson, J. E., Norlen, B. J., et al. (2002). Scandinavian Prostatic Cancer Group Study Number 4: Quality of life after radical prostatectomy or watchful waiting. *New England Journal of Medicine, 347,* 790–796.

Tay, H. P., Juma, S., & Joseph, A. C. (1996). Psychogenic impotence in spinal cord injury patients. *Archives of Physical Medicine and Rehabilitation, 77*, 391–393.

Tinkler, S. D., Howard, G. C. W., & Kerr, G. R. (1992). Sexual morbidity following radiotherapy for germ cell tumors of the testis. *Radiotherapy and Oncology: Journal of the European Society for Therapeutic Radiology and Oncology, 25*, 207–212.

van Basten, J. P., Jonker-Pool, G., van Driel, M. F., Sleijfer, D. T., Droste, J. H., van de Wiel, H. B., et al. (1997). Sexual functioning after multimodality treatment for disseminated nonseminomatous testicular germ cell tumor. *Journal of Urology, 158*, 1411–1416.

van Basten, J. P., Koops Schraffordt, H. S., Sleijfer, D. T., Pras, E., van Driel, M. F., & Hoekstra, H. J. (1997). Current concepts about testicular cancer. *European Journal of Surgical Oncology: Journal of the European Society of Surgical Oncology and the British Association of Surgical Oncology, 23*, 354–366.

van Tulder, M. W., Aaronson, N. K., & Bruning, P. F. (1994). The quality of life of long-term survivors of Hodgkin's disease. *Annals of Oncology: Official Journal of the European Society for Medical Oncology, 5*, 153–158.

Wiegerink, D. J. H. G., Roebroeck, M. E., Donkervoort, M., Stam, H. J., & Cohen-Kettenis, P. T. (2006). Social and sexual relationships of adolescents and young adults with cerebral palsy: A review. *Clinical Rehabilitation, 20*, 1023–1031.

Windhal, T., Skeppner, E., Andersson, S. O., & Fugl-Meyer, K. S. (2004). Sexual function and satisfaction in men after laser treatment for penile carcinoma. *Journal of Urology, 172*, 648–651.

Wise, T. N. (1983). Sexual dysfunction in the medically ill. *Psychosomatics, 24*, 787–805.

Wood, R. L., & Yurdakul, L. K. (1997). Change in relationship status following traumatic brain injury. *Brain Injury, 11*, 491–501.

Wyndaele, M., & Wyndaele, J. J. (2006). Incidence, prevalence and epidemiology of spinal cord injury: What learns a worldwide literature survey? *Spinal Cord: The Official Journal of the International Medical Society of Paraplegia, 44*, 523–529.

Yang, C. C., Bowen, J. D., Kraft, G. H., Uchio, E. M., & Kromm, B. G. (2001). Physiologic studies of male sexual dysfunction in multiple sclerosis. *Multiple Sclerosis: Clinical and Laboratory Research, 7*, 249–254.

Yang, C. C., Bowen, J. R., Kraft, G. H., Uchio, E. M., & Kromm, B. G. (2000). Cortical evoked potentials of the dorsal nerve of the clitoris and female sexual dysfunction in multiple sclerosis. *Journal of Urology, 164*, 2010–2013.

Yellen, S. B., Cella, D. F., & Bonomi, A. (1993). Quality of life in people with Hodgkin's disease. *Oncology, 8*, 41–45.

Zagaja, G. P., Mhoon, D. A., Aikens, J. E., & Brendler, C. B. (2000). Sildenafil in the treatment of erectile dysfunction after radical prostatectomy. *Urology, 56*, 631–634.

Zelefsky, M. J., & Eid, J. F. (1998). Elucidating the etiology of erectile dysfunction after definitive therapy for prostatic cancer. *International Journal of Radiation Oncology, Biology, Physics, 40*, 129–133.

Zippe, C. D., Jhaveri, F. M., Klein, E. A., Kledia, S., Pasqualotto, F. F., Kedia, A., et al. (2000). Role of Viagra after radical prostatectomy. *Urology, 55*, 241–245.

Zorzon, M., Zivadinov, R., Monti Bragadin, L., Moretti, R., De Masi, R., Nasuelli, D., et al. (2001). Sexual dysfunction in multiple sclerosis: A 2-year follow-up study. *Journal of the Neurological Sciences, 187*, 1–5.

PART 11

GENDER IDENTITY DISORDERS

Part Editor: Kenneth J. Zucker

This part takes you in an entirely different direction, one which to a large extent reiterates the power of genetic and prenatal influences on how we look (sexually) and who we become (in terms of sexual/gender identity). As research continues to increase our understanding of this area, we come to realize that an endpoint as seemingly simple as our sex, while necessarily dichotomous for the purposes of procreation (at least in this stage of our evolution), represents a continuum consisting of many dimensions: the biological, the psychological, the social, and the cultural. What most of us have taken for granted has, perhaps, not been as simple and risk-free a journey as we might have assumed. Indeed, as you read the chapters on genetic sexual development and disorders of sex development, you may think at least twice about the essence of maleness and femaleness.

Important advances in the field of biosexual development have occurred over the past 50 years, incredible advances within the past 10. Yet, because variations outside the male-female dichotomy are fairly rare, and because these sometimes do not come to the attention of the professional community until adulthood, understanding how best to deal with persons afflicted with gender issues so as to ensure an "adjusted" developmental and life course process is still a work in progress. Nevertheless, given these problems, the chapters on child/adolescent and adult gender identity problems help untangle difficult findings based on heterogeneous samples, differing methodologies, and developing theoretical perspectives.

Lest we become too enthralled with our own sense of progress in this area—seeking typically Western style solutions to variations predating Euro-American culture—we have included a chapter (Chapter 15) that views gender variations from a cross-cultural perspective. Long before people turned to medicine to fix problems, to make the abnormal normal, to help the varied become less varied, cultures and societies had found ways to recognize, accept, and incorporate variation. Many such cultures are now changing, becoming more aligned with the medical models prevalent in Western societies, a process not without loss. This chapter strongly suggests how Western-centric approaches could benefit from assimilation of ideas from other cultures.

Genetics of Sexual Development and Differentiation

Eric J. N. Vilain

11

Chapter

Learning Objectives

In this chapter, we:

- Review the concept of sex and disorders of sex development.
- Review the process of sexual differentiation.
- Review genes responsible for sex determination.
- Review the role of Y and non-Y genes.
- Discuss genetic processes responsible for sexual differentiation.
- Discuss sexual differentiation of the brain.
- Discuss the genetics of sexual orientation.

"One is not born a woman, one becomes one," said Simone de Beauvoir (1949) in *The Second Sex*. From a geneticist's standpoint, it seems that during all stages of fetal development maleness is a permanent molecular fight. During the past decade, a number of genes responsible for the making of a male have been characterized. When altered or, to use a genetic terminology, mutated, these genes are responsible for "demasculinization" of fetuses carrying a male, XY, chromosomal constitution, resulting in individuals born "intersex" or females. The discovery of these sex-determining genes is the direct result of the study of patients with ambiguous genitalia, also known as "intersex" or "Disorders of Sex Development" or "DSD." These discoveries have led to a better understanding of the biological mechanisms underlying sexual development and behavior and, equally important, to a more refined and rapid molecular diagnosis of intersex conditions.

In October 2005, an international consensus conference on the management of intersexuality was held in Chicago, under the auspices of the Lawson Wilkins Pediatric Endocrine Society (United States) and the European Society for Pediatric Endocrinology. A panel of experts from diverse perspectives (surgeons, endocrinologists, psychologists, geneticists, and pediatricians) was convened to discuss various aspects of intersexuality (genetics, medical management, surgical management, psychosocial management, and outcome data). One of the main resulting proposals of this conference was to change the current nomenclature, perceived as socially harmful by patients (with the use of pejorative terms such as *hermaphrodite* or *pseudohermaphrodite*) and seen as confusing because of gender labels used in many of the diagnostic terms (i.e., with the use of male or female in the disorder's name). Intersexuality (which had a social connotation) was replaced by Disorders of Sex Development (DSD), defined as congenital conditions in which development of chromosomal, gonadal, or anatomical sex is atypical (Hughes, Houk, Ahmed, & Lee, 2006).

Intersexuality/DSD is not rare. In its traditional definition (conditions where it is impossible to distinguish whether the individual is male or female), the incidence is estimated at 1 in 4,500 births. If all minor variants of genital conformation are included in the definition of intersex, the incidence rises to close to 1%, due to the high frequency of hypospadias, an abnormal placement of the urethral opening (about 0.4%; EUROCAT Working Group, 1997; Pierik et al., 2002), and of cryptorchidism, undescended testicles (around 1% at 3 months of age; Kaleva et al., 2001). These numbers show that, although not discussed as openly as other medical conditions, intersexuality is present at a high frequency throughout the world.

Understanding DSDs from a biological perspective has been a challenge. The major cause for the slow rate of progress in this field is the tremendous heterogeneity associated with intersex conditions. More than a dozen medical diagnoses are associated with the same appearance of genitalia that taken alone gives the observer little or no clue to the underlying physiopathology. Analyzing the various causes of DSD is essential at many levels: to understand the fundamental biological events of sexual development, to better interpret long-term follow-up studies on intersex patients, and to better predict psychosexual outcomes and therefore improve the clinical management of intersex patients with DSD.

Several Sexes?

Sex is not a simple matter. In fact, sex may be defined biologically in many ways (see Sidebar 11.1). The *genotypic* sex of an individual is defined by the genetic information leading to the development of one sex or the other. Typically, chromosomal makeup determines the genotypic sex of a person. For instance, males are usually 46,XY, meaning that they have a normal number of chromosomes (46), including one X chromosome and one Y chromosome; females are typically 46,XX, carrying 46 chromosomes in each of their cells, including two X chromosomes and no Y chromosome. In a few instances, the chromosomal constitution, or karyotype, is more complex, such as in cases of mosaic individuals who carry a patchwork of XX and XY cells. In other situations, the karyotype appears to be normal, but the appearance of the individual is opposite the expectation. This disparity is caused by mutations in genes important for sex determination, thereby leading to XX males or XY females.

SIDEBAR 11.1

Definitions of Sex

- *Genotypic sex:* Defined by the genetic information leading to the development of one sex or the other, that is, chromosomal constitution (karyotype).
- *Gonadal sex:* Corresponds to the type(s) of gonad (testis, ovary) present in the individual.
- *Phenotypic sex:* Defined by the primary and secondary sexual characteristics of that individual.
- *Sex of rearing:* Denotes cultural characteristics ascribed to an individual.
- *Gender identity:* The complex result of all genetic, hormonal, and environmental factors.
- *Legal sex:* In most societies, consists only of male and female, despite the theoretically infinite spectrum of gender and sexual variations.

The *gonadal* sex of an individual corresponds to the type of gonad present in that individual, either testis or ovary. There are also rare situations in which patients, formerly known as true hermaphrodites—or patients with ovotesticular DSD under the new nomenclature—are born with both testicular and ovarian tissues. These individuals often have an internal (abdominal) testis on one side and an ovary on the other side of their body; alternatively they can have a mixed structure known as ovotestis.

The *phenotypic* sex of an individual is defined by the primary and secondary sexual characteristics of that individual. These characteristics, usually male or female, may in some instances be ambiguous. In these intersex conditions, usually detected at birth, it is impossible to visually assess whether the newborn is a boy or a girl. The labia may be masculinized, more resembling a scrotum and fused to a certain degree. The genital bud may look too big to be a normal clitoris, yet too small to be considered a typical penis.

Sex of rearing denotes the cultural characteristics that we ascribe to an individual. These characteristics include not only the physical appearance of the individual's body, but also cultural characteristics such as name and manner of dress.

Gender identity is the complex result of all the genetic, hormonal, and environmental influences discussed previously. However, despite a theoretically infinite spectrum of sexual and gender variations, the legal definition of sex offers no more than two choices in most societies: male or female.

Our purpose in this chapter is to identify and characterize the biological factors responsible for the development of an undifferentiated, bipotential—or should we say multipotential?—embryo into a human being with either a male or a female appearance. These biological factors comprise genetic and hormonal components that contribute, at varying degrees, to each individual's sex. The environmental factors are much too complex to appreciate. Their influence, while fundamentally important, is extremely difficult to study. Even in lower organisms, in which sex is principally determined by environmental variables—by the temperature of incubation of the egg for alligators or by the social rank in certain fish species—the molecular mechanisms are very poorly understood. In this chapter, the focus is on the simpler, but nonetheless complex, genetic influences on sexual development.

Defining Sex Determination

What is sex determination? This concept refers to the decision that directs, during fetal development, the orientation of the undifferentiated embryo into a sexually dimorphic individual. In mammals, this decision occurs during the development of the gonads. For instance, once the testes are formed in males, its sex is determined. This was demonstrated in the 1940s by the French physiologist, Alfred Jost, who established for the first time a modern perspective on sex determination. Before then, the most unusual theories were proposed to explain the making of men and women. Jost castrated (male and female) rabbit embryos early in their development and reimplanted them in the uterus of their mother. All the offspring appeared female at birth. The conclusion of this experiment was that the testes determined the sex of an individual. In contrast, the ovaries were not necessary to make a female phenotype at birth; they were necessary at a later time for a normal puberty and fertility, but not for the early development of normal female genitalia. Thus, if testes were present, the individual would become male; if testes were not present, the individual would become female. Following this sex-determining decision, sexual differentiation takes place, and testes produce the male hormones responsible for male sexual characteristics.

Before a certain embryonic age, human embryos are bipotential (for male or female development) at all levels of sexual differentiation, including the formation of the gonads and the differentiation of internal and external genitalia. Until the end of the seventh week of gestation, male and female gonads remain indistinguishable. At this time, the primordial germ cells (future sperm or eggs) migrate from the yolk sac to the developing gonad. Testicular formation occurs during the eighth and the beginning of the ninth week of gestation, and the male external genitalia are formed during the tenth and eleventh weeks of gestation. The ovary does not differentiate until approximately the third month of gestation (Grumbach & Conte, 1998). During the seventh week of gestation, the genital ducts remain bipotential with both Müllerian and Wolffian ducts present. In females, the Müllerian ducts will become uterus, fallopian tubes, and superior third of the vagina, while the Wolffian ducts will regress in the absence of a sufficient amount of testosterone. In males, the Wolffian ducts will form the epididymis, vas deferens, and seminal vesicles under the influence of testosterone secreted by the Leydig cells, while the Müllerian ducts will regress because of the secretion of Müllerian inhibiting substance (MIS) by the Sertoli cells.

Development of internal genitalia occurs during the third month of gestation. External genitalia remain undifferentiated until the eighth week of gestation. A urogenic slit is present, with urethral folds on either side, and lateral to this, labioscrotal swellings. Anterior to the slit is the genital tubercule. By the twelfth to fourteenth week of gestation, the urethral folds fuse completely in the midline in the male to form the scrotum. The differentiation of the male external genitalia requires the action of testosterone and its 5-α-reduced metabolite, dihydrotestosterone (DHT). While testosterone is mainly responsible for the differentiation of Wolffian ducts, DHT directs the development of the penis and scrotum, as well as the appearance of secondary sexual characteristics at puberty.

The genes involved in the formation of external and internal genitalia are well known. They code for enzymes responsible for the synthesis of testosterone, as well as for the androgen receptor on the cell surface. Mutations in these genes account for the majority of intersex situations that are reviewed later in this chapter. However, the genes involved in the initial sex determination step are still poorly understood and are under intense investigation.

Genes of Sex Determination

Two major concepts have led the quest for sex determining genes. The first one established that sex determination was equivalent to testis determination, since it is the presence of the testes that determines maleness, and their absence that determines femaleness (Jost, 1947). A genetic consequence of this concept, now verified in most mammalian species, was the assumption that a sex-determining gene responsible for the formation of the testes must therefore exist. This gene was named, before it was even discovered, TDF, for testis determining factor. The second major concept of sex determination was proposed when the karyotype of patients with Klinefelter syndrome (male 47,XXY; Jacobs & Strong, 1959) and with Turner syndrome (female 45,X; Ford, Jones, Polani, de Almeida, & Brigg, 1959) were discovered. *Turner* patients (incidence 1:2,500 live female births) typically lack one X chromosome; therefore they have a total of 45 chromosomes and are designated chromosomally as 45,X (Ford et al., 1959). They appear as females with short stature and have a delayed puberty, lack of menses, and a variety of congenital malformations including heart and kidney defects. Their ovaries are underdeveloped and composed essentially of fibrous tissue with no oocytes, which results in infertility and low levels of estrogens. *Klinefelter* patients (incidence 1:1,000) have an extra X chromosome (47,XXY; Jacobs & Strong, 1959) and present as tall males with small, dysgenetic testicles, and often exhibit a delayed puberty. Their testes are somewhat fibrous and do not contain sperm.

The identification of the chromosomal constitution of Turner and Klinefelter syndromes in 1959 showed that the Y chromosome contained a testis-determining factor (TDF). Consider that Klinefelter patients (47,XXY) appear male and Turner patients (45,X) appear female. This distinction indicates that the presence of the Y chromosome is necessary to produce a male genital phenotype, regardless of the number of X chromosomes associated with it. The presence of a Y chromosome causes the fetus to develop into a male, while the lack of a Y chromosome results in a female. In other words, in humans, it appears that the number of X chromosomes is irrelevant to sex determination. The combination of these two concepts led to the hypothesis that a sex-determining gene, TDF, had to be localized on the Y chromosome. Although the molecular era of sex determination had begun at the end of the 1950s, it took another 30 years to identify TDF, the first sex-determining gene.

The Hunt for the Male Gene

The identification of TDF was helped considerably by the study of patients affected by pathologies of sex determination. These rare disorders (about 1 in 20,000 births) have facilitated the understanding of the major biological mechanisms of sex determination. The condition was named *sex-reversed* by geneticists because the external sexual phenotype was opposite the chromosomal constitution. The gonads of such individuals are usually abnormally developed and are called dysgenetic. The variations include XX male syndrome (now named 46,XX testicular DSD), XX true hermaphroditism (now named 46,XX ovotesticular DSD), and XY females with gonadal dysgenesis.

Males who are XX have normal (male) genitalia, small testes that do not produce sperm, and no Müllerian structures, that is, no uterus or fallopian tubes. They may also present at birth with severe hypospadias or sexual ambiguity. Patients with XX ovotesticular DSD present with ambiguous genitalia and persistence of some Müllerian structures, typically on the side of the ovary, and they are defined by the presence of both ovarian and testicular tissue in their gonads. XY females with pure gonadal dysgenesis have normal female genitalia, including a normal uterus, and fibrous streak gonads in place of the ovaries. When the gonadal dysgenesis is partial, these patients may present with ambiguous genitalia at birth.

How did these rare pathologies allow the identification of TDF? In 1966, it was proposed that XX males and XX ovotesticular DSD individuals could be explained by the presence of a fragment of a Y chromosome, containing TDF displaced, or translocated in genetic terms, on one of the X chromosomes (Ferguson-Smith, 1966). The hypothesis was that an abnormal exchange of chromosomal material might have occurred between the X and the Y chromosome.

The two sex chromosomes, X and Y, are remarkable. They are very different in size and sequence, unlike all the other 22 pairs of autosomes. The Y chromosome is very small compared to the X chromosome, and it is completely different from the X chromosome except at its tip, where the two sex chromosomes are identical. This identical region is named the pseudoautosomal region and allows pairing of the X and Y chromosome at the time of cell division. Normally, there is an exchange of chromosomal material between the X and Y pseudoautosomal regions. However, should a mistake happen during this exchange, resulting in the transfer of Y-specific material to the X chromosome, and should the exchanged material contain TDF, then an X chromosome bearing TDF results; thus the XX individual develops as a male because of TDF lying on the X chromosome. Conversely, such an exchange of material could also result in a Y chromosome deleted for TDF, hence resulting in an XY individual developing as a female (see Figure 11.1).

In fact, this hypothesis has now been supported. Y material is detectable in most XX males (Ohno, 1979). As a result, the hunt for

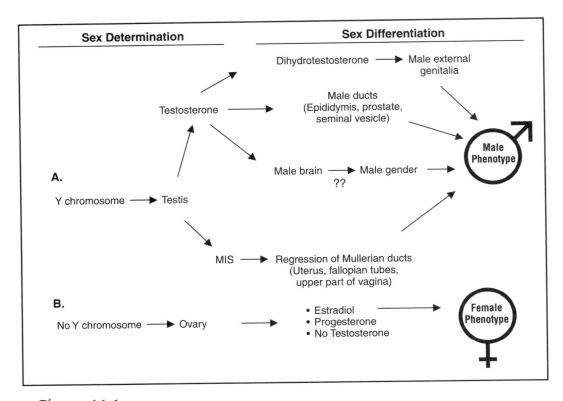

Figure 11.1

Schematic Strategy of Sexual Development in Humans

TDF could now begin, and the strategy was simple: to find the smallest region of the Y chromosome capable of inducing a male phenotype in an XX individual—this smallest region had to contain the TDF. In 1989, a very small fragment of the Y chromosome, about 35,000 base pairs, was detected on the X chromosome of 4 patients, XX males and individuals with ovotesticular DSD (Palmer et al., 1989). Within this small region, a gene, named SRY, was cloned (Sinclair et al., 1990), encoding a 204 amino acid protein with the ability to bind and bend DNA (Ferrari et al., 1992; Giese, Cox, & Grosschedl, 1992; Giese, Pagel, & Grosschedl, 1994; Harley et al., 1992). Several converging findings argued that SRY was indeed TDF. SRY protein has the biochemical properties of a factor important for gene expression, which is expected of a gene involved in an important developmental process such as sex determination (Harley et al., 1992); it is localized in the expected portion of the Y chromosome, that is, in the minimum portion of the Y chromosome capable of conferring a male phenotype to an XX individual (Sinclair et al., 1990); and its temporal profile of expression is appropriate, since the mouse Sry gene is turned on between 10.5

and 12.5 day of development, just prior to the appearance of a differentiated testis (Koopman, Munserberg, Capel, Vivian, & Lovell-Badge, 1990). The ultimate evidence that SRY was indeed TDF came from two genetic discoveries. An XX mouse transgenic for a small genomic Y chromosome fragment containing Sry was engineered. This mouse contained all the genes of a female except Sry that had then been transferred by microinjection of the egg—this mouse developed as a male. Since the only difference between a female mouse and this transgenic male mouse was the presence of Sry, this procedure demonstrated that Sry was sufficient to trigger the entire male pathway (Koopman, Gubbay, Vivian, Goodfellow, & Lovell-Badge, 1991). The other piece of evidence came from the identification of genetic mistakes—mutations—in XY females with gonadal dysgenesis. These mutations in SRY could divert the fate of the bipotential gonad of an XY fetus from testicular to ovarian tissue (Affara, Chalmers, & Ferguson-Smith, 1993; Berta et al., 1990; Brown et al., 1998; Domenice et al., 1998; Hawkins, Taylor, Berta, et al., 1992; Hawkins, Taylor, Goodfellow, et al., 1992; Jäger, Anvret, Hall, & Scherer, 1990; McElreavey, Vilain, Abbas, et al., 1992; McElreavey, Vilain, Boucekkine, et al., 1992; Müller, Schwartz, & Skakkebaek, 1992; Poulat et al., 1994; Tajima, Nakae, Shinohara, & Fujieda, 1994; Vilain, McElreavey, Jaubert, et al., 1992; Zeng et al., 1993). A change of only one base pair in the SRY gene was enough to make a female out of an XY individual, proving that SRY was the sex-determining gene TDF.

The identification of SRY as TDF in 1990 was only the beginning of an expanding field of investigations. A number of questions still remain unsolved. How does SRY work? In more specific terms, does SRY act as an activator or repressor? What controls SRY expression? What genes are controlled by SRY and what is its target? Can SRY explain all the human pathologies of sex determination? As of now, few of these questions have satisfactory answers.

We have suggested that SRY may antagonize a repressor of male-determining genes, based on the autosomal recessive pattern of inheritance of SRY-negative XX males (McElreavey, Vilain, Abbas, Herskowitz, & Fellous, 1993; Vilain, McElreavey, Herskowitz, et al., 1992). Instead of being an activator of a cascade of genes leading to male development, SRY would inhibit a repressor of male development. The end result would be identical: by inhibiting an "anti-testis" gene, SRY would ultimately lead to the formation of a male individual. However, a conceptual difference exists between SRY as an activator and SRY as an inhibitor. In the former model, the male pathway is dominant, and the female pathway would be the "default" pathway. In the latter model, the "anti-testis" gene inhibited by SRY could also be a "pro-ovary" gene. That is, an active female development pathway would actually have to be inhibited by a male gene. This latter model is supported by in vitro evidence that SRY can act as a repressor of transcription (Desclozeaux et al., 1998), as well as by the observation of dosage sensitive sex reversal in XY individuals (Arn et al., 1994; Bardoni et al., 1994). However, one report suggests that SRY may also act as an activator of transcription (Dubin & Ostrer, 1994).

SRY expression is controlled spatially and temporally very tightly. It is expressed specifically in the mouse genital ridges from days 10.5 to 12.5 (Koopman et al., 1990). In humans, expression of SRY in a variety of nongenital tissues has been noted, but its physiological significance remains elusive (Clépet et al., 1993). It is interesting to note, however, that SRY expression in the brain has been shown at the RNA level (Lahr et al., 1995) and at the protein level, in brain structures such as the substantia nigra, the mammillary bodies, and the cortex (Dewing et al., 2006). In the mouse, the expression of Sry in the substantia nigra influences the level of tyrosine hydroxylase, a key enzyme for the biosynthesis of dopamine. Whether the brain expression of SRY in the human also has a physiological relevance in terms of sexual behavior remains unknown. Control of SRY expression is also still unknown. Promoter studies have shown the existence of a GC-rich, TATA-less promoter, containing two Sp1 sites (Vilain, Fellous, McElreavey, 1992), but these studies did not demonstrate the binding of a specific transcription factor that could explain the precise regulation of SRY expression.

The target structure/site of action of SRY has also remained unclear so far. SRY contains a conserved protein motif named *HMG box* of 79 amino acids, similar to a group of nonhistone proteins that associate with DNA (Jantzen, Admon, Bell, & Tjian, 1990). The HMG box confers the ability to bind specifically to the sequences AACAAAG and AACAAT (Harley et al., 1992; Harley, Lovell-Badge, & Goodfellow, 1994; van de Wetering & Clevers, 1992; Waterman, Fisher, & Jones, 1991). SRY can also bind to DNA four-way junctions with no specific sequence requirement (Harley et al., 1994). SRY is also able to bend DNA by angles of 60 to 85 degrees, suggesting a role for SRY in the modification of chromatin structure, allowing the assembly of transcriptional regulators (Ferrari et al., 1992; Giese et al., 1992, 1994). However, no physiologically relevant target gene has been successfully identified so far.

One of the unsolved questions regarding SRY is the mechanism by which it interacts with its target, especially in the context of the existence of a large family of HMG proteins binding to similar sequences. This binding may be achieved via interaction with specific cofactors. One of these SRY cofactors may be SIP1, which contains a PDZ protein interaction domain and has been shown to interact with the last seven amino acids of SRY (Poulat et al., 1997). SRY's HMG box was also found to be a calmodulin binding domain, suggesting a possible interaction of SRY with calmodulin (Harley,

Lovell-Badge, Goodfellow, & Hextall, 1996). Finally, a variable stretch of glutamine is present in mouse Sry, but absent from its human homologue. Transgenic experiments revealed that this domain was necessary for murine Sry function, suggesting a potential interaction between the glutamine stretch and another protein in the murine system (Bowles, Cooper, Berkman, & Koopman, 1999).

Genetic studies of sex-reversed patients have shown that while SRY is present in 90% of XX testicular DSD (males) without ambiguities, it is detected in only 10% of patients with XX ovotesticular DSD and in only 10% of XX ambiguous males (McElreavey, Barbaux, Ion, & Fellous, 1995). Conversely, SRY mutations are found in only 25% of XY females with gonadal dysgenesis (McElreavey, Vilain, Abbas, et al., 1992). The variability of the phenotype observed in XX sex-reversed patients carrying SRY, from normal male to ambiguous, could be explained by differences in the pattern of X-inactivation between individuals (Abbas et al., 1993). Yet, SRY analysis is inadequate to explain the phenotype of all the patients with pathologies of sex determination. For instance, we have shown that a completely normal male phenotype could occur in an XX patient without any Y chromosome sequences including SRY (Vilain et al., 1994). This finding suggests that genes other than SRY are needed for normal male development. Identifying these other genes is the current focus of research in the field of sex determination, as such discoveries would help explain and diagnose most disorders of sexual development.

Non-Y Genes

The male development of an XX mouse transgenic for Sry (Koopman et al., 1991) showed not only that Sry was TDF, but also that all the other genes necessary for maleness had to be elsewhere than on the Y chromosome. The past 15 years have seen tremendous advances in the genetics of sex determination. New genes have been identified and have been shown to be involved in the development of the gonads. Table 11.1 summarizes all the genes currently known to be responsible for disorders of sex determination in humans. These genes can be classified into three categories.

First, genes involved in the organogenesis of the gonads are important for the development of the gonads in both sexes. They are not sex-determining per se, but if they are not functioning properly, gonads cannot develop. In humans, SF1 (Steroidogenic Factor 1) and WT1 (Wilms Tumor 1) belong to this category. Both genes are transcription factors that, when mutated, are responsible for a severe defect of gonad formation. In XY individuals, this results in a phenotype of XY female with gonadal dysgenesis. Mutations in these genes are associated with other malformations, such as adrenal defects for SF1, and kidney disorders for WT1.

Table 11.1 **Genes Involved in Human Sex Determination**

Gene	Localization	Gene Family	Putative Function	Phenotype of Mutation
SF-1	9q33	Nuclear receptor	Transcription factor	XY gonadal dysgenesis and adrenal insufficiency
WT-1	11p13	Zinc finger protein	Transcription factor	Denys-Drash and Fraiser syndromes
SRY	Yp11	HMG protein	Transcription factor	XY gonadal dysgenesis
DAX1	Xp21.3	Nuclear receptor	Transcription factor	*Duplication:* XY gonadal dysgenesis *Mutation:* Adrenal hypoplasia congenita
SOX9	17q24	HMG protein	Transcription factor	*Duplication:* XX sex reversal *Mutation:* Campomelic dysplasia with XY gonadal dysgenesis
Wnt-4	1p35	Wnt	Growth factor	*Duplication:* XY gonadal dysgenesis *Mutation*: XX sex reversal in mouse

From "Mammalian Sex Determination: From Gonads to Brain," by E. Vilain, and E. R. B. McCabe, 1998, *Molecular Genetics and Metabolism, 65,* 74–84. Adapted with permission.

Second, some genes are responsible for promoting male development, such as SRY and SOX9. Mutations in these genes result in XY gonadal dysgenesis, isolated in the case of SRY, and associated with a severe skeletal disorder (campomelic dysplasia) in the case of SOX9, or with a neuropathy in the case of Dhh.

Finally, some genes seem to antagonize male development, such as DAX1 and WNT-4. It is not entirely clear where these genes fit in the sex determination pathway. When DAX1 or WNT-4 are duplicated, and presumably expressed at a higher dosage than normal in XY individuals, the male pathway is inhibited and a female phenotype develops. Both genes are expressed preferentially in female gonads, but there is no evidence, besides their "anti-testis" role, that they are actively involved in ovarian development.

DAX1

Duplications of a region of the short arm of the X chromosome (Xp21.3) have been found in several XY females with gonadal dysgenesis (Arn et al., 1994; Bardoni et al., 1994). The shortest duplicated region of the X responsible for sex reversal was named DSS (Dosage Sensitive Sex reversal; Bardoni et al., 1994). Within DSS, DAX1, a gene also responsible when mutated for Adrenal Hypoplasia Congenita, was cloned (Guo, Burris, & McCabe, 1995; Zanaria et al., 1994). DAX1 encodes an unusual member of the nuclear hormone receptor superfamily, with a typical ligand-binding domain but a novel putative DNA-binding domain containing 3.5 repeats of 65 to 67 amino acids that may represent zinc finger structures (Zanaria et al., 1994). Although its actual target is unknown, DAX1 has been shown to bind to single-strand hairpin DNA motifs and to act as a repressor of transcription (Zazopoulos, Lalli, Stocco, & Sassone-Corsi, 1997). DAX1 expression in a mouse model is consistent with a role in sex determination. It is expressed at 11.5 days in gonads of both sexes in the mouse (Swain, Zanaria, Hacker, Lovell-Badge, & Camerino, 1996), which corresponds in males to the peak of expression of Sry and to the first signs of testis differentiation. At 12.5 days of mouse development, DAX1 is turned off in the testis, but remains on in the ovary (Swain et al., 1996), suggesting a possible role of DAX1 in ovarian formation. DAX1 could be part of a genetic cascade of successive inhibitions leading to testis formation. In addition, transgenic XY mice carrying additional copies of DAX1 develop as females, suggesting that DAX1 is involved in sex determination by antagonizing the action of Sry (Swain, Narvaez, Burgoyne, Camerino, & Lovell-Badge, 1998). DAX1 could be a switch between the male and the female pathway, activating the female pathway and inhibiting the male pathway. If SRY is present, as in normal males, DAX1 would be inhibited. Therefore, the female pathway would be turned off, but the male pathway would not be repressed by DAX1 anymore, and male development would occur. If SRY is absent, as in normal females, DAX1 would continue to activate the female pathway and inhibit the male pathway, leading to female development.

SOX9

Abnormalities in the structure of chromosome 17 have been observed in patients with campomelic dysplasia (Tommerup et al., 1993), a severe bone dysplasia in which a majority of XY patients are phenotypic females. This allowed demonstration of the role of SOX9, a member of a family of transcription factors—the SOX genes—that share the same HMG box as SRY (Foster et al., 1994; Wagner et al., 1994). Mutations of SOX9 were identified in XY females with campomelic dysplasia, demonstrating that it was part of the sex-determination pathway (Foster et al., 1994; Wagner et al., 1994). SOX9 binds to the same DNA targets as SRY in vitro (Bardoni et al., 1994; Bell et al., 1997), but, as for SRY, no physiological target of SOX9 has been clearly identified. There is, however, some evidence that this gene can regulate the transcription of Mullerian Inhibiting Substance (MIS) in association with SF1 (de Santa Barbara et al., 1998). Recently, an XX male patient was shown to carry a large duplication of chromosome 17 including SOX9 (Huang, Wang, Ning, Lamb, & Bartley, 1999). In 1994, we had already shown that it was possible to develop as a male without SRY (Vilain et al., 1994), but at the time, no viable molecular explanation existed. Now, with the data from Huang et al. (1999), we have a clear example of XX sex-reversal not caused by SRY in humans, but caused by a dysregulation of a non-Y gene, SOX9. These findings suggest that SOX9 and SRY are both activators of the male pathway, but via a series of inhibitions. We have proposed a model in which SRY would inhibit DAX1, which would in turn inhibit SOX9, an activator of testis development (Vilain & McCabe, 1998).

SF1 and WT1

Steroidogenic Factor 1 (SF1) and Wilms Tumor 1 (WT1) encode two transcription factors expressed very early in the development of the gonads (day 9 in the mouse). Both play a major role in the formation of the gonads of both sexes (Ikeda, Shen, Ingraham, & Parker, 1994; Pelletier, Bruening, Li, et al., 1991). When absent in a mouse knockout model, the observed phenotype is the absence of gonad development, associated with renal agenesis for WT-1 (Kreidberg et al., 1993), and adrenal agenesis for SF-1 (Luo, Ikeda, & Parker, 1994). In humans, mutations in WT-1 are observed in Denys-Drash and Frasier syndromes, consisting of severe renal disease and XY gonadal dysgenesis (Barbaux et al., 1997; Bardeesy, Zabel, Schmitt, & Pelletier, 1994; Pelletier, Bruening, Kashtan, et al., 1991). In addition, a mutation of SF-1 was identified in a patient with adrenal hypoplasia and XY gonadal dysgenesis (Achermann, Ito, Ito, Hindmarsh, & Jameson, 1999). These observations suggest that SF1 and WT1 are essential for the gonad development, but they are not sex determining in the sense of making a contribution toward male or female development. They appear to be important for both sexes.

Wnt-4

Wnt-4 is the only signaling molecule known to have a role in sex determination. It is a member of the Wnt family of locally acting signals. A targeted disruption of this gene in an XX mouse leads to a male phenotype (Vainio, Heikkilä, Kispert, Chin, & McMahon, 1999). Wnt-4 may therefore have a role in the development of Müllerian structures as well as in ovarian differentiation and may be the missing link between all the transcription factors presented above. As a signaling molecule, it may have a role in communicating information between the gonadal cells during development.

Sex Is Not Simple

All the sex-determining genes presented here are summarized in Table 11.1. They are undoubtedly part of a complex genetic pathway leading to gonad differentiation. These genes interact with each other via protein-DNA and protein-protein interactions. For instance, an SF1-response element was found in the DAX1 promoter (Burris, Guo, Le, & McCabe, 1995; Guo et al., 1996), and SF1 increases the expression of DAX1 (Vilain, Guo, Zhang, & McCabe, 1997). DAX1 and SF1 also interact at the protein level as part of a multiprotein complex (Ito, Yu, & Jameson, 1997). In fact, it has been demonstrated that SF-1 acts synergistically with WT-1 to upregulate MIS expression, and that this activation could be blocked by DAX1 (Nachtigal et al., 1998).

Genes of Sexual Differentiation

Most research in the field of sexual development is focused on the sex determination pathway. Many genes yet to be discovered are responsible for the proper development of the testes. In addition, very little is known about the genes involved in ovarian development. In contrast to sex determination, most genes involved in sexual differentiation are now known. The general strategy of sexual development is shown in Figure 11.1. The genes involved in sexual differentiation include all the genes encoding the enzymes for testosterone biosynthesis, the gene encoding the androgen receptor, and the genes encoding MIS and its receptor. Mutations in all these genes have been identified and are known to result in what was known as pseudohermaphroditism, a condition characterized by normally developed gonads and abnormal differentiation of internal and/or external genitalia. The term *pseudohermaphroditism* historically comes from the fact that affected patients typically have ambiguous genitalia, as is the case in true hermaphroditism, but have only one type of gonad, testis or ovary. True hermaphrodites, in contrast, have the simultaneous presence of testicular and ovarian tissue. These terms have been replaced by 46,XX DSD for female pseudohermaphroditism and 46,XY DSD for male pseudohermaphroditism.

We can distinguish two types of DSD (pseudohermaphroditism). In patients with 46,XY DSD (male pseudohermaphrodites), the presence of a normal Y chromosome, with a normal SRY, triggers a normal development of testes. The defect in sexual development occurs afterward, at the level of the production of testosterone or MIS, or more commonly, at the level of the receptor for testosterone (androgen resistance). The consequence is the development of an XY individual with normal testes who is not fully masculinized and may present either as a phenotypic female, or as intersex. In patients with 46,XX DSD (female pseudohermaphrodites), there is no Y chromosome and therefore normal formation of ovaries. But during fetal life, there is impregnation of the tissues with androgens, leading to a masculinized phenotype and ambiguous external genitalia. The source of the androgens can be maternal medications or an androgen-secreting tumor, but in the vast majority of the cases, the condition is caused by an overproduction of androgens by the fetal adrenals caused by a block in the synthesis of steroids (congenital adrenal hyperplasia or CAH). The most common intersex conditions are shown in Table 11.2.

The two most frequently encountered situations are androgen resistance (defects in the androgen receptor) and congenital adrenal hyperplasia (CAH). Mutations in the androgen receptor have been extensively studied in a large number of patients. These mutations result in a receptor that is not able to be effective (i.e., to have masculinizing effects) in the presence of testosterone or dihydrotestosterone. The diagnosis of androgen resistance by sequencing the gene for the androgen receptor has proved more precise than biochemical methods. However, the large size of the

Table 11.2 Characteristics of the Most Common Intersex Conditions

Karyotype	Diagnosis	Phenotype	Gonads	Genes
46,XY	Androgen resistance (complete)	Female external genitalia. No uterus	Testis	Androgen receptor
	Androgen resistance (partial)	Ambiguous genitalia	Testis	Androgen receptor
	Defect of testosterone biosynthesis	Ambiguous genitalia	Testis	Enzymes of testosterone synthesis pathway
	Gonadal dysgenesis	Female external genital-uterus	Streak gonad	SRY in 15% of cases
46,XX	Congenital adrenal hyperplasia	Ambiguous genitalia	Ovary	21-hydroxylase 11-hydroxylase 3-ß-hydroxysteroid dehydrogenase
	Fetal exposure to androgens (maternal tumor, androgen-containing medication)	Ambiguous genitalia	Ovary	
	Ovotesticular DSD	Ambiguous genitalia	Ovotestis	SRY in 10% of cases

gene and the large variety of mutations present in patients has hampered a systematic screening for mutations in XY females (Quigley et al., 1995).

Female pseudohermaphroditism (46,XX DSD) has been a showcase for the molecular diagnosis of intersex patients. Congenital adrenal hyperplasia (CAH) causes the vast majority of females with 46,XX DSD and accounts for most cases of ambiguous genitalia at birth. Eighty-five percent of CAH cases are caused by mutations in a gene coding for the enzyme 21-hydroxylase, essential for steroid synthesis. It is therefore relatively simple to identify the mutation responsible for CAH, when the diagnosis is suspected biochemically, through the detection of high levels of 17-hydroxyprogesterone in XX DSD patients. When a case of CAH has occurred in a family, the risk of recurrence is 25%. Molecular diagnosis allows prediction very early in pregnancy (6 weeks by chorionic villus sampling) of whether or not the fetus is affected. If the XX fetus is affected by CAH, it is possible to treat the mother early with steroids and thus prevent the appearance of ambiguous genitalia. The detection of mutations through genetic screening allows not only prediction, but also treatment in utero, of fetuses that would otherwise be born intersex (White, New, & Dupont, 1987).

Male pseudohermaphroditism (46,XY DSD) encompasses much more complex clinical situations. The appearance of the external genitalia is often ambiguous and does not contribute much to the diagnosis. A combination of endocrine and molecular investigations most often leads to the right diagnosis, the first step to better management of these patients. One possible cause for 46,XY DSD is a defect of testosterone biosynthesis, usually demonstrated by hormonal investigations and measurement of the level of precursors of testosterone. A more common cause of 46,XY DSD is an abnormal androgen receptor, resulting in androgen resistance.

There is a large variability of phenotypes of androgen resistance. The classical *complete* form is seen in patients with nonambiguous female external genitalia. They carry a Y chromosome and two testicles, producing high levels of testosterone and dihydrotestosterone that have no effect on the development of the genitalia because of defective androgen receptors on the target tissue. Partial resistance results in newborns with ambiguous genitalia. Finally, a third form of androgen resistance is seen in males with sterility. These three forms of androgen resistance are all caused by mutations in the gene encoding the androgen receptor. Androgen resistance can be diagnosed rapidly through detection of mutations in the androgen receptor gene. However, the large size of this particular gene and the vast number of different possible mutations responsible for androgen resistance have hampered this diagnostic approach.

Is There a Gonad in the Brain?

The next frontier in the field of sex determination is that of under-standing the biology of gender identity, that is, one's own percep-tion of one's sex. Gender identity is arguably the most important aspect of sex determination. Both from the basic scientific point of view and from a practical point of view for the management of DSD, understanding the biological and environmental factors that influence gender identity will certainly modify the current pat-tern of decision making for sex assignment for intersex patients. One way to get insight into the mechanisms responsible for the development of gender identity is to study the factors influencing brain sexual differentiation. Numerous and well-recognized sex-ual dimorphisms have been found in the mammalian brain, such as the sexually dimorphic nucleus of the preoptic area, the hypo-thalamic ventromedial nucleus, and the corpus callosum (Kawata, 1995). The classic view is that brain sexual differentiation is in-duced exclusively by gonadal steroids. According to this view, es-tablished by Jost in the 1940s (Jost, 1947, 1970; Jost, Vigier, Prepin, & Perchellet, 1973), mammalian sexual development (in-cluding brain sexual differentiation) is determined by testicular hormonal secretions. Hormonal control of sexual differentiation was shown to be active during brain development by exposure of female fetal guinea pigs to testosterone, resulting in a masculin-ization of their adult copulatory behavior (Phoenix, Goy, Gerall, & Young, 1959). Testosterone was shown to act, directly or via local conversion into estradiol, on brain sexual differentiation of rats (Arnold & Gorski, 1984). This hormone induces the formation of neural circuits involved in "masculine" behavior, that is, behav-iors performed more frequently by males, and it inhibits the for-mation of neural circuits responsible for "feminine" behavior. The sites and mode of action of testosterone and estradiol in the brain are well established (MacLusky & Naftolin, 1981; McEwen, 1981) and their masculinizing action has been widely demonstrated (Gorski, 1991). However, experimental evidence for exceptions to this view has since accumulated in mammals and birds. For in-stance, rat embryonic mesencephalic neurons have different characteristics when dissociated from a male or a female brain, even when harvested prior to fetal secretion of gonadal steroids (Beyer, Eusterschulte, Pilgrim, & Reisert, 1992; Beyer, Kolbinger, Froehlich, Pilgrim, & Reisert, 1992; Beyer, Pilgrim, & Reisert, 1991). Specifically, more neurons express tyrosine hydroxylase in female mesencephalon than in male, and this difference is not al-tered by sex steroids (Beyer, Eusterschulte, et al., 1992). In the zebra finch, male steroids are not entirely responsible for the sex-ually dimorphic neural song system. When females are manipu-lated to develop testicular tissue, and therefore secrete testicular hormones, they still have a feminine song circuit (Arnold, 1996; Wade, Gong, & Arnold, 1997). Such exceptions suggest that androgens and estrogens are not the only factors influencing brain sexual differentiation. Other factors may include environmental variables, which are difficult to specify, and genetic factors, which constitute a new field of investigation. Specifically, preliminary evidence now suggests that sex-determining genes themselves (such as SRY) are expressed in specific regions of the brain (Clépet et al., 1993; Guo et al., 1995; Harry, Koopman, Brennan, Graves, & Renfree, 1995; Lahr et al., 1995). This new evidence suggests that genetic influences play a role in the development of brain sexual dimorphism.

On the Topic of Genetics and Sex: Sexual Orientation

Another piece to the complex puzzle of brain sexual dimorphism is that of sexual orientation. Unlike the phenotypic sex, presence of testes or of a Y chromosome does not influence sexual orientation, which appears to be an independent outcome. Genetic studies of homosexuality have been highly controversial and publicized, and their results contradictory. In addition, obvious ethical issues come with research on the genetics of homosexuality. Finding genetic differences between "homosexual" and "heterosexual" may easily be construed as finding biological defects in lesbians and gay men, giving pseudo-scientific rationale for homophobia and discrimination. Others have argued that, to the contrary, such differences could increase the social acceptance of homosexuals by discouraging the idea of a "cure." Yet, the argument can be made that this moral dilemma should not prevent scientists from exploring genetic contributions to sexual orientation.

The first question relevant to the issue of genetics and sexual orientation was whether structural differences exist between the brains of homosexual and heterosexual individuals. LeVay (1991) showed small but significant differences, particularly in the anterior nucleus of the hypothalamus, smaller in homosexual than in heterosexual males. Despite the small number of individuals studied and the fact that all died of AIDS—a potential confounding factor that was eventually dismissed—the results of this study were generally persuasive (LeVay, 1991).

The next question to emerge was about the determinants of homosexuality: in particular, do genetic factors influence sexual orientation? Because of the involvement of a large number of social factors related to sexual orientation in humans, this question is difficult to answer. In the fruit fly, however, it has been demonstrated clearly that specific regions of the brain are important for sexual orientation, and that these regions are determined by a small number of genes. For instance, the genes "dissatisfaction," "fruitless," and "Voila" are responsible, when mutated, for a bisexual or a homosexual behavior in the fly (Balakireva, Stocker, Gendre, & Ferveur, 1998; Finley et al., 1998; Ryner et al., 1996).

Sexual orientation is obviously more complex in humans, combining social, familial, environmental, endocrine, and genetic factors. Geneticists became interested in sexual orientation when evidence began to suggest a genetic predisposition to homosexuality. In a landmark study, Bailey and Pillard (1991) showed that more than half (52%) of identical twins of homosexual men were gay, whereas only 22% of dizygotic twins and only 11% of adoptive brothers. Hamer, Hu, Magnuson, Hu, Pattatucci (1993) showed an increase in frequency of gay relatives on the maternal side of the families of homosexual men, suggesting a genetic factor on the X chromosome predisposing to homosexuality. Specifically, in this study of 40 pairs of gay brothers from families with gay maternal relatives, Hamer et al. (1993) demonstrated a significant association between their sexual orientation and genetic markers on the X chromosome, localized in the Xq28 region. A similar linkage study, performed by the same authors, has been repeated on 33 new pairs of gay brothers and has confirmed the initial findings for gay males, but not for lesbians (Hu et al., 1995). However, a recent study of 52 pairs of gay brothers by Rice, Anderson, Risch, and Ebers (1999) has been unable to replicate this association. Despite these conflicting results, a meta-analysis of all the genetic studies performed so far on humans provides support for genetic linkage to the X chromosome (Hamer, 1999).

Given the complexity of sexual orientation, it is likely to involve numerous genes, many of which are expected to be autosomal rather than sex-linked. Indeed, the modest levels of linkage that have been reported for the X chromosome can account for at most only a fraction of the overall heritability of male sexual orientation as deduced from twin studies. A genome-wide linkage scan to identify additional genetic regions contributing to variations in human sexual orientation was published recently (see Mustanski et al., 2005) and revealed some genetic association with 3 autosomal regions on 7q36, 8p12 and 10q26.

Although mounting evidence suggests that genetic factors do influence sexual orientation, precise genetic variations that might be associated with specific sexual orientations are yet a long way off.

Summary and Conclusions

Despite their complexity, the mechanisms of sexual development have been slowly deciphered during the last decade. This molecular understanding allows a new diagnostic approach to the intersex patient. The resulting molecular tools provide more rapid and more precise methods to establish a diagnosis and they allow pinpointing of the molecular variant responsible for the intersex condition.

Genetic mechanisms of sexual development demonstrate the large variability of possible sexual phenotypes and sexual behaviors present in humans. Instead of stigmatizing sexual variants, including intersex conditions and variants of sexual orientation, the genetic approach demonstrates the tremendous variability of human sexuality.

In summary, the following conclusions may be drawn:

- Evidence of DSD is present in about 1% of the population.
- Genetic and hormonal factors contribute to both the sex of the individual and his or her gender identity.
- Before the seventh week of embryonic age, human embryos are bipotential at all levels of sexual differentiation.
- A small region of the Y chromosome, named the SRY gene, is responsible for testis formation.
- Some non Y-genes appear to antagonize male development.
- Genes involved in sexual differentiation are those that encode enzymes for testosterone biosynthesis, the androgen receptor, and MIS (Mullerian Inhibiting Substance) and its receptor.
- Lack of androgen in a male fetus or, conversely, the presence of androgen in a female fetus, will result in disparity between genetic and phenotypic sex.
- Androgens, partly through conversion to estradiol, are responsible for masculinizing the brain and inducing the neural circuits of masculine behavior.
- The genetic contribution to sexual orientation remains largely unknown at this point.

References

Abbas, N., McElreavey, K., Leconiat, M., Vilain, E., Jaubert, F., Berger, R., et al. (1993). Familial case of 46,XX male and 46,XX true hermaphrodite associated with a paternal-derived SRY-bearing X chromosome. *Comptes Rendus de L Academie des Sciences. Serie III, Sciences de la Vie, 316*, 375–383.

Achermann, J. C., Ito, M., Ito, M., Hindmarsh, P. C., & Jameson, J. L. (1999). A mutation in the gene encoding steroidogenic factor-1 causes XY sex reversal and adrenal failure in humans. *Nature Genetics, 22*, 125–126.

Affara, N. A., Chalmers, I. J., & Ferguson-Smith, M. A. (1993). Analysis of the SRY gene in 22 sex-reversed XY females identifies four new point mutations in the conserved DNA binding domain. *Human Molecular Genetics, 2*, 785–789.

Arn, P., Chen, H., Tuck-Muller, C. M., Mankinen, C., Wachtel, G., Li, S., et al. (1994). SRVX, a sex reversing locus in Xp21.2. p22.11. *Human Genetics, 93*, 389–393.

Arnold, A. P. (1996). Genetically triggered sexual differentiation of brain and behavior. *Hormones and Behavior, 30*, 495–505.

Arnold, A. P., & Gorski, R. A. (1984). Gonadal steroid induction of structural sex differences in the central nervous system. *Annual Review of Neuroscience, 7,* 413–442.

Bailey, J. M., & Pillard, R. C. (1991). A genetic study of male sexual orientation. *Archives of General Psychiatry, 48*(12), 1089–1096.

Balakireva, M., Stocker, R. F., Gendre, N., & Ferveur, J. F. (1998). Voila, a new drosophila courtship variant that affects the nervous system: Behavioral, neural, and genetic characterization. *Journal of Neuroscience, 18*(11), 4335–4343.

Barbaux, S., Niaudet, P., Gubler, M. C., Grunfeld, J. P., Jaubert, F., Kuttenn, F., et al. (1997). Donor splice-site mutations in WT1 are responsible for Frasier syndrome. *Nature Genetics, 17,* 467–470.

Bardeesy, N., Zabel, B., Schmitt, K., & Pelletier, J. (1994). WT1 mutations associated with incomplete Denys-Drash syndrome define a domain predicted to behave in a dominant-negative fashion. *Genomics, 21,* 663–664.

Bardoni, B., Zanaria, F., Guioli, S., Floridia, G., Worley, K. C., Tonini, G., et al. (1994). A dosage sensitive locus at chromosome Xp21 is involved in male to female sex reversal. *Nature Genetics, 7,* 497–501.

Bell, D. M., Leung, K. K., Wheatley, S. C., Ng, L. J., Zhou, S., Ling, K. W., et al. (1997). SOX9 directly regulates the type-II collagen gene. *Nature Genetics, 16,* 174–178.

Berta, P., Hawkins, J. R., Sinclair, A. H., Taylor, A., Griffiths, B., Goodfellow, P. N., et al. (1990). Genetic evidence equating, SRY and the testis-determining factor. *Nature, 348,* 448–450.

Beyer, C., Eusterschulte, B., Pilgrim, C., & Reisert, I. (1992). Sex steroids do not alter sex differences in tyrosine hydroxylase activity of dopaminergic neurons in vitro. *Cell and Tissue Research, 270,* 547–552.

Beyer, C., Kolbinger, W., Froehlich, U., Pilgrim, C., & Reisert, I. (1992). Sex differences of hypothalamic prolactin cells develop independently of the presence of sex steroids. *Brain Research, 593,* 253–256.

Beyer, C., Pilgrim, C., & Reisert, I. (1991). Dopamine content and metabolism in mesencephalic and diencephalic cell cultures: Sex differences and effects of sex steroids. *Journal of Neuroscience: Official Journal of the Society for Neuroscience, 11,* 1325–1333.

Bowles, J., Cooper, L., Berkman, J., & Koopman, P. (1999). SRY requires a CAG repeat domain for male sex determination in Mus musculus. *Nature Genetics, 22,* 405–408.

Brown, S., Yu, C., Lanzano, P., Heller, D., Thomas, L., Warburton, D., et al. (1998). A de novo mutation (Gln2Stop) at the 5′ end of the SRY gene leads to sex reversal with partial ovarian function. *American Journal of Human Genetics, 62,* 189–192.

Burris, T. P., Guo, W., Le, T., & McCabe, E. R. B. (1995). Identification of a putative steroidogenic factor-1 response element in the DAX-1 promoter. *Biochemical and Biophysical Research Communications, 214,* 576–581.

Clépet, C., Schafer, A. J., Sinclair, A. H., Palmer, M. S., Lovell-Badge, R., & Goodfellow, P. N. (1993). The human SRY transcript. *Human Molecular Genetics, 2,* 2007–2012.

de Beauvoir, S. (1949). *Le deuxième sexe* [The second sex]. Paris: Gallimard.

de Santa Barbara, P., Bonneaud, N., Boizet, B., Desclozeaux, M., Moniot, B., Sudbeck, P., et al. (1998). Direct interaction of SRY-related protein SOX9 and steroidogenic factor 1 regulates transcription of the human anti-Müllerian hormone gene. *Molecular and Cellular Biology, 18,* 6653–6665.

Desclozeaux, M., Poulat, F., de Santa Barbara, P., Capony, J. P., Turowski, P., Jay, P., et al. (1998). Phosphorylation of an N-terminal motif enhances DNA-binding activity of the human SRY protein. *Journal of Biological Chemistry, 273,* 7988–7995.

Dewing, P., Chiang, C., Sinchak, K., Sim, H., Chesselet, M. F., Micevych, P., et al. (2006). Direct regulation of adult brain function by the male-specific factor SRY. *Current Biology, 16*(4), 415–420.

Domenice, S., Yumie Nishi, M., Correia Billerbeck, A. E., Latronico, A. C., Aparecida Medeiros, M., et al. (1998). A novel missense mutation (S18N) in the 5′ non-HMG box region of the SRY gene in a patient with partial gonadal dysgenesis and his normal male relatives. *Human Genetics, 102,* 213–215.

Dubin, R. A., & Ostrer, H. (1994). SRY is a transcriptional activator. *Molecular Endocrinology, 8,* 1182–1192.

EUROCAT Working Group. (1997). 15 years of surveillance of congenital anomalies in Europe 1980–1994 (Report 7). In *Scientific Institute of Public Health-Louis Pasteur.* Brussels, Belgium.

Ferguson-Smith, M. A. (1966). X-Y chromosomal interchange in the aetiology of true hermaphroditism and of XX Klinefelter's syndrome. *Lancet II,* 475–476.

Ferrari, S., Harley, V. R., Pontiggia, A., Goodfellow, P. N., Lovell-Badge, R., & Bianchi, M. E. (1992). SRY, like HMG1, recognizes sharp angles in DNA. *EMBO Journal, 11,* 4497–4506.

Finley, K. D., Edeen, P. T., Foss, M., Gross, E., Ghbeish, N., Palmer, R. H., et al. (1998). Dissatisfaction encodes a tailless-like nuclear receptor expressed in a subset of CNS neurons controlling drosophila sexual behavior. *Neuron, 21*(6), 1363–1374.

Ford, C. E., Jones, K. W., Polani, P. E., de Almeida, J. C., & Brigg, J. H. (1959). A sex chromosome anomaly in a case of gonadal dysgenesis (Turner syndrome). *Lancet II,* 711–713.

Foster, J. W., Dominguez-Steglich, M. A., Guili, S., Kowk, G., Weller, P. A., Stefanovic, M., et al. (1994). Campomelic dysplasia and autosomal sex reversal caused by mutations in an SRY-related gene. *Nature, 372,* 525–529.

Giese, K., Cox, J., & Grosschedl, R. (1992). The HMG domain of lymphoid enhancer factor 1 bends, D. N. A., & facilitates assembly of functional nucleoprotein structures. *Cell, 69,* 185–195.

Giese, K., Pagel, J., & Grosschedl, R. (1994). Distinct DNA-binding properties of the high mobility group domain of murine and human SRY sex-determining factors. *Proceedings of the National Academy of Sciences of the United States of America, 91,* 3368–3372.

Gorski, R. (1991). Sexual differentiation of the endocrine brain and its control. In M. Motta (Ed.), *Brain endocrinology* (2nd ed., pp. 71–104). New York: Raven Press.

Grumbach, M. M., & Conte, F. A. (1998). Disorders of sex differentiation. In D. Wilson, D. W. Foster, H. M. Kronenberg, & P. R. Larsen (Eds.), *Williams textbook of endocrinology* (9th ed.). Philadelphia: Saunders.

Guo, W., Burris, T. P., & McCabe, E. R. B. (1995). Expression of DAX-1, the gene responsible for X-linked adrenal hypoplasia congenita and hypogonadotropic hypogonadism, in the hypothalamic-pituitary-adrenal/gonadal axis. *Biochemical and Molecular Medicine, 56,* 8–13.

Guo, W., Burris, T. P., Zhang, Y. H., Huang, B. L., Mason, J., Copeland, K. C., et al. (1996). Genomic sequence of the DAX1 gene: An orphan nuclear receptor responsible for X-linked adrenal hypoplasia congenita and hypogonadotropic hypogonadism. *Journal of Clinical Endocrinology and Metabolism, 81,* 2481–2486.

Hamer, D. H. (1999). Genetics and male sexual orientation. *Science, 285,* 803.

Hamer, D. H., Hu, S., Magnuson, V. L., Hu, N., & Pattatucci, A. M. (1993). A linkage between DNA markers on the X chromosome and male sexual orientation. *Science, 261*(5119), 321–327.

Harley, V. R., Jackson, D. I., Hextall, P. J., Hawkins, J. R., Berkovitz, G. D., Sockanathan, S., et al. (1992). DNA binding activity of recombinant SRY from normal males and XY females. *Science, 255,* 453–455.

Harley, V. R., Lovell-Badge, R., & Goodfellow, P. N. (1994). Definition of a consensus DNA binding site for SRY. *Nucleic Acids Research, 22,* 1500–1501.

Harley, V. R., Lovell-Badge, R., Goodfellow, P. N., & Hextall, P. J. (1996). The HMG box of SRY is a calmodulin binding domain. *FEBS Letters, 391,* 24–28.

Harry, J. L., Koopman, P., Brennan, F. E., Graves, J. A., & Renfree, M. B. (1995). Widespread expression of the testis-determining gene SRY in a marsupial. *Nature Genetics, 11,* 347–349.

Hawkins, J. R., Taylor, A., Berta, P., Levilliers, J., Van der Auwera, B., & Goodfellow, P. N. (1992). Mutational analysis of SRY: Nonsense and missense mutations in XY sex reversal. *Human Genetics, 88,* 471–474.

Hawkins, J. R., Taylor, A., Goodfellow, P. N., Migeon, C. J., Smith, K. D., & Berkovitz, G. D. (1992). Evidence for increased prevalence of SRY mutations in XY females with complete rather than partial gonadal dysgenesis. *American Journal of Human Genetics, 51,* 979–984.

Hu, S., Pattatucci, A. M., Patterson, C., Li, L., Fulker, D. W., Cherny, S. S., et al. (1995). Linkage between sexual orientation and chromosome Xq28 in males but not in females. *Nature Genetics, 11*(3), 248–256.

Huang, B., Wang, S., Ning, Y., Lamb, A. N., & Bartley, J. (1999, October). Autosomal XX sex reversal caused by duplication of SOX9. Proceedings of the 49th meeting of the American Society of Human Genetics, San Francisco. *American Journal of Human Genetics, 65,* A6.

Hughes, I. A., Houk, C., Ahmed, S. F., & Lee, P. A. (2006). LWPES Consensus Group; ESPE Consensus Group: Consensus statement on management of intersex disorders. *Archives of Disease in Childhood, 91*(7), 554–563.

Ikeda, Y., Shen, W.-H., Ingraham, H. A., & Parker, K. L. (1994). Developmental expression of mouse steroidogenic factor-1, an essential regulator of the steroid hydroxylases. *Molecular Endocrinology, 8,* 654–662.

Ito, M., Yu, R., & Jameson, J. L. (1997). DAX-1 inhibits SF-1-mediated transactivation via a carboxy-terminal domain that is deleted in adrenal hypoplasia congenita. *Molecular and Cellular Biology, 17,* 1476–1483.

Jacobs, P. A., & Strong, J. A. (1959). A case of human DSD having a possible XXY sex-determining mechanism. *Nature, 183,* 302–303.

Jäger, R. J., Anvret, M., Hall, K., & Scherer, G. (1990). A human XY female with frame shift mutation in the candidate sex determining gene, SRY. *Nature, 348,* 452–454.

Jantzen, H. M., Admon, A., Bell, S. P., & Tjian, R. (1990). Nucleolar transcription factor hUBF contains a DNA-binding motif with homology to HMG proteins. *Nature, 344,* 830–836.

Jost, A. (1947). Recherches sur la différenciation sexuelle de l'embryon de lapin: III. Rôle des gonades foetales dans la différenciation sexuelle somatique. *Archives d'anatomie microscopique et de morphologie expérimentale, 36*, 271–315.

Jost A. (1970). Hormonal factors in the sex differentiation of the mammalian foetus. *Philosophical Transactions of the Royal Society: B. Biological Sciences, 259*, 119–130.

Jost, A., Vigier, B., & Prepin, J., & Perchellet, J. P. (1973). Studies on sex differentiation in mammals. *Recent Progress in Hormonal Research, 29*, 1–41.

Kaleva, M., Virtanen, H., Haavisto, A. M., Main, K., Skakkebaek, N. E., & Toppari, J. (2001). Incidence of cryptorchidism in Finnish boys. *Hormone Research, 55*, 54.

Kawata M. (1995). Roles of steroid hormones and their receptors in structural organization in the nervous system. *Neuroscience Research, 24*, 1–46.

Koopman, P., Gubbay, J., Vivian, N., Goodfellow, P. N., & Lovell-Badge, R. (1991). Male development of chromosomally female mice transgenic for SRY. *Nature, 351*, 117–121.

Koopman, P., Munserberg, A., Capel, B., Vivian, N., & Lovell-Badge, R. (1990). Expression of a candidate sex-determining gene during mouse testis differentiation. *Nature, 348*, 450–452.

Kreidberg, J. A., Sariola, H., Loring, J. M., Maeda, M., Pelletier, J., Housman, D., et al. (1993). WT-1 is required for early kidney development. *Cell, 74*, 679–691.

Lahr, G., Maxson, S. C., Mayer, A., Just, W., Pilgrim, C., & Reisert, I. (1995). Transcription of the Y chromosomal gene SRY in adult mouse brain. *Molecular Brain Research, 33*, 179–182.

LeVay, S. (1991). A difference in hypothalamic structure between heterosexual and homosexual men. *Science, 253*, 1034–1037.

Luo, X., Ikeda, Y., & Parker, K. L. (1994). A cell-specific nuclear receptor is essential for adrenal and gonadal development and sexual differentiation. *Cell, 77*, 481–490.

MacLusky, N. J., & Naftolin, F. (1981). Sexual differentiation of the central nervous system. *Science, 211*, 1294–1303.

McElreavey, K., Barbaux, S., Ion, A., & Fellous, M. (1995). The genetic basis of murine and human sex determination: A review. *Heredity, 75*, 599–611.

McElreavey, K., Vilain, E., Abbas, N., Costa, J.-M., Souleyreau, N., Kucheria, K., et al. (1992). XY sex-reversal associated with a deletion 5' to the SRY HMG-box in the testis-determining-region. *Proceedings of the National Academy of Sciences of the United States of America, 89*, 11016–11020.

McElreavey, K., Vilain, E., Abbas, N., Herskowitz, I., & Fellous, M. (1993). A regulatory cascade hypothesis for mammalian sex determination: SRY represses a negative regulator of male development. *Proceedings of the National Academy of Sciences of the United States of America, 90*, 3368–3372.

McElreavey, K., Vilain, E., Boucekkine, C., Vidaud, M., Jaubert, F., Richaud, F., et al. (1992). XY sex reversal associated with a nonsense mutation in SRY. *Genomics, 13*, 838–840.

McEwen, B. S. (1981). Neural gonadal steroid actions. *Science, 211*, 1303–1311.

Müller, J., Schwartz, M., & Skakkebaek, N. E. (1992). Analysis of the sex determining region of the Y chromosome (SRY) in sex reversed patients: Point mutation in SRY causing sex reversion in a 46,XY female. *Journal of Clinical Endocrinology and Metabolism, 75*, 331–333.

Mustanski, B. S., Dupree, M. G., Nievergelt, C. M., Bocklandt, S., Schork, N. J., & Hamer, D. H. (2005). A genomewide scan of male sexual orientation. *Human Genetics, 116*(4), 272–278.

Nachtigal, M. W., Hirokawa, Y., Enyeart-VanHouten, D. L., Flanagan, J. N., Hammer, G. D., Ingraham, H. A., et al. (1998). Wilms' tumor 1 and Dax-1 modulate the orphan nuclear receptor SF-1 in sex-specific gene expression. *Cell, 93*, 445–454.

Ohno, S. (1979). *Major sex-determining genes*. New York: Springer Verlag.

Palmer, M. S., Sinclair, A. H., Berta, P., Ellis, N. A., Goodfellow, P. N., Abbas, N. E., et al. (1989). Genetic evidence that ZFY is not the testis-determining factor. *Nature, 342*, 937–939.

Pelletier, J., Bruening, W., Kashtan, C. E., Mauer, S. M., Manivel, J. C., Striegel, J. E., et al. (1991). Germline mutations in the Wilms' tumor suppressor gene are associated with abnormal urogenital development in Denys-Drash syndrome. *Cell, 67*, 437–447.

Pelletier, J., Bruening, W., Li, F. P., Glaser, T., Haber, D. A., & Housman, D. (1991). WT1 mutations contribute to abnormal genital system development and hereditary Wilm's tumor. *Nature, 353*, 431–434.

Phoenix, C. H., Goy, R. W., Gerall, A. A., & Young, W. C. (1959). Organizing action of prenatally administered testosterone propionate on the tissues mediating mating behavior in the female guinea pig. *Endocrinology, 65*, 369–382.

Pierik, F. H., Burdof, A., Nijman, J. M. R., de Muinck Keizer-Schrama, S. M. P. F., Juttmann, R. E., & Weber, R. F. A. (2002). A high hypospadias rate in The Netherlands. *Human Reproduction, 17*, 1112–1115.

Poulat, F., de Santa Barbara, P., Desclozeaux, M., Soullier, S., Moniot, B., Bonneaud, N., et al. (1997). The human testis determining factor SRY binds a nuclear factor containing PDZ protein interaction domains. *Journal of Biological Chemistry, 272,* 7167–7172.

Poulat, F., Soullier, S., Goze, C., Heitz, F., Calas, B., & Berta, P. (1994). Description and functional implications of a novel mutation in the sex-determining gene SRY. *Human Mutation, 3,* 200–204.

Quigley, C. A., De Bellis, A., Marschke, K. B., el-Awady, M. K., Wilson, E. M., & French, F. S. (1995). Androgen receptor defects: Historical, clinical, and molecular. *Endocrine Reviews, 16,* 271–321.

Rice, G., Anderson, C., Risch, N., & Ebers, G. (1999). Male homosexuality: Absence of linkage to microsatellite markers at Xq28. *Science, 284,* 665–667.

Ryner, L. C., Goodwin, S. F., Castrillon, D. H., Anand, A., Villella, A., Baker, B. S., et al. (1996). Control of male sexual behavior and sexual orientation. In drosophila by the fruitless gene. *Cell, 87*(6), 1079–1089.

Sinclair, A. H., Berta, P., Palmer, M. S., Hawkins, J. R., Griffiths, B. L., Smith, M. J., et al. (1990). A gene from the human sex-determining region encodes a protein with homology to a conserved DNA binding motif. *Nature, 346,* 240–244.

Swain, A., Narvaez, V., Burgoyne, P., Camerino, G., & Lovell-Badge, R. (1998). DAX1 antagonizes SRY action in mammalian sex determination. *Nature, 391,* 761–767.

Swain, A., Zanaria, E., Hacker, A., Lovell-Badge, R., & Camerino, G. (1996). Mouse DAX1 expression is consistent with a role in sex determination as well as in adrenal and hypothalamus function. *Nature Genetics, 12,* 404–409.

Tajima, J., Nakae, J., Shinohara, N., & Fujieda, K. (1994). A novel mutation localized in the 3' non-HMG box region of the SRY gene in 46,XY gonadal dysgenesis. *Human Molecular Genetics, 3,* 1187–1189.

Tommerup, N., Schempp, W., Meinecke, P., Pedersen, S., Bolund, L., Brandt, C., et al. (1993). Assignment of an autosomal sex reversal locus (SRA1) and campomelic dysplasia (CMPD1) to 17q24.3-q25.1. *Nature Genetics, 4,* 170–174.

Vainio, S., Heikkilä, M., Kispert, A., Chin, N., & McMahon, A. P. (1999). Female development in mammals is regulated by Wnt-4 signaling. *Nature, 397,* 405–409.

van de Wetering, M., & Clevers, H. (1992). Sequence-specific interaction of the HMG box proteins TCF-1 and SRY occurs within the minor groove of a Watson-Crick double helix. *EMBO Journal, 11,* 3039–3044.

Vilain, E., Fellous, M., & McElreavey, K. (1992). Characterization and sequence of the 5'-flanking region of the human testis determining factor SRY. *Methods in Molecular and Cellular Biology, 3,* 128–134.

Vilain, E., Guo, W., Zhang, Y. H., & McCabe, E. R. (1997). DAX1 gene expression upregulated by steroidogenic factor 1 in an adrenocortical carcinoma cell line. *Biochemical and Molecular Medicine, 61,* 1–8.

Vilain, E., Lefiblec, B., Morichon-Delvallez, N., Brauner, R., Dommergues, M., Dumez, Y., et al. (1994). SRY-negative XX fetus with complete male phenotype. *Lancet II, 343,* 240–241.

Vilain, E., & McCabe, E. R. B. (1998). Mammalian sex determination: From gonads to brain. *Molecular Genetics and Metabolism, 65,* 74–84.

Vilain, E., McElreavey, K., Herskowitz, I., & Fellous, M. (1992). La détermination du sexe: Faits et nouveaux concepts. *Médecine/Sciences, 8,* I–VII.

Vilain, E., McElreavey, K. D., Jaubert, F., Raymond, J.-P., Richaud, F., & Fellous, M. (1992). Familial case with sequence variant in the testis-determining region associated with two sex phenotypes. *American Journal of Human Genetics, 50,* 1008–1011.

Wade, J., & Arnold, A. P. (1992). Functional testicular tissue does not masculinize development of the zebra finch song system. *Proceedings of the National Academy of Sciences of the United States of America, 93,* 5264–5268.

Wade, J., Gong, A., & Arnold, A. P. (1997). Effects of embryonic estrogen on differentiation of the gonads and secondary sexual characteristics of male zebra finches. *Journal of Experimental Zoology, 278,* 405–411.

Wagner, T., Wirth, J., Meyer, J., Zabel, B., Held, M., Zimmer, J., et al. (1994). Autosomal sex reversal and campomelic dysplasia are caused by mutations in and around the SRY-related gene SOX9. *Cell, 79,* 1111–1120.

Waterman, M. L., Fischer, W. H., & Jones, K. A. (1991). A thymus-specific member of the HMG protein family regulates the human T cell receptor C alpha enhancer. *Genes and Development, 5,* 656–669.

White, P. C., New, M. I., & Dupont, B. (1987). Congenital adrenal hyperplasia. *New England Journal of Medicine, 316,* 1519–1524.

Zanaria, E., Muscatelli, F., Bardoni, B., Strom, T. M., Guioli, S., Guo, W., et al. (1994). An unusual member of the nuclear hormone receptor superfamily responsible for X-linked adrenal hypoplasia congenita. *Nature, 372,* 635–641.

Zazopoulos, E., Lalli, E., Stocco, D. M., & Sassone-Corsi, P. (1997). DNA binding and transcriptional repression by DAX-1 blocks steroidogenesis. *Nature, 390,* 311–315.

Zeng, Y. T., Ren, Z. R., Zhang, M. L., Huang, Y., Zeng, F. Y., & Huang, S. Z. (1993). A new de novo mutation (A113T) in HMG box of the SRY gene leads to XY gonadal dysgenesis. *Journal of Medical Genetics, 30,* 655–657.

Disorders of Sex Development and Atypical Sex Differentiation

Vickie Pasterski

Learning Objectives

In this chapter, we review:

- Typical sex differentiation.
- Behavioral effects of gonadal steroids.
- A changing nomenclature around disorders of sex development.
- 46,XY disorders of sex development.
- 45,XY disorders of sex development.
- Chromosomal anomaly in disorders of sex development.
- Clinical management of disorders of sex development.

Gender development involves complex physiological, psychological, and psychosocial processes. This cascade of events progresses from the fertilization of an egg to a newborn baby who is either male or female and ultimately to an adult with a gender identity, gender-role behavior, and sexual orientation. If development proceeds typically, the individual differentiates gender-related characteristics that are in alignment with both genotypic (i.e., sex chromosomes) and phenotypic (i.e., external genitalia) sex. If development does not proceed typically, as with disorders of sex development (DSD),* there is misalignment of genotypic and phenotypic sex often resulting in physical ambiguity and a multitude of variation in gender identity, gender role behavior, and sexual orientation. This chapter addresses sex differentiation as it occurs in DSD, as well as etiologies, physiological presentations, clinical management, and psychological outcomes.

Typical Sexual Differentiation

Sex differentiation refers to the physiological component of gender development that takes place beginning very early prenatally. The complete process of sex determination and differentiation involves a series of sequential events and is considered to occur as specific development within four stages:

1. *Chromosomal sex:* Genetic material including sex chromosomes is contributed from two parents. The female parent contributes the female sex chromosome, X, the male parent contributes either the female sex chromosome, X, or the male chromosome, Y, thus determining the genotypic sex of the fetus: 46,XX female or 46,XY male.

2. *Gonadal sex (sex determination):* Genetic males and females begin with the same bipotential gonadal structures. The presence of the testis-determining gene SRY on the Y chromosome determines gonadal sex of an embryo by directing the development of the bipotential embryonic gonad into testes (see Figure 12.1). Without the influence of the sex-determining gene, the embryonic gonad will differentiate as the corresponding female reproductive structure, or ovaries.

3. *Differentiation of external and internal genitalia:* The gonadal sex of a fetus directs the differentiation of external genitalia and internal reproductive structures (i.e., phenotypic sex). Testosterone, along with the by-product dyhydrotestosterone (DHT), secreted by the testes directs the development of the bipotential genital tubercle, genital swellings, and

---

*Until very recently, the term *intersex* was used to generally describe conditions involving genital ambiguity or genotypic and phenotypic incongruity. However, in the most recent consensus statement on management of intersex disorders (see Hughes et al., 2006), the proposal was made to move away from using the term intersex as it was perceived to be pejorative by patients and possibly confusing to practitioners and parents. The term *disorders of sex development* should now be used to refer to congenital conditions in which development of chromosomal, gonadal, or anatomical sex is atypical (Hughes et al., 2006).

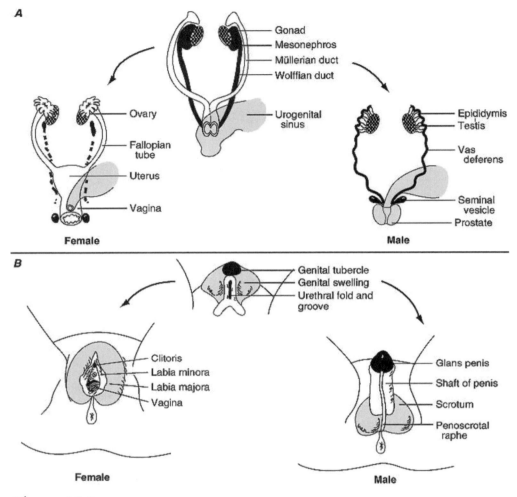

Figure 12.1

Sex Determination. Sexual differentiation of the internal reproductive tract (A) and the external genitalia (B). Males and females begin with the same bipotential structures (center A and center B). Development of testes, directed by the testis-determining factor SRY on the Y chromosome, results in the production of Müllerian Inhibiting Substance (MIS) and testosterone (T). MIS causes the female reproductive structures (Müllerian ducts) to regress, while T directs the development of the male reproductive structures (Wolffian ducts). Both T, and its by-product dyhydrotestosterone (DHT), are responsible for the development of the bipotential genital structures as male genitalia. Female genitalia will differentiate: (a) in the absence of T as in normal female development; (b) if T fails to convert to DHT as with 5 α-RD-2; or (c) as a result of androgen receptor failure as with AIS.

Source: Harrison's Principles of Internal Medicine, fourteenth edition, A. Fauci, E. Braunwald, K. Isselbacher, J. Wilson, J. Martin, D. Kasper, et al., (Eds.), 1998, New York: McGraw-Hill. Copyright 1998 by McGraw-Hill. Reprinted with permission.

urethral fold into a scrotum and penis (see Figure 12.2), producing the male phenotype. In the absence of testosterone, the same genital structures will develop into labia and clitoris, the female phenotype. Internally, Müllerian Inhibiting Substance (MIS) secreted by the testes will direct the development of male (Wolffian) reproductive structures and cause the female (Müllerian) reproductive structures to regress. The reverse occurs in the absence of testosterone (i.e., Wolffian structures regress and Müllerian structures develop). Differentiation of the external genitalia and the internal reproductive structures takes place beginning in week 7 of gestation.

4. *Secondary sexual differentiation:* The final stage of sex differentiation occurs when hormones produced by the gonads further direct the development of the full complement of secondary sex characteristics at puberty. Such characteristics include breast growth and menarche in girls and increases in body hair and muscle mass as well as penile and testicular growth in boys. Sexual reproduction becomes possible at this stage.

In this sequence of events, it is clear that the impact of sex chromosomes on differentiation is indirect. While genetic sex directs the development of the bipotential gonad, the male phenotype is strictly determined by gonadal hormones. The female phenotype is considered to be the "default" pathway in that the differentiation of female somatic sex structures is independent of gonadal hormones and can take place even in the absence of ovaries (see Grumbach, Hughes, & Conte, 2003). Errors occurring at any stage in this cascade may result in ambiguity of the external

Figure 12.2

Ambiguity of External Genitalia. Example of genital ambiguity in a 40-day-old, 46,XX female infant with congenital adrenal hyperplasia. The clitoris is enlarged (clitoromegaly) and the labia majora have fused forming a labioscrotal sac.

Photograph courtesy of Ira Shah. Reprinted with permission.

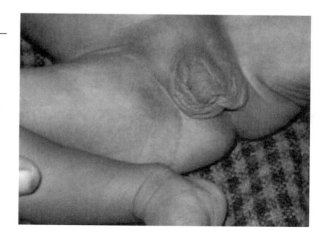

genitalia (see Figure 12.2) and/or incomplete or malformed internal reproductive structures.

In essence, ambiguity of the external genitalia at birth caused by errors in sex determination/differentiation is indicative of hormonal anomaly, whatever the cause. Given that hormones that masculinize the genitalia also masculinize and defeminize certain sex-dimorphic brain structures and behaviors (see Hines, 2004), assessments and, indeed, gender assignment, are quite concerned with concentrations of gonadal hormones during critical periods of fetal development. Decisions about gender assignment are largely informed by two sources in particular: (1) by experimental work on the development of sex-dimorphic neural and behavioral characteristics in mammalian species; and (2) by outcomes in previous clinical DSD cases with a similar diagnosis or presentation. Historically, the primary focus of investigations concerning the development of sex-dimorphic characteristics has centered on the effects of gonadal steroids; though, current research trends have seen a great increase in studies identifying specific gene mutations involved in various disruptions of sex determination and differentiation.

Behavioral Effects of Gonadal Steroids

Effects of gonadal steroids are not limited to the differentiation of internal and external somatic sex structures. The mammalian brain appears also to be bipotential and develops in the masculine or feminine direction under the influence of gonadal steroids (see Hines, 1998). The majority of knowledge about specific mechanisms of action of these hormones has come from studies of rodents and nonhuman primates. Rodents, for example, show sex differences in reproductive behaviors as well as in play behaviors, activity level, aggressive behavior, and maze learning, and these behaviors can be experimentally manipulated by altering androgens in the prenatal or early postnatal period (Collaer & Hines, 1995; Goy & McEwen, 1980; Hines & Gorski, 1985). Genetically female rats treated early postnatally* with testosterone show male-typical reproductive behaviors such as mounting and fail to show the female-typical sexual receptivity stance, lordosis. Likewise, a male rodent castrated at birth will show lordosis in re-

---

*Because of differences in gestational periods, early *postnatal* effects in rodents are analogous to *prenatal* effects in humans.

sponse to treatment with estradiol and progesterone and will not mount sexually receptive females (Goy & McEwen, 1980). These effects have also been demonstrated in other rodent species including mice, hamsters, gerbils, and guinea pigs, and in nonhuman primates including rhesus macaques (Hines, 1982).

Some sexually dimorphic behaviors in humans also appear to be influenced by hormones during early life. Behavioral outcomes related to prenatal androgen exposure have been well documented for toy, activity, and playmate preferences in children (Berenbaum & Hines, 1992; Dittmann, Kappes, Kappes, Börger, Stegner, et al., 1990; Ehrhardt & Baker, 1974; Hines & Kaufman, 1994; Pasterski et al., 2005; Pasterski et al., 2007; Slijper, 1984; Zucker et al., 1996), as well as for erotic preferences in adolescence/adulthood (Dittmann, Kappes, Kappes, Börger, Stegner, et al., 1990; Hines, Brook, & Conway, 2004; Money & Schwartz, 1976; Zucker et al., 1996).

Because it is unethical to administer hormones to developing human fetuses for experimental purposes, the majority of evidence regarding the effects of androgens on sex dimorphic behaviors in humans has come from studies of individuals having prenatal hormonal abnormalities due either to endocrinopathies (e.g., DSD) or to the administration of exogenous hormones as a medical treatment (Berenbaum & Hines, 1992; Berenbaum & Resnick, 1997; Dittmann, Kappes, Kappes, Börger, Meyer-Bahlburg, et al., 1990; Dittmann, Kappes, Kappes, Börger, Stegner, et al., 1990; Ehrhardt & Baker, 1974; Hines & Kaufman, 1994; Meyer-Bahlburg & Ehrhardt, 1982; Pasterski et al., 2005; Reinisch, 1981; Slijper, 1984). In this context, the most commonly studied endocrine disorder is the DSD, 21-hydroxylase deficiency (21-OHD) or classical congenital adrenal hyperplasia (CAH). For a more detailed discussion, see the section on classical CAH later in this chapter.

In addition to masculinized external genitalia at birth (due to exposure to excess androgens), females with classical CAH display increases in some male-typical behaviors from early childhood, suggesting that prenatal androgen may have an effect on neural as well as physical development. As noted, many reports have documented alterations in sex-typical childhood play interests and styles, particularly toy and playmate preferences (Berenbaum & Hines, 1992; Hines & Kaufman, 1994; Nordenstrom, Servin, Bohlin, Larsson, & Wedell, 2002; Pasterski et al., 2005; Pasterski et al., 2007; Slijper, 1984). Compared to unaffected sisters, girls with classical CAH are more likely to prefer boys' toys, boys as playmates, and a more active, rough, outdoor play style.

Thus, sex steroids appear to be a critical component for the differentiation of sex-dimorphic characteristics, both somatic and behavioral. It is not surprising, then, that during the course of typical gender development most individuals will differentiate

physical and behavioral features that are in alignment with gonadal sex and that gonadal dysfunction can disrupt psychosexual
development.

Disorders of Sex Development

Before commencing with a discussion of specific DSD, a note
on nomenclature is appropriate. Because of the sensitive nature of
and potential stigmatization surrounding DSD, scientists,
practitioners, and others should take care when referring to conditions and sufferers who bear them. In the latest consensus statement on the management of *intersex* disorders (Hughes, Houk,
Ahmed, & Lee, 2006), the term *DSD* was proposed to replace *intersex*, along with a nomenclature that abolishes other potentially
stigmatizing terms. Such terminology includes *pseudohermaphroditism, hermaphroditism,* and *sex reversal.* Additionally, Hughes et al.
(2006) recommend the classifications for DSD that will be used
here. Note that while the most common DSD are covered here, for
practical reasons the discussion is not exhaustive. See Grumbach
et al. (2003) for a more thorough and detailed discussion.

DSD can be divided into three general categories, 46,XY
DSD, 46,XX DSD, and sex chromosome DSD. By far, the majority
of DSD—and genital ambiguities—occur with the 46,XY karyotype. DSD concomitant with the full chromosomal complement
of 46,XY include androgen insensitivity syndrome, both complete
(CAIS) and partial (PAIS); 5 α-reductase-2 deficiency (5 α-RD-2);
17 ß-hydroxysteroid dehydrogenase-3 deficiency (17 ß-HSD-3);
gonadal dysgenesis; and micropenis. Classical CAH due to 21-
OHD is the most common DSD concomitant with the full chromosomal complement of 46,XX; and Turner syndrome (TS) is the
most common sex chromosome DSD.

Often, DSD first presents with ambiguous genitalia at birth.
For example, PAIS, 17 ß-HSD-3, micropenis, and CAH entail
some degree of ambiguity. Determining the etiology of the ambiguity is important for decisions about assigning gender. The karyotype of the individual gives a good indication of the source of
ambiguity. For example, 46,XX karyotype likely suggests female
internal reproductive structures with external virilization due to
excess androgen production, while 46,XY suggests male internal
reproductive structures with external undervirilization due to errors of androgen synthesis or receptor availability. By contrast, patients with DSD such as CAIS, 5 α-RD-2, gonadal dysgenesis, and
TS may not present with any degree of genital ambiguity at birth.
Symptoms such as virilization at puberty (5 α-RD-2), primary
amenorrhea at puberty (CAIS), or other somatic anomalies (TS)
are diagnostic indicators. Table 12.1 provides a summary of the

Table 12.1 Clinical Features of Disorders of Sex Development

Syndrome (Karyotype)	Internal Reproductive Tract	External Genitalia	Prenatal T Exposure	Assigned Gender	Identity	Behavior	Gender Change
cAIS (46,XY)	Testes develop Rudimentary Wolffian development Müllerian ducts regress	Female	N[a]	F	F	Feminine	N
pAIS (46,XY)	Testes develop Minimal Wolffian development Müllerian ducts regress	Ambiguous	Y	Mostly F	As reared	As reared	Y
5 α-RD-2 (46,XY)	Testes develop Wolffian ducts develop Müllerian ducts regress	Ambiguous	Y[b]	Both	M[c]	Masculine	Y
17 ß-HSD-3 (46,XY)	Testes develop Partial Wolffian duct development Müllerian ducts regress	Female/Ambiguous	N	Mostly F	M	Masculine	Y
Complete gonadal dysgenesis (46,XY)	Gonadal streaks Wolffian ducts regress Müllerian ducts develop	Female	N	F	F	Feminine	N
Micropenis	Testes develop Wolffian ducts develop Müllerian ducts regress	Extremely small penis	Y	Both	As reared	As reared	N
CAH (46,XX)	Ovaries develop Wolffian ducts regress[d] Müllerian ducts develop[e]	Ambiguous	Y	Mostly F	F	Masculine	N
Turner syndrome (46,XX)	Gonadal streaks Wolffian ducts regress Müllerian ducts develop	Female	N	F	F	Feminine	N

[a] No internal or external masculinization despite the presence of functioning testes and production of T. Thus there is effectively no prenatal T.
[b] Functional T is not converted to DHT, which is required for the prenatal development of the external genitalia.
[c] Approximately 60% of female-assigned and all male-assigned individuals with 5 α-RD identify as male.
[d] Wolffian ducts develop into the male internal reproductive structures of the epididymis, vas deferens, and seminal vesicles.
[e] Müllerian ducts develop into the female internal reproductive structures of the uterus and fallopian tubes.

361

clinical features and summary of findings of psychosexual outcome studies for each of the DSD discussed next.

46,XY Disorders of Sex Development

Androgen Insensitivity Syndrome

Androgens (T and DHT) exert their influences on specific tissues where functioning receptor cells are present (Lubahn et al., 1988). Errors in androgen biosynthesis or receptor availability lead to insensitivity, and sex differentiation is disrupted. Androgen insensitivity syndrome (AIS) is an X-linked disorder that results when a mutation of the androgen receptor gene (AR) renders the individual incapable of responding to circulating androgens. There are two variants of AIS, complete and partial. In the more severe, complete variant (CAIS), the end tissues of the body are not able to respond to androgen despite functioning testes. Due to the presence of MIS, the Müllerian ducts of the internal reproductive tract regress as do the Wolffian structures due to receptor failure; though, in some cases, rudimentary development of the Wolffian structures (epididymus and vas deferens) have been found (Hannema et al., 2004). Because the external genitalia are completely feminine in appearance, all newborns with CAIS are assigned the female gender and raised as girls. In addition, feminizing puberty partially progresses as testosterone is converted to estrogen, thereby promoting spontaneous breast development, though axillary and pubic hair are sparse. As such, the diagnosis of CAIS is usually not made until (late) adolescence when the individual fails to menstruate. At that time, using ultrasound, testes along with a blind-ending vagina may be detected. Removal of the testes is indicated because they pose a risk for malignancy, and lifelong hormone replacement therapy is initiated.

Partial androgen insensitivity (PAIS) occurs when there is a less severe mutation of the AR gene, and partial virilization of the end tissues ensues. Appearance of the external genitalia is highly variable. The genital tubercle is intermediate between a clitoris and a penis and the labioscrotal folds are often only partially fused with frequent perineal hypospadias. Internally, there is variable development as well. Most Müllerian structures regress; however, remnants of some of these structures have been reported. Wolffian structures may develop minimally and the testes may or may not descend (Hannema et al., 2004). Individuals with PAIS experience normal breast development at puberty as well as minimal axillary and pubic growth.

Limited data suggest that individuals with CAIS usually differentiate a female gender identity and assume a typical female gender role. Generally, these individuals are satisfied with their physical development, intimate relationships, and sexual functioning (Hines, Ahmed, & Hughes, 2003; Wisniewski et al., 2000).

Satisfaction with assigned gender is not as common in cases of PAIS. Mazur (2005) reviewed data on 99 individuals with PAIS and found that 9 initiated gender change later in life. Five individuals changed from female to male and four male to female (two of whom had experienced gender change from female to male once testes were detected at 18 months and 3 months, respectively; Diamond & Watson, 2004; Gooren & Cohen-Kettenis, 1991; Minto, Liao, Woodhouse, Ransley, & Creighton, 2003). Finally, AIS (complete and partial together) is intermediate in prevalence rates relative to other DSD. One report suggests that AIS occurs 1:99,000 live births (Boehmer et al., 1999).

5 α-Reductase-2 Deficiency (5 α-RD-2)

5 α-RD-2 is an autosomal recessive disorder caused by an enzyme deficiency consequent to a deletion or mutation of the relevant underlying gene. During typical fetal development, the genital tubercle, genital swelling, and urethral fold virilize upon exposure to DHT, which is converted from testosterone by the enzyme 5 α-reductase-2. The deficiency of this enzyme (i.e., 5 α-RD-2) results in under-virilization of the external genitalia. The disorder affects only males, and because internal reproductive structures are testosterone-dependent, not DHT-dependent, the development of the Wolffian structures (epididymus, vas deferens, and seminal vesicle) proceeds normally. The result is a newborn 46,XY male with functioning testes, normally formed male internal reproductive structures, a penis that resembles a clitoris, and a scrotum that resembles labia majora.

Detection of 5 α-RD-2 at birth is usually the result of genital ambiguity or presence of descended testicles in the female-appearing labioscrotal folds. In cases where under-virilization is complete, the diagnosis may be missed and the child incontrovertibly assigned to the female gender and unambiguously raised as a girl (Sobel & Imperato-McGinley, 2004). However, because secondary sexual development at puberty is dependent on testosterone, and DHT that has been converted by 5 α-reductase-1, individuals with 5 α-RD-2 will virilize in adolescence (Wilson, 2001). Such characteristics include increased muscle mass and hair growth, lowering of the voice, and growth of the penis (though it is unlikely to reach normal male size).

In a review of the published cases of female assigned and raised 5 α-RD-2 patients, Cohen-Kettenis (2005) found gender role change from female to male in 63% of cases; though, it is likely that the number of individuals who experience significant gender dissatisfaction short of gender change (perhaps due to cultural considerations) is even higher. No cases were reported of male-assigned 5 α-RD-2 cases who exhibited significant female-typical behavior or wished to change gender from male to female (Cohen-Kettenis, 2005). Furthermore, about half of the individuals studied who had feminine appearing genitalia differentiated a male gender identity and about half of the individuals with ambiguous genitalia differentiated a male gender identity. These data indicate that the degree of genital virilization at birth is not an indicator of future gender identity, at least in the case of 5 α-RD-2. Cohen-Kettenis (2005) suggests that general masculine appearance, along with masculine gender role behavior, may be more important than genital appearance for differentiating a male gender identity.

17 β-Hydroxysteroid Dehydrogenase-3 Deficiency (17 β-HSD-3)

17 ß-HSD-3 is an autosomal recessive disorder caused by mutations in the HSD17B3 gene (Grumbach et al., 2003). The fault lies with impaired ability to convert androstenedione to testosterone. As a consequence, this male form of pseudohermaphroditism is diagnostically identical to AIS in infancy. That is, patients with the disorder have testes and normally developed Wolffian ducts derivatives; however, they show severe to complete undervirilization of the external genitalia, often with normal appearing clitoris and labia majora (Grumbach et al., 2003). The prevalence of 17 ß-HSD-3 in the general population has been approximated at 1:147,000 (Boehmer et al., 1999). Due to the autosomal recessive nature, one would expect a higher incidence in isolated communities, such as the Gaza strip, where the prevalence has been reported to be as high as 1:100 or 1:150 (Kohn et al., 1985).

Individuals with 17 ß-HSD-3 are primarily raised as females and do not present with symptoms until the onset of puberty, at which time virilization occurs (most likely due to extratesticular conversion of androstenedione to testosterone; Andersson, Russell, & Wilson, 1996). For this reason, it is preferable to make the diagnosis before the onset of puberty at which time a gonadectomy is indicated. In cases of partial undervirilization, diagnosis should be made as soon as possible after birth. Due to the nature of the genital ambiguity (i.e., extratesticular conversion of androstenedione to testosterone), treatment with exogenous androgens may result in a nearly normal male phenotype in adulthood (Farkas & Rösler, 1993; Gross et al., 1986). Similar to 5 α-RD-2, individuals with 17 ß-HSD-3 typically differentiate male gender role behavior and many change their gender to male after puberty (Cohen-Kettenis, 2005), suggesting that assignment to the male gender as early as possible will likely accord the best possible psychosexual development.

Complete Gonadal Dysgenesis

During early stages of typical fetal development, the differentiation of the bipotential gonad into testis requires the action of certain transcription factors (e.g., SRY, DAX-1, SOX9). Errors in the action of any of a number of such factors can result in the deficiency of Sertoli and Leydig cells which are necessary for the development of the gonad into testis (Migeon & Wisniewski, 2003). By definition, gonadal dysgenesis is a DSD due to lack of the Sertoli and Leydig cells. In contrast to AIS, in which affected individuals cannot respond to androgens produced by functioning testes, patients with gonadal dysgenesis can respond to androgens; however, they develop abnormal testes incapable of producing androgens.

Complete gonadal dysgenesis affects 46,XY individuals and is characterized by streak gonads that do not fully differentiate on the pathway to becoming testes. Because of this malformation, the gonads do not produce T, DHT, or MIS, and the development of the internal reproductive tract follows the feminine pathway. That is, Müllerian ducts develop and Wolffian ducts regress. Individuals with complete gonadal dysgenesis are always assigned to the female gender and raised as girls. Diagnosis often occurs at puberty when sexual maturation fails to occur. At this stage, the streak gonads are removed due to high risk of malignancy, and hormone replacement therapy is initiated. No cases of gender change or gender dysphoria have been reported in female-raised 46,XY individuals with complete gonadal dysgenesis.

Micropenis

Androgens exert their influences on the development of male genitalia during two critical stages of fetal development. Early in gestation, androgens direct the development of the genital tubercle, genital swellings, and urethral fold into a fully formed penis and fused scrotum. It is believed that a second dose of androgens is required to enlarge the penis. Micropenis is the condition where the penis has fully differentiated from the bipotential genital structures, but is very small, possibly because of undervirilization at the second critical stage.

The diagnostic criteria of micropenis are the following: (a) 46,XY karyotype; (b) either descended or undescended testes; (c) completely formed penis, with no perineal hypospadias and an appropriately located urethral opening; and (d) stretched penile length at or below 2.5 SD of the population mean, adjusted for age (Lee et al., 1980). In a newborn, the criterion for inclusion for stretched penile length is ≤ 1.9 cm. Individuals with micropenis have been assigned as male and female, largely depending on circumstantial factors (i.e., policy of medical staff, parental wishes, cultural proscriptions). Mazur (2005) reports on 89 cases of micropenis, 10 of which were assigned and raised as female. Regardless of the sex of rearing, none of these cases initiated a gender change later in life, and only one male of 13 reported symptoms of gender dysphoria (Wisniewski et al., 2001). Wisniewski et al. also reported that, while two female-assigned individuals were unhappy with surgical outcomes, all female-assigned individuals in their study were feminine in their gender role behavior and happy with sex of assignment.

See Sidebar 12.1 for overview of 46,XY disorders of sexual development.

46,XY Disorders of Sex Development

- *Androgen insensitivity syndrome (AIS):* Mutation of androgen receptor gene (AR) renders individual unable to respond to circulating androgens; can be partial or complete; occurs 1 : 99,000 live births.
- *5 α-reductase-2 deficiency (5 α-RD-2):* Autosomal recessive disorder caused by enzyme deficiency consequent to deletion or mutation of underlying gene; affects males only; results in male newborn with functioning testes and normally formed internal male reproductive structures, a penis that resembles a clitoris, and a scrotum that resembles the labia majora.
- *17 β-hydroxysteroid dehydrogenase-3 deficiency (17 β-HSD-3):* Autosomal recessive disorder caused by mutations in the HSD17B3 gene, leading to impaired ability to convert androstenedione to testosterone; individuals with this disorder are often raised as females and do not present symptoms until onset of puberty; prevalence approximated at 1 : 147,000 in the general population.
- *Complete gonadal dysgenesis:* Errors in the action of any number of transcription factors during early stages of fetal development result in the deficiency of Sertoli and Leydig cells that are necessary for the development of the gonad into testis; individuals develop abnormal testes incapable of producing androgens; individuals raised as females; diagnosis often occurs at puberty.
- *Micropenis:* Penis has fully differentiated from the bipotential genital structures but is very small; possibly caused by undervirilization during second stage of androgen release in gestation.

46,XX Disorders of Sex Development

Congenital Adrenal Hyperplasia

Congenital adrenal hyperplasia (CAH) refers to a group of autosomal recessive disorders of adrenal steroid biosynthesis that results in excess androgen production beginning prenatally (Miller & Levine, 1987). 21-OHD accounts for 95% of cases and is caused by mutations of the CYP21 gene. Given the incidence rate of 1 : 15,000 births, CAH is the most common DSD and cause of genital ambiguity (Pang & Shook, 1997).

Cortisol is a corticosteroid hormone necessary for normal homeostasis. As part of a negative feedback system, several enzymatic steps are required for the conversion of cholesterol to cortisol. Deficiency of the enzyme 21-OH results in cortisol precursors being shunted into a path of least resistance, leading to the production of testosterone. Because this negative feedback system is never shut down, the production of testosterone is continual. The exposure begins as early as week 8 of gestation and continues until diagnosis and treatment with corticosteroid replacement therapy. Additionally, there are two variants of the disorder, the simple-virilizing (SV) variant, and the salt-wasting (SW) variant. The SW occurs in more than 75% of cases and is associated with inadequate aldosterone production. Individuals with the SW variant are at risk for life-threatening salt-wasting crises, due to insufficiency of aldosterone, unless appropriately regulated with mineralocorticoid replacement.

Females with 21-OHD are typically born with ambiguous genitalia involving varying degrees of clitoral enlargement, partial or total fusion of the labioscrotal folds, and development of a urogenital sinus (see Figure 12.2). Formation of a uterus and fallopian tubes from the Müllerian ducts progresses normally as CAH does not result in the production of anti-Müllerian hormone. Because the androgens produced by individuals with CAH come from the adrenal, and not the testes, the testicular hormone dependant Wolffian ducts regress. Virilization of the external genitalia has historically been measured using the Prader Scale (Prader, 1954), which ranges from 1 (normal female appearing genitalia) to 5 (normal male appearing genitalia).

Female infants with classical CAH are almost always assigned and reared as females and the external genitalia may be surgically feminized early in life. As mentioned elsewhere in this chapter, girls with CAH also show behavioral masculinization subsequent to prenatal androgen exposure. Behaviors that are affected include toy, playmate, and activity preferences, aggressive behavior, and, in adolescence and adulthood, sexual orientation. Compared to unaffected sisters, girls with CAH are more likely to prefer boys' toys, boys as playmates, a more active, rough, outdoor play style, and are more likely to show increased erotic attractions to females in adulthood (Berenbaum & Hines, 1992; Hines & Kaufman, 1994; Hines et al., 2004; Nordenstrom et al., 2002; Pasterski et al., 2005; Slijper, 1984).

By contrast, male fetuses are normally exposed to androgen from their testes during prenatal development and the excess androgen production resulting from 21-hydroxylase deficiency does not alter the physical appearance of boys with CAH. As a result, these individuals are usually diagnosed when the infant experiences a salt-wasting crisis in the presence of the more severe, salt-wasting (SW) variant of CAH, or as a result of premature sexual development in the case of the less severe, simple-virilizing (SV) variant. As such, while CAH is a DSD, the disorder does not alter sex differentiation and is not considered a DSD per se as it occurs in males. Additionally, by most accounts, the behavior of boys with CAH does not appear to be altered (Collaer & Hines, 1995), although some reports indicate that boys with CAH show reduced male-typical development, reflected in reduced rough-and-tumble play (Hines & Kaufman, 1994) and reduced visuospatial ability (Hampson, Rovet, & Altmann, 1998; Hines, Fane, et al., 2003).

Classical CAH is currently the only disorder of sex development amenable to prenatal diagnosis and intervention. Because of the autosomal recessive nature, it is possible to test the developing genetic offspring of a known carrier or affected individual. In such cases, mothers may be prescribed the synthetic cortisol, dexamethasone, which prevents virilization of the external genitalia by influencing the negative feedback system and shutting down the excess production of adrenal androgens. It is as yet unclear whether or not treatment with dexamethasone prevents behavioral masculinization. It is also possible that synthetic steroid administration may have detrimental effects on developing brain structures such as the hypothalamus. Further studies are needed to determine if this is a desirable intervention.

See Sidebar 12.2 for overview of 46,XX disorders of sex development.

SIDEBAR 12.2

46,XX Disorders of Sex Development

- *Congenital adrenal hyperplasia (CAH):* Group of autosomal recessive disorders of adrenal steroid biosynthesis resulting in excess androgen production; incidence rate of 1:15,000 births; 21-OHD, caused by mutations of the CYP21 gene, accounts for 95% of cases of CAH.
- *Turner syndrome (TS):* A class of chromosomal anomalies, most commonly monosomy X or the 45,XO karyotype; involves complete or partial deletion of the second sex chromosome; incidence rate is approximately 1 in 2,500 live female births; most commonly occurring features include short stature, primary gonadal failure, and infertility.

Chromosome DSD

Turner Syndrome

Turner syndrome (TS) is the term given to a class of chromosomal anomalies, the most common of which is monosomy X, or the 45,XO karyotype. In all types of TS there is a complete or partial deletion of the second sex chromosome, and characteristic physical features must be present for a diagnosis (Bondy, 2007). The incidence rate is approximately 1 in 2,500 live female births, making it one of the most common genetic disorders affecting girls and women (Nielsen & Wohlert, 1991). The deletion of the second sex chromosome in TS is associated with a wide variety of physical features, not all of which occur in all cases. The most commonly occurring features include short stature, primary gonadal failure, and infertility. Less frequent physical features include webbing of the neck, low-seated ears, and a broad, shield-like chest (Grumbach et al., 2003; Lippe, 1991). The most life-threatening consequence of the 45,XO karyotype involves defects in cardiac and aortic development associated with an increased fetal mortality rate (Bondy, 2007). Lifelong cardiac monitoring is indicated for many individuals with TS.

TS has also been associated with certain neurological deficits. Although verbal intelligence and reading skills show normal to above normal distributions in girls and women with TS (Garron, 1977; Reiss et al., 1993; Temple & Carney, 1996), other abilities appear to be compromised. Many patients have difficulty with tests of memory and attention, numerical ability, visuomotor function, and visuoperceptual skills (Collaer, Geffner, Kaufman, Buckingham, & Hines, 2002; Ross et al., 2002; Rovet, Berch, & Bender, 1990). Altered neural development, perhaps as a result of insufficient ovarian steroids, associated with TS is thought to play a role in cognitive deficiencies (Elliott, Watkins, Messa, Lippe, & Chugani, 1996). Even with typical development, prenatal levels of ovarian hormones appear quite low in comparison to those produced by the testes; however, postnatal levels of certain ovarian steroids and gonadotropins appear to be elevated (Bidlingmaier, Strom, Dörr, Eisenmenger, & Knorr, 1987; Bidlingmaier, Versmold, Knorr, Forest, & Bertrand, 1974). Given that sex steroids are known to alter behaviors that show sex differences (Collaer & Hines, 1995), the paucity of ovarian hormones beginning early in life may have influences on the cognitive and neural alterations that characterize TS.

Because TS, by definition, only affects females, and because genital ambiguity is not an associated feature (Bondy, 2007), gender assignment at birth is not required. In addition, girls and women with TS typically differentiate female-typical behavior and female gender identity, and engage in heterosexual relationships, although these individuals often reach romantic and sexual milestones later than their peers (Pavlidis, McCauley, & Sybert, 1995). This pattern is likely partly a reflection of lower levels of self-esteem, but may also reflect underlying genetic or hormonal influences on behavior (Carel et al., 2006).

TS presents with a wide array of genetic, developmental, endocrine, psychosocial, and reproductive issues. Specialized care for TS patients can be lifelong, often involving surgery to correct physical malformations, gonadectomy to avoid potential effects from failure of the gonads to differentiate properly, and courses of treatment with growth hormone (GH) during childhood and adolescence to increase final adult stature. However, considering the varied complications and alterations associated with TS, girls and women with the disorder, in general, function well and live fulfilling lives. In a recent study of girls and women with TS, respondents indicated that struggling with their infertility was the greatest challenge in adapting to life with TS (Sutton et al., 2005).

Clinical Management of Disorders of Sex Development

The birth of a child with a DSD necessitates a long-term management strategy that involves multidisciplinary teams of specialists. Careful consideration should be given to correct and timely diagnosis, appropriate hormone treatments, potential surgical interventions, and psychosocial monitoring, with the goal of optimal psychosexual development. Thus, the differentiation of sex-dimorphic features such as gender role behavior, gender identity, and sexual orientation are of great concern when considering gender assignment.

Gender dissatisfaction in the context of gender assignment in DSD is poorly understood and outcome data are limited. Dissatisfaction, and even gender change, have been linked to factors such as prenatal hormonal milieu and parental psychopathology (Meyer-Bahlburg, 2005; Zucker & Bradley, 1995), though it is difficult to say whether these are causal in nature. Outcome studies point to potential indicators such as karyotype, androgen exposure, degree of genital virilization, and environmental factors surrounding sex of rearing as indicators of gender satisfaction (Bradley, Oliver, Chernick, & Zucker, 1998; Mazur, 2005; Meyer-Bahlburg, 2005). Behavioral outcomes such as gender identity, gender role behavior, and sexual orientation are measured. However, Hughes et al. (2006) emphasize the separability of these three behavioral features and suggest that cross-sex gender role behavior or homosexual orientation is not necessarily an indicator of incorrect gender assignment. For example, although dose effects of prenatal androgens have been linked to the degree of behavioral masculinization in girls with CAH (Nordenstrom et al., 2002), and decreased heterosexual interest has been reported (Hines et al., 2004), the majority of girls and women with CAH do not experience gender dissatisfaction per se. Conclusions from studies where gender satisfaction is not measured explicitly or comprehensively should be taken with an element of caution. Zucker (2005) offers a comprehensive review of clinical tools that measure psychosexual differentiation that can be employed in cases of gender identity disorder (GID) as well as DSD.

Complexities such as timing and type of hormone exposure, receptor availability and temporal sensitivity, and modification by social environments are all considerations that must be taken into account when considering psychosexual development in cases of individuals with DSD (Goy, Bercovitch, & McBrair, 1988; Grumbach et al., 2003; Hines, 1998; Hughes et al., 2006; Nordenstrom et al., 2002; Wallen, 2005). Though excellent progress has been made in understanding biological and environmental factors that contribute to healthy psychosexual development, it is still the case that variability in behavioral outcomes makes it difficult to be certain of optimal sex assignment and cautious and careful planning is always indicated.

Summary and Conclusions

A number of conclusions may be drawn regarding the development of sex disorders:

- While sex chromosomes direct the differentiation of the gonads as ovaries or testes, it is the gonadal hormones produced from the testes that direct the phenotypic differentiation of the fetus in the male direction. In the absence of these hormones, development proceeds in the female direction.

- Gonadal hormones appear to masculinize certain brain structures and observable behaviors in addition to physical features. Exposure to androgens during critical periods of development results in masculinization and defeminization of behaviors that typically show sex differences. These effects have been found in most mammals including nonhuman primates and humans.

- As many DSD are the result of errors in gonadal steroid synthesis and/or errors of receptor availability, there is potential for variability in behaviors that are influenced by steroids as well as in physical characteristics such as internal reproductive structures and external genitalia.

- Even though research has demonstrated a critical role for prenatal androgens in masculinization of behaviors that show sex differences, these factors do not appear to be a reliable predictor of core gender identity. Thus, psychosocial factors likely also play a significant role.

- Regarding early gender assignment, the consensus among experts is that gender should be assigned to an ambiguous newborn as soon as possible, even if surgical intervention is to be delayed.

- Despite the publicity of a few cases of sex re-assignment in later life, most individuals with DSD do not experience such drastic effects and ultimately identify with their gender of rearing.
- Mindful clinical management of a child with DSD is critical and should involve an interdisciplinary team with careful consideration of proper diagnosis, appropriate hormone treatments, potential surgical interventions, and psychosocial monitoring, with the goal of optimal psychosexual development.

References

Andersson, S., Russell, D. W., & Wilson, J. D. (1996). 17 ß-Hydroxysteroid dehydrogenase-3 deficiency. *Trends in Endocrinology and Metabolism, 7,* 121–126.

Berenbaum, S. A., & Hines, M. (1992). Early androgens are related to childhood sex-typed toy preferences. *Psychological Science, 3,* 203–206.

Berenbaum, S. A., & Resnick, S. M. (1997). Early androgen effects on aggression in children and adults with congenital adrenal hyperplasia. *Psychoneuroendocrinology, 22,* 505–515.

Bidlingmaier, F., Strom, T. M., Dörr, G., Eisenmenger, W., & Knorr, D. (1987). Estrone and estradiol concentrations in human ovaries, testes, and adrenals during the first two years of life. *Journal of Clinical Endocrinology and Metabolism, 65,* 862–867.

Bidlingmaier, F., Versmold, H., Knorr, D., Forest, M., & Bertrand, J. (1974). Plasma estrogens in newborns and infants. In *Sexual endocrinology of the perinatal period* (pp. 299–314). Paris: Inserm.

Boehmer, A. L. M., Brinkmann, A. O., Sandkuijl, L. A., Halley, D. J. J., Niermeijer, M. F., Andersson, S., et al. (1999). 17 ß-Hydroxysteroid dehydrogenase-3 deficiency: Diagnosis, phenotypic variability, population genetics, and worldwide distribution of ancient and de novo mutations. *Journal of Clinical Endocrinology and Metabolism, 84*(12), 4713–4721.

Bondy, C. A. (2007). Care of girls and women with Turner syndrome: A guideline of the Turner syndrome study group. *Journal of Clinical Endocrinology and Metabolism, 92*(1), 10–25.

Bradley, S. J., Oliver, G. D., Chernick, A. B., & Zucker, K. J. (1998). Experiment of nurture: Ablatio penis at 2 months, sex reassignment at 7 months and a psychosexual follow-up in young adulthood. *Pediatrics, 102,* 102–101.

Carel, J. C., Elie, C., Ecosse, E., Tauber, M., Leger, J., Cabrol, S., et al. (2006). Self-esteem and social adjustment in young women with Turner syndrome: Influence of pubertal management and sexuality: Population-based cohort study. *Journal of Clinical Endocrinology and Metabolism, 91,* 2972–2979.

Cohen-Kettenis, P. T. (2005). Gender change in 46,XY persons with 5alpha-reductase-2 deficiency and 17 ß-hydroxysteroid dehydrogenase-3 deficiency. *Archives of Sexual Behavior, 34,* 399–410.

Collaer, M. L., Geffner, M., Kaufman, F. R., Buckingham, B., & Hines, M. (2002). Cognitive and behavioral characteristics of Turner syndrome: Exploring a role for ovarian hormones in female sexual differentiation. *Hormones and Behavior, 41,* 139–155.

Collaer, M. L., & Hines, M. (1995). Human behavioral sex differences: A role for gonadal hormones during early development? *Psychological Bulletin, 118,* 55–107.

Diamond, M., & Watson, L. A. (2004). Androgen insensitivity syndrome and Klinefelter's syndrome: Sex and gender considerations. *Adolescent Psychiatric Clinics of North America, 13,* 623–640.

Dittmann, R. W., Kappes, M. H., Kappes, M. E., Börger, D., Meyer-Bahlburg, H. F. L., Stegner, H., et al. (1990). Congenital adrenal hyperplasia: Pt. II. Gender-related behavior and attitudes in female salt-wasting and simple virilizing patients. *Psychoneuroendocrinology, 15,* 421–434.

Dittmann, R. W., Kappes, M. H., Kappes, M. E., Börger, D., Stegner, H., Willig, R. H., et al. (1990). Congenital Adrenal Hyperplasia I: Gender-related behavior and attitudes in female patients and sisters. *Psychoneuroendocrinology, 15,* 401–420.

Ehrhardt, A. A., & Baker, S. W. (1974). Fetal androgens, human central nervous system differentiation, and behavior sex differences. In R. C. Friedman, R. M. Richart, & R. L. van de Wiele

(Eds.), *Sex differences in behavior* (pp. 33–52). New York: Wiley.

Elliott, T. K., Watkins, J. M., Messa, C., Lippe, B., & Chugani, H. (1996). Positron emission tomography and neuropsychological correlations in children with Turner's syndrome. *Developmental Neuropsychology, 12,* 365–386.

Farkas, A., & Rösler, A. (1993). Ten years experience with masculinizing genitoplasty in male pseudohermaphroditism due to 17 ß-hydroxysteroid dehydrogenase deficiency. *European Journal of Pediatrics, 152*(Suppl. 2), 88–90.

Fauci, A., Braunwald, E., Isselbacher, K., Wilson, J., Martin, J., Kasper, D., et al. (Eds.). (1998). *Harrison's principles of internal medicine* (14th ed.). New York: McGraw-Hill.

Garron, D. C. (1977). Intelligence among persons with Turner's Syndrome. *Behavior Genetics, 7,* 105–127.

Gooren, L., & Cohen-Kettenis, P. T. (1991). Development of male gender identity/role and a sexual orientation towards women in a 46,XY subject with an incomplete form of androgen insensitivity syndrome. *Archives of Sexual Behavior, 20,* 459–470.

Goy, R. W., Bercovitch, F. B., & McBrair, M. C. (1988). Behavioral masculinization is independent of genital masculinization in prenatally androgenized female rhesus macaques. *Hormones and Behavior, 22,* 552–571.

Goy, R. W., & McEwen, B. S. (1980). *Sexual differentiation of the brain.* Cambridge, MA: MIT Press.

Gross, D. J., Landau, H., Kohn, G., Farkas, A., Elrayyes, E., El Shawwa, R., et al. (1986). Male pseudohermaphroditism due to 17 ß-hydroxysteroid dehydrogenase deficiency: Gender reassignment in early infancy. *Acta Endocrinologica (Copenhagen), 112*(2), 238–246.

Grumbach, M. M., Hughes, I. A., & Conte, F. A. (2003). Disorders of sex differentiation. In P. R. Larsen, H. M. Kronenberg, S. Melmed, & K. S. Polonsky (Eds.), *Williams textbook of endocrinology* (Vol. 10, pp. 842–1002). Philadelphia: Saunders.

Hampson, E., Rovet, J., & Altmann, D. (1998). Spatial reasoning in children with congenital adrenal hyperplasia due to 21-hydroxylase deficiency. *Developmental Neuropsychology, 14*(2), 299–320.

Hannema, S. E., Scott, I. S., Hodapp, J., Martin, H., Coleman, N., Schwabe, J. W., et al. (2004). Residual activity of androgen receptors explains Wolffian duct development in the complete androgen insensitivity syndrome. *Journal of Clinical Endocrinology and Metabolism, 89,* 5815–5822.

Hines, M. (1982). Prenatal gonadal hormones and sex differences in human behavior. *Psychological Bulletin, 92,* 56–80.

Hines, M. (1998). Abnormal sexual development and psychosexual issues. In I. A. Hughes, G. M. Besser, H. G. Burger, R. D. Cohen, M. B. Ranke, S. Reichlin, & J. D. Wilson (Eds.), *Balliere's clinical endocrinology and metabolism: International practice and research* (Vol. 12:1, pp. 173–187). London: Harcourt Brace Publishers International.

Hines, M. (2004). *Brain gender.* New York: Oxford University Press.

Hines, M., Ahmed, S. F., & Hughes, I. (2003). Psychological outcomes and gender-related development in complete androgen insensitivity syndrome. *Archives of Sexual Behavior, 32,* 93–101.

Hines, M., Brook, C., & Conway, G. S. (2004). Androgen and psychosexual development: Core gender identity, sexual orientation and recalled childhood gender role behavior in women and men with Congenital Adrenal Hyperplasia (CAH). *Journal of Sex Research, 41,* 1–7.

Hines, M., Fane, B. A., Pasterski, V. L., Mathews, G. A., Conway, G. S., & Brook, C. (2003). Spatial abilities following prenatal androgen abnormality: Targeting and mental rotations performance in individuals with Congenital Adrenal Hyperplasia (CAH). *Psychoneuroendocrinology, 28,* 1010–1026.

Hines, M., & Gorski, R. A. (1985). Hormonal influences on the development of neural asymmetries. In D. F. Benson & E. Zaidel (Eds.), *The dual brain: Hemispheric specialization in humans* (pp. 75–96). New York: Guilford Press.

Hines, M., & Kaufman, F. R. (1994). Androgen and the development of human sex-typical behavior: Rough-and-tumble play and sex of preferred playmates in children with Congenital Adrenal Hyperplasia (CAH). *Child Development, 65,* 1042–1053.

Hughes, I. A., Houk, C., Ahmed, S. F., & Lee, P. A. (2006). Consensus statement on management of intersex disorders. *Journal of Pediatric Urology, 2,* 148–162.

Kohn, G., Lasch, E. E., El-Shawwa, E., Elrayyes, E., Litvin, Y., & Rösler, A. (1985). Male pseudohermaphroditism due to 17 ß-Hydroxysteroid dehydrogenase deficiency in a large Arab kinship: Studies on the natural history of the defect. *Journal of Pediatric Endocrinology, 2,* 29–37.

Lee, P. A., Mazur, T., Danish, R., Amrhein, J. A., Blizzard, R. M., Money, J., et al. (1980). Micropenis: Pt. I. Criteria, etiologies, and classification. *Johns Hopkins Medical Journal, 145,* 156–163.

Lippe, B. (1991). Turner syndrome. *Endocrinology and Metabolism Clinics of North America, 20,* 121–152.

Lubahn, D. B., Joseph, D. R., Sullivan, P. M., Willard, H. F., French, F. S., & Wilson, E. M. (1988). Cloning of human androgen receptor complementary DNA and localization to the X chromosome. *Science, 240,* 327–330.

Mazur, T. (2005). Gender dysphoria and gender change in androgen insensitivity or micropenis. *Archives of Sexual Behavior, 34,* 411–421.

Meyer-Bahlburg, H. F. L. (2005). Gender identity outcome in female-raised 46,XY persons with penile agenesis, cloacal exstrophy of the bladder, or penile ablation. *Archives of Sexual Behavior, 34*(4) 423–438.

Meyer-Bahlburg, H. F. L., & Ehrhardt, A. A. (1982). Prenatal sex hormones and human aggression: A review, and new data on progestogen effects. *Aggressive Behavior, 8,* 39–62.

Migeon, C. J., & Wisniewski, A. (2003). Human sex differentiation and its abnormalities. *Best Practice and Research in Clinical Obstetrics and Gynecology, 17*(1), 1–18.

Miller, W. L., & Levine, L. S. (1987). Molecular and clinical advances in congenital adrenal hyperplasia. *Journal of Pediatrics, 111,* 1–17.

Minto, C. L., Liao, L. M., Woodhouse, C. R. J., Ransley, P. G., & Creighton, S. M. (2003). The effect of clitoral surgery on sexual outcome in individuals who have intersex conditions with ambiguous genitalia: A cross-sectional study. *Lancet, 361,* 1252–1257.

Money, J., & Schwartz, M. (1976). Fetal androgens in the early treated adrenogenital syndrome of 46,XX hermaphroditism: Influence on assertive and aggressive types of behavior. *Aggressive Behavior, 2,* 19–30.

Nielsen, J., & Wohlert, M. (1991). Chromosome abnormalities found among 34,910 newborn children: Results from a 13-year incidence study in Arhus, Denmark. *Human Genetics, 87,* 81–83.

Nordenstrom, A., Servin, A., Bohlin, G., Larsson, A., & Wedell, A. (2002). Sex-typed toy play behavior correlates with the degree of prenatal androgen exposure assessed by CYP21 genotype in girls with congenital adrenal hyperplasia. *Journal of Clinical Endocrinology and Metabolism, 87,* 5119–5124.

Pang, S., & Shook, M. K. (1997). Current status of neonatal screening for congenital adrenal hyperplasia. *Current Opinion in Pediatrics, 9,* 419–423.

Pasterski, V. L., Geffner, M. E., Brain, C., Hindmarsh, P., Brook, C., & Hines, M. (2005). Prenatal hormones and postnatal socialization by parents as determinants of male-typical toy play in girls with congenital adrenal hyperplasia. *Child Development, 76,* 264–278.

Pasterski, V. L., Hindmarsh, P., Geffner, M., Brook, C., Brain, C., & Hines, M. (2007). Increased aggression and activity level in 3- to 11-year-old girls with congenital adrenal hyperplasia (CAH). *Hormones and Behavior, 52,* 368–374.

Pavlidis, K., McCauley, E., & Sybert, V. P. (1995). Psychosocial and sexual functioning in women with Turner syndrome. *Clinical Genetics, 47,* 85–89.

Prader, A. (1954). Der genitalbefund beim pseudohermaphroditismus femininus des kongenitalen adrenogenitalen syndroms. *Helvetica Paediatrica Acta, 3,* 231–240.

Reinisch, J. M. (1981). Prenatal exposure to synthetic progestins increases potential for aggression in humans. *Science, 211,* 1171–1173.

Reiss, A. L., Freund, L., Plotnick, L., Baumgardner, T., Green, K., Sozer, A. C., et al. (1993). The effects of X monosomy on brain development: Monozygotic twins discordant for Turner's syndrome. *Annals of Neurology, 1*(34), 95–107.

Ross, J. L., Stefanatos, G. A., Kushner, H., Zinn, A. R., Bondy, C., & Roeltgen, D. (2002). Persistent cognitive deficits in adult women with Turner syndrome. *Neurology, 58,* 218–225.

Rovet, J. F., Berch, D. B., & Bender, B. G. (1990). The cognitive and neuropsychological characteristics of females with Turner syndrome. In *Sex chromosome abnormalities and human behavior* (pp. 38–77). Boulder, CO: Westview.

Slijper, F. M. E. (1984). Androgens and gender role behaviour in girls with Congenital Adrenal Hyperplasia (CAH). In G. J. De Vries, J. P. C. De Bruin, H. B. M. Uylings, & M. A. Corner (Eds.), *Progress in brain research* (pp. 417–422). Amsterdam: Elsevier.

Sobel, V., & Imperato-McGinley, J. (2004). Gender identity in XY intersexuality. *Child and Adolescent Psychiatric Clinics of North America, 13,* 609–622.

Sutton, E. J., McInerney-Leo, A., Bondy, C. A., Gollust, S. E., King, D., & Biesecker, B. (2005). Turner syndrome: Four challenges across the lifespan. *American Journal of Medical Genetics, 139,* 57–66.

Temple, C. M., & Carney, R. (1996). Reading skills in children with Turner's syndrome: An analysis of hyperlexia. *Cortex, 32,* 335–345.

Wallen, K. (2005). Hormonal influences on sexually differentiated behavior in nonhuman primates. *Frontiers in Neuroendocrinology, 26,* 7–26.

Wilson, J. D. (2001). Androgens, androgen receptors and male gender role behavior. *Hormones and Behavior, 40,* 358–366.

Wisniewski, A. B., Migeon, C. J., Gearhart, J. P., Rock, J. A., Berkovitz, G. D., Plotnick, L. P., et al. (2001). Congenital micropenis: Long-term medical, surgical, and psychosexual follow-up of individuals raised male or female. *Hormone Research, 56,* 3–11.

Wisniewski, A. B., Migeon, C. J., Meyer-Bahlburg, H. F. L., Gearhart, J. P., Berkovitz,

B., Brown, T. J., et al. (2000). Complete androgen insensitivity syndrome. Long-term medical, surgical, and psychosexual outcome. *Journal of Clinical Endocrinology and Metabolism, 85*, 2664–2669.

Zucker, K. J. (2005). Measurement of psychosexual differentiation. *Archives of Sexual Behavior, 34*(4), 375.

Zucker, K. J., & Bradley, S. J. (1995). *Gender identity disorder and psychosexual problems in children and adolescents.* New York: Guilford Press.

Zucker, K. J., Bradley, S. J., Oliver, G., Blake, J., Fleming, S., & Hood, J. (1996). Psychosexual development of women with congenital adrenal hyperplasia. *Hormones and Behavior, 30*, 300–318.

Kenneth J. Zucker and
Peggy T. Cohen-Kettenis

13
Chapter

Learning Objectives

In this chapter, we discuss:

- A brief history of the field and presentation of relevant terminology.
- Children with Gender Identity Disorder (GID) and its prevalence.
- Diagnosis and assessment of children with GID.
- Associated psychopathologies and developmental trajectories of childhood GID.
- Therapeutic strategies for childhood GID, including parental considerations.
- Adolescent GID, epidemiology, and prevalence.
- Diagnosis and assessment of adolescent GID.
- Associated psychopathologies and developmental trajectories of adolescent GID.
- The treatment strategies for adolescent GID.
- Legal issues and conclusions.

Clinical care and research pertaining to children and adolescents who would now be deemed to have a gender identity disorder (GID) began slowly, starting in the 1950s and 1960s (e.g.,

Green & Money, 1960; Stoller, 1968). In many respects, attention given to children and adolescents lagged behind the clinical care and research that focused on adults with GID, which was "jump-started" by the establishment of hospital- and university-based gender identity clinics in the 1960s (see Chapter 14, this volume). Because the prevalence of GID in children and adolescents is low, only a small number of clinician-researchers have directed their attention to this population, but, beginning in the mid-1960s, several specialty clinics or programs were established in the United States, Canada, The Netherlands, and England. Thus, in a gradual manner, a fair bit of knowledge has accumulated about children and adolescents with GID. In the past few years, GID has become a topic of fascination in the mass media: both print and television media have provided a great deal of coverage, including articles in the *New York Times* (Brown, 2006) and *Newsweek* (Rosenberg, 2007) and widely watched television programs, such as the *Oprah Winfrey Show* (May 12, 2004) and *ABC's 20/20* (April 27, 2007). In addition, there are now several web sites that focus on children and adolescents who are struggling with their gender identity (www .dcchildrens.com/dcchildrens/about/subclinical/subneuroscience /subgender/guide.aspx; www.transkidspurplerainbow.org/index .htm; http://imatyfa.org).

Terminology

Several terms used throughout this chapter are briefly described. These are: (a) sex, (b) gender, (c) gender identity, (d) gender role (masculinity-femininity), (e) sexual orientation, and (f) sexual identity. Further consideration of these terms is provided in Chapters 11 and 12 in this volume.

Sex

Sex refers to attributes that collectively, and usually harmoniously, characterize biological maleness and femaleness. In humans, the most well-known attributes that constitute biological sex include the sex-determining genes, the sex chromosomes, the H-Y antigen, the gonads, sex hormones, the internal reproductive structures, and the external genitalia (Migeon & Wisniewski, 1998). Over the past couple of decades, there has, of course, also been great interest in the possibility that the human brain has certain sex-dimorphic neuroanatomic structures that, perhaps, emerge during the process of prenatal physical sex differentiation (for recent developments in understanding aspects of physical sex differentiation, see Arnold, 2003; Grumbach, Hughes, & Conte, 2003; Haqq & Donahoe, 1998; Vilain, 2000; and Chapter 11, this volume).

Gender

Gender is used to refer to psychological or behavioral characteristics associated with males and females (Ruble, Martin, & Berenbaum, 2006). From a historical perspective, gender as a technical term is much younger than the technical term sex (Haig, 2004). Fifty years ago, for example, the term gender was not even part of the professional literature that purported to study psychological similarities and differences between males and females. In fact, the first terminology introduced to the literature was *gender role,* not gender (Money, 1955).

There has been a tendency to conflate the usage of the terms *sex* and *gender,* so that it is not always clear if one is referring to the biological or the psychological characteristics that distinguish males from females (Gentile, 1993). The use of these terms has also been related to assumptions about causality in that the former is used to refer exclusively to biological processes and the latter is used to refer exclusively to psychological or sociological processes (for critiques of this division, see Maccoby, 1988; Money, 1985). As a result, some researchers who study humans employ such terms as *sex-typical, sex-dimorphic,* and *sex-typed* to characterize sex differences in behavior, since terms of this kind are descriptively more neutral with regard to putative etiology.

Gender Identity

Gender identity was introduced into the professional lexicon by Hooker and Stoller almost simultaneously in the early 1960s (see Money, 1985). Stoller (1964), for example, used the slightly different term *core gender identity* to describe a young child's developing "fundamental sense of belonging to one sex" (p. 453). This term was later adopted by cognitive-developmental psychologists, such as Kohlberg (1966), who defined gender identity as the child's ability to accurately discriminate males from females and then to identify his or her own gender status correctly—a task considered by some to be the first "stage" in gender constancy development, the end state of which is the knowledge of gender invariance (Martin, Ruble, & Szkrybalo, 2002).

Gender Role

Gender role has been used extensively by developmental psychologists to refer to behaviors, attitudes, and personality traits that a society, in a given culture and historical period, designates as masculine or feminine, that is, more "appropriate" to or typical of the male or female social role (Ruble et al., 2006). It should be recalled, however, that defining gender roles in this way assumes that they are completely arbitrary and social in origin, a view not universally shared by researchers in the field. In any case, from a descriptive point of view, the measurement of gender role behavior in young children includes several easily observable phenomena, including affiliative preference for same-sex versus opposite-sex peers, roles in fantasy play, toy interests, dress-up play, and interest in rough-and-tumble play. In older children or adolescents, gender role has also been measured using personality attributes with stereotypic masculine or feminine connotations or with regard to recreational and occupational interests and aspirations (Ruble et al., 2006; Zucker, 2005).

Sexual Orientation

Sexual orientation can be defined by a person's relative responsiveness to sexual stimuli. The most salient dimension of sexual orientation is probably the sex of the person to whom one is attracted sexually. This stimulus class is obviously how one defines a person's sexual orientation, or erotic partner preference, as heterosexual, bisexual, or homosexual. In contemporary sexology, sexual orientation is often assessed by psychophysiological techniques such as penile plethysmography or vaginal photoplethysmography (Chivers, Rieger, Latty, & Bailey, 2004; Rosen & Beck, 1988). Although, structured interview assessments have become increasingly common, particularly when respondents do not have a compelling reason to conceal their sexual orientation (Schrimshaw, Rosario, Meyer-Bahlburg, & Scharf-Matlick, 2006).

Sexual Identity

It is important to uncouple the construct of sexual orientation from the construct of *sexual identity*. A person may, for example, be predominantly aroused by homoerotic stimuli, yet not regard himself or herself to be gay or lesbian. Indeed, a substantial body of evidence indicates disjunctions among markers of sexual orientation and sexual identity, including behavioral experience, attraction, and self-labeling (Laumann, Gagnon, Michael, & Michaels, 1994; Savin-Williams & Ream, 2007).

Sociologists, particularly those of the *social scripting* and *social constructionist* schools, have articulated the sexual orientation-sexual identity disjunction most forcefully, arguing that the incorporation of sexual orientation into one's sense of identity is a relatively recent phenomenon, culturally variable, and the result of a complex interplay of sociohistorical events (Gagnon, 1990). Nowadays, in postmodern Western culture, individuals with a minority sexual orientation frequently choose from a multiplicity of labels in characterizing their sexual identity (e.g., gay, pomo homo [postmodern homosexual], queer, questioning). Indeed, Rust (1999) reported no less than 21 different sexual identity labels generated by women who had had bisexual sexual experiences.

Children with Gender Identity Disorder

Phenomenology

Boys and girls diagnosed with GID as described in the *Diagnostic and Statistical Manual of Mental Disorders,* fourth, edition, text revision (*DSM-IV-TR;* American Psychiatric Association, 2000), the comparable diagnosis of gender identity disorder of childhood in *ICD-10* (World Health Organization, 1992), display an array of sex-typed behavior signaling a strong psychological identification with the opposite sex. These behaviors include (a) identity statements, (b) dress-up play, (c) toy play, (d) roles in fantasy play, (e) peer relations, (f) motoric and speech characteristics, (g) statements about sexual anatomy, and (h) involvement in rough-and-tumble play. In general, they show a strong preference for sex-typed behaviors more characteristic of the opposite sex and a rejection or avoidance of sex-typed behaviors more characteristic of one's own sex. There are also signs of distress and discomfort about one's status as a boy or a girl, including verbal expressions of dislike or disgust about one's genital anatomy. The behaviors that characterize GID in children occur in concert, not in isolation. It is this behavioral patterning that is of clinical significance, and recognition of the patterning is extremely important in conducting a diagnostic assessment.

The onset of most of the behaviors occurs during the preschool years (2 to 4 years), if not earlier. Clinical referral often occurs when parents begin to feel that the pattern of behavior is no longer a "phase," a common initial parental appraisal, that their child will "grow out of" (Stoller, 1967; Zucker, 2000). From a developmental perspective, the onset occurs during the same period that more typical sex-dimorphic behaviors can be observed in young children (Ruble et al., 2006). For a more detailed account of phenomenology, see Green (1974), Cohen-Kettenis and Pfäfflin (2003), and Zucker and Bradley (1995).

Epidemiology

Prevalence
None of the numerous contemporary epidemiological studies on the prevalence of psychiatric disorders in children has examined GID. Accordingly, estimates of prevalence have had to rely on less sophisticated approaches. For example, one estimate of prevalence might be inferred from the number of persons attending

clinics for adults that serve as gateways for hormonal and surgical sex reassignment. Because not all gender dysphoric adults may attend such clinics, this method may well underestimate the prevalence of GID; in any case, the number of adult transsexuals is small (see Chapter 14).

Another approach in gauging crude prevalence estimates can be gleaned from studies of children in whom specific cross-gender behaviors have been assessed (see Zucker, 1985). For example, one source of information comes from the widely used Child Behavior Checklist (CBCL; Achenbach & Edelbrock, 1983), a parent-report behavior problem questionnaire with excellent psychometric properties. It includes two items (out of 118) that pertain to cross-gender identification: "behaves like opposite sex" and "wishes to be of opposite sex." On the CBCL, ratings are made on a 3-point scale (0 = not true, 1 = somewhat or sometimes true, and 2 = very true or often true). In the standardization study, endorsement of both items was more common for girls than for boys, regardless of age and clinical status (referred versus nonreferred).

As reported by Zucker, Bradley, and Sanikhani (1997), among nonreferred boys (ages 4 to 11 years), 3.8% received a rating of a 1 and 1.0% received a rating of a 2 for the item "behaves like opposite sex," but only 1.0% received a rating of a 1 and 0.0% received a rating of a 2 for the item "wishes to be of opposite sex." The comparable percentages among nonreferred girls were 8.3%, 2.3%, 2.5%, and 1.0%, respectively. These findings suggest a sex difference in the occurrence of mild displays of cross-gender behavior, but not with regard to more extreme cross-gender behavior. These findings were replicated in a recent large-scale study of Dutch twins ($N = 23,393$) at ages 7 and 10 (van Beijsterveldt, Hudziak, & Boomsma, 2006). At both ages and for both sexes, behaving like the opposite sex was more common than wishing to be of the opposite sex (ratings of 1 and 2 combined); in general, more girls than boys were rated as showing these behaviors. Again, the percentage of both boys and girls who wished to be of the opposite sex was quite low (range, 0.9% to 1.7% by sex and age).

The main problem with such data is that they do not adequately identify patterns of cross-gender behavior that would be of use in determining "caseness." Thus, such data may be best viewed as screening devices for more intensive evaluation.

Sex Differences in Referral Rates

Among children between the ages of 3 to 12, boys are referred clinically more often than girls for concerns regarding gender identity. From the first author's clinic in Toronto, Canada, Cohen-Kettenis, Owen, Kaijser, Bradley, and Zucker (2003) reported a sex ratio of 5.75:1 ($N = 358$) of boys to girls based on consecutive referrals from 1975 to 2000. Comparative data were available on children evaluated at the second author's clinic in The Netherlands.

Although the sex ratio was significantly smaller at 2.93:1 ($N =$ 130), it still favored referral of boys over girls.

How might this disparity in the sex ratio be best understood? One possibility is that it reflects accurately the prevalence of GID in boys and girls, but because prevalence data from the general population are lacking, this remains a matter of conjecture. Another possibility is that social factors play a role. For example, in childhood, it is well-established that parents, teachers, and peers are less tolerant of cross-gender behavior in boys than in girls, which might result in a sex-differential in clinical referral (Zucker & Bradley, 1995). Another factor that could affect sex differences in referral rates pertains to the relative salience of cross-gender behavior in boys versus girls. For example, it has long been observed that the sexes differ in the extent to which they display sex-typical behaviors; when there is significant between-sex variation, it is almost always the case that girls are more likely to engage in masculine behaviors than boys are to engage in feminine behaviors (Zucker, 2005). Thus, the base rates for cross-gender behavior, at least within the range of normative variation, may well differ between the sexes.

Age at Referral

In the Cohen-Kettenis et al. (2003) study, the age distribution at referral showed some remarkable differences. The Toronto sample had a substantially higher percentage of referrals between the ages of 3 to 4, 4 to 5, and 5 to 6 years than did the Dutch sample (40.5% versus 13.1%) and these differences were even more pronounced for the age intervals of 3 to 4 and 4 to 5 years (22.6% versus 2.3%). Cohen-Kettenis et al. noted that the "delay" in referral to the Dutch clinic could not readily be accounted for by differences in natural history, including degree of cross-gender behavior, base rates of cross-gender behavior in the two countries, or financial factors (such as insurance coverage). It was speculated that cultural factors might account for the cross-national difference in age at referral, in that North American parents become concerned about their child's cross-gender behavior at an earlier age than do Dutch parents.

Diagnosis and Assessment

The *DSM-IV* Diagnosis of Gender Identity Disorder

Relative to earlier versions of the manual, the *DSM-IV* introduced some changes in the conceptualization of GID and in the diagnostic criteria. For example, there was a reduction of diagnoses from three to one between the *DSM-III-R* and the *DSM-IV.* The *DSM-IV*

Subcommittee on Gender Identity Disorders (Bradley et al., 1991) took the position that the *DSM-III-R* diagnoses of gender identity disorder of childhood, transsexualism, and gender identity disorder of adolescence or adulthood, nontranssexual type, were not qualitatively distinct disorders, but reflected differences in both developmental and severity parameters. As a result, the *DSM-IV* Subcommittee recommended one overarching diagnosis, "gender identity disorder" that could be used, with appropriate variations in criteria, across the life cycle (see also Chapter 14, this volume). Table 13.1 shows the *DSM* criteria for GID for children and adolescents.

In the *DSM-IV,* three criteria are required for the diagnosis and one exclusion criterion is also noted. The Point A criterion reflects the child's cross-gender identification, indexed by five behavioral characteristics, of which at least four must be present. The Point B criterion reflects the child's rejection of his or her anatomic status and/or rejection of same-sex stereotypical activities and behaviors. Point D specifies that the "disturbance . . . causes clinically significant distress or impairment in social, occupational, or other important areas of functioning" (American Psychiatric Association, 2000, p. 581). Point C is an exclusion criterion and pertains to the presence of a physical intersex condition (for discussion on this point, see Meyer-Bahlburg, 1994).

Reliability and Validity

The clinical research literature has paid very little attention to the reliability of diagnosis for GID in children. One study showed that clinicians can reliably make the diagnosis (Zucker, Finegan, Doering, & Bradley, 1984); however, a clinician judgment study by Ehrbar, Witty, and Bockting (in press) showed that nonspecialist clinicians often "under-diagnosed" GID when reading vignettes about children who met the complete *DSM* criteria for GID.

A much more extensive literature has examined evidence pertaining to discriminant validity. Over the past 30-plus years, a variety of measurement approaches have been developed to assess the sex-typed behavior in children referred clinically for GID, including observation of sex-typed behavior in free play tasks, on semi-projective or projective tasks, and on a structured Gender Identity Interview schedule. In addition, several parent-report questionnaires pertaining to various aspects of sex-typed behavior have been developed. In this line of research, several comparison groups have typically been utilized: siblings of GID probands, clinical controls, and nonreferred (or "normal") controls (for a summary and review of measures, see Zucker, 1992, 2005).

The results of these studies have demonstrated strong evidence for the discriminant validity of the various measures. Two examples are provided. The first is the Gender Identity Interview for Children

Table 13.1   *DSM-IV* Diagnostic Criteria for Gender Identity Disorder (Children)

A. A strong and persistent cross-gender identification (not merely a desire for any perceived cultural advantages of being the other sex).

   In children, the disturbance is manifested by at least four (or more) of the following:

   1. Repeatedly stated desire to be, or insistence that he or she is, the other sex.

   2. In boys, preference for cross-dressing or simulating female attire; in girls, insistence on wearing only stereotypical masculine clothing.

   3. Strong and persistent preferences for cross-sex roles in make-believe play or persistent fantasies of being the other sex.

   4. Intense desire to participate in the stereotypical games and pastimes of the other sex.

   5. Strong preference for playmates of the other sex.

B. Persistent discomfort with his or her sex or sense of inappropriateness in the gender role of that sex.

   In children, the disturbance is manifested by any of the following:

   1. In boys, the assertion that his penis or testes are disgusting or will disappear or the assertion that it would be better not to have a penis, or aversion toward rough-and-tumble play and rejection of male stereotypical toys, games, and activities.

   2. In girls, rejection of urinating in a sitting position, assertion that she has or will grow a penis, or assertion that she does not want to grow breasts or menstruate, or marked aversion toward normative feminine clothing.

C. The disturbance is not concurrent with a physical intersex condition.

D. The disturbance causes clinically significant distress or impairment in social, occupational, or other important areas of functioning.

Source: Diagnostic and Statistical Manual of Mental Disorders, fourth edition, text revision, by the American Psychiatric Association, 2000, Washington DC: Author. Copyright 2000 American Psychiatric Association. Reprinted with permission.

(GIIC), which contains 11 items. Each item is coded on a 3-point response scale. Based on factor analysis, Zucker et al. (1993) identified two factors, which were labeled *Affective Gender Confusion* (7 items) and *Cognitive Gender Confusion* (4 items), and which accounted for 38.2% and 9.8% of the variance, respectively. An item example from the first factor is "In your mind, do you ever think that you would like to be a girl (boy)?" and an item example from the second factor is "Are you a boy or a girl?" Both mean factor scores significantly differentiated gender-referred probands ($n = 85$)

from controls (*n* = 98). Cutoff scores of either three or four deviant responses yielded high specificity rates (88.8% and 93.9%, respectively), but lower sensitivity rates (54.1% and 65.8%, respectively).

In a second study, Wallien, Cohen-Kettenis, Owen-Anderson, Bradley, and Zucker (2007) examined the psychometric properties of the GIIC in a cross-national study of gender-referred children from Toronto (*n* = 376) and The Netherlands (*n* = 228), along with a control group of 180 children from Toronto. In this study, a one-factor solution containing all 12 items of the GIIC was obtained, accounting for 32.4% of the total variance. The gender-referred children from both clinics had a significantly higher mean deviant total score than did the controls; in addition, the Dutch gender-referred children had a significantly higher mean total score than did the Toronto gender-referred children. It was also shown that the gender-referred children from both clinics who had received a clinician diagnosis of GID had a significantly higher mean score on the GIIC than did the gender-referred children who were sub-threshold for the GID diagnosis.

The second is the Gender Identity Questionnaire for Children (GIQC), a parent-report questionnaire (Johnson et al., 2004). The GIQC consists of 16 items pertaining to various aspects of sex-typed behavior that are reflected in the GID diagnostic criteria, each rated on a 5-point response scale. A factor analysis based on 325 gender-referred children and 504 controls (siblings, clinic-referred, and nonreferred), with a mean age of 7.6 years, identified a one-factor solution containing 14 items, accounting for 43.7% of the variance. The gender-referred children had a significantly greater total deviant score than did the controls, with a large effect size of 3.70, using Cohen's *d*. With a specificity rate set at 95% for the controls, the sensitivity rate for the probands was 86.8%.

In a second study, Cohen-Kettenis et al. (2006) compared parent ratings on the GIQC for gender-referred children in Toronto (*n* = 338) and in The Netherlands (*n* = 175). Gender-referred boys from The Netherlands had a significantly higher total score (indicating more cross-gender behavior) than did gender-referred boys from Toronto, but there was no significant difference for girls. In the Toronto sample, the gender-referred girls had a significantly higher total score than the gender-referred boys, but there was no significant sex difference in the Dutch sample. Across both clinics, gender-referred children who met the complete *DSM* criteria for GID had a significantly higher cross-gender score than the gender-referred children who were subthreshold for the diagnosis.

Distress and Impairment

As noted by Zucker (1992), the *DSM-III-R* did not provide guidelines regarding the assessment of distress in the Point A criterion ("persistent and intense distress" about being a boy or a girl) or the ways in which it might be distinct from other operationalized components in the criteria (namely the "desire" to be of the other sex). In the *DSM-IV,* this problem persists, except that it is now located in Point D, with the additional problem of defining "impairment." The inclusion of a distress/impairment criterion ("a clinical significance criterion"; American Psychiatric Association, 2000, p. 8) is not unique to GID; in fact, this criterion now appears in most of the *DSM-IV* diagnoses. Very little empirical work preceded the introduction of the criterion (Spitzer & Wakefield, 1999). Indeed, the *DSM-IV* states that the assessment of distress and impairment "is an inherently difficult clinical judgment" (American Psychiatric Association, 2000, p. 8).

There are theoretical disagreements about the nature of distress and impairment in children with GID. Stoller (1968), for example, argued that GID in boys was ego-syntonic, but these boys become distressed only when their cross-gender fantasies and behaviors are interfered with. Stoller's conceptualization was, however, a *psychodynamic* formulation: he believed that GID was ego-syntonic because the familial conditions that produced it were systemically syntonic. Thus, it is likely that Stoller would have argued that the *DSM*'s conceptualization of distress was, and is, too narrow. Other theorists, however, have argued otherwise. For example, Coates and Person (1985) claimed that GID was a "solution" to specific forms of psychopathology in the child, particularly separation anxiety and "annihilation" anxiety, which were induced by familial psychopathology. It is conceivable that either the "primary" and "secondary" views are correct or that one or the other better fits individual cases.

One difficulty that remains to be sorted out is how best to operationalize the concept of distress, but this holds true not only for GID but also for all of the other childhood psychiatric conditions that include the distress/impairment criterion. A simple example of this is Separation Anxiety Disorder (SAD). If a 5-year-old with SAD shows chronic distress at having to attend kindergarten and hence be away from his or her attachment figure, is the distress simply secondary to the socially imposed requirement of attending school or is it inherent to the condition? The common distinction between socially induced and "in the person" distress may simply be a false dichotomy.

Associated Psychopathology

Comorbidity—the presence of two or more psychiatric disorders—occurs frequently among children referred for clinical evaluation. Assuming that the putative comorbid conditions actually represent distinct disorders, it is important to know, for various reasons, whether one condition increases the risk for the other condition or if the conditions are caused by distinct or overlapping factors (Caron & Rutter, 1991).

An interesting new example of comorbidity comes from several case reports describing GID's co-occurrence with Pervasive Developmental Disorders (PDD; Mukaddes, 2002; Perera, Gadambanathan, & Weerasiri, 2003; Williams, Allard, & Sears, 1996). These case reports mesh with our own recent clinical experience. In the first author's clinic, for example, about 10% of boys with GID seen over the past 7 years have also met criteria for PDD (including PDD-NOS). One 6-year-old boy, for example, who had many of the classic features of PDD, including intense behavioral rigidity and obsessional preoccupations (e.g., with vacuum cleaners), had been insisting that he was a girl for the past 3 years and would introduce himself to other children using a girl's name. He would have catastrophic temper tantrums if reminded that he was really a boy. It is, of course, highly unlikely that GID "causes" PDD or the other way round. Rather, it is conceivable that the relation between GID and PDD is linked by traits of behavioral rigidity and obsessionality.

The most systematic information on general behavior problems in children with GID comes from parent-report data using the CBCL. On the CBCL, clinic-referred boys and girls with GID show, on average, significantly more general behavior problems than do their siblings and nonreferred children (Cohen-Kettenis et al., 2003; Zucker & Bradley, 1995). When pair-matched to clinical controls on demographics variables, boys with GID were shown to have similar levels of behavior problems (Zucker & Bradley, 1995). Only one study has systematically assessed the presence of other *DSM* diagnoses using a structured interview schedule (Wallien, Swaab, & Cohen-Kettenis, 2007). In that study, 52% of children with GID met criteria for at least one other *DSM* diagnosis. This percentage was comparable to that of a control group of children with attention-deficit/hyperactivity disorder, 60% of whom met criteria for at least one other *DSM* diagnosis. Both clinical groups had a higher percentage of *DSM* diagnoses compared to a nonreferred reference group.

Patterns and Correlates of Behavior Problems

On the CBCL, boys with GID have a predominance of internalizing (as opposed to externalizing) behavioral difficulties whereas girls with GID do not (Cohen-Kettenis et al., 2003; Zucker & Bradley, 1995). Edelbrock and Achenbach (1980) used cluster analysis to develop a taxonomy of profile patterns from CBCL data. Intraclass correlations were calculated and then subjected to centroid cluster analysis, from which profile types were identified and labeled. Intraclass correlations can range from −1.00 to 1.00 and a score of .00 represents the mean of the referred sample in the standardization study.

Using this system, there was evidence for a clear internalizing pattern for boys with GID (Zucker & Bradley, 1995). For 3- to 5-year-old boys, the mean intraclass correlation for *Depressed-Social Withdrawal* was .04. For 6- to 11-year-old boys, the mean intraclass correlations for *Schizoid-Social Withdrawal* and *Schizoid* were .04 and .16, respectively. For both age groups, there was considerable "distance" from externalizing profile types; for example, for the 4- to 5-year-old boys, the mean intraclass correlation for *Aggressive-Delinquent* was −.42 and for the 6- to 11-year-old boys, the mean intraclass correlation for *Hyperactive* was −.33.

Two other studies have shown that boys with GID show high rates of separation anxiety traits (Coates & Person, 1985; Zucker, Bradley, & Lowry Sullivan, 1996). In a recent study, Wallien, van Goozen, and Cohen-Kettenis (2007) provided some evidence that children with GID showed more negative emotions and a tonically elevated skin conductance level response to a stress challenge than did normal controls. Wallien et al. concluded that their data provided some support for the idea that children with GID are more prone to anxiety than unaffected controls.

Zucker and Bradley (1995) found that increasing age was significantly associated with the degree of behavior problems in boys with GID (depending on the metric, *r*s ranged from .28 to .42, all *p*s < .001). This finding was replicated in the cross-national, cross-clinic comparative study by Cohen-Kettenis et al. (2003). One explanation for these age effects pertains to the role of peer ostracism; that children with GID experience significant difficulties within the peer group has been noted for some time. Using a composite index of poor peer relations derived from three CBCL items (Cronbach's alpha = .81), Zucker et al. (1997) showed that children with GID had significantly more peer relationship difficulties than did their siblings, even when controlling for overall number of behavior problems. Cohen-Kettenis et al. found that both Toronto and The Netherlands boys with GID had significantly poorer peer relations than girls with GID, consistent with normative studies showing that cross-gender behavior in boys is subject to more negative social pressure than is cross-gender behavior in girls. Nonetheless, Cohen-Kettenis et al. found that poor peer relations was the strongest predictor of CBCL behavior problems in *both* GID boys and girls, accounting for 32% and 24% of the variance, respectively, suggesting that social ostracism within the peer group may well be a potential mediator between cross-gender behavior and behavior problems.

An observational study by Fridell (2001) provided more direct support for the idea that the cross-sex-typed behavior of boys with GID may influence how well they are liked by other children.

Fridell created 15 age-matched experimental play groups consisting of one boy with GID, two nonreferred boys, and two nonreferred girls (age range, 3 to 8 years). During these sessions, the children in the playgroups had the opportunity to play with masculine, feminine, and neutral toys. After two 60-minute play sessions, conducted a week apart, each child was asked to select his or her favorite playmate from the group. The nonreferred boys chose most often the other nonreferred boy as their favorite playmate, thus indicating a distinct preference over the boy with GID. The nonreferred girls chose the other girl as their favorite playmate, thus showing a relative disinterest in either the boy with GID or the two nonreferred boys.

In summary, children with GID show, on average, as many other behavioral problems as do other clinic-referred children. Although these general behavior problems may contribute to their difficulties in the peer group, like other children with behavior problems, it is likely the case that their marked cross-gender behavior is particularly salient in eliciting negative reactions from their peers.

Although we have shown that poor peer relations are an important correlate of general behavior problems in children with GID, this finding is not meant to imply that it is the only source of these difficulties. Other research, for example, has shown that CBCL behavior problems in GID boys are associated with a composite index of maternal psychopathology, which may reflect generic, nonspecific familial risk factors in producing behavior problems in general (Zucker & Bradley, 1995). Furthermore, the predominance of internalizing psychopathology may reflect familial risk for affective disorders and temperamental features of the boys (Marantz & Coates, 1991). Thus, it is likely the case that there are both specific and general risk factors involved in accounting for the general behavioral problems of children with GID.

Developmental Trajectories

Follow-Up Studies of Boys

Green's (1987) study constitutes the most comprehensive, long-term follow-up of behaviorally feminine boys, the majority of whom would likely have met *DSM* criteria for GID. His study contained 66 feminine and 56 control boys (unselected for gender identity) assessed initially at a mean age of 7.1 years (range, 4 to 12). Forty-four feminine boys and 30 control boys were available for follow-up at a mean age of 18.9 years (range, 14 to 24). The majority of the boys were not in therapy between assessment and follow-up. Sexual orientation in fantasy and behavior was assessed by means of a semi-structured interview. Kinsey ratings were made on a 7-point continuum, ranging from exclusive heterosexuality (a Kinsey 0) to exclusive homosexuality (a Kinsey 6). Depending on the measure (fantasy or behavior), 75% to 80% of the previously feminine boys were either bisexual or homosexual (Kinsey ratings between 2 to 6) at follow-up versus 0% to 4% of the control boys. Green also reported on the gender identity status of the 44 previously feminine boys. He found that only one youth, at the age of 18 years, was gender-dysphoric to the extent of considering sex-reassignment surgery.

Data from six other follow-up reports on 55 boys with GID were summarized by Zucker and Bradley (1995). At follow-up (range, 13 to 26 years), 5 of these boys were classified as transsexual (with a homosexual sexual orientation), 21 were classified as homosexual, 1 was classified as a (heterosexual) transvestite, 15 were classified as heterosexual, and 13 could not be rated with regard to sexual orientation. If one excludes the 13 "uncertain" cases in these six studies, then 27 (64.2%) of the remaining 42 cases had "atypical" (i.e., homosexual, transsexual, or transvestitic) outcomes. In these studies, the percentage of boys who showed persistent GID was higher than that reported by Green (11.9% versus 2.2%, respectively), but the percentage who were homosexual (62.1%) was somewhat lower.

Zucker and Bradley (1995) reported preliminary follow-up data on their own sample of 40 boys first seen in childhood (M age at assessment, 8.2 years; range, 3 to 12). At follow-up, these boys were, on average, 16.5 years (range, 14 to 23). Gender identity was assessed by means of a semi-structured clinical interview and by questionnaire. Sexual orientation (for a 12-month period prior to the time of evaluation) was assessed for fantasy and behavior using the Kinsey scale in a manner identical to Green's study.

Of the 40 boys, 8 (20%) were classified as gender-dysphoric at follow-up. The remaining 80% had a "normal" gender identity. Regarding sexual orientation in fantasy, 20 (50%) were classified as heterosexual, 17 (42.5%) were classified as bisexual/homosexual, and 3 (7.5%) were classified as "asexual" (i.e., they did not report any sexual fantasies). Regarding sexual orientation in behavior, 9 (22.5%) were classified as heterosexual, 11 (27.5%) were classified as bisexual/homosexual, and 20 (50.0%) were classified as "asexual" (i.e., they did not report any interpersonal sexual experiences).

In the most recent follow-up study of boys with GID, Wallien and Cohen-Kettenis (2007) reported that 20% showed persistence of GID in mid-adolescence. Thus, the rate of GID persistence, at least into adolescence, was higher than that reported by Green (1987) and comparable to the rate obtained by Zucker and Bradley (1995), as noted earlier.

In taking stock of these outcome data, Green's (1987) study clearly shows that boys with GID were disproportionately, and substantially, more likely than the control boys to differentiate a bisexual/homosexual sexual orientation. The other follow-up studies yielded somewhat lower estimates of a bisexual/homosexual sexual orientation. In this regard, at least one caveat is in order. In the Zucker and Bradley (1995) follow-up, for example, the boys were somewhat younger than were the boys followed-up by Green, so their lower rate of a bisexual/homosexual sexual orientation outcome should be interpreted cautiously, as one would expect, if anything, these youth to underreport an atypical sexual orientation due to social desirability considerations. But even these lower rates of a bisexual/homosexual sexual orientation are substantially higher than the currently accepted base rate of about 2% to 3% of a homosexual sexual orientation in men identified in recent epidemiological studies (Laumann et al., 1994).

A more substantive difference between Green's (1987) study and the other follow-up reports pertains to the persistence of gender dysphoria. Both Zucker and Bradley (1995) and Wallien and Cohen-Kettenis (2007), for example, found higher rates of persistence than Green. At present, the explanations for this are unclear. One possibility pertains to sampling differences. Green's study was carried out in the context of an advertised research study whereas the Zucker and Bradley and Wallien and Cohen-Kettenis samples were clinic-referred. Thus, it is conceivable that their samples may have included more extreme cases of childhood GID than in the sample ascertained by Green. Indeed, Wallien and Cohen-Kettenis found that persistence was associated with more cross-gender behavior (based on three measures) at the time of assessment in childhood. This kind of information is very helpful in understanding the variation in gender identity and sexual orientation outcomes within a population of children referred for gender identity problems.

Follow-Up Studies of Girls

Unfortunately, the long-term follow-up of girls with GID remains very patchy. In part, this reflects the comparatively lower rate of referred girls to referred boys with GID in child samples (Cohen-Kettenis et al., 2003). In the first author's clinic, Drummond, Bradley, Badali-Peterson, and Zucker (in press) evaluated 25 girls, originally assessed at a mean age of 8.8 years (range, 3 to 12), at a follow-up mean age of 23.2 years (range, 15 to 36). Of these 25 girls, three (12%) had persistent GID (at follow-up ages of 17, 21, and 23 years, respectively), two of whom had a homosexual sexual orientation and the third was asexual. The remaining 22 (88%) girls had a "normal" gender identity. In the second author's clinic, Wallien and Cohen-Kettenis (2007) reported that 50% of their girl patients showed persistence of GID in mid-adolescence.

Regarding sexual orientation in fantasy (Kinsey ratings) for the 12 months preceding the follow-up assessment, Drummond et al. reported that 15 (60%) girls were classified as exclusively heterosexual, 8 (32%) as bisexual/homosexual, and 2 (8%) as "asexual" (i.e., they did not report any sexual fantasies). Regarding sexual orientation in behavior, 11 (44%) girls were classified as exclusively heterosexual, 6 (24%) as bisexual/homosexual, and 8 (32%) as "asexual" (i.e., they did not report any interpersonal sexual experiences).

Taken together, these two follow-up reports show a range of outcomes, but the rates of GID and a bisexual/homosexual sexual orientation without co-occurring gender dysphoria are likely to be higher than the base rates of these two aspects of psychosexual differentiation in an unselected population of women. For example, using Bakker, van Kesteren, Gooren, and Bezemer's (1993) estimation of GID prevalence in females, the odds of persistent gender dysphoria in Drummond et al.'s (in press) sample were 4,084 times the odds of gender dysphoria in the general population. Using prevalence estimates of bisexuality/homosexuality in fantasy among biological females (anywhere between 2% to 5%), the odds of reporting bisexuality/homosexuality in fantasy was 8.9 to 23.1 times higher than in the general population.

GID Persistence and Desistance in a Comparative-Developmental Perspective

A key challenge for developmental theories of psychosexual differentiation is to account for the disjunction between retrospective and prospective data with regard to GID persistence: only a minority of children followed prospectively shows a persistence of GID into adolescence and young adulthood.

In some respects, the situation is comparable to that found for other child psychiatric disorders. For example, adults with antisocial personality disorder (APD) invariably will have had a childhood history of oppositional defiant disorder (ODD) and conduct disorder (CD), an example of retrospective continuity (Robins, 1978). Yet, the vast majority of children with ODD and the majority of children with CD followed prospectively will not be diagnosed with APD in adulthood (Lahey, McBurnett, & Loeber, 2000; Zoccolillo, Pickles, Quinton, & Rutter, 1992).

Regarding children with GID, then, we need to understand why, for the majority, the disorder apparently remits by adolescence, if not earlier. One possible explanation concerns referral bias. Green (1974) argued that children with GID who are referred for clinical assessment (and then, in some cases, therapy) may come from families in which there is more concern than is the case for adolescents and adults, the majority of whom did not receive a clinical evaluation and treatment during childhood. Thus, a clinical evaluation and subsequent therapeutic intervention during childhood may alter the natural history of GID. Of course, this is only one account of the disjunction and there may well be additional factors that distinguish those children more strongly at risk for the disorder's continuation from those who are not. One possibility is that the diagnostic criteria for GID, at least as they are currently formulated, simply are not sharp enough to distinguish children who are more likely to show a persistence in the disorder from those who are not. An additional clue comes from consideration of the concepts of developmental malleability and plasticity. It is possible, for example, that gender identity shows relative malleability during childhood, with a gradual narrowing of plasticity as the gendered sense of self consolidates as one approaches adolescence. Some support for this idea comes from follow-up studies of adolescents with GID, who appear to show a much higher rate of GID persistence as they are followed into young adulthood (see the discussion that follows).

Therapeutics

Ethical Considerations

Consider the following clinical scenarios:

- A mother of a 4-year-old boy calls a well-known clinic that specializes in sexuality throughout the life span. She describes behaviors consistent with the *DSM* diagnosis of GID. The clinician tells the mother: "Well, we don't consider it to be a problem." The mother then contacts a specialty clinic for children and adolescents and asks, "What should I do?"

- A mother of a 4-year-old boy calls a well-known clinic that specializes in gender identity problems. She describes behaviors consistent with the *DSM* diagnosis of GID. She says that she would like her child treated so he does not grow up to be gay. She also worries that her child will be ostracized within the peer group because of his pervasive cross-gender behavior. What should the clinician say to this mother?

- The parents of a 6-year-old boy (somatically male) conclude that their son is really a girl, so they seek the help of an attorney to institute a legal name change (from Zachary to Aurora) and inform the school principal that their son will attend school as a girl. The local child protection agency is notified and the child is removed from his parents' care (Cloud, 2000). If a clinician was asked to evaluate the situation, what would be in the best interest of the child and family?

Any contemporary developmental clinician responsible for the therapeutic care of children with GID will quickly be introduced to complex social and ethical issues pertaining to the politics of sex and gender in postmodern Western culture and will have to think them through carefully. The scenarios described, as well as many others, require the clinician to think long and hard about theoretical, ethical, and treatment issues (Zucker, 2007).

Rationales for Treatment

The treatment literature on children with GID contains five rationales for treatment: (1) reduction in social ostracism, (2) treatment of underlying psychopathology, (3) treatment of the underlying distress, (4) prevention of transsexualism in adulthood, and (5) prevention of homosexuality in adulthood (Zucker, 2007).

In our view, the first four rationales are clinically defensible, but the fifth is not. So, on this last point, further explication is warranted. Some critics have argued that clinicians, consciously or unconsciously, accept the prevention of homosexuality as a legitimate therapeutic goal (Pleak, 1999; see also Zucker & Spitzer, 2005). Others have asserted, albeit without empirical documentation, that treatment of GID results in harm to children who are homosexual or prehomosexual (Isay, 1997). In response to these and other concerns, the Human Rights Commission of the city and county of San Francisco passed a resolution on September 12, 1996, that condemned "any treatment designed to manipulate a young person's . . . gender identity."

The various issues regarding the relation between GID and homosexuality are complex, both clinically and ethically. Three points, albeit brief, can be made. First, until it has been shown that any form of treatment for GID during childhood affects later sexual orientation, Green's (1987) discussion of whether parents have the right to seek treatment to maximize the likelihood of their child becoming heterosexual is moot. From an ethical standpoint, however, the treating clinician has an obligation to inform parents about the state of the empirical database. Second, we have argued elsewhere that some critics incorrectly conflate gender identity and sexual orientation, regarding them as isomorphic phenomena, as do some parents (Zucker, 1999). Psychoeducational work with parents can review the various explanatory models regarding the statistical linkage between gender identity and sexual orientation (Bailey & Zucker, 1995), but also discuss their distinctness as psychological constructs. Third, many contemporary child clinicians emphasize that the primary goal of treatment with children with GID is to resolve the conflicts that are associated with the disorder per se, regardless of the child's eventual sexual orientation.

If the clinician is to provide treatment for a child with GID, a variety of interventions are available and they are summarized in Sidebar 13.1. In appraising this literature, however, it is important to bear in mind the following: one will find not a single randomized controlled treatment trial. There have, however, been some treatment-effectiveness studies, although much is lacking in these investigations. In general, the practitioner must rely largely on the "clinical wisdom" that has accumulated in the case report literature and the conceptual underpinnings that inform the various approaches to intervention.

SIDEBAR 13.1

Types of Treatments and Interventions

- *Behavior therapy:* Gender-typical behaviors are rewarded while no rewards are given for cross-gender behavior; includes differential social attention or social reinforcement, self-regulation or self-monitoring, potential future treatments of behavior therapy that emphasize cognitive structures regarding gender.
- *Psychotherapy:* Includes psychoanalysis, psychoanalytic psychotherapy, and psychotherapy; includes varied approaches to understanding the etiology of GID including classical, object relations, and self-psychology; clinicians generally emphasize oedipal issues, developmental phenomena, overall adaptive functioning, and gender-specific perspectives on development.
- *Treatment of parents:* Addresses parents' potential influence on GID as well as daily management issues in the child's therapeutic plan; can support and encourage both the children being treated as well as the parents involved in the therapeutic plan.
- *Limit setting:* Encourages implementation of limits regarding cross-gender activity while also considering contextual and conceptual issues and systemic factors that contribute to symptom perpetuation; encourages parents to set limits but also encourage alternative activities, including same-sex peer group relationship-building; must also account for child's individual temperamental characteristics and examine initial parental dynamics.
- *Supportive treatments:* Stems from belief that GID is constitutional or congenital, thus potentially limiting the role of psychosocial or psychodynamic factors; main goal is to help parents in a supportive role and encourage opportunities for child's adjustment to accepting the child's authentic gender identity or role; differs from more traditional interventions in that it is supportive of cross-gender affirmation in its approach.

Behavior Therapy

The literature contains 13 single-case reports that employed a be-havior therapy approach to the treatment of GID in children (re-viewed in Zucker, 1985). The classical behavioral approach assumes that children learn sex-typed behaviors much as they learn any other behaviors and that sex-typed behaviors can be shaped, at least initially, by encouraging some and discouraging others. Accordingly, behavior therapy for GID systematically arranges to have rewards follow gender-typical behaviors and to have no rewards (or perhaps punishments) follow cross-gender behaviors.

One type of intervention employed has been termed *differential social attention* or *social reinforcement*. This type of intervention has been applied in clinic settings, particularly to sex-typed play behaviors. The therapist first establishes with baseline measures that the child (either when alone or in the presence of a noninter-acting adult) prefers playing with cross-sex toys or dress-up ap-parel rather than same-sex toys or dress-up apparel. A parent or stranger is then introduced into the playroom and instructed to at-tend to the child's same-sex play (e.g., by looking, smiling, and verbal praise) and to ignore the child's cross-sex play (e.g., by looking away and pretending to read). Such adult responses seem to elicit rather sharp changes in play behavior.

There have been two main limitations to the use of social at-tention or reinforcement in treating cross-gender behavior. First, at least some of the children studied reverted to cross-sex play patterns in the adult's absence or in other environments, such as the home—a phenomenon known as *stimulus specificity* (Rekers, 1975). Second, there was little generalization to untreated cross-sex behaviors—a phenomenon known as *response specificity.*

The problems of stimulus and response specificity have led behavior therapists to seek more effective strategies of promoting generalization. One such strategy, *self-regulation* or *self-monitoring*, has the child reinforce himself or herself when engaging in a sex-typical behavior. Although self-monitoring also resulted in sub-stantial decreases in cross-sex play, the evidence is weak that generalization is better promoted by self-regulation than by social attention (Zucker, 1985).

One final word about the behavioral approach to treatment is in order: The behavior therapy literature has produced no new case reports for over 20 years although its principles are often used in broader treatment approaches that involve the parents. This publication gap is curious because more contemporary be-havioral approaches, such as cognitive-behavior therapy, are now used so widely with other disorders.

Behavior therapy with an emphasis on the child's cognitive structures regarding gender could be an interesting and novel approach to treatment. A fairly large literature on the development of cognitive gender-schemas now exists in nonreferred children (Martin et al., 2002). It is possible that children with GID have more elaborately developed cross-gender schemas than same-gender schemas and that more positive affective appraisals are differentiated for the latter than for the former (e.g., in boys, "girls get to wear prettier clothes" versus "boys are too rough"). A cognitive approach to treatment might help children with GID develop more flexible and realistic notions about gender-related traits (e.g., "boys can wear pretty cool clothes too" or "there are lots of boys who don't like to be rough"), which may result in more positive gender feelings about being a boy or being a girl.

Psychotherapy

There is a large case report literature on the treatment of children with GID using psychoanalysis, psychoanalytic psychotherapy, or psychotherapy, some of which is quite detailed and rich in content (for references, see Zucker, 2001, 2007). The psychoanalytic treatment literature is more diverse than the behavior therapy literature, including varied theoretical approaches to understanding the putative etiology of GID (e.g., classical, object relations, and self psychology); nevertheless, a number of recurring themes can be gleaned from this case report literature.

Psychoanalytic clinicians generally emphasize that the cross-gender behavior emerges during the preoedipal years; accordingly, they stress the importance of understanding how the GID relates to other developmental phenomena salient during these years (e.g., attachment relations and the emergence of the autonomous self). Oedipal issues are also deemed important, but these are understood within the context of prior developmental interferences and conflicts. Psychoanalytic clinicians also place great weight on the child's overall adaptive functioning, which they view as critical in determining the therapeutic approach to the specific referral problem.

Apart from the general developmental perspective inherent to a psychoanalytic understanding of psychopathology, one might also add to this a gender-specific perspective on development (Martin et al., 2002). Many developmentalists, for example, note that the first signs of normative gender development appear during the toddler years, including the ability to correctly self-label oneself as a boy or a girl. Some authors have even postulated a sensitive period for gender identity formation (Money, Hampson, & Hampson, 1957), which suggests a period of time in which there is a greater malleability or plasticity in the direction that gender identity can move. Thus, early gender identity formation intersects quite neatly with analytic views on the early development of the sense of self in more global terms. It is likely, therefore, that the putative pathogenic mechanisms identified in the development of GID are likely to have a greater impact only if they occur during the alleged sensitive period for gender identity formation.

An overall examination of the available case reports suggests that psychotherapy, like behavior therapy, does have some beneficial influence on the sex-typed behavior of children with GID. However, the effectiveness of psychoanalytic psychotherapy, like that of behavior therapy, has never been demonstrated in an outcome study comparing children randomly assigned to treated and untreated conditions. Moreover, many of the cases cited above did not consist solely of psychoanalytic treatment of the child. The parents were often also in therapy, and, in some of the cases, the child was an inpatient and thus exposed to other interventions. It is impossible to disentangle these other potential therapeutic influences from the effect of the psychotherapy alone.

Parental Involvement in Treatment

Two rationales have been offered for parental involvement in treatment. The first emphasizes the hypothesized role of parental dynamics and psychopathology in the genesis or maintenance of the disorder. From this perspective, individual therapy with the child will probably proceed more smoothly and quickly if the parents are able to gain some insight into their own contribution to their child's difficulties. Many clinicians who have worked extensively with gender-disturbed children subscribe to this rationale (Newman, 1976; Zucker, 2001, 2007). In this context, a treatment plan requires as much of an assessment of the parents as it does of the child, as is the case with many child psychiatric disorders. Assessment of psychopathology and the marital relationship in the parents of children with GID reveals great variability in adaptive functioning, which may well prove to be a prognostic factor.

The second rationale is that parents will benefit from regular, formalized contact with the therapist to discuss day-to-day management issues that arise in carrying out the overall therapeutic plan. Work with parents can focus on the setting of limits with regard to cross-gender behavior, such as cross-dressing, cross-gender role and fantasy play, and cross-gender toy play and, at the same time, attempting to provide alternative activities (e.g., encouragement of same-sex peer relations and involvement in more gender-typical and neutral activities). In addition, parents can work on conveying to their child that they are trying to help him or her feel better about being a boy or a girl and that they want their child to be happier in this regard. Some parents, especially the well-functioning and intellectually sophisticated ones, are able to carry out these recommendations relatively easily and without ambivalence. Many parents, however, require ongoing support in implementing the recommendations, perhaps because of their own ambivalence and reservations about gender identity issues.

Technical Aspects of Limit Setting

Some technical aspects of limit setting are misunderstood. Thus, the role of limit setting in treatment requires some consideration of conceptual and contextual issues. A common error committed by some clinicians is to simply recommend to parents that they impose limits on their child's cross-gender behavior without attention to context. This kind of authoritarian approach is likely to fail, just like it will with regard to any behavior, because it does not take into account systemic factors, both in the parents and in the child, that contribute to symptom perpetuation. At the very least, a psychoeducational approach is required, but, in many cases, limit setting needs to occur within the context of a more global treatment plan. From a psychoeducational point of view, one rationale for limit setting is that if parents allow their child to continue to engage in cross-gender behavior, the GID is, in effect, being tolerated, if not reinforced. Another rationale for limit setting is to alter the GID from the outside in, while individual therapy for the child can explore the factors that have contributed to the GID from the inside out. At the same time that they attempt to set limits, parents also need to help their child with alternative activities that might help consolidate a more comfortable same-gender identification. As noted earlier, encouragement of same-sex peer group relations can be an important part of such alternatives. Some boys with GID develop an avoidance of male playmates because they are anxious about rough-and-tumble play and fantasy aggression. Such anxiety may be fueled by parent factors (e.g., where mothers conflate real aggression with fantasy aggression), but may also be fueled by temperamental characteristics of the child (Coates & Wolfe, 1995). Efforts on the part of parents to be more sensitive to their child's temperamental characteristics may be quite helpful in planning peer group encounters that are not experienced by the child as threatening and overwhelming. It is not unusual to encounter boys with GID who have a genuine longing to interact with other boys but, because of their shy and avoidant temperament, do not know how to integrate themselves with other boys, particularly if they experience the contextual situation as threatening. Over time, with the appropriate therapeutic support, such boys are able to develop same-sex peer group relationships and, as a result, begin to identify more with other boys.

Another important contextual aspect of limit setting is to explore with parents their initial encouragement or tolerance of the cross-gender behavior. Some parents will tolerate the behavior initially because they have been told, or believe themselves, that the behavior is "only a phase" that their child will grow out of or that "all children" engage in such behavior. For such parents, they become concerned about their child once they begin to recognize that the behavior is not merely a phase. For other parents, the tolerance or encouragement of cross-gender behavior can be linked to some of the systemic and dynamic factors described earlier. In these more complex clinical situations, one must attend to the underlying issues and work them through. Otherwise, parents may not be comfortable in shifting their position.

Although many contemporary clinicians have stressed the importance of working with the parents of children with GID, one can ask if empirical evidence supports its effectiveness. Again, systematic information on the question is scant. The most relevant study found some evidence that parental involvement in therapy was significantly correlated with a greater degree of behavioral change in the child at a 1-year follow-up, but this study did not make random assignment to different treatment protocols, so one has to interpret the findings with caution (Zucker, Bradley, Doering, & Lozinski, 1985).

Supportive Treatments

In the past few years, clinicians critical of conceptualizing marked cross-gender behavior in children as a disorder have provided a dissenting perspective to the treatment approaches described so far (e.g., Menvielle & Tuerk, 2002; Menvielle, Tuerk, & Perrin, 2005; see also Lev, 2005; Saeger, 2006). These clinicians conceptualize GID or pervasive gender-variant behavior from an essentialist perspective, that is, that GID is fully constitutional or congenital in origin and thus the clinicians are skeptical about the role of psychosocial or psychodynamic factors. As an example, Bockting and Ehrbar (2005) argued "instead of attempts to change the child's gender identity or role, treatment should assist the family to accept the child's authentic gender identity and affirm a gender role expression that is most comfortable for that child" (p. 128). Along similar lines, Menvielle and Tuerk (2002) noted that, while it might be helpful to set limits on pervasive cross-gender behaviors that may contribute to social ostracism, their primary treatment goal (offered in the context of a parent support group) was "not at changing the children's behavior, but at helping parents to be supportive and to maximize opportunities for the children's adjustment" (p. 2002). Menvielle et al. (2005) have taken a somewhat stronger position, arguing that "[t]herapists who advocate changing gender-variant behaviors should be avoided" (p. 45). This perspective, however, appears to be encouraging some parents to take an approach that is rather different from the more "traditional" therapeutic models: several examples are now reported in the media in which parents of very young children enforce a social gender change (e.g., registering a biological male child in school as a girl; see, e.g., Santiago, 2006).

Because comparative treatment approaches are not available, it is not possible to say whether or not this supportive or "cross-gender affirming" approach will result in both short-term and long-term outcomes any different from the more traditional approaches to treatment. The supportive approach does, however, highlight a variety of theoretical and clinical disagreements, which will only be resolved by more systematic research on therapeutics.

Adolescents with Gender Identity Disorder

Phenomenology

Adolescents with GID show a strong psychological identification with the opposite sex. More importantly, they also verbalize a strong desire to become a member of the opposite sex and indicate an extreme unhappiness about being male or female. The subjective experience of such youth can be characterized by the term *gender dysphoria* (see Fisk, 1973). In its full form, the clinical picture includes several characteristics: (a) a frequently stated desire to be a member of the opposite sex; (b) verbal or behavioral expressions of anatomic dysphoria (e.g., in girls, stating a desire to have a penis; to masculinize their bodies via contrasex hormones; and to have bilateral mastectomy; for sophisticated adolescents, they will also express the desire for both a hysterectomy and oophorectomy; in boys, stating a desire to have their penis and testes removed and to have the surgical creation of a neovagina and clitoris; to feminize their bodies via contrasex hormones, electrolysis, and reduction in size of the Adam's apple); (c) a strong desire to pass socially as a member of the opposite sex, which is often attempted via modification of phenotypic social markers of gender, such as hair and clothing style, and the adoption of a stereotypical name associated with the opposite sex.

It is commonly the case that adolescents with extreme forms of GID had an onset of their cross-gender behavior in early childhood. After elementary school, their cross-gender behavior and feelings continue and some start high school having transitioned into the gender role of the opposite sex. Adolescents who do not fulfill all criteria for GID are, however, a heterogeneous group. They may have a request for sex-reassignment (SR) but are ambivalent about it; have a strong SR wish during an initial assessment phase, but change their minds later; have no real SR request, but are merely confused about their gender feelings; or have questions regarding their gender identity that is secondary to other psychopathology (e.g., PDD). In these late-onset cases, there is generally no clear indication of pervasive cross-gender behavior during childhood.

Epidemiology

Prevalence

As in the case for children with GID, there are really no good estimates of GID prevalence for adolescents. On metrics like the CBCL, however, the percentage of adolescent boys and girls (ages 12 to 16) whose parents endorsed the item "Wishes to be of opposite sex" was extremely low; indeed, for some sex by age cells, the percentage was 0 (see Achenbach & Edelbrock, 1983, p. 33). Thus, against base rates, even a periodic desire to become a member of the opposite sex is quite atypical.

Sex Differences in Referral Rates

Compared to children with GID, the sex ratio of adolescents with GID is much smaller: among adolescents between the ages of 13 to 20, the sex ratio in the first author's clinic currently stands at 1.40:1 ($N = 139$) of males to females (see also Zucker, Owen, Bradley, & Ameeriar, 2002). This ratio is remarkably similar to the sex ratio of 1.20:1 ($N = 133$) in the second author's clinic (Cohen-Kettenis & Pfäfflin, 2003).

How might this narrowing of the sex ratio be best understood? One possibility is that it reflects accurately the change in prevalence of GID in males and females between childhood and adolescence. In adolescence, it may also be that extreme cross-gender behavior is subject to more equivalent social pressures across sex and thus there is a lowering in the bias toward a greater referral of boys. Along similar lines, it is possible that gender dysphoria in adolescent girls is more difficult to ignore than it is during childhood, as the intensification of concerns with regard to physical sex transformation becomes more salient to parents and other adults (e.g., teachers) involved in the life of the adolescent (see, e.g., Cohen-Kettenis & Everaerd, 1986; Streitmatter, 1985). However, in a community sample of adolescents, Young and Sweeting (2004) found that, like in childhood, cross-gender behavior was reacted to more harshly in boys than in girls.

Diagnosis and Assessment

To our knowledge, no study has evaluated the reliability of the GID diagnosis for adolescents. This may reflect the general dearth of empirical research when compared to their child counterparts (Cohen-Kettenis & Pfäfflin, 2003). If we consider the diagnostic criteria as they pertain to adolescents and adults (see Table 13.2), the Point A criterion contains four possible indicators of a "strong and persistent cross-gender identification": a stated desire to be the other sex, frequent passing as the other sex, desire to live or be treated as the other sex, and the conviction that he or she has the typical feelings and reactions of the other sex. The Point B criterion contains two possible indicators of a "persistent discomfort with [one's sex] or sense of inappropriateness in the gender role of that sex": preoccupation with getting rid of primary and secondary sex characteristics or the belief that one was born the wrong sex.

From a clinical practice perspective, we could argue that the application of the diagnostic criteria is not particularly difficult because it is relatively uncommon, at least in specialized child and adolescent gender identity clinics, to encounter an adolescent who has only very mild gender dysphoria. But this may well not be the

Table 13.2 *DSM-IV-TR* **Criteria for Gender Identity Disorder (Adolescents)**

A. A strong and persistent cross-gender identification (not merely a desire for any perceived cultural advantages of being the other sex).

   In adolescents, the disturbance is manifested by symptoms such as a stated desire to be the other sex, frequent passing as the other sex, desire to live or be treated as the other sex, or the conviction that he or she has the typical feelings and reactions of the other sex.

B. Persistent discomfort with his or her sex or sense of inappropriateness in the gender role of that sex.

   In adolescents, the disturbance is manifested by symptoms such as preoccupation with getting rid of primary and secondary sex characteristics (e.g., request for hormones, surgery, or other procedures to physically alter sexual characteristics to simulate the other sex) or belief that he or she was born the wrong sex.

C. The disturbance is not concurrent with a physical intersex condition.

D. The disturbance causes clinically significant distress or impairment in social, occupational, or other important areas of functioning.

   Specify if (for sexually mature individuals):
   – Sexually attracted to males
   – Sexually attracted to females
   – Sexually attracted to both
   – Sexually attracted to neither

Source: Diagnostic and Statistical Manual of Mental Disorders, fourth edition, text revision, by the American Psychiatric Association, 2000, Washington DC: Author. Copyright 2000 American Psychiatric Association. Reprinted with permission.

case in general clinical practice. Thus, it is important to keep in mind that the indicators of GID are meant to capture a "strong and persistent cross-gender identification" (Point A) and a "persistent discomfort" with one's gender (Point B), not transient feelings. Unfortunately, the *DSM* criteria are somewhat vague in assisting the clinician in making this distinction. Consider two examples from the Point A criterion. Note, for example, that the first indicator of the Point A criterion refers to a "stated desire" to be the other sex and that the third indicator refers to a "desire to live or be treated as the other sex." It is unlikely that these indicators were intended to reflect an episodic desire to be of the other sex or to live as the other sex but, for some reason, neither indicator included a specific reference to persistence or intensity. From a practical perspective, however, it could be argued that the odds of making a misdiagnosis of GID are probably not that high, primarily because, as noted above, normative data suggest that the frequent wish to be of the opposite sex in both referred and nonreferred samples is quite rare.

The *DSM-IV* criterion with regard to the "preoccupation" with one's primary and secondary sex characteristics (Point B-2) reflects well the adolescent expression of gender dysphoria as it pertains to discomfort with somatic sex, since the distress over physical sex markers is so pervasive. Nonetheless, even here, one has to exert some caution in making the diagnosis. For example, a study by Lee (2001) found a great deal of overlap in feelings of "anatomic dysphoria" among female-to-male transsexual women and self-identified "butch" lesbians. Similarly, the recently described phenomenon of "tranny boys" among young lesbian women (see McCarthy, 2003) in which, for example, there appears to be a desire for "partial" sex reassignment (e.g., mastectomy, but not masculinizing hormone treatment or the reverse), calls for caution in differential diagnosis.

In the *DSM,* the clinician can specify for "sexually mature individuals" information about sexual attraction (orientation) to males, females, both, or neither (see Table 13.2). In the clinical sexology literature on adults with GID, these categories have been termed, in relation to the patient's *birth sex,* heterosexual, homosexual, bisexual, or asexual (Blanchard, Clemmensen, & Steiner, 1987; see also Chapter 14, this volume).

For at least two reasons it is important to consider the sexual orientation of an adolescent with GID: theoretical reasons (not reviewed here) and clinical reasons. Most adolescents with GID who have an early onset, that is, starting in childhood, are sexually attracted to members of their birth sex and this is also the case with adults with GID (Blanchard et al., 1987). In contrast, most youth with GID who have a late onset, that is, starting in adolescence, are usually bisexual or heterosexual, and commonly have a co-occurring diagnosis of Transvestic Fetishism (TF) or autogynephilia (sexual arousal at the thought of being a woman; see Chapter 14, this volume).

In contrast to the empirical state of affairs for children, the development of reliable and valid assessment techniques for adolescents has lagged behind. Both authors have developed assessment protocols, but much of this material has not yet been published. In both our clinics, protocols include an assessment of general intelligence, behavior problems, dimensional evaluation of gender identity/gender dysphoria, and sexual orientation. Table 13.3 summarizes some of the more commonly used assessment methods.

Table 13.4 shows data from the Recalled Childhood Gender Identity/Gender Role Questionnaire (Zucker et al., 2006), a 23-item questionnaire designed to measure recalled sex-typed behavior during childhood. Factor analysis identified a two-factor solution: Factor 1 contains 18 items pertaining to childhood gender role and gender identity. It can be seen in Table 13.4 that both male and female adolescents with GID recalled significantly more

Table 13.3 **Methods of Assessment**

Variable	Measure	References
Gender identity	Draw-a-person test	Jolles (1952)
	Utrecht Gender Dysphoria Scale	Cohen-Kettenis & van Goozen (1997)
	Gender Identity/Gender Dysphoria Questionnaire for Adolescents and Adults	Deogracias et al. (in press)
	Body image	Lindgren & Pauly (1975)
Gender role	Gender Identity/Role Questionnaire (parental report)	Zucker & Bradley (1995)
	Recalled Childhood Gender Identity/Role Scale (self-report)	Zucker et al. (2006)
Sexual orientation	Erotic Response and Sexual Orientation Scale	Storms (1980)
	Modified Zuckerman Heterosexual and Homosexual Experiences Scale	Zucker et al. (1996)
	Kinsey Interview Ratings (fantasy, behavior)	Kinsey, Pomeroy, & Martin (1948)

Table 13.4 **Factor Score on the Recalled Childhood Gender Identity/Gender Role Questionnaire of Adolescents with Gender Identity Disorder or Transvestic Fetishism**

Group	GID Males (N = 55)	GID Females (N = 44)	TF (N = 41)
Factor 1*			
M	2.53	2.00	4.19
SD	0.84	0.66	0.38

* Absolute range = 1.00–5.00.

cross-gender behavior during childhood than did the adolescents with TF.

Table 13.5 shows data from the 27-item Gender Identity/ Gender Dysphoria Questionnaire for Adolescents and Adults (GIDYQ-AA), a newly developed dimensional measure (Deogracias et al., in press). Principal axis factor analysis identified a strong one-factor solution, accounting for 61.3% of the total variance, in which the median factor loading was .86. It was designed to complement the previously developed GIIC (see above) by capturing a range of developmentally sensitive markers indicative of cross-gender identification and gender dysphoria. In the Deogracias et al. study, the GIDYQ-AA showed strong evidence for discriminant validity in that the 73 gender identity patients studied had significantly more gender dysphoria than both the heterosexual and nonheterosexual university students (n = 389). Using a cut-point of 3.00, sensitivity was 90.4% for the gender identity patients and specificity was 99.7% for the controls.

As shown in Table 13.5, the mean GIDYQ-AA strongly discriminated both male and female adolescents with GID from a group of adolescent males with TF. Using the cut-point of 3.00, 90% of the male and 100% of the female GID adolescents were classified as a "case" compared to 0% of the TF adolescents. It ap-

Table 13.5 **Factor Score on the Gender Identity/Gender Dysphoria Questionnaire for Adolescents and Adults of Adolescents with Gender Identity Disorder or Transvestic Fetishism**

Group	GID Males (N = 30)	GID Females (N = 27)	TF (N = 16)
Factor 1*			
M	2.58	2.13	4.64
SD	0.52	0.26	0.43

* Absolute range = 1.00–5.00.

pears, therefore, that this dimensional measure holds a great deal of clinical utility.

Associated Psychopathology

The assessment of associated behavior and emotional problems in adolescents with GID has relied on several measurement approaches, including standardized parent-report questionnaires, personality tests, self-report questionnaires of emotional disturbance, and projective tests.

In the first author's clinic, the CBCL and the Youth Self-Report Form (YSR; Achenbach & Edelbrock, 1987) have been utilized to assess general behavior problems. As reported elsewhere (Zucker, 2006; Zucker et al., 2002), GID adolescents had, on average, levels of behavioral disturbance on the CBCL comparable to the standardization sample of referred adolescents and considerably higher levels of behavioral disturbance when compared to the nonreferred adolescents. Using cut-off scores provided by Achenbach and Edelbrock (1983, Table 7–6, p. 63), 74.2% of 105 GID adolescents had a sum score that was in the clinical range (> 90th percentile; Zucker, unpublished raw data). On the YSR (Zucker, unpublished raw data), 39.6% of 106 GID adolescents had a sum score that was in the clinical range, which was comparable, if not somewhat higher, than the referred sample of youth in the standardization study and about 4.5 times higher than that of the nonreferred sample.

Several studies of Dutch adolescents from the second author's clinic have also examined general psychologic and psychiatric functioning. For example, Smith, van Goozen, and Cohen-Kettenis (2001) compared 20 adolescents (M age, 16.6 years) who later received both hormonal and surgical sex-reassignment with 14 adolescents (M age, 17.3 years) for whom the request for sex-reassignment was rejected. The "rejected" group consisted of adolescents who were not "transsexuals despite the fact that some did have gender identity problems" (p. 473). At the time of initial assessment, Smith et al. reported that both the treated and untreated groups had, on average, elevated scores on the Dutch version of the Symptom Checklist 90. At follow-up, the treated group (M age, 21.0 years), that is, those who underwent sex-reassignment, showed a greater diminution in SCL-90 symptomatology than did the untreated group (M age, 21.6 years). Smith et al. also reported that more than half of the untreated group had, at the time of initial assessment, at least one clinician-diagnosed *DSM* disorder; unfortunately, comparable psychiatric diagnostic data on the treated group were not provided. Interestingly, the treated group showed a substantial reduction in mean scores on the Utrecht Gender Dysphoria Scale (UGDS; Cohen-Kettenis & van Goozen, 1997), whereas the untreated group showed a much more modest reduction on the UGDS and remained significantly higher than the mean score of a standardization referent group.

In another study, Cohen, de Ruiter, Ringelberg, and Cohen-Kettenis (1997) evaluated the presence of psychological disturbance using the Rorschach Comprehensive System. Adolescents with GID were found to be intermediate between clinic-referred adolescents and nonpatients on an index of perceptual inaccuracy, but did not differ from nonpatients with regard to thought disturbance or negative self-image (see also Smith, Cohen, & Cohen-Kettenis, 2002). Two methodological aspects of the Cohen et al. (1997) study deserve comment: first, only a subgroup of the GID patients was administered the Rorschach and this subgroup was likely better functioning than the subgroup that was excluded (see Smith et al., 2002); second, the clinical controls included youth for whom "a Rorschach protocol was available," raising the possibility that such youth were more disturbed than referred youth in general because a clinical decision had been made to administer a projective test. Taken together, then, the method of subject recruitment for the study may have led to an underestimation of psychological disturbance in the GID group and an overestimation of psychologic disturbance in the clinical controls.

In summary, adolescents with GID appear to show, on average, about as many behavioral difficulties as other referred youth and more than nonreferred youth. It is likely that multiple factors contribute to their difficulties, including risk factors common to many referred youth (Zucker et al., 2002). But, it is also likely that adolescents with GID have risk factors specific to their unique minority status (i.e., a markedly atypical gender identity) and, in this regard, likely share the same risk factors that have been identified in gay and lesbian adolescents, including stigmatization, rejection by the peer group, and discrimination (see, e.g., D'Augelli, 2002; Lombardi, Wilchins, Priesing, & Malouf, 2001; Mathy, 2002; Meyer, 2003; Sadowski & Gaffney, 1998; Savin-Williams & Ream, 2003).

Developmental Trajectories

The most systematic data on long-term outcome on adolescents with GID come from the second author's clinic. In contrast to the emerging data on children, in which the majority appear to show a desistance of gender dysphoria by adolescence or adulthood, a majority of adolescents appears to show a persistence of gender dysphoria as they are followed into later adolescence or young adulthood (unless the gender dysphoria is treated by physical means; see the discussion that follows).

Cohen-Kettenis and van Goozen (1997) reported that 22 (66.6%) of 33 adolescents went on to receive sex reassignment surgery (SRS). At initial assessment, the mean age of the 22 adolescents who received SRS was 17.5 years (range, 15 to 20). Of the 11 who did not receive SRS, eight were not recommended for it because they were not diagnosed with transsexualism (presumably the *DSM-IV* diagnosis of GID); the three remaining patients were given a diagnosis of transsexualism but the "real-life test" (i.e., living for a time as the opposite sex prior to the institution of contrasex hormonal treatment and surgery) was postponed because of severe concurrent psychopathology and/or adverse social circumstances. These data suggest a very high rate of GID persistence, which is eventually treated by SRS. It should be noted that the persistence rate could be even higher than 66% because Cohen-Kettenis and van Goozen did not provide follow-up information on the 11 patients who were not recommended to proceed with the real-life test or were unable to implement it.

In another study, Smith et al. (2001) reported that 20 (48.7%) of 41 other adolescent patients went on to receive SRS. At initial assessment, the mean age of the 20 adolescents who received SRS was 16.6 years (range, 15 to 19). Of the 21 who did not receive SRS (M age, 17.3 years; range, 13 to 20), the reasons were similar to that reported in the earlier study. Data from Smith et al. suggest that a substantial number of the patients who did not receive SRS were still gender-dysphoric at the time of a follow-up assessment that occurred, on average, 4.3 years later.

Less is known about the persistence of gender dysphoria among adolescents who do not have a childhood onset of their GID. For example, in the Dutch studies, virtually all of the probands likely had an early onset of their gender dysphoric feelings. In the first author's clinic, a small subgroup of adolescents have a late-onset of their gender dysphoria, but, like late-onset adults, clinical impression suggests that many of these youth also show GID persistence (see also Chapter 14, this volume). Accordingly, it is not entirely clear to what extent age-of-onset will prove to be prognostic of desistance versus persistence (see also Smith, van Goozen, Kuiper, & Cohen-Kettenis, 2005a, 2005b).

Treatment

If GID in adolescence is not responsive to psychosocial treatment, should the clinician recommend the same kinds of physical interventions that are used with adults (Beh & Diamond, 2005; Cohen-Kettenis, 2005; Meyer et al., 2001)? Prior to such a recommendation, most clinicians will encourage adolescents with GID to consider alternatives to this invasive and expensive treatment. One area of inquiry can, therefore, explore the meaning behind the adolescent's desire for sex-reassignment (SR) and if there are viable alternative lifestyle adaptations. In this regard, the most common area of exploration pertains to the patient's sexual orientation. As noted earlier, many adolescents with GID recall that they always felt uncomfortable growing up as boys or as girls; however, for some adolescents the idea of a sex change did not begin to crystallize until they became aware of homoerotic attractions. For some of these youngsters, the idea that they might be gay or homosexual is abhorrent. For some such adolescents, psychoeducational work can explore their attitudes and feelings about homosexuality. Group therapy, in which such youngsters have the opportunity to meet gay adolescents, can be a useful adjunct in such cases. In some cases, the gender dysphoria will resolve and a homosexual adaptation ensues (Zucker & Bradley, 1995). For others, however, a homosexual adaptation is not possible and the gender dysphoria does not abate. In the following paragraphs, we summarize the protocol for treatment of GID in adolescents that has been developed at the second author's clinic. This procedure follows the Standards of Care of the World Professional Association of Transgender Health (WPATH), in which decisions about SR proceed in several sequential steps. In the first phase, an applicant has to fulfill *DSM* or *ICD* criteria for GID or transsexualism. The next phase includes three elements. The elements consist of a real-life experience in the desired role, hormones of the desired gender, and surgery to change the genitals and other sex characteristics (see Sidebar 13.2 for an overview).

SIDEBAR 13.2

Protocol for Treatment of GID in Adolescents Desiring Sex-Reassignment (SR)

- *Pre-protocol:* Adolescents are often encouraged to consider alternatives to SR (i.e., psychoeducational work, group therapy).
- *First (diagnostic) phase:* Information is attained from adolescent and parents; adolescent is thoroughly informed of possibilities and limitations of SR and other treatments; differential diagnosis occurs to most specifically pinpoint the nature or presence of GID and related issues.
- *Second phase:* Psychological interventions may be implemented for those for whom SR is not the best option; any psychotherapy must be supportive; time and therapy may help address issues that surfaced in the First Phase; potential for hormone therapy discussed.

- *Real life experience (RLE) phase:* SR applicants must live permanently in the role of the desired sex; significant persons in the applicant's life must be notified of the impending change; applicants experience the familial, interpersonal, educational, and legal consequences of the change in gender role.
- *RLE and hormones/physical interventions:* Fully reversible physical interventions can include puberty-delaying hormones, often given after the second stage of puberty has begun to be experienced (this hormone therapy can happen before RLE); partially reversible interventions include cross-sex hormonal therapy (estrogens/androgens) and generally require mental health and parental support; irreversible interventions include actual SR surgical procedures but are not carried out before adulthood.

The First (Diagnostic) Phase

In this phase, information must be obtained from both the adolescent and the parents (when they are available for evaluation) on various aspects of the general and psychosexual development of the adolescent. Information is also needed about current cross-gender feelings and behavior, current school functioning, peer relations, and family functioning. With regard to sexuality, the subjective meaning of cross-dressing, the type of cross-dressing, sexual experiences, sexual behavior and fantasies, sexual attractions, and body image have to be explored.

This diagnostic phase does not only focus on gaining information. In order to prevent unrealistically high expectations as regards their future lives, the adolescent also has to be thoroughly informed about the possibilities and limitations of sex reassignment and other kinds of treatment. This information should be given soon after the first sessions. The way a patient responds to the reality of SR can also be informative diagnostically.

Differential Diagnosis

As noted earlier, not all transgendered adolescents have a clear and explicit wish for SR. Some may simply be confused regarding aspects of their gender. For example, young male homosexuals may have a history of stereotypical feminine interests and cross-dressing. In some cases, they mistake their homosexuality for a GID, despite a drastic postpubertal reduction or disappearance of their cross-gender interests and activities. In ego-dystonic homosexuals, it is not confusion but lack of acceptance of their homosexuality that makes them consider SR a solution to their problem.

Transvestic fetishism occurs in heterosexual or bisexual male adolescents who become sexually aroused by cross-dressing. Boys with TF may also be confused about their wish to cross-dress.

Usually they hope that SR will "solve" their sexual excitement when cross-dressed; however, some such youth show a pattern of behavior now known as *autogynephilia* (see Chapter 14, this volume) and they present with a strong desire for SR. In very rare cases, a wish for SR exists in persons who prefer to be sexless, but have no cross-gender identity, as in Skoptic syndrome (Money, 1988; see also Wassersug, Zelenietz, & Squire, 2004). They want to be rid of their sex organs, but do not wish to acquire the sex characteristics of the other sex. Individuals with transient stress-related cross-dressing may mistake their interest in cross-dressing for a need for SR. This may also happen in patients suffering from severe psychiatric conditions (e.g., schizophrenia) accompanied by delusions of belonging to the opposite sex (American Psychiatric Association, 2000). Some individuals with gender problems do not seek complete SR. Instead they try to integrate masculine and feminine aspects of the self and only want hormones or some form of surgery.

The Second Phase

The Desirability of Sex Reassignment for Adolescents

The desirability of SR as a resolution for the psychological suffering of transsexuals, irrespective of age, has been controversial since the first sex change operations were performed. Many psychotherapists feel that one should try to help transsexuals resolve emotional conflicts underlying their wish for sex change by no other means than psychotherapy. However, the existing case reports generally do not provide convincing evidence for complete and long-term reversal of cross-gender identity by means of psychotherapy (see also Chapter 14, this volume).

Outcome studies on extremely gender-dysphoric SR applicants, who have been randomly assigned to either SR or psychotherapeutic treatment and with very long-term follow-ups, do not exist. Considering the lack of motivation for psychotherapy of most transsexuals, one may wonder whether it will ever be possible to conduct such studies. The absence of evidence that psychotherapy is the treatment of choice has led clinicians to look for other solutions to the problem. Because a once firmly established cross-gender identity appeared virtually impossible to change, the only rational solution to the problem seemed to be the adaptation of the sex characteristics to the cross-gender identity. This solution was supported by the results of studies showing no apparent psychological disturbance in transsexuals, which would make SR a hazardous enterprise (see Chapter 14, this volume). This does not mean that psychopathology would be completely absent in an unselected sample of transsexuals. It has become clear that transsexualism is a heterogeneous phenomenon and that psychopathology is more likely in some subtypes (e.g., late-onset group) than in others. Young applicants are more likely to belong to the early onset group. It is, therefore, likely that their psychological functioning is relatively favorable.

Because an extreme cross-gender identity in most individuals seems to be fixed after puberty, and psychological treatments are not particularly successful in solving the problems of these individuals, SR seems to be the treatment of choice for very gender dysphoric adults. However, even if one agrees with SR as a (palliative) treatment form for adult transsexuals, one could argue that adolescents should never be allowed to start (the hormonal part of) SR, because they are still in a rapidly changing developmental process. Currently, clinicians are faced with increasing numbers of youngsters who powerfully express that they find their lives unbearable without hormonal interventions (Cohen-Kettenis & Pfäfflin, 2003).

One argument in favor of early hormone treatment is that an eventual arrest in emotional, social, and intellectual development can be warded off more successfully when the ultimate cause of this arrest has been taken care of. Another is that early hormone treatment might be beneficial in adolescents because their secondary sex characteristics have not yet fully developed. Young male-to-female transsexuals (MFs) will, as adults, pass much more easily as females when they have never grown a beard or developed a low voice. If the bodily changes of puberty are not interrupted and a child still wants SR in adulthood, major physical interventions will be required to remove the unwanted physical characteristics. Yet, despite these obvious advantages, early hormone treatment for adolescents with GID touches sensitive strings. In the absence of evidence that transsexualism can be treated in adolescence by psychotherapy alone, a few centers have started, in carefully selected cases, with hormonal therapy before adulthood (Delemarre-van de Waal & Cohen-Kettenis, 2006; Gooren & Delemarre-van de Waal, 1996).

Psychological Interventions

Persons who are merely gender-confused or whose wish for SR seems to originate from factors other than a genuine and complete cross-gender identity are served best by psychological interventions. Such interventions may help them to better understand and cope with gender issues, and to try out alternative solutions to their problem, such as part-time cross-gender living. For individuals who want to explore their options for coping with gender dysphoria, group therapy has also been advocated. The information coming from members who are in different phases of understanding their gender problem, and the support in finding ways to deal with the problem seem to be particularly beneficial to group members. Family therapy may help to solve conflicts between family members rather than intrapsychic conflicts. These conflicts are quite common in cross-gendered adolescents. For instance, it regularly happens that a transsexual adolescent wants to be more open about his or her condition than the other family members. Conversely, when they already live permanently in the opposite gender role, parents fear aggressive reactions when friends who are not informed discover the truth.

Psychotherapy is not only useful for applicants that do not fulfill GID criteria. For transsexual adolescents, the first (diagnostic) phase is lengthy and intensive. Besides gathering information to make the diagnosis, any relevant issue that comes up in the first phase has to be explored. This means that the diagnostic phase often contains therapeutic elements. Patients need time to reflect on any unresolved personal issues or doubts regarding SR before embarking on somatic treatment. It is paramount that any form of psychotherapy offered to GID patients is supportive. The more the patient is confronted with doubts on the part of the therapist, the less chance he or she has to explore his or her own doubts if they exist. Therapists also need to be knowledgeable about hormone treatment, surgery, and the legal consequences of the treatment to compare the SR solution in a balanced way with other options for living with the gender problem (e.g., part-time living in the opposite role). Other issues that may come up in the first phase are anxieties concerning the loss of family or friends, uncertainties whether passing in the opposite role is feasible, and whether it will be possible to have satisfying intimate relationships.

When hormone treatment has started, psychotherapy may still be of use. Some patients indeed have to deal with loss or negative reactions from the environment. Others can only work on certain personal issues after they no longer need to worry about their masculinizing or feminizing bodies. For these reasons, some clinics offer postsurgical psychotherapy. Whether patients accept this depends largely on the individual needs of the patient and the quality of earlier therapist-patient contact.

Real Life Experience

In the real life experience (RLE) phase, applicants have to live permanently in the role of the desired sex, if they were not already doing so. Significant persons have to be informed about the impending changes. The underlying idea of this requirement is that applicants should have had ample opportunity to appreciate in fantasy or in vivo the familial, interpersonal, educational, and legal consequences of the gender role change. During the RLE phase, cross-sex hormone treatment is usually started. Feelings of dysphoria generally decline as a result of both the first bodily changes and the possibility to live in the new social role. During the real-life experience, the social transformation is a major focus of the discussions, when an adolescent starts to live in the desired role after the diagnostic phase. This is obviously less the case when the adolescent has already lived in the desired role before applying for SR.

Physical Interventions: Hormone Treatment

A diagnosis of GID alone is not sufficient for the decision to start the next treatment phase (RLE and hormones). Despite the fact that formal criteria are applicable to an individual patient, the actual extremeness of the GID may vary. Thus, one should take potential risk factors into account when making decisions on the eligibility of early interventions. For adolescents, the guidelines of the Royal College of Psychiatrists (Di Ceglie, Sturge, & Sutton, 1998), as well as the HBIGDA Standards of Care, make a distinction among three stages of physical interventions:

1. The fully reversible interventions
2. Partially reversible interventions
3. Irreversible interventions

FULLY REVERSIBLE INTERVENTIONS As soon as pubertal changes have begun, adolescents with extreme forms of GID may be eligible for puberty-delaying hormones. However, they should be able to make an informed decision about pubertal delay. Therefore, it is preferable if they experience the onset of puberty, at least to the second phase of pubertal development, Tanner Stage Two. Allowing adolescents with GID to take puberty delaying hormones is justified by two goals. One is to gain time to further explore the gender identity and other developmental issues in psychotherapy. The second is to make passing easier if the adolescent continues to pursue SR. GID adolescents eligible for any form of hormone treatment are required to meet the following criteria:

- Throughout childhood the adolescent has demonstrated an intense pattern of cross-gender behaviors and identity.
- Gender discomfort has significantly increased with the onset of puberty.
- The family consents and participates in the therapy.

Puberty delaying hormone treatment should not be viewed as a first step of the cross-sex treatment, but as a diagnostic help. Therefore, a period of cross-gender living, the RLE, is not necessarily required, when only these hormones are taken. It is difficult to give a general rule for the start of the RLE, as the personalities and life circumstances of adolescents are so different. Some wait until they are 16 or have graduated from high school. They start the RLE when they start to take cross-sex hormones, because they want to look "really convincing" at the moment of their social role change. Some think, correctly, that they already look convincing enough and begin living in the desired role even before they have started with puberty-delaying hormones.

PARTIALLY REVERSIBLE INTERVENTIONS Adolescents eligible for cross-sex hormone therapy (estrogens for MFs or androgens for FMs) usually are around 16 or older. In many countries, 16-year-olds are legal adults for medical decision making. Although parental consent is not required, it is preferred, as adolescents need the support of their parents in this complex phase of their lives. Mental health professional involvement, for a minimum period of 6 months, is another eligibility requirement for hormonal interventions of adolescents. The objective of this involvement is that treatment is thoughtfully and recurrently considered over time.

IRREVERSIBLE INTERVENTIONS Surgery is not carried out prior to adulthood. The Standards of Care emphasize that the "threshold of 18 should be seen as an eligibility criterion and not an indication in itself for active intervention." If the RLE supported by the cross-sex hormones has not resulted in a satisfactory social role change or if the patient is not satisfied with or is ambivalent about the hormonal effects, the applicant should not be referred for surgery.

EFFECTS OF FULLY REVERSIBLE INTERVENTIONS Luteinizing hormone-releasing hormone (LHRH) agonists block further progress of puberty. These compounds bind so strongly to the pituitary that the secretion of luteinizing hormone (LH) and follicle-stimulating hormone (FSH) no longer takes place. Eventually, the gonadal production of sex steroids discontinues and a prepubertal state is (again) induced.

Adolescents that have gone into puberty at a very young age or have started with LHRH agonists at a relatively late age will already have developed certain secondary sex characteristics. Some cannot be reversed by hormone treatment. Because facial hair growth is very resistant to anti-androgen therapy, additional mechanic hair removal techniques may sometimes be necessary. Speech therapy is sometimes needed, because the vocal cords will not shorten once they have grown, and the MF has to learn to use his voice in a female fashion. Surgical techniques to shorten the vocal cord exist but are as yet rarely employed, because there are still concerns about the safety and effectiveness of such voice modification techniques.

EFFECTS OF PARTIALLY REVERSIBLE INTERVENTIONS To induce female sex characteristics in MFs (such as breasts and a more female-appearing body shape due to a change of body fat around waist, hips, shoulders and jaws), estrogens are used. Other physical effects are decreased upper body strength, softening of the skin, a decreased testicular size and fertility, and less frequent less firm erections.

In female-to-male transsexuals (FMs), androgens are used for the induction of male body features, such as a low voice, facial and body hair growth, and a more masculine body shape. Other physical changes are a mild breast atrophy and clitoral enlargement, though the size will never reach the size of a penis by means of androgen treatment only. Reversible changes are increased upper body strength, weight gain, and decreased hip fat.

EFFECTS OF IRREVERSIBLE INTERVENTIONS In MFs, female-looking external genitals are created by means of vaginoplasty, clitoroplasty and labiaplasty. In cases of insufficient responsiveness of breast tissue to estrogen therapy, breast enlargement may also be performed. After surgery, intercourse is possible. Arousal and orgasm are also reported postsurgically, though the percentages differ between studies.

For FMs, a mastectomy is often performed as the first surgery to successfully pass in the desired role. When skin needs to be removed, this will result in fairly visible scar tissue. Considering the still continuing improvements in the field of phalloplasty, some FMs do not want to undergo genital surgery until they have a clear reason for it or choose to have a neoscrotum with a testical prosthesis with or without a metaidoioplasty, which transforms the hypertrophic clitoris into a microphallus. Other genital procedures may include removal of the uterus and ovaries. Whether FMs can have sexual intercourse using their neo-penis depends on the technique and quality of the phalloplasty. Although some patients who had a metaidoioplasty report that they are able to have intercourse, the hypertrophic clitoris usually is too small for coitus. In most cases, the capacity for sexual arousal and orgasm remains intact.

Legal Issues

In many countries that derive their law from Napoleon's *Code Civil* of 1804, the birth certificate is the source for all other personal documents. Therefore, it is essential to change the sex in this document to endow a person with the full rights of his or her new gender. In Anglo-American countries, it is easier to adopt a new first name. However, registration of official documents is not centralized. As a result, a person can be male according to one and female according to another document. Nowadays, many countries either have specific laws or administrative solutions, implying that SR has become a fairly well accepted treatment.

The current guidelines for the treatment of adolescents with GID that distinguish between three types of physical interventions (wholly reversible, partly reversible, and irreversible ones) do not give defined ages for the physical interventions. Only for surgery the age of 18 is mentioned, as this is the age of legal adulthood in many Western countries. The rationale of this age limit is somewhat arbitrary. Outside Europe and the United States, the ages of legal maturity vary between 16 in Iceland and Nepal to 21 in many African and Latin American countries, while some countries do not even have a fixed age. Though the fixed age limits are an attempt to protect children from maltreatment, in the case of adolescents with GID it often seems to work against them. The age of psychological and somatic maturity varies largely interindividually. Adhering to such limits would severely hamper the development of a mature adolescent and may even facilitate fast routine decision making when a still immature 18-year-old wants to have surgery. Adolescents are probably better protected when all those involved in their treatment closely observe the guidelines of The Royal College of Psychiatrist and WPATH, and extensively discuss and weigh the pros and cons of SR for an individual patient.

References

Achenbach, T. M., & Edelbrock, C. (1983). *Manual for the Child Behavior Checklist and Revised Child Behavior Profile.* Burlington: University of Vermont, Department of Psychiatry.

Achenbach, T. M., & Edelbrock, C. (1987). *Manual for the Youth Self-Report and Profile.* Burlington: University of Vermont, Department of Psychiatry.

American Psychiatric Association. (2000). *Diagnostic and statistical manual of mental disorders* (4th ed., text rev.). Washington, DC: Author.

Arnold, A. P. (2003). The gender of the voice within: The neural origin of sex differences in the brain. *Current Opinion in Neurobiology, 13,* 759–764.

Bailey, J. M., & Zucker, K. J. (1995). Childhood sex-typed behavior and sexual orientation: A conceptual analysis and quantitative review. *Developmental Psychology, 31,* 43–55.

Bakker, A., van Kesteren, P. J. M., Gooren, L. J. G., & Bezemer, P. D. (1993). The prevalence of transsexualism in The Netherlands. *Acta Psychiatrica Scandinavica, 87,* 237–238.

Beh, H., & Diamond, M. (2005). Ethical concerns related to treating gender nonconformity in childhood and adolescence: Lessons from the Family Court of Australia. *Health Matrix: Journal of Law-Medicine, 15,* 239–283.

Blanchard, R., Clemmensen, L. H., & Steiner, B. W. (1987). Heterosexual and homosexual gender dysphoria. *Archives of Sexual Behavior, 16,* 139–152.

Bockting, W. O., & Ehrbar, R. D. (2005). Commentary: Gender variance, dissonance, or identity disorder? *Journal of Psychology and Human Sexuality, 17*(3/4), 125–134.

Bradley, S. J., Blanchard, R., Coates, S., Green, R., Levine, S. B., Meyer-Bahlburg, H. F. L., et al. (1991). Interim report of the DSM-IV subcommittee on gender identity disorders. *Archives of Sexual Behavior, 20,* 333–343.

Brown, P. L. (2006, December 2). Supporting boys or girls when the line isn't clear. *New York Times,* pp. A1–AX.

Caron, C., & Rutter, M. (1991). Comorbidity in child psychopathology: Concepts, issues and research strategies. *Journal of Child Psychology and Psychiatry, 32,* 1063–1080.

Chivers, M. L., Rieger, G., Latty, E., & Bailey, J. M. (2004). A sex difference in the specificity of sexual arousal. *Psychological Science, 15,* 736–744.

Cloud, J. (2000, September). His name is Aurora. *Time,* pp. 90–91.

Coates, S., & Person, E. S. (1985). Extreme boyhood femininity: Isolated behavior or pervasive disorder? *Journal of the American Academy of Child Psychiatry, 24,* 702–709.

Coates, S., & Wolfe, S. (1995). Gender identity disorder in boys: The interface of constitution and early experience. *Psychoanalytic Inquiry, 15,* 6–38.

Cohen, L., de Ruiter, C., Ringelberg, H., & Cohen-Kettenis, P. T. (1997). Psychological functioning of adolescent transsexuals: Personality and psychopathology. *Journal of Clinical Psychology, 53,* 187–196.

Cohen-Kettenis, P. T. (2005). Gender identity disorders. In C. Gillberg, R. Harrington, & H.-C. Steinhausen (Eds.), *A clinician's handbook of child and adolescent psychiatry* (pp. 695–725). Cambridge: Cambridge University Press.

Cohen-Kettenis, P. T., & Everaerd, W. (1986). Gender role problems in adolescence. *Advances in Adolescent Mental Health, 1*(Pt. B), 1–28.

Cohen-Kettenis, P. T., Owen, A., Kaijser, V. G., Bradley, S. J., & Zucker, K. J. (2003). Demographic characteristics, social competence, and behavior problems in children with gender identity disorder: A cross-national, cross-clinic comparative analysis. *Journal of Abnormal Child Psychology, 31,* 41–53.

Cohen-Kettenis, P. T., & Pfäfflin, F. (2003). *Transgenderism and intersexuality in childhood and adolescence: Making choices.* Thousand Oaks, CA: Sage.

Cohen-Kettenis, P. T., & van Goozen, S. H. M. (1997). Sex reassignment of adolescent transsexuals: A follow-up study. *Journal of the American Academy of Child and Adolescent Psychiatry, 36,* 263–271.

Cohen-Kettenis, P. T., Wallien, M., Johnson, L. L., Owen-Anderson, A. F. H., Bradley, S. J., & Zucker, K. J. (2006). A parent-report Gender Identity Questionnaire for children: A cross-national, cross-clinic comparative analysis. *Clinical Child Psychology and Psychiatry, 11,* 397–405.

D'Augelli, A. R. (2002). Mental health problems among lesbian, gay, and bisexual youths ages 14 to 21. *Clinical Child Psychology and Psychiatry, 7,* 433–456.

Delemarre-van de Waal, H. A., & Cohen-Kettenis, P. T. (2006). Clinical management of gender identity disorder in adolescents: A protocol on psychological and paediatric endocrinology aspects. *European Journal of Endocrinology, 155,* S131–S137.

Deogracias, J. J., Johnson, L. L., Meyer-Bahlburg, H. F. L., Kessler, S. J., Schober, J. M., & Zucker, K. J. (in press). The Gender Identity/Gender Dysphoria Questionnaire for Adolescents and Adults. *Journal of Sex Research.*

Di Ceglie, D., Sturge, C., & Sutton, A. (1998). *Gender identity disorders in children and adolescents: Guidelines for management* (Council Report CR63). London: Royal College of Psychiatrists.

Drummond, K. D., Bradley, S. J., Badali-Peterson, M., & Zucker, K. J. (in press). A follow-up study of girls with gender identity disorder. *Developmental Psychology.*

Edelbrock, C., & Achenbach, T. M. (1980). A typology of Child Behavior Profile patterns: Distribution and correlates in disturbed children age 6 to 16. *Journal of Abnormal Child Psychology, 8,* 441–470.

Ehrbar, R. D., Witty, M. C., & Bockting, W. O. (in press). Clinician judgment in the diagnosis of gender identity disorder in children. *Journal of Sex and Marital Therapy.*

Fisk, N. (1973). Gender dysphoria syndrome (the how, what, and why of a disease). In D. Laub & P. Gandy (Eds.), *Proceedings of the second Interdisciplinary Symposium on Gender Dysphoria Syndrome* (pp. 7–14). Palo Alto, CA: Stanford University Press.

Fridell, S. R. (2001). *Sex-typed play behavior and peer relations in boys with gender identity disorder.* Unpublished doctoral dissertation, University of Toronto, Ontario, Canada.

Gagnon, J. H. (1990). The explicit and implicit use of the scripting perspective in sex research. *Annual Review of Sex Research, 1,* 1–43.

Gentile, D. A. (1993). Just what are sex and gender, anyway? A call for a new terminological standard. *Psychological Science, 4,* 120–122.

Gooren, L., & Delemarre-van de Waal, H. (1996). The feasibility of endocrine interventions in juvenile transsexuals. *Journal of Psychology and Human Sexuality, 8*(4), 69–84.

Green, R. (1974). *Sexual identity conflict in children and adults.* New York: Basic Books.

Green, R. (1987). *The "sissy boy syndrome" and the development of homosexuality.* New Haven, CT: Yale University Press.

Green, R., & Money, J. (1960). Incongruous gender role: Nongenital manifestations in prepubertal boys. *Journal of Nervous and Mental Diseases, 131,* 160–168.

Grumbach, M. M., Hughes, I. A., & Conte, F. A. (2003). Disorders of sex differentiation. In P. R. Larsen, H. M. Kronenberg, S. Melmed, & K. S. Polonsky (Eds.), *Williams textbook of endocrinology* (10th ed., pp. 842–1002). Philadelphia: Saunders.

Haig, D. (2004). The inexorable rise of gender and the decline of sex: Social change in academic titles. *Archives of Sexual Behavior, 33,* 87–96.

Haqq, C. M., & Donahoe, P. K. (1998). Regulation of sexual dimorphism in mammals. *Physiological Reviews, 78,* 1–33.

Isay, R. A. (1997, November). Remove gender identity disorder in DSM. *Psychiatric News, 3*(2), 9, 13.

Johnson, L. L., Bradley, S. J., Birkenfeld-Adams, A. S., Radzins Kuksis, M. A., Maing, D. M., Mitchell, J. N., et al. (2004). A parent-report Gender Identity Questionnaire for Children. *Archives of Sexual Behavior, 33,* 105–116.

Jolles, I. (1952). A study of validity of some hypotheses for the qualitative interpretation of the H-T-P for children of elementary school age: Pt. I. Sexual identification. *Journal of Clinical Psychology, 8,* 113–118.

Kinsey, A. C., Pomeroy, W. B., & Martin, C. E. (1948). *Sexual behavior in the human male.* Philadelphia: Saunders.

Kohlberg, L. A. (1966). A cognitive-developmental analysis of children's sex-role concepts and attitudes. In E. E. Maccoby (Ed.), *The development of sex differences* (pp. 82–173). Stanford, CA: Stanford University Press.

Lahey, B. B., McBurnett, K., & Loeber, R. (2000). Are attention-deficit/hyperactivity disorder and oppositional defiant disorder developmental precursors to conduct disorder. In A. J. Sameroff, M. Lewis, & S. M. Miller (Eds.), *Handbook of developmental psychopathology* (2nd ed., pp. 431–446). New York: Kluwer Academic/Plenum Press.

Laumann, E. O., Gagnon, J. H., Michael, R. T., & Michaels, S. (1994). *The social organization of sexuality: Sexual practices in the United States.* Chicago: University of Chicago Press.

Lee, T. (2001). Trans(re)lations: Lesbian and female to male transsexual accounts of identity. *Women's Studies International Forum, 24,* 347–357.

Lev, A. I. (2005). *Transgender emergence: Therapeutic guidelines for working with gender-variant people and their families.* New York: Haworth Press.

Lindgren, T. W., & Pauly, I. B. (1975). A body image scale for evaluating transsexuals. *Archives of Sexual Behavior, 4,* 639–656.

Lombardi, E. L., Wilchins, R. A., Priesing, D., & Malouf, D. (2001). Gender violence: Transgender experiences with violence and discrimination. *Journal of Homosexuality, 42,* 89–101.

Maccoby, E. E. (1988). Gender as a social category. *Developmental Psychology, 24,* 755–765.

Marantz, S., & Coates, S. (1991). Mothers of boys with gender identity disorder: A comparison of matched controls. *Journal of the American Academy of Child and Adolescent Psychiatry, 30,* 310–315.

Martin, C. L., Ruble, D. N., & Szkrybalo, J. (2002). Cognitive theories of early gender development. *Psychological Bulletin, 128,* 903–933.

Mathy, R. M. (2002). Transgender identity and suicidality in a nonclinical sample: Sexual orientation, psychiatric history, and compulsive behaviors. *Journal of Psychology and Human Sexuality, 14*(4), 47–65.

McCarthy, L. (2003). *Off that spectrum entirely: A study of female-bodied transgender-identified individuals.* Unpublished doctoral dissertation, University of Massachusetts, Amherst.

Menvielle, E. J., & Tuerk, C. (2002). A support group for parents of gender non-conforming boys. *Journal of the American Academy of Child and Adolescent Psychiatry, 41,* 1010–1013.

Menvielle, E. J., Tuerk, C., & Perrin, E. C. (2005). To the beat of a different drummer: The gender-variant child. *Contemporary Pediatrics, 22*(2), 38–39, 41, 43, 45–46.

Meyer, I. H. (2003). Prejudice, social stress, and mental health issues in lesbian, gay, and bisexual populations: Conceptual issues and research evidence. *Psychological Bulletin, 129,* 674–697.

Meyer, W., Bockting, W. O., Cohen-Kettenis, P., Coleman, E., DiCeglie, D., Devor, H., et al. (2001). The Harry Benjamin International Gender Dysphoria Association's Standards of Care for Gender Identity Disorders, Sixth version. *Journal of Psychology and Human Sexuality, 13*(1), 1–30.

Meyer-Bahlburg, H. F. L. (1994). Intersexuality and the diagnosis of gender identity disorder. *Archives of Sexual Behavior, 23,* 21–40.

Migeon, C., & Wisniewski, A. B. (1998). Sexual differentiation: From genes to gender. *Hormone Research, 50,* 245–251.

Money, J. (1955). Hermaphroditism, gender and precocity in hyperadrenocorticism: Psychologic findings. *Bulletin of the Johns Hopkins Hospital, 96,* 253–264.

Money, J. (1985). The conceptual neutering of gender and the criminalization of sex. *Archives of Sexual Behavior, 14,* 279–290.

Money, J. (1988). The skoptic syndrome: Castration and genital self-mutilation as an example of sexual body-image pathology. *Journal of Psychology and Human Sexuality, 1,* 113–128.

Money, J., Hampson, J. G., & Hampson, J. L. (1957). Imprinting and the establishment of gender role. *Archives of Neurology and Psychiatry, 77,* 333–336.

Mukaddes, N. M. (2002). Gender identity problems in autistic children. *Child Care, Health, Development, 28,* 529–532.

Newman, L. E. (1976). Treatment for the parents of feminine boys. *American Journal of Psychiatry, 133,* 683–687.

Perera, H., Gadambanathan, T., & Weerasiri, S. (2003). Gender identity disorder presenting in a girl with Asperger's disorder and obsessive compulsive disorder. *Ceylon Medical Journal, 48,* 57–58.

Pleak, R. (1999). Ethical issues in diagnosing and treating gender-dysphoric children and adolescents. In M. Rottnek (Ed.), *Sissies and tomboys: Gender nonconformity and homosexual childhood* (pp. 34–51). New York: New York University Press.

Rekers, G. A. (1975). Stimulus control over sex-typed play in cross-gender identified boys. *Journal of Experimental Child Psychology, 20,* 136–148.

Robins, L. N. (1978). Sturdy childhood predictors of adult antisocial behaviour: Replication from longitudinal studies. *Psychological Medicine, 8,* 611–622.

Rosen, R. C., & Beck, J. G. (1988). *Patterns of sexual arousal: Psychophysiological processes and clinical applications.* New York: Guilford Press.

Rosenberg, D. (2007, May 21). (Rethinking) gender. *Newsweek,* pp. 50–57.

Ruble, D. N., Martin, C. L., & Berenbaum, S. A. (2006). Gender development. In W. Damon & R. M. Lerner (Series Eds.) & N. Eisenberg (Vol. Ed.), *Handbook of child psychology: Vol. 3. Social, emotional, and personality development* (6th ed., pp. 858–932). Hoboken, NJ: Wiley.

Rust, P. C. (1999, June). *Lesbianism and bisexuality: Cultural categories and the distortion of human sexual experience.* Paper presented at the meeting of the International Academy of Sex Research, Stony Brook, NY.

Sadowski, H., & Gaffney, N. (1998). Gender identity disorder, depression, and suicidal risk. In D. Di Ceglie (Ed.), *A stranger in my own body: Atypical gender identity development and mental health* (pp. 126–136). London: Karnac Books.

Saeger, K. (2006). Finding our way: Guiding a young transgender child. *Journal of GLBT Family Studies, 2*(3/4), 207–245.

Santiago, R. (2006). 5-year-old "girl" starting school is really a boy. *Miami Herald.* Retrieved July 11, 2006, from www.miami.com/mld/miamiherald/living/education/15003026.htm.

Savin-Williams, R. C., & Ream, G. L. (2003). Suicide attempts among sexual-minority male youth. *Journal of Clinical Child and Adolescent Psychology, 32,* 509–522.

Savin-Williams, R. C., & Ream, G. L. (2007). Prevalence and stability of sexual orientation components during adolescence and young adulthood. *Archives of Sexual Behavior, 36,* 385–394.

Schrimshaw, E. W., Rosario, M., Meyer-Bahlburg, H. F. L., & Scharf-Matlick, A. A. (2006). Test-retest reliability of self-reported sexual behavior, sexual orientation, and psychosexual milestones among gay, lesbian, and bisexual youths. *Archives of Sexual Behavior, 35,* 225–234.

Smith, Y. L. S., Cohen, L., & Cohen-Kettenis, P. T. (2002). Postoperative psychological functioning of adolescent transsexuals: A Rorschach study. *Archives of Sexual Behavior, 31,* 255–261.

Smith, Y. L. S., van Goozen, S. H. M., & Cohen-Kettenis, P. T. (2001). Adolescents with gender identity disorder who were accepted or rejected for sex reassignment surgery: A prospective follow-up study. *Journal of the American Academy of Child and Adolescent Psychiatry, 40,* 472–481.

Smith, Y. L. S., van Goozen, S. H. M., Kuiper, A. J., & Cohen-Kettenis, P. T. (2005a). Sex reassignment: Outcomes and predictors of treatment for adolescent and adult transsexuals. *Psychological Medicine, 35,* 89–99.

Smith, Y. L. S., van Goozen, S. H. M., Kuiper, A. J., & Cohen-Kettenis, P. T. (2005b). Transsexual subtypes: Clinical and theoretical significance. *Psychiatry Research, 137,* 151–160.

Spitzer, R. L., & Wakefield, J. C. (1999). *DSM-IV* diagnostic criterion for clinical significance: Does it help solve the false positives problem? *American Journal of Psychiatry, 156,* 1856–1864.

Stoller, R. J. (1964). The hermaphroditic identity of hermaphrodites. *Journal of Nervous and Mental Diseases, 139,* 453–457.

Stoller, R. J. (1967). "It's only a phase": Femininity in boys. *Journal of the American Medical Association, 201,* 314–315.

Stoller, R. J. (1968). *Sex and gender: On the development of masculinity and femininity* (Vol. 1). New York: Aronson.

Storms, M. D. (1980). Theories of sexual orientation. *Journal of Personality and Social Psychology, 38,* 783–792.

Streitmatter, J. L. (1985). Cross-sectional investigations of adolescent perception of gender roles. *Journal of Adolescence, 8,* 183–193.

van Beijsterveldt, C. E. M., Hudziak, J. J., & Boomsma, D. I. (2006). Genetic and environmental influences on cross-gender behavior and relation to behavior problems: A study of Dutch twins at ages 7 and 10 years. *Archives of Sexual Behavior, 35,* 647–658.

Vilain, E. (2000). Genetics of sexual development. *Annual Review of Sex Research, 11,* 1–25.

Wallien, M. S. C., & Cohen-Kettenis, P. T. (2007, September). *Prediction of adult GID: A follow-up study of gender-dysphoric children.* Paper presented at the meeting of the World Professional Association of Transgender Health, Chicago.

Wallien, M. S. C., Cohen-Kettenis, P. T., Owen-Anderson, A., Bradley, S. J., & Zucker, K. J. (2007). *Cross-national replication of the gender identity interview for children.* Manuscript submitted for publication.

Wallien, M. S. C., Swaab, H., & Cohen-Kettenis, P. T. (2007). Psychiatric comorbidity among children with gender identity disorder. *Journal of the American Academy of Child and Adolescent Psychiatry, 46,* 1307–1314.

Wallien, M. S. C., van Goozen, S. H. M., & Cohen-Kettenis, P. T. (2007). Physiological correlates of anxiety in children with gender identity disorder. *European Child and Adolescent Psychiatry, 16,* 309–315.

Wassersug, R. J., Zelenietz, S. A., & Squire, G. F. (2004). New age eunuchs: Motivation and rationale for voluntary castration. *Archives of Sexual Behavior, 33,* 433–442.

Williams, P. G., Allard, A. M., & Sears, L. (1996). Case study: Cross-gender preoccupations in two male children with autism. *Journal of Autism and Developmental Disorders, 26,* 635–642.

World Health Organization. (1992). *International statistical classification of diseases and related health problems* (10th rev.). Geneva, Switzerland: Author.

Young, R., & Sweeting, H. (2004). Adolescent bullying, relationships, psychological well-being, and gender atypical behavior: A gender diagnosticity approach. *Sex Roles, 50,* 525–537.

Zoccolillo, M., Pickles, A., Quinton, D., & Rutter, M. (1992). The outcome of childhood conduct disorder: Implications for defining adult personality disorder and conduct disorder. *Psychological Medicine, 22,* 971–986.

Zucker, K. J. (1985). Cross-gender-identified children. In B. W. Steiner (Ed.), *Gender dysphoria: Development, research, management* (pp. 75–174). New York: Plenum Press.

Zucker, K. J. (1992). Gender identity disorder. In S. R. Hooper, G. W. Hynd, & R. E. Mattison (Eds.), *Child psychopathology: Diagnostic criteria and clinical assessment* (pp. 305–342). Hillsdale, NJ: Erlbaum.

Zucker, K. J. (1999). Gender identity disorder in the *DSM-IV* [Letter to the editor]. *Journal of Sex and Marital Therapy, 25,* 5–9.

Zucker, K. J. (2000). Gender identity disorder. In A. J. Sameroff, M. Lewis, & S. M. Miller (Eds.), *Handbook of developmental psychopathology* (2nd ed., pp. 671–686). New York: Kluwer Academic/Plenum Press.

Zucker, K. J. (2001). Gender identity disorder in children and adolescents. In G. O. Gabbard (Ed.), *Treatments of psychiatric disorders* (3rd ed., Vol. 2, pp. 2069–2094). Washington, DC: American Psychiatric Press.

Zucker, K. J. (2005). Measurement of psychosexual differentiation. *Archives of Sexual Behavior, 34,* 375–388.

Zucker, K. J. (2006). Gender identity disorder. In D. A. Wolfe & E. J. Mash (Eds.), *Behavioral and emotional disorders in adolescents: Nature, assessment, and treatment* (pp. 535–562). New York: Guilford Press.

Zucker, K. J. (2007). Gender identity disorder in children, adolescents, and adults. In G. O. Gabbard (Ed.), *Gabbard's treatments of psychiatric disorders* (4th ed., pp. 683–701). Washington, DC: American Psychiatric Press.

Zucker, K. J., & Bradley, S. J. (1995). *Gender identity disorder and psychosexual problems in children and adolescents.* New York: Guilford Press.

Zucker, K. J., Bradley, S. J., Doering, R. W., & Lozinski, J. A. (1985). Sex-typed behavior in cross-gender-identified children: Stability and change at a one-year follow-up. *Journal of the American Academy of Child Psychiatry, 24,* 710–719.

Zucker, K. J., Bradley, S. J., & Lowry Sullivan, C. B. (1996). Traits of separation anxiety in boys with gender identity disorder. *Journal of the American Academy of Child and Adolescent Psychiatry, 35,* 791–798.

Zucker, K. J., Bradley, S. J., Lowry Sullivan, C. B., Kuksis, M., Birkenfeld-Adams, A., & Mitchell, J. N. (1993). A gender identity interview for children. *Journal of Personality Assessment, 61,* 443–456.

Zucker, K. J., Bradley, S. J., Oliver, G., Blake, J., Fleming, S., & Hood, J. (1996). Psychosexual development of women with congenital adrenal hyperplasia. *Hormones and Behavior, 30,* 300–318.

Zucker, K. J., Bradley, S. J., & Sanikhani, M. (1997). Sex differences in referral rates of children with gender identity disorder: Some hypotheses. *Journal of Abnormal Child Psychology, 25,* 217–227.

Zucker, K. J., Finegan, J. K., Doering, R. W., & Bradley, S. J. (1984). Two subgroups of gender-problem children. *Archives of Sexual Behavior, 13,* 27–39.

Zucker, K. J., Mitchell, J. N., Bradley, S. J., Tkachuk, J., Cantor, J. M., & Allin, S. M. (2006). The Recalled Childhood Gender Identity/Gender Role Questionnaire: Psychometric properties. *Sex Roles, 54,* 469–483.

Zucker, K. J., Owen, A., Bradley, S. J., & Ameeriar, L. (2002). Gender-dysphoric children and adolescents: A comparative analysis of demographic characteristics and behavioral problems. *Clinical Child Psychology and Psychiatry, 7,* 398–411.

Zucker, K. J., & Spitzer, R. L. (2005). Was the Gender Identity Disorder of Childhood diagnosis introduced into *DSM-III* as a backdoor maneuver to replace homosexuality? An historical note. *Journal of Sex and Marital Therapy, 31,* 31–42.

Gender Identity Disorders in Adults: Diagnosis and Treatment

Anne A. Lawrence

14
Chapter

Learning Objectives

In this chapter we review:

- The history and definitions of important terms.
- Summary of diagnostic categories and criteria.
- Typology and epidemiology.
- Clinical course and associated features.
- Diagnosis and assessment.
- Treatment options and outcomes.
- Treatment of families.

History

Persons who express discomfort or dissatisfaction with their anatomic sex or with the social roles associated with their sex have been reported since antiquity in many different cultures (Green, 1969). German sexologists Krafft-Ebing (1903/1965) and Hirschfeld (1910/1991) described persons who would now be recognized as transsexuals, and the first modern operations for surgical sex reassignment were performed in Germany in the 1930s (Abraham, 1931). The publicity surrounding Christine Jorgensen's sex reassignment in 1952 brought the phenomenon of transsexualism to public attention (Meyerowitz, 2002). In 1966, surgeons at Johns Hopkins Hospital began performing sex reassignment surgery (SRS) in the United States; in the same year, Harry Benjamin (1966), an endocrinologist who worked extensively with transsexual patients, published his groundbreaking book, *The Transsexual Phenomenon.* In 1979, the Harry Benjamin International Gender Dysphoria Association (HBIGDA), an organization of physicians, psychologists, and other professionals involved in treating gender identity problems, published the first Standards of Care for the treatment of gender identity disorders.

Terminology

Terminology related to the gender identity disorders has evolved over time and has not always been used consistently. The term *transsexualism* first appeared in the writings of Hirschfeld (1923), but only began being used in its contemporary sense in the 1950s, to describe persons who desired to live as members of the opposite sex and to undergo hormonal and surgical sex reassignment, or who had actually done so. Transsexualism was believed to represent a *gender identity disorder,* reflecting discordance between anatomic sex and *gender identity,* "a person's inner conviction of being male or female" (*Diagnostic and Statistical Manual of Mental Disorders,* fourth, edition, text revision [*DSM-IV-TR*]; American Psychiatric Association, 2000, p. 823). The term *gender identity* has been used in various ways.

It sometimes denotes the fundamental sense of being male, female, or of indeterminate sex that usually develops in children between ages 18 to 30 months and that is generally regarded as immutable thereafter; Stoller (1968) called this *core gender identity.* *Gender identity* can also denote a person's *current* sense of him or herself as being male, female, or of indeterminate sex (Money, 1986); gender identity in this latter sense can change over time and may not be identical to a person's core gender identity. Persons with gender identity disorders often experience their current gender identity as incongruent with their core gender identity (Stoller, 1968).

By the early 1970s, clinicians recognized that many persons who sought sex reassignment had histories and clinical presentations that were inconsistent with prevailing professional beliefs about "classical" or "true" transsexualism. As a result, the term *gender dysphoria syndrome* was coined to describe persons who sought sex reassignment, regardless of their diagnoses (Fisk, 1974). Over time, the term *gender dysphoria* lost its original association with the desire for sex reassignment and came to denote simply an "aversion to some or all of those physical characteristics or social roles that connote one's own biological sex" (American Psychiatric Association, 2000, p. 823).

The *gender identity disorders* first appeared as diagnoses in the third edition of the *Diagnostic and Statistical Manual of Mental Disorders* (*DSM-III;* American Psychiatric Association, 1980), denoting psychopathological conditions involving "an incongruence between anatomic sex and gender identity" (American Psychiatric Association, 1980, p. 261). Two categories of gender identity disorders were recognized in adults: *transsexualism,* applicable to persons who desired to live as members of the opposite sex and who sought genital conversion surgery; and a residual category, *atypical gender identity disorder,* without specific criteria. This general scheme, involving principal and residual adult diagnostic categories, continued in subsequent editions of the *DSM.* In the *DSM-III-R* (American Psychiatric Association, 1987), the principal diagnosis of transsexualism was retained but the residual category was expanded to include two diagnoses: gender identity disorder of adolescence or adulthood, nontranssexual type (GIDAANT), applicable to persons who met most criteria for transsexualism but who did not have a persistent wish to acquire the anatomic characteristics of the opposite sex; and gender identity disorder not otherwise specified (GIDNOS), without specific criteria. In the *DSM-IV* (American Psychiatric Association, 1994), the new diagnosis of gender identity disorder (GID) in adults subsumed the previous diagnoses of transsexualism and GIDAANT in adults, leaving only one adult residual category, GIDNOS. The *DSM-IV-TR* (American Psychiatric Association, 2000) retained the *DSM-IV* adult categories.

The adoption of GID as a replacement for transsexualism was perhaps logical, in that the latter term technically refers to a method of treating or coping with a gender identity problem (i.e., by "crossing sex"), not the gender problem itself (Money, 1986). Nevertheless, transsexualism remains an official diagnosis in the most recent edition of the *International Statistical Classification of Diseases and Related Health Problems* (*ICD-10;* World Health Organization, 1992) and the terms *transsexualism* and *transsexual* remain widely used clinically to describe persons who experience severe gender dysphoria or who request or have completed sex reassignment. In this chapter, I use *transsexualism* as synonymous with GID and *transsexual* as synonymous with "person with GID," reflecting the way these terms are ordinarily used in clinical practice.

The term *transvestism,* which denotes dressing in the clothing of the opposite sex, is sometimes used purely descriptively, but more often denotes cross-dressing associated with current or past sexual arousal, a condition more accurately called *transvestic fetishism.* Professional opinions concerning the relationship between transvestic fetishism and transsexualism have changed over time. The *DSM-III* and *DSM-III-R* recognized that Transvestism (i.e., transvestic fetishism) could sometimes evolve into transsexualism but specified that transsexualism (and GIDAANT in the *DSM-III-R*) excluded a concurrent diagnosis of transvestism. The

DSM-IV and *DSM-IV-TR*, in contrast, specified that persons could be diagnosed with both transvestic fetishism and GID.

The terms *transgender* and *transgenderism* are useful for referring to persons who display varying degrees of cross-gender identity or behavior but who may or may not meet diagnostic criteria for a gender identity disorder or for transvestic fetishism. Such issues, and the extent to which they are culture bound, are discussed in Chapter 15.

Diagnostic Criteria

DSM-IV-TR Diagnoses

The diagnostic criteria for the *DSM-IV-TR* diagnoses of GID, GIDNOS, and transvestic fetishism are summarized in Table 14.1. In males, it is useful to think of GID, GIDNOS and transvestic fetishism as domains within a spectrum of symptomatic male-to-female (MtF) transgender expression, rather than as discrete entities.

For the diagnosis of GID, criterion B requires either discomfort with one's anatomic sex or with the gender role associated with one's sex. Most persons with GID experience both, although in some cases either anatomic or gender role dysphoria will predominate. Anatomic dysphoria is believed by some experts (e.g., Bower, 2001) to be the sine qua non of GID. Criterion C for GID specifies that a physical intersex condition excludes the diagnosis, reflecting the observation that gender identity disturbances in persons with intersex conditions are often qualitatively different from those in persons without such conditions (Meyer-Bahlburg, 1994).

The diagnosis of GIDNOS also implies a criterion of "clinically significant distress or impairment in social, occupational, or other important areas of functioning," as is true for other *DSM-IV-TR* diagnoses. The diagnosis of GIDNOS is nonspecific and could potentially be applied to a wide variety of disturbances in persons' senses of themselves as male or female. The second example provided in the discussion of GIDNOS suggests that cross-dressing behavior per se may be regarded as presumptive evidence of a gender identity disturbance (cf. Levine, 1993).

The diagnosis of transvestic fetishism includes a specifier for the presence of gender dysphoria. A significant minority of nonhomosexual men who engage in erotic cross-dressing use cross-sex hormones to feminize their bodies or express a desire to do so (Docter & Fleming, 1992; Docter & Prince, 1997), suggesting that gender dysphoria not uncommonly accompanies transvestic fetishism.

Table 14.1 *DSM-IV-TR* **Criteria for Gender Identity Disorders in Adults and Transvestic Fetishism**

Gender Identity Disorder in Adults (GID; 302.85)

A. A strong and persistent cross-gender identification (not merely a desire for any perceived cultural advantages of being the other sex).

In . . . adults, the disturbance is manifested by symptoms such as a stated desire to be the other sex, frequent passing as the other sex, desire to live or be treated as the other sex, or the conviction that he or she has the typical feelings and reactions of the other sex.

B. Persistent discomfort with his or her sex or sense of inappropriateness of the gender role of that sex.

In . . . adults, the disturbance is manifested by symptoms such as preoccupation with getting rid of primary and secondary sex characteristics (e.g., requests for hormones, surgery, or other procedures to physically alter sexual characteristics to simulate the other sex) or belief that he or she was born the wrong sex.

C. The disturbance is not concurrent with a physical intersex condition.

D. The disturbance causes clinically significant distress or impairment in social, occupational, or other important areas of functioning. Specify if:
   –Sexually attracted to males
   –Sexually attracted to females
   –Sexually attracted to both
   –Sexually attracted to neither

Gender Identity Disorder Not Otherwise Specified (GIDNOS; 302.6)

This category is included for coding disorders in gender identity that are not classifiable as a specific Gender Identity Disorder. Examples include:

1. Intersex conditions (e.g., partial androgen insensitivity syndrome or congenital adrenal hyperplasia) and accompanying gender dysphoria.
2. Transient, stress-related cross-dressing behavior.
3. Persistent preoccupation with castration or penectomy without a desire to acquire the sex characteristics of the other sex.

Transvestic Fetishism (302.3)

A. Over a period of at least 6 months, in a heterosexual male, recurrent, intense, sexually arousing fantasies, sexual urges, or behaviors involving cross-dressing.

B. The fantasies, sexual urges, or behaviors cause clinically significant distress or impairment in social, occupational, or other important areas of functioning.

Specify if, with Gender Dysphoria, if the person has persistent discomfort with gender role or identity.

Source: Diagnostic and Statistical Manual of Mental Disorders, fourth edition, text revision, by the American Psychiatric Association, 2000, Washington DC: Author. Copyright 2000 American Psychiatric Association. Reprinted with permission.

Levine (1993) proposed that erotic cross-dressing always implies some degree of cross-gender identity, suggesting that many persons who meet diagnostic criteria for transvestic fetishism would also meet diagnostic criteria for GIDNOS. Although the diagnosis of transvestic fetishism is limited to heterosexual males, it is clear that many men who experience sexual arousal with cross-dressing engage in sexual activity with other men when cross-dressed, fantasize about doing so, or identify as bisexual (Docter & Prince, 1997).

ICD-10 Diagnoses

The criteria for the *ICD-10* diagnoses of transsexualism; dual-role transvestism; other gender identity disorders; gender identity disorder, unspecified; and fetishistic transvestism are summarized in Table 14.2. Although the description of fetishistic transvestism might imply that it is excluded by a diagnosis of transsexualism, this is never explicitly stated in the *ICD-10*.

Table 14.2 *ICD-10* Criteria for Gender Identity Disorders in Adults and Fetishistic Transvestism

Transsexualism (F64.0)
A desire to live and be accepted as a member of the opposite sex, usually accompanied by a sense of discomfort with, or inappropriateness of, one's anatomic sex, and a wish to have surgery and hormonal treatment to make one's body as congruent as possible with one's preferred sex.

Dual-Role Transvestism (F64.1)
The wearing of clothes of the opposite sex for part of the individual's existence in order to enjoy the temporary experience of membership of the opposite sex, but without any desire for a more permanent sex change or associated surgical reassignment, and without sexual excitement accompanying the cross-dressing.
Excludes: Fetishistic Transvestism (F65.1)

Other Gender Identity Disorders (F64.8)
(No description or diagnostic criteria are provided for this diagnosis.)

Gender Identity Disorder, Unspecified (F64.9)
(No description or specific criteria are provided for this diagnosis.)

Fetishistic Transvestism (F65.1)
The wearing of clothes of the opposite sex principally to obtain sexual excitement and to create the appearance of a person of the opposite sex. Fetishistic transvestism is distinguished from transsexual transvestism by its clear association with sexual arousal and the strong desire to remove the clothing once orgasm occurs and sexual arousal declines. It can occur as an earlier phase in the development of transsexualism.

Source: International Statistical Classification of Diseases and Related Health Problems, tenth revision, by World Health Organization, 1992, Geneva, Switzerland: Author. Copyright 1992 World Health Organization. Reprinted with permission.

Transsexual Typology

It has long been recognized that transsexualism is a "heterogeneous disorder" (American Psychiatric Association, 1980, p. 261). Consistent with Money's (1986) observation that transsexualism defines a treatment, not a syndrome, it is useful to think of transsexualism as representing a heterogeneous group of only marginally related psychological conditions for which sex reassignment seems to be—and often is—an appealing solution.

Two key features explain much of the diversity among adults who seek sex reassignment: (1) anatomic sex and (2) sexual orientation. Adult transsexualism occurs in both males (MtF transsexuals) and females (female-to-male [FtM] transsexuals); while MtF and FtM transsexualism have many features in common, they are not isomorphic phenomena. MtF transsexuals have received a disproportionate amount of clinical attention (Cromwell, 1998), but the presentations and issues of FtM transsexuals are sufficiently different that they are best considered separately and on their own terms.

Beginning with Hirschfeld (1910/1991), most attempts to construct clinically relevant typologies for MtF transsexualism have considered sexual orientation to be a key variable (for a review, see Blanchard, 1989a). The inclusion of specifiers for sexual orientation or sexual attraction in the *DSM* diagnoses for both transsexualism (American Psychiatric Association, 1980, 1987) and GID (American Psychiatric Association, 1994, 2000) reflected the belief that sexual orientation was an important diagnostic and prognostic feature in transsexualism. This belief has been confirmed in subsequent research: a large and growing body of evidence argues that homosexual MtF transsexuals, who are exclusively sexually attracted to members of their own biological sex, differ in important ways from nonhomosexual MtF transsexuals, who may be attracted to members of the opposite biological sex, to both sexes, or to neither sex. Homosexual and nonhomosexual FtM transsexuals also appear to differ in important ways, although the evidence for these differences is less extensive.

MtF Transsexual Subtypes

Sexual orientation in adult males, including MtF transsexuals, is strongly categorical, either homosexual or heterosexual (Chivers, Rieger, Latty, & Bailey, 2004; Lawrence, Latty, Chivers, & Bailey, 2005; Rieger, Chivers, & Bailey, 2005). Accordingly, there appear to be two and only two categories of MtF transsexuals based on sexual orientation, with intermediate or indeterminate cases likely to be rare or nonexistent. The key features of these categories are summarized across the upper tier of Table 14.3.

Table 14.3 **Transsexual Subtypes**

	Homosexual	Nonhomosexual
Male-to-female	Exclusively attracted to men	May be attracted to women, women and men, or neither sex
	Overtly feminine during childhood	Not overtly feminine during childhood
	Rated as more feminine by observers	Rated as less feminine by observers
	Not sexually aroused by cross-dressing	Sexually aroused by cross-dressing, currently or in the past
	Usually transition in 20s	Usually transition in 30s or later
Female-to-male	Almost exclusively attracted to women	May be primarily attracted to men or women and men
	Overtly masculine during childhood	Usually less overtly masculine during childhood
	Sexual attitudes are more male-typical	Sexual attitudes are less male-typical
	Greater desire for phalloplasty	Less desire for phalloplasty
	Less comorbid psychopathology	More comorbid psychopathology
	Usually transition in 20s	Usually transition in 20s

Homosexual MtF Transsexuals

MtF transsexuals who are exclusively sexually attracted to men resemble the popular stereotype of MtF transsexuals in many respects: usually overtly feminine as children and adolescents and extremely feminine as adults (Blanchard, 1988; Whitam, 1987, 1997), they are judged by observers to be more feminine in their appearance and behavior than their nonhomosexual counterparts (Smith, van Goozen, Kuiper, & Cohen-Kettenis, 2005b). Moreover, they usually do not find cross-dressing or presenting themselves as women to be sexually arousing (Blanchard, 1985, 1989b), although many of these persons probably would have met diagnostic criteria for GID during childhood and adolescence (see Chapter 13, this volume).

Because homosexual MtF transsexuals resemble the most feminine of gay men, their natural, pervasive femininity and exclusive attraction to male partners make it easier and more satisfying for them to live in the world as women than as men. Homosexual MtF transsexuals usually seek sex reassignment in their 20s (Blanchard, Clemmensen, & Steiner, 1987; Smith et al., 2005b), only rarely at later ages. Thirty years ago, most males who applied for sex reassignment were probably of the homosexual type. More recently, they appear to constitute only a minority of persons who request or undergo MtF SRS in the United States, Canada, and the

United Kingdom (Blanchard & Sheridan, 1992; Lawrence, 2003; Levine, 1993; Muirhead-Allwood, Royle, & Young, 1999).

Nonhomosexual MtF Transsexuals

MtF transsexuals who are not exclusively sexually attracted to men may choose women, women and men, or persons of neither sex as sexual partners, but their primary sexual attraction is to women. They are also sexually attracted, however, to the thought or image of *themselves* as women, a paraphilic sexual interest called *autogynephilia* ("love of oneself as a woman"; Blanchard, 1989a). Nonhomosexual MtF transsexuals therefore can accurately be described as autogynephilic transsexuals (Blanchard, 1989b). The most common manifestation of autogynephilia is cross-dressing; most nonhomosexual MtF transsexuals have a history of sexual arousal with cross-dressing or cross-gender fantasy (Blanchard, 1985), and there is evidence that such arousal is almost universal in MtF transsexuals (Blanchard, Racansky, & Steiner, 1986). Many of these persons would have met diagnostic criteria for transvestic fetishism in the past. Anatomic autogynephilia, in which the person is sexually aroused by the idea of having female somatic features (e.g., breasts or a vulva), is especially characteristic of men who seek SRS (Blanchard, 1993). It is conceptually useful to think of nonhomosexual MtF transsexuals as heterosexual men who have an unusual and powerful paraphilic sexual interest that leads them to want to *become what they love,* by turning their bodies into facsimiles of what they find sexually desirable, that is, women (Freund & Blanchard, 1993; see also Lawrence, 2007a). Some of these persons develop a secondary interest in men as sexual partners, not because they are attracted to men per se, but because they are attracted to the idea of taking a woman's sexual role in relationship to a man, thereby having their "physical attractiveness as women validated by others" (Blanchard, 1989b, p. 622; see also Lawrence, 2004). It is not unusual for nonhomosexual MtF transsexuals to display other paraphilic sexual interests, especially sexual masochism (e.g., Bolin, 1988; Walworth, 1997).

Nonhomosexual MtF transsexuals usually were not overtly feminine during childhood and typically they are not remarkably feminine as adults (Blanchard, 1990; Whitam, 1997). They sometimes give a history of mild or moderate gender nonconformity during childhood (e.g., avoidance of rough-and-tumble play or a preference for girls as playmates; e.g., Buhrich & McConaghy, 1977), but this is usually less overt and less pervasive than the gender nonconformity of homosexual MtF transsexuals. Nonhomosexual MtF transsexuals are judged by observers to be less feminine in their appearance and behavior than their homosexual MtF counterparts (Smith et al., 2005b). They usually seek sex reassignment in their mid-30s or later (Blanchard et al., 1987;

Smith et al., 2005b) and not uncommonly in their 50s and 60s (Lawrence, 2003). Typically these persons have been married to women and have struggled with their cross-gender feelings for decades before they finally decide that sex reassignment offers them their best hope for happiness. Thirty years ago, persons in this category were often considered unfavorable candidates for sex reassignment (e.g., Wålinder, Lundström, & Thuwe, 1978). Currently, they appear to constitute the majority of persons who request and undergo MtF SRS in the United States, Canada, and the United Kingdom.

Similarities between MtF Subtypes

Despite their many differences, homosexual and nonhomosexual MtF transsexuals report that they first wished to be the opposite sex or to change sex at similar ages, about 8 years on average (Lawrence, 2005), and they report similar intensities of gender dysphoria in adulthood. They are also about equally likely to experience comorbid psychological problems (Smith et al., 2005b).

FtM Transsexual Subtypes

There are also two distinct categories or subtypes of FtM transsexualism, again reflecting differences in sexual orientation. Differences between FtM transsexual subtypes appear to be less pronounced than is true of MtF subtypes, perhaps in part because sexual orientation in adult females is less categorical and more fluid than in males (Chivers et al., 2004; Diamond, 2003, 2005). Nevertheless, the homosexual-nonhomosexual distinction appears to be valid and clinically useful for FtM transsexuals as well. The key features of the two FtM transsexual subtypes are summarized across the lower tier of Table 14.3.

Homosexual FtM Transsexuals
FtM transsexuals who are exclusively sexually attracted to women were almost always overtly masculine in their behavior and attitudes as children (Smith et al., 2005b) and they tend to be very masculine adults. Probably most would have met diagnostic criteria for GID during childhood and adolescence. Their sexual attitudes tend to be male-typical in many respects: they prefer feminine partners, display greater sexual than emotional jealousy, and report more sexual partners, greater sexual assertiveness, more interest in visual sexual stimuli, and a more intense desire for phalloplasty than their nonhomosexual FtM counterparts (Chivers & Bailey, 2000). At one time, nearly all FtM transsexuals were believed to be homosexual (Blanchard et al., 1987); recent studies suggest that about 70% are (Smith, van Goozen, Kuiper, & Cohen-Kettenis, 2005a; Smith et al., 2005b).

Nonhomosexual FtM Transsexuals

According to Smith et al. (2005b), nonhomosexual FtM transsexuals "may have been girls with neutral interests or with some tomboy characteristics" (p. 159), but they rarely report the overt and pervasive childhood masculinity characteristic of their homosexual FtM counterparts, nor is arousal to cross-dressing or cross-gender fantasy a significant factor in the development of nonhomosexual FtM transsexualism (Smith et al., 2005b). Nonhomosexual FtM transsexuals prefer masculine, not feminine, male partners and report sexual attitudes that are more female-typical than their homosexual FtM counterparts (Chivers & Bailey, 2000). They are significantly more likely to report psychological problems than are homosexual FtM transsexuals (Smith et al., 2005b). At one time, nonhomosexual FtM transsexuals were rare enough to result in case reports; now they comprise about 30% of FtM transsexuals who are approved for (Smith et al., 2005b) or who complete sex reassignment (Smith et al., 2005a).

Similarities between FtM Subtypes

Homosexual and nonhomosexual FtM transsexuals report comparable degrees of gender dysphoria, apply for sex reassignment at similar ages (Smith et al., 2005b), and are about equally likely to have been married to men (Smith et al., 2005b). With the exception of phalloplasty, they do not differ significantly in their desire for physical masculinization (Chivers & Bailey, 2000).

Epidemiology

Prevalence and Sex Ratio

The best estimates of the prevalence of transsexualism and GID in Western societies come from population-based data from European countries. The most recent estimates, from Belgium (De Cuypere et al., 2007), reveal a prevalence of about 1:12,900 for MtF transsexualism (defined as having undergone SRS) and 1:33,800 for FtM transsexualism. Earlier data from the Netherlands (Bakker, van Kesteren, Gooren, & Bezemer, 1993) were similar: 1:11,900 for MtF transsexualism and 1:30,400 for FtM transsexualism. Survey data obtained from primary care physicians in Scotland (Wilson, Sharp, & Carr, 1999) showed similar results: The prevalence of patients with gender dysphoria who were either being treated with cross-sex hormone therapy or had completed SRS was 1:12,800 for MtF patients and 1:52,100 for FtM patients. In the same survey, when all persons diagnosed with gender dysphoria were included, regardless of treatment status, the prevalence was significantly higher: 1:7,400 for males and 1:31,200 for females. Most published reports from Western countries indicate that MtF transsexualism is about two to three times more prevalent than FtM transsexualism (Garrels et al., 2000; Landén, Wålinder, & Lundström, 1996).

The prevalence of transsexualism appears to be increasing. Studies conducted in Sweden and the United States in the 1960s reported prevalence figures of 1:37,000 to 1:100,000 for MtF transsexualism and 1:103,000 to 1:400,000 for FtM transsexualism (Landén et al., 1996), roughly an order of magnitude lower than current estimates. Reported increases in the prevalence of transsexualism probably reflect an increased number of persons who regard themselves as appropriate candidates for sex reassignment.

In one recent survey, 2.8% of adult males reported having experienced sexual arousal in association with cross-dressing (Langstrom & Zucker, 2005), suggesting that cross-dressers probably comprise the largest transgender subgroup. Many of these persons, however, probably do not experience sufficient gender dysphoria to meet diagnostic criteria for GID or GIDNOS, nor sufficient distress or impairment in functioning to meet diagnostic criteria for GID, GIDNOS, or transvestic fetishism in the *DSM-IV-TR.*

Age of Onset

Some persons with GID report that they were aware of their transgender feelings from their earliest memories. The cross-gender behaviors and interests of homosexual transsexuals, both MtF and FtM, are often evident in early childhood (see Chapter 13, this volume) and sexual arousal with cross-dressing, the most common precursor of nonhomosexual MtF transsexualism, has been reported in children younger than age 3 years (Stoller, 1985; Zucker & Blanchard, 1997). Adult MtF transsexuals typically report that they experienced their first desire to be of the opposite sex or to change sex in middle childhood (Lawrence, 2005). FtM transsexuals and homosexual MtF transsexuals usually apply for sex reassignment in their 20s; nonhomosexual MtF transsexuals usually apply significantly later, especially if they have married or have fathered children (Blanchard, 1994).

Clinical Presentation and Course

Clinical Presentation

In most clients with known or suspected gender identity disorders seen by mental health professionals, gender identity problems—or approval for an associated treatment, such as hormone therapy or SRS—is the presenting concern. Levine (1993) noted, however, that men with gender identity disorders sometimes present with other concerns, including paraphilias, sexual dysfunctions, or general psychiatric conditions such as depression.

Persons with gender dysphoria may desire the anatomy, the sexuality, or the social role of the opposite sex, or any combination of these (Carroll, 1999). Some experts regard intense dysphoria associated with the sexed body—the feeling of being "trapped in the wrong body"—as the essential feature of transsexualism or GID (e.g., Bower, 2001; Prosser, 1998). Persons with the anatomic type of gender dysphoria typically present with a request to be rapidly approved for cross-sex hormone therapy and surgical treatment. Intense anatomic dysphoria is not, however, invariably present in GID, although it is characteristic of most FtM transsexuals and nonhomosexual MtF transsexuals. In other persons, however, including many homosexual MtF transsexuals, gender dysphoria is primarily related to a desire for the gender role and the sexuality of the opposite sex. These persons may present to the clinician to request help in facilitating social transition, such as obtaining appropriate identity documents or dealing with family members or significant others.

Clinical Course

The course of GID is variable and incompletely understood. Meyer et al. (2001) observed that, even among carefully evaluated persons, the diagnosis of GID does not inevitably lead to a single predictable outcome. Carroll (1999) outlined four possible outcomes in severe gender dysphoria: (1) unresolved, (2) acceptance of natal gender, (3) part-time cross-gender behavior, and (4) full-time cross-living and sex reassignment.

Unresolved Outcomes

It is estimated that as many as 50% of persons who undergo evaluation or psychotherapy for GID leave treatment. Some drop out because they become impatient with the evaluation process, perceive their caregivers as uninformed or unempathetic, are unable to afford the expense of treatment, or are ambivalent about achieving resolution of their gender problem. Little is known about what subsequently happens to these clients, but some of them return to treatment months or years later.

Acceptance of Natal Gender

In the past, most clinicians regarded acceptance of natal gender as the preferred outcome in gender identity disorders and often recommended psychodynamic psychotherapy as the treatment most likely to achieve this outcome. However, rigorous studies demonstrating that psychotherapy can reduce or eliminate gender dysphoria or promote acceptance of natal gender are lacking.

Nevertheless, some individuals with gender identity disorders appear to achieve acceptance of their natal gender (e.g., Marks, Green, & Mataix-Cols, 2000), albeit not always with complete remission of gender dysphoria. Acceptance of natal gender is sometimes observed in persons whose comorbid psychological problems are effectively treated, whose religious beliefs are inconsistent with sex reassignment, whose anatomic characteristics (e.g., extreme height or size in men) make passing as a member of the preferred sex impossible, or who fear losing their spouses, children, or other significant relationships. Blanchard (1994) demonstrated that nonhomosexual men with gender dysphoria can sometimes successfully postpone treatment until they have completed parental or other family obligations. The Standards of Care (Meyer et al., 2001) list several "options for gender adaptation" for persons with gender identity disorders who decide not to live full- or part-time in cross-gender role.

Part-Time Cross-Gender Behavior

Some persons with GID choose to live part-time as members of their natal gender and part-time as members of their preferred gender, sometimes with the help of masculinizing or feminizing hormone therapy or surgical procedures. Docter and Fleming (1992), in a survey of 682 cross-dressing adult males, found that 11% referred to themselves as "transsexuals," but cross-dressed only episodically and did not live full-time as women. In a subsequent survey of 1,032 periodic heterosexual cross-dressers, Docter and Prince (1997) found that 17% identified as transsexual and would seek sex reassignment if possible, 28% regarded their feminine self as their preferred gender identity, 4% were currently using feminizing hormones, and another 43% would have liked to do so. These persons arguably had a strong and persistent cross-gender identity and plausibly experienced gender dysphoria in many cases, but chose to live only part-time as women. Part-time cross-living appears to occur in adult females with GID as well, but has not been as extensively documented.

Full-Time Cross-Living and Sex Reassignment

This outcome is sought by most clients with a presenting complaint of GID or transsexualism and the one that has been most extensively studied. It should be noted, however, that the boundary between this outcome and part-time cross-gender behavior is not always clearly demarcated. Some persons who live full-time in cross-gender role do not undergo SRS or may not use cross-sex hormone therapy; and some persons who use cross-sex hormones and undergo SRS do not present themselves unambiguously as members of the opposite gender, but instead present as androgynous, gender-ambiguous, or visibly transgender persons.

The process of undertaking full-time cross-living and sex reassignment typically occurs in stages, similar to the stages of "coming out" for lesbians and gay men. Several stage theories of transsexual coming-out have been proposed (Devor, 2004; Gagne, Tewksbury, & McGaughey, 1997; Lev, 2004; Lewins, 1995); most of these theories involve stages of awareness of gender dysphoria, questioning and information gathering, assumption of a transsexual identity, disclosure to significant others, cross-living, surgical reassignment, and posttransition identity evolution. For many clients, the course of gender transition involves emotional, psychological, and identity changes that continue for years or decades following sex reassignment.

Associated Features

Comorbid Mental Health Problems

Axis I Disorders
The prevalence of comorbid Axis I mental health problems in persons with gender identity disorders appears to be elevated. Hoenig and Kenna (1974) reported that roughly half of the MtF and FtM transsexuals they studied displayed significant current comorbid psychopathology, including about 12% with schizophrenia or affective psychosis. Bodlund and Armelius (1994) diagnosed 44% of a group of MtF and FtM transsexuals as having another current Axis I disorder, about half of which were merely adjustment disorders; however, 82% of persons with a diagnosis of GIDAANT had another Axis I disorder, only one third of which were adjustment disorders. De Cuypere, Jannes, and Rubens (1995) diagnosed a current comorbid Axis I disorder in none of their FtM transsexual patients but in 23% of their MtF transsexual patients. Haraldsen and Dahl (2000) observed that 33% of a group of MtF and FtM undergoing hormone therapy had a current Axis I disorder. Verschoor and Poortinga (1988) found that 21% of MtF transsexuals and 33% of FtM transsexuals reported a lifetime history of treatment for another psychiatric disorder; De Cuypere et al. (1995) reported figures of 45% and 38%, respectively.

Substance Abuse
Substance abuse is often considered separately from other Axis I disorders. Prevalence estimates for substance abuse among transsexuals vary widely. Cole, O'Boyle, Emory, and Meyer (1997) reported lifetime histories of substance abuse in 29% of MtF transsexuals and 26% of FtM transsexuals. De Cuypere et al. (1995) found higher figures, 50% in MtF transsexuals and 62% in FtM transsexuals, but Verschoor and Poortinga (1988) reported

much lower figures, 11% among MtF transsexuals and 4% among FtM transsexuals.

Personality Disorders

Comorbid personality disorders are common among persons with gender identity disorders. Hoenig and Kenna (1974) observed personality disorders in 18% of their MtF and FtM transsexual patients; Haraldsen and Dahl (2000) reported a similar figure, 20%. Personality disorders appear to be more common in persons with gender identity disorders other than transsexualism: Bodlund and Armelius (1994) found that 33% of their transsexual patients had a personality disorder, but this was true of 73% of their patients with GIDAANT. Similarly, Miach, Berah, Butcher, and Rouse (2000) reported personality disorders in 27% of their transsexual patients but in 65% of their patients with GIDAANT.

Comorbid Medical Problems

Suicide and Self-Harm

Van Kesteren, Asscheman, Megens, and Gooren (1997) found that, in the Netherlands, 13 (1.6%) of 816 MtF transsexuals receiving hormone therapy had died of suicide—a percentage more than nine times that of the general population—while none of 293 FtM transsexuals receiving hormone therapy had died of suicide. Dixen, Maddever, Van Maasdam, and Edwards (1984) reported a history of suicide attempts in about 25% of MtF applicants for sex reassignment and 19% of FtM applicants. Verschoor and Poortinga (1988) reported such a history in about 19% of both MtF and FtM transsexuals. Cole et al. (1997) observed that 12% of MtF transsexuals and 21% of FtM transsexuals had attempted suicide. Clements-Nolle, Marx, Guzman, and Katz (2001) documented attempted suicide in 32% of both MtF and FtM transsexuals; De Cuypere et al. (1995) observed even higher figures, 55% in MtF transsexuals and 46% in FtM transsexuals.

Some persons with gender identity disorders engage in self-mutilation of their genitals and breasts: Dixen et al. (1984) found that 9.4% of MtF applicants for sex reassignment and 2.4% of FtM applicants had done so. Cole et al. (1997) reported comparable percentages, 8% among MtF transsexuals and 1% among FtM transsexuals. Case reports of self-castration in MtF transsexuals are not uncommon, especially among persons who are unable to undergo SRS or who anticipate long waiting times.

Violence

Persons with gender identity disorders may be at increased risk for assault, sexual assault, and rape. In a survey of 402 transgender persons, most of whom were transsexuals or cross-dressers but not all of whom necessarily met diagnostic criteria for a gender identity disorder, Lombardi, Wilchins, Priesing, and Malouf (2001) found that 16% of respondents reported an assault within the past year and 3% reported a rape or attempted rape.

Sexually Transmitted Infections

Some MtF transgender persons in the United States, many of whom would probably meet diagnostic criteria for a gender identity disorder, have a disproportionately high prevalence of HIV infection. Reported HIV seropositivity figures, based on studies conducted with convenience samples of MtF transgender persons, include: 25% in New York City (McGowan, 1999); 19% in Philadelphia (Kenagy, 2002); 35%, 16%, and 48% in San Francisco (Clements-Nolle et al., 2001; Kellogg, Clements-Nolle, Dilley, Katz, & McFarland, 2001; Nemoto, Luke, Mamo, Ching, & Patria, 1999); 32% in Washington, DC (Xavier, 2000); and 22% in Los Angeles (Simon, Reback, & Bemis, 2000). HIV infection is especially prevalent among MtF transgender persons who engage in sex work and in MtF persons of color, particularly African Americans. Reported HIV seropositivity figures in FtM transgender persons are much lower: 0% in Philadelphia and New York City (Kenagy, 2002; McGowan, 1999), 2% in San Francisco (Clements-Nolle et al., 2001), and 5% or less in Washington, DC (Xavier, 2000). MtF transgender persons also report a high lifetime prevalence of sexually transmitted infections (STIs) other than HIV. Kenagy (2002) found that 41% of a convenience sample of MtF transgender persons in Philadelphia reported having been diagnosed with a STI other than HIV at some time in their lives; among FtM transgender persons, only 6% reported this.

Diagnosis and Assessment of Gender Identity Disorders

The diagnosis and assessment of persons known or suspected to have gender identity disorders is summarized in Table 14.4. Diagnosis and assessment typically involves: (a) determining the presence or absence of a gender identity disorder, including ruling out alternative diagnostic possibilities; (b) assessing the nature and intensity of the gender identity disorder, if present; and (c) evaluating comorbid conditions.

Determining the Presence or Absence of a Gender Identity Disorder

In adults, gender identity disorders are diagnosed almost entirely based on self-report. Diagnosis is made during one or more

Table 14.4 **Typical Processes and Considerations in the Diagnosis and Treatment of Gender Identity Disorders in Adults**

Process	Principal Considerations
Initial evaluation and diagnosis: –Is there a gender identity disorder? –What is its nature and severity? –Are there comorbid conditions?	Differential diagnosis: GID, GIDNOS, transvestic Fetishism, psychoses, dissociative identity disorder, personality disorders, gender nonconformity Is gender dysphoria related to anatomy, sexuality, or role? Is there a recent loss or crisis? Affective, adjustment, substance, or personality disorders? Suicidality? HIV in MtFs?
Psychotherapy: –Individual –Group	Individual psychotherapy is not required for later treatment steps under the Standards of Care, but is encouraged. Typical issues: evolving identity, relationships, employment concerns, treatment options. Group therapy can reduce feelings of isolation and provide opportunities to receive and give support.
Evaluation for hormone therapy	Clear rationale for hormones? Comorbid conditions controlled? Informed consent?
Hormone therapy	Relieves gender dysphoria; usually well tolerated, but significant complications possible.
Real-life experience	Better quality of life in new gender role? Can client cope with stigma and discrimination?
Evaluation for sex reassignment surgery	One year of successful real-life experience and hormone therapy? Informed consent?
Sex reassignment surgery	Vaginoplasty usually very successful; no entirely satisfactory phalloplasty technique.

Note: Many clients will not desire all of the treatment processes described.

clinical interviews, based on the client's self-reported history of psychosexual development, gender identification, sexual orientation, and feelings concerning his or her sexed body characteristics and the social role of his or her sex of assignment. Information about the client's social support system and occupational functioning is also obtained. Clients often self-diagnose gender dysphoria and typically volunteer much of the relevant information. Clinicians should be aware that clients sometimes deliberately or unintentionally give distorted accounts of their histories or feelings, especially if they are eager to be approved for sex reassignment.

Questionnaires and interviews for the assessment of gender identity, gender dysphoria, and sex-typed behaviors and interests in adults exist (see Zucker, 2005, p. 385), but many are either unpublished or have not been cross-validated. Two exceptions are the Feminine Gender Identity Scale for Males (Freund, Langevin, Satterberg, & Steiner, 1977) and the Masculine Gender Identity Scale for Females (Blanchard & Freund, 1983), but these are not widely used outside of research settings. The Gender Identity/Gender Dysphoria Questionnaire for Adolescents and Adults (Deogracias et al., in press) appears to be a promising instrument but has not been cross-validated. Usually the gender-related scales of the Minnesota Multiphasic Personality Inventory-2 (*Mf, GM,* and *GF;* Butcher et al., 2001) provide the most practical objective measure of a client's gender-atypical attitudes and interests.

Differential diagnostic considerations for the diagnosis of GID include GIDNOS, transvestic fetishism, schizophrenia and related psychotic conditions, dissociative identity disorder, Cluster B personality disorders, and gender nonconformity. As previously noted, distinguishing between GID and GIDNOS is somewhat arbitrary, except in the case of physical intersex conditions, which preclude the former diagnosis. In practice, the treatment implications of a diagnosis of GID versus GIDNOS may be minimal. Transvestic fetishism and GID can co-occur; however, the absence of either a strong and persistent cross-gender identification or persistent discomfort with one's sexed body characteristics or gender role excludes the latter diagnosis.

Patients with schizophrenia, bipolar disorder, and other psychotic disorders may sometimes experience delusions of being or becoming the opposite sex during acute psychotic episodes (e.g., Habermeyer, Kamps, & Kawohl, 2003; Manderson & Kumar, 2001); in these cases, cross-gender identity usually resolves with treatment of the psychotic condition, but occasionally both diagnoses may co-occur. Patients with dissociative identity disorder may display cross-gender ideation (Modestin & Ebner, 1995; Saks, 1998), but dissociative identity disorder and GID can also co-occur (Brown, 2001). Laub and Fisk (1974) reported that persons with antisocial personality disorder sometimes seek sex reassignment for reasons unrelated to gender dysphoria; and some experts propose that gender dysphoria may be a symptom of the identity diffusion associated with borderline personality disturbances (e.g., Lothstein, 1984; Person & Ovesey, 1974), suggesting that borderline personality disorder might be a differential diagnostic consideration in some cases. Some gender-nonconforming persons with significant cross-gender identifications or strong preferences for the gender role of the other sex may not experience enough distress or impairment in functioning to meet diagnostic criteria for any gender identity disorder (see Chapter 15, this volume).

Assessing the Nature and Intensity of the Gender Identity Disorder

Gender dysphoria may involve dissatisfaction with the sexed body characteristics, the sexuality, or the gender role of the person's sex of assignment. Often all three dissatisfactions are significant, but sometimes only one or two are; this may have important implications for treatment planning. Persons with GID also differ in the intensity and chronicity of their gender dysphoria. Gender dysphoria sometimes intensifies when clients experience significant crises or losses (Levine, 1993; Lothstein, 1979; Roback, Fellemann, & Abramowitz, 1984) and may moderate or remit when these resolve or have been addressed.

Evaluating Comorbid Conditions

As previously noted, comorbid mental health problems and related medical problems are not uncommon in persons with gender identity disorders. Comorbid psychotic, affective, and anxiety disorders sometimes must be assessed and treated before the presence or absence of a gender identity disorder can be confidently diagnosed. Satisfactory control of comorbid mental health problems is considered a precondition for approval for SRS (Meyer et al., 2001).

Treatment

Standards of Care for Gender Identity Disorders

HBIGDA, which was recently renamed the World Professional Association for Transgender Health, formulates and promotes Standards of Care, updated regularly, for the treatment of gender identity disorders. The most recent edition of the Standards of Care was published in 2001 (Meyer et al., 2001). The Standards of Care reflect the consensus opinions of experienced professionals but are not always evidence-based (e.g., Lawrence, 2001, 2003). They nevertheless provide an important resource for professionals who treat clients with gender identity concerns.

Typical elements in the treatment of GID are summarized in Table 14.4. In addition to psychotherapy, the Standards of Care describe three principal treatment modalities: (1) cross-sex hormone therapy, (2) full-time, real-life experience in the desired gender role, and (3) SRS, a term that usually refers specifically to feminizing or masculinizing genitoplasty. These three modalities are sometimes called the components of *triadic therapy* (Meyer et al., 2001). The Standards of Care recognize some patients with GID will not want all of the elements of triadic therapy or may conclude that the costs or negative consequences of some elements outweigh the benefits. For example, some FtM transsexuals and homosexual MtF transsexuals persons appear to be satisfied using cross-sex hormone therapy and living socially as members of their preferred sex, but without undergoing SRS. Similarly, some non-homosexual MtF persons with GID or GIDNOS appear to be satisfied using cross-sex hormone therapy and living part-time as members of their preferred sex. The Standards of Care support the provision of hormone therapy and the undertaking of a real-life experience separately or in combination, but state that SRS should ordinarily be provided only to persons who have used cross-sex hormone therapy for a minimum of 1 year and who have successfully completed a minimum of 1 year of real-life experience in the desired gender role (Meyer et al., 2001).

Psychotherapy for Gender Identity Disorders

Although not an element of triadic therapy, individual and group psychotherapy can be beneficial to persons with GID. Individual psychotherapy is unlikely to lead to remission of gender dysphoria, but it can provide clients with a safe and supportive setting in which to discuss difficult or ambivalent feelings, explore evolving identity, examine relationship and employment concerns, and consider various treatment options. Individual psychotherapy during the real-life experience, while not required by the Standards of Care, is encouraged (Meyer et al., 2001).

Group psychotherapy can also be helpful to persons with GID (Lev, 2004; Stermac, Blanchard, Clemmensen, & Dickey, 1991). Interacting with other persons who also experience gender dysphoria can reduce clients' feeling of isolation by allowing them to see that they are not alone and providing opportunities for them to receive and give support. Group settings allow clients to share advice about grooming and other aspects of social presentation. Sometimes group members will confront one another about issues of shame and denial, a process that can be valuable but that is often difficult to accomplish in individual psychotherapy (Lev, 2004).

Hormone Therapy

Cross-sex hormone therapy helps persons with gender identity disorders look and feel more like members of their preferred sex by stimulating the development of secondary sex characteristics of the preferred sex and suppressing secondary sex characteristics of the birth sex. Several recent comprehensive reviews address the management of cross-sex hormone therapy (Levy, Crown, & Reid, 2003; Michel, Mormont, & Legros, 2001; Moore, Wisniewski, & Dobs, 2003; Tangpricha, Ducharme, Barber, & Chipkin, 2003).

Guidelines and eligibility criteria for cross-sex hormone therapy are discussed in the HBIGDA Standards of Care (Meyer et al., 2001). Eligibility criteria primarily involve a thorough professional evaluation of the gender identity disorder; the existence of a clear rationale for hormone treatment; reasonable psychological stability, including satisfactory control of comorbid conditions; and the ability of the client to give informed consent. Smith et al. (2005a) observed that approval for hormone therapy is more likely to be given to persons who display more intense gender dysphoria and whose physical appearance is more congruent with their preferred sex. Hormone therapy is prescribed primarily for persons diagnosed with GID or transsexualism; prescribing for persons not meeting diagnostic criteria for these conditions was once regarded as "deeply controversial" (Levine et al., 1998, p. 32). The latest version of the Standards of Care (Meyer et al., 2001) emphasizes that hormone therapy can appropriately be prescribed for transgender persons who do not wish to live full-time in a cross-gender role or who do not desire feminizing or masculinizing genital surgery, which would include many persons with GIDNOS or transvestic fetishism.

Cross-sex hormone therapy is ideally prescribed based on the recommendation of an experienced mental health professional, but persons with gender identity disorders commonly acquire and use hormones without such recommendations and without medical supervision (Clements-Nolle et al., 2001; McGowan, 1999: Xavier, 2000). The most recent version of the Standards of Care (Meyer et al., 2001) authorized the prescription of hormones without the recommendation of a mental health professional in selected cases to persons engaging in unsupervised hormone use, in order to encourage medically monitored therapy.

Feminizing Hormone Therapy

Estrogens are the principal medications used in feminizing hormone therapy for MtF transsexuals. Estrogens can be administered orally, intramuscularly, or transdermally. Antiandrogens, medications that block the synthesis or the effects of testosterone and related androgens, are often prescribed as well, to reduce the dosage of estrogen required. Spironolactone is the most commonly prescribed antiandrogen in the United States. Medications with progesterone-like activity are sometimes prescribed, either to promote breast development or for their antiandrogenic effects; one such medication, cyproterone acetate, is not available in the United States but is often prescribed in other countries.

Desired effects of feminizing hormone therapy include breast growth, redistribution of body fat to a more female-typical pattern, decreased muscle mass and increased subcutaneous fat, softening of the skin, reduction in the rate of growth of facial and body hair, reduction or cessation of scalp hair loss, decreased testicular size, and elimination of spontaneous erections. Feminizing hormone therapy does not significantly affect vocal pitch or penile length. Potential side effects of feminizing hormone therapy include weight gain, reduced red cell mass, decreased libido, and infertility. Most of the effects of feminizing hormones are reversible if hormones are discontinued, but breast growth is permanent.

Feminizing hormones have emotional and psychological effects as well as physical effects. Leavitt, Berger, Hoeppner, and Northrop (1980) reported that a group of MtF transsexuals taking feminizing hormones displayed better psychological adjustment than a comparable group not using hormones and that longer duration of hormone use was associated with better psychological adjustment. Van Kemenade, Cohen-Kettenis, Cohen, and Gooren (1989) found that treatment with an antiandrogen increased feelings of relaxation and energy in MtF transsexuals and Slabbekoorn, van Goozen, Gooren, and Cohen-Kettenis (2001) observed that feminizing hormone therapy increased positive emotions and nonverbal emotional expressivity in MtF transsexuals.

Van Kesteren et al. (1997) found no evidence of increased mortality among hormone-treated MtF transsexuals in the Netherlands. Feminizing hormone therapy sometimes can be associated, however, with serious or life-threatening medical complications. The most significant of these are venous thrombosis and pulmonary embolism. Other potential medical complications include gallstones, liver disease, insulin resistance and glucose intolerance, and increased prolactin levels, rarely accompanied by pituitary gland enlargement. Feminizing hormone therapy results in infertility, although the time course and reversibility of this effect is poorly understood (Lawrence, 2007b). In an Internet survey, a significant number of MtF transsexuals expressed an interest in sperm preservation before beginning feminizing hormone therapy (De Sutter, Kira, Verschoor, & Hotimsky, 2003). Therefore, MtF transsexuals should be counseled about sperm preservation before beginning hormone therapy (Meyer et al., 2001).

Masculinizing Hormone Therapy

Testosterone is the only medication usually prescribed to induce masculinization in FtM transsexuals and is usually administered by intramuscular injection. Progesterone is occasionally prescribed with testosterone to suppress menses. Testosterone therapy causes deepening of the voice, clitoral enlargement, increased muscle mass, decreased subcutaneous fat, slight reduction in breast size, increased facial and body hair, male pattern scalp hair loss, and suppression of menses. Some of these changes are reversible if testosterone is discontinued, but the effects on voice, facial and body hair, and clitoral size are permanent.

Masculinizing hormone therapy has emotional and psychological effects as well as physical effects. Van Goozen, Cohen-Kettenis, Gooren, Frijda, and Van de Poll (1995) reported that testosterone treatment increased aggressiveness, anger-proneness, and sexual interest in FtM transsexuals. Slabbekoorn et al. (2001) found that testosterone treatment decreased the intensity of positive and negative emotions in FtM transsexuals, but increased sexual feelings and behaviors and anger-readiness.

Masculinizing hormone therapy is not associated with increased mortality (van Kesteren et al., 1997). However, significant side effects and complications can occur; these include acne, weight gain, increased red cell mass with possible polycythemia, liver disease, insulin resistance, fluid retention, and edema. Testosterone treatment decreases arterial reactivity and shifts lipid profiles toward a more male-typical pattern, potentially increasing cardiovascular risk.

Testosterone treatment often produces changes in the ovaries similar to those found in polycystic ovarian syndrome; because polycystic ovaries may be more likely to undergo malignant changes (Gooren, 1999), some experts recommend that FtM transsexuals who are treated with testosterone have their ovaries surgically removed after successful transition to the male gender role. Testosterone treatment can also cause endometrial hyperplasia, a known risk factor for endometrial carcinoma; consequently, some experts recommend that FtM transsexuals who are treated with testosterone undergo hysterectomy as soon as their emotional and clinical progress permits. At present, the only practical fertility preservation option available to FtM transsexuals is cryopreservation of fertilized embryos.

Real-life Experience in the Preferred Gender Role

The real-life experience provides an opportunity for the client to decide whether cross-living offers a better quality of life than living in the original gender role. Although the real-life experience is considered an element of triadic therapy, it is an element that the client can decide to undertake on his or her own; in fact, some clients will already be living full-time in their desired gender role when seen by the clinician. The real-life experience was formerly called the real-life *test*, with the implication that the cross-living experience provided a test of the appropriateness of the diagnosis of GID and of the client's suitability for a referral for irreversible SRS. In practice, the real-life experience may have irreversible social and economic consequences of its own, which may be perceived by clients to be more severe than the potential consequences of SRS. For this reason, some clients, especially nonhomosexual MtF transsexuals, do not want a full-time real-life experience and believe that they should be allowed to undergo SRS without one (Lawrence, 2001).

Being regarded and treated as a member of one's preferred gender during the real-life experience is usually easier for FtM transsexuals than for MtF transsexuals. As Kessler and McKenna (1978) observed, attribution of male status to a person results from observing signs of maleness, whereas attribution of female status occurs by exclusion, when few or no signs of maleness are detected. While it is difficult for both MtF and FtM transsexuals to eradicate all evidence of their birth sex, residual signs of maleness in MtF transsexuals can often interfere with their being considered female, while residual signs of femaleness in FtM transsexuals may interfere little if at all with their being considered male.

A successful real-life experience is considered an eligibility criterion for SRS in the Standards of Care (Meyer et al., 2001), but the meaning of success is open to interpretation. One measure of success in the real-life experience might be an improvement in social and psychological functioning in the preferred gender role. This may sometimes be difficult to demonstrate, however, because the negative psychological, social, and economic effects of discrimination against persons believed to be transsexual may counteract the benefits of living in a gender role that is more consistent with one's sense of self (Levy et al., 2003). In some cases, it may be difficult to decide whether a client is genuinely living in his or her preferred gender role, especially if that gender role is a nontraditional one: The Standards of Care do not require clients to present themselves as typical members of the opposite gender, but merely to present themselves in the gender role that is congruent with their gender identity.

Surgery

SRS in MtF Transsexuals

SRS for MtF transsexuals has been performed for over 70 years and has reached a high level of technical refinement. When performed by experienced surgeons, it yields good cosmetic and functional results and favorable subjective outcomes (Green & Fleming, 1990; Lawrence, 2003; Muirhead-Allwood et al., 1999). MtF SRS usually involves orchiectomy, penectomy, vaginoplasty, and vulvoplasty. Typically, the neovagina is lined with the inverted skin of the penis, which is widely regarded as the technique of choice (Karim, Hage, & Mulder, 1996). Most surgeons construct a sensate clitoris from part of the glans penis (Giraldo, Mora, Solano, Gonzáles, & Smith-Fernández, 2002).

While all the elements of MtF sex reassignment appear to provide relief of gender dysphoria (Kuiper & Cohen-Kettenis, 1988), MtF SRS offers particular social and psychological benefits. In a prospective, randomized, controlled study of outcomes of MtF SRS, Mate-Kole, Freschi, and Robin (1990) found that, compared to a wait-list control group, MtF transsexuals who received SRS on an expedited basis reported better psychosocial outcomes, including greater engagement in social activities and fewer neurotic symptoms.

Complications of MtF SRS can include vaginal stenosis, genital pain, clitoral necrosis, urethral stenosis, and rectovaginal or vesicovaginal fistulas (Krege, Bex, Lümmen, & Rübben, 2001; Lawrence, 2006). Good surgical results and an absence of complications are associated with better psychosocial outcomes and higher levels of patient satisfaction (Lawrence, 2003; Muirhead-Allwood et al., 1999; Ross & Need, 1989; Schroder & Carroll, 1999).

Other Surgical Procedures for MtF Transsexuals

MtF transsexuals often feel that hormone-induced breast development is inadequate and many request breast augmentation surgery. About three quarters of patients express satisfaction after breast augmentation; dissatisfied patients most commonly complain that their breasts were not made large enough (Kanhai, Hage, & Mulder, 2000).

SRS in FtM Transsexuals

At present, there are no entirely satisfactory masculinizing genitoplasty techniques available to FtM transsexuals. This situation led Green and Fleming (1990) to observe that "those [FtM transsexuals] with a weak interest in [phalloplasty] have a better prognosis" (p. 172). Two FtM SRS techniques have achieved the widest acceptance. In *metoidioplasty* (or *metaidoioplasty*), the hypertrophied clitoris is released from its suspensory ligament, creating a microphallus that retains sexual sensation (Hage, 1996); urethral lengthening is often performed as part of this procedure. The limited size of the resulting phallus, problems with urethral narrowing and leakage, and the frequent need for additional operations are the principal disadvantages of this technique (Hage & van Turnhout, 2006). In *radial forearm flap phalloplasty* (e.g., Gottlieb, Levine, & Zachary, 1999), a flap of skin from the forearm is used to create a tube-within-a-tube neophallus that permits voiding while standing and that often has sexual as well as protective sensation. A hydraulic penile prosthesis can provide rigidity (Hoebeke, de Cuypere, Ceulemans, & Monstrey, 2003). Disadvantages of the radial forearm flap technique include frequent problems with urethral narrowing and leakage, a cosmetically unattractive donor site, and often-prohibitive expense. In metoidioplasty and phalloplasty, the labia majora are typically brought together to create a neo-scrotum, in which testicular prostheses are inserted; dislocation or loss of these prostheses is a frequent complication of this procedure (Hage & van Turnhout, 2006).

Other Surgical Procedures for FtM Transsexuals

Reduction mammaplasty, more often called chest reconstruction, is the surgical procedure that FtM transsexuals most frequently undergo. It is often performed early in the FtM sex reassignment process. The principal techniques and aesthetic considerations have been outlined by Hage and van Kesteren (1995). The most frequent complication of chest reconstruction is cosmetically unacceptable scarring, which can occur despite careful placement and orientation of the incisions.

Results of Sex Reassignment

Most studies of the outcomes of sex reassignment have involved postoperative transsexuals, that is, MtF transsexuals who have undergone SRS and FtM transsexuals who have undergone chest reconstruction, with or without SRS. The consensus of most experts is that sex reassignment generally, and SRS specifically, is associated with a high degree of patient satisfaction, a low prevalence of regrets, significant relief of gender dysphoria, and aggregate psychosocial outcomes that are usually no worse and are often substantially better than before sex reassignment. Pfäfflin and Junge (1992/1998) reviewed the results of over 70 studies of SRS, involving over 2,000 patients, published between 1961 and 1991. They found that subjective satisfaction was high in most studies, that patients' mental health improved more often than it declined, that effects on socioeconomic functioning were generally positive (albeit with some instances of decline in employment status and social isolation among MtF transsexuals), and that patients' sexual satisfaction generally improved (see Sidebar 14.1).

SIDEBAR 14.1

Outcomes of Sex Reassignment for Patients and Their Families

Pfäfflin and Junge (1992/1998) found that subjective satisfaction with SRS was high, mental health improved more than declined, and socioeconomic functioning was generally positive.

Green and Fleming (1990) found in their study of SRS outcome studies since 1980 that satisfactory results were achieved in about 87% of MtF transsexuals and 97% of FtM transsexuals.

Two recent follow-up surveys involving 232 and 140 MtF patients found no reports of outright regret and only 6% reporting occasional regret.

Families of SRS patients often experience the same stages of emotional responses as those that accompany the death of a loved one: denial, anger, bargaining, depression, and acceptance.

Psychotherapy can be helpful to children, spouses, partners, and other family members of those undergoing SRS.

Green and Fleming (1990), in a review of SRS outcome studies conducted since 1980, found that satisfactory results were obtained in about 87% of MtF transsexuals and 97% of FtM transsexuals. They observed that it would be difficult to imagine any other major life decision—whether to have married a specific person, whether to have had children, whether to have pursued a specific occupation—that would yield such positive subjective outcomes. In two recent follow-up surveys of MtF SRS involving 232 and 140 patients, no respondents reported outright regret and only 6% expressed even occasional regret (Lawrence, 2003; Muirhead-Allwood et al., 1999).

In general, FtM transsexuals appear to achieve somewhat better results with sex reassignment than do MtF transsexuals, despite the absence of a truly satisfactory phalloplasty procedure. Other reported positive prognostic factors for SRS include presurgical emotional stability, availability of social support, and absence of surgical complications. Some studies have suggested that regrets after SRS are more common in nonhomosexual than in homosexual MtF transsexuals (e.g., Blanchard, Steiner, Clemmensen, & Dickey, 1989), but other reports have not confirmed this impression (e.g., Lawrence, 2003).

Treatment of Families of Persons with Gender Identity Disorders

Many transsexuals who undergo sex reassignment are married or partnered and some are parents. Sex reassignment of a spouse, partner, or parent is frequently a source of stress, anxiety, anger, or depression. Emerson and Rosenfeld (1996) observed that the family members of transsexuals typically experience the same sequence of emotional responses—denial, anger, bargaining, depression, and acceptance—that accompanies the death of a loved one. Among married transsexuals, sex reassignment commonly results in divorce. Even when partnerships are maintained, non-transsexual partners usually have to deal with questions about their sexual orientations and the meanings of their changed relationships. Psychotherapy can help spouses and partners adjust to these changes (see Sidebar 14.1).

The effects of sex reassignment on transsexuals' children are incompletely understood, but there is no evidence that the gender identity of the children is affected and their peer relationships are usually maintained without extensive conflict (Green, 1998). Based on a survey of experienced gender therapists, White and Ettner (2004) concluded that the preschool-age and adult children of transsexuals experience the most favorable immediate and long-term adjustment to a parent's gender change, whereas adolescent children are likely to experience the most difficult adjustment. Favorable prognostic factors include ongoing contact and close emotional relationships with both parents, parental cooperation, and support from the extended family; negative prognostic factors include high levels of parental conflict, abrupt separation from either parent, and a personality disorder in either parent (White & Ettner, 2004). Psychotherapy can be beneficial for children whose parents undergo sex reassignment (Sales, 1995).

Summary and Conclusions

The gender identity disorders comprise a heterogeneous group of conditions involving dissatisfaction with the body, the sexuality, or the gender role associated with a person's natal sex, or any combination of these. Important considerations in the diagnosis and treatment of persons with gender identity disorders, usually referred to as transsexuals, include the following:

- Biologic sex (male versus female) and sexual orientation (homosexual versus nonhomosexual) define four transsexual subtypes; these subtypes have some similarities but also many important differences.
- Possible outcomes for persons with gender identity disorders include acceptance of natal gender, part-time cross-gender behavior, and full-time cross-living and sex reassignment.
- Persons with gender identity disorders appear to be at increased risk for comorbid Axis I and Axis II psychiatric disorders, self-harm and suicide, and sexually transmitted infections, including HIV.

- Individual and group psychotherapy can benefit persons with gender identity disorders and their families.
- Hormonal and surgical sex reassignment results in high levels of satisfaction, significant relief of gender dysphoria, and favorable psychosocial outcomes for carefully selected patients.

References

Abraham, F. (1931). Genitalumwandlungen an zwei männlichen Transvestiten [Genital conversion in two male transvestites]. *Zeitschrift für Sexualwissenschaft und Sexualpolitik, 18,* 223–226.

American Psychiatric Association. (1980). *Diagnostic and statistical manual of mental disorders* (3rd ed.). Washington, DC: Author.

American Psychiatric Association. (1987). *Diagnostic and statistical manual of mental disorders* (3rd ed., rev.). Washington, DC: Author.

American Psychiatric Association. (1994). *Diagnostic and statistical manual of mental disorders* (4th ed.). Washington, DC: Author.

American Psychiatric Association. (2000). *Diagnostic and statistical manual of mental disorders* (4th ed., text rev.). Washington, DC: Author.

Bakker, A., van Kesteren, P. J., Gooren, L. J. G., & Bezemer, P. D. (1993). The prevalence of transsexualism in The Netherlands. *Acta Psychiatrica Scandinavica, 87,* 237–238.

Benjamin, H. (1966). *The transsexual phenomenon.* New York: Julian.

Blanchard, R. (1985). Typology of male-to-female transsexualism. *Archives of Sexual Behavior, 14,* 247–261.

Blanchard, R. (1988). Nonhomosexual gender dysphoria. *Journal of Sex Research, 24,* 188–193.

Blanchard, R. (1989a). The classification and labeling of nonhomosexual gender dysphorias. *Archives of Sexual Behavior, 18,* 315–334.

Blanchard, R. (1989b). The concept of autogynephilia and the typology of male gender dysphoria. *Journal of Nervous and Mental Diseases, 177,* 616–623.

Blanchard, R. (1990). Gender identity disorders in adult men. In R. Blanchard & B. Steiner (Eds.), *Clinical management of gender identity disorders in children and adults* (pp. 49–76). Washington, DC: American Psychiatric Press.

Blanchard, R. (1993). Varieties of autogynephilia and their relationship to gender dysphoria. *Archives of Sexual Behavior, 22,* 241–251.

Blanchard, R. (1994). A structural equation model for age at clinical presentation in nonhomosexual male gender dysphorics. *Archives of Sexual Behavior, 23,* 311–320.

Blanchard, R., Clemmensen, L. H., & Steiner, B. W. (1987). Heterosexual and homosexual gender dysphoria. *Archives of Sexual Behavior, 16,* 139–152.

Blanchard, R., & Freund, K. (1983). Measuring masculine gender identity in females. *Journal of Consulting and Clinical Psychology, 51,* 205–214.

Blanchard, R., Racansky, I. G., & Steiner, B. W. (1986). Phallometric detection of fetishistic arousal in heterosexual male cross-dressers. *Journal of Sex Research, 22,* 452–462.

Blanchard, R., & Sheridan, P. M. (1992). Sibship size, sibling sex ratio, birth order, and parental age in homosexual and nonhomosexual gender dysphorics. *Journal of Nervous and Mental Disease, 190,* 40–47.

Blanchard, R., Steiner, B. W., Clemmensen, L., & Dickey, R. (1989). Prediction of regrets in postoperative transsexuals. *Canadian Journal of Psychiatry, 34,* 43–45.

Bodlund, O., & Armelius, K. (1994). Self-image and personality traits in gender identity disorders: An empirical study. *Journal of Sex and Marital Therapy, 20,* 303–317.

Bolin, A. (1988). *In search of Eve: Transsexual rites of passage.* New York: Bergin & Garvey.

Bower, H. (2001). The gender identity disorders in the *DSM-IV* classification: A critical evaluation. *Australian and New Zealand Journal of Psychiatry, 35,* 1–8.

Brown, G. (2001, November). *Sex reassignment surgery in a patient with gender identity disorder and dissociative identity disorders: Report of a successful case.* Paper presented at the 17th Harry Benjamin International Symposium on Gender Dysphoria, Galveston, TX. Retrieved April 20, 2007, from www.symposion.com/ijt/hbigda /2001/61_brown.htm.

Buhrich, N., & McConaghy, N. (1977). Can fetishism occur in transsexuals? *Archives of Sexual Behavior, 6,* 223–235.

Butcher, J. N., Graham, J. R., Ben-Porath, Y. S., Telligen, A., Dahlstrom, W. G., & Kaemmer, B. (2001). *MMPI-2 (Minnesota Multiphasic Personal-*

ity Inventory-2) manual for administration, scoring, and interpretation (Rev. ed.). Minneapolis, MN: University of Minnesota Press.

Carroll, R. A. (1999). Outcomes of treatment for gender dysphoria. *Journal of Sex Education and Therapy, 24,* 128–136.

Chivers, M. L., & Bailey, J. M. (2000). Sexual orientation of female-to-male transsexuals: A comparison of homosexual and nonhomosexual types. *Archives of Sexual Behavior, 29,* 259–278.

Chivers, M. L., Rieger, G., Latty, E., & Bailey, J. M. (2004). A sex difference in the specificity of sexual arousal. *Psychological Science, 15,* 736–744.

Clements-Nolle, K., Marx, R., Guzman, R., & Katz, M. (2001). HIV prevalence, risk behaviors, health care use, and mental health status of transgender persons: Implications for public health intervention. *American Journal of Public Health, 91,* 915–921.

Cole, C. M., O'Boyle, M., Emory, L. E., & Meyer, W. J., III. (1997). Comorbidity of gender dysphoria and other major psychiatric diagnoses. *Archives of Sexual Behavior, 26,* 13–26.

Cromwell, J. (1998). Fearful others: Medico-psychological constructions of female-to-male transgenderism. In D. Denny (Ed.), *Current concepts in transgender identity* (pp. 117–144). New York: Garland.

De Cuypere, G., Jannes, C., & Rubens, R. (1995). Psychosocial functioning of transsexuals in Belgium. *Acta Psychiatrica Scandinavica, 91,* 180–184.

De Cuypere, G., Van Hemelrijck, M., Michel, A., Carael, B., Heylens, G., Rubens, R., et al. (2007). Prevalence and demography of transsexualism in Belgium. *European Psychiatry, 22,* 137–141.

Deogracias, J. J., Johnson, L. L., Meyer-Bahlburg, H. F. L., Kessler, S. J., Schober, J. M., & Zucker, K. J. (in press). The Gender Identity/Gender Dysphoria Questionnaire for Adolescents and Adults. *Journal of Sex Research.*

De Sutter, P., Kira, K., Verschoor, A., & Hotimsky, A. (2003). The desire to have children and the preservation of fertility in transsexual women: A survey. *International Journal of Transgenderism, 6*(3). Retrieved April 18, 2007, from www .symposion.com/ijt/ijtvo06no03_02.htm.

Devor, A. H. (2004). Witnessing and mirroring: A fourteen stage model of transsexual identity formation. *Journal of Gay and Lesbian Psychotherapy, 8*(1/2), 41–67.

Diamond, L. M. (2003). What does sexual orientation orient? A biobehavioral model distinguishing romantic love and sexual desire. *Psychological Review, 110,* 173–192.

Diamond, L. M. (2005). A new view of lesbian subtypes: Stable versus fluid identity trajectories

over an 8-year period. *Psychology of Women Quarterly, 29,* 119–128.

Dixen, J. M., Maddever, H., Van Maasdam, J., & Edwards, P. W. (1984). Psychosocial characteristics of applicants evaluated for surgical gender reassignment. *Archives of Sexual Behavior, 13,* 269–276.

Docter, R. F., & Fleming, J. S. (1992). Dimensions of transvestism and transsexualism: The validation and factorial structure of the Cross-Gender Questionnaire. *Journal of Psychology and Human Sexuality, 5*(4), 15–31.

Docter, R. F., & Prince, V. (1997). Transvestism: A survey of 1032 cross-dressers. *Archives of Sexual Behavior, 26,* 589–605.

Emerson, S., & Rosenfeld, C. (1996). Stages of adjustment in family members of transgender individuals. *Journal of Family Psychotherapy, 7*(3), 1–12.

Fisk, N. M. (1974). Gender dysphoria syndrome: The conceptualization that liberalizes indications for total gender reorientation and implies a broadly based multi-dimensional rehabilitative program. *Western Journal of Medicine, 120,* 386–391.

Freund, K., & Blanchard, R. (1993). Erotic target location errors in male gender dysphorics, paedophiles, and fetishists. *British Journal of Psychiatry, 162,* 558–563.

Freund, K., Langevin, R., Satterberg, J., & Steiner, B. (1977). Extension of the Gender Identity Scale for Males. *Archives of Sexual Behavior, 6,* 507–519.

Gagne, P., Tewksbury, R., & McGaughey, D. (1997). Coming out and crossing over: Identity formation and proclamation in a transgender community. *Gender and Society, 11,* 478–508.

Garrels, L., Kockott, G., Michael, N., Preuss, W., Renter, K., Schmidt, G., et al. (2000). Sex ratio of transsexuals in Germany: The development over three decades. *Acta Psychiatrica Scandinavica, 102,* 445–448.

Giraldo, F., Mora, M. J., Solano, A., Gonzáles, C., & Smith-Fernández, V. (2002). Male perineogenital anatomy and clinical applications in genital reconstructions and male-to-female sex reassignment surgery. *Plastic and Reconstructive Surgery, 109,* 1301–1310.

Gooren, L. J. G. (1999). Hormonal sex reassignment. *International Journal of Transgenderism, 3*(3). Retrieved April 18, 2007, from www .symposion.com/ijt/ijt990301.htm.

Gottlieb, L. J., Levine, L. A., & Zachary, L. S. (1999). Radial forearm free flap for phallic reconstruction. In R. M. Ehrlich & G. J. Alter (Eds.), *Reconstructive and plastic surgery of the external genitalia* (pp. 294–300). New York: Saunders.

Green, R. (1969). Mythological, historical, and cross-cultural aspects of transsexualism. In R. Green & J. Money (Eds.), *Transsexualism and sex reassignment* (pp. 13–22). Baltimore: Johns Hopkins Press.

Green, R. (1998). Transsexuals' children. *International Journal of Transgenderism, 2*(4). Retrieved April 20, 2007, from www.symposion.com/ijt /ijtc0601.htm.

Green, R., & Fleming, D. T. (1990). Transsexual surgery follow-up: Status in the 1990s. *Annual Review of Sex Research, 1,* 163–174.

Habermeyer, E., Kamps, I., & Kawohl, W. (2003). A case of bipolar psychosis and transsexualism. *Psychopathology, 36,* 168–170.

Hage, J. J. (1996). Metaidoioplasty: An alternative phalloplasty technique in transsexuals. *Plastic and Reconstructive Surgery, 97,* 161–167.

Hage, J. J., & van Kesteren, P. J. (1995). Chest-wall contouring in female-to-male transsexuals: Basic considerations and review of the literature. *Plastic and Reconstructive Surgery, 96,* 386–391.

Hage, J. J., & van Turnhout, A. A. (2006). Long-term outcome of metaidoioplasty in 70 female-to-male transsexuals. *Annals of Plastic Surgery, 57,* 312–316.

Haraldsen, I. R., & Dahl, A. A. (2000). Symptom profiles of gender dysphoric patients of transsexual type compared to patients with personality disorders and healthy adults. *Acta Psychiatrica Scandinavica, 102,* 276–281.

Hirschfeld, M. (1923). Die intersexuelle konstitution [The intersexual constitution]. *Jahrbuch für sexuelle Zwischenstufen, 23,* 3–27.

Hirschfeld, M. (1991). *Transvestites: The erotic drive to cross-dress* (M. A. Lombardi-Nash, Trans.). Buffalo, NY: Prometheus Books. (Original work published 1910)

Hoebeke, P., de Cuypere, G., Ceulemans, P., & Monstrey, S. (2003). Obtaining rigidity in total phalloplasty: Experience with 35 patients. *Journal of Urology, 169,* 221–223.

Hoenig, J., & Kenna, J. C. (1974). The nosological position of transsexualism. *Archives of Sexual Behavior, 3,* 273–287.

Kanhai, R. C., Hage, J. J., & Mulder, J. W. (2000). Long-term outcome of augmentation mammaplasty in male-to-female transsexuals: A questionnaire survey of 107 patients. *British Journal of Plastic Surgery, 53,* 209–211.

Karim, R. B., Hage, J. J., & Mulder, J. W. (1996). Neovaginoplasty in male transsexuals: Review of surgical techniques and recommendations regarding eligibility. *Annals of Plastic Surgery, 37,* 669–675.

Kellogg, T. A., Clements-Nolle, K., Dilley, J., Katz, M. H., & McFarland, W. (2001). Incidence of human immunodeficiency virus among male-to-female transgendered persons in San Francisco. *Journal of Acquired Immune Deficiency Syndrome, 28,* 380–384.

Kenagy, G. P. (2002). HIV among transgendered people. *AIDS Care, 14,* 127–134.

Kessler, S. J., & McKenna, W. (1978). *Gender: An ethnomethodological approach.* Chicago: University of Chicago Press.

Krafft-Ebing, R. (1965). *Psychopathia sexualis* (F. S. Klaf, Trans.). New York: Stein and Day. (Original work published 1903)

Krege, S., Bex, A., Lümmen, G., & Rübben, H. (2001). Male-to-female transsexualism: A technique, results, and long-term follow-up in 66 patients. *BJU International, 88,* 396–402.

Kuiper, B., & Cohen-Kettenis, P. T. (1988). Sex reassignment surgery: A study of 141 Dutch transsexuals. *Archives of Sexual Behavior, 17,* 439–457.

Landén, M., Wålinder, J., & Lundström, B. (1996). Prevalence, incidence, and sex ratio of transsexualism. *Acta Psychiatrica Scandinavica, 93,* 221–223.

Langstrom, N., & Zucker, K. J. (2005). Transvestic fetishism in the general population: Prevalence and correlates. *Journal of Sex and Marital Therapy, 31,* 87–95.

Laub, D. R., & Fisk, N. M. (1974). A rehabilitation program for gender dysphoria syndrome by surgical sex change. *Plastic and Reconstructive Surgery, 53,* 388–403.

Lawrence, A. A. (2001, November). *SRS without a one-year RLE: Still no regrets.* Paper presented at the 17th Harry Benjamin International Symposium on Gender Dysphoria, Galveston, TX.

Lawrence, A. A. (2003). Factors associated with satisfaction or regret following male-to-female sex reassignment surgery. *Archives of Sexual Behavior, 32,* 299–315.

Lawrence, A. A. (2004). Autogynephilia: A paraphilic model of gender identity disorder. *Journal of Gay and Lesbian Psychotherapy, 8*(1/2), 69–87.

Lawrence, A. A. (2005). Sexuality before and after male-to-female sex reassignment surgery. *Archives of Sexual Behavior, 34,* 147–166.

Lawrence, A. A. (2006). Self-reported complications and functional outcomes of male-to-female sex reassignment surgery. *Archives of Sexual Behavior, 35,* 717–727.

Lawrence, A. A. (2007a). Becoming what we love: Autogynephilic transsexualism conceptualized as an expression of romantic love. *Perspectives in Biology and Medicine, 50,* 506–520.

Lawrence, A. A. (2007b). Transgender health concerns. In I. H. Meyer & M. E. Northridge (Eds.), *The health of sexual minorities: Public health perspectives on lesbian, gay, bisexual and transgender populations* (pp. 473–505). New York: Springer.

Lawrence, A. A., Latty, E. M., Chivers, M., & Bailey, J. M. (2005). Measurement of sexual arousal in postoperative male-to-female transsexuals using vaginal photoplethysmography. *Archives of Sexual Behavior, 34,* 135–145.

Leavitt, F., Berger, J. C., Hoeppner, J.-A., & Northrop, G. (1980). Presurgical adjustment in male transsexuals with and without hormonal treatment. *Journal of Nervous and Mental Disease, 168,* 693–697.

Lev, A. (2004). *Transgender emergence: Therapeutic guidelines for working with gender-variant people and their families.* Binghamton, NY: Haworth Clinical Practice Press.

Levine, S. B. (1993). Gender-disturbed males. *Journal of Sex and Marital Therapy, 19,* 131–141.

Levine, S. B., Brown, G., Coleman, E., Cohen-Kettenis, P., Hage, J. J., Van Maasdam, J., et al. (1998). *The standards of care for gender identity disorders* (5th ed.). Düsseldorf, Germany: Symposion.

Levy, A., Crown, A., & Reid, R. (2003). Endocrine intervention with transsexuals. *Clinical Endocrinology, 59,* 409–418.

Lewins, F. (1995). *Transsexualism in society: A sociology of male-to-female transsexuals.* South Melbourne, Australia: MacMillan Education Australia.

Lombardi, E. L., Wilchins, R. A., Priesing, D., & Malouf, D. (2001). Gender violence: Transgender experiences with violence and discrimination. *Journal of Homosexuality, 42*(1), 89–101.

Lothstein, L. M. (1979). The aging gender dysphoria (transsexual) patient. *Archives of Sexual Behavior, 8,* 431–444.

Lothstein, L. M. (1984). Psychological testing with transsexuals: A 30-year review. *Journal of Personality Assessment, 48,* 500–507.

Manderson, L., & Kumar, S. (2001). Gender identity disorder as a rare manifestation of schizophrenia. *Australian and New Zealand Journal of Psychiatry, 35,* 546–547.

Marks, I., Green, R., & Mataix-Cols, D. (2000). Adult gender identity disorder can remit. *Comprehensive Psychiatry, 41,* 273–275.

Mate-Kole, C., Freschi, M., & Robin, A. (1990). A controlled study of psychological and social change after surgical gender reassignment in selected male transsexuals. *British Journal of Psychiatry, 157,* 261–264.

McGowan, C. K. (1999). *Transgender needs assessment.* New York: HIV Prevention Planning Unit, New York City Department of Health.

Meyer, W., III, Bockting, W. O., Cohen-Kettenis, P., Coleman, E., DiCeglie, D., Devor H., et al. (2001). *The standards of care for gender identity disorders* (6th ed.). Düsseldorf, Germany: Symposion.

Meyer-Bahlburg, H. F. (1994). Intersexuality and the diagnosis of gender identity disorder. *Archives of Sexual Behavior, 23,* 21–40.

Meyerowitz, J. (2002). *How sex changed: A history of transsexuality in the United States.* Cambridge, MA: Harvard University Press.

Miach, P. P., Berah, E. F., Butcher, J. N., & Rouse, S. (2000). Utility of the MMPI-2 in assessing gender dysphoric patients. *Journal of Personality Assessment, 75,* 268–279.

Michel, A., Mormont, C., & Legros, J. J. (2001). A psycho-endocrinological overview of transsexualism. *European Journal of Endocrinology, 145,* 365–376.

Modestin, J., & Ebner, G. (1995). Multiple personality disorder manifesting itself under the mask of transsexualism. *Psychopathology, 28,* 317–321.

Money, J. (1986). *Lovemaps: Clinical concepts of sexual/erotic health and pathology, paraphilia, and gender transposition in childhood, adolescence, and maturity.* New York: Irvington.

Moore, E., Wisniewski, A., & Dobs, A. (2003). Endocrine treatment of transsexual people: A review of treatment regimens, outcomes, and adverse effects. *Journal of Clinical Endocrinology and Metabolism, 88,* 3467–3473.

Muirhead-Allwood, S. K., Royle, M. G., & Young, R. (1999, August). *Sexuality and satisfaction with surgical results in male-to-female transsexuals.* Poster session presented at the 16th Biennial Symposium of the Harry Benjamin International Gender Dysphoria Association, London.

Nemoto, T., Luke, D., Mamo, L., Ching, A., & Patria, J. (1999). HIV risk behaviours among male-to-female transgenders in comparison with homosexual or bisexual males and heterosexual females. *AIDS Care, 11,* 297–312.

Person, E., & Ovesey, L. (1974). The transsexual syndrome in males, I. Primary transsexualism. *American Journal of Psychotherapy, 28,* 4–20.

Pfäfflin, F., & Junge, A. (1998). *Sex reassignment: Thirty years of international follow-up studies after sex reassignment surgery: A comprehensive review, 1961–1991* (R. B. Jacobson & A. B. Meier, Trans.). Retrieved December 14, 2006, from www.symposion.com/ijt/pfaefflin/1000.htm. (Original work published 1992)

Prosser, J. (1998). *Second skins: The body narratives of transsexuality.* New York: Columbia University Press.

Rieger, G., Chivers, M. L., & Bailey, J. M. (2005). Sexual arousal patterns of bisexual men. *Psychological Science, 16,* 579–584.

Roback, H. B., Fellemann, E. S., & Abramowitz, S. I. (1984). The mid-life male sex-change applicant: A multiclinic survey. *Archives of Sexual Behavior, 13,* 141–153.

Ross, M. W., & Need, J. A. (1989). Effects of adequacy of gender reassignment surgery on psychological adjustment: A follow-up of fourteen male-to-female patients. *Archives of Sexual Behavior, 18,* 145–153.

Saks, B. M. (1998). Transgenderism and dissociative identity disorder: A case study. *International Journal of Transgenderism, 2*(2). Retrieved April 20, 2007, from www.symposion.com/ijt/ijtc0404.htm.

Sales, J. (1995). Children of a transsexual father: A successful intervention. *European Child and Adolescent Psychiatry, 4,* 136–139.

Schroder, M., & Carroll, R. (1999). New women: Sexological outcomes of male-to-female gender reassignment surgery. *Journal of Sex Education and Therapy, 24,* 137–146.

Simon, P. A., Reback, C. J., & Bemis, C. C. (2000). HIV prevalence and incidence among male-to-female transsexuals receiving HIV prevention services in Los Angeles County. *AIDS, 14,* 2953–2955.

Slabbekoorn, D., van Goozen, S., Gooren, L., & Cohen-Kettenis, P. (2001). Effects of cross-sex hormone treatment on emotionality in transsexuals. *International Journal of Transgenderism, 5*(3). Retrieved April 18, 2007, from www.symposion.com/ijt/ijtvo05no03_02.htm.

Smith, Y. L. S., van Goozen, S. H. M., Kuiper, A. J., & Cohen-Kettenis, P. T. (2005a). Sex reassignment: Outcomes and predictors of treatment for adolescent and adult transsexuals. *Psychological Medicine, 35,* 89–99.

Smith, Y. L. S., van Goozen, S. H. M., Kuiper, A. J., & Cohen-Kettenis, P. T. (2005b). Transsexual subtypes: Clinical and theoretical significance. *Psychiatry Research, 137,* 151–160.

Stermac, L., Blanchard, R., Clemmensen, L. H., & Dickey, R. (1991). Group therapy for gender-dysphoric heterosexual men. *Journal of Sex and Marital Therapy, 17,* 252–258.

Stoller, R. J. (1968). *Sex and gender* (pp. 93–136). New York: Science House.

Stoller, R. J. (1985). A child fetishist. In *Presentations of gender* (pp. 93–136). New Haven, CT: Yale University Press.

Tangpricha, V., Ducharme, S. H., Barber, T. W., & Chipkin, S. R. (2003). Endocrinologic treatment of gender identity disorders. *Endocrine Practice, 9,* 12–21.

van Goozen, S. H., Cohen-Kettenis, P. T., Gooren, L. J. G., Frijda, N. H., & Van de Poll, N. E. (1995). Gender differences in behaviour: Activating effects of cross-sex hormones. *Psychoneuroendocrinology, 20,* 343–363.

van Kemenade, J. F. L. M., Cohen-Kettenis, P. T., Cohen, L., & Gooren, L. J. G. (1989). Effects of the pure antiandrogen RU 23.903 (anandron) on sexuality, aggression, and mood in male-to-female transsexuals. *Archives of Sexual Behavior, 18,* 217–228.

van Kesteren, P. J., Asscheman, H., Megens, J. A., & Gooren, L. J. (1997). Mortality and morbidity in transsexual subjects treated with cross-sex hormones. *Clinical Endocrinology (Oxford), 47,* 337–342.

Verschoor, A. M., & Poortinga, J. (1988). Psychosocial differences between Dutch male and female transsexuals. *Archives of Sexual Behavior, 17,* 173–178.

Wålinder, J., Lundström, B., & Thuwe, I. (1978). Prognostic factors in the assessment of male transsexuals for sex reassignment. *British Journal of Psychiatry, 132,* 16–20.

Walworth, J. R. (1997). Sex-reassignment surgery in male-to-female transsexuals: Client satisfaction in relation to selection criteria. In B. Bullough, V. L. Bullough, & J. Elias (Eds.), *Gender blending* (pp. 352–369). Amherst, NY: Prometheus Books.

Whitam, F. L. (1987). A cross-cultural perspective on homosexuality, transvestism, and trans-sexualism. In G. D. Wilson (Ed.), *Variant sexuality: Research and theory* (pp. 176–201). Baltimore: Johns Hopkins University Press.

Whitam, F. L. (1997). Culturally universal aspects of male homosexual transvestites and transsexuals. In B. Bullough, V. L. Bullough, & J. Elias (Eds.), *Gender blending* (pp. 189–203). Amherst, NY: Prometheus Books.

White, T., & Ettner, R. (2004). Disclosure, risks, and protective factors for children whose parents are undergoing a gender transition. *Journal of Gay and Lesbian Psychotherapy, 8*(1/2), 129–145.

Wilson, P., Sharp, C., & Carr, S. (1999). The prevalence of gender dysphoria in Scotland: A primary care study. *British Journal of General Practice, 49,* 991–992.

World Health Organization. (1992). *International statistical classification of diseases and related health problems* (10th rev., Vol. 1). Geneva, Switzerland: Author.

Xavier, J. (2000). *Final report of the Washington transgender needs assessment survey.* Washington, DC: Administration for HIV and AIDS, Government of the District of Columbia.

Zucker, K. J. (2005). Measurement of psychosexual differentiation. *Archives of Sexual Behavior, 34,* 375–388.

Zucker, K. J., & Blanchard, R. (1997). Transvestic fetishism: Psychopathology and theory. In D. R. Laws & W. O'Donohue (Eds.), *Sexual deviance* (pp. 253–279). New York: Plenum Press.

Cross-Cultural Issues

Serena Nanda

15

Chapter

Learning Objectives

In this chapter, we review:

- Cultural alternatives that challenge the Western sex/gender system.
- Neither man nor woman: the *hijras* of India.
- Men and not men: the sex/gender system in Brazil.
- Multiple discourses, multiple identities: gender diversity in Thailand.
- Binaries to blurred categories: transgenderism in the United States.
- Some cultural contexts for understanding sex/gender diversity.

Most of those organizations of personality that seem to us most . . . abnormal have been used by different civilizations in the very foundation of their institutional life. Conversely, the most valued traits of our normal individuals have been looked on in differently organized cultures as aberrant. Normality, in short, within a very wide range, is culturally defined . . . a term for the socially elaborated segment of human behavior in any culture, and abnormality a term for the segment that that particular civilization does not use. (Benedict, 1934, p. 73–74)

Deep thanks to all my colleagues whose field studies of cross-cultural sex/gender systems have made such an important contribution to understanding human sex/gender diversity. Special thanks to Jasper Burns and Joan Gregg for their insights and support.

457

Every society contains individuals who do not fit into the culture's dominant sex/gender categories—persons born intersexed (hermaphrodites), those who exhibit behavior or desires deemed appropriate for the "opposite" sex/gender, or those who, while conforming outwardly to culturally normative gender roles, experience themselves in conflict with these roles in some fundamental ways. A cross-cultural perspective makes it clear that societies organize their thinking about sex, gender, sexuality, and gender identity in many different, but perhaps not unlimited ways (see Quinn & Luttrell, 2004). Gender diversity, or gender variation, refers to the fact that cultures have constructed different sex/gender systems, and that these systems deal with these challenges differently.

In this chapter, I describe four different sex/gender systems: (1) an alternative sex/gender role in India that is neither man nor woman, but contains elements of both; (2) a man/not man dichotomy in Brazil; (3) changing sex/gender roles in Thailand as influenced by Western psychology and globalization; and (4) the movement toward dissolving the sex/gender binary as part of the transgender movement in the United States. At the conclusion of the chapter, I describe some cultural contexts, such as religion, ideas about the person, the homosexual/heterosexual divide, and social attitudes, within which sex/gender variation operates, with a view toward provoking a rethinking of the dominant Western sex/gender system. The ethnographic record makes it clear that no simple correspondence exists between sex, sexual orientation, gender role, and gender identity and that sex/gender subjective positions, or identities, are also variable. Indeed, a cross-cultural perspective creates problems for every aspect of sex/gender issues that Western culture takes for granted. Because sex, gender, and sexuality are at the very core of the Western understanding of individual identity, it is not easy to dislodge thinking about these issues, particularly in the context of our own culture. Examples of sex/gender diversity, of which only a few are included here, challenge intellectual understandings about what is natural, normal, and morally right, and also challenge thinking at deeper, emotional levels.

The cross-cultural record of sex/gender diversity provokes a reexamination of the nature and assumptions of the dominant sex/gender system: the cultural basis of its categories, the relations between sex/gender and other aspects of culture, and how those who do not fit into the culture's dominant sex/gender paradigms are defined and treated by society. The cross-cultural perspective enables fresh thinking about behavior, attitudes, and perceptions of sex/gender within cultural worlds that are not part of a person's experience. This perspective is useful for those who deal professionally with individuals with various forms of sex/gender dysphoria and also for those experiencing dsyphoria who are seeking meaning and models for experiences not satisfactorily addressed by a binary sex/gender system.

The representation and discourses surrounding sex/gender systems in other cultures have been influenced by European moral ethnocentrism since the earliest encounters between Europeans and other peoples. The nomenclature is confusing since early European travelers often translated indigenous transgender categories as hermaphrodite, even when these instances did not involve intersexuality. They also often referred to male mixed-gender roles as homosexuality, even when sexuality was only one aspect of these roles or when there was no evidence to support their perceptions. In ethnography, the term *transvestite* does not refer to fetishistic cross-dressing, but rather to the many alternative gender roles in different cultures in which cross-dressing is part of the role enactment. For insightful discussions on the difficulties of applying Western terminology regarding sex, gender, gender identity, and sexuality to other cultures, see introduction sections of Boellstorff (2005) and Blackwood and Wieringa (1999).

The imposition of European religions, cultures, law, and economies on non-Western societies in most cases resulted in the marginalization or disappearance of indigenous alternative sex/gender roles (Jacobs, Thomas, & Lang, 1997; Lang, 1999; Matzner, 2001; Roscoe, 1995); this has also occurred with the spread of Islam to places like West Africa (Matory, 1994) and Indonesia (Boellstorff, 2005). Currently, however, there is a reemergence of interest in these systems by ethnographers, medical and psychological professionals, sex/gender variant individuals, and in the wider society as part of constructing national identities or a cultural renaissance within the context of modernity.

The global diffusion of cross-cultural information and perspectives has had an important impact in modifying sex/gender systems in all cultures. Western medical and psychological sciences, internationally diffused gay and transgender activist agendas and networks, an increasingly global media, international tourism, and the Internet have all contributed to a broadening of cultures and an acknowledgment of the importance of culture as a context for examining and treating individuals in different sex/gender systems (Jackson, 1999; Matzner, 2001; Winter, 2006). This historical and modern globalization means that in all societies today, several sex/gender systems—with sources in traditional cultures, colonial cultures, and modern cultural influences—may operate simultaneously. While the sex/gender system of Western culture is influencing other cultures, knowledge of the sex/gender systems of other cultures is also influencing the United States.

In this chapter, I touch on only a small part of the great diversity of sex/gender systems in the world's cultures. I have chosen these particular examples because they are well documented in the ethnographic literature; they represent a diverse geographical and cultural scope; and in spite of some commonalities, they each represent a distinct cultural pattern in their understanding of sex, gender, and sexuality and the relationship of these to gender identity (see Sidebar 15.1 for an overview).

Examples of Sex/Gender Diversity

- *Hijra:* In India, culturally conceptualized as neither man nor woman, impotent men who are "like females" but not female take on traditional *hijra* roles in Indian society. Hinduism has an influence on the role and treatment of *hijras* in society. *Hijras* are believed to have powers to both bless and curse. They are treated with a mixture of "fear, mockery, and respect" in Indian society. Traditional Indian culture provides a context for positive meaning and self-esteem for those with variant sex/gender identities, including *hijras.*
- *Travesti or Pasivo:* In Brazil, they are culturally conceptualized as men who take the passive, receptive role in sexual interaction—conceptualized through practice, not sexual orientation. They are identifed as "nonmen" in a system of either men or nonmen, not as an alternative or "in-between" gender. Based on sexual practice, not anatomy, these people are closely associated with Afro-Brazilian religions called *candomble,* which can provide a powerful, meaningful context to the lives of variant sex/gender individuals.
- *Kathoey:* In Thailand, this category was culturally conceptualized as one of three sex/genders in traditional Thai society until the mid-twentieth century (male/female/*kathoey* or hermaphrodite). Contemporary attitudes toward *kathoey* in Thailand are influenced by Western biomedical thought, now they are defined as "a male who breaches biological and/or cultural norms of masculinity" or a man who appropriates women's characteristics, including hermaphrodites, transsexuals, transvestites, and effeminate homosexual men. Identity and treatment in society is influenced by contemporary views of *kathoey* as thoroughly feminine. *Kathoey* are being more constrained by contemporary Thai society, though this exists alongside older, more tolerant and compassionate views and treatment.
- *Transgenderism:* In the United States, this is conceptualized as the movement to identify gender as a continuum as opposed to the traditional binary categories of male or female. Unlike transsexualism and gender reassignment, transgenderism emphasizes not assignment to an opposing gender category but the idea that, rather than viewed as categories, gender can be viewed as a vary-

ing spectrum of desires, behaviors, and characteristics ranging from androgynous to transsexual. The goal is "not so much to do away with maleness and femaleness as to de-naturalize them, that is, take away their privileged status in relation to all other possible combinations of behaviors, roles, and identities."

The Hijras: An Alternative Gender Role in India

The *hijra*, an alternative gender role in India, are culturally conceptualized as neither man nor woman. Multiple sexes and genders are recorded very early in Indian religion and mythology, many of them primarily considered to be sexually impotent males (Zwilling & Sweet, 2000), as is believed true of the *hijras* today. *Hijras* are not merely defective males, however, but are culturally institutionalized as an alternative, mixed sex/gender role, neither man nor woman, neither male nor female (Nanda, 1999; Reddy, 2005). Their traditional occupation is to collect payment for their performances at weddings and the birth of a male child; today they also perform for the birth of girl children, collect alms from shopkeepers, act as tax collectors, and run for political office. They also are widely known as prostitutes, both in the past and present.

Hijras are "not-men" because they cannot function in the male sexual role and cannot reproduce. *Hijras* often define themselves as "men who have no (sexual) desire for women," though they do frequently, perhaps universally, act as anal receptive sexual partners for men, who are not, however, defined as homosexuals. Indeed, although the sex "work" of *hijras* is widely, though not universally known and/or acknowledged, *hijras* are perceived as quite different from other effeminate men or gay men in India (Cohen, 1995; Reddy, 2005, p. 53).

The main legitimacy of the *hijra* identity as an alternative sex/gender, both for themselves and their audiences, is found within the religious context of Hinduism though Reddy (2005) notes that, in a typically Indian paradox, Islam is also a major context for their identities. *Hijras* are devotees of Bahuchara Mata, one of the many versions of the Mother Goddess worshiped throughout India. Men who are sexually impotent are called on by Bahuchara Mata to dress and act like women and to undergo emasculation. This operation, called *nirvan,* or rebirth, involves the removal of the penis and testicles and endows *hijras* with the divine powers of the goddess (*shakti*). It is as vehicles of the Mata's divine power that *hijras* perform at weddings and births, receive alms as servants of the goddess at her temple, and are given alms by shopkeepers and the general public.

By virtue of their impotence, *hijras* are "man minus man," but they are also "man plus woman." *Hijras* wear women's dress, keep their hair long, imitate women's walk and gestures, voice and facial expressions and language; they take feminine names as part of their gender transformations; and they use female kinship terms for their relationships within the *hijra* community. But although *hijras* are "like women," they are also not women, partly because their feminine presentations are perceived as caricatures, but most essentially because *hijras* do not have female reproductive organs and cannot bear children. The cultural definition sketched here does not do justice to the multiplicity of identities they experience (Reddy, 2005). Some *hijras* self-identify as women, others as *hijras;* and their life stories, both constructed and factual, reveal many gender identity changes over a lifetime. *Hijra* gender identity is significantly influenced by socialization within the *hijra* community (Nanda, 1996, 1999; Reddy, 2005), just as the importance of socialization for American transsexuals as adult members of transsexual (or potentially transsexual) communities has also been noted (Bolin, 1996). This evidence of learning a new gender identity stands in contrast to the cultural construction of the term *transsexual* as someone who has always been convinced of being a member of the gender opposite that of one's anatomical sex.

In spite of their public presentations as women, two symbolic acts unique to the *hijra* community immediately identify them as outside the Indian binary sex/gender frame of reference. One is the distinctive hand-clap by which they announce their public presence and the other is the actual or threatened lifting of their saris to expose their genitalia (or lack thereof) as a rebuke to an audience who insults them, either by refusing to pay in response to their demands, or by questioning their authenticity as "true *hijras*," implying they are "merely" effeminate homosexuals (Reddy, 2005, p. 136).

Hinduism, in contrast to most Western religions, embraces contradictions without the need to resolve them (O'Flaherty, 1973). Male and female are viewed as natural categories, embodying qualities of both sex and gender in complementary opposition to each other. In spite of the importance of this dichotomy, sex and gender variations, interchanges, and transformations are meaningful and positive themes in Hindu mythology, ritual, and art (Humes, 1996; O'Flaherty, 1980). In Hinduism, impotence can be transformed into the power of generativity through the ideal of *tapasya*, the practice of asceticism, or the renunciation of sex. *Tapas*, the power that results from ascetic practices and sexual abstinence, becomes an essential feature in the process of creation. Ascetics appear throughout Hindu mythology in procreative roles; of these, Shiva is the greatest creative ascetic. Like Shiva, whose self-emasculation became the source of his creative power, so too, the *hijras* as emasculated men become vehicles for the creative power of the Mother Goddess, and, through her, with Shiva (Hiltelbeitel, 1980). Ancient Hindu texts refer to alternative sexes and genders among humans as well as deities, and the Kama Sutra, the classical Hindu manual of love, specifically refers to eunuchs and the particular sexual practices they should engage in. The ancient Hindu depiction of alternative genders among humans and deities is reinforced by the historical role of the eunuch in ancient Hindu, and more particularly, Muslim court culture, which has a 500-year history in India. This historical role has merged with those described in Hindu texts as a source of contemporary *hijra* identification.

Hijras are viewed with ambivalence in Indian society and are treated with a combination of mockery, fear, and respect. Although *hijras* have an auspicious presence, they also have an inauspicious potential. The loss of virility the *hijras* represent is a major source of the fear they inspire. The *hijras'* power to bless a family with fertility and fortune is joined to their power to curse a family with infertility and misfortune; a *hijra* who raises her skirt and displays her mutilated genitals is both a source of shame and insult to the audience, as well as a curse by which the *hijras* contaminate the potentially fertile with a loss of reproductivity.

The cultural anxiety surrounding the *hijras* draws on the Hindu concept that eroticism and asceticism both have divine power, yet both can also lead to social chaos. *Hijras* express this paradox in their bodies and their behavior. As eunuchs, *hijras* embody the "cool" ascetic male quality of the renunciation of desire, while in their behavior, they display "hot" uncontrolled feminine sexuality that also makes them "sacred, female, men" (Bradford, 1983). Like other ascetics, *hijras* are thus very much "creatures of the outside," powerful though they may be. As persons who do not marry and who renounce family life, *hijras* are also outside the social roles and relationships of caste and kinship that define the person in Hindu culture and that exercise control over an individual's behavior. Thus, like other ascetics, *hijras* are regarded as potential threats to the social order.

But within Hinduism, the concept of *karma* provides a path for incorporating *hijras* into the social fabric. Only through marriage and reproduction are Indian men and women granted full personhood, and an impotent man or a woman who does not menstruate is normally considered an incomplete person. Yet the ascetic, or renouncer (of sexuality, among other things), is a meaningful role that transcends conventional sex/gender roles and behaviors. In identifying—and being identified with—the ascetic role, individuals who are "betwixt and between" with regard to their sex and/or gender can transform their incomplete personhood into the *hijra* role, which transcends the stigma associated with their sex/gender deficiencies. The Hindu belief in *dharma,* the view that every individual has his or her own life path that he or she must follow, because every individual has a different innate essence, moral qualities, and special abilities, leads to an acceptance in India of many different occupations, behaviors, identities, and personal styles as legitimate life paths. This is particularly so when the behavior is sanctified by tradition, formalized in ritual, and practiced within a group as is true with the *hijras* (Kakar, 1982, p. 163).

Thus, in vivid contrast to the Judeo-Christian religions, which strenuously attempt to resolve, repress, or dismiss as jokes or trivia, sexual contradictions and ambiguities, in India, conscious and unconscious anxieties relating to transgenderism have not given way to a culturally institutionalized phobia or narrowly confined the sex/gender system to an exclusive system of opposites (Kakar, 1982). Hinduism thus affords the individual personality wide latitude in behavior, including that which Euro-American cultures label criminal or pathological and attempt to punish or cure. In accommodating the role of the *hijra*, traditional Indian mythology, drama, and history provide a context for positive meaning and self-esteem for those with variant sex/gender identities.

Men and Not-Men: A Sex/Gender Dichotomy in Brazil

In the sex/gender system in Brazil, the most significant dichotomy is between men and not-men, a dichotomy that is found in many cultures. Traditionally, in Brazil, men and women are viewed as opposite in every way, as a natural result of the biological differences between males and females. Men are considered superior, characterized by strength, virility, activity, potential for violence, and the legitimate use of force. Masculine virility is manifested in aggressive sexuality, having many children, and by the ability to control the sexuality of women, that is, daughters and wives. Women are defined as inferior and weak, yet also beautiful and desirable, and subject always to the control of men; a persistent underlying threat to masculinity is the loss of control over women and inherent in their beauty is the threat of sexual betrayal (Parker, 1991, p. 49). Unlike other Euro-American cultures where biological sex is the basis of gender classification crosscut by the homosexual/heterosexual divide, in Brazil the core gender opposition is based on sexuality, that is, the position taken in sexual intercourse. Brazilian gender ideology is based on the distinction between those who penetrate—the active (*atividade*) defined as masculine, and those who are penetrated—the passive (*passividade*) defined as feminine. The superiority of the active is reflected in language: the active penetration of the male is used in different contexts as a synonym for "to possess" and applied to many areas of life, such as sports and politics, as well as religion.

Males who take the passive, receptive position in sex are defined as not-men, called *travesti* (cross-dresser), *viado* (deer), or *bicha* (bug, female animal). Although *travestis* readily self-identify as homosexual, this term is not applied to the male-acting and penetrating partner in the same-sex sexual relationship. Thus, *travestis* are "produced" through the application of the distinction between *atividade* and *passividade* to individuals in same sex relationships, by practice and not by sexual orientation. The active, penetrating male in the relationship does not regard himself as homosexual and is not so regarded by society. Same-sex sexual practices are reported as a common introduction to sexual activity for many Brazilian men during adolescence and those in the active role are not stigmatized. Indeed, penetrating another male may even be claimed as indication of a super virile masculine identity (Parker, 1995, p. 245).

Like other "gender-organized" cultural systems (i.e., Thailand and the Philippines), the sexually receptive partner is expected to enact other aspects of the feminine gender role. The imputation of this femininity unalterably transforms and degrades a man as he becomes a symbolic female through his sexual role. *Travestis* not only dress and act like women, they also ingest or inject female hormones in order to give their bodies feminine contours (Kulick, 1997, 1998). In a seeming contradiction, however, in spite of the desire to achieve womanly breasts, buttocks, and thighs, *travesties* do not wish to get rid of their penises. Indeed, they value them and "gasp in horror" at the thought of an amputation, which would mean the loss of their ability to have an erection and achieve orgasm. In contrast to Western transsexuals, *travestis* believe that though they are like women, they are not and can never become women because their (male) sex can never be changed. They also believe that without a penis, semen cannot leave the body and thus trapped, will travel eventually to the brain and cause madness. For *travestis*, sex-change operations do not produce women but only castrated homosexuals (Kulick, 1997). The core of the *travestis'* self-identification is their sexual position, and their relationships with males are best characterized as "heterogenderal," rather than homosexual. Unlike the *hijras*, *travestis* do not identify as an "in-between," or "mixed" sex or gender, but rather as "not-men" in a cultural system whose opposing categories are "men" and "not-men," a category that also includes women, and is based on sexual practice, not anatomy.

In Brazil, the variant sex/gender role of the *travesti*, or *pasivo*, is closely associated with the Afro-Brazilian religions usually called *candomble* or *macumba*. While women and *pasivos* are generally stigmatized in Latin America, they dominate in these religions, which are focused on possession trance and on providing good health and good fortune for the leaders and spiritual help and protection for their followers. *Candomble* is organized into "houses" hierarchically structured around a male or more frequently, a female or *pasivo,* leader, called the mother or father of the particular saint that the house focuses on. The importance of *pasivo* leadership in *candomble* is consistent with the gender ambiguous nature of many Yoruba spirit possession priests in West Africa, who are marked by their transvestism, feminine gestures, and feminine occupations (Matory, 1994, p. 170). Possession trances, in which an initiate "receives" his or her special orixas in ritual séances (Hayes, 1996, p. 15), are particularly important and the meanings of penetration and possession in *candomble* reinforces the dominant gender system in Brazil. The relationship between spirits and humans—between the gods and the followers who incorporate them—is analogically associated with that of male to female through the metaphor of penetration. The term describing possession is *dar santo,* to "give saint" and the role of the person possessed, whether man or woman, is that applied to females who give themselves over to sexual penetration by males. The *candomble* priests who are possessed are called "horses" or "mounts" of the gods, who "ride" them, again identifying them with the passive sexual role of women. During possession, the god "mounts" the priest as a rider does his horse, and the spirits are viewed as penetrating their followers in order to express their desires, give advice, or merely to "play." Thus, a male who is penetrated by the spirits is identified with males who are sexually penetrated by other males; spirit penetration is the equivalent to sexual penetration. When humans go into possession trance they "give" offerings so that the spirits may "eat" in the same way as these verbs, "to give" and "to eat" are used to characterize sexual relations between men and women (Wafer, 1991, p. 18). Thus Brazil, like India, though different in many respects, also provides an accommodation for sex/gender diversity within a religious context, which gives both power and meaning to the lives of sex/gender variant individuals.

Kathoey and Gay: The Changing Sex/Gender System in Thailand

Thailand today is characterized by a complex and multiple system of sex/gender identities, which incorporates traditional cultural meanings, a Western biomedical view, and diffusion of various Western concepts of gay. Ancient Buddhist texts indicate that biological sex, culturally ascribed gender, and sexuality are not clearly distinguished. Thai Buddhist origin myths describe three original human sex/genders—male, female, and *kathoey*, or hermaphrodite, defined as a third sex, a variant of male or female, having characteristics of both (Jackson, 1997a). Linguistic evidence suggests, however, that *kathoey* may also have connoted "a person whose gender is different from other males" or a male who acts like a woman, a meaning consistent with the predominant contemporary usage.

The system of three human sexes remained prevalent in Thailand until the mid-twentieth century. At that time, the diffusion of various Western influences resulted in the proliferating variety of alternative or variant sex/gender roles and gender identities, and a fluctuating attitude toward sex/gender diversity, which characterizes contemporary Thailand (Costa & Matzner, 2007; Jackson, 1999; Matzner, 2006b; Morris, 1994).

Today, the term *kathoey* most commonly refers to a "deficient male," or a *male* transgender category, that is, a male who breaches biological and/or cultural norms of masculinity (Jackson, 1997b, p. 60). Put another way, "a *kathoey* is [viewed as] a man who appropriates female form [feminine attributes and behavior] without becoming a woman and without ceasing to be a man" (Morris, 1994, p. 25). This concept variously refers to hermaphrodites, transvestites, transsexuals, or effeminate homosexual men. Almost all *kathoey* cross-dress and undergo hormone replacement therapy; most have breast implants, and some also undergo genital reassignment surgery as well as other surgical procedures to feminize their appearance, for example, reducing their Adam's apple (Matzner, 2006b). At the same time, somewhat contradictorily, *kathoey* are still sometimes viewed as "midway" between men and women, or a second kind of woman (Jackson, 1997a, p. 312), a definition that contains cultural traces of the historical Buddhist position. This traditional concept is also reflected in the Royal Institute Thai language dictionary that defines a *kathoey* as "A person who has both male and female genitals; a person whose mind (i.e., psychology) and behavior are the opposite of their sex/gender," which (theoretically) applies to males and females.

In the 1950s, a Western, "scientific," biomedical sex/gender discourse was introduced into Thailand. This perpetuated the view within Thai academic circles that *kathoey* are hermaphrodites: persons whose biological characteristics—sex glands, genitals, and secondary sex characteristics—combined those of a male and a female to the extent that they could not be clearly assigned to one or the other sex/gender (Jackson, 1997b, p. 61).

The role of sexual orientation and sexual practice in identifying the *kathoey* has also changed. In traditional Thai culture, *kathoey* sexuality was peripheral to their identity. Indeed, in Thai culture, sexual orientation and sexual practices were not the basis of any personal or social identity, and the modern Western opposition of homosexual/heterosexual as types of persons did not exist. The influence of Western biomedical discourse, however, led to an emphasis on the feminine attributes of the *kathoey*, and particularly their sexuality, a view that converged with the Thai understanding of gay in the 1970s to the 1990s.

Although homoeroticism has long been recognized in Thailand, historically it was not religiously condemned as a sin, criminalized, or prosecuted by the state, and no efforts were made to "correct" or "cure" it. Homoerotic relations between masculine identified men (or between women), called "playing with a friend," *were* distinguished, however, from sex between a man and a feminine *kathoey*. These latter relations were viewed as less stigmatizing than sexual relations between two men because homoeroticism is not a man's fate, but it is the fate of a *kathoey*. And, unlike the sexual relationships between a male and a *kathoey*, relationships between two men were considered inauspicious, resulting in natural disasters, like droughts or being struck dead by lightning or madness (Jackson, 1997b, pp. 63–64).

Until the influence of Western biomedical paradigms in the 1950s, distinctive homosexual or heterosexual *identities* for homoerotic males and females who in other respects adhered to normative masculine and feminine gender roles were not culturally or linguistically noted in Thailand. The weight of the pejorative American pychoanalytical perspective on homosexuality, however, led to the perception in Thai academic circles that homosexuality was a form of pathology. This reinforced the traditional Thai view that the "natural" (biologically based) status of the *kathoey* had more legitimacy than the homosexuality of gender normative men that was considered "abnormal" or "unnatural." This biomedical approach implicitly continued the Buddhist view that *kathoey* were natural phenomena whose condition was a result of karmic fate preordained from birth and thus beyond their capacity to alter, a view still largely held by the Thai public. The Buddhist and biomedical paradigms, which share the view that *kathoey* status is predetermined, in the former case through karma and in the latter through genes, had an important effect on Thai social attitudes toward the *kathoey*.

While in the late 1970s, the English term "gay" entered Thai culture as a reference mainly to a cross-dressing or effeminate homosexual male, by the 1990s, the Thai image of "gay" became increasingly masculinized. This new "gay" identity again showed cultural traces from an earlier, implicit subcategory of masculine status: a man who is gender normative in all but his homoerotic preferences. In Thai culture, the category "man" could and did accommodate homoerotic preference as simply a variation of masculine sexuality, as long as it remained private. Taking the feminine, receptive sexual role, however, was stigmatized, if publicly known, and defined a man as socially deficient, ranked even lower than a *kathoey*.

The contemporary category of a masculinized gay identity in Thailand blurs the earlier distinction between "masculine" and "feminine" sexual practices, which are now viewed not as a defining marker of sex/gender identity, but rather as mere personal preferences. Gay men in Thailand now self-identify with a strong masculine body image and a strong preference for male heterosexual partners (Jackson, 1995). This masculine gay identity, which strongly disassociates itself from an imputed feminine status, is well established among educated and middle-class Thais, and increasingly among the lower and working classes. A Thai male who dresses, talks, and acts in ways expected of a Thai man, who is not known to take the woman's role in sexual relations, and who fulfils his social obligations by marrying and fathering a family is honored by being considered a man, even if he has, or has had, male sexual partners.

At the same time, however, that the contemporary meaning of "gay" offers a new, positive, sex/gender identity to Thai men, the Thai academic research establishment continues its attempt to locate the causes of homosexuality and find ways to intervene to prevent its occurrence and even to eliminate it from Thai society. This community (consistent with an earlier Western perspective) criticizes homosexuality as a pathological condition, but also seeks understanding, compassion, and acceptance of the homosexual as an individual, a value more consistent with traditional Thai culture.

Kathoey (sometimes called ladyboys) are now much more thoroughly identified as feminine, with their sexuality (though not that of their sexual partners) as well as their feminine behavior viewed as central to their identity. While the term *kathoey* today applies to a wide range of transgendered persons, including effeminate homosexuals, some *kathoey* also self-identify as women. Culturally, they have become the "other" against whom gay men construct their masculine identities. The categories of man and *kathoey* are now polar opposites in the sex/gender system, as a Thai man regards himself as *either* a man or a *kathoey* (Jackson 1997a, p. 172).

A *kathoey* is not a man in dress, speech, or demeanor; he is subordinate to another man in sexual relations; and he rejects the strongly sanctioned expectation that all men other than Buddhist monks should marry and become fathers. Indeed, the stigmatized demasculinized position of the *kathoey* (who are ritually barred from ordination as Buddhist monks) contrasts with that of the Buddhist monk who renounces sexuality but who is considered a type of Thai man (Jackson, 1997a, p. 312). The feminine sexual orientation, speech, behavior, and dress of the *kathoey* today defines their social and gender identity. In a patriarchal society like Thailand where women are devalued, this has increased the public stigma attached to the *kathoey*.

Simultaneously, Thai academic sex/gender discourse attempts to distinguish *kathoey* from homosexuals, for example, by linguistically distinguishing "genuine *kathoey*" or hermaphrodites from "false" or "artificial" *kathoey*, that is, males who (merely) exhibit cross-gender characteristics and engage in homoerotic practices, and who are sometimes defined as sexual perverts (a perspective also found frequently in India with regard to the *hijra*). By the 1970s and 1980s, the categories of transvestites and transsexuals were also distinguished from (biological) hermaphrodites, with only the latter considered true *kathoey*. The former began to be viewed as "false" *kathoey* who, like homosexual men, were considered to suffer from a psychological disorder. This distinction, which retains traces of the traditional *kathoey* as a distinctive intermediate sex/gender category of men born with the mind of a woman, is still sometimes used in the popular media, though it contrasts with the dominant popular view of the *kathoey* as a male who makes himself up as a woman or as an alternative category of maleness (Jackson, 1997a, p. 312; Morris, 1994).

Thailand's changing sex/gender system, in which the meaning of *kathoey* has changed from biological hermaphrodite to effeminate homosexual, or a "deficient kind of male," has resulted in increasing social and sexual stigmatization and marginalization of *kathoey* (Jackson, 1997b, p. 171, 1999). While the ethical principles of Buddhism, along with a generally noninterventionist state, are important factors in the international perception of Thailand as a "tolerant," and even accommodating place for sex/gender diversity, the most recent research suggests that attitudes toward transgendered persons are far from homogenous, even, or especially, within their families (Costa & Matzner, 2007), and more so for the public—Thai and non-Thai—at large. Despite the popular Western view that transgenderism is "accepted" in Thailand, in fact *kathoey* and other transgendered persons are becoming increasingly constrained by the contemporary Thai state. They are prevented from changing their status legally, must take out passports in their male identities, and as a result of some recent media sensationalism, are now prohibited from some occupations such as teaching (Matzner, 2006b). Homosexuality and male transgenderism are both now considered "social problems" by the Thai scientific community and, to some extent, by the state, somewhat negating an earlier view that the aim should be to help *kathoey* to live "happy and productive lives in society" through sex change operations and legal reforms that recognized the changed gender status of postoperative transsexuals. With transgenderism now being politically redefined as a perversion, there has been a rise of anti-*kathoey* and anti-sex change rhetoric that now exists alongside older, more tolerant, sympathetic, and noninterventionist discourses that, at one time, recognized *kathoey* as spirit mediums (Matzner, 2007; Winter, 2006).

What partly accounts for the Western view that *kathoey* and other transgender persons are "accepted" in Thailand is their high visibility. *Kathoey* are found in all social strata except at the highest levels of Thai nobility. They live and work openly both in rural and urban areas. Like the *waria* in Indonesia and the *bakla* in the Philippines, *kathoey* are particularly associated with feminine beauty and glamour and widely admired for their feminine grace and elegance. They are well-known performers in beauty contests and musical female impersonator revues, both critical sites of the enactment of the *kathoey*'s nonnormative sex/gender role. At the same time, although many *kathoeys* work at ordinary jobs and run their own businesses, they have the reputation of being sexual libertines, prostitutes, and sometimes crude and vulgar, which is very un-Thai behavior. This contributes to their marginal and generally derided position, even subjecting them to sexual attack.

Current attitudes toward gender diversity in Thailand must be viewed against the core Thai cultural value that how one acts is more important than how one feels. Integrating one's diverse public and private personae into a single "identity," or the public expression of one's "true self," are not strong Thai cultural values; however, they are so for the United States, a fact significantly affects the current movement toward transgenderism (see the section that follows). Leading a double life is a generally accepted feature of Thai culture, not necessarily equated with duplicity or deception as in the West. Thus it is not only the cultural ideologies of sex/gender diversity that must be considered in understanding the place of that diversity within a society, but the whole system of cultural values.

Blurring Categories: From Sex/Gender Binaries to Transgenderism in the United States

> *And God said unto Noah . . . [W]ith thee will I establish my covenant; And of every living thing of all flesh, two of every sort shalt thou bring into the ark to keep them alive with thee; they shall be male and female. (Genesis 6:3–19, as cited in Geertz, 1975, p. 10)*

In Western culture, nothing seems more natural, unchangeable, or desirable than that "human beings are divided without remainder into two biological sexes," male and female (Geertz, 1975, p. 10). The key cultural feature of the dominant American sex/gender system is the commitment to binaries—nature/culture; male/female, man/woman, homosexual/heterosexual. That system is well known, but here I emphasize a different vision of the future—one in which the lines demarcating the American sex/gender binary categories become blurred. As noted earlier, this vision needs to be understood in the context of a contemporary American cultural pattern that places a high value on the "authentic self" and on integrating the inner person with external actions. A cross-cultural perspective demonstrates that neither the Western sex/gender binaries nor the transgenderist vision is universal, but each is just one of many different cultural sex/gender paradigms.

In spite of the accumulating ethnographic evidence to the contrary, the view that sex, gender roles including sexuality, and gender identities are exclusively dichotomous, oppositional, and permanent, continues to be central in Western thought and highly resistant to alternative cultural constructions of reality. Given this cultural pattern, the dilemma for American culture and society is how to deal with persons who desire to be of a sex and gender class into which they were not born, when the American "incorrigible proposition" tells us that sex and gender, and the roles and identities associated with them, are ascribed and permanent.

The pioneering work of anthropologist Margaret Mead (1935/1963), whose cross-cultural studies demonstrated widely differing sex role patterns in different societies, made an important contribution to the distinction between (anatomical) sex and (cultural) gender. With the development of sex reassignment surgical techniques, the separation of sex and gender along with the associated concept of gender identity proved to be a useful formulation in treating some gender dysphoric individuals who experienced their bodies (their sex) as incongruent with their gendered sense of self. These persons, called *transsexuals,* could be treated by sex reassignment surgery and accompanying medical and psychological strategies aimed at bringing their sex and their gender identity into alignment. Transsexuals were defined as "biologically normal persons of one sex who were convinced that they were members of the *opposite* sex" (Stoller, cited in Kessler & McKenna, 1978, p. 115). The aim of sex reassignment surgery and the psychological and medical treatments (such as hormone therapy) that accompanied it was the transformation of an individual from one sex into the other. An important aspect of the treatment required individuals to show evidence to psychological and medical professionals that they were committed to, and were able to, make this transition. This construction of the transsexual was consistent with the American cultural dichotomy of sex and gender and was supported in the larger culture by permitting various legal changes as part of a revised life story (Bolin, 1988).

In spite of the many cultural and even legal supports of the construct of the transsexual as someone who crosses over completely to the "opposite" sex, some judges are skeptical. In a case in which a transsexual claimed the estate of her deceased spouse, the

Kansas Supreme Court stated that both science and the courts are divided on whether transsexuals are more appropriately defined in terms of their birth sex status or their postoperative sex/gender status (In *re Marshall G. Gardiner,* deceased, 2002). The court held that, while "through surgery and hormones, a transsexual can be made to look like a woman . . . the sex assignment surgery does not create the sexual organs of a woman." The court further held that while the plaintiff (a male-to-female transsexual) "wants and believes herself to be a woman [and] . . . has made every conceivable effort to make herself a female . . . her female anatomy, however, is still all man-made. The body [the plaintiff] inhabits is a male body in all aspects other than what the physicians have supplied. . . . From that the court has to conclude, that . . . as a matter of law [the plaintiff] is a male" (cited in Norgren & Nanda, 2006, p. 200; see also Currah, 1997).

In the past 30 years, the emphasis on transsexualism as a major theme in treating sex/gender dysphoria has been challenged by the emergence of transgenderism. The term *transgenderism* covers a wide variety of subjective experiences and identities that range widely over a sex/gender continuum, from androgynous to transsexual. Increasingly, persons defining themselves as transpeople see transgenderism as a way "out of the constraints imposed by a dichotomous sex/gender system [with the aim] . . . not to mandate anything, but to . . . be able to play with the categories, . . . to challenge the reductionism and essentialism that has accompanied these [binary] categories for so many millennia" (Ducat, 2006, p. 48).

Contemporary transgender communities do not necessarily aim at creating a third gender but rather creating space for multiple gender identities within the American binary sex/gender system. In spite of the many differences among individuals experiencing transgender identities, one repeated theme is that gender and sex categories are improperly imposed by society and its "sexual identity gatekeepers," referring here to the gender identity professionals who accept and work within the binary American system (Bolin, 1996, p. 447).

Transgenderists are challenging and stretching the boundaries of the American bipolar system of sex/gender oppositions and renouncing the American definition of gender as dependent on a consistency of genitals, body type, identity, role behaviors, and sexual orientation (Cromwell, 1997; Jervis, 2006). Contemporary transgender communities include a continuum of people, from those who wish to undergo sex reassignment surgery to those who wish to live their lives androgynously (Winter, 2006). The previous split between transsexuals who viewed surgery as the only authentic expression of a feminine nature, as opposed to "part time" gender crossers who did not wish to have sex reassignment surgery, has to some extent been reconciled by the emergence of a transgender community that attempts to validate a whole range of gender roles and identities. As one transgenderist expressed it, "you no longer have to fit into a box . . . it is okay to be transgendered. You can now lay [sic] anywhere on the spectrum from nongendered to full transsexual" (Bolin, 1996, p. 475). Transgenderists are trying not so much to do away with maleness and femaleness as to de-naturalize them, that is, take away their privileged status in relation to all other possible combinations of behaviors, roles, and identities (Jervis, 2006, p. 48). The point for some transpeople is that gender categories should be something that individuals can construct for themselves, through self-reflection and observation (Cromwell, 1997).

The dynamism of the transgender movement, which includes both transgender activists and mental health professionals, has most recently been acknowledged in a proposal by the New York City Board of Health to allow people to alter the sex on their birth certificate even if they have not had sex-change surgery (Cave, 2006a, p. A1). In introducing this proposal, the Board of Health emphasized the importance of separating anatomy from what it means to be a man or a woman (in short, eliminating anatomical considerations when defining gender), thus reducing discrimination against men and women who do not conform to gender stereotypes. Although the proposal was ultimately scrapped (Cave, 2006b, p. B12), New York has adopted other measures aimed toward blurring the lines of gender identification; for example, it allows beds in shelters to be distributed according to appearance, whether the individual is a postoperative transsexual, cross-dresser, or person perceived to be androgynous, and it has adopted a Metropolitan Transit Authority policy that allows people to define their own gender when deciding whether to use men's or women's restrooms. These new radical policies are just one of the many aspects of current debates over transgenderism in which an increasing number of mental health professionals are beginning to think of gender variance as a naturally occurring phenomenon rather than a disorder, and in which schools and parents are taking steps to support children who do not want to conform to current gender norms. In the process, they not only work to protect the rights of transgender students but also to dismantle gender stereotypes (Brown, 2006, p. A1).

Sam Winter, director of Transgender Asia web site (2006), suggests that treating gender disorders as a mental illness, as in *DMS-IV,* while useful for Western transsexuals in obtaining medical services, extracts too high a price by substantially contributing to transphobia. Winter perhaps best summarizes the views of contemporary transpeople when he says, "transgender is one aspect of human diversity. . . . It is a difference, not a disorder. . . . If we can speak to any gender identity disorder at all, it is in the inability of many societies to accept the particular gender identity difference we call transgender" (see also Richmond, 2004).

Unlike transsexualism, *transgenderism* is culturally subversive: it calls into question the exclusive rightness of the binary gender categories while providing a wider range of individual possibilities for those who experience distress by trying to conform to the dominant, exclusively binary American sex/gender system. The American transgender movement has been empowered by knowledge about alternative sex/gender systems throughout the world. Some of these sex/gender systems have offered American transpeople a source of meaning, and especially spiritual meaning, that they do not find in the transphobic, dichotomous sex/gender system currently dominating American society. Those sex/gender systems that include more than two sex/genders have thus attracted increasing interest in both the popular culture and among the medical and psychological communities.

Cultural Patterns and Sex/Gender Diversity

Sex/gender variation exists in many different cultural contexts and takes many different forms (see Sidebar 15.2). Many societies regard sex/gender variants as merely natural, albeit unusual, phenomena (Geertz, 1975), while other societies make accommodation for sex/gender variants through the construction of alternative sex/gender roles, as described earlier (Costa & Matzner, 2007; Graham, 2006; Herdt, 1996a, 1996b; Lang, 1999; Matzner, 2001; Nanda, 1999, 2000; Ramet, 1996). Native American cultures appear to be particularly associated with multiple genders, for both men and women (Brown, 1997; Jacobs et al., 1997; Lang, 1999; Roscoe, 1996; Williams, 1986). These roles (formerly called *berdache*, now called *two-spirit*) varied greatly: in some cultures the alternative sex/gender roles were assigned to hermaphrodites, in others they were associated with sexual orientation or practice, in others with cross-dressing, and in still others, with occupation, or a combination of all of these; in any case they were regarded as alternative and autonomous genders with a status equal to that of men or women (see Lang, 1998; Roscoe, 1996; Thomas, 1997). Gender variant individuals did not become members of the "opposite" sex or gender but rather enacted alternative gender roles that were distinguished from both man and woman, often comprising a "mixture" of masculine and feminine qualities. In some societies, the sex/gender variant was seen as uniting male and female within himself (Williams, 1986, p. 41,), an integration of sex/gender found in many cultures (see, for example, Marcos, 2002). Sometimes the male two-spirit person did not wear women's clothing but rather a mixture of men's and women's clothing (Williams, 1986, pp. 73–76); their other activities also symbolized their dual sex/gender integration.

Cultural Patterns and Sex/Gender Diversity

Sex/gender variation exists in many cultural contexts in various forms.

The Western understanding of an exclusive homosexual/heterosexual divide is culturally constructed, not universal, and often inappropriately imposed on other cultures.

Sexual orientation is not necessarily tied to sex/gender classification in many cultures; rather, sexual practices can be key in sex/gender classification, while in other cases, sexual orientation may have little to no bearing on gender identity.

Individuals expressing nonnormative gender behaviors may be treated with fear or disrespect in contemporary society; however, such individuals were often traditionally considered to have power and were given prestigious social roles (examples include Native American societies, India, Brazil, precontact Hawaii, and Indonesia).

Because sex/gender roles can only be understood within the context of specific cultures, one's individuality and identity and its relation to sex/gender vary cross-culturally.

While most recorded alternative gender roles are associated with males, others, like the "sworn virgin" of the Balkans (Grémaux, 1996), the *tombois* of Indonesia (Blackwood, 1998), the *sadhin* of India (Humes, 1996; Phillimore, 1991), or the Mohave *hwame* (Devereux, 1937) are associated with females. Still others, like the Hawaiian *mahu* (Matzner, 2001), the Thai *kathoey*, or the Indonesian *bissu* (Boellstorff, 2005) originally applied to both males and females, though they now refer mainly to feminine males. While anthropological debate continues on whether some of these roles were genuine or autonomous alternative genders (Blackwood & Wieringa, 1999; Boellstorff, 2005), roles transcending sex/gender binaries are clearly a widespread cultural phenomenon.

Culture and the Homosexual/Heterosexual Divide

Cross-cultural data strongly challenge the Western understanding of an exclusive homosexual/heterosexual divide, which associates sexual orientation with essentialized identities. The culturally constructed homosexual/heterosexual divide is not universal and has frequently been inappropriately imposed on other cultures.

Sexuality (sexual desire and practice) in many cultures is not viewed as either permanent or as an important component in gender, or it may be associated with other elements of culture in ways that stand in great contrast to Western understandings. In Brazil, as noted earlier, and in other cultures (Wikan, 1977), sexual practice, not sexual orientation, is the key element in the sex/gender system; in still other cultures, sexual orientation has little or no relevance to gender identity. While many of the male alternative gender roles described in the ethnographic literature are associated with gendered sexuality, in Thailand, as noted, and in Indonesia, these roles are definitively differentiated from "gay," and the sexual relations with males characteristic of such roles are defined as heterogenderal rather than homosexual (Boellstorff, 2004, p. 170).

Among the Sambia of New Guinea, what we call homosexual practice is culturally central in the sex/gender system, not as an aspect of a sexual orientation, but as a core ritual in male initiation considered essential for the development of adult masculinity (Herdt, 1981, 1996a, pp. 431–436). In Sambia culture, women are viewed as dangerous creatures that pollute men, deplete them of their masculinity substance, and are inferior in every way, except for reproduction. The Sambia believe that women are naturally fertile and mature naturally without external aid, whereas males do not naturally mature as fast or as competently as females. In Sambia belief, males cannot attain puberty or secondary sex characteristics such as body hair, or become "strong men" without semen. As the Sambia believe that their (male) bodies do not naturally produce semen, it must be externally and artificially introduced into the body through magical ritual treatments. A core element of the initiation of adolescent boys thus involves the ritual function of homosexual fellatio, in which the boys consume semen from adult men, which will thereby produce maleness. Only repeated inseminations of this kind are considered capable of conferring on the young boy the reproductive competence that results in manliness and fatherhood.

As a criterion of sex/gender classification, sexual orientation varies cross culturally. While many (male) alternative sex/gender roles in various cultures involve sexual relations with men, in none of those cultures is this, in itself, a sufficient condition of alternative gender status. Indeed, contrary to the Euro-American system, in which sexual orientation comes closest to defining the alternative gender of "homosexual" in other cultures, the sexual partner of the alternatively gendered person is not considered homosexual or gender divergent and is not even culturally acknowledged as different. Even in Western culture, the current sex/gender system of oppositions between homosexual and heterosexual as essential identities has waxed and waned in different eras and societies and emerged in its contemporary, exclusively binary form only in the last several hundred years (Trumbach, 1996). In premodern Europe, homosexuality was not a criterion of gender, and "the homosexual" as a sex/gender category did not exist.

Same-sex desire in women is often not culturally acknowledged, for example in Suriname, although intimate relations between women are known to be commonplace (Wekker, 1999). In other societies, such as Lesotho, female/female sexual relations are a regular feature of a growing girl's development that may cease in later life but may also be a normal feature of relations between adult women. These same-sex desires and practices have no cultural relevance to feminine gender identities or adult gender roles (Gay, 1985, as cited in Kendall, 1999). "Mummy-baby" relationships between younger and older girls and women involve mentoring on issues of sex and courtship and also involve intimacy and romance, such as the exchange of love letters and sexual relations. This relationship has become a substitute for older initiation rites that declined partly as a result of Western missionary activity. As the girls get older, they may become mummies to their own babies and begin to have boyfriends as well. The intensity of these relationships usually ends with marriage when women become more focused on domestic responsibilities.

Further, while the American concept of "homosexual" includes both men and women with a same-sex orientation regardless of other aspects of their gender role performance, in much of the world sexual orientation is only culturally acknowledged as relevant in gender identity for those men and women who enact their role "opposites," that is, effeminate homosexual men or masculine lesbian women. In West Sumatra, Indonesia, in contrast to the West, women's same-sex desires do not determine their gender roles or gender identities. Whereas both partners in a female-female relationship in the United States are labeled lesbians, in Sumatra, two females in a sexual relationship are viewed as occupying different gender roles and the relationship is called *cowok-cewek* (guy/girl). A *cowok* is expected to exhibit masculine behavior and dress, exhibit manly qualities such as bravery, and desire sex only with women while a *cewek* is expected to dress and comport herself as a woman, have sexual desires for men, and show feminine abilities to cook and keep house. *Cowoks* express masculine gender identities while *cewaks* express feminine gender identities; the overriding Western concept of lesbian as it applies to both women in a relationship is rejected in this context (Blackwood, 1998; Boellstorff, 2005, p. 159).

Social Attitudes toward Sex/Gender Diversity

While in many contemporary societies, individuals exhibiting non-normative or transgressive gender behaviors and/or identities may be treated with ridicule, fear, or disrespect, not all cultures make gender identity as central, as stable, or as unvarying as it is in Western culture. Traditionally such individuals were often believed to have sacred powers and superior skills and occupied special prestigious social roles. In many Native American societies, two-spirit persons received special recognition as healers and shamans, as well as occupying special roles such as go-betweens in marriage for which their mixed gender roles particularly suited them (Greenberg, 1985; Thayer, 1980; Williams, 1986). Also in India and Brazil, as noted earlier, individuals on the margins because of their sex/gender status are associated with powerful ritual capacities. Indeed, it is not surprising that transgressive sex/gender individuals like the *hijra* and the *pasivo* who have the power to undermine social conventions and cause social disorder should be linked to prodigious magical and other powers (Fry, 1995).

In precontact Hawaii also, feminine men and masculine women called *mahu* (literally, hermaphrodite) were not only accepted but were valued caregivers for children and the elderly and considered highly skilled in traditional arts. Male *mahu* particularly were associated with teaching hula and chants and were keepers of cultural tradition. As the term *mahu* changed to refer to male-to-female transgendered people as well as effeminate and gender-normative gay men, it became increasingly a term of derision; more recently, however, with the renaissance of Hawaiian culture, it is resuming its older meanings. *Mahu* oral histories indicate that some transgendered Native Hawaiians now increasingly identify with the traditional Hawaiian role, experiencing themselves, and seen by others, as especially skilled in traditional Hawaiian cultural patterns like hula, lei-making, chanting, singing, and sewing. As *mahu*, they feel a strong responsibility to pass these skills on to future generations (Matzner, 2001, pp. 14–15).

In Thailand, Brazil, the Philippines, and other cultures, the association of alternative gendered males with sex work has resulted in negative public images and to some extent hostile treatment by the state toward the alternatively gendered. Conversely, alternatively gendered males may also achieve prestige through their ability to transform themselves into glamorous and stylish women, adopting personae that, as with the *kathoey* in Thailand, are particularly associated with entertainment and beauty contests (Johnson, 1997).

The importance of accommodating differently gendered persons into civic life has become an explicit issue of national debate in Indonesia. One of the several gender variant roles in Indonesia, the *waria* (Boellstorff, 2004, 2005; Graham, 2006), is highly visible and significantly defined by their public performances as entertainers. Like the *bakla* of the Philippines or the Thai *kathoey*, the *waria* widely engage in sex work, but they also work in beauty salons (Boellstorff, 2004). Like other transgendered persons throughout the world today, the *waria* are much concerned with respect and with their incorporation into the larger civil society. In an attempt to increase this respect, the *waria* seek to make specific contributions to the Indonesian nation. One of the ways they do this is through their work in bridal salons. Through their expertise in creating wedding costumes, make up, and hair styles that project a "true Indonesian image" that transcends the many ethnic and regional divisions in the nation, the *waria* make an important contribution to furthering the unity of the Indonesian state. This contribution has been recognized by the state, which also provides financial and other assistance to *waria* in the fields of beauty and bridal culture.

Sex/Gender Systems and the Cultural Idea of the Person

To repeat, sex/gender concepts and roles can only be understood in the context of specific cultures. One of the most significant cultural patterns that shapes a society's attitudes toward sex/gender variation is its culturally constructed idea of the person. Thus, while the sex/gender systems of other societies have provided some alternative identifications for transgendered persons in American society, these identifications can be problematic, as the notion of the person in which they are embedded is not easily transferable between cultures.

The concept of identity as the sameness, unity, and persistence of one's individuality, especially as experienced in self-awareness and behavior, and its relation to gender and sexuality varies cross culturally. Not all cultures make gender identity as central, as stable, or as unvarying as it is in Western culture (Wekker, 1999, p. 120). In many societies, gender competes with other identities, such as age, ethnicity, kinship status, and class as a significant basis for self-identification and action. As ethnographic researchers increasingly incorporate the individual voices of transgendered persons into their ethnographies, they reveal that the gender identities of such individuals vary from each other, may change over a lifetime, and are associated with different degrees of negatively experienced internal conflict (see, e.g., Costa & Matzner, 2007; Matzner, 2001; Nanda, 1996).

In India, as noted earlier, gender roles and gender identities are not necessarily permanent. Gender transformations are not only part of Indian mythology, but are also permitted and occur in society. One of my *hijra* consultants, Salima, a hermaphrodite and a "born" *hijra*, referred to other *hijras* as "converts," a term that nicely illustrates the Indian view that people can either retain the gender they were born into or they can change their gender, just as one converts to a different religion. These possibilities for gender transformation are related to Hindu concepts of the person, as also noted earlier. Because Hinduism explicitly recognizes that humans achieve their ultimate goals by following many different paths, it affords the individual temperament the widest latitude in behavior, including what Western psychology might call compulsive extremes (Lannoy, 1975). This results in a greater tolerance for individual diversity, especially in matters of sexuality, than Western culture practices. Within this framework of the Indian concept of the person, *hijras* can find meaning in their ambiguous gender.

In Oman, also, beliefs regarding the alternative sex/gender role of the *xanith* can be understood only in the context of the Omani construct of the person. The *xanith,* a mixture of man and woman and known for playing the female sexual role, can become men if they marry and prove their sexual potency as males. Then they are reclassified as men for all social purposes, no matter how effeminate they remain. Wikan (1977) suggests that the Omani accommodation of the *xanith* role is directly related to their concept of the person. Homosexuality is considered shameful behavior in Oman because in sex acts males take the passive role associated with being a woman. However, Omanis acknowledge that the sexual deviant cannot be suppressed, and they let him practice his deviance in peace. The sexually different person is given a publicly acknowledged social status and participates in the full life of the society in his specialized role. In the Omani view of life the world is imperfect. People are created with dissimilar natures and are likewise imperfect. Thus, the passive, effeminate homosexual is acknowledged and reclassified as a *xanith.*

While it is difficult to generalize with regard to the alternative gender roles which existed in many Native American societies in North America, in a reexamination of these roles, Whitehead (1981) suggests that Native American cosmologies give wide scope to individual differences, institutionalizing them in social roles, rather than driving them underground. Such societies, she says, seem less concerned in general with why individuals become the way they are or why they change from one role to another; indeed, changes in sexuality and gender identity over a lifetime may be viewed as quite natural (Lang, 1998). Devereux (1937), noting that the Mohave believed an element of predestination or fate is involved in gender transformations, suggests that this feature inhibits negative moral evaluations or sanctions of gender variant individuals.

In Tahiti, too, concepts of the person appear to be relevant in understanding the creation of, and community response to, the *mahu* role. Levy (1973) found that traditionally oriented Tahitians considered the *mahu* a natural phenomenon and had little interest in how or why the *mahu* developed. Nor is the *mahu* subject to any negative moral evaluations or sanctions. People say that the *mahu* "is born like that," and he is simply accepted. In Tahiti generally, Levy (1973) reports, people are reluctant to generalize about the

quality of an individual's character based on his or her membership in a gender category; such reluctance inhibits generalizations
about ordinary men and women as well as *mahu*. In Tahiti, the
self is seen as a natural state of being and not easily changeable,
which inhibits not only a curiosity about the cause of becoming a
mahu, but any desire to correct or cure him, although this ready
acceptance does not hold true in all of Polynesia (Besnier, 1996).

Finally, in an interesting contrast to the American emphasis
on the unity of the self and the importance of the integration of its
private and public aspects, in Thailand the public expression of
one's "true self" is not as valued as it is in the West. This significantly impacts on an individual's experience of sex/gender dysphoria. "Coming out" as a homosexual in Thailand still brings
shame or "loss of face," but without the compensation of the high
value on "being oneself" so essential in American culture. A similar point was made by a Filipino *bakla* living in New York, in expressing a contrast between American and Filipino gay men to
ethnographer Martin Manalansan (2003):

> The Americans are different, darling. Coming out is their drama.
> When I was studying at [a New England college] the queens had noth-
> ing better to talk about than coming out. Maybe their families were
> very cruel. Back home, who cared? But the whites, my God, shedding
> tears, leaving the family. The stories are always so sad. (p. 27)

By itself, a cross-cultural perspective will not do away with
the trans- and homophobia that makes the lives of countless individuals throughout the world so difficult. But it can open our eyes
and offer us broader possibilities, and perhaps most importantly, in
our own culture, teach us to be cautious about drawing conclusions
in regard to the relationship of sex/gender variation and mental
health problems (see Summary and Conclusions). As anthropolo-
gists, our task is to continually weave between the particular and
the general as we try to understand—and to help communities understand—both the similarities and differences among individuals
and among cultures that are part of our common humanity.

Summary and Conclusions

- A cross-cultural perspective makes it clear that societies organize their thinking about sex/gender, sexuality, and identity
  in many different ways and construct different sex/gender
  systems.
- The *hijra* of India, the *travesti* or *pasivo* of Brazil, the *kathoey* of
  Thailand, and the transgenderists of America provide examples and insights into alternative sex/gender systems and

challenge us to reexamine our own assumptions regarding sex/gender as well as its cultural basis and the treatment of those who do not fit into our culture's sex/gender paradigms.

- Sex/gender-related categories are culturally constructed and not universal.

- Sexual orientation is not necessarily a factor in constructing sex/gender identity in various cultures.

- Sex/gender definitions do not necessarily centrally define a person's identity in various cultures as these definitions tend to do in many Western cultures.

- A cross-cultural perspective regarding sex/gender, sexuality, and identity can open our eyes and offer broader possibilities for understanding sex/gender variation as well as creating new ways to discuss and contemplate sex and gender in our own culture.

References

Benedict, R. (1934). Anthropology and the abnormal. *Journal of General Psychology, 10,* 59–82.

Besnier, N. (1996). Polynesian gender liminality through time and space. In G. Herdt (Ed.), *Third sex third gender: Beyond sexual dimorphism in culture and history* (pp. 285–328). New York: Zone Books.

Blackwood, E. (1998). Tombois in West Sumatra: Constructing masculinity and erotic desire. *Cultural Anthropology, 13,* 491–513.

Blackwood, E., & Wieringa, S. (Eds.). (1999). *Female desires: Same-sex relations and transgender practices across cultures.* New York: Columbia University Press.

Boellstorff, T. (2004). Playing back the nation: Waria Indonesian transvestites. *Cultural Anthropology, 19,* 159–195.

Boellstorff, T. (2005). *The gay archipelago: Sexuality and nation in Indonesia.* Princeton, NJ: Princeton University Press.

Bolin, A. (1988). *In search of Eve: Transsexual rites of passage.* South Hadley, MA: Bergin and Garvey.

Bolin, A. (1996). Transcending and transgendering: Male-to-female transsexuals, dichotomy and diversity. In G. Herdt (Ed.), *Third sex third gender: Beyond sexual dimorphism in culture and history* (pp. 447–485). New York: Zone Books.

Bradford, N. J. (1983). Transgenderism and the cult of Yellamma: Heat, sex, and sickness in South Indian ritual. *Journal of Anthropological Research, 39*(3), 307–322.

Brown, P. L. (Ed.). (1997). *Two spirit people: American Indian lesbian women and gay men.* Binghamton, NY: Haworth Press.

Brown, P. L. (2006, December 2). Supporting boys or girls when the line isn't clear. *New York Times,* p. A1.

Cave, D. (2006a, November 7). New York plans to make gender personal choice. *New York Times,* p. A1.

Cave, D. (2006b, December 6). No change in definition of gender: City drops plan involving choice. *New York Times,* p. B12.

Cohen, L. (1995). The pleasures of castration: The postoperative status of hijras, jankhas and academics. In P. R. Abramson & S. D. Pinkerton (Eds.), *Sexual nature, sexual culture* (pp. 276–304). Chicago: University of Chicago Press.

Costa, L., & Matzner, A. (2007). *Male bodies, women's souls: Personal narratives of Thailand's transgendered youth.* Binghamton, NY: Haworth Press.

Cromwell, J. (1997). Traditions of gender diversity and sexualities: A female-to-male transgendered perspective. In S. Jacobs, W. Thomas, & S. Lang (Eds.), *Two spirit people: Native American gender identity, sexuality, and spirituality* (pp. 119–142). Urbana, IL: University of Illinois Press.

Currah, P. (1997, August). Defending genders: Sex and gender non-conformity—The civil rights strategies of sexual minorities. *Hastings Law Journal, 48,* 1363–1385.

Devereux, G. (1937). Institutionalized homosexuality of the Mohave Indians. *Human Biology, 9,* 498–587.

Ducat, S. (2006, Summer). Slipping into something more comfortable: Towards a liberated continuum of gender. *LiP,* 46–51.

Fry, P. (1995). Male homosexuality and Afro-Brazilian possession cults. In S. O. Murray (Ed.), *Latin American male homosexualities* (pp. 193–220). Albuquerque, NM: University of New Mexico.

Geertz, C. (1975). Common sense as a cultural system. *Antioch Review, 33*(1), 5–26.

Graham, S. (2006). *Challenging gender norms: The five genders of Indonesia.* Belmont, CA: Wadsworth.

Greenberg, D. F. (1985). Why was the berdache ridiculed? *Journal of Homosexuality, 11,* 179–190.

Grémaux, R. (1996). Woman becomes man in the Balkans. In G. Herdt (Ed.), *Third sex third gender: Beyond sexual dimorphism in culture and history* (pp. 241–84). New York: Zone Books.

Hayes, K. (1996). *Meu querido viado: Gender and possession trance in candomble.* Unpublished manuscript.

Herdt, G. (1981). *Guardians of the flute: Idioms of masculinity.* New York: McGraw-Hill.

Herdt, G. (1996a). Mistaken sex: Culture, biology and the third sex in New Guinea. In G. Herdt (Ed.), *Third sex third gender: Beyond sexual dimorphism in culture and history.* New York: Zone Books.

Herdt, G. (Ed.). (1996b). *Third sex third gender: Beyond sexual dimorphism in culture and history.* New York: Zone Books.

Hiltelbeitel, A. (1980). Siva, the goddess, and the disguises of the Pandavas and Draupadi. *History of Religions, 20*(1/2), 147–174.

Humes, C. A. (1996). Becoming male: Salvation through gender modification in Hinduism and Buddhisim. In S. P. Ramet (Ed.), *Gender reversals and gender cultures: Anthropological and historical perspectives* (pp. 123–137). London: Routledge.

Jackson, P. (1995). *Dear Uncle Go: Male homosexuality in Thailand.* Bangkok: Bua.

Jackson, P. (1997a). Kathoey<>Gay><Man: The historical emergence of gay male identity in Thailand. In L. Manderson & M. Jolly (Eds.), *Sites of desire: Economies of pleasure: Sexualities in Asia and the Pacific* (pp. 166–190). Chicago: University of Chicago Press.

Jackson, P. (1997b). Thai research on male homosexuality and transgenderism and the cultural limits of Foucaultian analysis. *Journal of the History of Sexuality, 8*(1), 52–85.

Jackson, P. (1999). *Lady boys, tom boys, rentboys: Male and female homosexualities in contemporary Thailand.* Binghamton, NY: Haworth Press.

Jacobs, S., Thomas, W., & Lang, S. (Eds.). (1997). *Two spirit people: Native American gender identity, sexuality, and spirituality.* Urbana: University of Ilinois Press.

Jervis, L. (Ed.). (2006, Summer). Slipping into something more comfortable: Towards a liberated continuum of gender. *LiP,* 46–51.

Johnson, M. (1997). *Beauty and power: Transgendering and cultural transformation in the Southern Philippines.* New York: Berg.

Kakar, S. (1982). *Shamans, mystics and doctors: A psychological inquiry into India and its healing traditions.* New York: Alfred A. Knopf.

Kendall. (1999). Women in Lesotho and the (Western) construction of homophobia. In E. Blackwood & S. Wieringa (Eds.), *Female desires: Same-sex relations and transgender practices across cultures* (pp. 157–180). New York: Columbia University Press.

Kessler, S. J., & McKenna, W. (1978). *Gender: An ethnomethodological approach.* New York: Wiley.

Kulick, D. (1997). The gender of Brazilian transgendered prostitutes. *American Anthropologist, 99*(3), 574–585.

Kulick, D. (1998). *Travesti: Sex, gender and culture among Brazilian transgendered prostitutes.* Chicago: University of Chicago Press.

Lang, S. (1998). *Men as women, women as men: Changing gender in Native American cultures* (J. L. Vantine, Trans.). Austin: University of Texas Press.

Lang, S. (1999). Lesbians, men-women, and two-spirits: Homosexuality and gender in Native American cultures. In E. Blackwood & S. E. Wieringa (Eds.), *Female desires: Same-sex relations and transgender practices across cultures* (pp. 91–118). New York: Columbia University Press.

Lannoy, R. (1975). *The speaking tree.* New York: Oxford University Press.

Levy, R. (1973). *Tahitians: Mind and experience in the Society Islands.* Chicago: University of Chicago Press.

Manalansan, M. F. (2003). *Global divas: Filipino gay men in the diaspora.* Durham, NC: Duke University Press.

Marcos, S. (2002). Beyond binary categories: Mesoamerican religious sexuality. In S. Ellingson & M. C. Green (Eds.), *Religion and sexuality in cross-cultural perspective* (pp. 111–136). New York: Routledge.

Matory, J. L. (1994). *Sex and the empire that is no more: Gender and the politics of metaphor in Oyo Yoruba religion.* Minneapolis: University of Minnesota Press.

Matzner, A. (2001). *'O au no keia: Voices from Hawai'i's Mahu and transgender communities.* Philadelphia: Xlibris.

Matzner, A. (2006a). *The iron ladies: 14 questions.* Retrieved November 13, 2006, from www.goldenscene.com/ironladies/reviews/questions.html.

Matzner, A. (2006b). *Kathoey.* Retrieved April 11, 2006, from http://en.wikipedia.org/wiki/kathoey/.

Matzner, A. (2007). *Transgenderism and Northern Thai spirit mediumship.* Retrieved January 6, 2007, from http://web.hku.hk/~sjwinter/TransgenderASIA/TGinThailandSpirit.htm.

Mead, M. (1963). *Sex and temperament in three primitive societies.* New York: Dell. (Original work published 1935)

Morris, R. C. (1994). Three sexes and four sexualities: Redressing the discourses on sexuality and gender in Thailand. *Positions, 2,* 15–43.

Nanda, S. (1996). Hijras: An alternative sex and gender role in India. In G. Herdt (Ed.), *Third sex third gender: Beyond sexual dimorphism in culture and history* (pp. 373–418). New York: Zone Books.

Nanda, S. (1999). *Neither man nor woman: The hijras of India* (2nd ed.). Belmont, CA: Wadsworth.

Nanda, S. (2000). *Gender diversity: Crosscultural variations.* Prospect Heights, IL: Waveland.

Norgren, J., & Nanda, S. (2006). *American cultural pluralism and law* (3rd ed.). Westport, CT: Praeger/Greenwood.

O'Flaherty, W. D. (1973). *Siva: The erotic ascetic.* New York: Oxford University Press.

O'Flaherty, W. D. (1980). *Women, androgynes, and other mythical beasts.* Chicago: University of Chicago Press.

Parker, R. C. (1991). *Bodies, pleasure, and passions: Sexual culture in contemporary Brazil.* Boston: Beacon Press.

Parker, R. C. (1995). Changing Brazilian constructions of homosexuality. In S. O. Murray (Ed.), *Latin American male homosexualities* (pp. 241–255). Albuquerque, NM: University of New Mexico Press.

Phillimore, P. (1991). Unmarried women of the Dhaula Dhar: Celibacy and social control in Northwest India. *Journal of Anthropological Research, 47*(3), 331–350.

Quinn, N., & Luttrell, W. (2004). Psychodynamic universals, cultural particulars in feminist anthropology: Rethinking Hua gender beliefs. *Ethos, 32,* 493–513.

Ramet, S. P. (Ed.). (1996). *Gender reversals and gender cultures: Anthropological and historical perspectives.* London: Routledge.

Reddy, G. (2005). *With respect to sex: Negotiating hijra identity in south India.* Chicago: University of Chicago Press.

Richmond, M. (2004, Winter). Opinion: Review of the book *The man who would be queen: The science of gender-bending and transsexualism. TransgenderTapestry, 104,* 1–2. Retrieved May 29, 2006,

from www.ifge.org/index.php?name=News&file=article&sid=238/.

Roscoe, W. (1995). Cultural anesthesia and lesbian and gay studies. *American Anthropologist, 97,* 448–452.

Roscoe, W. (1996). How to become a berdache: Toward a unified analysis of gender diversity. In G. Herdt (Ed.), *Third sex, third gender: Beyond sexual dimorphism in culture and history* (pp. 329–372). New York: Zone Books.

Thayer, J. S. (1980). The berdache of the northern plains: A socioreligious perspective. *Journal of Anthropological Research, 36,* 287–293.

Thomas, W. (1997). Navajo cultural constructions of gender and sexuality. In S. Jacobs, W. Thomas & S. Lang (Eds.), *Two-spirited people* (pp. 156–173). Urbana, IL: University of Illinois Press.

Trumbach, R. (1996). London's sapphists: From three sexes to four genders in the making of modern culture. In G. Herdt (Ed.), *Third sex third gender: Beyond sexual dimorphism in culture and history* (pp. 111–136). New York: Zone Books.

Wafer, J. (1991). *The taste of blood: Spirit possession in Brazilian candomble.* Philadelphia: University of Pennsylvania Press.

Wekker, G. (1999). "What's identity got to do with it?": Rethinking identity in light of the *Mati* work in Suriname. In E. Blackwood & S. Wieringa (Eds.), *Female desires: Same-sex relations and transgender practices across cultures* (pp. 119–138). New York: Columbia University Press.

Whitehead, H. (1981). The bow and the burden strap: A new look at institutionalized homosexuality in Native North America. In S. B. Ortner & H. Whitehead (Eds.), *Sexual meanings: The cultural construction of gender and sexuality* (pp. 80–115). Cambridge: Cambridge University Press.

Wikan, U. (1977). Man becomes woman: Transsexualism in Oman as a key to gender roles. *Man, 12,* 304–319.

Williams, W. (1986). *The spirit and the flesh.* Boston: Beacon Press.

Winter, S. (2006). *Transphobia: A price worth paying for gender identity disorder?* Retrieved June 1, 2006, from http://web.hku.hk/~sjwinter/TransgenderASIA/index.htm.

Zwilling, L., & Sweet, M. (2000). The evolution of third sex constructs in ancient India: A study in ambiguity. In J. Leslie (Ed.), *Constructing ideologies: Religion, gender, and social definition in India* (pp. 99–133). New Delhi, India: Oxford University Press.

PARAPHILIAS AND ATYPICAL SEXUAL BEHAVIORS

Most of us undoubtedly heard or read about, in introductory level psychology and sociology textbooks, the various paraphilias. We probably regarded this seemingly disconnected array of disorders with little more than prurient curiosity, wondering who these people might be and what made them that way and consigning them to the "other" or "not-me" realm. Now, as students of sexology, we understand that variation *is* the norm, and that the question must be reframed in terms of at what point variation becomes a disorder, violates socially acceptable boundaries, and/or interferes with a person's functioning in society.

On a generic level, the paraphilias are not difficult to understand. Sex, and the intimacy that accompanies it, are powerful human drives with the potential under some circumstances to become obsessions, as suggested by Chapter 19 on sexual addictions. As these drives seek fulfillment with an object (person) of desire, most individuals express them through appropriate behaviors and toward appropriate objects that conform to established social norms. Yet in people's more private lives, these drives often lead to ideations and behaviors that show some deviation from the prevailing norms: sexual fantasizing, extramarital affairs, exhibitionism and voyeurism (e.g., strip shows), anal sex, prostitution, sadomasochism, and bondage. Since most of these are now no longer criminalized or are permitted in controlled situations in the United States and Europe, at what point, then, do certain behaviors—driven by strong and recurring urges—cross a boundary and become unacceptable, unlawful, or unhealthy. As the authors in this section note, according to contemporary Western mores, sexual behaviors become problematic (and usually unlawful) when they are carried out with individuals who do not or cannot give consent. What compels some to cross this line of consent, and others not, is among the major unsolved issues in the study of the paraphilias.

At the individual level, the paraphilias continue to puzzle sexologists. Why do some people become rapists, why do others have sex with minors, why does this person become an exhibitionist and that person a voyeur? Specifically, what developmental experiences, what personality traits, what biological dispositions, what circumstances are likely to lead to specific kinds of paraphilias?

As of now, many of these questions remain unsatisfactorily answered, although researchers are honing their classification systems, developing new assessment tools, accessing larger and "cleaner" study populations, and posing new theoretical frameworks to help understand these disorders. However, unlike the sexual dysfunctions and the gender identity disorders, the paraphilias carry with them moral and criminal implications that muddle the issues (e.g., confounding effects of incarceration) and make the understanding of effective treatment more difficult. And, unlike the other sexual disorders, classification, terminology, assessment, and treatment of the paraphilias from a legal/criminal standpoint, noted in the final chapter of this volume (Chapter 20), is carried out not for the good of the individual with the problem, but rather for the good of society.

Paraphilia and Paraphilia-Related Disorders: An Introduction

Luk Gijs

16

Chapter

Learning Objectives

In this chapter, we discuss:

- Problems in defining "normal" and "abnormal" sexual behaviors.
- Paradigmatic approaches to abnormal sexual behaviors.
- The definition and prevalence of the paraphilias.
- Theoretical perspectives on paraphilias: pathology versus normal variations of behavior.
- Assessment for persons with paraphilias.
- Treatments: psychotherapeutic and biomedical.
- Effectiveness of interventions.
- Paraphilia-related disorders.

People vary in the way in which they experience sex, as well as in their sexual behavior, as has been found both in clinical practice and in many surveys (e.g., Kinsey, Pomeroy, & Martin, 1948; Kinsey, Pomeroy, Martin, & Gebhard, 1953; Laumann, Gagnon, Michael, & Michaels, 1994; see also Bogaert, 2006). In fact, on nearly all aspects of sexuality, variation is found, with some such variations judged differently from others. For example, some people are of the opinion that only heterosexual behavior between married persons is acceptable or "normal"; others

think that consent is the crucial element to classify a sexual behavior as "normal"; and still others have the view that only "natural" sexual behavior should be considered "normal" (e.g.,
Karasic & Drescher, 2005).

Whatever one's view on what constitutes "normal" sexual
behavior, judgment of a particular sexual behavior (e.g., masturbation, homosexuality, rape, or pedophilia) as "(ab)normal" is
made from a normative perspective that defines certain sexual behaviors as deviant (Laws & O'Donohue, 1997; Wakefield, 2005).
Just as in society at large, there are different views in the field of
sexology as to what constitutes sexual normality and abnormality
(Osborne & Wise, 2005). Fundamentally, two dominant paradigms exist in sexology, each of which defines abnormal sexuality
quite differently: (1) the (psycho)pathological paradigm and the
(2) interpersonal social-psychological or sociological paradigm
(Kelly & Lusk, 1992; Kleinplatz & Moser, 2005; Moser & Kleinplatz, 2005; Spitzer, 2005; Verhaeghe, 2002). Sometimes a third
paradigm is added: (3) the statistical paradigm, which defines abnormality of a behavior by its deviation from the mean. However,
as has been argued convincingly by Bancroft (1989) and Wakefield (1992) along with others, the statistical norm is of little use
in defining abnormality because "statistical criteria tell us nothing
of the value or of the problems associated with a particular form
of behaviour" (Bancroft, 1989, p. 332). Consequently, the statistical paradigm is not considered in this chapter.

The psychopathological paradigm defines deviant sexuality
as a symptom of a psychopathological disorder of an individual. In
doing so, the assumption is made that there exists a "natural,"
evolutionary grounded and, at the core, cross-culturally invariant
sexual development, which results in a normal sexual object
choice with another adult human being (e.g., Spitzer, 2005). The
most influential prototype for this approach is the *Diagnostic and
Statistical Manual of Mental Disorders* (*DSM*; American Psychiatric
Association, 2000). The *DSM* classifies paraphilias—or disorders in
the sexual object choice—as "mental disorders," which are thus
defined as: "a clinically significant behavioral or psychological
syndrome or pattern that occurs in an individual and that is associated with present distress (e.g., a painful symptom) or disability
(i.e., impairment in one or more important areas of functioning)
or with a significant increased risk of suffering death, pain, disability, or an important loss of freedom. In addition, this syndrome or pattern must not be merely an expectable and culturally
sanctioned response to a particular event, for example the death
of a loved one. Whatever its original cause, it must currently be
considered a manifestation of a behavioral, psychological, or biological dysfunction in the individual. Neither deviant behavior
(e.g., political, religious, or sexual) nor conflicts that are primarily

between the individual and society are mental disorders unless the deviance or conflict is a symptom of a dysfunction in the individual" (*DSM-IV-TR*, p. xxxi).

The interpersonal, social-psychological, or sociological paradigm defines deviant sexuality not as a disorder of an individual, but as a transgression or violation of a social norm that is adhered to by a specific social group, institutions (e.g., the law), or societies as a whole (Plummer, 1975). The basic assumption is that "natural" or "normal" sexuality is not directed toward one clear class of sexual objects, but can have many forms of expression. Deviance is nothing more than the result of a social agreement by which a rule is stated that identifies some sexual behaviors as "normal" and other behaviors as "abnormal." In contrast with the psychopathological paradigm that supposes a biologically based and invariant development of sexuality, the sociological paradigm stresses judicial, cross-cultural, and historical variance in the definitions and classifications of abnormal sexuality (e.g., Green, 2002; Kleinplatz & Moser, 2005; Moser & Kleinplatz, 2005).

The influence of the two dominant paradigms has waxed and waned. In the 1960s, 1970s, and early 1980s, many sexologists adhered to the interpersonal, social-psychological, or sociological paradigm. Ever since, the psychopathological paradigm has regained significant influence (e.g., Bradford, 2000, 2006; Kafka, 2003, 2007; see also, Blanchard, Cantor, & Robichaud, 2006), possibly associated with a growing medicalization and pharmacologization of sexology in Western societies in particular. Furthermore, in recent years, the viewpoint that the paraphilias are the result of biopathology has become stronger (e.g., Blanchard et al., 2006; Kafka, 2007). This viewpoint has been expressed eloquently by Blanchard and colleagues (2006): "For many decades, anomalous sexual behavior has been widely viewed as the product of anything but anomalous brain development: classical conditioning, operant conditioning, psychodynamic processes, sexual politics, deficient social skills, reenactment of childhood traumas, and so on. In this context, the simple proposition that abnormal brains may produce abnormal sexual behavior is a relatively radical one, with the potential to energize a whole new generation of more sophisticated and more powerful research studies" (p. 100).

Despite their differences, a certain rapprochement between the two paradigms over the past 35 years has occurred (Gijs, 1994). Since the American Psychiatric Association has normalized homosexuality by a democratic referendum in 1974, "sex with consent" has become the norm of the psychopathological paradigm, a norm that is currently also the social and judicial norm in many societies. That norm can be violated by "unwillingness" or by "powerlessness." "Unwillingness" refers to violent sexual behavior in which the norm of consent is instrumentally violated; "powerlessness," on the other hand, refers to the impossibility to comply with the norm of consent as a consequence of a "mental disorder."

Nevertheless, much confusion remains about the difference between "paraphilic deviance" and "violent sexual behavior" (Maletzky, 2002; Marshall, 2007; Studer & Aylwin, 2006). Although some experts conceptualize violent sexual behavior as a result or even a symptom of a paraphilia, others disagree and think of violent sexual behavior as an unacceptable social and interpersonal behavior that can be caused by many different factors (Laws & Marshall, 2003; Marshall & Laws, 2003). This conceptual confusion is further increased by the simultaneously and often not well differentiated use of terms such as "sexual obsessive-compulsive disorder," "sexual impulse disorder," "sex addiction," "perversion," and "paraphilia."

This chapter provides an introductory overview of current sexological thinking and clinical practice about the paraphilias. In doing so, the psychopathological paradigm is used as a guiding framework because, in our opinion, there are good arguments to classify the paraphilias as a psychopathological disorder. However, the viewpoint that (some) paraphilias are atypical, but not disordered, sexual variation (e.g., Baumeister & Butler, 1997; Reiersøl & Skeid, 2006), will not be neglected. Furthermore, separate attention is given to the so-called "paraphilia related disorders" (e.g., Kafka, 2007). For an overview of current sexological thinking regarding sexual violence the reader is referred to Ward, Polashek, and Beech (2005) as well as Knight and Guay (2006) and Malamuth, Huppin, and Paul (2005).

Definition, Prevalence, Incidence, and Phenomenology

Definition

Originating from the Greek "para" (beyond, alongside of) and "philia" (love), the term *paraphilia* was already in use by the psychiatrist Stekel in the first quarter of the twentieth century. The term however was not popularized until the *Diagnostic and Statistical Manual of Mental Disorders*, third edition (*DSM-III*) preferred the term *paraphilia* over "sexual deviation" because the first term "correctly emphasizes that the deviation (para) is in that to which the individual is attracted (philia)" (*DSM-III*, American Psychiatric Association, 1980, p. 267). The most recent version of the *DSM*, the *Diagnostic and Statistical Manual of Mental Disorders*, fourth edition, text revision (*DSM-IV-TR*; American Psychiatric Association, 2000, p. 566) defines paraphilias by using two criteria:

1. "Recurrent, intense sexually arousing fantasies, sexual urges, or behaviors generally involving (1) nonhuman objects,

(2) the suffering or humiliation of oneself or one's partner, or (3) children or other nonconsenting persons that occur over a period of at least 6 months (Criterion A)."

2. The paraphilic fantasies, urges, and behaviors "cause clinically significant distress or impairment in social, occupational, or other important areas of functioning (Criterion B)."

In contrast with *DSM-IV,* the B criterion is no longer deemed necessary in *DSM-IV-TR* in order to diagnose the following paraphilias: pedophilia, voyeurism, exhibitionism, and sexual sadism (with a nonconsenting partner). In other words, if the person has acted on his sexual impulses, the diagnosis of pedophilia, voyeurism, exhibitionism, or sexual sadism (with a nonconsenting partner) is justified. Hilliard and Spitzer (2002) have rightfully signaled that this change is conceptually incongruent with the definition of a mental disorder in the *DSM,* which assumes suffering as a defining characteristic of a mental disorder. The reasons for this change have not been explained by the *DSM* (see Sidebar 16.1).

SIDEBAR 16.1

Sexual and Gender Identity Disorders in DSM-IV-TR (2000): Paraphilias

Paraphilias: The essential features . . . are . . . recurrent, intense sexually arousing fantasies, sexual urges, or behaviors generally involving (1) nonhuman objects, (2) the suffering or humiliation of oneself or one's partner, or (3) children or other nonconsenting persons that occur over a period of at least 6 months (Criterion A).

For Pedophilia, Voyeurism, Exhibitionism, and Frotteurism, the diagnosis is made if the person has acted on these urges or the urges or sexual fantasies cause marked distress or interpersonal difficulty. For Sexual Sadism, the diagnosis is made if the person has acted on these urges with a nonconsenting person or the urges, sexual fantasies, or behaviors cause marked distress or interpersonal difficulty. For the remaining Paraphilias, the diagnosis is made if the behavior, sexual urges, or fantasies cause clinically significant distress or impairment in social, occupational, or other important areas of functioning (Criterion B).

Types of Paraphilia and Paraphilic Focus

302.4 Exhibitionism: the exposure of one's genitals to a stranger.

302.1 Fetishism: the use of nonliving objects (the "fetish").

302.89 Frotteurism: touching and rubbing against a nonconsenting person.

302.2 Pedophilia: a sexual activity with a prepubescent child (generally age 13 years or younger) and the individual with pedophilia must be age 16 years or older and at least 5 years older than the child.

302.83 Sexual Masochism: the act (real, not stimulated) of being humiliated, beaten, bound, or otherwise made to suffer.

302.84 Sexual Sadism: acts (real, not stimulated) in which the individual derives sexual excitement from the psychological or physical suffering (including humiliation) of the victim.

302.3 Transvestic Fetishism: cross-dressing by a male in women's attire.

302.82 Voyeurism: the act of observing unsuspecting individuals, usually strangers, who are naked, in the process of disrobing, or engaging in sexual activity.

302.9 Paraphilia not otherwise specified: do not meet the criteria for any of the specific categories (e.g., telephone scatologia, necrophilia, partialism, zoophilia, coprophilia, klismaphilia, urophilia).

Although the influence of the *DSM* is significant, a number of important critiques of the definition and the diagnostic criteria of paraphilia by the *DSM* have been offered (Green, 2002; Kleinplatz & Moser, 2005; Marshall, 1997, 2007; Moser, 2001; Moser & Kleinplatz, 2005; O'Donohue, Regev, & Hagstrom, 2000; Studer & Aylwin, 2006). The two most important criticisms are that the *DSM* classification of paraphilias lacks reliability and validity. The reliability of the diagnostic criteria used by the *DSM* is not satisfactory. Various studies have found that the interrater reliability of paraphilic diagnoses remains far below the psychometric norm of a kappa coefficient of .90 (Marshall, 2007, for a review). As a consequence, different clinicians are not reaching the same diagnosis on the basis of the same information. The validity problem can be explained as follows: the *DSM* is classifying some sexual variations as paraphilias unrightfully; in other words, these sexual variations are not a "manifestation of a behavioral, psychological, or biological dysfunction in the individual." Through the present, there has been debate about the (lack of validity of the) classifications of homosexuality, rape, sadomasochism, transvestic fetishism, and pedophilia as paraphilias. Homosexuality was deleted from the *DSM* in 1974 by a democratic vote of the American Psychiatric Association. Interestingly, rape had been removed from the *DSM* since 1980. Some experts have argued that this change is correct while others disagree.

In light of the expected publication of the *DSM-V* in 2010, the debate about the inclusion of rape in the *DSM* has recently intensified (see Prentky, Janus, Barbaree, Schwartz, & Kafka, 2006). Up to the present, rape has not been included as a psychiatric disorder in the *DSM-IV-TR*. In contrast, and despite vigorous controversy, sadomasochism, transvestic fetishism, and pedophilia are still classified as paraphilias in the *DSM*. Although proposals to delete the paraphilias from the *DSM* (e.g., Moser & Kleinplatz, 2005) may seem unrealistic or sound like "a bridge too far," the *DSM* classification of paraphilias yet has many problems and is urgently in need of revision and validation (e.g., Kingston, Firestone, Moulden, & Bradford, 2007; Marshall, 1997, 2007; Moser & Kleinplatz, 2005). Furthermore, the incorrect inclusion of some sexual variations as paraphilias runs the risk of medicalizing, pathologizing, and stigmatizing some sexual variations (Irvine, 1995).

As a psychiatric classification system, the *DSM* has only one competitor: the much less popular *ICD-10* (1992, 1993). The conceptualization of the paraphilias by the *ICD-10* is much the same as that of the *DSM*. However, instead of the term *paraphilias*, the *ICD-10* prefers the term *disorders of sexual preference*.

The *DSM* has until now been a syndromal categorical system. As is the case for many disorders—and especially for the so-called personality disorders (e.g., Clark, 2007; Widiger & Trull, 2007)—there is an alternative dimensional conceptualization called "the sexual preference hypothesis" or "the sexual orientation conceptualization" (Barbaree & Seto, 1997). In this conceptualization, a paraphilia is viewed as a trait that can be nearly absent or very strong and that predisposes a person toward (paraphilic) behavior. The markers of this disposition or trait are paraphilic sexual fantasies, paraphilic sexual attraction, and paraphilic sexual arousal. However, a (paraphilic) predisposition is conceptually not the same as (paraphilic or unlawful) behavior, which is mostly multidetermined. In other words, it is conceptually possible that a person with a paraphilia (e.g., pedophilia) is not acting on that paraphilia (e.g., child molesting behavior) (Barbaree & Seto, 1997; Seto, 2004).

Prevalence and Incidence

The prevalence of most paraphilias in the Western world is unknown due to an absence of representative epidemiological studies of paraphilias in the general population (Långström & Seto, 2006; Quinsey, Rice, Harris, & Reid, 1993). Recently, however, Långström and colleagues reported the prevalence of exhibitionism, voyeurism, and transvestic fetishism in a representative sample of the Swedish population between 18 and 74 years of age (Långström & Seto, 2006; Långström & Zucker, 2005; see also: Långström & Hanson, 2006). They found that 4.1% of men and 2.1% of women had at least one episode of exhibitionistic behavior. The lifetime prevalence for voyeuristic behavior was 11.5% for men and 3.9% for women. At least one episode of transvestic fetishism was experienced by 2.8% of men and by 0.4% of women.

Research into the prevalence or incidence of paraphilias in the nonWestern world is nonexistent. Bhugra (2000) has put forward the interesting hypothesis that the paraphilias are culture bound western syndromes. Nevertheless, case reports of paraphilias in nonWestern-cultures (e.g., Bhardwaj, Rautji, Sharma, & Dogra, 2004; Dewaraja & Money, 1986) suggest that paraphilias are not unique to Western cultures. However, research into the cross-cultural prevalence of paraphilias is virtually nonexistent. Neither is there research into factors that might mediate or moderate the cross-cultural prevalence of paraphilias.

From a developmental perspective, it is not clear when paraphilias first begin. The frequent assumption is that the crucial developmental period is approximately between 12 and 18 years of age (puberty and/or adolescence) (e.g., Bradford & Fedoroff, 2006). Congruent with this view is the fact that children can fall in love from their fourth or fifth year of life (Hatfield, Schmitz, Cornelius, & Rapson, 1988), but that people remember their first sexual fantasies at the age of 12 or 13 (Leitenberg & Henning, 1995). Also congruent with this view is research on sex offenders indicating that paraphilias often start in (early) adolescence (e.g., Abel, Osborn, & Twigg, 1993). However, as a consequence of a lack of prospective and representative data, it is premature to draw any conclusions regarding the onset of paraphilias. Furthermore, theoretical models assume different critical periods for the development of various paraphilias (see below the paragraph on theoretical models).

The prevalence of paraphilias is much higher in men than women. Abel and Osborne (2000) estimate the sex ratio of 30 to 1. Although there may be differences among specific paraphilias—for example, lust murder or sex killing is much less prevalent in women (e.g., Bradford, 2006)—and the ratio 30 to 1 is probably an overestimate, all indications suggest that the prevalence of paraphilia is much higher in men than in women. In the previously cited studies of Långström and colleagues, the sex ratio was 2:1 for exhibitionistic behavior, 3:1 for voyeuristic behavior, and 7:1 for transvestic fetishism (Långström & Hanson, 2006; Långström & Seto, 2006; Långström & Zucker, 2005). Four hypotheses have been proposed to explain the differences in prevalence between men and women: (1) men have a greater biological sexual plasticity and as a consequence are more easily conditioned to a wider range of "sex objects"; (2) as a consequence of their greater visual sexual sensitivity, men are more vulnerable to develop a paraphilia; (3) because men have to de-identify with their first "love object," namely their mother, they are more vulnerable than girls to develop a paraphilia; or, in contrast to the previous three, (4) there is no difference between the sexual preferences of men and women, but only men are culturally allowed to express their varied sexual preferences. None of these hypothetical explanations has been empirically validated, and the causes of the sex differences in the prevalence of paraphilias between men and women remain an enigma.

Phenomenology

DSM-IV-TR (American Psychiatric Association, 2000) differentiates nine paraphilias. With the exception of "frotteurism," which is not mentioned in *ICD-10*, *ICD-10* lists nearly the same paraphilias as the *DSM*. However, two additional categories of the *ICD-10* not listed in the *DSM* are: "Multiple disorders of sexual preference" and "Other disorders of sexual preference."

In contrast with the short lists of the *DSM* and the *ICD*, some authors describe dozens of other paraphilias (e.g., Milner & Dopke, 1997; Money, 1986). Some are relatively benign (e.g., infantilism); others are very dangerous (e.g., asphyxiophilia and sex killings: see Petrunik & Weisman, 2005). Most such unusual paraphilias are rare (Langevin, 1983). However, some of them (such as asphyxiophilia, sex killing, or necrophilia) are encountered on a more regular basis in the forensic practice (e.g., Bauer, Tatschner, & Patzelt, 2007; Briken, Habermann, Berner, & Hill, 2005; Hill, Habermann, Berner, & Briken, 2006; Purcell & Arrigo, 2006; Sauvageau & Racette, 2006).

In general, we are struck by the great variety of the paraphilias, which then leads to the question of whether they represent distinct versus correlated categories. Opinions differ greatly. The *DSM*, for example, assumes that different paraphilias are correlated rather strongly, and some empirical studies have corroborated this view (e.g., Abel & Osborn, 2000; Freund, Seto, & Kuban, 1997; Price, Kafka, Commons, Gutheil, & Simpson, 2002). However, Marshall and Eccles (1991) have not found evidence that exhibitionists and child molesters have other paraphilias as well. Until now, we have no sound explanation for these different results (Marshall, 2007).

An important clinical consequence is that a diagnostic assessment should try to make an inventory of all the different paraphilias in one client/patient. Money has proposed to differentiate between a simple and a multiplex paraphilia (Lehne & Money, 2003). A multiplex paraphilia is defined as "a paraphilia having many parts or elements, each interconnected around a primary fixation" (p. 62) and is seen as the result of one underlying disorder. It is this central disorder that should be targeted by therapeutic intervention. Although not identified specifically with the terminology of multiplex paraphilia, a similar view on the therapeutic consequences of the occurrence of different paraphilias in one person has recently been stated by Marshall (2007): "Surely our goal in treatment is not to train our clients to concretely deal with each paraphilia independently, or to see each identified risk factor as fixed and as involving a fixed unchangeable set of problems. What we need to do in assessment and treatment is to encourage sexual offenders to develop an understanding of why it is they seek deviant ways to meet their needs and provide them with the skills and attitudes necessary to meet their needs in prosocial ways." In contrast with the view of Marshall and Money, Abel and colleagues (Abel & Rouleau, 1990; Abel & Osborn, 2000) favor the conceptualization that different paraphilias in one person should be viewed as discrete categories and should be treated as such.

Finally, there is currently a debate about the (phenomenological) relations between transvestic fetishism and transsexuality, and between autogynephilia and transsexuality. Bailey (2003; see also Blanchard, 2005; Lawrence, 2004, 2006), for example, has suggested that at least in some male-to-female transsexuals, autogynephilia—in which a biological male has the image of himself as a female as "his" erotic object or preference—is a precursor or determinant of the development of transsexuality. Unfortunately, little research exists to support or refute this hypothesis.

Theoretical Models

Theoretical explanations of paraphilia can be divided into the pathological approach and the normality-theory approach (see Figure 16.1; Kelly & Lusk, 1992). The pathological view begins with the assumption that a paraphilia is (a symptom of) a disorder. In contrast, a normality-theory emanates from the idea that a

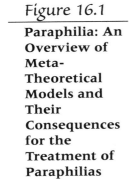

Figure 16.1

Paraphilia: An Overview of Meta-Theoretical Models and Their Consequences for the Treatment of Paraphilias

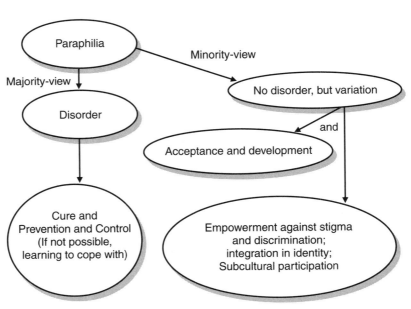

paraphilia is a normal variant of sexual variation. The pathological paradigm is clearly dominant in the literature. However, little research has empirically tested either theoretical assumption, and during the past 2 decades little theoretical innovation on the topic of paraphilias has occurred. The reasons for this stagnation are not clear. Perhaps it results from the strong influence of forensic approaches, which focus less on a theoretical understanding of the paraphilias and more on controlling paraphilic (and unlawful) behavior (Verhaeghe, 2002).

Normality Theories

Normality theories conceptualize sexual desire not as a "naturally" determined trait, but as an empty potential for the experience of lust (e.g., Foucault, 1976; Plummer, 1975; Simon, 1994). The content and object of sexual desire is shaped by interaction with the social environment (Plummer, 1975; Simon, 1994). This social environment also decides what is sexually allowed or not and what is sexually normal and abnormal. Historically, among the first proponents of a normality perspective were Kinsey and colleagues (1949) who argued: "In the light of these accumulated data, we must conclude that current concepts of normality and abnormality in human sexual behavior represent what are primarily moral evaluations. They have little if any biologic justification. The problem presented by the so-called sexual perversions is a product of the disparity between the basic biologic heritage of the human animal, and the traditional, cultural codes. It is society's reaction to the individual who departs from the code, or the individual's fear of social reaction if his departure from the code is discovered, which is most often responsible for his personality disturbances. The problem of the so-called sexual perversions is not so much one of psychopathology as it is a matter of adjustment between an individual and the society in which he lives" (p. 32). In the more social-psychological oriented variants of this approach, it is assumed that the personal self has a rather strong regulatory influence on sexuality (e.g., Baumeister & Butler, 1997).

A prototypical exponent of this normality perspective is Baumeister (e.g., 1989). His hypothesis is that a too strong explicit emphasis on the development of a personal and individualized self—as, for example, is the case in the Western world—is dysfunctional and will lead to feelings of unhappiness and overburdening. In response to these feelings, people try to escape the burden of an overvalued personal self by activating some coping-mechanism to delete or at least diminish, temporarily, the focus on the personal self by generating very intense physical sensations in the here and now. One of those coping-mechanisms is sexual masochism. Sexual masochism not only diminishes the attention for the personal self, but is also at the same time sexually pleasurable. More precisely, the experience of sexual pain prevents the activation of (attention for) the (schema of the) personal self, and the experience of loss of control deletes the personal self as an autonomous decision maker. The historical fact that sexual masochism is practiced much more in higher socioeconomic classes and emerged after 1500 is interpreted by Baumeister as strong evidence for his theory (Baumeister & Butler, 1997). Higher socioeconomic classes emphasize the personal self much stronger than lower classes, and before 1500, the concept of a personal self in Western societies was absent. Aside from Baumeister's own research, very little research has empirically tested this escape-from-self theory. However, Cross and Matheson's (2006) Internet study with a group of 93 self-identified sadomasochists did not corroborate Baumeister's theory because—among other things—sadists were not from lower social classes than masochists.

Although theoretically not very connected to Baumeister's theoretical view, research has been done on sadomasochism from a normality perspective. The focus of this research has been on the development of a personal identity as a "sadomasochist" and on the development of and integration in sadomasochistic subcultures (Dancer, Kleinplatz, & Moser, 2006; Nordling, Sandnabba, Santtila, & Alison, 2006; Plante, 2006; Weinberg, 2006). With the exception of sadomasochism, little theory-building or research from the normality-perspective has occurred. In most cases, authors who defend the normality-perspective have offered this perspective as an alternative to pathological and social-oppressive views.

Psychopathological Theories

Psychoanalytical Conceptualizations

The psychoanalyst Freud (1905) was of the opinion that the sexual instinct strives for heterosexual coitus, thus making it the normal goal or aim of sexuality. By implication, a person of the other sex is the normal object of the sexual instinct. The normal goal is, however, not automatically present from birth on, but is the result of a developmental trajectory. At birth a person is "polymorf pervers," meaning that different erogenic zones of the human body, or the partial components of human sexuality, are not yet integrated. That integration is achieved by passing unconsciously, but adequately, through the different phases of sexual development in approximately the first 5 years of life. As a result of a successful development, the different components of the sexual instinct are integrated under the umbrella of the so called genital primate, by which coitus becomes the primary mean to achieve sexual gratification. To reach such a successful development, the different developmental tasks of the different phases should be solved sufficiently. In the traditional Freudian theory, these phases are: the oral, the anal, and the phallic stadium (and for the determination of the object choice, the oedipal phase). If the passing of a developmental phase is not sufficiently successful, paraphilic symptoms or a full blown paraphilia may result. These effects are seen as an unsuccessful—pathological—attempt to cope with the suffering from an underlying unconscious developmental conflict. In its manifestation, the paraphilic symptomatology concerns sexual activities with body parts or impersonal objects that allow no normal union and no normal contact with a person of the other sex (e.g., fetishism), or that result in sexual activities that are only a "prestage" to the normal aim of sexuality (e.g., voyeurism, exhibitionism, sexual sadism, sexual masochism).

Since Freud's original conceptualization, many different psychoanalytical theories have been formulated (e.g., Rosen, 1996; Socarides, 1988; Stoller, 1975; see also Osborn & Wise, 2005). They differ in their view as to which conflicts in which developmental phases lead to the development of a paraphilia, but they share the idea that a paraphilia is an unconscious symptom of an insufficiently solved developmental task in the first 6 years of life. The core themes of these conflicts are: the development and separation of the self, the development of gender identity, and object relations.

Learning Theory and Social-Cognitive Views
Learning and sociocognitive theories have evolved from single factor conditioning theories to multidimensional biopsychosocial conceptualizations of paraphilias (Figures 16.2 and 16.3). Originally, a paraphilia was seen as the result of classical conditioning. Due to accidental but sufficiently frequent association between sexual arousal and especially orgasm, any stimulus could become the object of sexual desire (e.g., McGuire, Carlisle, & Young,

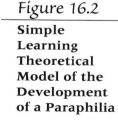

Figure 16.2

Simple Learning Theoretical Model of the Development of a Paraphilia

Note: Based on the work of McGuire et al. (1965).

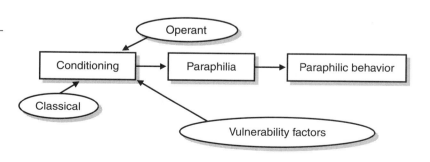

Figure 16.3

Multifactorial (Social-Cognitive) Learning Model of the Development of a Paraphilia

Note: Based on the work of Abel and Rouleau, 1990; Abel and Osborn, 2000; and Laws and Marshall (1990).

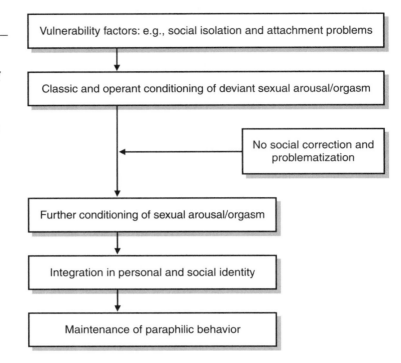

1965). In particular, the pairing of orgasm during masturbation with paraphilic fantasies was seen as a crucial determinant in the development of a paraphilia. When, for example, an adolescent masturbates on a fantasy of leather boots, these boots will later become the object of sexual desire (see, e.g., the early research of Rachman, 1966; Rachman & Hodgson, 1968).

Recent learning and social-cognitive views attribute the development of a paraphilia to three key processes (Abel & Osborn, 2000; Laws & Marshall, 1990). The first one is the conditioning of a paraphilic preference or orientation; second, the reinforcement of a developing paraphilia by the continuing association of a deviant stimulus with the pleasure of orgasm, if the paraphilia is not negatively socially sanctioned and problematized; and finally, the paraphilia will be incorporated into the personal and social identity so that a life-pattern takes shape that contributes to the maintenance of the paraphilia.

Finally, it is important to note that learning and sociocognitive theories increasingly emphasize the importance of vulnerability factors. Presumably, as a consequence of our evolutionary history, some sexual stimuli are conditioned more easily than others and some persons are more vulnerable due to attachment problems or social isolation (e.g., Marshall, 1989).

Money's Theory of Love-Map Disorders

Based on phylogenetic considerations, Money (1986, 1999) assumes that heterosexual coitus is the typical outcome of normal sexual development. A necessary prerequisite to reach that normal developmental outcome is sexual rehearsal play in childhood, because during normal sexual rehearsal play children form a love-map. A love-map is defined as a "developmental representation synchronously existent in the mind and the brain (the mindbrain) depicting the idealized lover, the idealized love and sexual affair, and the idealized solo or partnered program of sexuoerotic activity projected in private imagery and ideation or in observable performance" (Money, 1997, p. 101). Once such a love-map has been formed, it is, according to Money, nearly unchangeable. Based on his clinical experience, Money has put forward the hypothesis that the critical period for the (eventually disordered) development of a love-map lies between the ages of 5 and 10. Money hypothesized further that in that 5-year span the age period between 8 and 10 years may be the most influential, because in that same period androgen levels rise due to the adrenarche (initial functioning of the adrenal glands). The love-map formed in the period between 5 and 8 will be sexualized by puberty so that prototypically a normal sexual orientation is the result. Such a normal development can become distorted—or in Money's terminology "vandalized"—when normal sexual rehearsal play is distorted by sexual repression, sexual abuse, or sexual exposure at too early an age. The result of such a pathological development is a paraphilia. In other words, a paraphilia is the result of the sexualization by puberty of a pathological love-map, by which sexual arousal and orgasm become dependent on an atypical and/or unacceptable stimulus (see Figure 16.4). As a result of this pathological development, a

Figure 16.4

Money's View of the Development of a Paraphilia

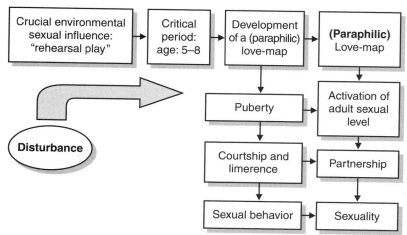

paraphilia creates a structural psychological distance toward a sexual partner. As a consequence, a reciprocal sexual union with a partner becomes impossible.

Based on clinical experience, Money posits that paraphilias have several specific characteristics: (a) they are characterized by an altered state of consciousness, the paraphilic fugue state, which shows parallels with dissociation and epilepsy; (b) between episodes of paraphilic behavior, the paraphilic person fantasizes obsessively and isolates himself socially; (c) a cyclic pattern between the paraphilic fugue state and obsessive fantasizing arises; and (d) the paraphilic exhibits hyperorgasm, as many as 4 to 10 orgasms a day. To our knowledge, there have been no empirical tests of Money's theoretical views.

Although Money (2002) views a paraphilia as a disorder, he offers the following clinical guideline: "Diagnostically, paraphilias range from nonpathological in degree to pathological—in other words from playful (ludic) to harmless, to harmfully self-injurious, to assaultive and homicidal. Provided the players are in concordance with one another, harmless paraphilias do not necessitate intervention, either disciplinary or ostensibly curative" (pp. 90–91). It would be interesting to know how many clinicians agree with Money's view and treat their patients accordingly.

Freund's Theory of Courtship Disorders

Freund and his colleagues distinguish four phases in the normal sexual interpersonal sequence: the perception of a potential partner, pretactile interaction, tactile interaction, and genital union (Sidebar 16.2; Freund, 1990; Freund et al., 1997). Courtship disorders are defined by Freund as distortions of the normal sexual interpersonal sequence, so that the different phases are deformed or intensified. Voyeurism is a distortion of the first phase. Exhibitionism is a disturbance of the second phase. Frotteurism is a dysregulation of the third phase. Preferential rape is a disorder of the last phase. Based on the correlations (depending on the specific association measure, roughly between .15 and .54) among these paraphilias, with the exception of preferential rape (Freund et al., 1997), Freund concluded that they are caused by the same underlying disorder. A different symptomatology (e.g., exhibitionism versus frotteurism) is conceptualized as a consequence of differences in the severity of the underlying disorder. And, possibly, a progression may occur from more mild forms of courtship disorder to more severe ones (e.g., Sugerman, Dughn, Saad, Hinder, & Bluglass, 1994). The key element of the underlying problem in the courtship disorders is "the preference of these patients for a virtually instant conversion of sexual arousal into orgasm" (Freund et al., 1997, p. 113).

SIDEBAR 16.2

Freund's Model of the Courtship Disorders

Perception of a potential partner	Pretactile interaction	Tactile interaction	Genital union
Voyeurism	Exhibitionism	Frotteurism	Preferential rape

Biopathological Theories

The central biopathological hypothesis is that the paraphilias are the result of a genetic, hormonal, or brain defect (Blanchard et al., 2006; Gaffney & Berlin, 1984; Gaffney, Lurie, & Berlin, 1984; Kafka, 2003, 2007; see also Giotakos, Markianos, Vaidakis, & Christodoulou, 2004). This defect either directly causes the paraphilia or increases the person's vulnerability to the development of a paraphilia. Until now, the evidence for a genetic or hormonal influence on the development of a paraphilia has been weak (Blanchard et al., 2006; Osborn & Wise, 2005), although Gaffney et al. (1984) have shown higher rates of pedophilia in first-degree relatives of persons with pedophilia and higher rates of nonpedophilic paraphilias in the first-degree relatives of nonpedophilic paraphiles. As Blanchard and colleagues (2006) have remarked, this study still awaits replication. Recently, the following factors have received the most attention in biopathological theories of paraphilias: the monoamine hypothesis, the number and meaning of older brothers, the influence of brain injuries, and the influence of our evolutionary history.

Inspired by the positive outcomes of treatments with selective serotonin reuptake inhibitors (SSRIs) and the clinical parallels between the paraphilias and obsessive-compulsive and impulse control disorders, Kafka (e.g., 2003) hypothesized most influentially that paraphilias are the result of a disturbance of the cerebral regulation of sexuality by the neurotransmitters dopamine, serotonin, and norephinephrine. As a consequence of this cerebral dysregulation, the following symptoms are caused: an extension or intensification of a paraphilic interest, a (much) higher frequency of sexual desire and behavior, and a dysregulation of the control of impulses. Maes and colleagues (Maes, De Vos, et al., 2001; Maes, van West, et al., 2001) reported that persons with pedophilia were, in comparison to a normal control group, characterized by lower baselines of cortisol and prolactin, higher levels of catecholamines, in particular ephinephrine, and higher body temperature. These results were interpreted as support for the hypothesis that disturbed regulation of serotonin causes the development of a paraphilia.

Blanchard and colleagues (Blanchard et al., 2003; Bogaert, Bezeau, Kuban, & Blanchard, et al., 1997; Cantor et al., 2004; see also the review of Blanchard et al., 2006) attempted to discover what factors differentiate persons with pedophilia from those without pedophilia. They found that homosexual pedophile persons have a later birth order than heterosexual pedophile persons; in other words, the former group has, on average, a higher number of older brothers. Pedophilic people also have lower average IQ, they are more likely to be left-handed, and they reported more head injuries before the age of 13 (and not later) than control subjects. These investigators concluded that unknown prenatal or postnatal neuro-hormonal or neuro-developmental factors influence the development of a (pedophilic) paraphilia.

One final biological model posits that paraphilia is the result of a disorder of the evolutionary-determined mechanism to find sexual partners (Figure 16.5; Quinsey, 2003; see also Epstein, 1975; Wilson, 1987). The underlying assumption of this model is that men will have an evolutionary-shaped preference for healthy and fertile women. The evolutionary advantage is that men can maximize their genetic reproductive success by impregnating as many healthy women as possible. In other words, evolution has shaped a specific male sexual preference system that includes specific neurobiological modules to select and interact adequately with partners of the correct evolutionary sex and age. As of now, specific empirical tests of this model have not been conducted. However, Quinsey (2003) interpreted the available evidence on proximate biological determinants of a paraphilia as congruent with his evolutionary based model.

Figure 16.5

Quinsey's Evolutionary Model

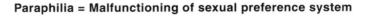

Paraphilia = Malfunctioning of sexual preference system

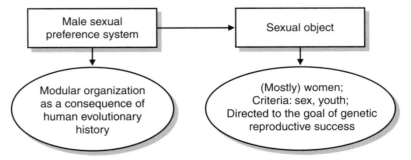

Care for Persons with Paraphilia

A subgroup of people with paraphilias consults the health care system. For therapists, it appears that the most important reasons to do so are suffering by the person him- or herself or pressure by others or society to change a negatively valued paraphilia.

Theoretically, persons with a paraphilia can be treated from two paradigms (Figure 16.1). On the one hand, the health care professional can attempt through treatment to optimize, to the extent possible, an egosyntonic development of a paraphilia. Important goals of such treatment are: acceptance of the paraphilia, integration of the paraphilia into one's identity and learning to give the paraphilia a prosocial place in personal and social life, and acquiring skills to cope with stigma and discrimination (e.g., Nichols, 2006; see also Kolmes, Stock, & Moser, 2006). This approach resembles affirmative therapy with lesbian, gay, and bisexual clients (Kolmes et al., 2006). The dominant view of most health care professionals, however, is that one tries to cure or control the paraphilia as much as possible (e.g., Bradford, 2000; Kafka, 2007; Osborne & Wise, 2005).

However, when clients explicitly ask to learn to accept and develop their paraphilia and there is no risk for abuse, or violent or unlawful behavior as, for example, is the case with fetishism, transvestic fetishism, and (consensual) sado-masochism, some therapists choose to work from a paraphilia affirmative viewpoint (Kolmes et al., 2006). Unfortunately, few reports have described paraphilia-affirmative interventions and research into their efficacy or effectiveness is nonexistent.

In view of the different opinions on how to treat paraphilias, clients/patients have the right to be informed on the normative views of their therapists, and therapists have the duty to explore very thoughtfully and carefully the goals of their clients in order to determine if they can accept the goals of their clients.

In the twentieth century, the care for people with paraphilias has been dominated by psychoanalytic (cognitive-) behavior, and biomedical treatments (Gijs, 1994; Laws & Marshall, 2003; Marshall & Laws, 2003). During the past 30 years, cognitive-behavioral therapies have been the most popular interventions (Maletzky, 2002). Since about 1990, biomedical interventions have gained substantial influence. Remarkably, the ever-increasing influence of biomedical interventions has not been based on controlled research (Kafka, 2007). To the contrary, very few controlled studies regarding the effectiveness of pharmacological interventions with paraphilias have been conducted (e.g., Bancroft, Tennent, Lucas, & Cass, 1974; Kruesi, Fine, Valladares, Phillips, & Rapoport, 1992; Schober et al., 2005; Tennent, Bancroft, & Cass,

1974). Three reasons might account for the growing popularity of biomedical interventions: (1) a general trend in Western societies toward the medicalization of problems and the growing popularity of pharmacological interventions, (2) the realization that the effectiveness of cognitive-behavioral therapies is less than what was hoped for since those therapies came to the fore in the 1970s, and (3) the conclusion that, despite being based on approximately 200 to 300 case studies rather than on well-controlled research, pharmacological interventions are effective (Bradford, 2000; Bradford & Fedoroff, 2006; Kafka, 2003, 2007).

Assessment and Diagnosis

Ideally, assessment aims to answer the question "what is going on," not only in a descriptive and classificatory way, but also by diagnosing the determinants and processes that have led to the problem. Based on the results of the assessment, specific therapeutic interventions are indicated. Moreover, procedures for arriving at a diagnosis are explicated in the ideal diagnostic protocol. In the field of paraphilias, descriptions of such an ideal assessment process are rare. The impression clearly exists that the past 20 years have seen movement away from individualized assessment, and toward the application of standard omnibus treatment programs for people with paraphilias. This has especially been the situation within a forensic context (Marshall, 2007).

In our opinion, crucial dimensions in the assessment of the paraphilias are (a) the phenomenological dimension, (b) the biological dimension, (c) the (psycho)pathological dimension, and (d) the social dimension. In principle, two other dimensions can be added, although they are not relevant for all paraphilias: (e) the forensic dimension, and (f) the dangerousness dimension.

With regard to all these dimensions—the importance and interpretation of which depend on the theoretical orientation of the clinician—it is imperative to inventory which factors or determinants facilitate or inhibit the paraphilia. For a list of concrete questions to inventory the different dimensions, see Sidebar 16.3.

SIDEBAR 16.3

Diagnostic Questions for the Assessment of Paraphilias

1. What is the phenomenology of the paraphilia?
   a. What is the onset, intensity and frequency of the paraphilic sexual desire?
   b. Is the paraphilia experienced as ego-syntonic or dystonic?
   c. How is the paraphilia put in practice?

    d. What are the consequences of the paraphilia/paraphilic behavior?

    e. To what extent is the activation or the expression of the paraphilia situation specific?

2. Is there biological pathology?

    a. Are there indications for a genetic, hormonal, or brain deviation/defect?

    b. Is there other medical comorbidity that is relevant for the paraphilia?

3. Which psychopathology is present?

    a. What is the severity of the paraphilia?

    b. Which psychopathological comorbidity is present?

    c. What is the place of the paraphilia in the personal identity or self?

4. What is the social world of the client/patient?

    a. What is the social identity?

    b. What are the social skills of the person?

    c. What is the social network of the person?

    d. How is the social environment treating the paraphilic person and what are the consequences for the intensity/frequency of the paraphilia and for the comorbidity?

    e. Is the person embedded in a (criminal) subculture?

5. Are there forensic aspects involved?

    a. Is a judicial dimension involved?

    b. If so, what are the consequences for treatment?

6. Dangerousness-taxation?

    a. Is there suicide risk?

    b. Is there danger for other persons?

Before discussing specific diagnostic instruments, it is useful to pay attention to psychiatric and neurological comorbidity in people with paraphilias. Some clinicians suggest that comorbidity is low (e.g., Maletzky, 2002) whereas others argue a high rate of comorbidity. For example, Raymond, Coleman, Ohlerking, Christenson, and Miner (1999) reported that 93% of their mostly ambulant treated pedophilic patients had another Axis-I disorder and that 60% had a personality disorder. Specifically, affective and anxiety disorders, ADHD and conduct disorders, and alcohol and substance abuse are frequently encountered in persons with a paraphilia (Kafka, 2003; Lehne & Money, 2003). Nevertheless, the variance in comorbidity in the different studies is remarkable, as illustrated by three examples borrowed from a recent review by Marshall (2007). The comorbidity of mood disorders varies between 3% and 95%, that of anxiety disorders between 2.9% and 38.6%, and that of personality disorders between 33% and 52%.

At times, a paraphilic symptomatology may be a precursor to or signal of a vulnerability for psychotic disorders (Frost &

Chapman, 1987). However, in recent studies on clinical populations, the lifetime prevalence of psychotic and schizoaffective disorders was low: for example, 2.2% reported by Raymond et al. (1999) and 5.6% reported by Kafka and Hennen (2002).

It is important to note that paraphilic symptomatology and syndromes have been reported as a consequence of neurologic trauma to the frontal lobes and the hippocampus and as a correlate of diseases such as multiple sclerosis, dementia, and tumors (e.g., Burns & Swerdlow, 2003; Casanova, Mannheim, & Kruesi, 2002; Dhikav, Anand, & Aggarwal, 2007; Frohman, Frohman, & Moreault, 2002). A neuropsychological and neurologic assessment should be integral parts of the global assessment procedure of paraphilias (see also, Abel & Osborn, 2000). Finally, it is important to mention that in some cases paraphilic symptoms and/or hypersexuality is the result of the pharmacological treatment of Parkinson's disease by pergolide, selegiline, or dopamine agonists (Cannas et al., 2006; Klos, Bower, Josephs, Matsumoto, & Ahlskog, 2005; Riley, 2002; Shapiro Chang, Munson, Okun, & Fernandez, 2006).

Many different diagnostic instruments have been used for the assessment of paraphilias (Maletzky, 2002; Seto, 2004). These include: the clinical interview, the sexological interview, psychological tests and, in some Anglo countries, penile plethysmography (Abel & Osborn, 2000; Maletzky, 2002). Furthermore, the use of the polygraph and the "Abel screen" has been explored in North America. Unfortunately, few validation studies have been carried out on these diagnostic strategies, and the few that have been conducted reveal significant problems (Maletzky, 2002).

Psychotherapeutic Interventions

Cognitive-Behavioral Treatments

As mentioned previously, behavioral and social-cognitive conceptualizations of the etiology of paraphilias have evolved from single factor to multifactorial theories. According to these conceptualizations, the key determinants of the development of a paraphilia are (a) the (classical and operant) conditioning of sexual arousal and orgasm; (b) the lack of social correction, by which the enjoyment of the paraphilic orgasm is not problematized or corrected; (c) the inclusion of the paraphilia in the personal and social identity; and (d) factors involving biological and/or psychological vulnerability. Closely associated with these conceptualizations, cognitive-behavioral treatment programs also changed from single to multifactorial treatment packages. In contrast with the dominance of aversion therapy in the 1960s, current cognitive-behavioral treatment packages include typically six modules (see Sidebar 16.4). For introductory reviews of specific cognitive-behavioral techniques, see Maletzky (2002) and Marshall, Anderson, and Fernandez (1999).

SIDEBAR 16.4

An Overview of the Six Typical Modules of Cognitive-Behavioral Treatment Packages

1. The reduction of deviant sexual arousal and acquisition of normative sexual arousal.
2. Acquisition or amelioration of social skills.
3. The challenge and reparation of cognitive processes as values, attitudes, and schemas that facilitate a paraphilic expression.
4. Acquisition or amelioration of relational skills (with special attention for intimacy and attachment).
5. Acquisition of problem-solving and coping skills to tackle life span and social tasks (e.g., unemployment or boredom).
6. Relapse-prevention by recognition and handling of lapses by means of adequate coping strategies.

Ideally, for each client the clinician carries out a functional analysis that precisely describes the paraphilia and explains its current existence by means of a detailed analysis of the controlling variables of the paraphilia and associated problems. However, in current standard clinical practice, individual functional analyses are made infrequently. Instead standard and homogeneous treatment packages are used for most clients with paraphilias (Marshall, 2007).

During the past 10 to 15 years, very few new developments in cognitive-behavioral treatments of paraphilias have occurred. Remarkably, attention to the sexual aspects of the paraphilias has diminished since the 1960s and 1970s, although the reason for this is not clear. It may be that the greater attention to nonsexual determinants of sexual deviant and sexual violent behavior has marginalized the role of sexual motivation, sexual arousal, and orgasm. Because deviant sexual arousal is clearly a risk factor for recidivism of sexual deviant and violent behavior (Hanson & Morton-Bourgon, 2005; Hildebrand, de Ruiter, & Vogel, 2004), renewed attention for paraphilic sexuality by cognitive-behavioral therapists is warranted.

The most important development in this field is related to the importance of the therapeutic relationship in the cognitive-behavioral treatment of paraphilias. In the 1960 to 1970s, cognitive-behavioral therapists did not consider the therapeutic relationship very important, but since then, two main views have been developed: (1) An aggressive confrontational style that holds the person accountable for his paraphilic behavior is a necessary component of the treatment and (2) A supportive but firmly challenging style that respects the person, but sets firm boundaries on deviant behavior, is most effective (Marshall et al., 2003). Based on an extensive literature review, Marshall and colleagues concluded that the second approach is much more effective.

Psychoanalytic Treatments

Although psychoanalytic treatments of paraphilias have lost predominance over the last 30 years and research from this perspective is almost nonexistent, psychoanalytic approaches remain influential in clinical practice. The many variants of this intervention model (e.g., Rosen, 1996; Socarides, 1988; Stoller, 1975) share the same core assumption that a paraphilia can be cured when the (assumed) underlying developmental psychological conflict is solved.

Despite differences in psychoanalytic approaches, the common core of their treatment of paraphilias has been described well by Van de Putte (1994). First, the therapist should determine if there is a valid indication for the start of an ambulant psychoanalytic therapy. Thus is the case if a person suffers from a paraphilia and realizes that it is causing harm, when there has been no violent behavior, and when there are enough possibilities for insight and introspection along with a motivation to change. Secondly, the therapist should create a holding environment, that is, a therapeutic climate in which the patient can feel safe to relive traumas and to problematize his paraphilia without too much anxiety. The next step is the analysis of the general personality pathology (e.g., narcissistic disorders), which forms the general developmental foundation of the paraphilia. Finally, there is the analysis of the paraphilia itself, which aims to give insight into the erotic function of the paraphilia in order to "cure" (the dependency of) the paraphilic gratification itself.

Biomedical Interventions

In the twentieth century, three biomedical interventions have been used to treat paraphilias: castration, neurosurgery, and pharmacological interventions. The first two are no longer used in most countries due to ethical concerns (Gijs & Gooren, 1996). Pharmacological interventions, which have long been quite controversial, have acquired a clear place in the treatment of paraphilias over the last 25 years (Allen & Hollander, 2006; Bradford, 2000; Bradford & Fedoroff, 2006; Briken, Hill, & Berner, 2003; Kafka, 2007; Maletzky, Tolan, & McFarland, 2006; Schober, Byrne, & Kuhn, 2006).

Pharmacological interventions are used mostly as an adjunctive strategy in combination with psychotherapy for two reasons: because no empirical evidence supports the idea that the use of pharmacological interventions alone can cure a paraphilia and because the specific (biological) factors involved in the etiology of paraphilias are currently unknown (Bradford & Fedoroff, 2006; Gijs & Gooren, 1996; Osborne & Wise, 2005; Hunsel van & Cosyns, 2002).

Two classes of drugs have been used to treat paraphilias: hormonal interventions that target the facilitative influence of androgens on sexuality; and psychotropic medications that target the (dys)regulation of sexuality by the brain.

Hormonal Interventions

Gijs and Gooren (1996) have argued that hormonal interventions are indicated for severe paraphilias that strongly predispose the individual toward paraphilic behavior; psychopharmacological interventions are indicated for the treatment of people with paraphilias with comorbid depression and obsessive-compulsive or impulse disorders. However, a somewhat different approach has been proposed by Bradford (Figure 16.6; 2000; Bradford & Fedoroff, 2006).

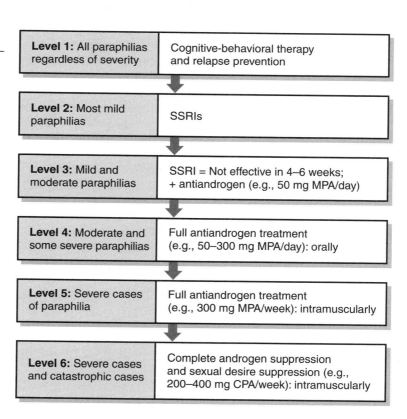

Figure 16.6

Bradford's Algorithm for the Hormonal and Pharmacological Treatment of Paraphilia's

Note: Based on the work of Bradford (2000); Bradford and Federoff (2006).

Level 1: All paraphilias regardless of severity	Cognitive-behavioral therapy and relapse prevention
Level 2: Most mild paraphilias	SSRIs
Level 3: Mild and moderate paraphilias	SSRI = Not effective in 4–6 weeks; + antiandrogen (e.g., 50 mg MPA/day)
Level 4: Moderate and some severe paraphilias	Full antiandrogen treatment (e.g., 50–300 mg MPA/day): orally
Level 5: Severe cases of paraphilia	Full antiandrogen treatment (e.g., 300 mg MPA/week): intramuscularly
Level 6: Severe cases and catastrophic cases	Complete androgen suppression and sexual desire suppression (e.g., 200–400 mg CPA/week): intramuscularly

Based on the severity and the dangerousness of the paraphilia, he proposed an algorithm for the pharmacological treatment of paraphilias. Bradford categorizes severity into four classes: mild, moderate, severe, and catastrophic (see Bradford & Fedoroff for further specifications on the definition of these classes).

Hormonal interventions are based on the empirical fact that a minimal amount of androgen is necessary in order to function sexually. When testosterone levels drop below a critical threshold, sexual functioning is minimized. So, it is logical to reduce the intensity and frequency of the paraphilic desire by the use of anti-androgens. Since medroxyprogesterone acetate (MPA) and cyproterone acetate (CPA) have been on the market since the end of the 1960s, both products have been used regularly in the treatment of paraphilias (Allen & Hollander, 2005; Bradford & Fedoroff, 2006; Gijs & Gooren, 1996; Rösler & Witztum, 2000). Because CPA has not been approved by the U.S. Food and Drug Administration (FDA), MPA is used primarily in the United States and CPA primarily in Europe (Allen & Hollander, 2005; Gijs & Gooren, 1996; see also Bradford, 2000; Bradford & Fedoroff, 2006). Since the early 1990s, interest in the use of LH-RH-agonists and the anti-androgen flutamide as alternatives to CPA and MPA has increased (Gijs & Gooren, 1996; for reviews: Allen & Hollander, 2006; Bradford & Fedoroff, 2006; Briken et al., 2003). For specific guidelines for the clinical application and dosages of the hormonal interventions in the treatment of paraphilias, see the following reviews: Bradford and Fedoroff (2006); Gijs and Gooren (1996); Osborne and Wise (2005).

The application of hormonal agents to control paraphilias requires careful medical monitoring in light of the reported side-effects of these drugs: reduced erections, reduced ejaculate, reduced spermatogenesis, fatigue, sleepiness, depressive episodes, weight gain, dry skin from decreased production of sebum, varicose veins, cramping in the legs, breast formation, hair loss, Cushing's syndrome and adrenal insufficiency, and in the long run osteoperosis (see further: Bradford & Fedoroff, 2006; Gooren, Lips, & Gijs, 2001; Grasswick & Bradford, 2003; Krueger, Hembree, Hill, 2006). Medical contra-indications for the use of CPA or MPA in the treatment of a paraphilia are: thrombo-emolic antecedents and diseases that affect the production of testosterone, such as renal failure, liver diseases, protein malnutrition, hypothalamic-pituitary dysfunction, and cancer chemotherapy (Gijs & Gooren, 1996)

Based on numerous case studies and a few controlled studies, hormonal agents appear to be effective in reducing the intensity and severity of paraphilias (Bradford & Fedoroff, 2006; Gijs & Gooren, 1996). Nevertheless, even after approximately 40 years of use of MPA and CPA, the need to evaluate these drugs in controlled research studies remains great. But as Bradford and Fedoroff (2006) recently remarked, it will not be easy to conduct such research, because governments and the pharmaceutical industry have very little interest in financing such controlled research.

Psychopharmacological Interventions

In the 1960s to 1970s, a small number of clinical case studies suggested that the use of such drugs as benperidol, thioridazine, carbamazepine, haloperidol, lithium carbonate, and tryciclic antidepressants reduces paraphilic symptoms (Gijs & Gooren, 1996). However, their use never became popular. Besides the prevailing "zeitgeist," the absence of outcome research and the rather severe side effects of these agents likely contributed to their limited use. However, by the end of the 1980s, interest in the use of psychopharmacological drugs for the treatment of paraphilias was renewed, partly because some authors reported clinical cases that were treated successfully by drugs. For example, Fedoroff (1988) successfully treated a 40-year-old married man with transvestic fetishism, generalized anxiety disorder, and alcohol dependence with buspirone. This treatment not only reduced the level of anxiety, but also stopped the cross-dressing behavior. Cesnik and Coleman (1989) treated a 26-year-old single man suffering from depression, suicidal thoughts, contact problems, and asphyxia with psychotherapy and lithium carbonate. Since those initial studies, although a great many case studies have been reported, almost no controlled studies have been carried out (Allen & Hollander, 2005; Bradford & Fedoroff, 2006; Kafka, 2007).

Currently, the most frequently used psychotropic medications are: fluoxetine, fluvoxamine, sertraline, imipramine, clomipramine, desipramine, buspirone, and lithium carbonate. And the use of many others has been suggested on the basis of single case studies (Bradford & Fedoroff, 2006; Coleman, 2005; Kafka, 2007). For example, Shiah, Chao, Mao, and Chuang (2006) successfully used topiramate, an anticonvulsant, to treat a 23-year-old male with fetishism. However, well controlled studies are needed before reliable conclusions about the effect of any of these medications on paraphilias can be drawn. For specific guidelines on the dosages and clinical application of psychotropic drugs in the treatment of paraphilias, see the reviews of Bradford and Feodroff (2006), Gijs and Gooren (1996), Kafka (2007), and Osborn and Wise (2005).

In contrast with hormonal interventions, few side effects from treatment with the SSRIs have been reported (Kafka, 2007). Kafka (2007) mentioned apathy and fatigue as possible side-effects, adding that "there are no known long-term consequences associated with remaining on these medications as long as a beneficial effect continues to be sustained" (p. 469).

Effectiveness of Interventions

Few controlled studies have investigated the effectiveness of treatments of paraphilia (Emmelkamp, 2004; Maletzky, 2002). For example, only a few controlled studies of psychopharmacological interventions with paraphilias have been reported (Bancroft et al., 1974; Kruesi et al., 1992; Schober et al., 2005; Tennant et al., 1974) and no controlled studies of psychological treatments of paraphilias have been reported since the early 1990s (Emmelkamp, 2004; Osborn & Wise, 2005). If we accept the assumption that the results of outcome research of treatments of sexual violence can be generalized to treatments of paraphilias—as sexual violence and paraphilias show similarities—only cognitive-behavioral therapies and hormonal interventions have been proven effective: both these interventions reduce recidivism significantly (Bradford & Fedoroff, 2006; Gijs & Gooren, 1996; Maletzky, 2002; Marshall, 2006). However, a significant reduction of recidivism does not equate with full effectiveness or a "cure." And many methodological problems remain. Follow-up research is almost nonexistent and the following topics have been neglected in outcome research: in- and exclusion criteria for treatment, refusal rates; drop-out; differences between different paraphilias; and the possible role of a partner. Judicial influences have not necessarily been negative on the outcome of treatments of paraphilias (Maletzky, 1980).

Based on these shortcomings, Rice and Harris (2003) have concluded that no evidence whatsoever proves that treatments for paraphilias (and sex offenders) reduce recidivism. Although this represents a radical conclusion, and has been so argued by Marshall (2006), the (empirical study of the) effectiveness of treatments for paraphilias is clearly in great need of improvement.

Paraphilia-Related Disorders

In the *DSM,* paraphilias are defined as disorders of the sexual object choice. However, sometimes there is no abnormal object choice, but rather sexual response is dysregulated by becoming hypersexual or obsessive-compulsive, that is, the person has lost control of self-regulation. As a result, the frequency of sexual desire and behavior rises strongly and sexuality is experienced as aversive. Furthermore, the person who suffers from such dysregulation has the feeling that he has lost control and cannot stop his deviant sexuality. Typical examples are: hypersexual and compulsive masturbation, hypersexual consumption of pornography; telephone sex dependence, uncontrollable promiscuity, hypersexual desire and behavior within a relationship, and hypersexual use of the Internet.

Unfortunately, the terminology surrounding these issues is confusing. Some professionals use the term "sexual addiction" (e.g., Carnes, 1983) or "sexual (obsessive-) compulsive disorders" (e.g., Coleman, 2005; Coleman, Raymond, & McBean, 2003) or "sexual impulse disorders" (e.g., Kafka, 1995; see also Allen & Hollander, 2006). Others use the term "paraphilia-related disorders" (e.g., Kafka, 2003, 2007) or "hypersexual desire" (Vroege, Hengeveld, & Gijs, 1998).

The preferred terminology seems to depend on the hypothesized etiology of the dysregulation of sexuality. Carnes defines sexual addiction in the following terms: "The sexual addict substitutes a sick relationship to an event or process for a healthy relationship with others" (1983, p. 4). In his view, sex addiction is a disease with particular symptoms: the loss of control over sexuality, the use of sex to cope with pain and stress and to reach intimacy. The effects of this disease are conflict and endangerment of relations, work, health and safety. In contrast, Coleman (1987) describes the sexual compulsive person as follows: He "is obsessively preoccupied with certain patterns of sexual behavior and as a result of this preoccupation, experiences negative consequences following engaging in this behavior. Yet, despite the negative consequences, the individual experiences great difficulty and many frustrated attempts to change his or her behavior" (pp. 142–143). Coleman emphasized that every sexual behavior can become compulsive. Kafka (1995) is of the opinion that paraphilia-related disorders are impulse control disorders, and defined them as: "the failure to resist an impulse, drive, or temptation to perform an act that is harmful to the person or to others" (*DSM-IV-TR*, p. 663). Just as with the paraphilias, it has been hypothesized that this dysregulation of sexuality is caused by a cerebral monoaminergic dysregulation that disturbs the neurotransmission of norephinephrine, dopamine, and serotonin, with hypersexuality as a symptomatic effect. Antisocial impulsivity and anxiety and affective disorders are frequent comorbidities. Kafka (2003, 2007) operationally defines hypersexuality as at least seven orgasms during 1 week for at least a period of 6 months after the age of 15. That frequency of orgasm is reported by 3% to 8% of men in sexological surveys of the general male population (e.g., Laumann et al., 1994). Hypersexual men spend at least 1 to 2 hr per day to carry out their paraphilia-related disorder.

The terminological confusion in this field has led to many commentaries. Coleman (2005), for example, remarked with irony: "Despite the lack of consensus of terminology, there is consensus that just as there can be problems with hyposexuality, there are individuals who experience hypersexuality" (p. 147). And Gold and Heffner (1998)—and we agree with them—commented that the termination of the terminological confusion remains impossible as long as there is no sound research into the etiology of this sexual behavior. Stemming from these terminological debates, Kafka proposed a descriptive terminology, strongly informed by the descriptive classification of the *DSM* (e.g., Kafka, 2007). Paraphilia are defined by Kakfa according to the *DSM-IV-TR,* and paraphilia-related disorders are defined as: "sexually arousing fantasies, urges, or activities involving culturally sanctioned sexual interests and behaviors that increase in frequency or intensity (for at least a 6-month duration) so as to interfere with the capacity for reciprocal affectionate activity" (Kafka & Prentky, 1994, p. 482). The core element of this definition is the dysregulation of the (growing) frequency, intensity, and control of "normal" sexuality. In the strictest sense, this definition assumes consensus about the parameters of normal sexuality, about which no consensus exists. Or as Groneman (2001, p. 187) asked in her history of nymphomania: "How much is too much? How much is enough? And who decides?" These questions have not been answered satisfactorily.

It is no surprise then, that (the conceptualizations of) the concepts "sexual addiction," "sexual (obsessive-) compulsive disorder," and "sexual impulse disorder" have been heavily criticized (Irvine, 1995). The criticisms are double-sided: (a) by using concepts as "sexual addiction," normal sexual variations become medicalized; and (b) the cultural norms that support and inspire that medicalization are not called into question and problematized. Although this critique is on target, clinicians have argued against disposing of the concepts entirely because some people who consult them suffer from their sexual preoccupations, because these patients cannot control their sexual behavior, because they experience the frequency and or intensity of their sexual behavior as aversive, and because their behavior has a negative impact on their well-being, relationships, work, and health.

Some clinicians believe that paraphilia-related disorders run a progressive course. Carnes (1983, 1989) and Coleman (2005) have pointed out that a paraphilia-related disorder functions as an (inadequate) coping-mechanism that dulls negative emotions. With the progression of time, the effects of this coping mechanism become less and less successful, so that a stronger sexual experience becomes necessary. Carnes (1983) suggests a cyclical pattern with three levels of severity: (1) masturbation, multiple heterosexual and homosexual relations, pornography and prostitution; (2) exhibitionism, voyeurism, and telephone-scatologia; and (3) sexual abuse of children, incest, and rape. Carnes "cyclus of dysregulation" has six phases: (1) initiation phase, (2) establishment phase, (3) contingent phase: escalation mode, (4) contingent phase, (5) acute phase, and (6) chronic phase (Carnes, 1989).

Coleman (2005; Coleman et al., 2003) provides a different view. They conceptualize compulsive sexual behavior as an obsessive-compulsive or as an impulse-disorder without any presuppositions about a typical course. This view is shared by Kafka (2003, 2007; Kafka & Hennen, 2002) but he classifies paraphilia-related disorders as ones involving the affective spectrum, arguing that dysregulation of the monoaminergic neurotransmission in the brain is the source of this disorder.

At the moment there has been no documentation of a typical course for paraphilia-related disorders. However, it may take years before clients/patients with a paraphilia-related disorder consult a therapist. Kafka and Hennen (2002) have found that patients endured a paraphilia related disorder on average 12 years before consulting a clinician.

Three main treatment programs have been described in the literature to treat paraphilia-related disorders: Carnes 12-step program, and the approaches of Coleman and Kafka, that combine psychotherapy and psychopharmacological treatment.

Carnes' 12-step program is based on and analogous to Alcoholics Anonymous. Colemans' approach emphasizes learning to prevent or to cope with the negative emotions (such as anxiety and depression) that lead to paraphilia-related disorders, and the recognition and handling of triggers of these negative emotions to prevent relapse. Pharmacotherapy is used as an adjunctive strategy to psychotherapy. Coleman and colleagues have used mostly lithium carbonate and naltrexone (Coleman, 2005). Kafka's psychotherapeutic approach has many similarities with Coleman's treatment interventions but uses mostly SSRIs (Kafka, 2003, 2007). Currently, none of the therapeutic programs for paraphilia-related disorders has been tested empirically (Coleman, 2005; Kafka, 2007).

Summary and Conclusions

In this chapter, we noted that people show variation in sexual behaviors and that these variations are judged in different ways. A specific part of this variation is accounted for by paraphilias. How can these be described, be put in order, and be elucidated?

In sexology paraphilias are defined as "social deviance," as a "personal (psychopathological) disorder" or as a "personality trait." We prefer the last characterization. The stronger a trait, the more likely the individual will display the behavior belonging to it. Rightly, paraphilias such as pedophilia and sexual sadism are included as a risk factor in models of sexual aggressive behavior and abuse. However, this personality-trait conceptualization does not say anything about the significance of this trait in the personal life of the individual.

The atypical sexual variations or paraphilias can be considered as pathology or not. We suggest reserving the term "paraphilias" for pathological sexual orientations or preferences. The differentiation between atypical but normal sexual variations and paraphilias is, unfortunately, still not well validated. Until now, sexology has restricted the term *sexual orientation* for the homo-, hetero- or bisexual orientation. Other varieties are considered a priori pathological. We believe that a better validation of the psychopathological model of paraphilias, predominant in public health, deserves more attention.

The many theories about the etiology of paraphilias have not survived critical empirical testing. It is both striking and alarming that empirical research into the etiology of paraphilias has virtually come to a standstill, with the exception of a few investigations into potential biological etiologies. In summary, the etiology of paraphilias (and of sexual orientations in general) is still not understood (Gooren, 2006; Osborn & Wise, 2005). Futhermore, most theories have assumed that the paraphilias share a common pathogenesis, but it remains to be seen whether the large phenemomenological differences between different paraphilias, as for example infantilism, transvestic fetishism, asphyxiophilia, and sex killing, can be explained by one or a few common pathological mechanisms.

Only cognitive behavior-therapeutic, hormonal, and psychopharmalogical treatments have been shown to be clinically efficacious, but even these have only modest effects. It is unfortunate that controlled studies into the efficacy and effectiveness of psychotherapy have been lacking since the mid-1990s. The methodological quality of the empirical study of pharmacological interventions is also very weak, and well-controlled studies are rare.

In addition to these gaps and deficiencies, the validity of diagnostic procedures needs to be improved. And almost nothing has been published about therapies from the "normality perspective."

Some clinical topics associated with paraphilias deserve more scrutiny. For example, bereavement has never received serious attention in the treatment of paraphilias. Mourning, in light of the realization that a "normal" choice of partner and a "normal" sex life is seriously impeded by the paraphilia, seems unavoidable from a life-span perspective. Especially for adolescents who have come to realize that their paraphilia will seriously hamper the solution of (some) developmental tasks, attention to grief is warranted. And for those who have developed relationships, the involvement of partners in the therapeutic process has also not been adequately considered.

We also considered paraphilia-related disorders. These latter disorders are characterized by a strong loss of self regulation of sexuality and by hypersexuality (which is experienced as aversive). In general, this field suffers much confusion, much theoretical speculation, and a lack of empirical research. Treatment of paraphilia-related disorders currently resembles either Alcoholics Anonymous programs or traditional (cognitive-behavioral) psychotherapy, in combination with pharmacotherapy. Until now their efficacy and effectiveness is unknown.

References

Abel, G. G., & Osborn, C. (2000). The paraphilias. In M. C. Gelder, J. J. Lopez-Ibor, & N. C. Andreasen (Eds.), *New Oxford textbook of psychiatry* (pp. 897–913). New York: Oxford University Press.

Abel, G. G., Osborn, C. A., & Twigg, D. A. (1993). Sexual assault through the life span: Adult offenders with juvenile histories. In H. E. Barbaree, W. L. Marshall, & Hudson, S. M. (Eds.), *The juvenile sex offender* (pp. 104–117). New York: Guilford Press.

Abel, G. G., & Rouleau, J-L. (1990). The nature and extent of sexual assault. In W. L. Marshall, D. R. Laws, & H.E. Barbaree (Eds.), *Handbook of sexual assault: Issues, theories, and treatment of the offender* (pp. 9–21). New York: Plenum.

Allen, A., & Hollander, E. (2006). Sexual compulsions. In E. Hollander & D. J. Stein (Eds.), *Clinical manual of impulse control-disorders* (pp. 87–114). Washington, DC: American Psychiatric Press.

American Psychiatric Association. (1980). *Diagnostic and statistical manual of mental disorders* (3rd ed.). Washington, DC: Author.

American Psychiatric Association. (2000). *Diagnostic and statistical manual of mental disorders* (4th ed., text rev.). Washington, DC: Author.

Bailey, M. (2003). *The man who would be queen: The science of gender-bending and transsexualism*. Washington, DC: Joseph Henry Press.

Bancroft, J. (1989). *Human sexuality and its problems* (2nd ed.). London: Churchill Livingstone.

Bancroft, J., Tennent, G., Lucas, K., & Cass, J. (1974). The control of deviant sexual behaviour by drugs. *British Journal of Psychiatry, 125,* 310–315.

Barbaree, H. E., & Seto, M. C. (1997). Pedophilia: Assessment and treatment. In R. D. Laws & W. O'Donohue (Eds.), *Sexual deviance: Theory, assessment, and treatment* (pp. 175–193). New York: Guilford Press.

Bauer, M., Tatschner, T., & Patzelt, D. (2007). Digital imaging of the dissection and sexual abuse of a corpse: An exceptional case of necrophilia. *Legal Medicine, 9,* 143–146.

Baumeister, R. F. (1989). *Masochism and the self.* Hillsdale, NJ: LEA.

Baumeister, R. F., & Butler, J. L. (1997). Sexual masochism: Deviance without pathology. In D. R. Laws & W. O'Donohue (Eds.), *Handbook of sexual deviance* (pp. 225–239). New York: Guilford Press.

Bhardwaj, D. N., Rautji, R., Sharma, R. K., & Dogra, T. D. (2004). Suicide by a transvestite or sexual asphyxia? A case report. *Medicine, Science, and the Law, 44,* 173–175.

Bhugra, D. (2000). Disturbances in objects of desire: Cross-cultural issues. *Sexual Relations and Therapy, 15,* 67–78.

Blanchard, R. (2005). Early history of the concept of autogynephilia. *Archives of Sexual Behavior, 34,* 439–446.

Blanchard, R., Cantor, J. M., & Robichaud, L. K. (2006). Biological factors in the development of sexual deviance and aggression in males. In H. E. Barbaree & W. L. Marshall (Eds.), *The juvenile sex offender* (pp. 77–104). New York: Guilford Press.

Blanchard, R., Kuban, M. E., Klassen, P., Dickey, R., Christensen, B. K., Cantor, J. M., et al. (2003). Self-reported head injuries before and after age 13 in pedophilic and nonpedophilic men referred for clinical assessment. *Archives of Sexual Behavior, 32,* 573–581.

Bogaert, A. F. (2006). Toward a conceptual understanding of asexuality. *Review of General Psychology, 10,* 241–250.

Bogaert, A. F., Bezeau, S., Kuban, M., & Blanchard, R. (1997). Pedophilia, sexual orientation and birth order. *Journal of Abnormal Psychology, 106,* 331–335.

Bradford, J. M. W. (2000). The treatment of sexual deviation using a pharmacological approach. *Journal of Sex Research, 37,* 248–257.

Bradford, J. M. W. (2006). On sexual violence. *Current Opinion in Psychiatry, 19,* 527–532.

Bradford, J. M. W., & Fedoroff, P. (2006). Pharmacological treatment of the juvenile sex offender. In H. E. Barbaree & W. L. Marshall (Eds.), *The juvenile sex offender* (2nd ed., pp. 358–382). New York: Guilford Press.

Briken, P., Habermann, N., Berner, W., & Hill, A. (2005). The influence of brain abnormalities on psychosexual development, criminal history and paraphilias in sexual murderers. *Journal of Forensic Sciences, 50,* 1204–1208.

Briken, P., Hill, A., & Berner, W. (2003). Pharmacotherapy of paraphilias with long-acting agonists of luteinizing hormone-releasing hormone: A systematic review. *Journal of Clinical Psychiatry, 64,* 890–897.

Burns, J. M., & Swerdlow, R. H. (2003). Right orbitofrontal tumor with pedophilia symptom and constructional apraxia sign. *Archives of Neurology, 60,* 437–440.

Cannas, A., Solla, P., Floris, G., Tacconi, P., Loi, D., Marcia, E., et al. (2006). Hypersexual behavior, frotteurism and delusional jealousy in a young Parkinsonian patient during dopaminergic therapy with pergolide: A rare case of iatrogenic paraphilia. *Progress in Neuro-pharmacology and Biological Psychiatry, 30,* 1539–1541.

Cantor, J. M., Blanchard, R., Chirstensen, B. K., Dickey, R., Klassen, P. E., Beackstead, A. L., et al. (2004). Intelligence, memory, and handedness in pedophilia. *Neuropsychology, 18,* 3–14.

Carnes, P. (1983). *Out of the shadows: Understanding sexual addiction.* Minneapolis, MN: CompCare.

Carnes, P. (1989). *Contrary to love: Helping the sexual addict.* Minneapolis, MN: CompCare.

Casanova, M. F., Mannheim, G., & Kruesi, M. (2002). Hippocampal pathology in two mentally ill paraphiliacs. *Psychiatry Research Neuroimaging, 115,* 79–89.

Cesnik, J. A., & Coleman, E. (1989). Use of lithium carbonate in the treatment of autoerotic asphyxia. *American Journal of Psychotherapy, 43,* 277–286.

Clark, L. A. (2007). Assessment and diagnosis of personality disorder: Perennial issues and emerging reconceptualization. *Annual Review of Psychology, 58,* 227–257.

Coleman, E. (1988). Sexual compulsivity: Definition, etiology, and treatment considerations. In E. Coleman (Ed.), *Chemical dependency and intimacy dysfunction* (pp. 189–204). New York: Haworth Press.

Coleman, E. (2005). Neuroanatomical and neurotransmitter dysfunction and compulsive sexual behavior. In J. Hyde (Ed.), *Biological substrates of human sexuality* (pp. 147–169). Washington, DC: American Psychological Association.

Coleman, E., Raymond, N., & McBean, A. (2003). Assessment and treatment of compulsive sexual behavior. *Minnesota Medicine, 86,* 42–47.

Cross, P. A., & Matheson, K. (2006). Understanding sadomasochism: An empirical examination of four perspectives. *Journal of Homosexuality, 50,* 133–166.

Dancer, P. L., Kleinplatz, P. J., & Moser, C. (2006). 24/7 SM slavery. *Journal of Homosexuality, 50,* 81–101.

Dewaraja, R., & Money, J. (1986). Transcultural sexology: Formicophilia, a newly named paraphilia in a young Buddhist male. *Journal of Sex and Marital Therapy, 12,* 139–145.

Dhikav, V., Anand, K., & Aggarwal, N. (2007). Grossly disinhibited sexual behavior in dementia of Alzheimer's type. *Archives of Sexual Behavior, 36,* 133–134.

Emmelkamp, P. M. G. (2004). Behavior therapy with adults. In M. J. Lambert (Ed.), *Bergin and Garfield's psychotherapy and behavior change* (pp. 393–446). Hoboken, NJ: Wiley.

Epstein, A. W. (1975). The fetish object: Phylogenetic considerations. *Archives of Sexual Behavior, 4,* 303–308.

Fedoroff, J. P. (1988). Buspirone hydrochloride in the treatment of transvestic fetishism. *Journal of Clinical Psychiatry, 49,* 408–409.

Foucault, M. (1976). *La volonté de savoir* [The history of sexuality: An introduction]. Paris: Gallimard.

Freud, S. (1905). *Drei Abhandlungen zur Sexualtheorie.* [Three essays on the theory of sexuality]. Gesammelte Werke 5. Frankfurt am Main: Fisher Verlag.

Freund, K. (1990). Courtship disorder. In W. L. Marshall, D. R. Laws, & H. E. Barbaree (Eds.), *Handbook of sexual assault: Issues, theories, and treatment of the offender* (pp. 195–207). New York: Plenum Press.

Freund, K., Seto, M. C., & Kuban, M. (1997). Frotteurism and the theory of courtship disorder. In R. D. Laws & W. O'Donohue (Eds.), *Sexual deviance: Theory, assessment, and treatment* (pp. 111–130). New York: Guilford Press.

Frohman, E., Frohman, T., & Moreault, A. M. (2002). Acquired sexual paraphilia in patients with multiple sclerosis. *Archives of Neurology, 59,* 1006–1010.

Frost, L. A., & Chapman, L. J. (1987). Polymorphous sexuality as an indicator of psychosis proneness. *Journal of Abnormal Psychology, 96,* 299–304.

Gaffney, G. R., & Berlin, F. S. (1984). Is there a hypothalamic-pituitary-gonadal dysfunction in paedophilia? A pilot study. *British Journal of Psychiatry, 145,* 657–660.

Gaffney, G. R., Lurie, S. F., & Berlin, F. S. (1984). Is there familial transmission of pedophilia? *Journal of Nervous and Mental Diseases, 172,* 546–548.

Giotakos, O., Markianos, M., Vaidakis, N., & Christodoulou, G. N. (2004). Aggression, impulsivity, plasma sex hormones and biogenic amine turnover in a forensic population of rapists. *Journal of Sex and Marital Therapy, 29,* 215–225.

Gijs, L. (1994). Honderd jaar seksuologisch denken over seksueel deviant gedrag: Een paradigmatisch overzicht in vogelvlucht [One hundred years of thinking about sexual deviant behavior: A paradigmatic overview]. In W. Bezemer, L. Gooren, & H. Van Marle (Eds.), *Seksueel deviant gedrag* [Sexual deviant behavior] (pp. 6–32). Bussum: Medicom.

Gijs, L., & Gooren, L. (1996). Hormonal and psychopharmacological interventions in the treatment of paraphilias. *Journal of Sex Research, 33,* 272–290.

Gold, S. N., & Heffner, C. L. (1998). Sexual addiction: Many conceptions, minimal data. *Clinical Psychology Review, 18,* 367–381.

Gooren, L. (2006). The biology of human psychosexual differentiation. *Hormones and Behavior, 50,* 589–601.

Gooren, L. J. G., Lips, P., & Gijs, L. (2001). Osteoporosis and androgen-depleting drugs in sex offenders. *Lancet, 357,* 1208–1209.

Grasswick, L. J., & Bradford, J. M. W. (2003). Osteoporosis associated with the treatment of paraphilias: A clinical review of seven cases. *Journal of Forensic Science, 48,* 1–7.

Green, R. (2002). Is pedophilia a mental disorder? *Archives of Sexual Behavior, 31,* 467–471.

Groneman, C. (2001). *Nymphomania: A history.* London: Fusion Press.

Hanson, K. R., & Morton-Bourgon, K. E. (2005). The characteristics of persistent sexual offenders: A meta-analysis of recidivism studies. *Journal of Consulting and Clinical Psychology, 73,* 1154–1163.

Hatfield, E., Schmitz, E., Cornelius, J., & Rapson, R. L. (1988). Passionate love: How early does it begin? *Journal of Psychology and Human Sexuality, 1,* 35–52.

Hildebrand, M., de Ruiter, C., & Vogel, V. (2004). Psychopathy and sexual deviance in treated rapists: Association with sexual and nonsexual recidivism. *Sexual Abuse, 16,* 1–24.

Hill, A., Habermann, N., Berner, W., & Briken, P. (2006). Sexual sadism and sadistic personality disorder in sexual homicide. *Journal of Personality Disorders, 20,* 671–684.

Hilliard, R. B., & Spitzer, R. L. (2002). Change in criterion for paraphilias in DSM-IV-TR. *American Journal of Psychiatry, 159,* 1249.

Hunsel, F. van, & Cosyns, P. (2002). Biomedische interventies bij plegers van seksueel geweld [Biomedical interventions for sex offenders]. *Tijdschrift voor Seksuologie, [Journal of Sexology], 26,* 87–96.

Irvine, J. M. (1995). Reinventing perversion: Sex addiction and cultural anxieties. *Journal of the History of Sexuality, 5,* 429–450.

Kafka, M. P. (1995). Sexual impulsivity. In E. Hollander & E. Stein (Eds.), *Impulsivity and aggression* (pp. 201–228). New York: Wiley.

Kafka, M. P. (2003). The monoamine hypothesis for the pathophysiology of paraphilic disorders: An update. In R. A. Prentky, E. S. Janus, & M. C. Seto (Eds.), *Sexually coercive behavior: Understanding and management. Annals of the New York Academy of Sex Research, 989,* 86–94.

Kafka, M. P. (2007). Paraphilia-related disorders: The evaluation and treatment of nonparaphilic hypersexuality. In S. R. Leiblum (Ed.), *Principles and practice of sex therapy* (4th ed., pp. 442–467). New York: Guilford Press.

Kafka, M. P., & Hennen, J. (2002). A *DSM-IV* axis I comorbidity study of males (n = 120) with paraphilias and paraphilia-related disorders. *Sexual Abuse, 14,* 349–366.

Kafka, M. P., & Prentky, R. A. (1994). Preliminary observations of *DSM-III-R* axis I comorbidity in men with paraphilias and paraphilia-related disorders. *Journal of Clinical Psychiatry, 55,* 481–487.

Karasic, D., & Drescher, J. (Eds.). (2005). Sexual and gender diagnoses of the *Diagnostic and Statistical Manual (DSM):* A reevaluation [Special issue]. *Journal of Psychology and Human Sexuality, 17,* 1–154.

Kelly, R. J., & Lusk, R. (1992). Theories of pedophilia. In W. O'Donohue & J. H. Geer (Eds.), *The sexual abuse of children: Theory and research* (Vol. 1, pp. 168–203). Hillsdale, NJ: LEA.

Kingston, D. A., Firestone, P., Moulden, H. M., & Bradford, P. M. (2007). The utility of the diagnosis of pedophilia: A comparison of various classification procedures. *Archives of Sexual Behavior, 36,* 423–436.

Kinsey, A. C., Pomeroy, W. B., & Martin, C. E. (1948). *Sexual behavior in the human male.* Philadelphia: Saunders.

Kinsey, A. C., Pomeroy, W. B., Martin, C. E., & Gebhard, P. H. (1949). Concepts of normality and abnormality in sexual behavior. In P. H. Hoch & J. Zubin (Eds.), *Psychosexual development in health and disease* (pp. 11–32). New York: Grune & Stratton.

Kinsey, A. C., Pomeroy, W. B., Martin, C. E., & Gebhard, P. H. (1953). *Sexual behavior in the human female.* Philadelphia: Saunders.

Kleinplatz, P. J., & Moser, C. (2005). Politics versus science: An addendum and response to Drs. Spitzer and Fink. *Journal of Psychology and Human Sexuality, 17,* 135–139.

Klos, K. J., Bower, J. H., Josephs, K. A., Matsumoto, J. Y., & Ahlskog, J. E. (2005). Pathological hypersexuality predominantly linked to adjuvant dopamine agonist therapy in Parkinson's disease and multiple system atrophy. *Parkinsonism and Related Disorders, 11,* 381–386.

Knight, R. A., & Guay, J. (2006). The role of psychopathy in sexual coercion against women. In C. J. Patrick (Ed.), *Handbook of psychopathy* (pp. 512–532). New York: Guilford Press.

Kolmes, K., Stock, W., & Moser, C. (2006). Investigating bias in psychotherapy with BDSM clients. *Journal of Homosexuality, 50,* 301–324.

Krueger, R. B., Hembree, W., & Hill, M. (2006). Prescription of medroxyprogesterone acetate to a patient with pedophilia, resulting in Cushing's syndrome and adrenal insufficiency. *Sexual Abuse, 18,* 227–228.

Kruesi, M. P., Fine, S., Valladares, L., Phillips, R. A., & Rapoport, J. (1992). Paraphilias: A double blind cross-over comparison of clomipramine versus desipramine. *Archives of Sexual Behavior, 21,* 587–593.

Langevin, R. (1983). *Sexual strands: Understanding and treating sexual anomalies in men.* Hillsdale, NJ: LEA.

Långström, N., & Hanson, R. K. (2006). High rates of sexual behavior in the general population: Correlates and predictors. *Archives of Sexual Behavior, 35,* 37–52.

Långström, N., & Seto, M. C. (2006). Exhibitionistic and voyeuristic behaviour in a Swedish national populations study. *Archives of Sexual Behavior, 35,* 427–435.

Långström, N., & Zucker, K. J. (2005). Transvestic fetishism in the general population: Prevalence and correlates. *Journal of Sex and Marital Therapy,* 87–95.

Laumann, E. O., Gagnon, J. H., Michael, R. T., & Michaels, S. (1994). *The social organization of sexuality: Sexual practices in the United States.* Chicago: University of Chicago Press.

Lawrence, A. A. (2004). Autogynephilia: A paraphilic model of gender identity disorder. *Journal of Gay and Lesbian Psychotherapy, 8,* 69–87.

Lawrence, A. A. (2006). Clinical and theoretical parallels between desire for limb amputation and gender identity disorder. *Archives of Sexual Behavior, 35,* 263–278.

Laws, D. R., & Marshall, W. L. (1990). A conditioning theory of the etiology and maintenance of deviant sexual preference and behavior. In W. L. Marshall, D. R. Laws, & H. E. Barbaree (Eds.), *Handbook of sexual assault: Issues, theories,* *and treatment of the offender* (pp. 209–229). New York: Plenum Press.

Laws, D. R., & Marshall, W. L. (2003). A brief history of behavioral and cognitive behavioral approaches to sexual offenders: Pt. I. Early developments. *Sexual Abuse, 15,* 75–92.

Laws, D. R., & O'Donohue, W. (Eds.). (1997). *Handbook of sexual deviance.* New York: Guilford Press.

Lehne, G. K., & Money, J. (2003). Multiplex versus multiple taxonomy of paraphilia: Case Example. *Sexual Abuse, 15,* 61–72.

Leitenberg, H., & Henning, K. (1995). Sexual fantasy. *Psychological Bulletin, 117,* 469–496.

Maes, M., De Vos, N., van Hunsel, F., Van West, D., Westenberg, H., Cosyns, P., et al. (2001). Pedophilia is accompanied by increased plasma concentrations of catholamines in particular ephinephrine. *Psychiatry Research, 103,* 43–49.

Maes, M., van West, D., De Vos, N., Westenberg, H., van Hunsel, F., Hendriks, D. et al. (2001). Lower baseline plasma cortisol and prolactin together with increased body temperature and higher mCPP-induced cortisol responses in men with pedophilia. *Neuropsychopharmacology, 24,* 37–46.

Malamuth, N. M., Huppin, M., & Paul, B. (2005). Sexual coercion. In D. M. Buss (Ed.), *The handbook of evolutionary psychology* (pp. 394–418). Hoboken, NJ: Wiley.

Maletzky, B. M. (1980). Self-referred versus court-referred sexually deviant patients: Success with assisted covert sensitization. *Behavior Therapy, 11,* 306–314.

Maletzky, B. M. (2002). The paraphilias: Research and treatment. In P. E. Nathan & J. M. Gorman (Eds.), *A guide to treatments that work* (2nd ed., pp. 525–557). Oxford: Oxford University Press.

Maletzky, B. M., Tolan, A., & McFarland, B. (2006). The Oregon depo-Provera program: A five-year follow-up. *Sexual Abuse, 18,* 303–316.

Marshall, W. L. (1989). Intimacy, loneliness, and sexual offenders. *Behaviour Research and Therapy, 27,* 491–503.

Marshall, W. L. (1997). Pedophilia: Pathology and theory. In D. R. Laws & W. O'Donohue (Eds.), *Handbook of sexual deviance* (pp. 152–174). New York: Guilford Press.

Marshall, W. L. (2006). Appraising treatment outcome with sexual offenders. In W. L. Marshall, Y. M. Fernandez, L. E. Marshall, & G. E. Serran (Eds.), *Sexual offender treatment: Controversial issues* (pp. 255–273). Chichester, West Sussex, England: Wiley.

Marshall, W. L. (2007). Diagnostic issues, multiple paraphilias, and comorbid disorders in sexual offenders: Their incidence and treatment. *Aggression and Violent Behavior, 12,* 16–35.

Marshall, W. L., Anderson, D., & Fernandez, Y. (1999). *Cognitive behavioural treatment of sexual offenders.* Chichester, West Sussex, England: Wiley.

Marshall, W. L., & Eccles, A. (1991). Issues in clinical practice with sex offenders. *Journal of Interpersonal Violence, 6,* 68–93.

Marshall, W. L., Fernandez, T. M., Serran, G. A., Mulloy, R., Thornton, D., Mann, R. E., et al. (2003). Process variables in the treatment of sexual offenders: A review of the relevant literature. *Aggression and Violent Behavior, 8,* 205–234.

Marshall, W. L., & Laws, D. R. (2003). A brief history of behavioral and cognitive behavioral approaches to sexual offender treatment: Pt. 2. The modern era. *Sexual Abuse, 15,* 93–120.

McGuire, R. J., Carlisle, J. M., & Young, B. G. (1965). Sexual deviations as conditioned behaviour: A hypothesis. *Behaviour Research and Therapy, 2,* 185–190.

Milner, J. S., & Dopke, C. A. (1997). Paraphilia not otherwise specified. In D. R. Laws & W. O'-Donohue (Eds.), *Sexual deviance* (pp. 394–423). New York: Guilford Press.

Money, J. (1986). *Lovemaps: Clinical concepts of sexual/erotic health and pathology, paraphilias, and gender transposition in childhood, adolescence, and maturity.* New York: Irvington.

Money, J. (1997). *Principles of developmental sexology.* New York: Continuum.

Money, J. (1999). *The lovemap guidebook: A definitive statement.* New York: Continuum.

Money, J. (2002). *A first person history of pediatric psychoendocrinology.* New York: Kluwer Academic.

Moser, C. (2001). Paraphilia: A critique of a confused concept. In P. J. Kleinplatz (Ed.), *New directions in sex therapy: Innovations and alternatives* (pp. 91–108). Philadelphia: Brunner-Routledge.

Moser, C., & Kleinplatz, P. J. (2005). *DIS-IV-TR* and the paraphilias: An argument for removal. *Journal of Psychology and Human Sexuality, 17,* 91–109.

Nichols, M. (2006). Psychotherapeutic issues with "kinky" clients: Clinical problems, yours and theirs. *Journal of Homosexuality, 50,* 281–300.

Nordling, N., Sandnabba, N. K., Santtila, P., & Alison, L. (2006). Differences and similarities between gay and straight individuals involved in the sadomasochistic subculture. *Journal of Homosexuality, 50,* 41–57.

O'Donohue, W. T., Regev, L. G., & Hagstrom, A. (2000). Problems with the *DSM-IV* diagnosis of pedophilia. *Sexual Abuse: A Journal of Research and Therapy, 12,* 95–105.

Osborne, C. S., & Wise, T. N. (2005). Paraphilias. In R. Balon & R. T. Segraves (Eds.), *Handbook of sexual dysfunction* (pp. 293–330). London: Taylor & Francis.

Petrunik, M., & Weisman, R. (2005). Constructing Joseph Fredericks: Competing narratives of a child sex murderer. *International Journal of Law and Psychiatry, 28,* 75–96.

Plante, R. F. (2006). Sexual spanking, the self, and the construction of deviance. *Journal of Homosexuality, 50,* 59–79.

Plummer, K. (1975). *Sexual stigma: An interactionist account.* London: Routledge & Kegan Paul.

Prentky, R. A., Janus, E., Barbaree, H., Schwartz, B. K., & Kafka, M. P. (2006). Sexually violent predators in the courtroom; Science on trial. *Psychology, Public Policy, and Law, 12,* 357–393.

Price, M., Kafka, M. P., Commons, M. L., Gutheil, T. G., & Simpson, W. (2002). Telephone scatologia: Comorbidity with other paraphilias and paraphilia-related disorders. *International Journal of Law and Psychiatry, 25,* 37–49.

Purcell, C. E., & Arrigo, B. A. (2006). *The psychology of lust murder: Paraphilia, sexual killing and serial homicide.* New York: Academic Press.

Putte, D., van de (1994). De psychoanalytische behandeling van parafilieën [The psychoanalytic treatment of paraphilias]. *Tijdschrift voor Seksuologie, 18,* 46–55.

Quinsey, V. L. (2003). The etiology of anomalous sexual preferences in men. *Annals of the New York Academy of Sciences, 989,* 105–117.

Quinsey, V. L., Rice, M. E., Harris, G. T., & Reid, K. S. (1993). The phylogenetic and ontogenetic development of sexual age preferences in males: Conceptual and measurement issues. In H. E. Barbaree, W. L. Marshall, & S. M. Hudson (Eds.), *The juvenile sex offender* (pp. 143–163). New York: Guilford Press.

Rachman, S. (1966). Sexual fetishism: An experimental analogue. *Psychological Record, 16,* 293–296.

Rachman, S., & Hodgson, R. J. (1968). Experimentally induced "sexual fetishism": Replication and development. *Psychological Record, 18,* 25–27.

Raymond, N. C., Coleman, E., Ohlerking, F., Christenson, G. A., & Miner, M. (1999). Psychiatric comorbidity in pedophilic sex offenders. *American Journal of Psychiatry, 156,* 786–788.

Raymond, N. C., Grant, J. E., Kim, S. W., & Coleman, E. (2002). Treatment of compulsive sexual behavior with naltrexone and serotonine reuptake inhibitors: Two case studies. *International Clinical Psychopharmacology, 17,* 201–205.

Reiersøl, O., & Skeid, S. (2006). The ICD diagnoses of fetishism and sadomasochism. *Journal of Homosexuality, 50,* 243–262.

Rice, M. E., & Harris, G. T. (2003). The size and sign of treatment effects in sex offender therapy. *Annals of the New York Academy of Sciences, 989,* 428–440.

Riley, D. E. (2002). Reversible transvestic fetishism in a man with Parkinson's disease treated with selegiline. *Clinical Neuropharmacology, 25,* 234–237.

Rosen, I. (Ed.). (1996). *Sexual deviation* (3rd ed.). Oxford: Oxford University Press.

Rösler, A., & Witztum, E. (2000). Pharmacotherapy of the paraphilias in the next millennium. *Behavioral Sciences and the Law, 18,* 43–56.

Sauvageau, A., & Racette, S. (2006). Autoerotic deaths in the literature from 1954 to 2004: A review. *Journal of Forensic Sciences, 51,* 140–146.

Schober, J. M., Byrne, P. M., & Kuhn, P. J. (2006). Leuprolide acetate is a familiar drug that may modify sex-offender behaviour: The urologist's role. *British Journal of Urology International, 97,* 684–686.

Schober, J. M., Kuhn, P. J., Kovacs, P., Earle, J., Byrne, P., & Fries, R. (2005). Leuprolide acetate suppresses pedophilic urges and arousability. *Archives of Sexual Behavior, 34,* 691–705.

Seto, M. C. (2004). Pedophilia and sexual offenses against children. *Annual Review of Sex Research, 15,* 321–361.

Shapiro, M. A., Chang, Y. L., Munson, S. K., Okun, M. S., & Fernandez, H. H. (2006). Hypersexuality and paraphilia induced by selegiline in Parkinson's disease: Report of 2 cases. *Parkinsonism and Related Disorders, 12,* 392–395.

Shiah, I., Chao, C., Mao, C., & Chuang, Y. (2006). Treatment of paraphilic sexual disorder: The use of topiramate. *International Clinical Psychopharmacology, 21,* 241–243.

Simon, W. (1994). Deviance as history: The future of perversion. *Archives of Sexual Behavior, 23,* 1–19.

Socarides, C. W. (1988). *The preoedipal origin and psychoanalytic therapy of sexual perversions.* Madison, WI: International Universities Press.

Spitzer, R. L. (2005). Sexual and gender identity disorders: Discussion of questions for *DSM-V. Journal of Psychology and Human Sexuality, 17,* 111–116.

Stoller, R. J. (1975). *Perversion: The erotic form of "hatred."* New York: Delta Book.

Studer, L. H., & Aylwin, S. (2006). Paraphilia: The problem with diagnosis and limitations of CBT in treatment. *Medical Hypotheses, 67,* 774–751.

Sugerman, P., Dughn, C., Saad, K., Hinder, S., & Bluglass, R. (1994). Dangerousness in exhibitionists. *Journal of Forensic Psychiatry, 5,* 287–296.

Tennent, G., Bancroft, J., & Cass, J. (1974). The control of sexual deviant behavior by drugs: A double-blind controlled study of benperidol, chlorpromazine and placebo. *Archives of Sexual Behavior, 3,* 261–271.

Verhaeghe, P. (2002). Perverse structuur versus perverse trekken: Wie behandelt wie [Perverse structure versus perverse traits: Who is treating whom?]. In M. Thys & M. Kinet (Eds.), *Liefdesverklaringen* [Love declarations] (pp. 33–59). Leuven: Acco.

Vroege, J. A., Hengeveld, M., & Gijs, L. (1998). Classification of sexual dysfunctions: Towards *DSM-V* and *ICD-11. Comprehensive Psychiatry, 39,* 333–337.

Wakefield, J. C. (1992). The concept of mental disorder: A conceptual critique of *DSM-III-R's* definition of mental disorder. *American Psychologist, 47,* 373–388.

Wakefield, J. C. (2005). Biological function and dysfunction. In D. M. Buss (Ed.), *The handbook of evolutionary psychology* (pp. 878–902). Hoboken, NJ: Wiley.

Ward, T., Polashek, D. L. L., & Beech, A. R. (2005). *Theories of sexual offending.* London: Wiley.

Weinberg, T. S. (2006). Sadomasochism and the social sciences: A review of the sociological and social psychological literature. *Journal of Homosexuality, 50,* 17–40.

Widiger, T. A., & Trull, T. J. (2007). Plate tectonics in the classification of personality disorder: Shifting to a dimensional model. *American Psychologist, 62,* 71–83.

Wilson, G. D. (1987). An ethological approach to sexual deviation. In G. D. Wilson (Ed.), *Variant sexuality: Research and Theory* (pp. 54–115). London: Croom.

World Health Organization. (1992). *The ICD-10 classification of mental and behavioural disorders: Clinical descriptions and diagnostic guidelines.* Geneva, Switzerland: Author.

World Health Organization. (1993). *The ICD-10 classification of mental and behavioural disorders: Diagnostic criteria for research.* Geneva, Switzerland: Author.

The Etiology of Sexual Deviance

Patrick Lussier, Kristie McCann,
and Eric Beauregard

17
Chapter

Learning Objectives

In this chapter, we discuss:

- General etiological models of sexual deviance.
- Comorbid disorders.
- Specific etiological models of sexual deviance.
- Co-occurrence of paraphilia.
- Theoretical integration and clinical implications.

Traditionally, etiological models of sexual deviance have been focused on the specific factors characterizing sexual offending. Furthermore, clinical researchers have emphasized the importance of elaborating specific etiological models for different types of paraphilia activity, as suggested by the nosological classifications proposed by the *DSM-IV-TR*. Empirical evidence regarding the comorbid disorders and co-occurrence of paraphilia suggests that we must reconceptualize the origins of sexual deviance and how it may develop over time. In this chapter, we review recent theoretical developments explaining sexual deviance, its specific manifestations as well as the empirical evidence supporting those, and the importance of appreciating the complexity of these behaviors and their origins. We focus this review on deviant sexual behaviors that involve interpersonal transgression (i.e., rape, pedophilia, courtship disorders, sadism).

General Etiological Models of Sexual Deviance

Biological/Neuropsychological Models

Various researchers have investigated the relationship between sexual deviance and testosterone, the hormone most responsible for male sexual behavior. In their review, Blanchard, Cantor, and Robichaud (2006) concluded that samples of sexually violent offenders and pedophiles may differ in testosterone levels from control samples, though each in opposite directions. In other words, sexually violent offenders tend to show higher testosterone and pedophiles lower testosterone than controls. These results might be interpreted as reflecting only a general link between level of testosterone and level of violence used in sexual deviance. A recent meta-analysis found that the link between general aggression and testosterone level was weak in a sample of young adults ($K = 14$ studies; $r = .08$; Archer, Graham-Kevan, & Davies, 2005; see also Book, Starzyk, & Quinsey, 2001). It has been argued that behaviors associated with high testosterone levels are situation-dependent, being influenced by the person's characteristics and the social circumstances surrounding the act (Rubinow & Schmidt, 1996). In that context, high main effect sizes are not expected.

It has also been proposed that sex offenders on average have lower intelligence than nonsex offenders. A meta-analysis of 236 studies and 25,146 offenders found that sex offenders have lower IQs than nonsex offenders, and this association was more specific for child molesters than for those targeting adult victims (Cantor, Blanchard, Robichaud, & Christensen, 2005). These differences might be specific to adult sex offenders because no differences in IQ were found in juvenile sex offenders. This disparity between age groups suggests that different processes might be associated with sex offending in adolescence versus in adulthood. The reasons explaining the possible link between low IQ and sexual offending against children in adulthood remain equivocal. Because meta-analyses can assess only bivariate relationships, this study was unable to determine whether the link might have been confounded by other factors such as school performance, school adaptation, impulsivity, self-control, socioeconomic background, and so on.

Kafka (2003) recently proposed that dysregulation of the monoamine (MA) neurotransmitters might lead to repetitive, socially deviant sexual behaviors. Monoamine neurotransmitters (i.e., norepinephrine, dopamine, and serotonin) presumably play a modulatory role in attention, learning, physiological functions, affective states, goal-motivated and motor behavior, and appetitive states (e.g., sleep, sex, thirst, and hunger). The general idea is that a dysfunctional neurotransmitter mechanism might increase sexual appetite and, consequently, make it more difficult for the individual to control his sexual urges. Levels of norepinephrine, dopamine, and serotonin have more generally been related to aggressive and violent behavior (Lösel & Bender, in press). Furthermore, Caspi and associates (2002) found that individuals with lower activity of the monoamine oxidase A (MAOA) gene were more likely to show evidence of antisocial behavior when severe maltreatment was experienced as a child.

Conditioning/Behavioral Model

In the 1960s, various researchers emphasized the role of deviant sexual preferences in deviant sexual behavior. The "sexual preference hypothesis" implies that: (a) strongest sexual arousal is associated with the strongest gratification; (b) the images and acts associated with such arousal will be most reinforcing; and (c) sexual preference is relatively stable over time (Hudson & Ward, 1997). Among others, McGuire, Carlisle, and Young (1965) observed that sexual victimization is often the first sexual experience of the child victim (see also, Abel & Blanchard, 1974). They further argued that this initial sexual experience could serve as a template for the development of sexual thoughts and fantasies that would later be used by the youth during masturbatory activities. These thoughts and fantasies, paired repetitively with the pleasurable consequences of masturbation, could lead to the development of specific sexual preferences. The main implication of this approach is that sexual offenders should therefore display deviant sexual preferences. Although a large-scale study of paraphilic men showed that close to 50% reported having deviant sexual interest prior to turning 18 (Abel & Rouleau, 1990), this finding has not been replicated (e.g., Marshall, Barbaree, & Eccles, 1991). Clearly, a more complex framework linking sexual arousal and sexual deviance is needed.

Using the key principles of social learning theory, many researchers have focused on the presence of sexual victimization in the developmental history of sexually deviant men (Burton, 2003; Laws & Marshall, 1990). It is now well established that sexual victimization during childhood is neither a necessary nor sufficient condition to explain sexually deviant behaviors (Hanson & Slater, 1988). Specifically, a meta-analytic study has shown that between 21% and 49% of victims of sexual abuse do not show clinical symptoms or behavior problems following their victimization (Kendall-Tackett, Williams, & Finkelhor, 1993). In fact, most victims of child sexual abuse do not become sex offenders (Salter et al., 2003), and victims are as likely to show nonsexual developmental problems and symptoms (e.g., conduct disorder, aggression, anxiety, depression, somatic complaints) as sexual problems (Kendall-Tackett, Williams, & Finkelhor, 1993). Nevertheless, high sexualization symptoms are more specific to child victims of sexual abuse than other forms of abuse (Kendall-Tackett, Williams, & Finkelhor, 1993). Even so, sexual behaviors of children such as unwanted sexual touching, rubbing, and exhibitionism do not require either sexual victimization or its conditioning mechanisms; these behaviors also occur in normative samples of children (see Sidebar 17.1). The lack of control for the timing and "dosage" of such victimization might well explain the inconsistent results across studies. Overall, however, these findings suggest that sexual victimization may play a role in the etiology of sexual deviance, but its role is still not clearly understood.

SIDEBAR 17.1

Sexual Behaviors in Children

The scientific literature on early sexual manifestations in children shows much variation across types of sexual behavior, the most prevalent manifestations being the touching of private parts, a behavior identified in more than half of the sample (Friedrich et al., 1992). Using mothers as informants, Friedrich, Grambsch, Broughton, Kuiper, and Beilke (1991) found that between age 2 and 6, a substantial proportion of American children manifest exhibitionism (e.g., undressing in front of others = 50%; shows sex parts to adults = 26%; showing sex parts to children = 16%) and voyeurism (e.g., trying to look at people when they are nude or undressing = 34%).

More aggressive sexual behaviors are relatively uncommon during that period (e.g., trying to undress other children or adults against their will = 4%) as well as those mirroring the behaviors of adults (e.g., putting their mouths on sex parts = 0.4%; imitating sexual intercourse = 0.8%). Similarly, acts of unwanted sexual touching appear to be relatively rare during childhood. Factors such as age and sexual victimization appear to be related to the prevalence of such manifestations. For example, Friedrich et al. (1991) showed that the prevalence of those overt sexual manifestations tends to decline from age 2 to age 12. However, prevalence rates of sexual touching as high as 46% have been reported in children who have been sexually victimized (Friedrich et al., 1992; Gray, Busconi, Houchens, & Pithers, 1997).

Another perspective receiving only minor attention is the "cumulative deficit" approach. Briefly, advocates of this framework postulate that it is not so much the nature of one type of childhood experience (e.g., sexual victimization) that explains later maladjustments but the *accumulation* of negative and inadequate childhood experiences. For example, reviews have highlighted the presence of various environmental and familial risk factors associated with sexual violence (Barbaree & Langton,

2006; Starzyk & Marshall, 2003). Among those most commonly reported are: a criminogenic environment (i.e., socioeconomic deprivations, parental neglect, and disruption of care; inadequate parent-child relationship; early physical and psychological abuse); early sexual victimization experiences and inadequate response to child sexual abuse; and parental deviance and early exposure to sexual material/behavior. Taken together, these criminogenic factors may increase the risk of various behavioral disturbances, including sexually deviant behaviors. For example, among males who were sexually abused during childhood, those exposed to physical violence, emotional rejection, and neglect are more likely to sexually abuse in adulthood (Salter et al., 2003). It has been hypothesized that one of the key experiences explaining the link between these risk factors and sexual deviance is an insecure attachment bond.

Attachment Models

Many researchers have relied on the concept of parent-child attachment to characterize the developmental background of sexually deviant individuals (Marshall & Barbaree, 1990). The main underlying hypothesis is that sex offenders suffer from difficulties in establishing and maintaining intimate relationships. Drawing from Bowlby's well-known (1969) description of the attachment process, Marshall (1989) first hypothesized that a lack of a secure attachment was an important precursor of sexual deviance. The argument is based on the observation that stressors activate an attachment behavioral system in the infant. When active, only physical contact with the attachment figure will de-activate this system. If the attachment needs are not met and the system persists for a long period, negative emotional states (such as anger) will occur. As a result, the parent-child relationship has been described as providing a template for all future relationships. A securely attached child is better equipped to develop self-confidence and skills that help to form effective relationships outside the family setting. Securely attached children learn that they have the qualities to be loved and that other people can be trusted and loved. Therefore, securely attached children are better prepared to cope with life's adversities and stressful events. Conversely, insecurely attached individuals lack the skills necessary to regulate their emotional states and develop positive and trusting relationships with others. Relying on Ainsworth's work on attachment (Ainsworth, Blehar, Waters, & Wall, 1978), Marshall et al. (1991) further distinguished two types of insecure attachments in children: (1) avoidant, where parents are perceived as distant and untrustworthy; and (2) anxious/ambivalent, where parents are seen as offering little or no support or encouragement to the child.

Marshall and Marshall (2000) proposed a stepping-stone approach whereby poor parent-child attachment makes a child prone to developing low self-esteem and poor interpersonal relationships. Vulnerable children, especially those with an anxious/ambivalent attachment, are described as being particularly responsive to physical attention from others, to the point of even tolerating sexual advances in exchange for emotional closeness with another person. Low self-esteem and the need for attention may allow these inappropriate sexual experiences with an adult to be perceived positively. Marshall and Marshall (2000) further postulated that these vulnerable youth use self-stimulation as a way to make themselves feel better and by doing so, might develop the tendency to use sex as a way to cope with daily life stresses. Through a negative reinforcement process, sexual response might become the preferred way of dealing with negative life events, especially because it is easier than confronting personal problems and because the outcome is pleasurable. To explain the occurrence of deviant sexual interests and fantasies, Marshall and Marshall hypothesized that repetitive masturbation and fantasizing could lead someone to increase their repertoire of sexual interests in order to avoid boredom. This series of processes is described as being the core of the propensity to act in a sexually deviant manner, especially when situational and contextual factors (i.e., availability of a victim) are interacting with such propensity. The empirical validation of this approach should be considered only tentative at this point, particularly in view of various methodological limitations. Specifically, these studies have been retrospective in nature, which might create biases toward stability of attachment styles over time and be affected by memory decay and distortion.

Self-Regulation Model

In a series of papers, Ward and Beech (2006) proposed a model to explain the onset, development, and maintenance of sexual offending. In their model, sexual offending results from the interplay of three sets of factors: (1) biological factors or those influenced by genetic inheritance and brain development; (2) ecological niche factors or those representing the cultural, social, and personal circumstances as well as the physical environment of the individual over time; and (3) the neuropsychological functioning of the individual. Their model also identified three types of vulnerabilities—genetic predisposition, social learning experiences and circumstances, and neuropsychological systems—that can generate additional situational and contextual precursors for sexual offending (i.e., deviant sexual arousal, deviant thoughts and fantasies, negative/positive emotional states, and social difficulties). The interactions among these factors may lead to clinical symptoms involving emotional, social, and cognitive dimensions, as well as deviant sexual interests (see Sidebar 17.2). The consequences of actually carrying out sexual offenses on the offenders' own environment and psychological functioning tend to entrench the offenders' vulnerabilities and consequently maintain and/or escalate sexually deviant acts. As recognized by Ward and Beech, their model is more a framework for understanding sexual deviance than a theoretical system and, as a result, conceptual limitations restrict empirical verification of its many assumptions.

SIDEBAR 17.2

The Clinical Symptoms of Sex Offenders

1. *Emotional problems,* reflecting impulsive acts, poor emotional control and emotional impulses. Sex offenders are characterized by emotional deficits (inability to dampen down, communicate their emotions in a healthy way) that are likely to produce powerful negative emotional states following particular circumstances (argument, stress). As a result, they tend to rely on sex to increase self-esteem.
2. *Social difficulties,* which imply emotional loneliness, inadequacy, low self-esteem, passive victim stance and suspiciousness. Those deficits result from attachment insecurity leading to problems establishing intimate relationship with others.
3. *Cognitive distortions,* or sex offense supporting cognitions—these cognitions serve to explain, predict and interpret interpersonal phenomena which can be described as "implicit theories"—in a way these cognitions serves to filter perceptual information.
4. *Deviant sexual interests,* which result from the difficulty to manage effectively attachment and mood in the presence of dysfunctional schema that may lead to the occurrence of deviant sexual fantasies. The failure to regulate sexual desire in conjunction with a high sex arousal driven by deviant sexual fantasies can lead to sexual offending when the circumstances are favorable (i.e., presence of triggering factors, presence of a victim, anger, hostility).

Note: Based on the work of Ward and Beech (2006).

Comorbidity

Most general etiological models of sexual deviance tend to focus on explanatory factors specifically linked to sexual deviance and paraphilic activity. Until recently, the issue of the comorbidity of sexual deviance with other disorders had been largely overlooked. But in a recent review, Marshall (2007) showed that the comorbid disorders in sexual offenders are considerable, the most frequent being: (a) mood disorder (3% to 95%; $n = 5$ studies); (b) psychosis (1.7% to 16%, $n = 3$ studies); (c) anxiety disorders (2.9% to 38.6%; $n = 3$ studies); (d) substance-related disorders (7.8% to 60%, $n = 3$ studies); (e) antisocial personality disorder (35% to 40%, $n = 2$ studies); and (f) any personality disorders (33% to 52%, $n = 2$ studies). These studies show much variation in prevalence rates, suggesting heterogeneity in the developmental antecedents of sexual offending.

It is possible to categorize the main comorbid disorders of sexual disorders into three clusters or syndromes: (1) externalization or antisociality, (2) internalization or negative emotionality, and (3) sexualization or hypersexuality. We briefly review the evidence supporting the relationship of these comorbid disorders to sexual deviance and offending.

Externalization or Antisociality

Evidence supports the hypothesis that deviant sexual behaviors are associated with externalization syndrome, and this link is important. Sex offenders do not restrict themselves to sexual crimes but engage in a wide variety of antisocial criminal behaviors (Lussier, 2005; Lussier, LeBlanc, & Proulx, 2005). Prospective studies using representative samples of the general population have shown that: (a) there are few differences between juvenile sexual offenders as a group and nonsexual violent offenders (Van Wijk et al., 2005); (b) as the frequency of general offending increases, so does the risk of committing a sexual crime (Tracy, Wolfgang, & Figlio, 1990); (c) early onset of manifestations of antisociality increases the risk of physical and sexual violence against women (Moffitt, Caspi, Harrington, & Milne, 2002); and (d) sexual assault is almost always preceded by nonsexual assault (Elliott, 1994). Several studies based on convenience samples of sexual offenders have confirmed the importance of behavioral manifestations of externalization to the development of antecedents of sexual aggression (see Sidebar 17.3). These studies have shown that manifestations of antisociality tend to be higher in sexual aggressors of women compared to aggressors of children (Bard et al., 1987; Kavoussi, Kaplan, & Becker, 1988; Lussier, LeBlanc, et al., 2005). Sexual aggressors with a more extensive history of antisocial manifestations tend to have an early age of onset and commit a higher number of sexual crimes (Lussier, LeBlanc, et al., 2005; Lussier, Proulx, & LeBlanc, 2005; Prentky & Knight, 1993). Furthermore, sexual aggressors with more extensive delinquency and criminal histories are more likely to sexually re-offend, this trend having been observed in both juvenile (McCann & Lussier, 2006) and adult sex offenders (Hanson & Bussière, 1998). Finally, anti-social tendency and its manifestations are associated with a high level of sexual coercion in sexual aggressors of women (Knight & Sims-Knight, 2003). All these findings point to links between be-havioral manifestations of antisociality and the onset, frequency, and seriousness of sex offending.

SIDEBAR 17.3

Externalization

Externalization refers to a wide spectrum of undercontrolled behav-iors (Achenbach & Edelbrock, 1984). Different labels have been used to refer to this set of conceptually related behaviors such as problem behaviors and conduct disorder in children, delinquency in adoles-cents and antisociality in adults. The presence of this construct has been empirically verified on many occasions in children, adoles-cents, and young adults (LeBlanc & Bouthillier, 2003).

Taken together, these studies have found four dimensions to the antisocial syndrome: (1) authority-conflict behaviors such as being defiant at home, at school, at work; (2) reckless and risky behaviors, or behaviors jeopardizing one's, or someone else's, health such as substance abuse, dangerous driving, gambling, unprotected sex and so on; (3) covert behaviors, or being sneaky, dishonest and deceitful toward others; and (4) overt behaviors, or being aggressive and vio-lent toward others or objects.

Confirmatory factor analyses have shown that these domains of an-tisociality share significant variance, but also demonstrate unique variance as well. These results are in agreement with the simultaneous presence of generality and specificity in deviance over time (LeBlanc & Bouthillier, 2003). While the syndrome of antisociality seems to be widely accepted among criminologists and psychologists, the develop-ment of this syndrome is still a point of debate. This is primarily be-cause there is both continuity and discontinuity in the behavioral manifestation of externalization over time (Farrington, 2005).

Internalization or Negative Emotionality

Research on sexual deviance has not directly addressed a possible role for the wide spectrum of internalizing disorders; never-theless, its behavioral manifestations are well known to clinical researchers. Descriptive studies have shown that anxiety, depres-sion, and social withdrawal are important precursors of sexual offenses (Pithers, 1990; Proulx, Perreault, & Ouimet, 1999), yet these factors have not been consistently related to sexual recidivism (Hanson & Bussière, 1998). Furthermore, laboratory studies have shown that experiencing negative emotional states, such as depression and loneliness, are associated with an increase in sexual fantasizing and masturbation activities in sexual aggressors (Proulx, McKibben, & Lusignan, 1996). It has been proposed that sex offenders have self-regulation problems, especially in regard to the management of negative emotional states (Beech & Ward, 2004) or, alternatively, that sex offenders use sexuality (deviant and nondeviant) as a way to cope with negative emotional states and interpersonal conflicts (Cortoni & Marshall, 2001). Also, retrospective studies have demonstrated that behavioral manifestations of internalization play a pivotal role in the development of child molesting (see Sidebar 17.4). Indeed, child molesters who report more symptoms of anxiety and depression show a preference for sexual and interpersonal relationships with children (Knight, 1992; Prentky, Knight, Rosenberg, & Lee, 1989). Individuals subject to such feelings in adolescence might feel alienated and insecure with their peers due to fear of being rejected and criticized. These youth might be at risk of turning to children to fulfill sexual and emotional needs. Congruently, recent studies have verified that early behavioral manifestations of anxiety, depression, and social withdrawal are related to sexual crimes against children (Hunter, Figueredo, Malamuth, & Becker, 2003) and pedophilic sexual interest measured phallometrically (Lussier, Beauregard, Proulx, & Nicole, 2005). Therefore, there is some continuity between manifestations of internalization and sexual deviance, but the continuity appears to be more specific to child molesters. The reasons for such a link, however, are not well understood.

SIDEBAR 17.4

Internalization

The construct of internalization has been described as representing a wide spectrum of over-controlled behaviors (Achenbach & Edelbrock, 1984). According to Acton and Zodda (2005), internalization refers to the combination of experiencing negative emotions and introversion. In that regard, the concept of internalization is somewhat similar to that of negative emotionality (Lahey & Waldman, 2003).

Researchers have usually described behavioral manifestations of internalization partly in terms of the following dimensions: anxiety, depression, somatic complaints, and social withdrawal. In addition, while there is some continuity in manifestations of internalization over time, this continuity is far from being consistent (Reitz, Dekovic, & Meijer, 2005). Furthermore, empirical studies have shown that manifestations of internalization and externalization tend to co-occur in a complex manner (Lansford et al., 2006; Reitz et al., 2005). This co-occurrence has been established, particularly with depression in youth where depression has the tendency to follow antisocial behavior over time (Lahey & Waldman, 2003).

However, the link between anxiety and criminal offending has been contradictory across studies. It has been hypothesized that when anxiety reflects shyness it tends to decrease the risk for offending, while when it reflects the tendency to experience negative emotional states, it increases the risk (Lahey & Waldman, 2003).

Sexualization or Hypersexuality

The concept of sexualization and the constructs therein have been studied primarily with samples of sexual aggressors of women. Such studies have generally supported the importance of sexualization to sexual offending. Evolutionary psychologists have focused on the role of impersonal sex or the tendency in some men to pursue a short-term mating strategy by maximizing the number of sexual partners, having a high quantity of offspring, and investing little in each in order to maximize their reproductive success (Malamuth, 1998). Evolutionary psychologists have argued for a role for hypersexuality in sex offending and have empirically demonstrated a link between increased mating effort and sexual coercion (Lalumière & Quinsey, 1996; Malamuth, 1998). Indeed, results show that sexually coercive men have an earlier age of onset of sexual intercourse, more sexual partners, and a preference for partner variety as opposed to monogamy. Other studies, mostly based in clinical/psychiatric settings, have focused on the compulsive dimension of hypersexuality. Kafka and Hennen (2002) reported that close to 74% of their sample of paraphilic men showed manifestations of hypersexuality, most commonly exhibited through compulsive masturbation. Sexualization or hypersexuality has also been related to sexual coercion (i.e., forced kissing, petting, oral sex, intercourse, and the like) in adult and juvenile sexual offenders (Knight & Sims-Knight, 2003). As well, measures of sexualization have been related to deviant sexual interest for sexual aggression against children (Lussier, Beauregard, et al., 2005) and sexual aggression against women (Beauregard, Lussier, & Proulx, 2004). On the other hand, Lussier, Proulx, et al. (2005) have shown that while measures of sexualization tend to be related to sexual crimes in adulthood, the relationship was modest after controlling for behavioral antecedents of externalization.

While most researchers have reported simply the level of comorbidity in sex offenders, Lussier, Leclerc, Cale, and Proulx (2007) investigated how the three main comorbid disorders (i.e., internalization, externalization, and sexualization) relate to sexual offending. Using a large sample of convicted sex offenders ($n = 553$), they found that while all three syndromes were significantly correlated to the frequency of sex crimes committed, the dimensions of sexualization and externalization appeared most strongly predictive of the frequency of sexual offending (Figure 17.1). In fact, the link between internalization and sexual offending disappeared after controlling for sexualization and externalization, suggesting that the tendency to experience negative moods/emotional states might be better understood as an important comorbid precipitator than as one of its developmental causes. Specifically, a high level of sexualization (i.e., hypersexuality) and externalization (i.e., antisociality) might favor the actualization of deviant sexual fantasies following episodic emotional dysregulation. Sexualization might become important following puberty, when sexual drive and sexual interactions increase (Abel, Osborn, & Twigg, 1993; Marshall & Barbaree, 1990). The

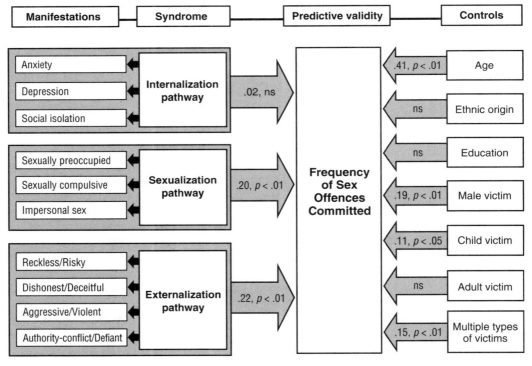

Figure 17.1

Developmental Pathways and Sexual Offending in Adulthood

Note: ns = Relationship is nonsignificant at $p < .01$. From "Developmental Pathways of Deviance in Sexual Aggressors," by P. Lussier, B. Leclerc, J. Cale, and J. Proulx, 2007, *Criminal Justice and Behavior, 34*, 1441–1462. Adapted with permission.

risk of committing a sex crime might increase as a function of the sexual drive and be facilitated by the presence of an antisocial tendency. High sexualization might especially lead to the development of deviant sexual interests if deviant sexual behaviors have been reinforced early and repeatedly (Laws & Marshall, 1990).

Specific Etiological Models of Sexual Deviance

Rape

There is no diagnostic category of rape (i.e., sexual assault) in the *Diagnostic and Statistical Manual of Mental Disorders,* fourth edition, text revision (*DSM-IV-TR;* American Psychiatric Association, 2000). Clinical researchers have criticized the *DSM* for this lack of inclusion (Abel & Rouleau, 1990; Laws & O'Donohue, 1997; Marshall, 2007). For example, Abel and Rouleau (1990) have argued that rapists should be considered sexual deviates since they tend to show other activity paraphilias such as exhibitionism, voyeurism, and frotteurism. In contrast, feminists and criminologists have argued the opposite viewpoint, emphasizing that rapists tend to commit other nonsexual criminal activity as well (Simon, 2000). Because important clinical considerations underlie this issue, this issue is more than just an empirical question. Currently, theoretical developments and empirical findings appear to favor the position that rape is a behavior that is part of a general tendency to act in an antisocial manner. The feminist/criminological perspective that supports this position has not adequately addressed the issue of persistence in rape, an integral part of the classification.

The Deviant Sexual Preference Hypothesis
Many laboratory investigations have examined the sexual preferences of sexual aggressors of women. These studies have yielded four main findings. First, as a group, sex offenders are more sexually aroused by rape stimuli than nonsex offenders, results consistent with observations from both clinical (Lalumière & Quinsey, 1994) and nonclinical settings (Lohr, Adams, & Davis, 1997). Second, differences between sex offenders and controls are accentuated by using explicit violent rape stimuli (Proulx, Aubut, McKibben, & Côté, 1994). Third, sexual arousal to stimuli depicting consensual sex does not distinguish between sex offenders and nonsex offenders (Earls & Proulx, 1987). Fourth, only about 25% of convicted sexual aggressors of women are equally or more sexually aroused by rape than by consenting sexual behavior (Looman, 2000). Therefore, a general model of sexual aggression based on the assumption that *all* individuals who commit coercive sex offenses have a sexual preference for rape cannot be accepted.

This observation, nevertheless, does not contradict the fact that sexual offenders' arousal patterns tend to be different from those of nonsexual offenders. The pattern observed is more congruent with a disinhibition model of sexual aggression (Barbaree & Marshall, 1991).

Psychopathological Model

In her "life-course persistent" model of antisocial behavior, Moffitt (1993) has proposed one of the most influential explanations of violence in recent years. According to this model, rape is described as being just another behavioral manifestation of the life-course persistent syndrome. Those manifestations change with the social context and opportunities as the individual gets older (e.g., behavior problems at 10, violent and nonviolent delinquency at 14, rape at 20, child abuse at 30). According to her model, the life-course persistent syndrome is the result of two main factors: neuropsychological deficits of the child and the presence of a criminogenic environment. Executive functioning in the individual has been associated with frontal lobe function as well as with many of the brain's cognitive abilities such as memory, learning, language, and problem-solving skills. Neurological deficits are hypothesized to be the result of either genetic predispositions or pre/perinatal factors (e.g., mother's smoking or consuming alcohol or drugs during pregnancy, malnourishment during infancy). Successive interaction between the criminogenic environment and the neuropsychologically impaired child limit his development of social and problem-solving skills, thus impeding the child's control over his behavior. Indeed, the "difficult" child is described as being at an increased risk of evoking antisocial and aggressive behavior. Furthermore, since neurological deficits may be inherited, chances are that one of the parents may be characterized by such deficits, thus further challenging the success of the socialization process. The association of early executive dysfunctions and antisocial behavior has been well documented (e.g., Farrington, 2005; Lösel & Bender, in press).

Sociocultural Approach

Building on key propositions of the sociobiological and feminist approaches, Malamuth (1998, 2003) proposed two interacting pathways leading to sexual coercion; (1) hostile masculinity; and (2) delinquency/sexual promiscuity. The hostile masculinity path describes individuals who value and are rewarded for male bonding, toughness, and interpersonal violence. These individuals are hostile toward women and endorse rape myths and attitudes supporting coercion and violence. Malamuth emphasized the role of society in reinforcing such myths, notably through pornography. Hostile masculinity is especially important in the perpetration of sexual coercion in disinhibiting the individual's behavior by being less sympathetic to the victim as well as being less anxious about the thought of being rejected by the victim.

The delinquency/sexual promiscuity path reflects the use of sexuality as a source of self-esteem. As a consequence, those following this path are likely to revert to coercive tactics in order to maximize their number of sexual partners. Sexually coercive college students tend to have more sexual partners and sexual experiences than nonsexually coercive men (Lalumière & Quinsey, 1996). Raymond Knight's work with convicted sexual aggressors in a psychiatric setting failed to replicate some of Malamuth's findings (Johnson & Knight, 2000; Knight & Sims-Knight, 2003). Indeed, Knight found that high sexualization (i.e., sexually preoccupied, sexually compulsive) and aggressive sexual fantasies are more strongly associated with sexual coercion than callous unemotional trait (i.e., lack of concern for others, lack of remorse), a concept similar to hostile masculinity proposed by Malamuth. Knight's results, however, might have more implications for the understanding of sadism rather than sexual coercion per se.

General Criminological Approach
The general criminological approach assumes that various forms of deviant activity and criminal activity share a common cause. This model suggests that one's developmental trajectory accounts for the various criminal activity patterns observed. Among others, Gottfredson and Hirschi (1990) argue that offenders can be distinguished by a latent construct—namely, low self-control—which reflects the propensity to commit a crime, given the opportunity. Individuals with low self-control can be described as having difficulties in resisting the immediate gratification that various criminal opportunities provide. Individuals lacking self-control have been described as impulsive, insensitive, physical, risk-taking, shortsighted, and nonverbal. The developmental background of these individuals has been characterized by early exposure to criminogenic models that prevented them from developing sufficient control over their behavior. Low self-control is relatively stable, beginning with early childhood as a result of inadequate socialization where parents did not supervise, recognize, and efficiently punish their child's deviant behavior.

Lussier, Proulx, and LeBlanc (2005) conducted a simultaneous empirical verification of different theoretical explanatory models of sexual aggression against women. Using structural equation modeling, they showed that the early onset and frequency of sexual offending were explained first and foremost by an early and persistent antisocial tendency. Sexual offending against women could thus be seen as part of a chronic and aggressive antisocial lifestyle.

Pedophilia

Many conceptual issues arise with the diagnostic of pedophilia, as defined by the *DSM-IV* and the *DSM-IV-TR* (Marshall, 1997, 2007). As a result, clinicians and researchers have not consistently used the same criteria to define pedophilia; others have simply dropped the term altogether in favor of the generic and rather imprecise term *child molester*. In fact, most empirical studies have been based on samples of child molesters, and thus, much of what we know applies more to child molesters than specifically to pedophiles. This lack of differentiation has severely limited theoretical developments on understanding pedophilia.

Biological or Neuropsychological Damage

It has been hypothesized that child molesting might be linked to early neuropsychological damage. For example, Blanchard et al. (2003) reported that men with a diagnosis of pedophilia were more likely to report a head injury before age 13 than nonpedophilic men. No differences in head injuries were found between these groups after age 13. At this stage, however, a causal link between head injuries and pedophilia remains tentative. Taking another approach, Quinsey (2003) has argued that causes of pedophilia might occur even earlier in the individual's development, showing a link between fraternal birth-order (i.e., having a higher number of older brothers) and homosexual pedophilia (but not heterosexual pedophilia). It has been argued that successive male fetuses help in sensitizing the maternal immune system against male specific proteins produced by the fetus. This, in turn, may affect the masculinization of the next fetus's brain (Quinsey, 2003).

Deviant Sexual Preference Hypothesis

The sexual preference hypothesis, as applied to child molesting, has received some empirical support. In laboratory studies using phallometric assessment, child molesters as a group show more sexual arousal to audiotape stimuli of sexual interactions involving children than controls. Methodological problems associated with the use of the phallometric device aside (see Marshall & Fernandez, 2000, for a discussion of those issues), sexual arousal to children is related to: (a) sexual recidivism (Hanson & Bussière, 1998); (b) early age of onset and higher number of sex crimes (Lussier, Beauregard, et al., 2005); (c) the use of violence in committing the offense (Avery-Clark & Laws, 1984); and (d) characteristics of the victims such as extrafamilial, prepubescent, and male (Seto & Lalumière, 2000). Yet, based on the current scientific literature, only a minority of convicted child molesters show a sexual preference for children (i.e., being more sexually aroused by children than by adults; Barbaree & Marshall, 1989). For example, one phallometric study has shown that only about 40% had such a preference (Lussier, Beauregard, & Proulx, 2001). Although the sexual preference hypothesis might have some potential in explaining child molestation, it has major shortcomings.

Taking this heterogeneity of response to sexual stimuli into account, Lussier, Beauregard, et al. (2005) investigated the developmental precursors of a sexual preference for children (i.e., pedophilia). Using retrospective data from a sample of convicted child molesters, they found two pathways leading to a sexual preference for children, which had been assessed phallometrically. The first was associated with psychosocial deficits, characterized by social isolation, anxiety, and depressive symptoms in childhood and adolescence. This pathway was associated with the presence of a nonviolent sexual preference for children. The second pathway, however, was associated with elements of an early sexualization, that is, early onset of sexual contact, compulsive masturbation, and early onset of deviant sexual behaviors. This pathway was more strongly related to a sexual preference for children with coercive and violent elements. Interestingly, these authors found no link between an antisocial tendency and the presence of a deviant sexual preference for children. Although preliminary, these results provide a foundation for investigating heterogeneity not only among child molesters in general, but among pedophiles more specifically.

Cognitive-Behavioral Model

Hall and Hirschman (1992) proposed a cognitive-behavioral model explaining sexual aggression toward children. The model involves four components: deviant sexual arousal, cognitive distortions, emotional dysfunctions, and personality disorders. The first three components—the physiological arousal, cognitive distortion, and emotional dysfunction—are state-dependent (i.e., situational and contextual factors), while the fourth is a trait-like characteristic (e.g., stable over time). Hall and Hirschman argued that deviant arousal has a cognitive support system that need not be true in order to be believed by the perpetrator. These cognitive distortions supporting sexual aggression tend to be idiosyncratic in child molesters (e.g., misinterpret children's behavior as indicating a sexual intent or interest). Furthermore, this model recognizes principles of the rational-choice approach by assuming that sexual aggression occurs when the appraised benefits of the aggression (e.g., sexual gratification) outweigh the risks of committing the act (e.g., getting caught). The presence of affective or emotional dyscontrol, such as occurs with depression, constitutes

the third component of the propensity to sexually aggress. This
lack of control acts as an important disinhibitor toward committing the offense. The fourth factor assumes that sexual aggressors are characterized by specific personality traits or disorders.
Unfortunately, Hall and Hirschman described this factor the least,
leaving many unanswered questions. For example, they do not
identify specific traits that might be relevant to the disorder.
Overall, while the factors presented in Hall and Hirschman's
model are theoretically grounded in a cognitive-behavioral approach, the model is more descriptive than explanatory.

Disinhibition Model
One of the more influential models explaining child molestation has
been proposed by Finkelhor (1984). This model is based on four
main factors: (1) emotional congruence, (2) sexual arousal to children, (3) blockage, and (4) disinhibition. Emotional congruence
refers to the person's motives for finding contact with children pleasurable and fulfilling. In other words, the personality characteristics
of the child are congruent with the emotional and sexual needs of
the perpetrator (e.g., the perpetrator as having childlike personality
traits, such as immaturity). Sexual arousal to children refers to the
origins of the sexual interest for children through behavioral and
conditioning mechanisms. The blockage component includes factors
that prevent child molesters from meeting their sexual needs with
adults due, for example, to poor social skills. Finally, the disinhibition component identifies various cognitive and emotional states
(i.e., impulsivity, intoxication, negative emotional states, mental retardation, stress, sexualization of children) favoring the sexual act.
These cognitive and emotional states help the individual overcome
personal inhibitions against the thought of having sex with a child
as well as external inhibitions to overcome the child's usual resistance and reluctance to take part in the acts. While Finkelhor's model
has been helpful in providing general guiding principles in the study
of child molestation, it is not grounded in theory, thus limiting its
ability to generate specific hypotheses and predictions about the origins and persistence of child molestation.

Courtship Disorder

Freund (1990) argued that acts of voyeurism, exhibitionism, frotteurism, and preferential rape should best be conceptualized
under the broader category of courtship disorders. These manifestations are aberrations of the typical behavioral interactions that
precede and initiate sexual intercourse: (a) the finding phase consisting of locating and appraising a potential partner (i.e.,
voyeurism); (b) an affiliative phase, characterized by nonverbal
and verbal overtures such looking, smiling, and talking to a potential partner (i.e., exhibitionism); (c) a tactile phase in which physical contact is made (i.e., frotteurism); (d) a copulatory phase in

which forced sexual intercourse occurs (i.e., rape). Freund, Seto, and Kuban (1997) have shown that paraphilic activities associated with the pretactile phase of courtship disorders (i.e., exhibitionism, voyeurism, and frotteurism) are more likely to occur together than they are with manifestations associated with the tactile phase, such as rape, sadism and masochism (see also Templeman & Stinnett, 1991). An important limitation of this conceptualization, however, is that acts of frotteurism tend to co-occur with paraphilic activity other than those found under the umbrella term of courtship disorder (Abel & Rouleau, 1990).

Biological and Neuropsychological Factors

Using retrospective file reviews of a large sample of adult males and females in an inpatient/outpatient hospital for individuals with traumatic brain injury (TBI; $n = 445$), Simpson, Blaszczynski, and Hodgkinson (1999) found that 29 males (6.5%) had committed at least one "sexually aberrant behavior" (i.e., exhibitionism, frotteurism, toucherism, sexual assault). The most common inappropriate sexual behavior was frotteurism, which accounted for more than 64% of all the inappropriate sexual behaviors committed by the patients, the hospital staff being the primary target of such behaviors. Bivariate statistical analyses showed that those who committed a sexually aberrant act sustained more severe brain injuries at a younger age. Further analyses (Simpson, Tate, Ferry, Hodgkinson, & Blaszczynski, 2001) showed that failure to return to work, substance abuse, and nonsexual criminal behavior postinjury were correlated with the presence of inappropriate sexual behaviors. Overall, however, neuroradiological (type of injury, site of brain injury) and neuropsychological factors did not appear to be strong correlates of aberrant sexual behaviors.

Social Incompetency Hypothesis

This approach tends to describe individuals with a courtship disorder as having certain psychosocial disturbances leading to social incompetence and thus limiting their access to a consenting partner (e.g., Allen, 1969). Different forms of incompetence have been described, such as being shy and inhibited (Brockman & Bluglass, 1996), uncertainty about one's virility in the presence of women (Krafft-Ebing, 1886/1965, 1886/1998), and severe psychological impairment such as Asperger's syndrome, mental retardation, and developmental delay (Fedoroff, 2003). To date, few empirical studies have examined personality characteristics and mental disorders of individuals with a courtship disorder, and this lack of research makes it difficult to draw any strong conclusions about the role of social incompetency.

High Sexual Drive Hypothesis

Many researchers have emphasized the strong sexual drive of individuals with a courtship disorder. For example, Krafft-Ebing (1886/1965, 1889/1998) first suggested that frotteurs might be hypersexual individuals having difficulty controlling their masturbatory urges. We found no evidence, however, supporting such a claim. From an evolutionary standpoint, Thornhill and Palmer (2000) have argued that many sexual behaviors are by-products of the intense sexual desires of males and the sexual choosiness of human females. They described acts of exhibitionism, frotteurism, and voyeurism as a means of giving sexual stimulation to male perpetrators by circumventing female choice. It is not clear, however, if the tendency to circumvent female choice is attributable to individual traits such as egocentrism, impulsivity, hostile masculinity, or a lack of empathy. Along the same line, Freund et al. (1997) argued that courtship disorders may reflect the preference for a rapid conversion of sexual arousal into orgasm at an early phase within the courtship sequence. It is not clear from the account by Freund et al. (1997), however, why some individuals would become fixated at one phase of the courtship rather than another (Lussier & Piché, in press).

Sadism

The diagnosis of sexual sadism remains somewhat elusive for clinical practitioners. Despite high discriminant validity revealed in studies using *DSM* diagnostic criteria, Marshall and Yates (2004) expressed reservations about this method of identifying sexual sadism. Marshall, Kennedy, Yates, and Serran (2002) illustrated how even internationally renowned forensic psychiatrists, all known for their work on sexual sadists, could not agree precisely on who was and who was not a sadist. Consequently, the generalization of theoretical developments and the validity of empirical studies on sexual sadism are limited by the absence of a consensus on the definition of sexual sadism.

Biological and Neuropsychological Model
Krafft-Ebing (1886/1965, 1886/1998) believed that sexual sadism constitutes an atavistic expression engraved in our genes. Contemporary authors such as Chessick (1997) defended a similar position: that "all humans are born with a primal biological archaic aggressive-destructive drive, the gratification of which gives satisfaction just like the sexual drive" (p. 612). Nevertheless, the predominant point of view in recent studies stipulates that this innate capacity to destroy others expresses itself only if specific developmental factors favor its emergence (Marmor & Gorney, 1999). As for the biological causes of sexual sadism, physiopathologies of the right frontal lobe are frequent in sadistic offenders (Hucker, 1997; Hucker et al., 1988; Langevin et al., 1985; Money, 1990) but it has not been confirmed if cerebral damages cause sexual sadism. The role of these damages, whether genetic or the result of a trauma, is an unresolved question requiring further investigation.

Deviant Sexual Preferences

Phallometric studies of sadists indicate that they prefer sexually coercive activities (Barbaree, Seto, Serin, Amos, & Preston, 1994; Fedora et al., 1992; Proulx, 2001). Marshall, Kennedy, and colleagues (2002) reported that sexual offenders identified by psychiatrists as nonsadistic had a more pronounced sexual preference for rape than those identified as sadists. Finally, the results of studies by Seto and Kuban (1996) and Langevin et al. (1985) have not suggested any significant difference between sexual offenders identified as sadists and nonsadists. These inconsistent results may be due to discrepancies in the definitions of sadists or they may result from the different samples studied.

Developmental Approach

Developmental factors appear to contribute to the emergence of sadism in sexual offenders. Brittain (1970) concluded that the early childhood of sexual sadists was characterized by overprotective and controlling behaviors by the mother, and by acts of violence by an authoritarian father. In response to these inadequate relationships with their parents, sexual sadists developed an insecure attachment style that expresses itself through attitudes of withdrawal. MacCulloch, Snowden, Wood, and Mills (1983) indicated that all the subjects in their sample of sadistic sexual offenders ($N = 13$) reported difficulties in their interpersonal relationships and sociosexual interactions during adolescence. The authors interpreted these relational failures as responsible for the development of low self-esteem among sexual sadists and also as aggravating their social isolation. In such conditions, sadistic sexual fantasies and paraphilic behaviors (voyeurism, exhibitionism, and fetishism) become established as a surrogate source of emotional and sexual gratification in these offenders.

Psychopathology and Personality Disorders

Regarding the personality traits of sadists, Brittain (1970) described them as shy, anxious, introverted, and socially isolated, but of superior intelligence. He depicts the sadist as someone who is studious, punctual, meticulous, prudish, and does not consume alcohol. He has little sexual experience and has difficulty achieving an erection with a partner, thus often considering himself inferior to other more virile men where sex is concerned. The only aspect of the sadist's life in which he is triumphant is his secret world, which is dominated by sadistic sexual fantasies, paraphilic behaviors, the torture of animals, and ultimately, the commission of sexual aggression and sexual murder. The sadist is seen as well-mannered, effeminate, pedantic, and as having problems openly expressing anger. Finally, Brittain claims sadists rarely have previous convictions, except for sexual nuisance offenses (e.g., exhibitionism, voyeurism, obscene phone calls). Most aspects of the clinical portrait provided by Brittain have been confirmed in empirical studies conducted by Dietz and colleagues (Dietz, Harry, & Hazelwood, 1986; Dietz, Hazelwood, & Warren, 1990; Hazelwood & Douglas, 1980; Warren, Hazelwood, & Dietz, 1996). However, they did identify some differences, with their subjects presenting alcohol/drug abuse problems (50%) and criminal records (35%). Moreover, their results showed the presence of other paraphilias (between 20% and 45%).

Regarding the psychopathological profile, some authors conclude that sexual sadists are psychopathic and narcissistic, based on the characteristics of the offense rather than on a careful evaluation of their personality (Dietz et al, 1986; Dietz et al., 1990; Smith & Brown, 1977). Contrary to Dietz et al.'s opinion (1990), the results of a study by Holt, Meloy, and Strack (1999) showed that there was no significant link between psychopathy—evaluated using the Psychopathy Checklist Revised (PCL-R; Hare, 1991)—and sexual sadism. Beauregard and Proulx (2002) as well as Proulx, Blais, and Beauregard (2006) suggested that sadistic sex offenders were characterized by schizoid and avoidant personality disorders. The different opinions regarding the personality disorders of sadistic sexual offenders presented above may be interpreted in several ways: (a) it may be that in their everyday interpersonal relationships, sexual sadists present a functioning mode characterized by avoidant (introversion, low self-esteem) and schizoid (solitary) personality features, but adopt a psychopathic functioning mode (lack of empathy) in their sexual fantasies and sexual offenses; (b) it may be that two or more types of sadistic sexual offenders exist (Siomopoulos & Goldsmith, 1976); and (c) it may be that given the paucity of evidence, sadists do not suffer from any type of personality disorder.

Proulx et al. (2006) suggested that Millon and Davis's (1996) model of personality disorder may help us weigh the respective value of these hypotheses. This model stipulates that individuals with an avoidant personality disorder have several features in common with those presenting with an antisocial-sadistic disorder. Both types have presumably suffered at the hands of violent parents and were exposed to models of violence during childhood. While avoidant personality types and sadists share the same mistrust and hostility as adults, their coping strategies differ. According to this view, the avoidant aggressor will express this propensity for violence only in his fantasies and sexual offenses, whereas the antisocial aggressor expresses it daily in his interpersonal relationships, including his consenting sexual activities. Millon and Davis's model is compatible with both a psychopathic way of functioning, as well as an avoidant personality disorder in sadistic sexual aggressors. Choosing what he sees as a weak victim (i.e., a woman) suits the avoidant aggressor because of his lack of self-confidence, whereas the antisocial sadist adopts a predatory mode with all people he considers inferior (Feister & Gay, 1991; Spitzer, Feister, Gay, & Pfohl, 1991).

Comparative Studies of Sadistic and Nonsadistic Offenders

Four studies comparing sadistic and nonsadistic offenders have been identified in the literature (Gratzer & Bradford, 1995; Langevin et al., 1985; Marshall et al., 2002; Proulx, Blais, & Beauregard, 2006). There have been relatively few empirical studies on sexual sadism and the existing ones suffer from certain limitations. Langevin et al.'s study (1985), as well as that by MacCulloch et al. (1983), both had a limited number of subjects. Moreover, samples of other studies were biased, with some composed in large part of serial sexual murderers (Dietz et al., 1990; Warren et al., 1996). Finally, several samples were composed of mixed groups of sexual aggressors of women and those who assaulted children (Dietz et al., 1990; Marshall et al., 2002). Overall, Proulx et al.'s (2006) results are in agreement with those of Gratzer and Bradford (1995), and show that sadistic sexual offenders differ from nonsadists on several levels. In both studies, *DSM* diagnostic criteria (American Psychiatric Association, 1987, 1994) were used in order to distinguish sexual sadists from nonsadists. Interestingly, most of the differences noted are congruent with the portrait of the sadistic offender described previously by Brittain (1970) and Dietz et al. (1990). Nevertheless, Marshall et al. (2002) found significant differences contradictory to the actual knowledge on sexual sadism. Specifically, compared with nonsadistic offenders, sadistic offenders were less likely to mutilate and torture their victim; they showed less sexual arousal to violent rapes; and they were less likely to be diagnosed with an additional personality disorder. It is important to recognize that the participants in this study were not representative of incarcerated sadistic and nonsadistic sexual offenders. In fact, this sample included only offenders for whom a psychiatric evaluation was conducted in order to assess their dangerousness. Moreover, the sadistic participants in this study committed less coercive offenses than has been generally reported in studies on sexual sadism.

Co-Occurrence of Paraphilia

Theoretical models of specific forms of deviant sexual behaviors have emphasized different sets of explanatory factors for rape (e.g., low self-control), pedophilia (e.g., emotional congruence between the individual's personality and the child's characteristic), courtship disorder (e.g., high sexual drive), and sadism (e.g., psychopathy). Those theoretical developments, however, have rarely taken into account the fact that different types of paraphilic activity tend to co-occur. Clinical studies have shown that persistent sex offenders tend not to restrict themselves to one type of deviant sexual behavior. For example, it has been shown that more than 40% of sex offenders had committed more than one paraphilic activity (Abel & Rouleau, 1990; Bradford, Boulet, & Pawlak, 1992). Abel and Rouleau (1990) attested that while 15% to 19% of extrafamilial pedophiles were characterized by only one paraphilia, about 40% were characterized by four or more. Similarly, Abel, Becker, Cunningham-Rathner, Rouleau, and Murphy (1987) reported that 20% of their sample offended against both males and females, 42% offended against more than one age category, and 23% offended against both intra- and extrafamilial victims. Weinrott and Saylor (1991) underlined the importance of using self-reported data to estimate sexual polymorphism: based on an official source of data, 84% of their sample restricted themselves to one victim type; this percentage fell to 47% when based on self-reported data. Even more drastic effects regarding the source and methodology for data have been presented by Heil, Ahlmeyer, and Simons (2003). Their study showed that 70% of offenders limit themselves to a single sex crime type using official records, but this number dropped to 20% using self-report data and 11% with polygraph testing. More specifically, sexual polymorphism regarding the gender of the victim increased from 9% to 36% using polygraph testing (as opposed to official data), from 7% to 70% regarding the victims' age, and from 7% to 57% regarding relationship of the victim (stranger versus nonstranger). In sum, these studies suggest that among sex offenders who tend to persist and re-offend, the tendency is to commit more than one type of deviant sexual behavior.

Theoretical Intergration and Clinical Considerations

Most theoretical models of sexual deviance are nondevelopmental and static in focus, emphasizing the description of the characteristics associated with the propensity to act in a sexually deviant manner. As such, they do not provide explanations for the most important dimensions of the *development* of sexual deviance (i.e., onset, persistence, desistance). Static models have not helped us devote attention to the consequences of deviant sexual behaviors on a person's sexual and nonsexual development or to the role of different life transitions (e.g., school entry, dating, marriage, parenthood). Those transitions and events may have profound implications on interpersonal relationships and sexual expressions. We believe that a more fruitful approach to the understanding of sexual deviance lies in the application of a developmental paradigm. A key argument of developmentalists is that quantitative and qualitative changes in the manifestations of deviance are related to age in an orderly and hierarchical way (Loeber & LeBlanc, 1990).

A Life-Course Developmental Approach to Sexual Deviance

Based on this review, three conclusions can be drawn about the etiology of sexual deviance; these have important implications for the assessment and treatment of sex offenders. First, researchers widely accept that different sets of factors play an integral part in the etiology of and propensity for sexual deviance (Marshall & Barbaree, 1990; Ward & Beech, 2006). Five main domains of risk factors seem especially relevant to the understanding of sexual deviance: (1) cognitive/neuropsychological, (2) interpersonal, (3) sexual, (4) the moral/social, and (5) cultural. Second, while early models focused on the early years of development (childhood) to explain this propensity, researchers are increasingly accepting the idea that other periods of development (e.g., adolescence, adulthood) are also important (Marshall & Marshall, 2000; Smallbone, 2006). In fact, psychological functioning and personality develop over the life-course and do not become stable until about mid-life (i.e., about 50 years old; Caspi & Roberts, 2001). Third, sex offenders show the presence of comorbid disorders as well as the co-occurrence of different paraphilic activities. In other words, sex offenders tend not to restrict themselves to one type of deviant sexual activity while presenting other nonsexual behavioral/psychological disturbances. According to this more complex, developmental model, sexual deviance is *multidetermined* (i.e., various risk factors), *multistages* (i.e., develops over different developmental periods), and *multifaceted* (i.e., if persistent, sexual deviance manifests itself in different ways across time and setting).

Although exceptions are evident (Marshall & Barbaree, 1990; Marshall & Marshall, 2000), existing theories of sexual deviance do not explain how the propensity to commit deviant sexual behavior develops over time. We propose a life-course framework that assumes the propensity to commit deviant sexual behaviors develops over time through a succession of stepping-stones from early infancy to adulthood (see Figure 17.2). This *cumulative-deficits model* is composed of five interrelated areas of functioning, where early deficits tend to spill over and cascade into the next developmental phase. Furthermore, each developmental period is associated with particular life transitions and

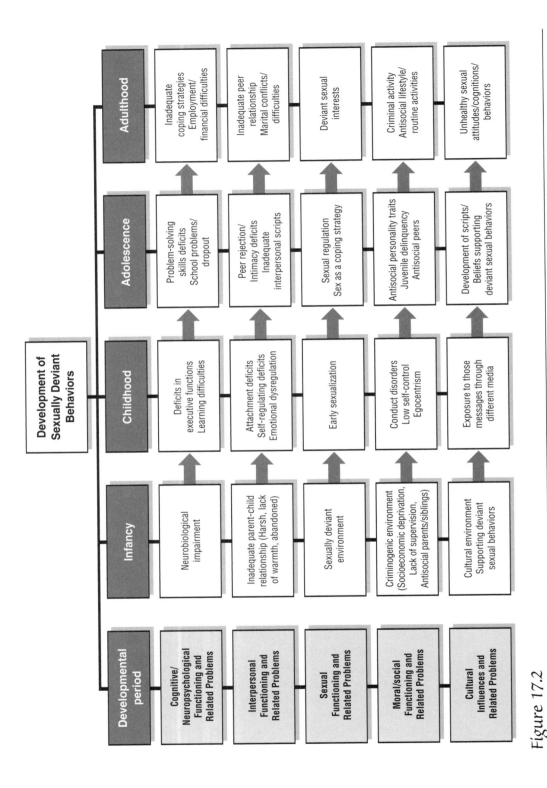

Figure 17.2

An Integrated Life-Course Developmental Explanatory Framework of Sexual Deviance

adaptations: (a) infancy (i.e., primary role of parents), (b) childhood (i.e., transition to school years), (c) adolescence (i.e., transition to peer influences), and (d) early adulthood (i.e., transition to work and intimate partner). Early deficits might thus limit the individual's ability to adapt effectively to the next developmental transition. Therefore, the earlier the risk factors, the higher the propensity to act in a sexually deviant manner. While practitioners in current treatment programs tend to emphasize mainly self-regulation deficits in interpersonal and sexual functioning (Beech & Ward, 2004; Ward & Marshall, 2004), we argue that treatment targets should incorporate these five domains of functioning and assess the extent to which such functioning is characterized by developmental excess/deficits.

First, the cognitive/neuropsychological functioning path implies that early neuropsychological damage can have long-lasting negative outcomes on cognitive abilities, problem solving skills, and coping skills (Moffitt, 1993). Those deficits can lead to learning difficulties and negative outcomes at school, which in turn might have negative implications later on at work. Second, the interpersonal functioning path, based mainly on the work of attachment theorists (Marshall & Marshall, 2000; Smallbone, 2006), rests on the assumption that early negative parent-child interactions may affect the ability to develop adequate peer-peer interactions during adolescence. Such difficulties might lead to peer rejection and inadequate interpersonal scripts (Marshall, 1989), thus limiting the ability of developing and maintaining mutually satisfying intimate relationships in adulthood. Third, exponents of the sexual functioning path suggest that a deviant sexual environment (i.e., sexually promiscuous parents, exposure to incest, sexual victimization) impedes the child in developing self-control of expression of sexual behavior. This promotes, among other things, the development of early sexualization in childhood (Friedrich et al., 1991). The inability to restrain sexual expression might lead to the use of sexuality as a way to obtain immediate gratifications when faced with life adversities (Cortoni & Marshall, 2001; Ward & Beech, 2006). The repetition of such processes might lead to the development and the maintaining of deviant sexual interests through conditioning/reinforcing mechanisms (Laws & Marshall, 1990). Fourth, the moral/social functioning path is based mainly on the criminological literature (among others, Gottfredson & Hirschi, 1990) suggesting that an early criminogenic environment (e.g., socioeconomic deprivation, lack supervision, antisocial values) will not help the child develop self-control over his behavior. Such children will lack the ability to delay immediate gratification despite longer-term, negative consequences. This inadequate socialization process may deter the child from moving from an egocentric and self-serving mode of functioning to one characterized by allocentrism (i.e., a genuine consideration of others and the surrounding environment) (LeBlanc, 2005). Finally, societal and cultural influences through various mechanisms and media can promote elements associated with deviant sexual behaviors such as beliefs supporting violence, pornography legitimizing sexual violence, sexualization of children and so on (Finkelhor, 1984; Marshall & Barbaree, 1990). The life-course process by which these ideas become personal beliefs and in turn lead to deviant sexual behaviors remains somewhat elusive.

This model emphasizes the stability and the continuity of deviance over time. Even so, empirical research studies on the sex offenders' rates of recidivism underscore how persistence in sexual offending is relatively low (Lussier, 2005; McCann & Lussier, 2006). A better understanding of the discontinuity of sexual deviance and desistance from deviant sexual behaviors remains among the most important challenges currently facing researchers.

Summary and Conclusions

The current state of empirical findings suggests that sexual deviance is multidetermined, develops in a multistage fashion, is manifested in various ways if it persists over time, and tends to co-occur with other behavioral disturbances. Currently, this developmental model of cumulative disadvantages is more theoretically and clinically intuitive than empirically based:

- In the past 30 years or so, several longitudinal cohort studies have been implemented to investigate the psychosocial development of children over the life-course.
- Much has since been learned about within-individual changes and associated risk/protective factors of many behavioral disturbances.
- One domain of functioning consistently overlooked in these studies is that of sexual development. A developmental framework has been proposed to document the activation, developmental course, and desistance from deviant sexual behavior over time (Lussier, 2005). In documenting the unfolding of deviant sexual manifestations through longitudinal analysis, we can secure valuable information about the trajectories of sexual deviance. Such analysis should not only obtain baseline information about the development of sexual behavior from early childhood to adolescence and adulthood, but also explore the biopsychosocial factors associated with sexual deviance and offending.

References

Abel, G. G., Becker, J. V., Cunningham-Rathner, J., Rouleau, J. L., & Murphy, W. D. (1987). Self-reported sex crimes of nonincarcerated paraphiliacs. *Journal of Interpersonal Violence, 2,* 3–25.

Abel, G. G., & Blanchard, E. B. (1974). The role of fantasy in the treatment of sexual deviation. *Archives of General Psychiatry,* 467–475.

Abel, G. G., Osborn, C. A., & Twigg, D. A. (1993). Sexual assault through the life span: Adult offenders with juvenile histories. In H. E. Barbaree, W. L. Marshall, & S. M. Hudson (Eds.), *The juvenile offender* (pp. 104–117). New York: Guilford Press.

Abel, G. G., & Rouleau, J.-L. (1990). The nature and extent of sexual assault. In W. L. Marshall, D. L. Laws, & H. E. Barbaree (Eds.), *Handbook of sexual assault: Issues, theories, and treatment of the offender* (pp. 9–21). New York: Plenum Press.

Achenbach, T. M., & Edelbrock, C. (1984). Psychopathology of childhood. *Annual Review of Psychology, 35,* 227–256.

Acton, G. S., & Zodda, J. J. (2005). Classification of psychopathology: Goals and methods in an empirical approach. *Theory and Psychology, 15,* 373–399.

Ainsworth, M. D. S., Blehar, M. C., Waters, E., & Wall, S. (1978). *Patterns of attachment: A psychological study of the strange situation.* Hillsdale, NJ: Erlbaum.

Allen, C. (1969). *A textbook of psychosexual disorders* (2nd ed.). Oxford: Oxford University Press.

American Psychiatric Association. (1987). *Diagnostic and statistical manual of mental disorders* (3rd ed., rev.). Washington, DC: Author.

American Psychiatric Association. (1994). *Diagnostic and statistical manual of mental disorders* (4th ed.). Washington, DC: Author.

American Psychiatric Association. (2000). *Diagnostic and statistical manual of mental disorders* (4th ed., rev.). Washington, DC: Author.

Archer, J., Graham-Kevan, N., & Davies, M. (2005). Testosterone and aggression: A reanalysis of Book, Starzyk, and Quinsey's (2001) study. *Aggression and Violent Behavior, 10,* 241–261.

Avery-Clark, C. A., & Laws, D. R. (1984). Differential erection response patterns of sexual child abusers to stimuli describing activities with children. *Behavior Therapy, 15,* 71–83.

Barbaree, H. E. & Langton, C. M. (2006). The effects of child sexual abuse and family environment. In H. E. Barbaree & W. L. Marshall (Eds.), *The juvenile sex offender* (pp. 58–76). New York: Guilford Press.

Barbaree, H. E., & Marshall, W. L. (1989). Erectile responses among heterosexual child molesters, father-daughter incest offenders, and matched non-offenders: Five distinct age preference profiles. *Canadian Journal of Behavioural Science, 21,* 70–82.

Barbaree, H. E., & Marshall, W. L. (1991). The role of male sexual arousal in rape: Six models. *Journal of Consulting and Clinical Psychology, 59,* 621–630.

Barbaree, H. E., Seto, M. C., Serin, R. C., Amos, N. L., & Preston, D. L. (1994). Comparisons between sexual and nonsexual rapists subtypes: Sexual arousal to rape, offense precursors and offense characteristics. *Criminal Justice and Behavior, 21,* 95–114.

Bard, L. A., Carter, D. L., Cerce, D. D., Knight, R. A., Rosenberg, R., & Schneider, B. (1987). A descriptive study of rapists and child molesters: Developmental, clinical, and criminal characteristics. *Behavioral Sciences and the Law, 5,* 203–220.

Beauregard, E., Lussier, P., & Proulx, J. (2004). An exploration of developmental factors related to deviant sexual preferences among adult rapists. *Sexual Abuse: A Journal of Research and Treatment, 16,* 151–162.

Beauregard, E., & Proulx, J. (2002). Profiles in the offending process of nonserial sexual murderers. *International Journal of Offender Therapy and Comparative Criminology, 46,* 386–399.

Beech, A. R., & Ward, T. (2004). The integration of etiology and risk in sexual offenders: A theoretical framework. *Aggression and Violent Behavior, 10,* 31–63.

Blanchard, R., Cantor, J. M., & Robichaud, L. K. (2006). Biological factors in the development of sexual deviance and aggression in males. In H. E. Barbaree & W. L. Marshall (Eds.), *The juvenile sex offender* (pp. 77–104). New York: Guilford Press.

Blanchard, R., Kuban, M. E., Klassen, P., Dickey, R., Christensen, B. K., Cantor, J. M., et al. (2003). Self-reported head injuries before and after age 13 in pedophilic and nonpedophilic men referred for clinical assessment. *Archives of Sexual Behavior, 32,* 573–581.

Book, A. S., Starzyk, K. B., & Quinsey, V. L. (2001). The relationship between testosterone and aggression: A meta-analysis. *Aggression and Violent Behavior, 6,* 579–599.

Bowlby, J. (1969). *Attachment and loss* (Vol. 1). London: Hogarth.

Bradford, J. M., Boulet, J., & Pawlak, A. (1992). The paraphilias: A multiplicity of deviant behaviours. *Canadian Journal of Psychiatry, 37,* 104–108.

Brittain, R. P. (1970). The sadistic murderer. *Medicine, Science and the Law, 10,* 198–207.

Brockman, B., & Bluglass, R. S. (1996). A general approach to sexual deviation. In I. Rosen (Ed.), *Sexual deviation* (3rd ed., pp. 1–42). New York: Oxford University Press.

Burton, D. L. (2003). The relationship between the sexual victimisation and the subsequent sexual abuse by male adolescents. *Child and Adolescent Social Work Journal, 20,* 277–296.

Cantor, J. M., Blanchard, R., Robichaud, L. K., & Christensen, B. K. (2005). Quantitative reanalysis of aggregate data on IQ in sexual offenders. *Psychological Bulletin, 131,* 555–568.

Caspi, A., McClay, J., Moffitt, T. E., Mill, J., Martin, J., Craig, I. W., et al. (2002). Role of genotype in the cycle of violence in maltreated children. *Science, 297,* 851–854.

Caspi, A., & Roberts, B. W. (2001). Personality development across the life course: The argument for change and continuity. *Psychological Inquiry, 12,* 49–66.

Chessick, R. D. (1997). Archaic sadism. *Journal of the American Academy of Psychoanalysis, 24,* 605–618.

Cortoni, F., & Marshall, W. L. (2001). Sex as a coping strategy and its relationship to juvenile sexual history and intimacy in sexual offenders. *Sexual Abuse: Journal of Research and Treatment, 13,* 27–43.

Dietz, P. E., Harry, B., & Hazelwood, R. R. (1986). Detective magazines: Pornography for the sexual sadists? *Journal of Forensic Sciences, 31,* 197–211.

Dietz, P. E., Hazelwood, R., & Warren, J. (1990). The sexually sadistic criminal and his offenses. *Bulletin of the American Academy of Psychiatry and the Law, 18,* 163–178.

Earls, C. M., & Proulx, J. (1987). The differentiation of francophone rapists and non-rapists using penile circumferential measures. *Criminal Justice and Behaviour, 13,* 419–429.

Elliott, D. S. (1994). Longitudinal research in criminology: Promise and practice. In E. G. M. Weitekamp & H.-J. Kerner (Eds.), *Cross-national longitudinal research on human development and criminal behavior* (pp. 189–201). Dordrecht, The Netherlands: Kluwer Academic.

Farrington, D. P. (2005). The integrated cognitive antisocial potential (ICAP) theory. In D. P. Farrington (Ed.), *Integrated life-course theories of offending: Advances in criminological theory* (Vol. 14, pp. 73–92). London: Transaction.

Fedora, O., Reddon, J. R., Morrison, J. W., Fedora, S. K., Pascoe, H., & Yeudall, L. (1992). Sadism and other paraphilias in normal controls and aggressive and nonaggressive sex offenders. *Archives of Sexual Behavior, 21,* 1–15.

Fedoroff, J. P. (2003). The paraphilic world. In S. B. Levine, C. B. Risen, & S. E. Althof (Eds.), *Hand-book of clinical sexuality for mental health professionals* (pp. 333–356). New York: Brunner-Routledge.

Feister, S. J., & Gay, M. (1991). Sadistic personality disorder: A review of data and recommendations for *DSM-IV. Journal of Personality Disorders, 5,* 376–385.

Finkelhor, D. (1984). *Child sexual abuse: New theory and research.* New York: Free Press.

Freund, K. (1990). Courtship disorders. In W. L. Marshall, D. R. Laws, & H. E. Barbaree (Eds.), *Handbook of sexual assault: Issues, theories, and treatment of the offender* (pp. 195–207). New York: Plenum Press.

Freund, K., Seto, M. C., & Kuban, M. (1997). Frotteurism and the theory of courtship disorder. In D. R. Laws & W. O'Donohue (Eds.), *Sexual deviance: Theory, assessment, and treatment* (pp. 111–130). New York: Guilford Press.

Friedrich, W. N., Grambsch, P., Broughton, D., Kuiper, J., & Beilke, R. L. (1991). Normative sexual behaviour in children. *Pediatrics, 88,* 456–464.

Friedrich, W. N., Grambsch, P., Damon, L., Hewitt, S. K., Koverola, C., Lang, R. A., et al. (1992). Child sexual behavior inventory: Normative and clinical comparisons. *Psychological Assessment, 4,* 303–311.

Gottfredson, M., & Hirschi, T. (1990). *A general theory of crime.* Stanford: Stanford University Press.

Gratzer, T., & Bradford, M. W. (1995). Offender and offense characteristics of sexual sadists: A comparative study. *Journal of Forensic Sciences, 40,* 450–455.

Gray, A., Busconi, A., Houchens, P., & Pithers, W. D. (1997). Children with sexual behavior problems and their caregivers: Demographics, functioning, and clinical patterns. *Sexual Abuse: A Journal of Research and Treatment, 9,* 267–290.

Hall, G. C. N., & Hirschman, R. (1992). Sexual aggression against children: A conceptual perspective of etiology. *Criminal Justice and Behavior, 19,* 8–23.

Hanson, R. K., & Bussière, M. T. (1998). Predicting relapse: A meta-analysis of sexual offender recidivism studies. *Journal of Consulting and Clinical Psychology, 66,* 348–362.

Hanson, R. K., & Slater, S. (1988). Sexual victimization in the history of sexual abusers: A review. *Annals of Sex Research, 1,* 485–499.

Hare, R. D. (1991). *Hare Psychopathy Checklist-Revised.* Toronto, Ontario, Canada: Multi-Health Systems.

Hazelwood, R. R., & Douglas, J. E. (1980). The lust murderer. *FBI Law Enforcement Bulletin, 49,* 18–22.

Heil, P., Ahlmeyer, S., & Simons, D. (2003). Crossover sexual offenses. *Sexual Abuse: A Journal of Research and Treatment, 15,* 221–236.

Holt, S., Meloy, J. R., & Strack, S. (1999). Sadism and psychopathy in violent and sexually violent offenders. *Journal of American Academy of Psychiatry and the Law, 27,* 23–32.

Hucker, S. J. (1997). Sexual sadism: Psychopathology and theory. In D. R. Laws & W. O'Donohue (Eds.), *Sexual deviance: Theory, assessment and treatment* (pp. 194–209). New York: Guilford Press.

Hucker, S. J., Langevin, R., Dickey, R., Handy, L., Chambers, J., & Wright, P. (1988). Cerebral damage and dysfunction in sexually aggressive men. *Annals of Sex Research, 1,* 33–47.

Hudson, S. M., & Ward, T. (1997). Rape: Psychopathology and theory. In D. R. Laws & W. O'-Donohue (Eds.), *Sexual deviance: Theory, assessment, and treatment* (pp. 332–355). New York: Guilford Press.

Hunter, J. A., Figueredo, A. J., Malamuth, N. M., & Becker, J. V. (2003). Juvenile sex offenders: Toward the development of a typology. *Sexual Abuse: A Journal of Research and Treatment, 15,* 27–48.

Johnson, G. M., & Knight, R. A. (2000). Developmental antecedents of sexual coercion in juvenile sexual offenders. *Sexual Abuse: A Journal of Research and Treatment, 12,* 165–178.

Kafka, M. P. (2003). Sex offending and sexual appetite: The clinical and theoretical relevance of hypersexual desire. *International Journal of Offender Therapy and Comparative Criminology, 47,* 439–451.

Kafka, M. P., & Hennen, J. (2002). A *DSM-IV* Axis I comorbidity study of males ($n = 120$) with paraphilias and paraphilia-related disorders. *Sexual Abuse: A Journal of Research and Treatment, 14,* 349–366.

Kavoussi, R. J., Kaplan, M., & Becker, J. V. (1988). Psychiatric diagnoses in adolescent sex offenders. *Journal of the American Academy of Child and Adolescent Psychiatry, 27,* 241–243.

Kendall-Tackett, K. A., Williams, L. M., & Finkelhor, D. (1993). Impact of sexual abuse on children: A review and synthesis of recent empirical studies. *Psychology Bulletin, 113,* 164–180.

Knight, R. A. (1992). The generation and corroboration of a taxonomic model for child molesters. In O'Donohue, W., & Geer, J. H. (Eds.), *The sexual abuse of children: Clinical issues* (Vol. 2, pp. 24–70). Hillsdale, NJ: Erlbaum.

Knight, R. A., & Sims-Knight, J. E. (2003). Developmental antecedents of sexual coercion against women: Testing of alternative hypotheses with structural equation modeling. In R. A. Prentky, E. S. Janus, & M. Seto (Eds.), *Sexual coercive behavior: Understanding and management* (pp. 72–85). New York: New York Academy of Sciences.

Krafft-Ebing, R. V. (1965). *Psychopathia sexualis.* New York: Stein & Day. (Original work published 1886)

Krafft-Ebing, R. V. (1998). *Psychopathia sexualis.* New York: Special Books. (Original work published 1886)

Lahey, B. B., & Waldman, I. D. (2003). A developmental propensity model of the origins of conduct problems during childhood and adolescence. In B. B. Lahey, T. E. Moffitt, & A. Caspi (Eds.), *Causes of conduct disorder and juvenile delinquency* (pp. 76–119). New York: Guilford Press.

Lalumière, M. L., & Quinsey, V. L. (1994). The discriminality of rapists from non-sex offenders using phallometric measures: A meta-analysis. *Criminal Justice and Behaviour, 21,* 150–175.

Lalumière, M. L., & Quinsey, V. L. (1996). Sexual deviance, antisociality, mating effort, and the use of sexually coercive behaviours. *Personality and Individual Differences, 21,* 33–48.

Langevin, R., Bain, J., Ben-Aron, M. K., Coulthard, R., Day, D., Handy, L., et al. (1985). Sexual aggression: Constructing a predictive equation. In R. Langevin (Ed.), *Erotic preference, gender identity and aggression in men: New research studies* (pp. 39–76). Hillsdale, NJ: Erlbaum.

Lansford, J. E., Malone, P. S., Stevens, K. I., Dodge, K. A., Bates, J. E., & Pettit, G. S. (2006). Developmental trajectories of externalizing and internalizing behaviors: Factors underlying resilience in physically abused children. *Development and Psychopathology, 18,* 35–55.

Laws, D. R., & Marshall, W. L. (1990). A conditioning theory of the etiology and maintenance of deviant sexual preference and behaviour. In W. L. Marshall, D. R. Laws, & H. E. Barbaree (Eds.), *Handbook of sexual assault: Issues, theories and treatment of the offender* (pp. 209–230). New York: Plenum Press.

Laws, D. R., & O'Donohue, W. (1997). *Sexual deviance: Theory, assessment, and treatment.* New York: Guilford Press.

LeBlanc, M. (2005). An integrative personal control theory of deviant behavior: Answers to contemporary empirical and theoretical developmental criminological issues. In D. P. Farrington (Ed.), *Integrated developmental and life-course theories of offending* (pp. 125–163). London: Transaction.

LeBlanc, M., & Bouthillier, C. (2003). A developmental test of the general deviance syndrome with adjudicated girls and boys using hierarchical confirmatory factor analysis. *Criminal Behaviour and Mental Health, 13,* 81–105.

Loeber, R., & LeBlanc, M. (1990). Toward a developmental criminology. *Crime and Justice: A Review of Research, 12,* 375–473.

Lohr, B. A., Adams, H. E., & Davis, J. M. (1997). Sexual arousal to erotic and aggressive stimuli in sexually coercive and noncoercive men. *Journal of Abnormal Psychology, 106,* 230–242.

Looman, J. (2000). Sexual arousal in rapists as measured by two stimuli sets. *Sexual Abuse: A Journal of Research and Treatment, 12,* 235–248.

Lösel F., & Bender, D. (in press). Risk factors for serious and violent antisocial behaviour in children and youth. In A. Hagell & R. Jeyarajah Dent (Eds.), *Dangerous behavior: Difficult decisions: Meeting the needs of children who harm.* London: Jessica Kingsley.

Lussier, P. (2005). The criminal activity of sexual offenders in adulthood: Revisiting the specialization debate. *Sexual Abuse: A Journal of Research and Treatment, 17,* 269–292.

Lussier, P., Beauregard, E., & Proulx, J. (2001, November). *Deviant sexual preferences for violent and non-violent sexual interactions in child molesters.* Paper presented at the annual meeting of the American Society of Criminology, Atlanta, GA.

Lussier, P., Beauregard, E., Proulx, J., & Nicole, A. (2005). Developmental factors related to deviant sexual preferences in child molesters. *Journal of Interpersonal Violence, 20,* 999–1017.

Lussier, P., LeBlanc, M., & Proulx, J. (2005). The generality of criminal behavior: A confirmatory factor analysis of the criminal activity of sexual offenders in adulthood. *Journal of Criminal Justice, 33,* 177–189.

Lussier, P., Leclerc, B., Cale, J., & Proulx, J. (2007). Developmental pathways of deviance in sexual aggressors. *Criminal Justice and Behavior, 34,* 1441–1462.

Lussier, P., & Piché, L. (in press). Frotteurism: Psychopathology and theory. In D. R. Laws & W. D. O'Donohue (Eds.), *Sexual deviance: Theory, assessment and treatment* (2nd ed.). New York: Guilford Press.

Lussier, P., Proulx, J., & LeBlanc, M. (2005). Criminal propensity, deviant sexual interests and criminal activity of sexual aggressors against women: A comparison of alternative explanatory models. *Criminology, 43,* 247–279.

MacCulloch, M. J., Snowden, P. R., Wood, P. J. W., & Mills, H. E. (1983). Sadistic fantasy, sadistic behaviour and offending. *British Journal of Psychiatry, 143,* 20–29.

Malamuth, N. M. (1998). An evolutionary-based model integrating research on the characteristics of antisocial men. In J. G. Adair & D. Belanger (Eds.), *Advances in psychological science* (pp. 151–184). Erlbaum, England: Psychology Press.

Malamuth, N. M. (2003). Criminal and noncriminal sexual aggressors: Integrating psychopathy in a Hierarchical-Mediational Confluence model. *Annals of the New York Academy of Sciences, 989,* 33–58.

Marmor, J., & Gorney, R. (1999). Instinctual sadism: A recurrent myth about human nature.

Journal of the American Academy of Psychoanalysis, 27, 1–6.

Marshall, W. L. (1989). Intimacy, loneliness, and sexual offenders. *Behaviour Research and Therapy, 27,* 491–503.

Marshall, W. L. (1997). Pedophilia: Psychopathology and theory. In D. R. Laws & W. O'Donohue (Eds.), *Sexual deviance: Theory, assessment, and treatment* (pp. 152–174). New York: Guilford Press.

Marshall, W. L. (2007). Diagnostic issues, multiples paraphilias, and comorbid disorders in sexual offenders: Their incidence and treatment. *Aggression and Violent Behavior, 12,* 16–35.

Marshall, W. L., & Barbaree, H. E. (1990). An integrated theory of the etiology of sexual offending. In W. L. Marshall, D. R. Laws, & H. E. Barbaree (Eds.), *Handbook of sexual assault: Issues, theories and treatment of the offender* (pp. 257–278). New York: Plenum Press.

Marshall, W. L., Barbaree, H. E., & Eccles, A. (1991). Early onset and deviant sexuality in child molesters. *Journal of Interpersonal Violence, 6,* 325–335.

Marshall, W. L., & Fernandez, Y. M. (2000). Phallometric testing with sexual offenders: Limits to its value. *Clinical Psychology Review, 20,* 807–822.

Marshall, W. L., Kennedy, P., Yates, P., & Serran, G. (2002). Diagnosing sexual sadism in sexual offenders: Reliability across diagnosticians. *International Journal of Offender Therapy and Comparative Criminology, 46,* 668–676.

Marshall, W. L., & Marshall, L. E. (2000). The origins of sexual offending. *Trauma, Violence, and Abuse, 1,* 250–263.

Marshall, W. L., & Yates, P. (2004). Diagnostic issues in sexual sadism among sexual offenders. *Journal of Sexual Aggression, 10,* 21–27.

McCann, K., & Lussier, P. (2006). *A meta-analysis of the risk factors of general and sexual recidivism in juvenile sex offenders.* Manuscript submitted for publication.

McGuire, R. J., Carlisle, J. M., & Young, B. G. (1965). Sexual deviations as conditioned behaviour: A hypothesis. *Behaviour Research and Therapy, 2,* 185–190.

Millon, T., & Davis, R. D. (1996). *Disorders of personality: DSM-IV and beyond.* New York: Wiley.

Moffitt, T. (1993). Adolescence-limited and life-course-persistent antisocial behavior: A developmental taxonomy. *Psychological Review, 100,* 674–701.

Moffitt, T. E., Caspi, A., Harrington, H., & Milne, B. J. (2002). Males on the life-course persistent and adolescence-limited antisocial pathways: Follow-up at age 26. *Development and Psychopathology, 14,* 179–206.

Money, J. (1990). Forensic sexology: Paraphilic serial rape (biastophilia) and lust murder (erotophonophilia). *American Journal of Psychotherapy, 44*, 26–36.

Pithers, W. D. (1990). Relapse prevention with sexual aggressors. In W. L. Marshall, D. R. Laws, & H. E. Barbaree (Eds.), *Handbook of sexual assault: Issues, theories and treatment of the offender* (pp. 343–362). New York: Plenum Press.

Prentky, R. A., & Knight, R. A. (1993). Age of onset of sexual assault: Criminal and life history correlates. In G. C. N. Hall, R. Hirschman, J. R. Graham, & M. S. Zaragoza (Eds.), *Sexual aggression: Issues in etiology, assessment, and treatment* (pp. 43–62). Washington, DC: Taylor & Francis.

Prentky, R. A., Knight, R. A., Rosenberg, R., & Lee, A. (1989). A path analytic approach to the validation of a taxonomic system for classifying child molesters. *Journal of Quantitative Criminology, 6*, 231–257.

Proulx, J. (2001). *Sexual preferences and personality disorders of MTC-R3 rapists subtypes.* Paper presented at the 20th Annual Research and Treatment Conference of the Association for the Treatment of Sexual Abusers, San Antonio, TX.

Proulx, J., Aubut, J., McKibben, A., & Côté, M. (1994). Peniule responses of rapists and nonrapists to rape stimuli involving physical violence or humiliation. *Archives of Sexual Behaviour, 23*, 295–309.

Proulx, J., Blais, E., & Beauregard, E. (2006). Sadistic sexual aggressors. In W. L. Marshall, Y. M. Fernandez, L. E. Marshall, & G. A. Serran (Eds.), *Sexual offender treatment: Controversial issues* (pp. 61–77). Chichester, West Sussex, England: Wiley.

Proulx, J., McKibben, A., & Lusignan, R. (1996). Relationship between affective components and sexual behaviors in sexual aggressors. *Sexual Abuse: A Journal of Research and Treatment, 8*, 279–289.

Proulx J., Perreault, C., & Ouimet, M. (1999). Pathways in the offending process of extrafamilial sexual child molesters. *Sexual Abuse: A Journal of Research and Treatment, 11*, 117–129.

Quinsey, V. L. (2003). The etiology of anomalous sexual preferences in men. *Annals of the New York Academy of Sciences, 989*, 105–117.

Reitz, E., Dekovic, M., & Meijer, A. M. (2005). The structure and stability of externalizing and internalizing problem behavior during early adolescence. *Journal of Youth and Adolescence, 34*, 577–588.

Rubinow, D. R., & Schmidt, P. J. (1996). Androgens, brain and behavior. *American Journal of Psychiatry, 153*, 974–984.

Salter, D., McMillan, D., Richards, M., Talbot, T., Hodges, J., Bentovim, A., et al. (2003). Development of sexually abusive behaviour in sexually victimized males: A longitudinal study. *Lancet, 361*, 471–476.

Seto, M. C., & Kuban, M. (1996). Criterion-related validity of a phallometric test for rape and sadism. *Behaviour Research and Therapy, 34*, 175–183.

Seto, M. C., & Lalumière, M. L. (2000). Psychopathy and sexual aggression. In C. Gacono (Ed.), *The clinical and forensic assessment of psychopathy* (pp. 333–350). Mahwah, NJ: Erlbaum.

Simon, L. M. J. (2000). An examination of the assumptions of specialization, mental disorder, and dangerousness in sex offenders. *Behavioural Sciences and the Law, 18*, 275–308.

Simpson, G., Blaszczynski, A., & Hodgkinson, A. (1999). Sex offending as a psychosocial sequela of traumatic brain injury. *Journal of Head Trauma Rehabilitation, 14*, 567–580.

Simpson, G., Tate, R., Ferry, K., Hodgkinson, A., & Blaszczynski, A. (2001). Social, neuroradiologic, medical, and neuropsychologic correlates of sexually aberrant behavior. *Journal of Head Trauma Rehabilitation, 16*, 556–572.

Siomopoulos, V., & Goldsmith, J. (1976). Sadism revisited. *American Journal of Psychotherapy, 30*, 631–640.

Smallbone, S. W. (2006). Social and psychological factors in the development of delinquency and sexual deviance. In H. E. Barbaree & W. L. Marshall (Eds.), *The juvenile sex offender* (2nd ed., 105–127). New York: Guilford Press.

Smith, S., & Brown, C. (1977). Necrophilia and lust murder: Report of a rare occurrence. *Bulletin of the American Academy of Psychiatry and the Law, 6*, 259–268.

Spitzer, R. L., Feister, S., Gay, M., & Pfohl, B. (1991). Results of a survey of forensic psychiatrists on the validity of the sadistic personality disorder diagnosis. *American Journal of Psychiatry, 148*, 875–879.

Starzyk, K. B., & Marshall, W. L. (2003). Childhood family and personological risk factors for sexual offending. *Aggression and Violent Behavior, 8*, 93–105.

Templeman, T. L., & Stinnett, R. D. (1991). Patterns of sexual arousal and history in a "normal" sample of young men. *Archives of Sexual Behavior, 20*, 137–150.

Thornhill, R., & Palmer, C. T. (2000). *A natural history of rape: Biological bases of sexual coercion.* Cambridge, MA: MIT Press.

Tracy, P. E., Wolfgang, M. E., & Figlio, R. M. (1990). *Delinquency careers in two birth cohorts.* New York: Plenum Press.

Van Wijk, A., Loeber, R., Vermeiren, R., Pardini, D., Bullens, R., & Doreleijers, T. (2005). Violent juvenile sex offenders compared with violent juvenile nonsex offenders: Explorative findings from the Pittsburgh Youth Study. *Sexual Abuse: A Journal of Research and Treatment, 17,* 333–352.

Ward, T., & Beech, A. (2006). An integrated theory of sexual offending. *Aggression and Violent Behavior, 11,* 44–63.

Ward, T., & Marshall, W. L. (2004). Good lives, aetiology and the rehabilitation of sex offenders: A bridging theory. *Journal of Sexual Aggression, 10,* 153–169.

Warren, J. I., Hazelwood, R. R., & Dietz, P. E. (1996). The sexually sadistic serial killer. *Journal of Forensic Sciences, 41,* 970–974.

Weinrott, M. R., & Saylor, M. (1991). Self-report of crime committed by sex offenders. *Journal of Interpersonal Violence, 6,* 286–300.

J. Paul Fedoroff

18

Chapter

Learning Objectives

In this chapter, we review:

- Reasons for the widespread view that paraphilic sexual disorders are untreatable.
- Behavioral strategies for treating paraphilias.
- The problems with the "relapse prevention model."
- Surgical treatments procedures and pharmacological anti-androgen approaches.
- Other pharmacological strategies.
- A method of integrating treatment approaches.

The Myth: Paraphilias Are Untreatable

Consumers of public media may be excused for coming to the conclusion that the prognosis for people with paraphilic disorders is hopeless or at least dismal. This conclusion is hardly surprising since the media understandably focuses on failure and sensationalism. A sex offender who commits an horrendous crime or who re-offends is much more newsworthy than the potential sex offender who has never committed a crime or one who has done so but has subsequently avoided any further problematic behaviors.

This point raises the questions of what professionals charged with the assessment and care of individuals with paraphilias should think, and on what basis. To provide an answer, treatment paradigms for paraphilias and the evidence to support them are reviewed. Suggestions for treatment of paraphilias are also presented, based in part on experience from the Sexual Behaviors Clinic of the Royal Ottawa Health Care Center, and research conducted within the University of Ottawa Institute of Mental Health Research.

The Issue(s)

A favorite courtroom question posed by lawyers is: "Doctor, isn't it true that paraphilias are incurable?"

Suppose a similar question was posed about some other medical condition, for example, gall bladder disease. The unfortunate expert could not possibly say this condition was definitely "curable," given highly publicized examples of disastrous outcomes such as Andy Warhol who died at age 49 on February 22, 1987, following surgery for cholecystitis (ref, http://en.wikipedia.org/wiki /Andy_Warhol/). Nor could she argue that surgery (removal of the gallbladder) corrects the underlying pathophysiologic processes that led to the formation of gallstones. In fact, even the prognostic risk factors associated with the development of gall bladder disease are not 100% reliable. Young, thin, childless men—those with the lowest risk factors—are also known to suffer from the disease.

Skeptics might argue that gall-bladder disease is not illegal and does not endanger the lives of others. What about a disease that does potentially endanger self and others, for example major depression? The degree of human suffering caused by mood disorders is astronomical and has been associated with suicide, homicide, parricide, and filicide. The current relapse rate for *treated* major depression is 50% after the first episode, 70% after the second episode, and 90% after three episodes (Blier, personal communication, 2006). One study of people with major depression reported the median time to relapse after thorough treatment was 7.4 years in 66% of patients; but in patients with residual symptoms, the relapse rate rose to 92% with a median time to relapse of 2 years (Judd et al., 2000). In spite of these sobering statistics, no practice guidelines recommend therapists to advise their patients that they have an incurable disease. What would happen if they did?

Suppose the surgeon defending treatment of gall bladder disease and the mental health practitioner describing treatment of mood disorders were asked to defend their practice with additional constraints. What problems would these experts face if the diseases they treated were illegal and socially abhorred? What if surgeons were asked to describe the prognosis not of patients with gall bladder disease but rather of those with pain in the stomach? What if psychiatrists were asked to defend the prognosis of depressed patients, some of whom received treatments that were 40 years old, some of whom received no treatment, and some of whom received inadequate treatment? Finally, suppose the patients who responded to treatment were suspected of having relapsed but were not yet detected?

The problem for advocates of modern treatment of paraphilic disorders is that the situation is much worse than the hypothetical problems faced by the defendants of treatment of gallbladder disease or mood disorders: therapists of patients with paraphilic disorders not only face all the questions listed above, they also face two other paradoxical problems. First, sex offenses are low-frequency events. Second, the known re-offense rates, even of untreated sex offenders, are low. This means that any proposed treatment must be exceptionally effective in order to demonstrate a treatment effect. While this is a fortunate position, it has contributed to the myth that paraphilias are untreatable (Fedoroff & Moran, 1997).

Can paraphilic disorders be cured? Cholecystectomy is considered to be a cure for gall bladder disease and this surgical procedure is one of the first operations surgery residents learn. However, cholecystectomies do require surgical knowledge and skill, and a trained surgical team including an anaesthesiologist, nurses, and (usually) surgical assistants. The prognosis becomes dramatically worse if any one of these components is eliminated. Cholecystectomy is considered to be a cure because it eliminates the signs and symptoms associated with gall bladder disease (though it does nothing to alter the biochemical pathophysiology that caused the formation of gallstones in the first place). Similarly, a patient with mood disorder who is successfully treated no longer reports symptoms of depression. While the relapse rates are high, successfully treated patients with depression often say they feel "cured." In perhaps 50% of first episode cases, they are right.

What about individuals with paraphilic disorders?

The Paraphilias

The assessment and diagnosis of paraphilic disorders has been discussed in previous chapters in this volume. These disorders are highly variable in their presentation, particularly when combined with "atypical sexual behaviors." Unfortunately, the heterogeneity of paraphilic disorders and atypical sexual behaviors makes definitive statements about their treatment difficult. This problem is compounded by the fact that most published treatment studies include "sex offenders." This lack of distinction makes interpretation of findings difficult because not all people with paraphilic sexual disorders become sex offenders and not all sex offenders have paraphilias (analogous to basing prognostic studies of gallbladder disease on patients who present with belly pain).

The *DSM-IV-TR* lists eight specific paraphilias and one "catchall" category of "paraphilia not otherwise specified" (American Psychiatric Association, 1994). The "essential" features of all paraphilic sexual disorders include "recurrent, intense sexually arousing fantasies, sexual urges, or behaviors generally involving 1) nonhuman objects, 2) the suffering or humiliation of oneself or one's partner, or 3) children or other nonconsenting persons that occur over a period of at least 6 months" (p. 566).

While any sexual behavior could conceivably be associated with a criminal offense, of the eight specific paraphilias listed in the *DSM-IV-TR*, only "exhibitionism" (*DSM-IV-TR* 302.4), "frotteurism" (302.89), "pedophilia" (302.2), "sexual sadism" (302.84), and "voyeurism" (302.82) involve (at least) problematic fantasy of criminal activity. In this chapter, treatment approaches apply to all paraphilic disorders unless otherwise specified.

Treatments

All psychiatric disorders, including paraphilic sexual disorders are complex and multifactorial (McHugh & Slavney, 1983). Extensive and comprehensive general reviews of treatment programs/strategies have been published (e.g., Abel, Osborn, Anthony, & Gardos, 1992; Grossman, Martis, & Fichtner, 1999; Kilmann, Sabalis, Gearing, Bukstel, & Scovern, 1982; Laws & O'Donohue, 1997). Although most contemporary treatment programs advocate a combination of treatment strategies, the primary modes of treatment are reviewed within the subcategories to which they have traditionally been assigned.

Psychological Treatments

Psychological treatments refer to those interventions that include no pharmacological or surgical procedures. These treatment approaches are not based on a "disease" perspective.

Behavioral Reconditioning
Many specific types of therapy based on behavioral conditioning paradigms (classical, operant or mixed) have been described (see Sidebar 18.1). These include: "covert sensitization" (McConaghy, Armstrong, & Blaszczynski, 1985); "imaginal desensitization" (McConaghy, Blaszczynski, & Kidson, 1988); "fantasy alteration"

(VanDeventer & Laws, 1978); "thematic shift" (W. L. Marshall, 1973); "orgasmic reconditioning" (Marquis, 1970); "masturbatory satiation" (W. L. Marshall, 1979); "verbal satiation" (Laws, 1995); "shame aversion" (Serber, 1970); "olfactory aversion" (Laws, 2001); and even "electrical" aversion (Marks, Gelder, & Bancroft, 1970). Papers describing variations on conditioning paradigms and combinations of behavioral conditioning strategies have also been published (Abel, Blanchard, & Jackson, 1974; Laws & O'Neil, 1981). Each of the behavioral treatments described involves one or more of the following strategies: (a) pairing nondeviant thoughts with a reward (usually orgasm), (b) pairing deviant fantasy with punishment (e.g., in olfactory aversion where a noxious odor is paired with the deviant stimulus), (c) altering the rewarding quality of the reinforcer (e.g., in covert sensitization where previously arousing fantasies are changed to ones with negative consequences like thoughts of being arrested), or (d) delaying of the reinforcement (e.g., masturbatory satiation in which the patient is encouraged to continue masturbating to deviant fantasies after he has reached orgasm).

SIDEBAR 18.1

Cognitive-Behavioral Treatments of Paraphilic Disorders

- *Covert sensitization:* Combination of imagined aversive consequences with imagined behavior to be changed.
- *Imaginal desensitization:* Imagined rehearsal of high-risk situations that aim to reduce anxiety and catastrophic thinking.
- *Fantasy alteration:* Intentional change in form or content of sexual fantasies.
- *Thematic shift:* Change in nature of sexual fantasies, often in conjunction with increased sexual arousal through other means (e.g., masturbation).
- *Orgasmic reconditioning:* Another name for masturbatory reconditioning; pairing normal sexual fantasies with orgasm.
- *Masturbatory satiation:* Continued prescribed masturbation after orgasm paired with the deviant fantasies.
- *Verbal satiation:* Lengthy dictation of deviant sexual fantasy immediately after orgasm.
- *Shame aversion:* Pairing of deviant behavior with induced shame or humiliation.
- *Olfactory aversion:* Pairing deviant thoughts or behaviors with aversive smells or compounds (e.g., rotting meat or ammonia).
- *Electrical aversion:* Pairing deviant thoughts or behaviors with electric shock either to the arm or genitals.

Regarding behavioral reconditioning strategies, a review of the efficacy of behavioral conditioning treatment paradigms (Laws & Marshall, 1991) concluded, "there is insufficient data meeting adequate empirical standards to permit us to conclude that masturbatory reconditioning, in any of the forms reviewed here, is clearly effective for sexual deviations of any kind" (p. 24). The review was particularly critical of "thematic shift" and "fantasy alteration" techniques about which the authors concluded, "if anything, the data would discourage their use" (p. 24). While aversive conditioning paradigms were not reviewed therein, a subsequent paper made similarly negative comments concerning the efficacy of treatment based on aversive conditioning (Laws, 1995).

There are at least four reasons why studies of treatment strategies of paraphilic disorders based on behavioral conditioning strategies have been so disappointing. The first is that much of the work in this area has included studies of gay men who wished to change their sexual orientation but who had no paraphilic disorders. Homosexuality is phenomenologically different from any of the paraphilias because, unlike paraphilic disorders, nothing about homosexuality or heterosexuality necessarily precludes the establishment of a reciprocal, mutually beneficial relationship. It is therefore not surprising that treatments designed to treat paraphilias show no efficacy when used with inappropriate "patients" such as gay men.

The second possible explanation for the poor efficacy of reconditioning treatment paradigms is that most are based on the assumption that orgasm is the single reinforcing stimulus. However, sexual activity prior to orgasm is highly reinforcing, particularly for women, many of whom enjoy sexual activity with no reliable experience or even expectation of orgasm (Shotly et al., 1984). In fact, in the case of individuals with paraphilic disorders, orgasm may become an aversive stimulus (punishment) due to its association with feelings of shame and guilt that such individuals often report immediately following orgasm.

Third, evidence based on animal research suggests that the conditioning of sexual behavior may be constrained by a "critical period," after which further conditioning has less effect on previously learned behaviors (Pfaus, Kippin, & Centeno, 2001). This last possibility is likely a good thing since as Albert Moll noted: "Were a single sexual experience, and, indeed, the first sexual experience to induce a lasting association between sex drive and the object of their first sexual experience, then we would have to find sexual perversion everywhere. Where are there to be found people who initially satisfied their sexual impulse in a normal manner?" (Moll, 1897, as cited in Sulloway, 1983, p. 304).

Finally, all behavioral treatment paradigms are based on the premise that the patient's response to behavioral treatment is normal. However, criminals, including sex offenders, may suffer from impairments in their ability to associate their actions with the consequences of their behaviors. Unfortunately, as Abel noted (1974) "a review of behavioral studies treating sexual fantasies as an independent variable, altering them directly during masturbation, still leaves a number of unanswered questions." (p. 474).

Relapse Prevention

Beginning in the early 1980s, therapists began to explicitly include innovations from the field of cognitive psychology that collectively have come to be known as cognitive-behavioral therapy. Cognitive-behavior treatment has become the most common (though not exclusive) mode of treatment, particularly within the subgroup of treatment programs with research interests. In a 43-study review that used stringent criteria for selecting outcomes, 63% were classified as having used some form of cognitive-behavioral therapy (Hanson et al., 2002). One of the most prominent of the many subtypes of cognitive-behavioral treatments is "relapse prevention" therapy (Pithers, Marques, Gibat, & Marlatt, 1983). This approach was based on modifications of methods used to assist individuals with alcohol dependency but also included innovations from "rational emotive therapy" (Ellis, 1984); "social learning" theory (Bandura, 1978; Bandura & Walters, 1974) and "social skills" training (D. S. Marshall & Suggs, 1971). Relapse prevention quickly became the treatment of choice in most sex offender treatment programs in North America, the United Kingdom, the Netherlands, Australia, and New Zealand (W. L. Marshall, Fernandez, Hudson, & Ward, 1998).

The most definitive review of "psychological treatments" involved a meta-analysis of 43 treatment studies (Hanson et al., 2002). Included were 21 studies conducted in the United States, 16 in Canada, 5 from the United Kingdom, and one from New Zealand. A total of 5,078 treated and 4,376 untreated sex offenders were compared in studies averaging 46 months of follow-up. Overall, there was a modest odds ratio = 0.81 (odds of recidivism in the treated group divided by the odds of recidivism in the untreated group) indicating a significant reduction in recidivism rates for treated sex offenders, though the effect was greatest in unpublished studies. Not surprisingly, offenders referred for treatment on the basis of "perceived need" had significantly higher sexual recidivism rates than those who were not believed to require treatment. The authors concluded that given the large numbers, the finding that recidivism rates of treated sex offenders were lower than the recidivism rates of untreated sex offenders "cannot seriously be disputed" (p. 186).

However, at the time of publication, only preliminary results were available from the California's sex Offender Treatment and Evaluation Project (SOTEP; Marques, Day, Nelson, & West, 1994).

Results of this project had been eagerly anticipated for many years since it represented one of the few randomized prospective treatment studies of "relapse prevention." Now reported by Marques, Wiederanders, Day, Nelson, & Van Ommeren (2005), the project involved 704 male sex offenders. Of these, 484 were volunteers who agreed to be randomly assigned to a 2-year relapse prevention program within a secure State Hospital, or to a "no treatment" condition within prison. Unfortunately, 55 men withdrew from the study when they discovered they were in the "no-treatment" condition and a further 14 withdrew before completing 1 year of the treatment program. Out of the 220 men who did not participate, the remainder were "nonvolunteer controls" who met study criteria but who "chose not to participate." Randomization of participants was stratified so as to match the groups on the basis of age, prior criminal history, and "type of offender" (presumably based on the nature of the sexual offense for which each man was most recently convicted). This methodological procedure was important since child molesters with only male victims were more likely to volunteer for the study than other offender types, especially rapists. Men in the study were followed for at least 5 years after release from either the hospital or prison, and the time of release was independent of participation in the study.

Based on survival analysis of the data, this study failed to find a significant effect of assigned treatment on either sexual re-offenses or nonsexual re-offenses. Specifically, the authors concluded "sexual offenders who were randomly assigned (to the) relapse prevention program did not reoffend at a lower rate than those who were randomly assigned to the in-prison groups" (p. 98).

Variations on a Theme

As a credit to the investigators in the SOTEP study, the negative results came as no surprise to investigators in the field who had had already received advance warning that relapse prevention was not as effective as had been hoped. Therefore, further modifications of the relapse prevention strategies are already being investigated.

Paradoxically, concerns with standard relapse prevention treatments appear to center on their similarity to the programs from which they derive: treatment of addictive disorders (Ward, Hudson, & Keenan, 1998). New behavioral treatment paradigms have moved from traditional addiction models in which individuals were told to abstain absolutely to models that expect occasional "lapses" or "relapses." In contrast, paraphilic disorders that are by definition sexually motivated refer to a group of disorders, the cause (or stimulus) of which simply cannot be "avoided." Further, the concept of "relapse" that, in the field of addictions has come to be an accepted event that needs to be worked through, is simply not an acceptable outcome when dealing with sex offend-

ers. New treatment programs based on these modifications of relapse prevention are currently under investigation (Hanson &
Harris, 2000).

Modifications of standard relapse prevention therapy are
characterized by a change from the view that sex offenses are an
almost inevitable event if the right circumstances are present to
the view that sex offenses are always avoidable given the correct
degree of determination. This concept is often novel for sex offenders who have been told by their therapists that they are certain to reoffend, especially if they let their guard down or are not
monitored closely enough by third parties. As a result of this information, sex offenders often state they are not sure whether or
not they will re-offend. However, asked if they know whether or
not they will rob a bank or jump off a cliff, they can answer no
with certainty.

Thus, treatments now focus on why the offender can be certain about not committing some crimes but not others. For example, while anyone can conceivably commit a bank robbery, and
while few have failed to fantasize about what life could be like
with a bank's worth of money, most people can state categorically
that they will never commit an armed bank robbery (even sex offenders). Current modifications of traditional relapse prevention
not only avoid presenting sex offenses as inevitable but also encourage offenders to own the position that the aim of treatment is
to ensure they are as unlikely to reoffend sexually as they are to
commit armed robbery.

Surgical Treatment

Surgical and pharmacological treatment of paraphilic disorders
rely on a disease model that assumes a physiological system or
anatomical structure is dysfunctional or "broken."

Surgical Antiandrogenic Interventions

Initial surgical interventions were based on the undisputed observation that more males than females committed sex crimes. If so,
then interventions and medications that mimicked female physiology should be helpful. Among the most successful treatments
are those involving surgical castration of sex offenders (Gaensbauer, 1973; Heim, 1981; Heim & Hursch, 1979; Hicks, 1993; Ortmann, 1980; Sturup, 1972).

A measure of the potential efficacy of this treatment is evident
from the report of Hanson et al. (2002), which observed that the efficacy of medical/hormonal treatments based on a meta-analytic review of treatments (Nagayama Hall, 1995) could be attributed to a
single study of surgical castration (Wille & Beier, 1989). In a review
specifically dealing with surgical castration (J. Bradford, 1997), the

mean long term recidivism rate across four studies was 2.9% with one 30-year follow-up study reporting a recidivism rate of 2.2% within a group of 900 rapists (Sturup, 1968). Some jurisdictions in the United States have enacted statutes requiring either "chemical" or "surgical" castration of convicted sex offenders, though not without controversy (Berlin, 1997).

However, surgical castration has not become the standard of treatment for sex offenders for three reasons:

1. Ethical concerns arise concerning the prescription of an irreversible surgical procedure, particularly in the case of men within the criminal justice system who might feel coerced into agreeing to surgery in exchange for leniency (Berlin, 2005).

2. Although surgical castration certainly decreases testosterone levels in men, there is no reliable evidence that men with paraphilic sexual disorders have higher than average sex drives or testosterone levels (Fedoroff & Moran, 1997; Freund, 1980). It may be that the low reported recidivism rate for sex offenders who volunteered to be surgically castrated is due to the degree of motivation demonstrated rather than the procedure itself. In addition, follow-up studies of sex offenders who underwent surgical castration in an age before medications like sildenafil were available found 10% were still able to have sexual intercourse 10 years after surgery (Cornu, 1973); furthermore, in a study of 101 healthy young adult men investigating the relationship between serum testosterone and sexual activity or interest, no correlation was found (Brown, Monti, & Corriveau, 1978).

3. In terms of the effectiveness of decreasing serum testosterone levels, surgical castration is less effective than "chemical castration," since not all testosterone is produced by the testes.

Pharmacologic Androgen Reduction

Three main classes of antiandrogens constitute the medications referred to as "chemical castration." These medications act to decrease the action of testosterone via at least one of three mechanisms: (1) the competitive inhibition of androgenic intracellular receptors, (2) the increased metabolism or breakdown of testosterone and its metabolites, or (3) the inhibition of luteinizing hormone (LH). These antiandrogens have been used medically, primarily in the treatment of testosterone dependent tumors, most notably prostate cancer (Sausville & Longo, 2001).

Cyproterone Acetate (CPA)
Cyproterone acetate is sometimes described as a testosterone receptor blocker. Although partly true, CPA's effectiveness in reducing testosterone is due to a combination of pharmacologic effects.

Testosterone is a potent inhibitor of LH production. Therefore, testosterone inhibition only (as for example by the nonsteroidal antiandrogen, flutamide) is compensated for by an increase in LH production and a compensatory increase in testosterone production (Chubner, Ryan, Luiz, Garcia-Carbonero, & Calabresi, 2001). However, CPA is a steroid that can lower serum testosterone because it is both a weak partial agonist and a competitive inhibiter of intracellular androgen receptors. In addition, CPA has progestational agonist activity sufficient to prevent a compensatory increase in LH production. While this combination of actions makes it an effective agent for the purpose of lowering circulating testosterone, it is also associated with gynecomastia in 20% of men (Neumann & Kalmus, 1991). Other possible adverse side effects include liver dysfunction and adrenal suppression, particularly in the case of (female) adolescents (J. Bradford, 1997; Cremonocini, Viginati, & Libroia, 1976). CPA is available in both oral and intramuscular injection formulations, but it is not currently available in the United States.

Summaries of the efficacy of this medication in the treatment of sex offenders have been published (J. Bradford, 1997; J. M. W. Bradford & Greenberg, 1996; Laschet & Laschet, 1971, 1975). In a review of seven studies involving 96 sex offenders treated with CPA and followed for up to 4.5 years (modal follow-up time was 3 years), six studies reported a recidivism rate of 0%, and the seventh reported a recidivism rate of 16.7% (one out of 6 men known to have re-offended after 1.5 years of follow-up; Appelt & Floru, 1974).

In a brief (3-month) double blind, placebo controlled study of 19 men with paraphilic disorders, CPA significantly reduced sexual arousal, fantasy, and most importantly, self-reported sexual activity (J. M. W. Bradford & Pawlak, 1993). Similar findings were reported in an independent study of 7 sex offenders who received placebo-controlled treatment with medroxyprogesterone acetate (MPA, see next) or CPA (Cooper, Sandhu, Losztyn, & Cernovsky, 1992). However, before the blind was broken, participants were asked which medication they preferred; 5 of 7 preferred MPA though, unfortunately, reasons why were not provided in the report. A subsequent study of 17 male pedophiles, using a 2 × 4 factorial design, compared men with high or low testosterone levels and treatment responses to pedophilic stimuli, coercive stimuli, assault stimuli, and adult consensual stimuli. For the high testosterone group, CPA preferentially decreased pedophilic interests relative to consensual sexual arousal to adults, which actually rose in this group (but not in the low testosterone group).

Medroxyprogesterone Aceatate (MPA)
In contrast to CPA, MPA's primary action occurs through induction of alpha-A-reductase in the liver, resulting in quicker metabolism

of testosterone (Southren, Gorodon, Vitteck, & Altman, 1977). Like CPA, it also has the important secondary action of inhibiting LH secretion, thereby preventing secondary upregulation of testosterone production.

In a review of eight studies of 452 male sex offenders treated with MPA and followed from 1 to 13 years, recidivism rates (defined in variety of ways across studies) ranged from 1% to as high as 17% (Grossman, Martis, & Fichtner, 1999). In a double-blind placebo controlled study of 11 pedophiles who completed a 3-month treatment trial, the five men treated with MPA reported fewer sexual fantasies. However, no difference in other factors such as frequency of orgasm or quality of penile erection was found between groups (Hucker, Langevin, & Bain, 1988).

Leuprolide and Triptorelin
A third means of decreasing circulating testosterone is by chronically stimulating the pituitary gland to reduce LH production. Several gonadotrophic releasing hormone (GNRH) partial agonists do this reliably, but the most well studied ones in sex offender research are leuprolide and triptorelin. One study involved non-blinded treatment of 30 men with paraphilias (25 of which included pedophilia) using triptorelin. All men reported complete elimination of deviant fantasies and deviant sexual activities. This effect persisted for all 25 men who continued in treatment for over a year. During the study, five men stopped treatment for a variety of reasons (including in two cases the wish to have children). Of the three who stopped due to "side effects," all were switched to CPA but two subsequently re-offended (Roesler & Witztum, 1995).

Similar results were found in two reports of six men with "severe" paraphilias (Thibaut, Cordier, & Kuhn, 1993, 1996). Of these, four had either failed to respond to treatment with CPA or had discontinued treatment with CPA. Treatment with triptorelin was reported to have "ended deviant sexual behavior in five cases" (p. 417). However, closer review indicated that in addition to "case 5" who continued to show active symptoms of pedophilia despite lowered testosterone levels, cases 3 and 4 also recidivated after antiandrogen treatment was stopped. Although the authors indicated the absence of a "selective effect" of tirptorelin on deviant sexual interests, the case reports indicate preservation and even possible augmentation of nondeviant sexual interests. This finding is supported by an independent study using LHRH ethylamate in combination with an androgen receptor blocker, flutamide, to achieve a "complete androgen blockade," in the case of a "severe" exhibitionist (Rousseau, Couture, Dupont, Labrie, & Couture, 1990). Despite complete suppression of exhibitionistic interests and activities, this man continued to have consensual sexual intercourse with his wife.

Two reports have described sequential treatment with a combination of placebo, CPA and (in the second paper) leuprolide in a hospitalized sex offender who was studied for 54 months (Cooper & Cernovsky, 1994; Cooper, Cernovsky, & Magnus, 1992). In this study, leuprolide "almost totally suppressed both self-report and phallometric measures of sexual arousal, and reduced testosterone levels to near 0" (p. 271). Improved efficacy of leuprolide over MPA in controlling sexual interest has also been reported in an open treatment study of a man with mixed paraphilic interests (Dickey, 1992).

Serotonergic Medications

Selective serotonergic reuptake inhibitors (SSRIs) have also been used in the treatment of paraphilic disorders and sex offenders (J. M. W. Bradford, 1996; Fedoroff, 1993; M. P. Kafka & Coleman, 1991), with the first description involving the serendipitous successful treatment of a man with transvestic fetishism with buspirone (Fedoroff, 1988). Buspirone is a partial agonist of alpha-1 presynaptic serotonergic auto-receptors and therefore has a different mechanism of action than that of the traditional SSRIs. Buspirone has been used clinically primarily as an anxiolytic medication, but it has also been described as having anti-obsessional characteristics and has been used to augment antidepressant medications. Possible mechanisms of action for buspirone in the treatment of paraphilias have been reviewed elsewhere (Fedoroff & Fedoroff, 1992). A significant aspect of the initial report was the claim by the patient (and verified by the man's wife) that nonparaphilic sexual activities were enhanced while paraphilic interests (cross-dressing) were suppressed. The effect was reversed when the medication was stopped and returned when it was resumed. The effect also appeared to be independent of any anxiolytic effect of the medication (Fedoroff, 1989). The results of studies involving serotonergic treatment of paraphilic disorders or sex offenders are summarized in Table 18.1.

A review of these studies reveals a consistent pattern of reduction in paraphilic interests for a wide variety of paraphilic disorders. Several studies also report improvement in nonparaphilic sexual interests and activities. This finding counters the common belief that SSRIs are effective because they suppress sex drive. If so, then other medications known to suppress sex drive, including other antidepressants, would be equally effective. Although treatment of paraphilic disorders with lithium has been reported (Cesnik & Coleman, 1989), lithium is less frequently associated with decreased sexual desire—it is a mood stabilizer, and its effectiveness in the treatment of paraphilias

Table 18.1 **Studies of Serotonergic Treatment of Paraphilias and Sex Offenders**

Paraphilia (Number of Cases)	Medication	Paraphilic Symptoms	Nonparaphilic Sex Interests	Reference
Transvestism (1)	Buspirone	Improved	Improved	Fedoroff (1988)
Exhibitionism (1)	Fluoxetine MPA	Improved No effect	Not reported Not reported	Bianchi (1990)
Voyeurism (1)	Fluoxetine	Improved	Not reported	Emmanuel, Lydiard, & Ballenger (1991)
Mixed Paraphilia NOS (10)	Fluoxetine Trazadone lithium	Improved	Improved	M. P. Kafka (1991a)
NOS (1)	Fluoxetine	Improved	Improved	M. P. Kafka (1991b)
NOS (1)	Fluoxetine	Improved	Improved	Kerbeshian & Burd (1991)
Pedophilia (1) Exhibitionism (1) Voyeurism (1)	Fluoxetine	Improved	Improved	Perilstein, Lipper, & Friedman (1991)
Muscle fetish (1)	Fluoxetine	Improved	Improved	Lorefice (1991)
Pedophilia (9) Exhibitionism (2) Voyeurism (3) NOS (2)	Fluoxetine	Improved	Not specifically reported	Coleman, Cesnick, Moore, & Dwyer (1992)
Exhibitionism (4) Transvestism (3) Scatalogia (4) Fetish (2) NOS (2)	Chlomipramine Desipramine Placebo	Improved Improved Improved for 4	Transient worsening	Kruesi, Fine, Valladares, Phillips, & Rapoport (1992)
NOS (1)	Buspirone	Improved	Improved	Fedoroff (1992)
Exhibitionism (1)	Buspirone	Improved	Improved	Pearson, Marshall, Barbaree, & Southmayd (1992)
Sadomasochism (3) Pedophilia (1) Fetish (1)	Fluoxetiine Fluoxetine and chomipamine	No change	Worse	Stein et al. (1992)
Exhibitionism (1)	Fluvoxamine Placebo Desipramine	Improved Ineffective Ineffective	No change No change No change	Zohar, Kaplan, & Benjamin (1994)
Mixed paraphilias (13)	Fluoxetine Sertraline	Improved Improved	Not reported	M. P. Kafka (1994)
Pedophilia (18)	Sertraline	Improved	Improved	J. M. W. Bradford & Greenberg (1996)
Mixed paraphilias (58)	Fluvoxamine Sertraline Fluoxetine	Improved	Not reported	Greenberg, Bradford, Curry, & O'Rourke (1996)

has been disputed (Balon, 2000). Furthermore, although sexual dysfunction, especially decreased sexual desire, is estimated to occur in 30% to 50% of people treated with antidepressants of all types (tricyclics, MAOIs, and SSRIs; Maurice, 2005), successful treatment of paraphilic disorders has not been reported with any other class of antidepressant. If fact, the efficacy of SSRIs in the treatment of paraphilias appears to decrease with higher doses. For example, the poor efficacy reported by Stein et al. (1992) is distinguished by the high dosages of the medications used in that study.

One explanation for the apparent decrease in efficacy of SSRIs with increasing doses has now been offered (Fedoroff, 1993; Fedoroff, Peyser, Franz, & Folstein, 1994). Specifically, increasing doses of SSRIs are associated with an increased incidence of inhibited orgasm (Waldinger, 2005). Some men report that, as a result, they have returned to paraphilic fantasies and behaviors when they were unable to reach orgasm through conventional fantasies or behaviors (Fedoroff, 2003). Thus, the side effects of the higher doses of the SSRIs on orgasm may be related to their decreased effectiveness relative to lower doses in the treatment of paraphilias.

Psychostimulants

The most recent class of medications explored in the treatment of individuals with unconventional sexual interests are psychostimulants, most notably methylphenidate and dextroamphetamine sulfate (M. P. Kafka & Hennen, 2000). Early reports are complicated by their combined treatment with SSRIs and by inclusion of so-called "sexual compulsives" or "sex addicts" with "paraphilia-related" syndrome. Sexual compulsivity and sexual addiction may include comparatively benign problems such as repeated masturbation; and it may be that people with such problems are more likely to have comorbid conditions such as attention deficit hyperactivity disorder (ADHD) and that their response to treatment is secondary to effective pharmacologic treatment of (adult) ADHD (M. P. Kafka & Prentky, 1998). (Sidebar 18.2 shows a protocol for the pharmacologic treatment of paraphilias.) Nevertheless, the acknowledgment of the importance of both traditionally accepted psychiatric disorders (e.g., substance abuse) as well as newer and more controversial disorders (e.g., paraphilia-*related* disorders) is important for several reasons. It is likely to lead to improvement in existing treatments, to provide new understandings and treatments of known "legitimate" paraphilias, and to result in improved assessment and risk assessment of more dangerous offenders (Habermann, Kafka, Berger, & Hill, 2006).

Protocol for Pharmacologic Treatment of Paraphilias

1. Assess and diagnose paraphilia and comorbid psychiatric and medical conditions.
2. Explain risks and benefits of accepting and declining pharmacologic treatments.
3. Obtain voluntary, informed consent.
4. Obtain base-line measures of normal and paraphilic interests.
5. If anti-androgens are prescribed:
   a. Obtain baseline liver function tests, blood pressure.
   b. Obtain baseline sex hormones: LH, FSH, free testosterone.
   c. Obtain baseline bone densitometry (especially in GNRH analogues are used).
6. Prescribe medication.
7. Re-assess at 1 month (items 4, 5a, and 5b).
   a. If satisfactory response, continue medication and go to 8.
   b. If unsatisfactory response:
      i. Reassess in 1 month, or
      ii. Increase dosage and reassess in 1 month, or
      iii. Switch to another medication in same class, reassess in 1 month, or
      iv. Add another medication from another class, reassess in 1 month, or
      v. If inhibited orgasm is present, consider trial with reduced dosage of medication, reassess in 1 month.
8. Reassess need for medication and dosage at 6-month intervals.
9. Repeat 5a and 5b at 6-month intervals until stable.
10. Repeat 5c yearly unless stable in which case repeat 5c every 2 years.

Putting It All Together

In reviewing the treatment modalities, a major theme emerges: treatment must be individualized and should not depend on a single paradigm. This principle has been reviewed on multiple occasions but perhaps most succinctly and clearly by Fagan (2004) who makes the case that sexual disorders (including paraphilic disorders) should be assessed and treated on the basis of four independent but mutually complementary "perspectives." The first is a "life story" perspective, which is based on an attempt to find a personal, meaningful explanation for the cause of the paraphilia. The second is a "dimensional" perspective that involves placement of problematic behaviors along a continuum (e.g., viewing pedophilic sexual interests as an extreme variant of the commonly observed sexual interest of the general population in "youthfulness"). A third perspective involves "behaviorism" and focuses on learned associations. The fourth perspective has been labeled a "disease" perspective and is based on a presumed pathophysiological disease or "broken part" that produces an alteration in sexual interest.

The way in which each of the four perspectives can interact and be used in successful therapy has previously been reviewed (Fedoroff, 2003). Both patients and therapists have a tendency to cling to favorite or comfortable paradigms. And while it is excusable for patients at the beginning of treatment to rely on a single paradigm (in fact, this may be the primary cause of their problem), not only must therapists be able to shift their patients' perspectives, but they themselves must also be adept at shifting paradigms. Importantly, none of the four perspectives excludes simultaneous analysis from each of the other perspectives. Skillful therapists can use alternative perspectives to help move a recalcitrant patient with problematic sexual behaviors into a "new way of looking at things." Table 18.2 summarizes the way in which patients often signal the perspective on which they are relying to explain or justify their paraphilic interests.

Although comprehensive reviews of specific treatments for *specific* paraphilic disorders have been published (e.g., Laws & O'Donohue, 1997), several general strategies appear relevant to the treatment of any paraphilic disorders. These include: (a) an accurate diagnosis of the paraphilia and comorbid disorders, (b) immediate cessation of the paraphilic behavior (especially if criminal), (c) vigorous treatment of the symptoms resulting from cessation of the paraphilic activities, and (d) establishment of noncoercive romantic and sexual relations. Thus, the twin aims of treatment are to stop or prevent danger to the community and to substitute paraphilic sexual activity with nonparaphilic sexual activity in combination with a "pro-social" lifestyle. In most cases, these aims are more easily achieved by programs that strive for "reintegration" as opposed to "isolation" from the community. While these goals are not always possible, no evidence exists to support the success of alternative "treatment" aims.

Summary and Conclusions

This chapter began with the question of whether paraphilic disorders can be cured. There no longer is any question that paraphilic disorders can and should be treated. The efficacy of treatment has not yet been finally determined; nor has the best means of treatment been documented, but this is hardly surprising since the

Table 18.2 **Perspectives by Paraphilic Disorders**

	Life Story	Dimensional	Behavioral	Disease
Exhibitionism	"It is my way of taking back control."	"I am just less ashamed about nudity."	"My first girlfriend taught me to do it."	"I only did it when I was using steroids."
Fetishism	"It means I can never be abandoned."	"I find high heels sexier than most men do."	"I used a shoe the first time I masturbated."	"It gets worse when I stop my anticonvulsant medication."
Frotteurism	"Women won't let me touch them any other way."	"Haven't you just wished you could touch a pretty woman?"	"When I touch someone without them knowing I get an erection."	"I touch everything exactly five times."
Pedophilia	"I love children."	"I admire youth and innocence."	"My mother abused me as a child."	"It started after my stroke."
Masochism	"It means I never have to take responsibility for what happens."	"I vowed to love honor and obey."	"When I am submissive I get more attention."	"The only way I can reach orgasm is when I hold my breath."
Sadism	"I have to be in control."	"I am more assertive than most."	"I was spanked when I was a child."	"When I am drunk I do things I can't believe."
Transvestic Fetishism	"Wearing dresses makes me feel like another person."	"Lingerie is a multibillion dollar industry."	"I was dressed as a girl for Halloween."	"I was in a coma after a car accident. When I woke up all I could think of was nylons."
Voyeurism	"The only way to know someone is to watch them without them knowing."	"Everyone like to look at sexy people."	"I learned about sex from spying on my sister and her boyfriend."	"I am deaf so I rely on my vision."
Primary Intervention	Reframe cognitive distortions.	Educate.	Reinforce healthy associations.	Pharmacotherapy.

etiology of paraphilic disorders is unknown. Given the variety of paraphilic disorders, it is likely that multiple etiologies exist and therefore that a variety of treatments will ultimately be established. An example of a multidimensional approach to the treatment of a paraphilic disorder is given in Sidebar 18.3.

SIDEBAR 18.3

Bradford Pharmacologic Treatment Algorithm

Level 1: Cognitive-behavioral and/or relapse prevention
Level 2: SSRI pharmacologic treatment

Level 3: If SSRI's are inadequate after 4 to 6 weeks, add low-dose anti-androgen (e.g., sertraline 200 mg daily) plus 50 mg MPA daily by mouth (p.o.)

Level 4: Full antiandrogen treatment given orally or by intramuscular (i.m.) injection (e.g., 50 to 300 MPA or CPA p.o. or i.m.)

Level 5: Full antiandrogen treatment by i.m. injection (e.g., 300 mg MPA by i.m. injection weekly or 200 mg. CPA by i.m. injection every 2 weeks)

Level 6: Complete androgen suppression and sex drive suppression: (e.g., CPA 200 to 400 mg by weekly i.m. injection or luprolide 7.5 mg by i.m. injection every 3 to 4 weeks)

Procedure

- In the Bradford treatment algorithm, all patients would receive Level 1 intervention(s) regardless of severity of presenting problem(s).
- Patients with mild degrees of symptom severity would receive Level 1 or 2 interventions.
- Patients with moderate to severe degrees of symptom severity would receive Level 1 to 3 Levels of intervention, possibly escalating to Levels 4 or 5.
- Patients with catastrophic degrees of symptom severity would receive Level 6 intervention.

Note: Based on the work of J. M. W. Bradford (2000).

In contrast to major depression, with at best a 50% success rate, reoffense rates for sex offenders (who include not only individuals with paraphilic disorders but also common criminals) are much lower. A meta-analysis including 23,393 sex offenders yielded an average sexual offense recidivism rate of 13.4% (Hanson & Bussière, 1998). Furthermore, sex offender reoffense rates have been dropping. For example, in Canada, the rate of sexual assaults on women dropped by 35% from 1993 to 2000; in the United States, the self-report data from the National Crime Victimization Survey found a 68% drop in sexual assaults from 1991 to 2001. Similar reductions in sex crimes have been found worldwide (data summarized in Lalumiere, Harris, Quinsey, & Rice, 2005).

Explanations for this dramatic reduction might focus on changes that have occurred worldwide during this same period. First, there has been an increased awareness about the consequences of sexual abuse and, as a result, much public education has ensued. Second, the ability to monitor the Internet has been associated with an increase in arrest rates of individuals who have collected or transmitted child pornography over that medium. Many of these offenders, while often highly pedophilic, appear to have no "hands-on" victims (i.e., they are unknown to have personally assaulted any children in real life; Fedoroff, Smolewska,

Selhi, Ng, & Bradford, 2001). Such people may represent a new, previously unstudied and, therefore, untreated population. If paraphilias are similar to other psychiatric conditions, prevention and early treatment of pedophilia should be even more effective than treatment of individuals who have committed "hands on" assaults. And third, SSRIs have become widely available. Recent warnings about possible adverse effects resulting from the prescription of SSRIs, particularly for adolescents, have actually provided a natural experimental situation (J. M. W. Bradford & Fedoroff, 2006): if SSRIs have decreased the incidence of sexual assaults, and if the prescription of SSRIs drops as the result of recent warnings, then an increase in sexual assaults would be predicted, with investigations underway.

When should clinicians refer patients for specialized treatment? Paraphilic disorders are rarely, if ever, included in medical or clinical psychology training curricula. They are sufficiently infrequent and symptoms sufficiently underreported such that most clinicians in general practice have only marginal experience with individuals with paraphilias who are seeking treatment. As a result, referral to an expert is always prudent. However, most paraphilias are reasonably easy to treat, with most complications surrounding treatment arising from unresolved legal issues. Usually, establishment of a working relationship with a specialized clinic is best, particularly if one of the aims is for the patient to assure a "healthy lifestyle" by continuing to reside in the community. Support for establishment of a healthy lifestyle for sex offenders (including those with paraphilias) has been reviewed elsewhere (W. L. Marshall, Marshall, Serran, & Fernandez, 2006). Ultimately, clinicians should welcome the opportunity to treat people with paraphilic disorders for the following reasons: (a) most patients with paraphilic disorders want treatment but think none is available, (b) the prognosis for people with paraphilic disorders is excellent, and (c) to withhold treatment without hope of cure as a goal is unethical.

References

Abel, G. G., Blanchard, E. B., & Jackson, M. (1974). The role of fantasy in the treatment of sexual deviation. *Archives of General Psychiatry, 30,* 467–475.

Abel, G. G., Osborn, C., Anthony, D., & Gardos, P. (1992). Current treatments of paraphiliacs. In J. Bancroft, C. M. Davis, & H. J. Ruppel (Eds.), *Annual review of sex research: An integrative and interdisciplinary review* (Vol. 3, pp. 255–290). Allentown, PA: Society for the Scientific Study of Sex.

American Psychiatric Association. (1994). *Diagnostic and statistical manual of mental disorders* (4th ed.). Washington, DC: Author.

Appelt, M., & Floru, L. (1974). Erfahmigen uberdie beemflussung der sexualital cyproteronacetat. *International Pharmaco-Psychiatry, 9,* 61–76.

Balon, R. (2000). Lithium for paraphilias? Probably not. *Journal of Sex and Marital Therapy, 26,* 361–363.

Bandura, A. (1978). Social learning theory of aggression. *Journal of Communication, 28,* 12–29.

Bandura, A., & Walters, R. H. (1974). Catharsis: A questionable mode of coping with violence. In S. K. Steinmetz & M. A. Straus (Eds.), *Violence in the family* (pp. 303–307). New York: Dodd, Mead.

Berlin, F. S. (1997). "Chemical castration" for sex offenders. *New England Journal of Medicine, 336*(14), 1030.

Berlin, F. S. (2005). Commentary: The impact of surgical castration on sexual recidivism risk among civilly committed sexual offenders. *Journal of the American Academy of Psychiatry and the Law, 33*(1), 37–41.

Bianchi, M. D. (1990). Fluoxetine treatment of exhibitionism. *American Journal of Psychiatry, 147*(8), 1089–1090.

Bradford, J. (1997). Medical interventions in sexual deviance. In D. R. Laws & W. O'Donohue (Eds.), *Sexual deviance: Theory, assessment, and treatment* (pp. 449–464). New York: Guilford Press.

Bradford, J. M. W. (1996). The role of serotonin in the future of forensic psychiatry. *Bulletin of the American Academy of Psychiatry and the Law, 24*(1), 57–72.

Bradford, J. M. W. (2000). The treatment of sexual deviation using a pharmacological approach. *Journal of Sex Research, 37*(3), 248–257.

Bradford, J. M. W., & Fedoroff, J. P. (2006). Pharmacologic treatment of the juvenile offender. In H. E. Barbaree & W. L. Marshall (Eds.), *The juvenile sex offender* (2nd ed., pp. 358–382). New York: Guilford Press.

Bradford, J. M. W., & Greenberg, D. M. (1996). Pharmacological treatment of deviant sexual behavior. *Annual Review of Sex Research, 7,* 283–306.

Bradford, J. M. W., & Pawlak, A. (1993). Double-blind placebo crossover study of cyproterone acetate in the treatment of the paraphilias. *Archives of Sexual Behavior, 22*(5), 383–402.

Brown, W. A., Monti, P. M., & Corriveau, D. P. (1978). Serum testosterone and sexual activity and interest in men. *Archives of Sexual Behavior, 7*(2), 97–103.

Cesnik, J. A., & Coleman, E. (1989). Use of lithium carbonate in the treatment of autoerotic asphyxia. *American Journal of Psychotherapy, 43*(2), 277–286.

Chubner, B. A., Ryan, D. P., Luiz, P.-A., Garcia-Carbonero, R., & Calabresi, P. (2001). Antineoplastic agents. In J. G. Hardman, L. E. Limbird, & A. G. Gilman (Eds.), *The pharmacologic basis of therapeutics* (10th ed., pp. 1389–1459). New York: McGraw-Hill.

Coleman, E., Cesnick, J., Moore, A., & Dwyer, S. N. (1992). An exploratory study of the role of psychotropic medications in the treatment of sex offenders. *Journal of Offender Rehabilitation, 18,* 75–88.

Cooper, A. J., & Cernovsky, Z. Z. (1994). Comparison of cyproterone acetate (CPA) and leuprolide acetate (LHRH agonist) in a chronic pedophile: A clinical case study. *Biological Psychiatry, 36,* 269–271.

Cooper, A. J., Cernovsky, Z., & Magnus, R. V. (1992). The long-term use of cyproterone acetate in pedophilia: A case study. *Journal of Sex and Marital Therapy, 18,* 292–302.

Cooper, A. J., Sandhu, S., Losztyn, S., & Cernovsky, Z. (1992). A double-blind placebo controlled trial of medroxyprogesternone acetate and cyproterone acetate with seven pedophiles. *Canadian Journal of Psychiatry, 37,* 6687–6693.

Cornu, F. (1973). Katamnesen bei kkastrierten. In F. Cornu (Ed.), *Katamnesen bei kkastrierten* (pp. 1–132). Verlag für Medizin und Naturwissenschaften, Basel, Switzerland: S. Karger, AG.

Cremonocini, C., Viginati, E., & Libroia, A. (1976). Treatment of hirsuitism and acne in women with two combinations of cyproterone acetate and thinyloestradiol. *Acta Europa Fertility, 7,* 299–314.

Dickey, R. (1992). The management of a case of treatment-resistant paraphilia with a long-acting LHRH agonist. *Canadian Journal of Psychiatry, 37,* 567–569.

Ellis, A. (1984). The essence of RET. *Journal of Rational-Emotive Therapy, 2,* 19–25.

Emmanuel, N. P., Lydiard, R. B., & Ballenger, J. C. (1991). Fluoxetine treatment of voyeurism. *American Journal of Psychiatry, 148*(7), 950.

Fagan, P. J. (2004). *Sexual disorders: Perspectives on diagnosis and treatment.* Baltimore: Johns Hopkins University Press.

Fedoroff, J. P. (1988). Buspirone hydrochloride in the treatment of transvestic fetishism. *Journal of Clinical Psychiatry, 49*(10), 408–409.

Fedoroff, J. P. (1989). Buspirone and transvestitic fetishism. *Journal of Clinical Psychiatry, 50,* 361.

Fedoroff, J. P. (1992). Buspirone hydrochloride in the treatment of an atypical paraphilia. *Archives of Sexual Behavior, 21*(4), 401–406.

Fedoroff, J. P. (1993). Serotonergic drug treatment of deviant sexual interests. *Annals of Sex Research, 6,* 105–121.

Fedoroff, J. P. (2003). The paraphilic world. In S. B. Levine, C. B. Risen, & S. E. Althof (Eds.), *Handbook of clinical sexuality for mental health professionals* (pp. 333–356). New York: Brunner-Routledge.

Fedoroff, J. P., & Fedoroff, I. C. (1992). Buspirone and paraphilic sexual behavior. *Journal of Offender Rehabilitation, 18*(3/4), 89–108.

Fedoroff, J. P., & Moran, B. (1997). Myths and misconceptions about sex offenders. *Canadian Journal of Human Sexuality, 6*(4), 263–276.

Fedoroff, J. P., Peyser, C., Franz, M. L., & Folstein, S. E. (1994). Sexual disorders in Huntington's disease. *Journal of Neuropsychiatry, 6*(2), 147–153.

Fedoroff, J. P., Smolewska, K., Selhi, Z., Ng, E., & Bradford, J. M. W. (2001). *Victimless pedophiles.* Paper presented at the International Academy of Sex Research Twenty-seventh annual meeting, Montreal, Quebec, Canada.

Freund, K. (1980). Therapeutic sex drive reduction. *Acta Psychiatrica Scandinavica, 62,* 3–38.

Gaensbauer, T. J. (1973). Castration in treatment of sex offenders: An appraisal. *Rocky Mountain Medical Journal, 70,* 23–28.

Greenberg, D. M., Bradford, J. M. W., Curry, S., & O'Rourke, A. (1996). A comparison of treatment of paraphilias with three serotonin reuptake inhibitors: A retrospective study. *Bulletin of the American Academy of Psychiatry and the Law, 24*(4), 525–532.

Grossman, L. S., Martis, B., & Fichtner, C. G. (1999). Are sex offenders treatable? A research overview. *Psychiatric Services, 50*(3), 349–361.

Habermann, N., Kafka, M. P., Berger, W., & Hill, A. (2006). The paraphilia-related disorders: An investigation of the relevance of the concept in sexual murderers. *Journal of Forensic Sciences, 51,* 683–688.

Hanson, R. K., & Bussière, M. T. (1998). Predicting relapse: A meta-analysis of sexual offender recidivism studies. *Journal of Consulting and Clinical Psychology, 66*(2), 348–362.

Hanson, R. K., Gordon, A., Harris, A. J. R., Marques, J. K., Murphy, W., Quinsey, V. L., et al. (2002). First report of the collaborative outcome data project on the effectiveness of psychological treatment for sex offenders. *Sexual Abuse: A Journal of Research and Treatment, 14*(2), 169–194.

Hanson, R. K., & Harris, A. (2000). The sex offender need assessment rating (SONAR): A method for measuring change in risk levels. In *Corrections Research: Manuals and Forms* (pp. 1–23). Ottawa, Ontario, Canada: Department of the Solicitor General of Canada.

Heim, N. (1981). Sexual behavior of castrated sex offenders. *Archives of Sexual Behavior, 10*(1), 11–19.

Heim, N., & Hursch, C. J. (1979). Castration for sex offenders: Treatment or punishment? A review and critique of recent European literature. *Archives of Sexual Behavior, 8*(3), 281–304.

Hicks, P. K. (1993). Castration of sexual offenders. *Journal of Legal Medicine, 14,* 641–667.

Hucker, S., Langevin, R., & Bain, J. (1988). A double-blind trial of sex drive reducing medication in pedophiles. *Annals of Sex Research, 1*(2), 227–242.

Judd, L. L., Paulus, M. J., Schettler, P. J., Akiskal, H. S., Endicott, J., Leon, A. C., et al. (2000). Does incomplete recovery from first lifetime major depressive episode herald a chronic course of illness? *American Journal of Psychiatry, 157,* 1501–1504.

Kafka, M. P. (1991a). Successful antidepressant treatment of nonparaphilic sexual addictions and paraphilias in men. *Journal of Clinical Psychiatry, 52*(2), 60–65.

Kafka, M. P. (1991b). Successful treatment of paraphilic coercive disorder (a rapist) with fluoxetine hydrochoride. *British Journal of Psychiatry, 158,* 844–847.

Kafka, M. P. (1994). Sertraline pharmacotherapy for paraphilias and paraphilia-related disorders: An open trial. *Annals of Clinical Psychiatry, 6,* 189–195.

Kafka, M. P., & Coleman, E. (1991). Serotonin and paraphilias: The convergence of mood, impulse, and compulsive disorders. *Journal of Clinical Psychopharmacology, 11*(3), 223–224.

Kafka, M. P., & Hennen, J. (2000). Psychostimulant augmentation during treatment with selective serotonin reuptake inhibitors in men with paraphilias and paraphilia-related disorders: A case series. *Journal of Clinical Psychiatry, 61*(9), 664–670.

Kafka, M. P., & Prentky, R. A. (1998). Attention-deficit/hyperactivity disorder in males with paraphilias and paraphilia-related disorders: A comorbidity study. *Journal of Clinical Psychiatry, 59*(7), 388–396.

Kerbeshian, J., & Burd, L. (1991). Tourette's syndrome and recurrent paraphilic masturbatory fantasy. *Canadian Journal of Psychiatry, 36*(2), 155–157.

Kilmann, P. R., Sabalis, R. F., Gearing, I. M. L., Bukstel, L. H., & Scovern, A. W. (1982). The treatment of sexual paraphilias: A review of the outcome research. *Journal of Sex Research, 18*(3), 193–252.

Kruesi, M. J. P., Fine, S., Valladares, L., Phillips, R. A., & Rapoport, J. L. (1992). Paraphilias: A double-blind crossover comparison of clomipramine versus desipramine. *Archives of Sexual Behavior, 21*(6), 587–593.

Lalumiere, M. L., Harris, G. T., Quinsey, V. L., & Rice, E. J. (2005). *The causes of rape: Understanding the differences in male propensity for sexual aggression.* Washington, DC: American Psychological Association.

Laschet, U., & Laschet, L. (1971). Psychopharmacotherapy of sex offenders with cyproterone acetate. *Pharmakopsychiatrie Neuropsychopharmakologic, 4,* 99–104.

Laschet, U., & Laschet, L. (1975). Antiandrogens in the treatment of sexual deviations of men. *Journal of Steroid Biochemistry, 6,* 821–826.

Laws, D. R. (1995). Verbal satiation: Notes on procedure, with speculations on its mechanism of effect. *Sexual Abuse: A Journal of Research and Treatment, 7*(2), 155–166.

Laws, D. R. (2001). Olfactory aversion: Notes on procedure, with speculations on its mechanism of effect. *Sexual Abuse: Journal of Research and Treatment, 13*(4), 275–287.

Laws, D. R., & Marshall, W. L. (1991). Masturbatory reconditioning with sexual deviates: An evaluative review. *Advances in Behavior Research and Therapy, 13,* 13–25.

Laws, D. R., & O'Donohue, W. (Eds.). (1997). *Sexual deviance: Theory, assessment, and treatment.* New York/London: Guilford Press.

Laws, D. R., & O'Neil, J. A. (1981). Variations on masturbatory reconditioning. *Behavioral Psychotherapy, 9,* 111–136.

Lorefice, L. S. (1991). Fluoxetine treatment of a fetish. *Journal of Clinical Psychiatry, 52*(1), 41.

Marks, I., Gelder, M., & Bancroft, J. (1970). Sexual deviants two years after electric aversion. *British Journal of Psychiatry, 117,* 173–185.

Marques, J. K., Day, D. M., Nelson, C., & West, M. A. (1994). Effects of cognitive-behavioral treatment on sex offender recidivism. *Criminal Justice and Behavior, 21*(1), 28–54.

Marques, J. K., Wiederanders, M., Day, D. M., Nelson, C., & Van Ommeren, A. (2005). Effects of a relapse prevention program on sexual recidivism: Final results from California's Sex Offender Treatment and Evaluation Project (SOTEP). *Sexual Abuse: A Journal of Research and Treatment, 17*(1), 79–107.

Marquis, J. (1970). Orgasmic reconditioning: Changing sexual object choice through controlling masturbation fantasies. *Journal of Behavior Therapy and Experimental Psychiatry, 1,* 263–271.

Marshall, D. S., & Suggs, R. C. (1971). Human sexual behavior. In D. S. Marshall & R. C. Suggs (Eds.), *Human sexual behavior* (pp. 3–294). New York: Basic Books.

Marshall, W. L. (1973). The modification of sexual fantasies: A combined treatment approach to the reduction of deviant sexual arousal. *Behavior Research and Therapy, 11,* 557–564.

Marshall, W. L. (1979). Satiation therapy: A procedure for reducing deviant sexual arousal. *Journal of Applied Behavior Analysis, 12,* 10–22.

Marshall, W. L., Fernandez, Y. M., Hudson, S. M., & Ward, T. (Eds.). (1998). *Sourcebook of treatment programs for sexual offenders.* New York and London: Plenum Press.

Marshall, W. L., Marshall, L. E., Serran, G. A., & Fernandez, Y. M. (2006). *Treating sexual offenders: An integrated approach.* New York: Routledge.

Maurice, W. L. (2005). Male hypoactive sexual disorder. In R. Balon & R. T. Segraves (Eds.), *Handbook of sexual dysfunction* (pp. 67–109). Boca Ratan, FL: CRC Press.

McConaghy, N., Armstrong, M. S., & Blaszczynski, A. (1985). Expectancy, covert sensitization and imaginal desensitization in compulsive sexuality. *Acta Psychiatrica Scandinavica, 72,* 176–187.

McConaghy, N., Blaszczynski, A., & Kidson, W. (1988). Treatment of sex offenders with imaginal desensitization and/or medroxyprogesterone. *Acta Psychiatrica Scandinavica, 77,* 199–206.

McHugh, P. R., & Slavney, P. R. (1983). The perspectives of psychiatry. In P. R. McHugh & P. R. Slavney (Eds.), *The perspectives of psychiatry* (2nd ed., pp. 1–332). Baltimore, MD: Johns Hopkins University Press.

Nagayama Hall, G. C. (1995). Sexual offender recidivism revisited: A meta-analysis of recent treatment studies. *Journal of Consulting and Clinical Psychology, 63*(5), 802–809.

Neumann, F., & Kalmus, J. (1991). Cyproterone acetate in the treatment of sexual disorders. *Pharmacological Base and Clinical Experience, 98*(2), 71–80.

Ortmann, J. (1980). The treatment of sexual offenders. *International Journal of Law and Psychiatry, 3,* 443–451.

Pearson, H. J., Marshall, W. L., Barbaree, H. E., & Southmayd, S. (1992). Treatment of a compulsive paraphiliac with buspirone. *Annals of Sex Research, 5*(4), 239–246.

Perilstein, R. D., Lipper, S., & Friedman, L. J. (1991). Three cases of paraphilias responsive to Fluoxetine treatment. *Journal of Clinical Psychiatry, 52*(4), 169–170.

Pfaus, J. G., Kippin, T. E., & Centeno, S. (2001). Conditioning and sexual behavior: A review. *Hormones and Behavior, 40,* 1–31.

Pithers, W. D., Marques, J. K., Gibat, C. C., & Marlatt, G. A. (1983). Relapse prevention with sexual aggressives: A self-control model of treatment and maintenance of change. In J. G. Greer & I. R. Stuart (Eds.), *The sexual aggressor: Current perspectives on treatment* (pp. 214–239). New York: Van Nostrand Reinhart.

Roesler, A., & Witztum, E. (1995). Successful treatment of paraphilic sex offenders with long acting GnRH analog triptorelin (decapeptyl-CR). *Hormone Research, 82.*

Rousseau, L., Couture, M., Dupont, A., Labrie, F., & Couture, N. (1990). Effect of combined androgen blockade with and LHRH agonist and flutamide in one severe case of male exhibitionism. *Canadian Journal of Psychiatry, 35,* 338–341.

Sausville, E., & Longo, D. L. (2001). Principles of cancer treatment. In E. Braunwald, S. L. Hauser, A. S. Fauci, D. L. Longo, D. L. Kasper & J. L. Jameson (Eds.), *Harrison's principles of internal medicine* (15th ed., pp. 543–544). New York: McGraw-Hill.

Serber, M. (1970). Shame aversion therapy. *Journal of Behavior Therapy and Experimental Psychiatry, 1,* 213–215.

Shotly, M., Ephross, P. H., Plaut, S. M., Fischman, S., H., Charnas, J. F., & Cody, C. A. (1984). Female orgasmic experience: A subjective study. *Archives of Sexual Behavior, 13,* 155–164.

Southren, A. L., Gorodon, G. G., Vitteck, J., & Altman, K. (1977). Effects of progestagens on androgen metabolism. In L. Martini & M. Motta (Eds.), *Androgens and antiandrogens* (pp. 263–279). New York: Raven Press.

Stein, D. J., Hollander, E., Anthony, D. T., Schneier, F. R., Fallon, B. A., Liebowitz, M. R., et al. (1992). Serotonergic medications for sexual obsessions, sexual addictions, and paraphilias. *Journal of Clinical Psychiatry, 53*(8), 267–271.

Sturup, G. K. (1968). Treatment of sexual offenders in Herstedvester, Denmark. *Acta Psychiatrica Scandinavica, 44,* 1–64.

Sturup, G. K. (1972). Castration: The total treatment. In H. L. P. Resnik & M. E. Wolfgang (Eds.), *Treatment of the sex offender* (Vol. 8, pp. 175–196). Boston: Little, Brown.

Sulloway, F. J. (1983). *Freud, biologist of the mind.* New York: Basic Books.

Thibaut, F., Cordier, B., & Kuhn, J.-M. (1993). Effect of a long-lasting gonadotrophin hormone-releasing hormone agonist in six cases of severe male paraphilia. *Acta Psychiatrica Scandinavica, 87,* 445–450.

Thibaut, F., Cordier, B., & Kuhn, J.-M. (1996). Gonadotrophin hormone releasing hormone agonist in cases of severe paraphilia: A lifetime treatment? *Psychoneuroendocrinology, 21*(4), 411–419.

VanDeventer, A. D., & Laws, D. R. (1978). Orgasmic reconditioning to redirect sexual arousal in pedophiles. *Behavior Therapy, 1978,* 748–765.

Waldinger, M. D. (2005). Male ejaculation and orgasmic disorders. In R. Balon & R. T. Segraves (Eds.), *Handbook of sexual dysfunction* (pp. 215–248). Boca Raton, FL: CRC Press.

Ward, T., Hudson, S. M., & Keenan, T. (1998). A self-regulation model of the sexual offense process. *Sexual Abuse: A Journal of Research and Treatment, 10*(2), 141–157.

Wille, R., & Beier, K. M. (1989). Castration in Germany. *Annals of Sex Research, 2,* 103–133.

Zohar, J., Kaplan, Z., & Benjamin, J. (1994). Compulsive exhibitionism successfully treated with fluvoxamine: A controlled case study. *Journal of Clinical Psychiatry, 55*(3), 86–88.

Matt O'Brien, Liam E. Marshall,
and W. L. Marshall

19

Chapter

Learning Objectives

In this chapter, we discuss:

- The classification and measurement of sexual addiction.
- The prevalence of sexual addiction and comorbidity with other addictions.
- Sexual behavior of those who are sexually addicted.
- Sexual addiction and psychopathy.
- Online sexual behavior problems and relationship with offending.
- Treatment of sexual addiction.

Sexual addiction has been described as a sexual desire that diminishes the capacity or wish to control sexual behaviors that persist despite significant harmful consequences (Carnes, 1983, 1989; Goodman, 1998). However, controversy surrounds the use of the term *sexual addiction* as the single descriptor for a cluster of behaviors associated with problematic sexual behavior. Other authors, for example, have used other terms to describe similar symptoms, and the specific terminology appears to depend on personal preference and reflect preferred treatment methodologies (see Sidebar 19.1). Attempts to reach consensus among sexual addiction researchers on the classification of sexual addiction are

587

ongoing. To date, the main descriptors used appear to be describing a broadly similar cluster of behaviors, yet to reflect preferred treatment methodologies. These descriptors include: sexually impulsive (Barth & Kinder, 1987), sexually compulsive (Coleman, 1987), hypersexual (Kafka, 1997; Kafka & Hennen, 1999), or sexually excessive (Manley & Koehler, 2001). Still others see these behaviors as variants of obsessive-compulsive disorder (Coleman, 1990; Leedes, 2001). Despite the difference in terminology, all describe the essential sexual behavior problems referred to in Carnes's (1983) conceptualization of sexual addiction: abrogation of control and persistence of behavior, despite harm. "Sexual addicts" view their problematic behavior as involving high rates of overt sexual contacts, excessive masturbation, or habitual use of the Internet to access sexual sites including pornography.

SIDEBAR 19.1

Terminology and Classification of Sexual Addiction

The construct of sexual addiction first appeared in the *Diagnostic and Statistical Manual of Mental Disorders*, third edition, revision (*DSM-III-R*; American Psychiatric Association, 1987); however, it was referred to under "Sexual Disorder Not Otherwise Specified" as an example of problematic sexual behavior. Under section 320.90, *DSM-III-R* describes one instance of a sexual disorder not otherwise specified as "distress about a pattern of repeated sexual conquests or other forms of nonparaphilic sexual addiction, involving a succession of people who exist only as things to be used" (p. 296). No specific criteria are given for diagnosing sexual addiction in *DSM III-R*, nor have subsequent editions made any further or expanded reference to sexual addiction. This static description reflects not only the fact of limited empirical research, but also a conflicted political climate surrounding sexual issues (Smith, 1994). Some attempt has been made to reach consensus about descriptions among sexual addiction researchers and theorists (American Foundation for Addiction Research [AFAR], 2001) on the classification of sexual addiction. This effort led to a research project intended to develop both a standardized measure to assess the construct and to provide further information on its classification. This project, however, is still in process.

Sexual Addiction in Sexual Offenders

In our treatment programs in two Canadian federal prisons, a number of sexual offenders exhibit behaviors similar to the features described by Carnes (1983, 1989) as indicative of sexual addiction. For example, some offenders indicate they are so preoccupied with sexual thoughts that they have problems interacting appropriately with prison staff. Or they disclose being bothered by inappropriate sexual fantasies or appear to enjoy listening to the offence details of other group participants, even after receiving feedback indicating the inappropriateness of this behavior. Some sexual offender clients report having attended a community sexual addiction program.

Through work in our programs, we have found features of sexual addiction that might be relevant to the treatment of sexual offenders, such as the lack of desire, or the inability to control sexual behavior, and the persistence of these behaviors despite negative consequences, both for the offender and even more importantly, for victims. As a result, in 1997, our team began a research program to examine the features and relevance of a sexual addiction diagnosis in such offenders. The following section presents our research on sexual addiction in incarcerated sexual offenders and socioeconomically matched community comparison groups (L. E. Marshall & Marshall, 1998, 2001, in press; L. E. Marshall, Marshall, & Moulden, 2000; L. E. Marshall, Moulden, Serran, & Marshall, 2004).

We present the findings in the following order: first, the psychometric properties of the Sexual Addiction Screening Test (SAST; Carnes, 1989), including the underlying factor structure; the observed incidence of sexual addiction in incarcerated sexual offenders and in a community comparison group; the comorbidity of sexual addiction with other addictions; the relationship between sexual addiction and clients' history of sexual outlets, as well as the inclination to use sex as a coping strategy; and finally, the possible relationship between psychopathy and sexual addiction. Unless otherwise stated, the information reported is based on the responses of the sexual offenders in our research program.

Measure of Sexual Addiction

The SAST (Carnes, 1989) has been used to measure sexual addiction in our research. In that research (L. E. Marshall & Marshall, 2001; in press; L. E. Marshall, Marshall, & Moulden, 2000), the SAST demonstrated good internal consistency, with alpha coefficients ranging from .89 to .93. We subjected the SAST to both an exploratory factor analysis, using principal axis factoring, and then a confirmatory factor analysis using the maximum likelihood method with promax rotation. Three-, two-, and one-factor solutions were tested for improvement of fit using Root Mean Square Error of Approximation (RMSEA; Steiger & Lind, 1980) and the Proportional Reduction in Error (PRE) method. These analyses revealed a one factor solution as the most satisfactory representation of our data, accounting for 39% of the variance in SAST scores. We concluded that the SAST measures a single latent factor that Carnes (1989) calls "sexual addiction" (but that might be described by any number of the other terms listed earlier). Consequently, any relationships found in our research ought to be indicative of sexual addiction as well as its correlates. Carnes (1989) reports that scores on the SAST do not predict dangerousness, or the consequences for either the addict or others. As a result, any over-representation of sexual addicts among sexual offenders will be a function of their responses to the SAST and not a result of their offending behavior.

Prevalence of Sexual Addiction

Based on clinical work with these problems, Carnes (1989) estimated the prevalence of sexual addiction in a middle-class community to be between 3% and 6%. Regrettably, little research has addressed important questions about the prevalence rates of sexual addiction, either in the general community or in special populations. In their study on sexual addiction using the Sexual Dependency Inventory-Revised (SDI-R), Delmonico, Bubenzer, and West (1998) reported that 33 (19.4%) of 170 respondents were sexually addicted. This study included self-identified sexual addicts ($N = 73$, 43%), sexual offenders ($N = 55$, 32%), and a comparison group that was identified neither as sexual offenders nor sexual addicts ($N = 42$, 25%). The specific distribution of sexual addicts within each of the three groups was unfortunately not reported. However, fewer subjects (19.4%) were classified as sexual addicts by the SDI-R than actually self-reported being a sexual addict (43%), indicating disparity between the assessment tool and self-report. This finding reinforced our decision to use the SAST rather than the SDI as the measure of sexual addiction in our research.

In our studies, matched community samples reported significantly lower rates of sexual addiction (12% to 15%) than did samples of sexual offenders (35% to 43%). Clearly then, the behaviors described in the SAST present a greater problem for incarcerated sexual offenders than for nonoffenders (see Sidebar 19.2). Another interesting feature about these findings was the higher rate of sexual addiction in our nonoffender, lower-socioeconomic comparison group relative to the rate of middle-class, nonoffenders estimated by Carnes. It is unknown whether this reflects a socioeconomic cohort difference or an underestimate by Carnes.

SIDEBAR 19.2

Sexual Addiction Prevalence and Comorbidity

Incarcerated sexual offenders reported higher rates of sexual addiction (35% to 43%) than did matched community controls (12% to

15%) as measured using the Sexual Addiction Screening Test (SAST; Carnes, 1989).

Comorbid Addictions

Carnes (1989) hypothesized that sexual addiction would be comorbid with other addictive behaviors. Schneider and Schneider (1991) did find comorbidity, with sexual addicts at greater risk for pathological gambling and eating disorders. Our studies, however, did not support comorbidity of sexual addiction with either drug or alcohol problems. Measures of alcohol (Michigan Alcoholism Screening Test [MAST], Selzer, 1971) and drug (Drug Abuse Screening Test [DAST], Skinner, 1982, 1998) problems were highly correlated with each other but not significantly related to sexual addiction. This finding was particularly surprising since other researchers have reported greater alcohol problems in sexual offenders than either nonsexual offenders or community comparison groups (Abracen, Looman, & Anderson, 2000; Looman, Abracen, DiFazio, & Maillet, 2004). In our studies, community respondents reported greater problems with nonalcohol drugs than did incarcerated sexual offenders, a finding supported by other research (Looman et al., 2004) in which sexual offenders had fewer problems with such drugs than nonsexual offender groups.

Sexual Behavior of Sexual Addicts

It is possible that sexual addicts, described as unwilling or unable to control their sexual behavior, engage in a higher frequency and diversity of sexual behaviors than nonaddicts. Yet, no significant difference between sexual addicts and nonaddicts in the age of onset of sexual activity or in the frequency or diversity of sexual behaviors was found (see Sidebar 19.3). Although sexual addicts report an inability to control their sexual desires, their overt sexual behavior does not significantly differ from that of nonaddicts, suggesting that although sexual addicts may be bothered by fantasies and urges, this strong sexual desire does not necessarily translate into overt sexual acts. Among sexually addicted sexual offenders, these unresolved fantasies and urges have led to attempts to meet sexual needs in inappropriate ways. This interpretation is supported by significant differences in self-reported sexual urges between sexual offending sexual addicts and sexual offending nonaddicts. Although sexual offending sexual addicts were more likely to report unconventional sexual thoughts, fantasies, and urges, they were no more likely to report engaging in these behaviors. In fact, sexual offending sexual addicts were less likely to engage in conventional sex with a partner, but more likely to masturbate to fantasies of unconventional sex than sexual offending nonaddicts. Thus, the problem for those sexual addicts who become sexual offenders is their withdrawal from appropriate sexual relationships and their retreat into deviant sexual fantasies which, ultimately, is expressed in an inappropriate way. Research on sexual offenders has shown an increase in deviant fantasizing when they are suffering from distress arising from various sources (Looman, 1995; McKibben, Proulx, & Lusignan, 1994; Proulx, McKibben, & Lusignan, 1996). It may be that a number of sexual offenders fantasize about previous sexual behaviors when under duress and, as a result, become so sexually preoccupied as to reach the threshold for sexual addiction.

SIDEBAR 19.3

Sexual Addiction as Coping

No significant differences between sexual addicts and nonaddicts were found in the age of onset of sexual activity, or in the frequency or diversity of sexual behaviors. Sexual addicts may be bothered by fantasies and urges, but this increased sexual desire does not necessarily translate into increased overt sexual acts.

Sexual offending sexual addicts were more likely to self-report using sex as a coping strategy than were sexual offending nonaddicts, but no relationship between sexual addiction and psychopathology was apparent.

Sexual Addiction and Using Sexual Activity to Cope

Sexual activity frequently functions as a coping strategy for sexual offenders (Cortoni & Marshall, 2001), that is, sexual offenders will use sexual activity of various kinds (both appropriate and deviant) as a way to cope with stress (see Sidebar 19.3). This finding matches research (Looman, 1995; McKibben, Proulx, & Lusignan, 1994; Proulx, McKibben, & Lusignan, 1996) demonstrating that sexual offenders, when in a negative mood, are more likely to engage in deviant sexual fantasizing. In our research, sexual offending sexual addicts were more likely to report using sex as a coping strategy than were sexual offending nonaddicts.

Sexual Addiction and Psychopathy

The issue of comorbid psychopathy is relevant to sexual offenders and thus has been widely examined. Based on Hare's (1991) Psychopathy Checklist-Revised (PCL-R), 7.8% of incarcerated sexual offenders meet criteria for psychopathy (Serin, personal communication, September 2006). Thus, given the high rates of sexual addiction in sexual offenders, we might expect correlations between scores on the PCL-R and measures of sexual addiction. Specifically, a number of aspects of psychopathy may be related to sexual addiction: failure to accept responsibility for one's own actions, impulsivity, and poor behavioral control. However, our research failed to find a relationship between sexual addiction and any of these variables (L. E. Marshall, Moulden, Serran, & Marshall, 2004). Higher levels of psychopathy were related to a higher number of orgasms per week, greater engagement in unconventional sex, and lower resistance toward engaging in inappropriate sex. However none of these features was specifically related to the measures of sexual addiction. Thus, from our limited research on incarcerated sexual offenders, no significant overlap occurs between sexual addiction and psychopathy.

Summary

The results of our research with sexual offenders suggest that sexual addiction is a significant problem for incarcerated sexual offenders: more than one-third of the sexual offenders in our studies could be classified as sexual addicts. Although a central feature of the use of the term sexual addiction is the expected presence of comorbid addictions, our research found no support for this hypothesis with respect to alcohol or drug addiction. Nor were sexual addicts found to have more overt sexual behavior problems than nonaddicts. However, they were bothered by a greater number of sexual thoughts, urges, and fantasies.

In a factor analysis of the sexual addiction measure (SAST), items loading most heavily on the underlying single factor were those related to sexual thoughts, in particular to feelings of shame and guilt about sexual behavior. This finding suggests that incarcerated sexual offending sexual addicts may have difficulties regarding the interpretation of their sexual desires: the more they try not to think about sex, the more intrusive such thoughts become (W. L. Marshall & Langton, 2004); and if they act on these thoughts when in a vulnerable state (see W. L. Marshall & Marshall, 2000, for a description of vulnerability in sexual offenders) they interpret their behavior as being out of their control both to rationalize and to explain it.

Online Sexual Behavior Problems

Easily available pornography on the Internet appears to have brought problems for some people. A number of our sexual offender clients have been incarcerated because they accessed illegal material online. Others have problems functioning due to their excessive use of the Internet for sexual purposes. Such clients may chat or engage in sexual activities online with others while essentially ignoring people in their immediate environment or neglecting their responsibilities, thereby disrupting key supportive relationships. The most common time for accessing the Internet for sexual purposes is between 9 a.m. and 5 p.m., or work time (Carnes, 2001; Cooper, Griffin-Shelley, Delmonico, & Mathy, 2001). Such behaviors may cause problems at work for these individuals, including the possibility of losing their jobs.

Sex has been one of the biggest factors in the development of, interest in, and activity on the Internet (Cooper, 1997; Cooper, Boies, Maheu, & Greenfield, 1999), to the extent that an estimated 20% of Internet users engage in some form of online sexual activity (Cooper, Delmonico, & Burg, 2000). According to Carr (2000), this number is rapidly increasing, not surprisingly, given that sexuality has been a significant financial engine driving the growth of the Internet since its inception (Hapgood, 1996; Stefanac, 1993). In fact, Sprenger (1999) suggests that 70% of money spent online is related to sexual pursuits. Sex, combined with the anonymity, speed, and capabilities of the Internet, has produced an effect so dramatic that some researchers claim it is heralding the next "sexual revolution" (Cooper, Boies, et al., 1999). Figures taken from www.sexual-addict.com estimate some 4.2 million pornographic web sites (about 12% of the total number) and 68 million daily pornographic search engine requests (about 25% of the total). As such, the Internet presents an unprecedented opportunity for individuals to have anonymous, cost-effective, and unfettered access to an essentially unlimited range of sexual stimuli. And many are taking advantage of this opportunity.

Cooper and his colleagues (Cooper, Boies, et al., 1999; Cooper, Scherer, Boies, & Gordon, 1999) suggest that despite the large number of people engaging in online sexual activity, the majority who visit sexual sites on the Internet do so in moderation and do not suffer any negative consequences. In fact, research by Cooper et al. (2000) found that nearly 83% of all users of sexual sites on the Internet reported no difficulties in their life related to their online activities.

The National Council on Sexual Addiction and Compulsivity (NCSAC, 2000) claims two million Internet users are sexually addicted, presumably a relatively small percentage of those who use the Internet for sexual purposes yet still a large number of people overall. Still, the overall impact of such usage is unclear. Based on the first large-scale study of online sexual activity, only 8.3% of those who used the Internet for sexual purposes 11 hours or more per week experienced difficulties in other areas of their lives (Cooper, Scherer, et al., 1999). Cooper et al. (2000), using an online survey with a measure of compulsivity to better understand those who had used the Internet for sexual purposes, report that

13% of the 9,265 respondents showed signs of moderate to severe problems of distress and compulsivity (see Sidebar 19.4). Carnes (2001) found that about 6% of Internet users have concerns about their use of the Internet for sex. All in all, then it appears that the perceived impact of Internet use for sexual purposes is limited if, at least, one accepts the validity of such self-report measures from self-selected samples of users.

SIDEBAR 19.4

Sexual Addiction and Online Access to Sexual Stimuli

In three separate large-scale studies of online sexual activity, concerns about the impingement of this activity on day-to-day living were expressed by 6% to 13% of respondents.

At least some men who access child pornography sites on the Internet are led there by previous access to other adult-oriented web sites.

Categorization of Online Sexual Behavior Problems

Three subtypes of online sexual compulsivity have been identified through research by Cooper, Griffin-Shelly, et al. (2001). The *Depressive* type uses Internet sex as an escape from depression; the *Stress-Reactive* type uses Internet sex as a way of relieving high levels of stress; the *Fiction and Fantasy* type uses Internet sex as an escape from the daily routine of life in order to fulfill sexual desires.

The behaviors of all three subtypes can rapidly accelerate. Schneider (2000) found that users initially accessed certain types of pornography out of curiosity, sites which quickly became the focus of interest. Clients frequently reported new sexual behaviors or obsessions that became part of their sexual repertoire as a result of accessing online sexual material. Some frequent users of the Internet, becoming desensitized to the material initially accessed, move on to progressively more eccentric, and finally to deviant sexual materials, with some few ultimately seeking out child pornography (Cooper, Golden, & Marshall, 2006). Of course, some Internet users who access child pornography go directly to those sites because they already have such sexual proclivities. In a large sample of men convicted for accessing child pornography on the Internet, all of whom denied throughout the criminal investigation and prosecution process that they had ever sexually touched a child, as many as 70% admitted after almost 2 years in treatment that they had indeed sexually abused children.

Etiology of Online Sexual Behavior Problems

Griffiths (2000), in a study of five cases of excessive sexual computer usage, concluded that use was symptomatic of other problems, and he highlighted the way subjects used the Internet to counteract other deficiencies. For example, those with psychological problems used the Internet to hide behind rather than face their sexual or social conflicts and fears. Higher rates of Internet sexual usage reflect increased levels of depression (Walther, Anderson, & Park, 1994; Young & Rogers, 1998), and Reed (1994) suggests one possible consequence of depression is that certain users become vulnerable to the sexually addictive use of the Internet.

Consequences of Online Sexual Compulsivity

Not only might depression increase vulnerability to sexually addictive use, Schneider (2000) reports that the adverse consequences of online sexual compulsivity include social isolation and depression, decreased job performance or job loss, and abandonment of other social activities. One key consequence reported in Schneider's study was a loss of interest in "ordinary" sex with their usual partner. Similarly, sexual offending sexual addicts in our research reported masturbating more frequently to unconventional fantasies, as well as engaging less frequently in conventional sex with a partner, than did sexual offenders who were deemed to be nonsexual addicts. One commonly expressed concern is that, as online sexual activity becomes more widespread, even more people will develop unrealistic expectations of their sexual relationships, thereby threatening them. Several authors (Greenfield, 1999; Kraut et al., 1998) have expressed the fear that long-term exposure to sexually explicit material may decrease attraction to one's primary partner or increase the desire for emotionally uncommitted sexual involvement. The research reviewed by Cooper et al. (2006) supports this possible consequence.

In a major study of nearly 1,000 people who engaged compulsively in online sexual activity, Carnes (1999) found that "by far the biggest losses recorded were in the workplace" (p. 87), with work time as the main loss: 86% reported acting out sexually in some way in the workplace and 80% reporting a loss of productivity. In a survey of almost 40,000 adults, 20% reported going online for sexual activities at work (Cooper, Scherer, & Mathy, 2001). Compulsive users with access at work may spend over 2.5 hours per day in online sexual activity during work hours (Cooper, Scherer, et al., 2001), a finding made plausible by Carnes' (2001) report that 70% of all adult content Internet traffic occurs during the workday.

Relationship to Offending

The need for sexual satiation can, for at least some, become an obsession that may escalate into a criminal act (see Sidebar 19.4). At least some men who access child pornography sites on the Internet are led there by previous access to other adult-oriented web sites (Cooper et al., 2000; Cooper et al., 2006; Cooper, Putnam, Planchon, & Boies, 1999; Greenfield, 1999; Schneider, 2000). Moreover, Zwicke (2000) reports that the distribution of online "child pornography" is rapidly increasing: specifically, Wyre (2003) reported that a half-year period in 2001 saw a 345% increase in sites containing child abusive images on the Internet.

Sexual preoccupation in general has been linked to reoffending (Hanson & Harris, 2000; Hanson & Morton-Bourgon, 2004); in fact, it was not only one of the strongest predictors of sexual offending, but also strongly related to violent reoffending, sexual and nonsexual. These authors suggested that for such offenders, sexual preoccupation may be accompanied by specific problems controlling sexual impulses, a general lack of self control (more common among young people and criminals), and a tendency to overemphasize sex in the pursuit of happiness. For some, sexual activity on the Internet will not constitute illegal behavior but will seriously interfere with pursuing a satisfying lifestyle, and quite possibly relate to future acts of criminality.

Involvement by Women and Children

Some recent findings suggest that women may be well represented among those with online sexual compulsivity (Cooper et al., 2000). According to Nielsen NetRatings, the number of women in Britain downloading Internet pornography has soared 30% to 1.4 million (Downloads of net porn, 2006). Research regarding young people and sexual activity on the Internet is also emerging. As for children, some evidence suggests that 90% of the 8- to 16- year age group have viewed pornography online (Ropelato, 2007), and according to Nielsen NetRatings more than half of all children admit to having viewed adult images "while looking for something else." The Internet Filter Review authored by Ropelato (2007) also reports that 11 years is the average age of first exposure to Internet pornographic images among users in the United States.

Longo, Brown, and Orcutt (2002) express concern about children's exposure to large amounts of inappropriate sexual material on the Internet, given that the American Psychological Association has determined that exposure to excessive amounts of television violence has a negative impact on children's aggressive behaviors. Boies (2002) reports that 3.5% of a sample of college students viewed sexually explicit material online and masturbated to it at least once a day. This finding suggests a potential for compulsivity in this subgroup, although whether this behavior actually leads to sexual offending is unknown.

Treatment of Sexual Addiction

A number of different approaches, both pharmacological and psychological, have been used in attempting to treat those with sexual addiction. For further information on the pharmacological treatment of hypersexuality, see Kafka (1997). To date, the most predominant psychological strategy for treating sexual addictions has been a 12-step approach, which emphasizes the need for the addict to admit to powerlessness over his or her behavior. Further information on this approach may be found in Carnes (1989).

In contrast with the 12-step approach, our cognitive-behavioral treatment requires sexual offender clients to accept at least some degree of responsibility for their behavior. The observed sexual recidivism rate in the 534 sexual offenders we have treated, released for a mean of 5.4 years, is just 3.2%, markedly lower than the rate reported in other studies, 16.8% (see W. L. Marshall, Marshall, Serran, & Fernandez, 2006 for a review of our treatment approach and outcome data). Although not an indicator of a change in clients' *sexual addictive behaviors,* but to the extent that these populations show some overlap, the fact that the program has so markedly reduced sexual offending suggests that it may contribute to the amelioration of sexual addiction as well.

Certain aspects of our treatment program may be effective in the treatment of sexual addiction. For example, therapists help clients learn to cope more competently with their problems without resorting only to the use of sex. For the many clients who have attempted to meet their sexual needs in inappropriate ways, therapists in our program help clients explore more suitable means. Focusing on understanding and achieving real intimacy may help those who have withdrawn from appropriate sexual relationships in the past. Therapists lead group discussions and exercises on sex, and on the role of sex in relationships, thus helping those who may have overemphasized sex in the pursuit of happiness. To this end, therapists also present the Good Lives model (Ward, 2002), asking clients to select purposeful and personal goals to help them maintain a satisfying and balanced lifestyle. Given the link between feelings of shame and guilt on the one hand, and sexual behavior and sex-related problems on the other, therapists lead discussions and exercises on normative sexual behaviors and on the restrictions to the enjoyment of these acts such unhelpful feelings can produce. Therapists also help clients deal with feelings of loneliness and low self-esteem in order to help them learn how to alleviate both social and emotional isolation.

The Future

This field is clearly young. The growth of the Internet over the past 15 years has required researchers and clinicians to examine new paradigms, but as Cooper (1998) correctly asserts, health professions have been relatively slow to respond to these new developments. Continued research is needed to fully understand, evaluate, and treat those with online sexual behavior problems. Once these problems are better understood, future research should focus on developing reliable and valid protocols for accurate evaluation and effective treatment. Such research is imperative, given that online access to sexually explicit materials in the future will only continue to expand.

Summary and Conclusions

Sexual addiction, as described by Carnes (1983, 1989) and outlined in his measure (SAST), appears to be more of a problem for sexual offenders than community comparison groups:

- Our research indicates that sexual offending sexual addicts are plagued by sexual preoccupation that reduces the number of conventional sexual outlets and increases the rate of masturbation to unconventional sexual outlets. These findings are consistent with other research reports on sexual addicts who have problems with online sexual activities: greater time spent online accessing sexual materials resulted in less interest in "ordinary" sexual behaviors with a partner.

- Sexual addiction probably results from inappropriate attempts to cope with deficits and problems in other areas of functioning and then effectively isolates the addict. This isolation further exacerbates the problem, resulting in an even greater dependence on the need to sexually cope and leading to a further increase in the use of sex to alleviate negative affect.

- The sexual offender field has been relatively slow to investigate sexual addiction among sexual offenders, quite possibly due to the association of addiction with 12-step treatment programs in which one goal is to have addicts admit to powerlessness over their behavior. Current approaches to treatment for sexual offenders require at least some degree of acceptance of responsibility by the clients for their behavior, an approach that appears to be in conflict with the 12-step approach. However, given our findings, it appears advisable that sexual offender researchers consider further examining the features of sexual addiction in sexual offenders.

- Respondents in our sexual offender research have come from our treatment program setting, a medium-security federal prison in Canada. In addition to the high rates of sexual addicts in these groups, our clients include a growing number of men convicted of accessing child pornography on the Internet. Since sexual preoccupation, also a characteristic of addiction, has been found to be a predictor of sexual recidivism, any program that manages to reduce this outcome among sexual offenders should prove effective for sexual addicts.

- Our treatment outcome data offer hope for the effective reduction of risk for recidivism, both sexual and nonsexual, in sexual offending sexual addicts. The observed sexual recidivism rate in 534 sexual offenders in our treatment program, released for a mean of 5.4 years, is just 3.2%, markedly lower than the expected rate of 16.8%.

- While we have not yet analyzed our outcome data to see if, indeed, our program reduced proclivities to sexual addiction, the fact that it reduced sexual offending suggests that it may contribute to the amelioration of sexual addiction as well. To the extent that our research samples are representative of the larger population of sexual addicts, this treatment approach may include features helpful in the treatment of sexual addiction more generally.

References

Abracen, J., Looman, J., & Anderson, D. (2000). Alcohol and drug abuse in sexual and nonsexual violent offenders. *Sexual Abuse: Journal of Research and Treatment, 12,* 263–274.

American Foundation for Addiction Research (AFAR) (2001, March). The Vanderbilt Symposium on the Nosology of Sexual Addiction, Nashville, TN. *Sexual Addiction and Compulsivity: Journal of Treatment and Prevention, 8,* 185–307.

American Psychiatric Association (APA) (1987). *Diagnostic and Statistical Manual of Mental Disorders* (3rd ed., rev.). Washington, DC: American Psychiatric Association.

Barth, R. J., & Kinder, B. N. (1987). The mislabeling of sexual impulsivity. *Journal of Sexual and Marital Therapy, 13,* 15–23.

Boies, S. C. (2002). University students' uses of and reactions to online sexual information and entertainment: Links to online and offline sexual behavior. *Canadian Journal of Human Sexuality, 11*(2), 77–89.

Carnes, P. (1983). *Out of the shadows: Understanding sexual addiction.* Minneapolis, MN: CompCare.

Carnes, P. (1989). *Contrary to love: Helping the sexual addict.* Minneapolis, MN: CompCare.

Carnes, P. (1999). Editorial: Cybersex, sexual health, and the transformation of culture. *Sexual Addiction and Compulsivity: Journal of Treatment and Prevention, 6,* 77–78.

Carnes, P. (2001). Cybersex, courtship, and escalating arousal: Factors in addictive sexual desire. *Sexual Addiction and Compulsivity: Journal of Treatment and Prevention, 8,* 45–78.

Carr, L. (2000). *Sizing up virtual vice: Porn and gambling are making more money than ever.* Available from http://thestandard.com/article /display/0,1151,1754900.html.

Coleman, E. (1987). Sexual compulsivity: Definition, etiology, and treatment considerations. *Journal of Chemical Dependency Treatment, 1,* 189–204.

Coleman, E. (1990). Toward a synthetic understanding of sexual orientation. In D. P. McWhirter & S. A. Sanders (Eds.), *Homosexuality/heterosexuality: Concepts of sexual orientation* (pp. 267–276). Oxford: Oxford University Press.

Cooper, A. (1997). The Internet and sexuality: Into the new millennium. *Journal of Sex Education and Therapy, 22,* 5–6.

Cooper, A. (1998). Sexuality and the Internet: Surfing into the new millennium. *CyberPsychology and Behavior, 1,* 187–193.

Cooper, A., Boies, S., Maheu, M., & Greenfield, D. (1999). Sexuality and the Internet: The next sexual revolution. In F. Muscarella & L. Szuchman (Eds.), *The psychological science of sexuality: A research based approach* (pp. 519–545). New York: Wiley.

Cooper, A., Delmonico, D. L., & Burg, R. (2000). Cybersex users, abusers, and compulsives: New findings and implications. *Sexual Addiction and Compulsivity: Journal of Treatment and Prevention, 7,* 5–29.

Cooper, A., Golden, G. H., & Marshall, W. L. (2006). Online sexuality. In W.L Marshall, Y. M. Fernandez, L. E. Marshall, & G. A. Serran (Eds.), *Sexual offender treatment: Controversial issues* (pp. 79–91). Chichester, West Sussex, England: Wiley.

Cooper, A., Griffin-Shelley, E., Delmonico, D. L., & Mathy, R. M. (2001). Online sexual problems: Assessment and predictive variables [Special issue]. *Sexual Addiction and Compulsivity: Journal of Treatment and Prevention, 8,* 267–285.

Cooper, A., Putnam, D. E., Planchon, L. A., & Boies, S. C. (1999). Online sexual compulsivity: Getting tangled in the net. *Sexual Addiction and Compulsivity: Journal of Treatment and Prevention, 6,* 79–104.

Cooper, A., Scherer, C., Boies, S. C., & Gordon, B. (1999). Sexuality on the internet: From sexual exploration to pathological expression. *Professional Psychology: Research and Practice, 30,* 154–164.

Cooper, A., Scherer, C., & Mathy, R. (2001). Overcoming methodological concerns in the investigation of online sexual activities. *Cyberpsychology and Behavior, 4,* 437–448.

Cortoni, F., & Marshall, W. L. (2001). Sex as a coping strategy and its relationship to juvenile sexual history and intimacy in sexual offenders. *Sexual Abuse: A Journal of Research and Treatment, 13,* 27–44.

Delmonico, D. L., Bubenzer, D. L., & West, J. D. (1998). Assessing sexual addiction using the Sexual Dependency Inventory-Revised. *Sexual Addiction and Compulsivity: Journal of Treatment and Prevention, 5,* 179–187.

Downloads of net porn hit record high. (2006, May 30). *Daily Mail.*

Goodman, A. (1998). *Sexual addiction: An integrated approach.* Madison, CT: International Universities Press.

Greenfield, D. N. (1999). *Virtual addiction: Help for netheads, cyberfreaks, and those who love them.* Oakland, CA: New Harbinger Publications.

Griffiths, M. (2000). Excessive internet use: Implications for sexual behavior. *Cyberpsychology and Behavior, 3,* 537–552.

Hanson, R. K., & Harris, A. J. R. (2000). Where should we intervene? Dynamic predictors of sex offence recidivism. *Criminal Justice and Behavior, 21,* 187–202.

Hanson, R. K., & Morton-Bourgon, K. (2004). *Predictors of sexual recidivism: An updated meta-analysis* (Report 02). Canada: Public Safety and Emergency Preparedness.

Hapgood, F. (1996). Sex sells, Inc. *Technology, 4,* 45–51.

Hare, R. D. (1991). *Manual for the Revised Psychopathy Checklist.* Toronto, Ontario, Canada: Multi-Health Systems.

Kafka, M. P. (1997). Hypersexual desire in males: An operational definition and clinical implications for men with paraphilias and paraphilia-related disorders. *Archives of Sexual Behavior, 26,* 505–526.

Kafka, M. P., & Hennen, J. (1999). The paraphilia-related disorders: An empirical investigation of nonparaphilic hypersexuality disorders in outpatient males. *Journal of Sex and Marital Therapy, 25,* 305–319.

Kraut, R., Lundmark, V., Patterson, M., Kiesler, S., Mukopadhyay, T., & Scherlis, W. (1998). Internet paradox: A social technology that reduces social involvement and psychological well-being? *American Psychologist, 53,* 1017–1031.

Leedes, R. (2001, March). *The three most important criteria in diagnosing sexual addiction unerringly: Obsession, obsession, and obsession.* Paper presented at the American Foundation for Addiction Research/Vanderbilt Symposium, Nashville, TN.

Longo, R. E., Brown, S. M., & Orcutt, D. P. (2002). Effects of Internet sexuality on children and adolescents. In A. Cooper (Ed.), *Sex and the internet: A guidebook for clinicians* (pp. 87–105). New York: Brunner-Routledge.

Looman, J. (1995). Sexual fantasies of child molesters. *Canadian Journal of Behavioral Science, 27,* 321–332.

Looman, J., Abracen, J., DiFazio, R., & Maillet, G. (2004). Alcohol and drug abuse among sexual and nonsexual offenders: Relationship to intimacy deficits and coping strategy. *Sexual Abuse: Journal of Research and Treatment, 16,* 177–189.

Manley, G., & Koehler, J. D. (2001, March). *Proposed diagnostic features of sexual behavior disorder.* Paper presented at the AFAR/Vanderbilt Symposium, Nashville, TN.

Marshall, L. E., & Marshall, W. L. (1998, October). *Sexual addiction and substance abuse in sexual offenders.* Paper presented at the 17th Annual Treatment and Research Conference of the Association for the Treatment of Sexual Abusers, Vancouver, British Columbia, Canada.

Marshall, L. E., & Marshall, W. L. (2001). Excessive sexual desire disorder among sexual offenders: The development of a research project. *Sexual Addiction and Compulsivity: Journal of Treatment and Prevention, 8,* 301–307.

Marshall, L. E., & Marshall, W. L. (in press). Sexual addiction in incarcerated sexual offenders. *Sexual Addiction and Compulsivity: Journal of Treatment and Prevention.*

Marshall, L. E., Marshall, W. L., & Moulden, H. (2000, November). *Sexual addiction, substance abuse, coping, and sexual history in sexual offenders.* Paper presented at the 19th Annual Treatment and Research Conference for the Association for the Treatment of Sexual Abusers, San Diego, CA.

Marshall, L. E., Moulden, H. M., Serran, G. A., & Marshall, W. L. (2004, October). *Sexual addiction and psychopathy in incarcerated sexual offenders.* Paper presented at the 23rd Annual Treatment and Research Conference of the Association for the Treatment of Sexual Abusers, Albuquerque, NM.

Marshall, W. L., & Langton, C. (2004). Unwanted thoughts and fantasies experienced by sexual offenders: Their nature, persistence, and treatment. In D. A. Clark (Ed.), *Intrusive thoughts in clinical disorders: Theory, research, and treatment* (pp. 199–225). New York: Guilford Press.

Marshall, W. L., & Marshall, L. E. (2000). The origins of sexual offending. *Trauma, Violence, and Abuse: A Review Journal, 1,* 250–263.

Marshall, W. L., Marshall, L. E., Serran, G. A., & Fernandez, Y. M. (2006). *Treating sexual offenders: An integrated approach.* New York: Routledge.

McKibben, A., Proulx, J., & Lusignan, R. (1994). Relationships between conflict, affect and deviant sexual behaviors in rapists and pedophiles. *Behavior Research and Therapy, 32,* 571–575.

National Council on Sexual Addiction and Compulsivity. (2000). *Cybersex and sexual addiction.* Retrieved April 13, 2000, from National Council on Sexual Addiction and Compulsivity www.ncsac.org/cybersex.htm.

Proulx, J., McKibben, A., & Lusignan, R. (1996). Relationships between affective components

and sexual behaviors in sexual aggressors. *Sexual Abuse: A Journal of Research and Treatment, 8,* 279–290.

Reed, M. D. (1994). Pornography addiction and compulsive sexual behavior. In D. Zillmann, J. Bryant, & A. C. Huston (Eds.), *Media, children and the family: Social scientific, psychodynamic and clinical perspectives* (pp. 249–269). Hillsdale, NJ: Erlbaum.

Ropelato, J. (2007). *Internet Pornography Statistics.* Retrieved October 25, 2007, from http://internet-filter-review.toptenreviews.com/internet-pornography-statistics.html.

Schneider, J. P. (2000). Effects of cybersex addiction on the family: Results of a survey. *Sexual Addiction and Compulsivity: Journal of Treatment and Prevention, 7,* 31–58.

Schneider, J. P., & Schneider, B. (1991). *Sex, lies, and forgiveness: Couples speaking out on healing from sex addiction.* New York: HarperCollins.

Selzer, M. L. (1971). The Michigan Alcoholism Screening Test (MAST): The quest for a new diagnostic instrument. *American Journal of Psychiatry, 127,* 1653–1658.

Skinner, H. A. (1982). Drug Abuse Screening Test. *Addictive Behaviors, 7,* 363–371.

Skinner, H. A. (1998). *Drug Abuse Screening Test (DAST): Guidelines for administration and scoring.* Toronto, Ontario, Canada: Addiction Research Foundation.

Smith, D. E. (1994). Response to Schneider. *Sexual Addiction and Compulsivity: Journal of Treatment and Prevention, 1,* 45.

Sprenger, P. (1999, October 9). Porn: Online pioneers. *Age Newspaper,* p. 10.

Stefanac, S. (1993). Sex and the new media. *New-Media, 3,* 38–45.

Steiger, J. H., & Lind, J. C. (1980, May). *Statistically based tests for the number of common factors.* Paper presented at the annual meeting of the Psychometric Society, Iowa City, IA.

Walther, J. B., Anderson, J. F., & Park, D. W. (1994). Interpersonal effects in computer-mediated interaction: A meta-analysis of social and antisocial communication. *Communication Research, 21*(4), 460–487.

Ward, T. (2002). Good lives and the rehabilitation of offenders: Promises and problems. *Aggression and Violent Behavior, 7,* 513–528.

Wyre, R. (2003, September). Child porn. *Community Care,* 11–17.

Young, K. S., & Rogers, R. C. (1998). The relationship between depression and internet addiction. *CyberPsychology and Behavior, 1,* 25–28.

Zwicke, L. (2000). *Crime on the superhighway: A guide to online safety.* Retrieved March 27, 2000, from www.geocities.com/CapitolHill/6647/.

Legal and Privacy Issues Surrounding Sexual Disorders

Renee Sorrentino

20

Chapter

Learning Objectives

In this chapter, we discuss:

- A brief historical perspective on sex offender legislation.
- Current sex offender legislation.
- The idea of civil commitment and its constitutionality.
- Psychiatric perspectives on sex offender legislation.
- Community notification laws.
- Sex offender evaluation for the court, including the role of the expert witness.
- Legal and ethical issues surrounding the treatment of sex offenders.

The treatment and evaluation of sex offenders is an important public safety concern. Psychiatrists have been enlisted as clinicians responsible for sex offender evaluation. As such, psychiatrists frequently encounter clinical situations that have legal implications. This chapter discusses the legal and ethical issues involved in the evaluation and treatment of sex offenders after a brief overview of the history of sex offender legislation, community notification of sex offenders, and sex offender evaluations and treatment.

History of Sex Offender Legislation

> *[T]he particular form of abomination which shocked the sensibilities of our forefathers.*

These words, stated by the Kansas Supreme Court in a 1925 sodomy case, sum up the historical attitude of the Anglo-American legal system toward nonprocreative eroticism (Painter, 2004). The first-generation of sex offender legislation originated in the 1930s when Michigan enacted the first sexual psychopath law in 1937 followed shortly thereafter by California in 1939 (Sreenivasan, Weinberger, & Garrick, 2003). This legislation used civil commitment procedures to commit sex offenders to treatment programs as an alternative to incarceration. The rationale for these laws was to provide community protection while rehabilitating sex offenders. By 1960, more than 25 states had enacted sex offender commitment laws, "sexual psychopath" laws, "sexually dangerous persons" acts, and "mentally disordered sex offender" acts (Brakel, Parry, & Weiner, 1985). Since the mid-1970s, most states have repealed their sexual psychopath laws because of skepticism about treatment effectiveness, an inability to predict dangerousness or diagnose sexual psychopathologies according to accepted medical standards, and public opinion that increasingly prefers punishment for sex offenders over treatment (Lieb, 1996).

The American Bar Association observed that sexual psychopath legislation rested on the following assumptions (American Bar Association, 1989):

- There is a specific mental disability called sexual psychopathy.
- Persons suffering from such a disability are more likely to commit serious crimes, especially dangerous sex offenses, than normal criminals.
- Such persons are easily identified by mental health professionals.
- The dangerousness of these offenders can be predicted by mental health professionals.
- Treatment is available for the condition.
- Large numbers of persons afflicted with the designated disabilities can be cured.

A study of the psychopathic offender law in Illinois published in 1948 detailed some cases prosecuted under it. One was a music teacher and church organist who had a long-standing habit of engaging in frottage with male students (Painter, 2004). Another was a 67-year-old man who had a long-standing relationship with a 9-year-old boy who became enraged when the man "transferred his affections to other children" and "informed on him" (Painter, 2004).

Individuals eligible for civil commitment under the first-generation sexual psychopath laws included persons who had been convicted of a crime—typically a sex crime, but not exclusively—and persons who were not charged with a crime but thought to be sexually dangerous. For example, Ohio Rev. Code Ann. 2947.25 and Baldwin (1958; as cited in Swanson, 1960) specify the following, "After conviction and before sentence, a trial court must refer for examination all persons convicted under [special sections] of the Revised Code, to the department of mental hygiene and correction or to a state facility designated by the department, or to a psychopathic clinic approved by the department." Additionally, Utah Code Ann. 77-49-1 (1953; as cited in Swanson, 1960) specifies, "Whenever any person is convicted of the offense of rape, sodomy, incest, lewdness, indecent exposure or carnal knowledge . . . the judge shall order a mental examination of such person." In some states, offenders were civilly committed in lieu of incarceration, while other states mandated completion of a criminal sentence if the offender no longer met the criteria for civil commitment.

Modern Sex Offender Legislation

The public's attitude toward sex offenders and sexual offenses became evident in the 1970s when the premature release of offenders hospitalized as sexual psychopaths resulted in sex offender recidivism. The sexual psychopath laws were rendered the subject of scrutiny in the 1970s and 1980s as a result of criticism of the sexual psychopath laws. After repeal of a Wisconsin statute permitting hospitalization of defendants convicted of sexual crimes, the percentage of sex offenders among persons hospitalized after being found not guilty by reason of insanity was found to increase (Miller, Stava, & Miller, 1988).

At this time, the Group for the Advancement of Psychiatry (GAP) recommended revision of the sexual psychopath laws. GAP concluded: "First and foremost, sex psychopath and sexual offender statutes can best be described as approaches that have failed. The discrepancy between the promises in sex statutes and performances have rarely been resolved. . . . The notion is naïve and confusing that a hybrid amalgam of law and psychiatry can validly label a person a 'sex psychopath' or 'sex offender' and then treat him in a manner consistent with a guarantee of community safety. The mere assumption that such a heterogeneous legal classification could define treatability and make people amenable to treatment is not only fallacious, it is startling. Our position is that the experiment was a form of well intentioned but misguided intervention. Its dual goals have often remained in conflict. After a given passage of time an experiment needs evaluation in terms of its demonstrable benefits and liabilities. If the assessment of the statute in terms of achieving certain goals, for whatever reasons, leads to the conclusion that an experiment has not been successful, it should be halted" (Group for the Advancement of Psychiatry, 1977).

The public criticized the sexual psychopath laws as ineffective because of widely publicized cases of sex offenders who reoffended on release from "treatment." The professional and public skepticism about treatment effectiveness resulted in a political climate that favored punishment of sex offenders over treatment. In response to this political climate, many states repealed the first-generation sexual psychopath laws. The first-generation sexual psychopath laws were replaced by the second-generation, modern psychopath laws that are rooted in the premise that sex offenders who are sexually dangerous should be civically committed to a treatment detention center after serving their prison sentence. Unlike the first-generation psychopath laws, second-generation laws were focused on punishment and detention. The modern psychopath laws established treatment for sex offenders after completion of incarceration, in contrast to the first-generation laws that provided treatment as an alternative to incarceration. The second-generation psychopath laws were appealing to the public because they served two purposes: retribution for criminal activity through incarceration, and confinement of dangerous persons through indeterminate commitment post incarceration.

Civil Commitment of Sexually Violent Predators

In 1990, Washington State enacted a law authorizing civil commitment of individuals found to be sexually violent predators at the end of their criminal sentence (Lieb, 1996). The civil commitment of sexually violent predators after incarceration reflected the societal view that sex offenders should be punished before they are eligible for treatment. The law establishes a civil commitment for those individuals determined to be "sexually violent predators." Individuals in this category were defined as those who have been convicted of or charged with a crime of sexual violence and suffer from a "mental abnormality or personality disorder which makes the person likely to engage in predatory acts of sexual violence" (Wash. Rev. Code Ann. §§71.09.060, West 1975 & Supp. 1991).

The enactment of a sexually violent predator law in Washington was the direct result of the public's outrage when Earl

Shriner, a convicted sex offender released into the community, raped and strangled a 7-year-old boy. In May 1987, Earl Shriner completed a 10-year sentence in Washington for kidnapping and assaulting two teenage girls. He had a 24-year history of killing, sexual assault, and kidnapping. During his last months in prison, Shriner designed plans to maim or kill children and made diary entries that identified apparatus he would use. In a conversation with a cellmate, he said he wanted a van customized with cages so he could pick up children, molest them, and kill them ("System Just," 1989). Prior to his discharge, prison officials learned that he intended to torture children after he was released, and they tried vigorously to detain him through the civil commitment laws covering mental illness (Leib, 1996). Nevertheless, the court released Shriner into the community because there was no substantial evidence of recent dangerousness. Two years after his release, he raped and strangled a 7-year-old boy in Tacoma, Washington, severed his penis, and left him in the woods to die.

Washington's sexually violent predator law reflects the public safety concerns that arose after the Shriner case. More specifically, the sexually violent predator law did not require a recent act of sexual violence. In addition, the sexually violent predator law did not require the presence of a major mental illness, as outlined in general civil commitment statutes, but rather a "mental abnormality." "Mental abnormality" as defined by the Washington law is "a congenital or acquired condition affecting the emotional or volitional capacity which predisposes the person to the commission of criminal sexual acts" (Wash. Rev. Code Ann. §§71.09.060, West 1975 & Supp. 1991).

By 1990, only 13 jurisdictions still had sexual psychopath laws in place (Gleb, 1991). As of 2007, 19 states had enacted civil commitment statutes for sex offenders (Davey & Goodnough, 2007). Several states modeled their civil commitment sex offender laws after Washington State. In addition to Washington's model of postconviction commitment, two additional models of sex offender commitment evolved. New Jersey's law for sexual predators relied on the existing mental health commitment laws. The definition of mental illness was amended so psychosis was not required for commitment, and special procedures to review prisoners were established (Leib, 1996). Illinois and Minnesota modeled their civil commitment sex offender laws after existing sexual psychopathy models. In this model, the state must choose between criminal prosecution and a sexual psychopath filing (Leib, 1996). The standard of proof required in sexual predator statutes varies by jurisdiction, with the majority of states favoring a "Beyond a reasonable doubt" standard over "Clear and convincing evidence." The duration of confinement for civically committed sex offenders is indeterminate in all states except for California. According to the California sexually violent predator statute, offenders are committed for 2 years, which can be extended by the court with a second petition and trial (Lieb, 1996).

Since enactment of the civil commitment statute in Arizona in 1995, Arizona has discharged the highest number of offenders at 81, while five states have never discharged an offender (Davey & Goodnough, 2007).

Constitutional Challenges

These legislative initiatives were passed despite a lack of evidence that such laws actually reduce sexual violence. The constitutionality of Washington's sexually violent predator law was challenged in 1993. In 1993, two repeat rapists, Andre Young and Vance Cunningham, appealed their civil commitments on the following constitutional arguments: The statute violated the double jeopardy clause of the Fifth Amendment and the prohibition of ex post facto laws; the statute violated substantive due process because it allowed the state to commit individuals without proving both mental illness and dangerousness; the statute violated the equal protection principles of the Fourteenth Amendment that requires the state to guarantee sexual predators procedural protections equivalent to those accorded in the ordinary civil commitment process (American Psychiatric Association, 1999). The Supreme Court ruled that the Washington sexually violent predator statute was constitutional based on the finding that the statute was civil in purpose, not criminal. As such, the statute did not violate the double jeopardy clause, the ex post facto law, or the substantive due process and equal protection principles instilled in the constitution.

The U.S. Supreme Court upheld the constitutionality of the Kansas sexually violent predator statute in the 1997 *Kansas v. Hendricks* ruling. In 1984, Hendricks, a pedophile, was convicted of sexually abusing two 13-year-old boys. After serving 10 years of his sentence, Hendricks was scheduled to be released from prison. Before his release, however, the state sought to have Hendricks committed as a sexually violent predator under the newly enacted law. Hendricks was psychiatrically evaluated and diagnosed with pedophilia. Hendricks agreed with the diagnosis of pedophilia and stated, if released, it was likely he would continue to molest children. The jury unanimously found that Hendricks was a sexually violent predator, and the court determined that Hendricks's pedophilia constituted a "mental abnormality" as outlined in the sexually violent predator statute.

Hendricks appealed to the Kansas Supreme Court on the basis that pedophilia did not meet the criteria for a mental abnormality, thereby rendering his civil commitment unconstitutional. The U.S. Supreme Court rejected Hendricks argument stating that:

The mental-disorder for civil commitment is a legal, as opposed to a medical, term. As all Members of the court seem to agree, then, the power of the state to confine persons who, by reason of a mental disease or mental abnormality, constitute a real, continuing, and serious danger to society is well established. Addington v. Texas, *441 U.S. 418, 426–427 (1979). Confinement of such individuals is permitted even if it is pursuant to a statute enacted after the crime has been committed and the offender has begun serving, or has all but completed serving, a penal sentence, provided there is no object or purpose to punish. See* Baxstrom v. Herold, *383 U.S. 107, 111–112 (1966). The Kansas law, with its attendant protections, including yearly review and review at any time at the instance of the person confined, is within this pattern and tradition of civil confinement. In this case, the mental abnormality—pedophilia—is at least described in the* DSM-IV, American Psychiatric Association, Diagnostic and Statistical Manual of Mental Disorders, *524–525, 527–528 (4th ed. 1994). Notwithstanding its civil attributes, the practical effect of the Kansas law may be to impose confinement for life. At this stage of medical knowledge, although future treatments cannot be predicted, psychiatrists or other professionals engaged in treating pedophilia may be reluctant to find measurable success in treatment even after a long period and may be unable to predict that no serious danger will come from release of the detainee. (Kansas v. Hendricks, 1997)*

The constitutionality of the Kansas sexually violent predator statue was rechallenged with *Kansas v. Crane* in 2002. Michael Crane was diagnosed with exhibitionism and antisocial personality disorder. He had a long history of arrests, some of which involved sexual assault, and since he was not exposed to therapy specific to his problems while in prison, he was eligible for consideration for commitment. A jury found him to meet the criteria for civil commitment as outlined in the Kansas sexually violent predator law. Crane appealed the civil commitment arguing that due process requires that a person suffer from a total lack of volitional control in order to be subject to involuntary commitment.

The U.S. Supreme Court upheld Kansas, ruling that Crane met the criteria for civil commitment articulated in the Kansas sexually violent predator statute. The court ruled that a total lack of control is not constitutionally required and there must be proof of serious difficulty in controlling one's behavior (*Kansas v. Crane*, 2002).

In summary, the second-generation psychopath laws were created in response to the public's fear of sex offender release into the community whereas the first-generation psychopath laws were aimed at providing treatment for offenders. As a result of the first-generation laws, some sex offenders were released into the community and reoffended. The public demanded a higher level of security and containment of these individuals, and as such, several states adopted sexual predator laws that established detainment of sex offenders postincarceration. The sexual predator laws are based on the principle that sex offenders should receive treatment after punishment. The constitutionality of these laws has been upheld on the tenet that sexual predator laws are civil, not criminal, in nature.

Psychiatric Opinion

An American Psychiatric Association task force declared that "sexual predator commitment laws establish a nonmedical definition of what purports to be a clinical condition without regard for scientific and clinical knowledge," and thus "distort the traditional meaning of civil commitment, misallocate psychiatric facilities and resources, and constitute an abuse of psychiatry" (American Psychiatric Association, 1999). The National Association of State Mental Health Program Directors (NASMHPD) believes that legislation allowing for the civil commitment of dangerous sex offenders who do not have a mental illness to psychiatric hospitals following completion of their prison sentences creates the following significant risks: Laws that provide for the civil commitment of dangerous sex offenders for purposes that are principally punitive or for the purpose of continuing confinement, rather than for the purpose of providing treatment or psychiatric services, disrupt the state's ability to provide services for people with treatable psychiatric illnesses and undermine the mission and integrity of the public mental health system (National Association of State Mental Health Program Directors, 1997). Furthermore, NASMHPD argues that commitment of sex offenders to psychiatric hospitals places other psychiatric patients, who may be vulnerable, at risk.

Community Notification

In 1996, President Clinton signed "Megan's Law," mandating all 50 states to develop requirements for convicted sex offenders to register with local law enforcement agencies and to notify communities when a sex offender lives in close proximity (Levenson, 2003). Community notification refers to the dissemination of identifying information to the public about convicted sex offenders who are released into the community. The conception of community notification of sex offenders can be traced to the state of Washington. In 1989, Washington Governor Booth Gardner appointed a task force to recommend changes to the state sex offender laws. The task force recommendations included registration and community notification (Matson, 2001). Similarly, other states reformed sex offender statutes to include community notification.

In addition to community notification laws, sex offender registry laws have been enacted. In 1994, Congress enacted the Jacob Wetterling Crimes against Children and Sex Offender Registration Act. This Act federally mandates states to create a program to register sex offenders and authorized discretionary community notification (Matson, 2001). The Wetterling Act has been amended three times to include the following: Megan's Law in 1996; The Pam Lychner Sexual Offender Tracking and Identification Act in 1996; and Section 115 of the General Provisions of Title 1 of the Departments of Commerce, Justice, and State, the Judiciary, and Related Agencies Appropriations Act (CJSA) of 1998 (Matson, 2001). The Pam Lychner Act's amendments to the Wetterling Act created a limited number of new requirements for state registration programs, including a requirement that the perpetrators of particularly serious offenses and recidivists be subject to lifetime registration. The CJSA amendments made extensive changes to the Wetterling Act, many of which afford states greater flexibility in achieving compliance. For example, the CJSA added provisions to promote registration of sex offenders in states where they work or attend school (as well as states of residence) and to promote registration of federal and military.

Constitutional Challenges

The procedural due process afforded in community notification statutes has been challenged. The Massachusetts Supreme Court found that provisions of the state's community notification law violated constitutional due process (Matson, 2001). The Massachusetts Supreme Court ruled that an offender should be allowed a hearing to challenge their sex offender risk classification. More specifically, the court stated "the appropriateness of an offender's risk classification must be proved by a preponderane of the evidence, and that the (Sex Offender Registry) board must make specific, written, detailed, and individualized findings to support the appropriateness of each offender's risk classfication" (*Doe v. Sex Offender Registry Board*, 1998).

Empirical Evidence

There is no empirical evidence to suggest that community notification has decreased sex offender recidivism and thereby instilled safer communities. The Washington State Recidivism Study compared the recidivism rates of adult sex offenders who were classified as Level III notification (highest risk) with sex offenders who were released prior to community notification laws. Data from the study revealed that at the end of 54 months the notification group did not have a statistically significant difference in rates of sexual recidivism when compared to the group not subject to community notification, the comparison group (Schram & Milloy, 1995). It was found that 63% of the new sex offenses occurred in the jurisdiction where notification took place, suggesting that notification did not deter offenders or motivate them to venture outside their jurisdictions (where they would be less likely identified) to commit crimes. Based on these findings, the authors concluded that community notification appeared to have little effect on sex offense recidivism (Schram & Milloy, 1995).

Caputo and Brodsky (2004) investigated citizen reactions to notifications of sex offenders in the neighborhood, in an effort to determine whether sex offender notification laws were accomplishing their goal of increased protective actions against sex offenses. Caputo et al. (2004) found that notification importance predicted fear of crime, which, in turn, predicted coping. In addition, the focus of control inherent in community notification did not moderate the relation between fear of crime and coping strategy. Zevitz and Farkas (2000) examined the relationship between community notification meetings and the collective response of the community. Their data suggested that the decision to notify and involve the public in a community notification meeting may come at the cost of increased community anxiety.

Societal Challenges

In April 2006, two registered sex offenders were shot and killed in their Maine homes by a Canadian man the police say had used the state's online registry to locate the men at their homes and kill them. The mother of one of the slain men testified before legislators last year that the registry had killed her son (Associated Press, 2006). Studies suggest that one-third to one-half of sex offenders subjected to community notification experience adverse events such as the loss of a job or home, threats, or harassment, or property damage (Levenson & Cotter, 2005). Society's efforts to decrease sexual offender recidivism by community notification laws may be counterproductive. Homelessness and unemployment are in part the result of community notification laws. Both homelessness and unemployment are independent risk factors for sexual offender recidivism.

Sex Offender Evaluations

Evaluations for the Court

A number of individuals charged with sex offenses are referred to mental health clinicians for psychiatric evaluation. Individuals are typically referred by the courts, but may seek evaluations independently or with the advice of their attorney. The type of evaluations commonly requested includes evaluations to determine the most appropriate disposition of the offender and risk of sexual offender recidivism. Evaluations of individuals who are not adjudicated are problematic. In the evaluation process, individuals are asked to recount their version of the alleged offense. Admissions of guilt or information recounted in individuals' evaluations may be used against them in the adjudication process. Evaluations present another set of problems associated with the validity of available assessment instrumentation to determine innocence or guilt, as there is no scientific basis for assuming that any currently available psychometric or psychophysiological measure of personality or sexual interest is valid for that purpose (Melton, Petrila, Poythress, & Sloborin, 1997). Clinicians are frequently asked to give an opinion about an individual's risk of sexual offender recidivism. The scientific literature supports the use of identified risk factors and risk assessment tools in the evaluation of risk. However, the field of sex offender risk assessment is not an exact science and risk assessments are merely clinical opinions, not hard facts.

The responsibilities of the evaluator in sex offender evaluations are distinct from the responsibilities of a treating clinician. In a treatment relationship, the clinician has a duty to maintain the evaluee's confidentiality. In other words, a treating clinician who discloses information about an evaluee without proper authorization is breaching confidentiality and subject to malpractice. In the purely evaluative relationship, however, the evaluator maintains confidentially to the extent possible given the legal context. Clinicians performing evaluations for the courts are required to give third parties information about the person evaluated regardless of that person's wishes (Melton et al., 1997). Clinicians performing evaluations are obligated to inform the evaluee about the limitations of confidentiality and the absence of a traditional "doctor-patient" relationship.

Role of the Expert Witness

Expert witnesses have a central role in the civil commitment proceedings of sex offenders. In order for an individual to meet criteria for civil commitment under the sexually violent predator or sexually dangerous persons statute, he or she must have a diagnosed mental disorder and a likelihood to engage in future sexual offenses. Experts testify about both of these issues. Competent experts are familiar with the controversies that surround the inclusion of the diagnosis of antisocial personality disorder (APD) as a qualifying mental disorder for civil commitment. Traditionally, the diagnosis of APD has been excluded as a qualifying mental illness for civil commitment. This rationale for exclusion is due to the belief among mental health professionals that this disorder does not readily fit into assumptions of the medical model of involuntary civil commitment, that is, the necessity to protect individuals when they are unable to recognize their need for treatment because of a serious mental illness (Sreenivasan et al., 2003). The differing opinion regarding the definition of a mental illness may impose ethical challenges to the expert witness. The expert witness must struggle with whether it is ethical to provide testimony that an individual with APD should be treated in a psychiatric facility. In fact, the clinical literature would support the opposite—the individual with APD should be discharged from a psychiatric facility.

The testifying expert must also give an opinion about the individual's likelihood to engage in future sexual offenses. The expert should emphasize that forensic risk assessment is not risk prediction (Sreenivasan et al., 2003). A competent risk assessment is based on evidence-based data. Thus, experts who testify solely on their clinical experience without applying evidence-based data are not practicing within the standard of care. These experts are subject to medical liability and impeachment by the courts.

Sex Offender Treatment

Legal and Ethical Issues in Treatment

The treatment of sex offenders is distinct from other clinical populations. As such, the traditional codes of ethics employed in medical treatment are not applicable to the treatment of sex offenders. The legal and ethical issues that arise in the course of sex offender treatment are outlined in Sidebar 20.1.

SIDEBAR 20.1

Legal and Ethical Issues in Treatment of Sexual Offenders

- *Beneficence:* The oath of beneficence in sex offender treatment gives priority of protection to the public, which may result in conflict with the Hippocratic Oath that states that the physician must do no harm and mental health ethical codes that state that the patient's interest is to receive highest priority.
- *Involuntary treatment:* Sex offender treatment is often court ordered; ethical and legal obligations are to the protection of the public, not

the patient, which may create conflict with mental health ethical codes; involuntary treatment raises the question of whether informed consent is truly being given.

- *Right to refuse treatment:* The right to refuse a treatment is based on the rights of privacy, due process, and self-determination; because courts treat sexual offenders as incompetent patients, they potentially compromise an individual's right to refuse treatment in favor of protecting the community.
- *Confidentiality and privilege:* Confidentiality can often be breached during the course of treatment and various reporting obligations.

Beneficence

Nearly all codes of ethics in mental health practice require the patient's interest to be paramount (Glaser, 2003). The Hippocratic Oath states that a physician should do no harm. In sex offender treatment, the oath of beneficence is to the public at large, not the individual patient. As such, the patient's interests and needs are secondary. At times, the treating clinician may engage in practices that directly harm the patient, such as reporting certain behaviors to the Parole Department.

Involuntary Treatment

Most sex offender treatment is court ordered as part of incarceration or community release. The identified "patient" in sex offender treatment is the public, not the individual receiving treatment. As such, the ethical and legal obligations in sex offender treatment are to the public, not the offender. Breaches in the traditional codes of mental health ethics are pervasive in all aspects of treatment programs for sex offenders (Glaser, 2003).

The concept of involuntary treatment raises the issue of whether informed consent is upheld in sex offender treatment. In order for consent for medical treatment to be valid, three conditions are required: the patient must have knowledge, the patient must be competent, and the consent must be voluntary.

Informed consent requires the understanding of (a) the medical condition for which the treatment is proposed, (b) the nature and effect of the proposed treatment, (c) the risks and benefits of the proposed treatment, (d) the likely result of refusing the proposed treatment, and (e) any alternative treatments.

Consent must be voluntary. In other words, a patient's decision regarding treatment should be made of his or her own free will, without constraint or expectation of reward. Obviously, court-ordered sex offender treatment is not voluntary. Individuals who choose not to participate in court-ordered therapy are subject to punishment imposed by the court. The typical punishment for refusal to attend court-ordered treatment is incarceration. In addition, the offender's choice of therapist is not voluntary. Sex offenders are required to complete particular programs, irrespective of any other treatment that they might be receiving, in order to gain parole or avoid imprisonment (Glaser, 2003). The rationale for this selective treatment is based on some empirical evidence that programs based on particular treatment methods (particularly cognitive-behavior therapy supplemented by pharmacological interventions) result in lower recidivism rates (Marshall, Anderson, & Fernandez, 1999).

The Association for the Treatment of Sexual Abusers (ATSA) has developed guidelines to attempt to address these deviations from traditional mental health ethical codes. Traditionally, courts recognize the following four exceptions to informed consent: (1) emergency; (2) incompetence or lack of capacity that would accompany decisions that must be made without the benefit of the court; (3) waiver; and (4) therapeutic privilege. Waiver refers to the patient's right to waive disclosure of information. Therapeutic privilege refers to a doctor's decision to withhold information from a patient because telling the patient would cause psychological damage or render the patient ineffective in decision making. Sex offender treatment is not formally recognized as an exception to informed consent. By construct, sex offenders cannot give informed consent for treatment due to the involuntariness of the relationship.

Right to Refuse Treatment

In the medical model, patients have a right to refuse various types of treatment, including life-saving surgery and chemotherapy. The right to refuse a treatment is based on the constitutional right to privacy and the right to due process. When an incompetent patient refuses psychiatric treatment, the court may become the vicarious decision maker. The court views sex offenders like incompetent patients, and as such the court becomes the decision maker regarding treatment. Specifically, the court decides whether to override a patient's treatment refusal based on the individual's risk of danger to the community. If an individual is deemed dangerous in the community without treatment, the court imposes treatment over refusal.

As part of treatment, individuals are required to adopt specific attitudes, values, and behaviors determined largely by the therapist (Glaser, 2003). Individuals must admit to guilt regarding their sex offenses. If individuals do not admit to guilt, they are considered treatment refusers and in violation of court-ordered treatment. This requirement violates the individual's right to self-determination.

Confidentiality and Privilege

Confidentiality refers to the physician's obligation to keep information learned in a professional relationship private from other parties. The concept of confidentiality can be traced to the Hippocratic Oath, that is: "What I may see or hear in the course of the treatment or even outside of the treatment in regard to the life of men, which on no account one must spread abroad, I will keep to myself, holding such things shameful to be spoken about." The American Medical Association, the American Psychiatric Association, and the federal HIPPA regulation have adopted a code of ethics that specifies the ethical responsibility to maintain confidentiality.

In the area of sex offender treatment, confidentiality is routinely breached. When individuals enter treatment, they are required to give permission for their cases to be discussed with both clinical and nonclinical personnel, correctional officers, members of their family, past and potential victims, and those associated with them and fellow offenders (Glaser, 2003).

Privilege refers to the patient's right to prevent a physician from providing testimony about personal medical information. The psychiatrist has a duty to honor the patient's privilege unless ordered to testify by a judge. Information gained in confidence about a patient may not be released without the authorization of the patient. However, a number of exceptions to this occur, including mandatory reporting (child abuse, elder abuse, and infectious disease), emergencies, court-ordered examinations, patient litigant exceptions (patient puts their mental condition at issue), and in some states commitment proceedings and treatment refusal hearings. As previously discussed, individuals entering sex offender treatment are required to waive their privilege by giving the treating clinician permission to contact both clinical and nonclinical personnel involved in the offender's care.

In response to the deviations from traditional ethical codes inherent in sex offender treatment, ethical and practice guidelines were developed by the Association for the Treatment of Sexual Abusers (ATSA). ATSA's code of ethics endorses standards of professional conduct that promote competent practice, and as such, they represent a public commitment to clients and society toward the goal of preventing sexual violence. The ATSA guidelines state that the ethical care of sex offenders is achieved by encouraging individuals to take responsibility for their behavior, that is, admitting their guilt. In addition, the ethical principle of beneficence is achieved in sex offender treatment when the public at large is the understood patient. Furthermore, ATSA maintains that the identification and collaborative management of risk and safety factors (waiver of privilege) are indeed in the best interests of both sex offender patients and potential victims due to the grave consequences incurred by sexual offense recidivism (Levenson & D'Amora, 2005).

Castration of Sex Offenders; Legal and Ethical Issues

The biologic treatment of sex offenders involves decreasing testosterone levels by surgical castration (removal of the testes) or chemical castration (use of medications to decrease testosterone). In 1996, California became the first state to authorize the use of either chemical or surgical castration for certain sex offenders who were being released from prison into the community. To date, an additional nine states authorize surgical or chemical castration for sex offenders, including Georgia, Montana, Oregon, Wisconsin, Florida, Iowa, Louisiana, and Texas. Some states do not require informed consent for surgical or chemical castration (see Sidebar 20.2). In other states, the informed consent procedure requires only that the offender be informed regarding the side effects (Scott & Holmberg, 2003). One could argue that informed consent for court-ordered castration is impossible due to the involuntariness of the treatment. In addition, in order to obtain informed consent, the patient should be educated about the indications, advantages, and disadvantages of treatment.

SIDEBAR 20.2

Sex Offender Legislation Key Points

- First-generation sex offender legislation used civil commitment procedures as an alternative to incarceration.

- Such legislation gave way to second-generation sex offender legislation, which calls for civil commitment for treatment after incarceration and focuses more heavily on punishment and detention.

- The constitutionality of such laws has been called into question, in part due to a lack of evidence that such laws reduce sexual violence, but such laws have ultimately been upheld by the courts.

- Second-generation laws grew from public fears over community release of sexual offenders, a contrast to the first-generation laws that focused on treatment for offenders.

- An American Psychiatric Association task force cited fears that civil commitment of sex offenders may drain resources from the system and may be improperly placed in mental facilities; the NASMHPD cited fears that commitment of sexual offenders with no medical mental illness may place other patients at risk.

- Various community notification laws and registry laws exist, some of which have been cited as causes for the harm, harassment, homelessness, and unemployment of sexual offenders in various communities; a lack of empirical evidence as to the efficacy of such legislation still exists, as do challenges in conducting research on the efficacy of such legislation.

- Psychiatric evaluation for the court presents a number of issues, including the admission of guilt and its consequences, the conflicts between obligations as an evaluator and a treating clinician, and the role of the expert witness in testimony, among others.

- Various ethical and legal issues in the treatment of sexual offenders exist, including issues of beneficence, involuntary treatment, voluntary consent, right to refuse treatment, and confidentiality and privilege; such issues are also involved in the consideration of castration of sexual offenders.

The efficacy of biologic treatment in sex offenders is poorly understood. The potential to use double-blinded, randomized controlled trials of treatment in sex offenders is limited by the risk to the public and the difficulty that would arise if a sex offender randomized to a nontreatment arm reoffended (Gordon & Grubin, 2004). Thus, it is difficult to provide a patient with information regarding the utility of such a treatment. The administration of a treatment in the absence of informed consent breaches ethical guidelines of health care.

The American Psychiatric Association (1999) stated "these laws, which predicate release from prison on chemical castration by surgery or antiandrogenic agents, are objectionable because they are not based on adequate diagnostic and treatment considerations. They also improperly link medical treatment with punishment and social control." What then is the liability of the individual who provides chemical or surgical castration? Some jurisdictions provide for immunity for the individual administering surgical or chemical castration. Providers in Georgia and Louisiana are not liable civilly or criminally if the provider acts in good faith. Physicians in Texas are "not liable for an act or omission relating to the procedure unless negligent" (Scott & Holmberg, 2003).

The U.S. Supreme Court has not addressed the constitutionality of court-ordered castration of sex offenders. The challenges to the constitutionality of court-ordered castration include infringement on the sex offender's First Amendment right to entertain sexual fantasies, violation of the Eighth Amendment ban on cruel and unusual punishment, and deprivation of the fundamental right to procreation (Scott & Holmberg, 2003).

Summary and Conclusions

Psychiatric involvement in the assessment and treatment of sex offenders has dramatically increased as a result of the second-generation psychopath laws. The role of psychiatrist as defined by the judicial system is in conflict with the traditional role of the psychiatrist physician. As a result, psychiatrists are asked to participate in sex offender treatment without regard to the traditional ethical guidelines inherent in the practice of medicine. The American Psychiatric Association created a specialized sex offender task force to educate the profession and the public about the current understanding of sexual disorders and developing treatments for sex offenders. In addition, the task force provided recommendations regarding the role of psychiatry in sex offender treatment. The task force offered the following recommendations:

- Increased investment in research on paraphilic disorders and in the clinical training of psychiatrists and other mental health professionals regarding assessment and treatment of persons with those disorders.
- With regard to sexual predator commitment laws, the task force opined that psychiatry must vigorously oppose these statutes in order to preserve the moral authority of the profession and to ensure continuing societal confidence in the medical model of civil commitment.
- Societal concerns about the need for punishment and incapacitation of dangerous sex offenders should be met through customary sentencing alternatives within the criminal justice system and not through involuntary civil commitment statutes.

In summary, psychiatrists have been identified as clinicians responsible for sex offender treatment and evaluation. Current sex offender legislation is predicated on the safety of the community. As such, the state's duty to maintain public safety frequently outweighs an offender's individual rights. Modern sex offender legislation was enacted in order to ensure public safety and allows for the civil commitment of sexually violent predators and community notification of released sex offenders. However, there is no empirical evidence that the civil commitment of sexually violent predators and the notification of released sex offenders affords public safety or directly decreases sexual offender recidivism. In contrast, there are some data that community notification increases sex offender recidivism by increasing independent risk factors for sexual offender recidivism such as homelessness and unemployment.

Clinicians are frequently asked to give an opinion about an individual's risk of sexual offender recidivism. Clinicians who treat sex offenders are confronted with legal and ethical challenges in the delivery of care. It is important for treating clinicians to understand the application and deviation of the traditional codes of ethics employed in medical treatment of sex offenders.

Successful sex offender legislation should be established on evidence-based knowledge rather than societal fears. The enactment of sex offender civil commitment laws, sentencing, and community notification should be based on scientific research in the field. Legislation informed by scientific data is more likely to result in the successful evaluation, treatment, and containment of sex offenders.

References

American Bar Association. (1989). *Criminal justice mental health standards: Commentary to Standard 7-8.1.* Washington, DC: Author. Available from www.abanet.org/crimjust/standards/mentalhealth .pdf.

American Psychiatric Association. (1999). *Dangerous sex offenders: A task force report of the American Psychiatric Association.* Washington DC: Author.

Associated Press. (2006, April 17). 2 sex offenders shot to death in their homes. *New York Times,* National Ed.

Brakel, S., Parry, J., & Weiner, B. (1985). *The mentally disabled and the law* (3rd ed.). Chicago, IL: American Bar Foundation.

Caputo, A., & Brodsky, S. (2004). Citizen coping with community notification of released sex offenders. *Behavioral Sciences and the Law, 22*(29), 239–252.

Davey, M., & Goodnough, A. (2007, March 4). Doubts rise as states hold sex offenders after prison. *New York Times.*

Doe v. Sex Offender Registry Board (Doe No. 4), 428 Mass. 90 (1998).

Gleb, G. (1991). Washington's sexually violent predator law: The need to bar unreliable psychiatric predictions of dangerousness from civil commitment proceedings. *UCLA Law Review, 39,* 213, 215.

Glaser, B. (2003). Therapeutic jurisprudence: An ethical paradigm for therapists in sex offender treatment programs. *Western Criminology Review, 4*(2), 143–154.

Gordon, H., & Grubin, D. (2004). Psychiatric aspects of the assessment and treatment of sex offenders. *Advances in Psychiatric Treatment, 10,* 73–80.

Group for the Advancement of Psychiatry. (1977). *Psychiatry and sex psychopath legislation: The 30's to the 80's.* New York: Author.

Kansas v. Crane, 534 U.S. 407, 122 S.Cir.867 (2002).

Kansas v. Hendricks, 521 U.S. 399 (1997).

Levenson, J. S. (2003). Policy interventions designed to combat sexual violence: Community notification and civil commitment. *Journal of Child Sexual Abuse, 12*(3/4), 17–52.

Levenson, J., & Cotter, L. (2005, April). The impact of sex offender residence restrictions: 1,000 feet from danger or one step from absurd? *International Journal of Offender Therapy and Comparative Criminology, 49*(2), 168–178.

Levenson, J., & D'Amora, D. (2005). An ethical paradigm for sex offender treatment: Response to Glaser. *Western Criminology Review, 6*(1), 145–453.

Lieb, R. (1996). *Washington's sexually violent predator law: Legislative history and comparisons with other states.* Washington State Institute for Public Policy. Retrieved May 20, 2007, from www.wsipp.wa.gov/rptfiles/WAsexlaw.pdf.

Marshall, W., Anderson, D., & Fernandez, Y. (1999). *Cognitive behavioral treatment of sexual offenders.* New York: Wiley.

Matson, S. (2001). Community notification and education. *Center for sex offender management.* Retrieved May 20, 2007, from www.csom.org /pubs/notedu.html.

Melton, G., Petrila, J., Poythress, N., & Sloborin, C. (1997). *Psychological evaluations for the courts* (2nd ed.). New York: Guilford Press.

Miller, R., Stava, L., & Miller, R. (1988). The insanity defense for sex offenders: Jury decisions after repeal of Wisconsin's Sex Crimes Law. *Psychiatric services.* Retrieved April 28, 2007, from http://psychservices.psychiatryonline.org/cgi/content/abstract/39/2/186/.

National Association of State Mental Health Program Directors. (1997, September 9). *Position statement on laws providing for the civil committment of sexually violent criminal offenders.* Available from www.nasmhpd.org/general_files/position_statement/sexpred.htm.

Painter, G. (2004). The history of sodomy laws in the United States-IL. *Sodomy laws.* Retrieved May 10, 2007, from www.sodomylaws.org/sensibilities/illinois.htm.

Schram, D., & Milloy, C. (1995). *Community notification: A study of offender characteristics and recidivism.* Olympia, WA: Washington State Institute for Public Policy.

Scott, C. L., & Holmberg, T. (2003). Castration of sex offenders: Prisoners' rights versus public safety. *Journal of the American Academy of Psychiatry and the Law, 31,* 502–509.

Sreenivasan, S., Weinberger, L., & Garrick, T. (2003). Expert testimony in sexually violent predator commitments: Conceptualizing legal standards of "Mental Disorder" and "Likely to Reoffend." *Journal of the American Academy of Psychiatry and the Law, 31,* 471–485.

Swanson, A. H. (1960, July/August). Sexual psychopath statutes: Summary and analysis. *The Journal of Criminal Law, Criminology, and Police Science, 51*(2), 215–235.

System just couldn't keep suspect. (1989, May 23). *Tacoma Morning News Tribune.*

Wash. Rev. Code Ann. §§71.09.060 (West 1975 & Supp. 1991).

Zevitz, R., & Farkas, M. (2002). Sex offender community notification: Examining the importance of neighborhood meetings. *Behavioral Sciences and the Law, 18*(2/3), 393–406.

Appendix

Dyspareunia (302.76)

A. Recurrent or persistent genital pain associated with sexual intercourse in either a male or a female.

B. The disturbance causes marked distress or interpersonal difficulty.

C. The disturbance is not caused exclusively by Vaginismus or lack of lubrication, is not better accounted for by another Axis I disorder (except another Sexual Dysfunction), and is not due exclusively to the direct physiological effects of a substance (e.g., a drug of abuse, a medication) or a general medical condition.

Specify Type:
   Lifelong Type
   Acquired Type

Specify Type:
   Generalized Type
   Situational Type

Specify Type:
   Due to Psychological Factors
   Due to Combined Factors

Exhibitionism (302.4)

A. Over a period of at least 6 months, recurrent, intense sexually arousing fantasies, sexual urges, or behaviors involving the exposure of one's genitals to an unsuspecting stranger.

B. The person has acted on these sexual urges, or the sexual urges or fantasies cause marked distress or interpersonal difficulty.

Female Orgasmic Disorder

A. Persistent or recurrent delay in, or absence of, orgasm following a normal sexual excitement phase. Women exhibit wide variability in the type or intensity of stimulation that triggers orgasm. The diagnosis of Female Orgasmic Disorder should be based on the clinician's judgment that the woman's orgasmic capacity is less than would be reasonable for her age, sexual experience, and the adequacy of sexual stimulation she receives.

B. The disturbance causes marked distress or interpersonal difficulty.

C. The orgasmic dysfunction is not better accounted for by another Axis I disorder (except another Sexual Dysfunction) and is not due exclusively to the direct physiological effects of a substance (e.g., a drug of abuse, a medication) or a general medical condition.

Specify Type:
   Lifelong Type
   Acquired Type

Specify Type:
   Generalized Type
   Situational Type

Specify Type:
   Due to Psychological Factors
   Due to Combined Factors

Female Sexual Arousal Disorder (302.72)

A. Persistent or recurrent inability to attain, or to maintain until completion of the sexual activity, an adequate lubrication-swelling response of sexual excitement.

B. The disturbance causes marked distress or interpersonal difficulty.

C. The sexual dysfunction is not better accounted for by another Axis I disorder (except another Sexual Dysfunction) and is not due exclusively to the direct physiological effects of a substance (e.g., a drug of abuse, a medication) or a general medical condition.

Specify Type:
   Lifelong Type
   Acquired Type

Specify Type:
   Generalized Type
   Situational Type

Specify Type:
   Due to Psychological Factors
   Due to Combined Factors

Fetishism (302.81)

A. Over a period of at least 6 months, recurrent, intense sexually arousing fantasies, sexual urges, or behaviors involving the use of nonliving objects (e.g., female undergarments).

B. The fantasies, sexual urges, or behaviors cause clinically significant distress or impairment in social, occupational, or other important areas of functioning.

C. The fetish objects are not limited to articles of female clothing used in cross-dressing (as in Transvestic Fetishism) or devices designed for the purpose of tactile genital stimulation (e.g., a vibrator).

Frotteurism (302.89)

A. Over a period of at least 6 months, recurrent, intense sexually, arousing fantasies, sexual urges, or behaviors involving touching and rubbing against a nonconsenting person.

B. The person has acted on these urges, or the sexual urges or fantasies cause marked distress or interpersonal difficulty.

Gender Identity Disorder (See below for number)

A. A strong and persistent cross-gender identification (not merely a desire for any perceived cultural advantages of being the other sex).

In children, the disturbance is manifested by four (or more) of the following:

(1) Repeatedly stated desire to be, or insistence that he or she is, the other sex.

(2) In boys, preference for cross-dressing or simulating female attire; in girls, insistence on wearing only stereotypical masculine clothing.

(3) Strong and persistent preferences for cross-sex roles in make-believe play or persistent fantasies of being the other sex.

(4) Intense desire to participate in the stereotypical games and pastimes of the other sex.

(5) Strong preference for playmates of the other sex.

In adolescents and adults, the disturbance is manifested by symptoms such as a stated desire to be the other sex, frequent passing as the other sex, desire to live or be treated as the other sex, or the conviction that he or she has the typical feelings and reactions of the other sex.

B. Persistent discomfort with his or her sex or sense of inappropriateness in the gender role of that sex.

In children, the disturbance is manifested by any of the following: in boys, assertion that his penis or testes are disgusting or will disappear or assertion that it would be better not to have a penis, or aversion toward rough-and-tumble play and rejection of male stereotypical toys, games, and activities; in girls, rejection of urinating in a sitting position, assertion that she has or will grow a penis, or assertion that she does not want to grow breasts or menstruate, or marked aversion toward normative feminine clothing.

In adolescents and adults, the disturbance is manifested by symptoms such as preoccupation with getting rid of primary and secondary sex characteristics (e.g., request for hormones, surgery, or other procedures to physically alter sexual characteristics to simulate the other sex) or belief that he or she was born the wrong sex.

C. The disturbance is not concurrent with a physical intersex condition.

D. The disturbance causes clinically significant distress or impairment in social, occupational, or other important areas of functioning.

Code based on current age:
302.6 Gender Identity Disorder in Children
302.85 Gender Identity Disorder in Adolescents or Adults

Specify if (for sexually mature individuals):
Sexually attracted to Males
Sexually attracted to Females
Sexually attracted to Both
Sexually attracted to Neither

Gender Identity Disorder Not Otherwise Specified (302.6)

This category is included for coding disorders in gender identity that are not classified as a specific Gender Identity Disorder. Examples include:

1. Intersex conditions (e.g., partial androgen insensitivity syndrome or congenital adrenal hyperplasia) and accompanying gender dysphoria.
2. Transient, stress-related cross-dressing behavior.
3. Persistent preoccupation with castration or penectomy without a desire to acquire the sex characteristics of the other sex.

Hypoactive Sexual Desire Disorder (302.71)

A. Persistently or recurrently deficient (or absent) sexual fantasies and desire for sexual activity. The judgment of deficiency or absence is made by the clinician, taking into account factors that affect sexual functioning, such as age and the context of the person's life.

B. The disturbance causes marked distress or interpersonal difficulty.

C. The sexual dysfunction is not better accounted for by another Axis I disorder (except another Sexual Dysfunction) and is not due exclusively to the direct physiological effects of a substance (e.g., a drug of abuse, a medication) or a general medical condition.

Specify Type:
   Lifelong Type
   Acquired Type

Specify Type:
   Generalized Type
   Situational Type

Specify Type:
   Due to Psychological Factors
   Due to Combined Factors

Male Erectile Disorder (302.72)

A. Persistent or recurrent inability to attain, or to maintain until completion of the sexual activity, an adequate erection.

B. The disturbance causes marked distress or interpersonal difficulty.

C. The erectile dysfunction is not better accounted for by another Axis I disorder (other than a Sexual Dysfunction) and is not due exclusively to the direct physiological effects of a substance (e.g., a drug of abuse, a medication) or a general medical condition.

Specify Type:
   Lifelong Type
   Acquired Type

Specify Type:
    Generalized Type
    Situational Type

Specify Type:
    Due to Psychological Factors
    Due to Combined Factors

Male Orgasmic Disorder (302.74)

A. Persistent or recurrent delay in, or absence of, orgasm following a normal sexual excitement phase during sexual activity that the clinician, taking into account the person's age, judges to be adequate in focus, intensity, and duration.

B. The disturbance causes marked distress or interpersonal difficulty.

C. The orgasmic dysfunction is not better accounted for by another Axis I disorder (except another Sexual Dysfunction) and is not due exclusively to the direct physiological effects of a substance (e.g., a drug of abuse, a medication) or a general medical condition.

Specify Type:
    Lifelong Type
    Acquired Type

Specify Type:
    Generalized Type
    Situational Type

Specify Type:
    Due to Psychological Factors
    Due to Combined Factors

Pedophilia (302.2)

A. Over a period of at least 6 months, recurrent, intense sexually arousing fantasies, sexual urges, or behaviors involving sexual activity with a prepubescent child or children (generally age 13 years or younger).

B. The person has acted on these sexual urges, or the sexual urges or fantasies cause marked distress or interpersonal difficulty.

C. The person is at least age 16 years and at least 5 years older than the child or children in Criterion A.

Note: Do not include an individual in late adolescence involved in an ongoing sexual relationship with a 12- or 13-year-old.

Specify if:
    Sexually Attracted to Males
    Sexually Attracted to Females
    Sexually Attracted to Both

Specify if:
  Limited to Incest

Specify Type:
  Exclusive Type (attracted only to children)
  Nonexclusive Type

Premature Ejaculation (302.75)

A. Persistent or recurrent ejaculation with minimal sexual stimulation before, on, or shortly after penetration and before the person wishes it. The clinician must take into account factors that affect duration of the excitement phase, such as age, novelty of the sexual partner or situation, and recent frequency of sexual activity.

B. The disturbance causes marked distress or interpersonal difficulty.

C. The premature ejaculation is not due exclusively to the direct effects of a substance (e.g., withdrawal from opioids).

Specify Type:
  Lifelong Type
  Acquired Type

Specify Type:
  Generalized Type
  Situational Type

Specify Type:
  Due to Psychological Factors
  Due to Combined Factors

Sexual Aversion Disorder (302.79)

A. Persistent or recurrent extreme aversion to, and avoidance of, all (or almost all) genital sexual contact with a sexual partner.

B. The disturbance causes marked distress or interpersonal difficulty.

C. The sexual dysfunction is not better accounted for by another Axis I disorder (except another Sexual Dysfunction).

Specify Type:
  Lifelong Type
  Acquired Type

Specify Type:
  Generalized Type
  Situational Type

Specify Type:
  Due to Psychological Factors
  Due to Combined Factors

Sexual Masochism (302.83)

A. Over a period of at least 6 months, recurrent, intense sexually arousing fantasies, sexual urges, or behaviors involving the act (real, not simulated) of being humiliated, beaten, bound, or otherwise made to suffer.

B. The fantasies, sexual urges, or behaviors cause clinically significant distress or impairment in social, occupational, or other important areas of functioning.

Sexual Sadism (302.84)

A. Over a period of at least 6 months, recurrent, intense sexually, arousing fantasies, sexual urges, or behaviors involving acts (real, not simulated) in which the psychological or physical suffering (including humiliation) of the victim is sexually exciting to the person.

B. The person has acted on these sexual urges with a nonconsenting person, or the sexual urges or fantasies cause marked distress or interpersonal difficulty.

Transvestic Fetishism (302.3)

A. Over a period of at least 6 months, in a heterosexual male, recurrent, intense sexually arousing fantasies, sexual urges, or behaviors involving cross-dressing.

B. The fantasies, sexual urges, or behaviors cause clinically significant distress or impairment in social, occupational, or other important areas of functioning.

   Specify if:
   With Gender Dysphoria: if the person has persistent discomfort with gender role or identity

Vaginismus (306.51)

A. Recurrent or persistent involuntary spasm of the musculature of the outer third of the vagina that interferes with sexual intercourse.

B. The disturbance causes marked distress or interpersonal difficulty.

C. The disturbance is not better accounted for by another Axis I disorder (e.g., Somatization Disorder) and is not due exclusively to the direct physiological effects of general medical condition.

   Specify Type:
   Lifelong Type
   Acquired Type

Specify Type:
Generalized Type
Situational Type

Specify Type:
Due to Psychological Factors
Due to Combined Factors

Voyeurism (302.82)

A. Over a period of at least 6 months, recurrent, intense sexually arousing fantasies, sexual urges, or behaviors involving the act of observing an unsuspecting person who is naked, in the process of disrobing, or engaging in sexual activity.

B. The person has acted on these sexual urges, or the sexual urges or fantasies cause marked distress or interpersonal difficulty.

AUTHOR INDEX

Aaron, L. A., 235
Aaronson, N. K., 291
Aass, N., 293
Abate, S., 295
Abbas, N., 336, 337, 339
Abbott, F. V., 227, 229, 232, 234, 235, 241
Abdel-Hamid, I. A., 91, 92, 93
Abdo, C., 92, 102, 117
Abel, G. G., 498, 499, 500, 504, 512, 531, 540, 541, 547, 552, 566, 567, 569
Abracen, J., 591
Abraham, F., 423
Abrahamson, D. J., 134
Abramovici, H., 241
Abramowitz, S. I., 442
Abu El-Magd, S., 25
Achenbach, T. M., 381, 387, 402, 407, 537, 538
Achermann, J. C., 342
Acton, G. S., 538
Acunzo, G., 257
Adaikan, G., 60, 61
Adams, C. G., 202
Adams, H. E., 541
Addis, M. E., 285
Adekunle, A. O., 261, 267
Adiakan, P. G., 14
Admon, A., 338
Adolfsson, J., 289
Adshead, J., 298
Affara, N. A., 337
Agarwal, A., 62, 231
Aggarwal, N., 512
Agmo, A., 155
Agnello, C., 195, 209, 257
Agras, K., 91, 92
Aguirre, O., 275
Ahlmeyer, S., 552
Ahlskog, J. E., 512
Ahmed, S. F., 330, 355, 360, 362, 370, 371
Ahn, T. Y., 49
Ahnadi, C. E., 140
Aikens, J. E., 290
Aimaretti, G., 146
Ainsworth, M. D. S., 533
Aizenberg, D., 200

Akiskal, H. S., 564
Aksaray, G., 200
Alarcon, G. S., 235
Albertsen, P. C., 289
Alessi, C. A., 18
Alexander, C. J., 197, 198
Alexander, J. L., 261, 262
Alexander, R. W., 235
Alison, L., 502
Allamaneni, S. S., 62
Allard, A. M., 387
Allen, A., 514, 516, 517, 519
Allen, C., 547
Allin, S. M., 405
Allsworth, J. E., 260, 261
Aloni, R., 312
Altay, B., 79, 161
Althof, S., 42, 57, 72, 74, 75, 82, 90, 95, 102, 109, 135, 136, 148
Altman, K., 574
Altmann, D., 368
Altwein, J., 106
Amar, E., 20, 21, 22
Amato, R. J., 296
Ameeriar, L., 402, 407, 408
Amichetti, M., 297
Amos, N. L., 549
Amrhein, J. A., 365
Amsel, R., 221, 224, 225, 227, 228, 229, 232, 234, 235, 236, 237, 241, 242
Amsterdam, A., 226
Anand, A., 348
Anand, K., 512
Andersen, B. M., 242
Andersen, K. V., 45
Andersen, M. L., 91, 92, 93
Anderson, B. L., 201
Anderson, C., 348
Anderson, D., 513, 591, 616
Anderson, G. L., 273
Anderson, J. F., 596
Anderson, M., 55
Anderson-Hunt, M., 194
Andersson, S., 293, 363, 364
Andrews, Z. B., 162
Andry, C., 46
Anglin, G., 22

Angst, J., 199
Angulo, J., 195
Annable, L., 198
Anthony, D., 566, 576, 577
Antunez, P., 14, 16
Anvret, M., 337
Aoki, Y., 291
Aouizerate, B., 75
Aparecida Medeiros, M., 337
Apaydin, E., 161
Apfelbaum, B., 104, 108, 109, 114
Appelt, M., 573
Apperloo, M. J., 159, 161, 179, 180
Apt, C., 171, 172, 176, 177, 199, 201
Aradna, C., 14, 16
Aragaki, A., 273
Arai, Y., 291, 297
Araujo, A. B., 22, 127
Archer, J., 25, 530
Arlt, W., 145, 159
Armelius, K., 437, 438
Armstrong, M. S., 566
Arn, P., 338, 340
Arnold, A. P., 346, 353, 377
Arrigo, B. A., 499
Arver, S., 144
Ashton, A. K., 180
Ashton, K., 24
Asscheman, H., 438, 445, 446
Atan, A., 91, 92
Atteya, A., 25
Aubin, S., 177, 179
Aubut, J., 541
Auriacombe, M., 75
Avall-Lundqvist, E., 169
Aversa, A., 23, 54, 93, 132
Avery-Clark, C. A., 544
Avis, N. E., 157, 164, 166, 202, 259, 260
Aviv, N., 132
Ayers, C., 209
Ayers, S., 242
Aylwin, S., 494, 496
Azadzoi, K., 44, 46, 49
Aziz, A., 260, 261
Azzoni, A., 168

633

Spanier, G. B., 86, 206
Sparice, S., 257
Sparks, R., 194
Spector, I. P., 12, 18, 171, 172, 226
Speer, J. J., 169
Spera, G., 23, 132
Speroff, L., 276
Spiering, M., 157, 158
Spitzer, R. L., 386, 394, 492, 495, 551
Sprenger, P., 594
Squire, G. F., 412
Sreenivasan, S., 604, 614
Srilatha, B., 14
Staehr, P., 90
Stam, H., 193, 210, 313
Stanford, J. L., 289
Stanton, S., 242
Starcevic, B., 140
Starkman, M. N., 16
Starkstein, S., 49
Starzyk, K. B., 530, 533
Stauber, P. M., 127
Stava, L., 605
Stecher, V. J., 315
Steege, J. F., 241
Steers, W. D., 40
Stefanac, S., 594
Stefanatos, G. A., 369
Stefanick, M. L., 273
Stefanovic, M., 341
Stegner, H., 359
Steidle, C., 23, 90, 128
Steiger, J. H., 589
Stein, D. J., 576, 577
Steinberg, A. C., 241
Steinberg, L., 12, 18, 171, 172
Steineck, G., 169, 289
Steiner, B., 441
Steiner, B. S., 128, 131
Steiner, B. W., 404, 430, 431, 432, 450
Steiner, M., 265
Stemhagen, A., 22
Stenager, E., 43
Stenberg, A., 255, 263
Stephenson, R. A., 289
Stermac, L., 443
Stern, D., 211
Steup, W. H., 295, 296
Steven, K., 294
Stevens, K. I., 539
Stewart, D. E., 277
Stewart, E. G., 206, 226, 227
Stinnett, R. D., 547
Stocco, D. M., 341
Stock, W., 509

Stocker, R. F., 348
Stodgell, C. J., 228
Stolar, Z., 241
Stoller, R. J., 377, 378, 380, 386, 424, 434, 503, 514
Storer, T. W., 127, 128, 132
Storms, M. D., 405
Strack, S., 550
Strain, G. W., 194
Strassberg, D., 90, 110, 199
Strauss, D., 199
Strauss, J. D., 40
Streitmatter, J. L., 402
Striegel, J. E., 342
Strigo, I. A., 232
Stringham, J. D., 127
Strollo, F., 138
Strom, T. M., 341, 369
Strong, J. A., 334
Stuart, F. M., 163
Stuckey, B., 91, 92, 93
Studer, L. H., 494, 496
Stulhofer, A., 164, 165, 166
Sturge, C., 415
Sturup, G. K., 571, 572
Sudbeck, P., 342
Sugerman, P., 506
Suggs, R. C., 569
Sugrue, D. P., 169
Sullivan, M. J., 235, 236
Sullivan, P. M., 362
Sulloway, F. J., 568
Sultan, F. E., 211
Summaria, V., 14
Summitt, R. L., Jr., 242
Sun, C. C., 299
Sun, Y., 123, 125
Sundwall, D. A., 275
Sutton, A., 415
Sutton, E. J., 370
Suzuki, H., 196
Svendsen, E., 49
Swaab, H., 387
Swain, A., 341
Swan, G. E., 130
Swanson, A. H., 605
Sweeney, M., 315
Sweet, M., 461
Sweeting, H., 402
Swerdloff, R., 21, 22, 124, 126, 128, 131, 139, 140, 142, 143, 144
Swerdlow, R. H., 512
Swieczkowski, J. B., 199
Sybert, V. P., 369
Symonds, T., 174, 269
Symons, J., 269
Szkrybalo, J., 378, 397

Tacconi, P., 512
Taddei, S., 49
Taffe, J., 256, 258, 259, 261, 263, 265
Tai, W., 73, 79, 81
Taieb, C., 138
Tajima, J., 337
Takamizawa, K., 46
Talakoub, L., 194, 226
Talbot, T., 531, 533
Tamboli, P., 296
Tan, P., 90
Tancredi, A., 140
Tang, C. S., 202
Tang, G. W., 266
Tang, W., 91, 92
Tangpricha, V., 444
Tassan, P., 241
Tate, R., 547
Tatschner, T., 499
Tauber, M., 369
Tay, H. P., 306
Taylor, A., 337
Taylor, J. A., 147
Taylor, J. F., 171, 172, 203
Taylor, M. J., 180
Taylor, T., 22
Tekdogan, U., 91, 92
Telligen, A., 441
Temple, C. M., 369
Templeman, T. L., 547
Tennent, G., 509, 518
Tenover, J. L., 44
Terada, N., 291
ter Kuile, M. M., 18, 224, 236, 237, 243, 244
Tessier, J., 46
Tewksbury, R., 437
Thakar, R., 242
Thase, M. E., 167
Thayer, J. S., 479
Thibaut, F., 574
Thijssen, J., 161
Thomas, G., 210, 276
Thomas, L., 337
Thomas, S., 106
Thomas, W., 459, 475
Thonneau, P., 296
Thorn, B., 235, 236
Thornhill, R., 548
Thornton, D., 514
Thranov, I., 197, 227, 299
Thuwe, I., 432
Tignol, J., 25, 75
Tilmann, A., 147
Tinkler, S. D., 297, 298
Tiret, E., 295
Tiryakioglu, O., 162, 197